Tennyson and the Doom of Romanticism

Tennyson and the Doom of Romanticism

HERBERT F. TUCKER

HARVARD UNIVERSITY PRESS
CAMBRIDGE, MASSACHUSETTS
LONDON, ENGLAND 1988

This book is printed on acid-free paper, and its binding materials
have been chosen for strength and durability.

Library of Congress Cataloging-in-Publication Data
Tucker, Herbert F.
    Tennyson and the doom of romanticism.
    Bibliography: p.
    Includes index.
    1. Tennyson, Alfred Tennyson, Baron, 1809–1892—
Criticism and interpretation. 2. Romanticism—
England. I. Title.
PR5592.R63T83 1988   821'.8   87–12978
ISBN 0–674–87430–7 (alk. paper)

11|20|00

Matri V.C.T. Carissimae
In Memoriam H.F.T. Patris

Acknowledgments

❧

M Y WORK ON TENNYSON has migrated through the 1980s to and from a number of academic harbors and publishers' ports of call, and I launch it at last across the bar with a full cargo of thanks. No project stays afloat as long as mine has done without much support, and support of many kinds. It gives me great pleasure to record the help of the colleagues and groups named below.

First, in an appropriately Tennysonian mode, I acknowledge a sponsor I cannot name: the anonymous donor of the annual MLA-ACLS Fellowship, of which I was recipient in 1982–83. Subsequent research expenses were defrayed in part by travel grants from the American Philosophical Society and the Faculty Research Committee of Northwestern University, where two chairmen, Gerald Graff and Martin Mueller, also made generous provision of teaching leaves and clerical support. With his usual grace under pressure John Knott, my chairman at the University of Michigan, found means of research assistance during one especially harried interval. At the University of Virginia the Center for Advanced Studies has blessed me with a bounty that has made the final revision as nearly pleasant as such an ordeal can ever be.

For permission to examine and cite a variety of Tennyson's manuscripts I am grateful to the following: Lord Tennyson on behalf of the Tennyson trustees; the Master and Fellows of Trinity

College Cambridge, the Syndics of the Fitzwilliam Museum; the Syndics of Cambridge University Library; the Tennyson Research Centre at Lincoln and the Lincolnshire County Library; the Houghton Library of Harvard University. Of the many research librarians on whom I made demands, Timothy Hobbes at Trinity and Susan Gates at Lincoln showed special hospitality and patience.

I thank the editors of *PMLA*, *Victorian Poetry*, and *The Victorian Newsletter* for permission to make use of articles that appear in revised form as Chapter 1 and as parts of Chapters 2 and 3. Portions of Chapters 3, 5, and 6, delivered as conference papers, have profited from the reactions of several astute yet friendly audiences. My thanks accordingly to those who took part in the 1982–83 English Department Colloquium at Northwestern, especially my respondent David Simpson; in the Critical Theory Colloquium at Michigan for 1984–85; in the session of the 1985 English Institute devoted to Victorian poetics and chaired by Carol Christ; and in the 1985–86 English Department lecture series at Virginia.

I have been fortunate in my students at each of the three universities that have employed me during the writing of this book. In the worst of times they have put up with my first attempts to expound ideas that are better developed in the pages that follow; in the best of times they have been less tolerant, offering instead the challenge of articulate resistance that inspires development. I gratefully remember Patricia O'Neill and Whitney Hoth as types of the student a teaching scholar most self-interestedly wants to find.

At sundry hours of need a series of generous colleagues—Peter Rogerson, Thomas Toon, William Ingram—volunteered cybernetic expertise that converted word-processing impasses into thoroughfares. And of the several professional computer folk on whose time my project had a claim, I especially salute Mark Weishan: but for his silicon spelunking, half of Chapter 2 might still be entombed in microcircuitry somewhere in Ann Arbor. With respect to older modes of word processing, my thanks go to Daniel Garrison for his impromptu tutorials in reading Latin, and to Mark Scowcroft for his in writing it.

Finally, a debt that would be imponderable but for the sunny disposition of my creditor. Not only has Timothy Peltason taught me much during the past decade about the subject of this book; at a crucial juncture he also read the manuscript in its entirety, indeed in a baggier incarnation that his comments helped me to reduce and shape. Our ten years' exchange—of conversation, of essays, and now of books—has time and again reminded me how, in the mainly solitary business of scholarship, collaboration really does work.

Contents

PART ONE   1809–1832

Introduction to Part One   3

1. The Measure of Doom   12
2. Keen Discoveries: Originality and Tradition in the   31
Juvenilia and *Poems, Chiefly Lyrical*
3. Emergencies: Crises of Relation in *Poems* (1832)   93

PART TWO   1833–1855

Introduction to Part Two   177

4. In Extremis: Margins of the Self in the Classical   191
Dramatic Monologues
5. In England: Arts of the Joiner in the Domestic Idylls   270
6. Pyrrhic Victorian: The Incorporated Imagination in   346
The Princess, *In Memoriam*, and *Maud*

Afterword   431

NOTES   437
WORKS CITED   457
INDEX   471

The most pathetic utterance in all history is that of Christ on the Cross, "It is finished."

—Tennyson to his son

A Note on Documentation

Throughout the text and notes I have provided parenthetical references that are keyed to the list of works cited, which gives full bibliographic particulars. I refer to a small number of frequently cited sources by the following abbreviated titles:

C.MS. Manuscripts at the University Library of Cambridge University

H.Nbk. Numbered notebooks from the Tennyson collections at the Houghton Library of Harvard University

Heath MS. Heath Commonplace Book at the Fitzwilliam Museum of Cambridge University

LH *The Letters of Arthur Henry Hallam*, ed. Jack Kolb (Columbus: Ohio State University Press, 1981)

LTJ *Lady Tennyson's Journal*, ed. James O. Hoge (Charlottesville: University Press of Virginia, 1981)

Letters *The Letters of Alfred Lord Tennyson*, ed. Cecil Y. Lang and Edgar F. Shannon, Jr., vol. I (Cambridge, Mass.: Harvard University Press, 1981)

Memoir Hallam Tennyson, *Alfred Lord Tennyson: A Memoir*, 2 vols. (New York: Macmillan, 1897)

PT *The Poems of Tennyson*, ed. Christopher Ricks (London: Longman, 1969)

T.Nbk. Numbered notebooks from the Tennyson collections at Trinity College of Cambridge University

WH *The Writings of Arthur Henry Hallam*, ed. T. Vail Motter (New York: Modern Language Association, 1943)

Part One

1809-1832

Introduction to Part One

*T*HE PREFATORY SURVEY of modern responses to a classic author, I realize even as I prepare to conduct my own here, is a modest scholarly convention that has come to lord it over critical studies of Alfred Tennyson. Bibliographic essays recording the ups and downs of the poet's stock abound, as they should for a writer of such prominence.[1] But in the case of Tennyson studies this normally specialist interest enjoys peculiarly general currency. Recapitulation of the posthumous estimate of the poet's works has become a well nigh obligatory prolegomenon to any newly published scrutiny of the works themselves. It is a rare book of Tennyson criticism that does not get under way, in ritual fashion, by offering up some anxious *Rezeptionsgeschichte*: a washing and wringing of hands at the threshold.

Something about Tennyson, or at least about working on Tennyson, must induce particularly deep disturbances in that stratum of professional self-consciousness which scholarly prefaces usually engage with some explicitness, even when the scholarly books they precede do not. To judge only from the vigilant retrospection that typifies the prefaces we write, it appears that students of this poet have to confront, with exceptional and often embarrassing directness, certain sources of unease that also vex literary studies at large. Some of this malaise, perhaps the worthiest part, arises from cultural questions about the place of literature in modern life. These questions are so immensely disquieting that I have done little more than glance at them in the Afterword, confident that their pressure will make itself felt locally in the explications that principally make up this book. Political and institutional questions aside, even within the professional discourse of scholarship a number of stress points might be identified as especially pertinent to Tennyson studies. Among them I would include our intermittent rage at Romanticism as the asylum of unkempt sentimentality, together with our abiding rage *for* Romanticism as the still-unmet challenge of the secular spirit; and our lovers' quarrel with classicism in matters of artistic form, together with our suspicion of any author who becomes, as Tennyson did, a classic in his own lifetime.

Sounding further along these and other fault lines, I would submit that the throat-clearing rumble which comes to the top of so many Tennyson studies arises, at intellectual bedrock, in a collision between historical and ahistorical modes of signification, or between conditionalist and essentialist apprehensions of value. This fundamental conflict—which troubles Victorianists more conspicuously than specialists in other areas of English literature— also underlies much recent debate over the principles and methods proper to literary scholarship in general. Furthermore, something very like this conflict increasingly informed Tennyson's career, the establishment of which furnishes this book with its chief narrative line. The familiar, checkered landscape of Tennyson's twentieth-century reputation, therefore, seems worth surveying once again, this time with an eye on the rivalry between history and eternity, between temporal and structural claims, which I suspect has done much to produce it.

Until the day when our theory can keep pace with our desires— until the synchronic, vertical thrust of imagination and the diachronic, horizontal pressures of historical contingency cease to seem mutually disruptive—we do well as scholarly readers to find those forces mutually corrective. The best criticism and literary historiography, of course, have always done just that. For Johnson or Ruskin historical and critical observations could mingle freely in the play of intelligent response to a literature that, being both document and testament, obviously invited exploration along both its dimensions. The late Victorian period, however, witnessed with the academic professionalization of literary study a segregation of criticism from literary history, which drove the old tacit eclecticism underground. There, as a matter of fact, it has done fairly well. In the richest analyses and appreciations by the formalist disciples of a Pater or a Croce, and in the best philological studies by the historicist descendants of a Taine or a Lowes, historical and critical arguments constantly poach on each other's terrain, despite their authors' evident belief that they are behaving with more theoretical and methodological consistency than that. The ensuing dissonance between stern preaching and flexible practice would be relatively harmless, if it did not have a way of inhibiting the congregation. The contraceptive effect of the theoretical sequestering of archival from interpretive scholarship is a fact of literary studies in this century; and it is a more than usually depressing fact of Tennyson studies, which enjoy the dubious privilege of exemplifying, in almost ideal form, the schism between historical and exegetical research. This privilege results from a historical coincidence: namely, that Tennyson died, and thus turned into scholarly property, at just the time when literary study was institutionalizing itself in the English-speaking world where his poetry would be mostly read.

Whether we survey literary-historical studies devoted to Tennyson or trace the changing critical estimates of the poet's signal achievements in artistic form, we encounter work of considerable acumen by scholars who have nevertheless confined themselves in intradisciplinary shackles. The situation emerges most clearly in studies of the historical kind. Where these rise above anecdotal small talk into scholarly analysis of backgrounds and genesis, too often the background swallows up the genesis. Even in the best such work there is something furtive about the scholar's break from documentation into explication. The amassed Tennysoniana dwarf the Tennyson who matters, the artist who made the poem; the Victoriana swamp the Victorian text whose intrinsic importance nevertheless seems to provide the fundamental justification for the scholar's work. Such work is less literary history than it is cultural history haunted by the specter of the literary criticism it severely circumscribes.

This self-limitation testifies to the persistence of a long-since questionable yet still overbearing historicist prohibition: Thou shalt not mix subjective literary response and objective historical research. This interdict, itself a legacy of Tennyson's Romantic century, has disfigured in equal degree both historicism and the opposite it has precipitated: that is, the phantom of an intrinsic, purely "literary" criticism. Finding literature expelled from the new republic of the sciences, I. A. Richards and Cleanth Brooks played Coriolanus and expelled science instead from the old republic of letters. They decreed a *cordon sanitaire* fencing off the literary work of art from history, and then they supplied the discipline that a banished history no longer could enforce with the different, apparently subtler rigors of the pseudostatement and with the tough-minded maturity whereby, in great art, wit and irony and paradox controlled feeling.

The theoretical abstraction of poet, text, and critic from history—theoretical because never achieved in practice, never achieved in practice because impossible—had, in the short term, disastrous consequences for the understanding of Tennyson's work, especially those portions of Tennyson's work that aspired to convene poet and reader on historical common ground. Early in the modernist period Harold Nicolson memorably and influentially articulated a developing consensus, also affirmed in more glancing ways by poets from Ezra Pound to W. H. Auden, which ran somewhat as follows. The public greatness thrust upon Tennyson toward the middle of the nineteenth century had ruined the career of a superbly gifted lyricist of melancholy. The works of this laureate *malgré soi*, ranging from his domestic idylls of 1842 to the *Idylls of the King* he presented complete to his sovereign over forty years later, had been benighted attempts to make poetry speak to broadly historical issues from a narrow emotional base, which was granted to be "deep," but unfathomably deep, and therefore unreliable in the practical terms a public poetry exacted. The demands of his age for the ennoblement of complacency and for a pious grandeur without risk had thus fissured Tennyson's oeuvre and fractured his imaginative power.

Some such fissure there undoubtedly was in Tennyson's oeuvre. Far from ruining him, however, it is precisely what kept him alive as a poet—longer alive, we now can see, than any of the modernists who scorned him. (W. B. Yeats may be an exception to this formulation, though the habit of saying unkind things about Tennyson fell from him as he entered his own mature phase of cultural responsibilities.) The point requiring notice here is that the modernist consensus depended for the terms of its critique on just the division between poetry and history, just the mutual exclusion of literary space and public arena, that it wished to claim had cracked

Tennyson in two and had pulled his public imagination away from his best, authentically poetical self. Tennyson's modernist detractors, and furthermore those twentieth-century admirers who have read and written about him in the undertowing wake of modernist assumptions, have approached Tennyson in this particularly prejudicial way because what for Tennyson had been a fissure between the privately poetic and the publicly historical has opened since into a chasm.

That such an oeuvre as Tennyson's might be at once historically and emotionally responsive, or that historicity and emotion might intensify each other's impact and interest, evidently were possibilities that ran too deeply counter to prevailing attitudes to get a serious hearing, during the first half of our century, in the critical line that runs from Nicolson (1923) to Baum (1948). The dissociation of sensibility; the movement to rewrite Romantic and Victorian literary history in the mode not of comprehension but of indictment; the symbolist aim to purify the dialect of the tribe; the imagist aim to effect a fusion of thought and feeling somewhere, anywhere, outside the field of a historical relevance: these were powerfully attractive, mutually supportive modernist myths. They allowed two generations of poets and critics to wink at Tennyson's authority among them—inescapable though it then was, and largely uncharted though it still is—by regarding the result of his path-breaking work in the integration of lyric impulse and public responsibility as, on balance, a road better not taken by poets in the modern world. The soil of history had defiled Tennyson's gift; and more was the pity exquisitely savored by a succession of patronizing heirs, whom we in our decades succeed, and now and then patronize, in turn. For the advocates of modernity, new poets and New Critics alike, the rewards of such polemical attitudinizing were not slight during the first half of the century, when for much of the literary vanguard to be up to date meant to be clean of history in a streamlined present. Nor are comparable rewards slight now; it would ill become our "postmodern" moment to pretend that we succeed as heirs to Tennyson's heirs under any less polemically blinkered conditions than obtained with them (Sale 1974, 450). Still, while the rewards of the dismissive pose are many, understanding does not rank high among them. It remains safe to say that we now can grasp Tennyson's achievement more fairly than could our twentieth-century predecessors, just as a coming generation of scholars will in all likelihood be fairer to modernist movements than we.

However historically determined the early twentieth-century reaction to Tennyson may have been, the immediate consequences of its ahistorical rigor for the understanding of Tennyson's Victorianism were unpropitious. At the same time, though, the modernist critical practice of close reading brought with it, in the case of Tennyson's reputation, its own corrective. Once history had been ruled out—once poet, text, and reader had been, in theory, quarantined from anything else—the intellectual discipline that fell to humane letters by default was exegetical: it practiced the painstaking husbandry of certain strains of secular yet ostensibly timeless meaning, cultivated and harvested with a set of brilliantly teachable analytic tools that by midcentury belonged to thousands of academically certified readers. By binding poet, text, and reader in unprecedented intimacy, this modernist and New Critical quarantine compelled an unprecedented degree of textual scrutiny. And such high-powered examination, given the excellence of Tennyson's craftsmanship and given sufficient occasion for its discovery by enough trained readers, in time furnished grounds for undoing the short-term consequences of the modernist reaction against him.

Method thus outlives theory and taste: the modernist flight from history was rectified by the pedagogy of the New Criticism to which it gave rise. Not the practice but the rather different principles of New Critical formalism, attractively laid out and strenuously defended with the formidable intelligence of an F. R. Leavis or a W. K. Wimsatt, played as large a role as did generational revolt in causing their immediate disciples to find Tennyson's poetry unpalatable. We know it was principles of taste and not procedures of reading that had this effect because for some time now a newer wave of critics have been admiring in Tennyson features of witty versification and delicate semantic complexity. And these very features are now discernible thanks largely to the procedures of close reading exemplified by Richards, Leavis, Brooks, and Wimsatt, no matter what canonical and methodological exclusions those masterly readers may have thought their teachings entailed.

So we may faintly trust the larger hope: in the long run, the best practice will prevail upon the best-laid plans of either critical or historical sorts. Meanwhile, as a check upon short-term astigmatism, it will be well to bear in mind that what we claim as the function of criticism at the present time is likely to be out of phase with what, at any present time, we actually do. This self-critical posture, with attendant vacillation between competing textualist and contextualist approaches, may offer the soundest means of getting history back into the texts we study without denying to those texts their legitimate, historically constitutive force as landmarks of the imagination. If historical research reduces literature to the fact, and critical interpretation reduces it to the idea, we should remember (as Tennyson did most of the time) that the idea itself has a history and that the fact itself always comes to us interpreted.

ONE AIM OF this book is to tell the story of the life in Tennyson's texts to midcareer, and thereby to practice specifically *literary* biography: a subgenre of literary historiography whose value derives from its proximity to the exegetical practice on which, in my view, the distinctiveness and the health of literary studies are likely to continue to depend. Prompted by the considerations outlined above, and doubtless also by some degree of allergic reaction to certain strains in my own scholarly education, I expressly set this kind of literary biography in opposition to the doggedly contextual historicism that has stood in the way of interpretation and disabled our estimate of a great writer's art. Analysis of Tennyson's poetry has been stalled at a mediocre level—too often, indeed, at a level that comparison with critical work on poets of comparable stature, in either of the periods flanking Tennyson's, should oblige us to call elementary. Given a choice between Victorian context-setting and exegesis of the poems Tennyson wrote, I unhesitatingly embrace exegesis.

Fortunately, however, the choice need not present itself in such terms. While the tendencies represented by the putative contrast between literary-historical fact and literary-critical meaning possess ample reality as facts in the history of criticism during the twentieth century, by now it should be apparent that the choice between them is a false one, grounded in the conditions of literary modernism and thus susceptible to a critique of a historical kind. I hope, in any case, to offer here a study that is both historical and critical. My exegetical ambition declares itself, for better or worse, in the overall design and on almost every page: the many close readings that follow, if they establish nothing else, will establish beyond question my zeal for the explication of Tennyson's poems. But I hope, too, that the salutary pull of history—the literary history to which Tennyson became so alert so early, the personal history that became art in Tennyson's hands, and the social history that presses on virtually all his work—will have preserved this book from the sterilities of that New Critical formalism which, only yesterday, thought Tennyson's formally faultless poetry too personally messy and historically contaminated to meddle with.

Here follow, then, chapters in the creative life of Alfred Tennyson. I approach my subject not in his capacity as a son, friend, lover, husband, or father, but as the poet whom an in many ways ordinary nineteenth-century man wrote his way to becoming—the maker of texts that were, among other things, predictions as well as reflections of the career they constituted. The unparalleled, often uncanny symbiosis between Tennyson's art and his celebrity becomes increasingly explicit across the decades of his long career; it becomes, accordingly, an increasingly explicit theme of this book. Part I moves from the earliest surviving manuscripts to the verge of the "ten years' silence" of 1832–1842. It was during that decade, I shall argue in introducing Part II, that Tennyson consolidated his public ambitions as a poet and formulated the genres wherein those ambitions would be realized during the decades to come. In the meantime, those poetically formative rather than transformative years on which this first part concentrates, for Tennyson the prospect of his future fame was more a hazy vista than a goal in sharp focus. His earliest writings show less interest in the historically concrete problems of established authorship than in the establishment of poetic authority as such.

Starting from an intensely verbal introversion whose privacy he quickly learned to thematize in a variety of ways, Tennyson authorized himself, at first and in a sense forever, through the sonorous and passional imagination of a distinctive form of command. Chapter 1 argues for the consistency of this authority across the poet's career; Chapters 2 and 3 trace its beginnings in the manuscript juvenilia and its development in Tennyson's first publications. I read these works as a series of experiments, hazardous if always controlled, which tested the young poet's authority by exposing it more and more urgently to challenges from without, whether through the imagination of fictive others or through poetic allusion, and often through both at once. These external challenges, as Tennyson conceived them from adolescence into his twenty-fourth year, disclose incipiently social concerns; yet the cultural and historical content of the work of Tennyson's youth remains predictably neutral and abstract. I have generally conformed my critical practice in Part I to his poetic practice during the period it treats, restricting myself as a rule to literary analyses of textually intrinsic and interpoetically comparative kinds. The reader who follows me patiently into Part II will witness, and I hope will confirm, my discovery that to read with care Tennyson's work from 1842 and thereafter is to find close reading of poetic texts expanding irresistibly into consideration of Victorian social texts as well.

The Measure of Doom

THIS BOOK ADDRESSES Tennyson's poetry from the un-published juvenilia through *Maud* (1855); and it will be an appropriate introduction to its argument if we start, as the poet so often did, at our destination. For Tennyson's account of the way he wrote *Maud*, at the midpoint of his career, can tell us something important about everything he wrote. Here is the report Aubrey de Vere left behind:

> Its origin and composition were, as he described them, singular. He had accidentally lighted upon a poem of his own which begins, "O that 'twere possible," and which had long before been published in a selected volume got up by Lord Northampton for the aid of a sick clergyman. It had struck him, in consequence, I think, of a suggestion made by Sir John Simeon, that, to render the poem fully intelligible, a preceding one was necessary. He wrote it; the second poem too required a predecessor: and thus the whole poem was written, as it were, *backwards*. (*PT*, 1037; Martin 1980, 226–228)

The backward genesis of an intricate work of over a thousand lines is indeed "singular." Yet the composition of *Maud* was not a freakish episode but a quite typical instance of Tennyson's approach to his art. *Idylls of the King* (1885), an epic-length work matured during the course of forty years and more, proceeds from King Arthur's mysterious birth, through the rise and decline of Camelot, to his no less mysterious death. But it was the last idyll, "The Passing of Arthur," that came first, published in 1842 as "Morte d'Arthur" and written nine years before that: in keying his epic to its foregone conclusion Tennyson wrote *Idylls of the King* backward, much as he had done with *Maud*.

Likewise, he composed the quatrain lyrics that make up *In Memoriam* (1850) over the better part of two decades; and the resolutions of the poem, the easiest and most easeful lyrics, were the ones that came to him first. His expansion of a handful of elegies into a poem of major proportions was largely a backing and filling maneuver—"if there were a blank space I would put in a poem" (*PT*, 859–860)—which supplied preparatory complications as afterthoughts to the emotional stabilities they precede in the text we read today. As an emblem of this compositional process, Tennyson prefaced the finished poem with a prologue dated "1849," a retrospective introduction that forecasts and summarizes the plot of the elegies that follow. "All, as in some piece of art, / Is toil coöperant to an end" (cxxviii.23–24). One reason why *In Memoriam* so pervasively implies a teleology may lie in the circumstances of its composition; the final vision of "One far-off divine event, / To which the whole creation moves" (Epilogue, 143–144) could describe the creatively ordained evolution of the poem as well as the evolving universe the poem has come to celebrate.[1]

Even when, to the best of our knowledge, the process of composition was straightforward, Tennyson delighted to enclose his poems in frames that give the illusion of retrospective return. Sometimes, as in *The Princess* (1847) or "Aylmer's Field" (1864), a scene of narration opens and closes a poem whose recounted events recede into the mythic or historical past. Sometimes, as in "The Lotos-Eaters" (1832) or "Lucretius" (1868), a past-tense narrative preface embeds and distances the present urgency of lyric voice. Even in such comparatively rare instances of naked lyric address as "Break, Break, Break" (1842), "The Eagle" (1851), and "Crossing the Bar" (1889), Tennyson's theme and imagery gravitate toward some inevitable ground in the power of God, the drift of nature, or a psychic fixation upon the days that are no more.

Whether we inspect the circumstances of textual composition, then, or the emotional texture of the verse, we find in Tennyson a poetry of aftermath. What drew him repeatedly to imagine terminal or retrospective lyric situations, and also fostered his curious retrograde approach to the composition of longer poems, was a fascination with inevitability. Although his was a century re-

markable for its faith in progress and hope for the future—currents
of the zeitgeist by which Tennyson could scarcely remain untouched—his genius gave its real allegiance to an older and darker
wisdom, which discerns in the present the determining hand of
the past (Gransden 1964, 11; Donoghue 1968, 93). This allegiance
explains why in the private realm his poems yield well to a psy-
choanalysis of desire, why his public poems disclose a fatalistic
politics or teleological view of history (Culler 1977, 14–15; Kozicki
1979), and why imitation and allusion form so large a part of his
work (Pattison 1979). Tennyson prized the past as the temporal
locus of a power more important to him than the past itself: the
power of what cannot be changed. His poetry is a coming to terms
with the inevitable, and to approach it as such is to appreciate the
relation between the notes of helplessness and authority that produce its distinctive tone. The following general remarks on Tennyson's handling of character, action, and atmosphere will
introduce the connections between his undeniable limitations and
his great strengths; they should also prepare us to see how the
shaggy mystic and the precise formalist in him can have consorted
together so well (Shaw 1976b, 285–287).

WRITING AT THE FIRST CREST of Tennyson's immense popularity,
Matthew Arnold described as definitively modern those situations
"in which there is everything to be endured, nothing to be done"
(1960, 2–3). We might read into this criticism of Arnold's own
Empedocles on Etna a sidelong glance at the works of his modern,
all too modern, contemporary. For there is something of an ethical
vacuum in Tennyson's poetry. He simply was not very interested
in investigating and assessing the interplay of motive and action,
and those who seek primarily these things in poetry will not read
him for long with much pleasure. We cannot overlook the moral
exhortation and argument in Tennyson's public set pieces, including those he produced years before gaining the laureateship.
But to set forth rules for conduct is not to imagine the ethical
crisis, the awareness of other minds, and the resultant dramatic
pressure of choice that have provided central themes for English
poets of character from Chaucer onward (Horne 1844, 157). The
interest of an absorbing poem like "The Two Voices" (1842)
scarcely inheres in the drama of the modern psychomachia, though
that is where Tennyson probably expected his readers to find it.

The heavy reliance on generalizing epigram and illustrative emblem, the virtual absence of context, the ultimate passivity of the speaker before the different injunctions he hears—all conspire against the credible formation of character in a poem that seeks, nevertheless, to render a character-forming crisis of faith. The monodramatic form of *Maud*, in contrast, makes a virtue of Tennyson's defects by dwelling on isolated moods and letting their serial juxtaposition do the work of dramatic development.

The irresistible comparison with his contemporary Browning shows that, while Tennyson could create character and sustain its moods, he could not dramatize it beyond a relatively narrow range of internal and external action—a range of action that is most compelling, in fact, when it addresses those conditions or psychological mechanisms that thwart change. Conservative in most respects, Tennyson was nowhere more so than in a psychology that embraced the determination of character, whether by the blood or by the unalterable past. His speakers are notable for their lack of pluck: they exhibit determination rarely and suffer it often. Typically they come into voice after the fact, once some irrevocable deed has been committed and its consequences are making themselves felt. Tennyson's voices bring to their postfactual situations a belated commentary, and it is the burden of his unsurpassed rhetoric to interest us in situations out of which a belated commentary is all that can be made (Ricks 1972, 293; Drew 1973, 142; Bayley 1978, 246).

A conviction of inevitability as profound as Tennyson's spells the death of a certain kind of ethical curiosity. His speakers are responsive but not responsible, at least inasmuch as responsibility implies the capacity for present or future action; and Tennyson makes them most convincing when he cleaves to his psychological conservatism and does not ask them to transform themselves. If Princess Ida and the hero of *Maud* undergo such transformation, it is precisely as something not achieved but undergone, through submission to overbearing forces beyond their own initiative. As Tennyson's characters are seldom responsible, so they are seldom guilty (Pitt 1962, 246; Golffing 1966, 226; Storch 1971, 293; Ricks 1972, 77). Though we may wish to charge Mariana or Ulysses with crimes against themselves, and against any other portion of humanity that impinges on their consciousness, we should observe that Mariana and Ulysses do not express guilt directly or practice the conscious arts of self-justification. Instead they baffle their guilt, projecting it into a landscape from which it returns with ominous alien authority. When for characters like Guinevere and Lancelot in the *Idylls* guilt is a given of the tale—that is, when for its author the inevitable takes the authoritative shape of antique legend—the behavior of Tennyson's characters is more revealing still. Guinevere and Lancelot, much like their poet, treat guilt as a given, and this acceptance of uncontested guilt is the equivalent, in character, of Tennyson's narrative elision of the moments of their fall and redemption.

Sometimes the drama of self-justification becomes explicit, but then it also becomes suspiciously schematic. Tennyson's guiltiest creature, St. Simeon Stylites (1842), uses the dogma of sin and atonement to avoid really grappling with the questionable state of his soul; his dramatic monologue, which may provide the best character sketch anywhere in Tennyson, characteristically finds its theme in the evasion of responsibility. One can only wish that the poet's awareness of such tendencies toward ethical abstractness had stayed with him, and stayed his hand, when he lent his support to King Arthur's formal and vacuous apologia in the eleventh of the *Idylls*. The guilt-ridden second part of *Maud* may serve as an exception that not only proves the rule of evasiveness but also suggests why Tennyson clung to it elsewhere. Here for once a character confronts guilt without stay or prop, and madness is the result: character itself dissolves into a welter of constituencies that can be brought to order only, it seems, through repeated submission to the inevitable, "the purpose of God, and the doom assigned" (III.vi.59).

Tennyson's career, I believe, makes sense as a series of just such submissions to an inevitable doom. When there is everything to be endured and nothing to be done, endurance will be a leading virtue; the index of a speaker's strength will be the deepening stasis of a mood; and action will take the strictly subordinate place it takes in Tennyson's poetry. Critics who contend that Tennyson could not tell a proper story must contend first with the enormous success of "The Gardener's Daughter" (1842), "Enoch Arden" (1864), and other tales among an audience whose taste for moving narration Tennyson manifestly knew how to meet. Still, anyone who reads widely in Tennyson's collected works will know what

these critics mean. Something about the stories he tells best, in
their climactic emphasis on inhibition or their diffuse sense of
breakdown, scandalizes the assumptions behind critical metaphors
of narrative "development" and "progression." Something opposes the thrust of narrative and deflects the poetry in an allegorical
direction that has made readers since Walter Bagehot suspect that,
whatever a Tennyson poem is ostensibly about, its real subject
lies elsewhere (1864, 343; Carr 1950, 51; Pitt 1962, 215; Lourie
1979, 22). When undertaking an actual story, Tennyson consistently opts for descriptive over narrative effects, and even then he
gives atmospheric or local description priority over physical description of characters or analysis of their minds (Shaw 1976b,
285–289; Sinfield 1976a; Sherry 1979). On a smaller scale, but with
similar effect, he habitually gives adjectival and adverbial modifiers
syntactic priority over main subjects and predicates (Boyd 1977,
30). For longer works, Tennyson goes out of his way to devise
narrative structures that deemphasize action and intensify mood.
In Memoriam and *Maud* are collections of lyrics in which narrative
continuity is only implied; the significantly plural *Idylls* disperse
what might have been epic unity into a series of discrete vignettes;
The Princess subordinates plot to plottiness, trumpeting its status
as an improvised "medley," a multimedia event for mixed voices.

The case against Tennyson's narrative ability can rest more
firmly on his disinclination than on his incompetence. He could
convey action with thrift and force when he wanted to, but he
did not often want to. We might say, recalling his determinist
notions about character, that Tennyson's imagination was reluctant to believe in the efficacy of human action. Thus, when his
characters conceive plots, their plots are always frustrated: the
frustration may be comic, as when the broken purposes of Princess
Ida and her suitor lead to a higher harmony; or it may be tragic,
as when the governing vision of Camelot decays. But in either
case some external power, in the guise of providence or inertia,
balks independent initiative.[2] Such instances of independence are
rare with Tennyson: far more often action begins as reaction,
where the proximate stimulus matters less than some distant final
cause, the call of the occult, the holy, the other. The Kraken (1830)
stirs only when stirred by the distant fire of apocalypse; from the
first the Lady of Shalott (1832) suffers under a curse that any course

of action seems doomed to fulfill; the poet himself anticipates crossing the bar only in response to "one clear call" (2) from beyond.

The voyage motif in "Crossing the Bar" suggests the relevance to Tennyson's other proclivities of his lifelong fondness for the imaginative pattern of the quest. As a plot motif the quest permits plenty of action, but action in which the actors obey some authority outside themselves. Consider the mingled vigor and acquiescence of Tennyson's questers. On their travels the Magus in *The Devil and the Lady* (1825?), Galahad, Percivale, and company in "The Holy Grail" (1869), and the thinly veiled figure of the poet in "Merlin and the Gleam" (1889) meet with the most marvelous things; but by the standards of romance they *do* remarkably little. They experience wonders without confronting them. Tennysonian experience, it appears, is not a mode of self-expression but a pressure exerted on the self from without. Even Odysseus, that archetypal Western adventurer, becomes in Tennyson a figure for whom "all experience" is somewhere out there, "an arch wherethrough / Gleams that untravelled world, whose margin fades / For ever and for ever when I move" ("Ulysses," 19–21). Tennyson's questers move through space and time, like Ulysses, in order that they may be moved inwardly. "When he wishes to represent movement," observed Henry James, "the phrase always seems to me to pause and slowly pivot upon itself, or at most to move backward" (1875, 171). Tennyson's figures do not actively adopt perspectives; they find themselves in contexts. And the backward movement of his phrases and plots, insisting on the belatedness of context, owns the inevitable power he enshrined in the past.

Tennyson put so little stock in action, and in the capacity of human character to conceive a plot and bring it to fulfillment, because his interest lay instead in *passion*, a term whose etymological connection to *passivity* his poetry consistently reinforces. It is this connection that explains his uncanny knack for making a landscape describe both an environmental and a mental state. This gift has been hailed retrospectively as an anticipation of Symbolism, but Tennyson's sense of landscape is both more literal and less merely technical than that. If for Tennyson experience is the pressure of events, very often scenic events, upon the self, then his renditions of inner and outer weather ought to coincide. They never do quite coincide, though, in Tennyson; it was left for later

generations to alloy perception and passion with the extreme sim-
plification of the pure poetic image.[3] But Tennyson helped cast
the crucible of imagism; for the atrophy of character and paralysis
of action in his poetry expose, as his prime achievements, the
rendition of unshakable moods in still and scenic imagery, and the
composition of a superb verbal music that for him is no mere
medium of rendition. So to the reader willing to tolerate a certain
ethical and practical poverty, Tennyson offers the twin compen-
sations of his richest gifts: the sustained evocation of an emotional
atmosphere, and the atmospheric and physical acoustics of one of
the most fulfilling voices in English tradition.

These gifts are profoundly allied, and we might approach their
alliance by positing a typical Tennysonian setting and pursuing a
few of its implications. His scenes are more literally "set" than
those of most writers: vivid, immediate details stand out like gems
against a shadowy background. The vacancy of the middle distance
probably owes something to the poet's myopia (Nicolson 1923,
278–279; Rosenberg 1974, 308; Joseph 1977). But his eye problems
and lifelong, never-realized fears of blindness suggest further that
for Tennyson visible detail served defensive ends. His lovingly
precise visualization of what was at hand arose in response to an
awareness of a threat from beyond, a sentence of doom that was
nearing its period (Abercrombie 1931, 66; Pitt 1962, 26; Millhauser
1971, 29; Ford 1977, 38). The face of his poetry turns westward,
to "a land / In which it seemèd always afternoon" ("The Lotos-
Eaters," 3–4)—and the longer after noon, the more evocative the
tension between foreground and encroaching depth. Indeed, the
time of day most in keeping with Tennyson's poetry of aftermath
is dusk—a scene bathed in the half-light after sunset, not
before dawn—a time of day that purchases its comprehensive overview at the sacrifice of any will to alter what past events have
rendered inevitable. When dawn does rise, more often than not it
rises on emphatically terminal situations: the deathbed figure in
"Tears, Idle Tears," the hopeless speaker of the seventh lyric from
In Memoriam, and especially Tithonus greet the dawn with the
poignant sense of discrepancy that engenders in Tennyson not
irony but its cousin melancholy. Tennysonian dusk is a liminal
hour, and its threshold has a clear sensory and psychic direction,
away from sight into sound and feeling, away from character into
passion, away from conscious will into mystic passivity. The field

of vision at this hour features what is precious in evanescence: a fugitive gleam, a glimmering ghost, a shape that pales into oceanic gloom—each, like the glint of the discarded brand Excalibur, the wraith of an abandoned intention.[4]

The greatest moments in Tennyson's poetry occur as sight drowns in darkness and the object world is whelmed in a tide of sound that moans round with many voices, voices that merge— as in the long view Tennyson's precariously achieved personae merge—into the roar or pulse of an inevitable, unutterable power. The haunt of this power Tennyson calls "the deep," a locality he approaches when the light of sense goes out and yields to auditory and kinesthetic evidences of a music that is both heard and felt, though hardly understood. When Tennyson wants an objective correlative to the power of the great deep, he habitually imagines the biggest and least objectlike thing in the world, the sea, which is less often briny or wine-dark than oral in its attributes: vocal, devouring, or both. Thus, to take a justly famous instance, at the close of "Ulysses" the "dark broad seas" first "gloom" afar, in the privation of sight (45), then acquire the blind, increasingly intimate power of voice and—finally, primally—of thirst, as they surround and ingest Tennyson's hungry-hearted speaker: "the deep / Moans round with many voices"; "It may be that the gulfs will wash us down" (55–56, 62). Yet even so persuasively em-bodied a sea is ultimately a figure for an inner wave of feeling that sweeps beyond individual emotions to an epiphany of the inevi-table, with a rhythm, at once cardiac and astral, to which the whole creation moves.

Tennyson was never comfortable about fixing this inevitable power to form or linking its manifestations to any inherited or devised intellectual system. Had he been able to do so more con-sistently he might have written the kind of poetry his Victorian public hoped they were reading when they pored over *In Memo-riam*. But his intuitions of the music of the deep remained too sensuously concrete for that—Hallam was right to class his friend among the poets of sensation—and Tennyson remains an essen-tially modern, which is to say an essentially Romantic, religious poet.[5] Tennyson makes the task of conceptualizing so sensuous an imagination unusually difficult, by keeping his intuitions of inevitable power as conceptually and even mythically vague as they are physically urgent. We do his imagination the least violence if we respect the temporality implied by his representation of power in musical terms. "The Mystic" of 1830 "hath heard / Time flowing in the middle of the night, / And all things creeping to a day of doom" (38–40). A dozen years later the resolutely unmystical speaker of "Locksley Hall" (1842) has likewise felt "the deep heart of existence beat for ever like a boy's" (140). The same speaker can be recognized a decade further on in *Maud*, and at one of the imaginative peaks of the poem he returns to the mystic measure of simultaneous intimacy and enormous distance: "Beat, happy stars, timing with things below" (I.xviii.679). The posthumously published "Akbar's Dream," where "the living pulse of Alla beats / Through all His world" and where the sun is conclusively hymned as a cosmic metronome, "the flame that measures Time" (39–40, 201), follows the oriental detour of Tennyson's final phase back to the same pulse that had fed the ear of the collegiate mystic of "Timbuctoo," in rapt attention to "the lordly music flowing from / The illimitable years" (214–215).

In these musical phrasings of "that which is," in the "deep pulsations" of an "Aeonian music" that measures out "The steps of Time—the shocks of Chance— / The blows of Death" (*In Memoriam*, xcv.39–43), Tennyson hears not a person or a proposition, but what he calls "Eternal process" (lxxxii.5); not timeless sublimity, but the sublime measure in and of time itself. His vision of transcendence is an audition of transience, and an audition made to measure (Brashear 1977, 32). Even when Tennyson registers the eternal process as a stream or tide, he takes care to break the flow into rhythmic units that creep or beat with a fundamentally musical organization. This is so whether those units are pulses or eons; indeed, one of the most disturbing features of this poet's imagination is its way of implying how little difference it makes what the time scale may happen to be. By the same token, he takes care to keep the eternal process from sounding much more concrete than such an elemental pulsation suggests. "Tithonus," in some ways Tennyson's most extreme poem, betrays an extraordinary lust for the concrete when it gives the weird music an anthropomorphic source and vocal shape: "That strange song I heard Apollo sing, / While Ilion like a mist rose into towers" (62–63). The otherwise comparable architectonic music of Camelot is, more typically, free of origin and contour: "the city is built / To music, therefore never built at all, / And therefore built

for ever" ("Gareth and Lynette," 272–274). What perennially recurs at points of imaginative climax for Tennyson is the sense of
eternal recurrence itself. By all contemporary accounts a marked
perception of rhythm dominated the poet's recitation of his own
works, and something like it should inform our discussion of the
effects of formal repetition in his verse. His metrical mastery, his
circling syntax, and his manipulation of stanzaic forms do different
jobs, of course, in different poems. But one way of seeing Tennyson whole is to grasp these repetitive devices as modes of approach to, or recession from, musical intuitions of an inevitable
burden—something he felt as a pressure and expressed in the half-
mimetic, half-protective mediations of song (Spitzer 1950, 197;
Dodsworth 1969; Kissane 1970, 32–33; Ricks 1972, 44–49).

Tennyson takes up the burden of eternal process as both a weight
and a shield, for its rhythmic movement bears an ambiguous relation to mortality and thus to human time generally. On the one
hand—the hand of Keats is discernible here—the process means
death to the individual self, and in two ways. Its measure enforces
the march of a life from youth through age to the grave; and those
who would listen to the music that drives them can do so only
through the "weird seizures" of *The Princess*, the trances known
by Arthur in "The Holy Grail," by the Ancient Sage, and by
Tennyson himself, possibly in the form of mild epilepsy (Culler
1977, 1–13; Martin 1980, 28–29; Kolb 1983, 171–181). On the
other hand—arguably the hand of Shelley—this figurative death
or self-annihilation discloses intimations of immortality: Tennyson
never represents the process as other than *eternal*, and in yielding
to its force he enjoys a state that knows no death.

Recognitions of the power, the process, the deep music of doom
came to Tennyson early and seem never to have deserted him for
long. Since these recognitions demanded nothing less than the
extinction of what he regarded as human personality, they came
to prompt in him an ambivalence almost as deep as the power
itself. This ambivalence manifests itself, for example, in his reliance
on binary devices for the structuring of individual poems and in
his corresponding habit of balancing complementary poems within
the volumes he published. It is more generally manifest in the
melancholy that typifies the Tennysonian spirit. The elegiac tone
and gesture of farewell that are hallmarks of his poetry have been
derided in our century as signs of an indulgent sentimentality; but

we understand this melancholy better once we recognize that it proceeds, however oddly, from a tough honesty. What Tennyson regrets is the self's passing away, an imaginative necessity imposed by a power whose authority he would not shirk yet could not accept without a murmur (Pitt 1962, 33). That murmur, the self's lament for the self, in counterpoint to the rhythmic ground swell of doom, generates Tennyson's poetic theme, by which I mean both his subject and his music. Passionately melancholic and authoritatively impassive, his speakers remain the victims of circumstance in a double sense: they regard themselves as heirs of a past they cannot control, and at the same time they invest the present scene of aftermath with an enveloping power that dissolves the will. Coming to terms with the inevitable, they lament what they know too well to resist it.

The close link between the atmospheric inevitability of Tennyson's poetic world and the formal inevitability of his poetic style appears in his talent for ending even undistinguished poems with an authority that makes it very hard to imagine how they might have ended otherwise. Tennyson is the most finished, the most inevitable of English poets, at least in the Romantic tradition; and the inevitability that marks his style also characterizes the attitude that lies behind the style. One reason Tennyson's poems create the impression that they have to conclude as they do is that their maker seems often to have been subject to that impression, not just about poetic events, but about events in the world as well. Finding imagined or actual events inevitable is a far cry from being in command of them, to be sure; but it can offer a semblance of command, one that Tennyson sees reflected in the command of poetic form. The elaboration of a verbal maestro's art, which gave him a hold on himself and on his world, also gave him a large measure of his hold on contemporary readers. Apropos of Tennyson's versification, W. H. Auden speculated that "the more conscious he is of an inner disorder and dread, the more value he will place on tidiness in the work as a defence, as if he hoped that through his control of the means of expressing his emotions, the emotions themselves, which he cannot master directly, might be brought to order" (1945, xviii).[6]

Composition as a means to composure: Auden half sneers at the idea; but readers taught by T. S. Eliot that poetry may be an escape from emotion, and that the peculiar grandeur of Tennyson's

poetry comes from emotions of doubt and dread it never did quite
escape (1950, 10, 289, 294), should be prepared to find in Tennyson's postfactual strategies and in the impeccability of his style
the marks of a disturbingly modern sensibility. As Tennyson once
declared to his son, with bardic modesty (and a craftsman's nod
to Goethe), "The artist is known by his self-limitation" (*Memoir*,
I, 118). Tennyson resorted to self-limitation as a means of self-
definition, in part because he wrote in and of a century that witnessed the disintegration of traditional limits. Well aware that the
great world around him was spinning down ringing grooves of
change, but fearfully ignorant of its destination, Tennyson defended against his ignorance by imagining terminal situations in
accomplished verse. Yet, in leaping to the ends of things, his
imagination was too honest not to import into its stronghold much
of the melancholy helplessness that characterized the present it
could only partially evade.

A poet's grammar is an aspect of imaginative form; and we
could describe the Tennysonian discrepancy between that which
is, and that which might have been, as a tension between indicative
and subjunctive moods (Puckett 1974; Sinfield 1976b). An attempt
to write the generative grammar of Tennyson's imagination might
indeed begin with his success in animating the latent ambiguity
of those past-tense forms that do double duty in English as sub-
junctives. Consider, for example, the lyric seed out of which he
bred *Maud*:

> O that 'twere possible
> After long grief and pain
> To find the arms of my true love
> Round me once again!   (II.iv.141–144)

"O that 'twere possible": the verb denotes a situation contrary to
fact. But through an emotionally trustworthy if philologically
shaky homonymy that is part of the traditional wisdom of the
language, the verb also invites us to conceive this hypothetical
situation as part of a story set in the past and to live through the
story, in imagination, to the end.[7] And, as we know, that is what
Tennyson did when he backed into the plot of *Maud*. In providing
a chain of antecedent action, he substantiated the yearning "that
'twere possible" with a narrative circumstance: once upon a time,
the consummation of this now-forbidden love *was* possible. The

postfactual and the contrafactual implications of Tennyson's verb mix the inevitabilities of memory and desire (Carr 1950, 48). Remorse enriches yearning, to produce the emotional complex, deep as first love and wild with all regret, that is the condition for Tennyson's idle tears: "to weep, and weep, and weep / My whole soul out to thee" (237–238).

A fuller consideration of Tennyson's historical position would return us to the central dilemma outlined above: his poetry is caught between the desires of the self and the demands of a power whose recognition exacts, in one way or another, the dissolution of the self. To the latter imperative Tennyson owes his utter authority of manner, to the former the submerged lyric drive whose strength surfaces in the classical monologues he drafted during the early 1830s, but whose persistence we must largely infer from his more habitual melancholy, which is a symptomatic response to the incompatibility of the two imperatives he faces. We cannot know whether Tennyson's authority or his melancholy had the greater appeal for contemporary readers, especially since after his earliest work the two are rarely found apart. But an important clue to his popularity is probably that, writing during a crisis of authority, he could simultaneously gratify conflicting needs. The seal of certitude allayed publicly a cultural malaise that the note of melancholy was secretly feeding all the while.

Tennyson was no hypocrite; a sense of scruple, if anything, produced his peculiarly undogmatic certitude and his vagueness about the object of his grief. Yet these very characteristics arguably made his dilemmas and resolutions the more available for public adoption. Apparently it did not strike de Vere as strange that a lament of erotic frustration like "O That 'Twere Possible" should occupy a place first in a volume got up "for the aid of a sick clergyman" and later in a long poem containing some of the bitterest social invective Tennyson ever published. Something in the poem's theme of loss, presumably, and in the peculiar kind of "aid" it offered through the expression of loss, struck a common chord that resounded through the multiple discontents of the age. Nowadays our analysis of Victorian malaise would include among its interlocking causes industrialization, and the consequent alienation of workers from traditional modes of labor; restratification both of the family and of social classes, with correlative shifts in the domestic and political bases of power; the crumbling of religious orthodoxy under scientific attack; and much more. Tennyson's special fitness for the role of Victoria's laureate appears in the inventive consistency with which he could let a reading public touched by any or all of these causes imagine that the situation was awful and that it was also, somehow, at last, all right (Preyer 1966, 350–351). His readers responded—as they can still respond—to the expression of an inconsolable loss beyond words, a content irreducible to form, and at the same time to a polished style offering a genuine consolation of its own, a reassuring message independent of substantial reference.

Auden's comment about the relation of formal to emotional control draws on the plausible assumption that a line rings true to a poet's ear when it speaks the truth to his mind. Tennyson's obiter dicta on poetic style disclose his sympathy for what a passage says, as often as his appreciation for its wording. He seems to have been moved especially by turns of phrase that emphasize the sense of aftermath we find in his own writing; and on more than one revealing occasion, he gave other writers' suggestive phrases emphatic twists in the direction of a Tennysonian doom. William Allingham's diary on two occasions (1967, 296, 324) records the laureate's expressions of admiration for the following two lines, from a text to which we shall have frequent occasion to refer in the following chapters, Keats's "Ode to a Nightingale" (69–70):

> Charm'd magic casements, opening on the foam
> Of perilous seas, in faery lands forlorn.

The words are quoted accurately (by Tennyson, too, we may presume), but Keats's syntax has been truncated to make the lines appear more Tennysonian than Keatsian. Keats wrote that, in hearing the voice of the nightingale, he heard the same song that had filled the ears of emperor, clown, and the biblical Ruth: "The same that oft-times hath / Charm'd magic casements . . . " Tennyson lops off the subject and auxiliary verb of Keats's clause and effectively transforms "Charm'd" into a past passive participle, which links up with "forlorn" to frame the active participle "opening." As Tennyson remembers them, Keats's lines suggest a magic that performs itself without the benefit of a magician, the work of an agency even more mysterious than the one the "Nightingale" ode addressed. Tennyson's memory, like much of his best poetry, avoids confrontation with the cause and relishes the effect instead.

At least two of the poet's best known pieces grew from the germ of a phrase taken, like Keats's, out of its context and transplanted into Tennyson's imagination. Hallam Tennyson writes, "My father's poems were generally based on some single phrase like 'Someone had blundered': and were rolled about, so to speak, in his head, before he wrote them down." The illustrative example, of course, is "The Charge of the Light Brigade," which the poet composed after reading in the *Times* for November 13, 1854, the phrase "some hideous blunder," and then submitting the phrase to his reverberant alchemy; "and this," records his son, "was the origin of the metre of his poem."[8] Bearing in mind the effect on Tennyson of Keats's "Charm'd magic casements," we suspect that the germinal phrase from the *Times* supplied him with more than a meter—a suspicion confirmed when we see how this unusually action-packed poem never does get back to the precipitating blunder, which remains the deed of an unspecified agent ensconced in the pluperfect: "Someone had blundered" (12). The Light Brigade horsemen are a heroic company for Tennyson in that they are doomed: accursed rather than charmed, but at all events "framed," performing the will of a power they cannot question (Adams 1979, 420). In describing the Light Brigade as "hurried to their doom by some inextricable error" and the British soldier as "not paralyzed by feeling that he is the victim of some hideous blunder," the *Times* evidently gave Tennyson an idea as well as a sound. That he remembered his debt as a metrical one betokens the indivisibility of idea from sound in the poet's mind. The compression of passivity into valor, together with the consonantal hum of doom ("victim of some hideous blunder"), presented him with what he so often needed in order to compose: an emotionally congenial subject and a tonic refrain to which he could build his battering stanzas (Conrad 1982, 530).

Occasionally, then, Tennyson might recall phrasing like Keats's verbatim but in such a way as to revise its sense; at other times he might find a rough-hewn phrase like "some hideous blunder" and roll it about in his head until he had smoothed its wording into consonance with his own internal measure (Anderson 1967, 62–63). This latter process apparently reached an extreme in the composition of the early lyric "Mariana," which begins with an epigraph attributed to Shakespeare's *Measure for Measure*: "Mariana in the moated grange." Strictly speaking, nothing in the play comes any closer to Tennyson's poetic epigraph than this prosy business from Duke Vincentio: "I will presently to St. Luke's; there at the moated grange resides this dejected Mariana" (III.i.256–258). The one common phrase, that "moated grange," is what drew Tennyson to Mariana's case. Like the other phrases just discussed, it is a past passive construction; and Tennyson based upon it his most evocative distillation of defensive victimage and fixation on the past. The power of this evocation, in turn, seems to have colored Tennyson's verbal memory. He wanted the suggestive force of a phrase, an image at most, and certainly not the manifold irrelevancies of a Shakespearean problem play. Accordingly he plucked Mariana and her grange from the Duke's declarative sentence, isolated them in a grammatical fragment, condensed Shakespeare's phrasing, and substituted "in" for "at." This revision immures Mariana yet further in a murmur of *m*'s and *n*'s that, seeming to proceed from her own name, implies a theme less Shakespearean than Romantic: the tyranny of Mariana over herself (*LH*, 433).

IN HIS CIVILIZED, often urbane authority, his unremitting estimate of the sacrifices a self-conscious life in civilization demands, and his painstaking elaboration of a verse that gives expression to both, Tennyson ranks as the most Virgilian of English poets. A principal difference between Augustus's imperial laureate and Victoria's is that, where Virgil faced Homer as his inevitable precursor, Tennyson faced the British Romantics. His work replaces Virgil's rationalized Olympian pantheon with a modern mythology of the divided psyche, under the regime of the irresistible power he spoke by but could not name. Typically Tennyson represents dilemmas rather of the Romantic imperial self than of political and cultural empire, although at midcareer he evinces a strongly Virgilian interest in the congruence between political and psychological spheres; and as a Victorian Romantic he tends to lyric and idyllic forms instead of the didactic and epic forms refined by Virgil. But when all is said, across two millennia the resemblance between these poets' sensibilities remains striking, particularly in their attitudes toward form itself.

In intellectual, cultural, and above all poetic terms, Romanticism was the destiny dealt Tennyson by his historical situation; and he received it in much the way he received whatever fell to him. With restive, brooding resignation he sought less to escape his confinement than to explore the prison, or furnish the shelter, in which he found himself. At once traditional and original, Tennyson perfected a consummate art through the themes, the images, and the very words that the Romantics left him. If there was something fundamentally anti-Romantic about such classic perfectionism, it did not suffice to finish off the movement: reports of the death of Romanticism are as greatly exaggerated now as ever; and in any case literary history could imagine nothing more Romantic than the demise of a cultural movement at the hands of a single genius. But while Romanticism outlasted Tennyson, it no less conspicuously passed through his hands. He substantially refinished its interior design (in both intentional and formal senses), and gave it a newly respectable, even imposing, civic facade. The strenuously sleek body of work that Tennyson produced, and the magnitude of the public image that he among living British poets uniquely attained, have made major differences in both the creative practice and the historical understanding of Romanticism in nineteenth- and twentieth-century literature. Here again the parallel with Virgil proves instructive. Virgil, by submitting his muse to Homer's while consolidating an intricately stable versecraft, became the principal transmitter of epic vision to an auditory so vastly exceeding Homer's that the Virgilian became the classic archetype—not just for later poets but for later readers even of Homer. In an admittedly foreshortened perspective not of two thousand years but two hundred, Tennyson's classic status within the modern tradition justifies a similar claim: if Romanticism was his doom, his work was also the doom of Romanticism.

Tennyson's late tribute "To Virgil" (1882) records the salute of one kindred spirit to another, sharing in melancholy sympathy a vision of the tears in things, Virgil's *lacrimae rerum*: "Thou that seëst Universal Nature moved by Universal Mind; / Thou majestic in thy sadness at the doubtful doom of human kind" (11–12). Yet Tennyson reserves highest praise for the Virgil who was "lord of language," who captured "All the charm of all the Muses often flowering in a lonely word" (3, 6).[9] Not a single word; a *lonely* word: it is as if the *lacrimae rerum* were also *lacrimae verborum*, as if the magical "charm" and the pathetic "charm" of poetic lan-

guage were one and the same. For Tennyson, Virgil expresses not
the pathos of a sublime isolation but the sublimity of a pathos that
words can approximate and poetic rhythm can convey. Across
vast space and time, the sympathetic vibration of an "ocean-roll
of rhythm" joins the poet of a perished empire with the spokesman
of "the Northern Island sundered once from all the human race"
(16, 18)—sundered once, but since redeemed into ethnocentric
community with the European culture, sown by Virgil, that had
led in England to the development of the accentual-syllabic prosody Tennyson was among the last great poets to cultivate. There
is an abyss in things, replenished first by tears and then by the
patient art of the poet as human communicant. Virgil's majesty,
like Tennyson's, inheres in the measure of his "sadness," and not
vice versa: tears well up from the depth of a despair that is divine,
and the poet's definitively human touch makes language of a cry,
shapes an idyll from idle tears. Thus it is as a touchstone of the
human, as the formalist artist who respects the ends of things and
"is known by his self-limitation," that Tennyson salutes Virgil
last: "Wielder of the stateliest measure ever moulded by the lips
of man" (20).

The focus on Virgil's "measure," as on the "metre" Tennyson
once heard in a newspaper article, shows again how poetic rhythm
serves him as a way of capturing and transmitting the deep music
of the doubtful doom of humankind: "Aeonian music measuring
out / The steps of Time—the shocks of Chance— / The blows of
Death." The point of this capture, the "use in measured language"
(*In Memoriam*, v.6), is for Tennyson mimetic and expressive at
once. His rhythms imitate the experience of unconditioned being,
which he feels as a pulse at the core of consciousness and intuits
at its outer limits as a patterned, governing force; they also express
the deep if restricted range of moods that arise in owning the fatal
necessity which that experience discloses. He hopes to achieve by
incantation—"The charm of all the Muses"—what cannot be
achieved, he is sure, by the reasoning mind (Bruns 1978, 248).
Tennyson aims not to master his doom but to take its measure,
in a music not intelligible, but perceptible and communicable, the
ground of a shared fate else unknown.

2

Keen Discoveries: Originality and Tradition in the Juvenilia and *Poems, Chiefly Lyrical*

THE FIRMAMENT OF English literature boasts more than its share of prodigious poets, but not many among them were also, like Tennyson, child prodigies in their art. In approaching the poet's extraordinary juvenilia, therefore, we might consider in general terms how rare a thing a poetry prodigy is. The immensely gifted child, in any field of endeavor, presents a spectacle that takes us aback: the imagination kindles at precocity, but the understanding also reckons up its hidden costs. If this holds true of the junior athlete (fading young, we fear) and of the math or music or chess whiz (humanly stunted, we suspect), the prospect of a prodigy in language—the subtlest and least manageable of human inventions—may be more disturbing still. In fiction and in drama such a prodigy has never appeared, finally not even to the better judgment of the Brontë enthusiast; and we may predict that none ever will. These arts require a breadth of social knowledge and a depth of psychological insight that only maturity and experience can give. But with poetry it is otherwise: an entire branch of the poet's art, some would say its root and trunk, involves mastery of certain abstract structures and paradigms that are, in matters of verbal form, analogous to the patterns of muscular coordination, logical consequence, or spatial configuration that challenge prodigies in other fields. In these strictly formal disciplines of language a youth of exceptional literary and lexical acquisition may, under the right circumstances, become amazingly adept amazingly early. Still, the same limitations that forbid precocity in the writing of a novel or a tragedy will constrain the poetry such a youth can produce. It will exhibit the highest possible ratio of form to content; it will take its subject matter from obviously literary sources and conventional topics; and its original energy will be devoted to an intensity of verbal design that may be boldly experimental but must also, if it is to obtain recognition at all, be prodigiously correct.

Alfred Tennyson was such a youth, and not only his juvenilia but all his works show it. Perhaps only Pope and Swinburne may stand beside Tennyson as marvelous boys who grew up in their art and matured a stunning early facility as versifiers into the fruits of canonical achievement. Temperamentally these three figures could hardly be more diverse, yet both their earliest writings and their adult masterpieces fit the profile of the precocious poet. The Tory Pope famously aspired to the wise child's sublimity, correctness; the radical Swinburne jealously guarded his prerogatives as an enfant terrible who required a steady supply of icons to smash; the progressive conservative Tennyson belonged somewhere in between, though with age he listed increasingly to the right. But the works of all three exhibit in high relief the characteristics of the poetry prodigy: markedly literary inspiration, with a lifelong interest in imitation and translation; extraordinary concern with the prevalent conventions governing literary (and other) behavior; devotion to verbal sound as the perfection and often the motive of poetic sense. All three won acclaim at a very impressionable age for doing consummately well the things that a poetry prodigy can do, and it is hard to banish altogether from a reading of their works some curiosity about the effects of early stunting upon their eventual development.

Unlike the diminutive and celibate Pope, and unlike the habitual dependent he took to calling "little Swinburne," Tennyson the man grew to a grandly handsome maturity and, after admittedly long delay, assumed social majority with the roles of husband and father. As a poet, however, he grew so fast in certain formal skills that by adolescence, when we meet him, there seemed no important growing left for him to do in the arts of versification.[1] The occurrence of this early growth spurt is necessarily an inference, since Tennyson left behind him not one scrap of technically sloppy juvenilia. But among its results we may note that Tennyson never *had* to grow thereafter at all. That he did so, extending his formal as well as thematic range in experiment after experiment, is one of the perennially prodigious facts about his career. And yet the habit of perfection, so early formed, took its toll. Tennyson astounds us more often by the executive excellence with which he does what he aims to do than by his conception of the aim itself. He is the least translatable of poets, as anyone will find who attempts to arouse the interest of a stranger to his works, by any means short of quotation.

This effect has many explanations, but one of them involves precocity. Like other prodigies, Tennyson received for his accomplishments in verse a warmth of approval that he came deeply to crave, and that in his case never seriously abated over the course of nearly seventy years. This approval came from within his family circle first, and most memorably from a cloudy quarter where approval was generally hard to win (Pyre 1921, 13). One of the later Trinity notebooks includes a telling reminiscence: "My father who was a sort of Poet himself thought so highly of my first epic that he prophecised I sd be the greatest Poet of the Time" (T.Nbk. 34, fol. 22). Tennyson may have destroyed the epic, but he kept a lifetime grip on the praise. As he fulfilled his father's prophecy to the letter and became indeed the greatest poet of the time, one wonders how far Tennyson's writing was governed by this rare paternal blessing, how far his thirst for a repetition of its approval—which Tennyson so consistently found from fellow students, reviewers, friends, and the public because he so consistently sought it—dictated the tonal consistency of his evolving work.

Curiosity about such questions is probably both the most natural and the most productive spirit in which to make acquaintance with Tennyson's principal unpublished juvenilia. We shall find him perfecting an art that generally gives the prodigy's skill in formal finish priority over the material on which it works, and that at its best does something more. The gifted teenager—"whelp," Benjamin Jowett called him in amazement upon reading some of these texts decades later—began a lifetime habit of discovering in his subject matter thematic equivalents for the very processes of creative detachment and technical continence that were to distinguish his subsequent publications, in both enabling and limiting ways.

Although Tennyson's earliest surviving poems ostensibly concern devils and gods, heaven and hell, and the battle of good against evil, they are remarkably amoral performances, explosions of a precocious verbal gift that may be most precocious in its cool

exploration of the sources of its peculiar power. The teenage son
of a country clergyman might be expected to find urgently apocalyptic themes in "The Rape of Proserpine," "The Coach of
Death," and "Armageddon." In the battery of adulterous prop-
ositions structuring *The Devil and the Lady*, such a young man
might be expected to find headier stimulants yet. But these poems,
which Tennyson left unpublished as "too much out of the common
for the public taste" (*Memoir*, I, 23), do not deliver quite the kind
of thrill one might expect. Their hubbub lies all on the surface:
the vitality of Tennyson's juvenilia proceeds less from the ecstatic
agonies of an adolescent's spiritual questionings or sexual fantasies
than from an almost exclusively verbal energy that, from the first,
sets this adolescent apart. Tennyson's first productions gauge not
the poet's self but the poet's relation to his medium. Beneath the
frivolous or awe-struck surface of the verse there resides, in detachment, an already accomplished craftsman who is concerned
both with the manufacture of appealing surfaces and with the very
condition of detachment, in one sense aesthetic and in another
anesthetic, that makes their manufacture possible. This detachment, once he had conceived it as culpable isolation, would become
an obsessive problem for the young poet; but the earliest Tennyson
we can read today remained refreshingly free from these worries.
He was occupying himself instead with a more fundamental poetic
problem, one whose solution would both precipitate and make
creatively affordable the luxury of all his subsequent self-criticism:
he was laying the bases of his own authority.

The basis of stylistic authority—authoritativeness to the ear—
he found in a poetic diction and cadence heavily derivative of
Milton and of later accommodations of the Miltonic pentameter
to couplet and stanzaic forms. It is hardly surprising that the juvenilia of so sound-intoxicated a poet should reverberate with
Miltonic echoes. But we might note in passing that this early
fixation on Milton marks the Tennyson of the mid-1820s as a very
junior scion of the Romantic line, half a generation behind Shelley
and Keats without knowing it. The corresponding basis of imaginative authority—the visionary aplomb behind his themes, genres, timbres of thought—Tennyson found in submitting his muse
to the measure of doom. In the rhythm of fatality he tapped a
power as imperturbable as Milton's God but even more distant in
its nameless, faceless indifference. Inevitability of event is the most

striking feature of Tennyson's earliest poetry, and it is bound up with the formal inevitability of tone and phrase that he had already taken as his poetic signature.

The Devil and the Lady: Brazen Fatality

Nothing about Tennyson's career seems stranger than that it should begin with a play, and a farcical comedy at that. At least *The Devil and the Lady* starts out as a play, though before its conclusion, which never does arrive, it finds the initial dramatic mode unserviceable or obsolete, and swerves into a quite different blank-verse narrative medium. This first original production of Tennyson's pen thus does by accident something the poet will often later do on purpose, taking a permanent detour from one genre into another that has become more fulfilling or opportune. Here the detour will interest us most, but the original generic intention matters as well. The play abounds in characters whose speeches and actions are doubly determined. First, they are stock types, prefabricated Jonsonian humors zanily adapted to their fixed stations in life. Tennyson's logic-chopping lawyer, tackle-bound seaman, wine-bibbing monk, and others all pursue their courses with just the predictable regularity that might let a youth of four-teen get on with his writing—albeit a canny youth who partially excuses his own deficiencies by having his Magus ask, "Who shall know man, or freely explicate / The many folds of character?" (I.iv.58–59). For these flat-ironed stereotypes, as for the more ambitiously imagined personae of his later monologues and idylls, the fixity of role blinkers perspective but stabilizes it, too, so as to permit within certain bounds a free yet consistent verbal ex-patiation. Each character's language bespeaks his given role, though it might be more accurate to say that his role speaks him. For the second determining agency in Tennyson's play is that of language itself as it holds character hostage and keeps action in perpetual abeyance. The play arouses expectations of an adulterous romp involving "the Lady," Amoret, and her various suitors, only to divert it permanently into a romp through the dictionary.[2]

In order to test the intentions of the professional men who call upon Amoret during her magician husband's absence, the Devil (conjured up by the Magus to play chaperone) receives the suitors' overtures behind her hood and veil. But the comic device of substituting one character for another carries less weight, in representative exchanges like the following, than does Tennyson's potentially endless substitution of one word for another, and of verbiage for action:

> *Stephanio*   Consider, prithee,
>   How shall the airy ardent kiss make way
>   Through the thick folds of that dark veil, which bars
>   All access to the fortress of thy soul.
> *Antonio*   Ay! Ay! unveil.
> *Angulo*   Disperse thy "nebulae."
> *Devil*   Ay and the *nebulones* that surround me.
> *Antonio*   Thou wert not used to such reservedness.
>   Veil versus BEAUTY is a case which will
>   Admit of many pleadings.
> *Devil*   'Troth, I dare not
>   Unveil lest ye should quarrel for my nose
>   [*Aside*] (No fear of that methinks) and make partition
>   Of all the other features of my face.
> *Angulo*   And think you that we would bisect your visage?
> *Antonio*   Will you not face us?
> *Devil*   Nay, I cannot countenance ye.
> *Antonio*   Prithee unveil! why, only double-faces
>   Do lurk beneath a veil.
> *Devil*   And said I not
>   You wished to halve my physiognomy?
>   You hint that I am double-faced and hence
>   'Tis plain you wish that half my face were off.
> *Angulo*   Equals from equals taken remain equals.
> *Devil*   Let me have no divisions on the point.
> *Angulo*   A point hath neither parts nor magnitude,
>   Thy face hath both and therefore is no point.
>
>   (III.i.56–78)

No point, indeed. This fertile game of verbal dominoes, which continues unabated for another dozen lines and more, neutralizes dramatic action as such. Neither the Devil's veil nor that of Tennyson's language is lifted; here the only potency is cant, the only consummation the mating of word with punning word. It would belie the rambunctiousness of *The Devil and the Lady* to seek too solemnly a correspondence between Tennyson's tactics here and his later tendency to diffuse erotic energies into descriptive wordscape. Still, what keeps Amoret and the suitors apart is neither moral scruple nor the machination of the Devil, but a diabolical inventiveness with words that threaten, in this unfinished play, to beget themselves interminably.

The nearest thing to a proper conclusion arrives in act III, scene ii, with the return of the Magus from the quest upon which he has embarked in act I. It is a conclusion that, I imagine, surprised Tennyson himself—surprised him into a sense of vocation that induced him to give up comic playwriting for more congenial modes. The Magus's departure and return constitute a time-honored framing device for the farcical sort of business that can develop while the cat's away, but with the tale of his quest an altogether different purpose cuts across the comedy to usurp its imaginative and verbal energies. The Magus narrates his adventures in seventy uninterrupted lines that have very little to do with the Devil, the Lady, or anything else in the plot, but a great deal to do with the future shape of Tennyson's career and with the kind of poetic texture that we have come to declare Tennysonian (Buckley 1960, 13). The blank verse attains a new, scarcely dramatic but compelling majesty of measure; the quest itself, and the natural landscape in which it takes place, convey a characteristically gratifying frustration; and the Magus, hitherto a comic *senex amans*, becomes instead a type of those old men who would be explorers in some of Tennyson's most moving later poetry.

The Magus's narrative functions to all intents as a soliloquy or fragmentary poem, and the impression that he is speaking more to himself than to the dumbstruck Devil may reflect the poet's sudden absorption in a new interest. Leaping *in medias res*, with visionary intensity and a battery of definite articles for which nothing has prepared the way, the Magus tells how a stormy trip through deep forests has led him to the seashore, whence he has sailed into a tempest peopled with mysterious shapes and voices. These manifestations he has warded off with a charmed scarf, the gift of "Mother Hecate" (116). But his magic has served him only for resistance, not for progress: three times the waves and weather have returned his "charmèd person" (120) untouched to the shore and then calmed themselves at once. Note that the sum of all his activity is precisely zero, a resumption of the status quo. Furthermore, this dramatically irrelevant quest seems as unmotivated as it is pointless. Although the Magus describes himself as "Foiled of my purpose" (135), at no time do we learn where he has pur-

posed to go or why. We can only observe that his quest is doomed
to failure and that, despite some angry blustering earlier in the
scene, he has received his doom with utter equanimity.

Like every other action in *The Devil and the Lady*, the Magus's
quest cancels itself out as action and leaves a residuum of language
instead. Or, more precisely, the quest is ruled out, by the bounding
power of fate:

> Half the powers o' the other world
> Were leagued against my journeying: but had not
> The irresistible and lawless might
> Of brazen-handed fixed Fatality
> Opposed me, I had done it.   (III.ii.68–72)

> Some unwholesome star,
> Some spells of darker Gramarie than mine,
> Ruled the dim night and would not grant me passage.
>   (III.ii.135–137)

These passages circumscribe the Magus's narrative, as the "fixed
Fatality" they name hems in his quest, and as the lesser power of
his magic envelops his scarf-wound body on its ride through the
surf. Two levels of supernatural power are at work here, the fatal
magic of the elements and the defensive magic of the scarf; although they seem to be working in opposition, the text also provides evidence of a deeper collusion between them. If we remark
that the girdling scarf, the "glassy arch" of the tempest (118), and
the dome of the heavens all describe concentric patterns around
the "charmèd person" of the Magus, and that both magics, despite
their opposition, serve the ends of static calm, the passage can
offer a very early glimpse of a dynamic alignment that is central
to much of what Tennyson went on to write. Wrapped in an
emblem of his power, the Magus is also rapt by a fate that lies
beyond his power, but that seems also to collaborate with it, to
produce a complex stalemate—the essential condition of Tennyson's early poetry and of much in the work of his maturity. The
individual exertions of the Magus disclose, and curiously correspond to, the working of a higher, not quite personal power that
contains them, in a manner that is frustrating and fulfilling at once.[3]

On several levels, then, the Magus's narrative is a tissue of
enclosures, a text that reports multiple submissions to an overarching authority. If the frustration of his purpose entails any

emotional frustration, it is evidently a frustration that pleases, rather like the emotion he has read into the seascape upon arriving at the shore:

> The mighty waste of moaning waters lay
> So goldenly in moonlight, whose clear lamp
> With its long line of vibratory lustre
> Trembled on their dun surface, that my Spirit
> Was buoyant with rejoicings.   (III.ii.78–82)

These lines derive their characteristic charm from the interplay of sound and light, as the trembling reflection joins the tidal moan in owning the sway of the moon.[4] Tennyson further complicates the synesthetic interplay by introducing kinesthesia as well, as the Magus takes the scene up into internal sensation and lets his spirit float in "buoyant" sympathy with the vibrant waters he beholds. The moaning of these submissive waters is both a delighted and a delighting sound, and Tennyson's Magus is at his happiest when his spirit's bark most resembles a cradle rocked by an inevitable force. We might say that the goal of the Magus's otherwise aimless quest is the revelation of the force that inhibits it, and that for Tennyson's purposes this revelation is the proper goal of his play—which peters out anyhow some hundred lines after the Magus concludes his narrative. Those hundred lines offer further confirmation, should we need it, of the fixative properties of job and jargon; but the quest of the Magus has already offered a vision of "fixed Fatality" itself as the source of the authentic Tennysonian melody.

The serenity that attends an ineluctably foiled purpose is manifested in the serenity of the text at this point, the first sustained passage in the collected works that beyond a doubt feels like Tennyson. The versification, especially the music of the vowels and voiced consonants, sheds on the Magus's narrative a tranquility that is at variance with the business he narrates but in harmony with the resignation in which his business concludes: "Came sounding o'er the lone Ionian" (114); "And all the moon-lit Ocean slumbered still" (131). Given Tennyson's theme of frustration, another poet would have crumpled things up more, if not torn the passion to tatters. But even this early in his career Tennyson's imagination characteristically seized upon frustration not for its explosive but for its composing power. As a worker of "magic spells" (125), the Magus resembles his poet, a potentate of language who is both exploring the limits of his craft and discovering the authority that results from an alignment of that craft with the mysterious external forces that constrain it. Although the verbal skill of the Magus cannot procure any significant advance against the "spells of darker Gramarie" that oppose him, it can insulate him admirably against the potential menace of those spells. And likewise his poetic creator: it is the binding capacity of language, whether to transfix character in a role or to transfigure it in the image of a distant fatality, that counts most, here and throughout the play to which the Magus's quest provides an apt conclusion.[5]

"Armageddon": Song of Myself

There is a miniature oral tradition that antedates Tennyson's career as a writer of verse: his son records as the poet's first fragment a line of perfect iambic pentameter uttered in early boyhood before he had learned how to read: "I hear a voice that's speaking in the wind" (*Memoir*, I, 11; II, 94). What that voice had to tell him the boy did not say—and in important respects neither did the mature poet he became—but *The Devil and the Lady* offers an early hint that its message had to do with the governance of "brazen-handed fixed Fatality" over human affairs. Tennyson's goal in that play was to put himself in touch with an indifferent power of doom, which he came to intuit at the core of every motive and at the circumference of every act. He hardly acknowledged such a goal in setting out, to be sure, but he wrote his way to it nevertheless with the Magus's quest and wisely put a halt to the play shortly thereafter. With his conviction of the inevitability of things—a conviction one would have thought incapacitating, especially to a beginning poet—in this as in his other earliest writings Tennyson made an astonishingly strong first step, by determining to join what he could not imagine beating.

Among the juvenilia both private and published, "Armageddon" represents the most ambitious and successful of Tennyson's early attempts to merge his poetry with the force of fatality. Its doomsday title suggests as much, and so does the persistent care Tennyson took with the poem. He first wrote it in 1824 or 1825, gave it thorough pruning and redirection in 1828 in the Trinity notebook, and after further revision submitted it under the title "Timbuctoo" at Cambridge, where it was published as the Chancellor's prize poem for 1829. "Armageddon" and "Timbuctoo" are significantly different poems; and much of the significance of the latter poem depends on their difference, since "Timbuctoo," as we shall see, enacts the poet's emergence from the shelter of his juvenilia into sophisticated engagement with the Romantic tradition. But in order to appreciate the decisive revisionism of "Timbuctoo," we should first assay "Armageddon" on its own phenomenally private terms. A prerequisite to sophisticated engagement with the Romantic tradition, in Tennyson and in most of his successors, seems to be the writing of naively Romantic poetry. "Armageddon" furnishes one of the finest examples of such naive poetry—highly imaginative, accomplished verse written in ignorance of its most recent and germane antecedents—that the last two centuries have witnessed.

"Armageddon" pursues the familiar Romantic theme of the poet's accession to power, a theme that Tennyson himself here confronts, head on, for the first time. The mode of the poem is visionary, though its modus operandi is to discredit mere vision in favor of a synesthetic and at best kinesthetic perception, in which deep sensation and cosmic rhythm pulse as one. Tennyson starts out smitten by an awareness of all that he lacks: the poet-prophet's traditional avowal that he cannot paint what then he was lets him pepper his text with words ending in "-able," which, along with such phrases as "mighty grasp," "subtle ken," and "mortal faculties," direct us to a crisis of power that is also a crisis of perception. The existence at Harvard of Tennyson's torn manuscript, which was until 1969 the only publishable source text for these lines (and which may still make for the best reading) fortuitously but most clearly brings out the poet's obsession with power (Ricks 1981, 79). The first eight lines, as printed in Ricks's edition from the Harvard manuscript, are headless torsos, laboratory specimens of the Burkean sublime. In the very naiveté of its concern with sensory perception "Armageddon" is the purest expression in Tennyson's oeuvre of what it is a mistake to call lightly his *sense* of doom. Since in the visionary mode what the poet says is identical with what he sees, for Tennyson to resolve his crisis of perception by integrating the fallen senses will be to resolve his crisis of poetic power as well. Thus the poem plots a movement from discrete, variously impeded experiences of sight and sound, through a successful blending of eye and ear, to a threshold state in which the poet sees and hears feelingly; finally he crosses this threshold into a condition of deep sensation that is at once private and universal.

At the outset the poem intimates the improvement of perception it seeks, by giving thanks to the power of prophecy, "Whose wondrous emanation hath poured / Bright light on what was darkest" (I. 10–11). The palpable influence of a light that can be "poured" represents the kind of power that Tennyson first discovered in the synesthetic description of the Magus's quest from *The Devil and the Lady*, and that he now aims to retrieve for his prophetic self in the course of this poem. That such light appears to have been siphoned off from Miltonic urns (as in *Paradise Lost*, III.1–8 and VII.359–365) suggests Tennyson's paradisal design, together with an almost Blakean conception of the Fall as the sundering of an original perceptual wholeness:

> Eve came down
> Upon the valleys and the sun was setting;
> Never set sun with such portentous glare
> Since he arose on that gay morn, when Earth
> First drunk the light of his prolific ray.   (I.30–34)

Evening comes down like Eve, fallen from a paradise that Tennyson again presents with imagery of a recollected liquid light.[6] Like Milton, he wants to trace a movement from paradise lost to paradise regained; but he means to trace this movement as the Romantics did, in perceptual terms. The comparison of this doomsday sunset to sunrise at the creation establishes a further point of kinship with the proud belatedness of Romantic poetry: Tennyson takes his postlapsarian stand on "the knowledge of the Latter Times" (I.13); and, if we compute by a biblical calendar, his is the latest Romantic poem of them all. As of 1825, ironically, he did not know just how belated he was, but by the time he produced "Timbuctoo" he did so under the fresh influence of Wordsworth, Coleridge, Shelley, and Keats. While he pulled the revised poem back from the apocalyptic date of "Armageddon" to the present hour, the burden of his revision was to accommodate a chastening awareness that, in interpoetic terms, the present hour was even later than he had thought.

For the time being, the simpler "Armageddon" grapples with more tractable obstacles. Once the vision is underway in part I its apparently random verse paragraphs follow a distinct logic of the senses, as they encounter various impediments to perception. Visual interference (I.35–54) is succeeded by auditory disturbance (I.55–70), leading to a short paragraph tidily twinned into three-line accounts of purged but distant light and sound:

> Nor did the glittering of white wings escape
> My notice far within the East, which caught
> Ruddy reflection from the ensanguined West;
> Nor, ever and anon, the shrill clear sound
> Of some aerial trumpet, solemnly
> Pealing throughout the Empyrean void.   (I.71–76)

Throughout this part of the poem the eye and the ear seem equally apt to catch what is near and what is far; the objects of Tennyson's perception are less important than the segmentation of his perceptual experience. Voyeur and auditor by turns, he suffers the plight of the narcissist turned against himself and therefore separated from what he loves. There is no surer token of the innocent Romanticism of this poem than the fact that its speaker's internal division will be healed at last with a self-absorption so strong as to transcend itself, in the perfection of narcissism and not, as in "Timbuctoo," its correction. Meanwhile, however, the segmentation of perception suggests that the faculties of the detached voyeur, Tennyson's habitual early persona, have now become detached from each other. When he interrupts his detailed visual description of the streams in the valley of Megiddo, it is to remark on their silence: "there awoke / No murmurs round them" (I.93–94). Even when the senses appear to mix, their mingling is only apparent; the rising moon looks

> Sickly, as though her secret eyes beheld
> Witchcraft's abominations, and the spells
> Of sorcerers, what time they summon up
> From out the stilly chambers of the earth
> Obscene, inutterable phantasies.   (I.103–107)

Tennyson's moon seems to "behold" a summoning "spell," to see an empowered voice. But the temporarily heartening synesthesia of this visible voice is doubly countered, by the "stilly" scene of the rite and by the implication that what the voice summons is in any case "inutterable"—another adjective of in-ability reinforcing Tennyson's serial confinement within noncommunicating compartments of the sensorium. From this point in part I he can hear only his own heartbeat (I.113) and must submit to the tyranny of the unassisted and insatiable eye.

It comes, then, as a genuine relief at the opening of part II no longer merely to see "the glittering of white wings" (I.71) but now to hear *and* see "A rustling of white wings!" A young seraph descends, like perceptual grace abounding to the chief of voyeurs, delivering Tennyson from his burdensome isolation and from the mutual isolation of his several senses. As the seraph tells him, "Thy sense is clogged with dull Mortality, / Thy spirit fettered with the bond of clay— / Open thine eyes and see!" (II.14–16). The seraph understands that paradise regained will involve a reclaiming of the physical, an integration of the fallen body into a spiritual vehicle. Tennyson, who has just thrown out both hands as a veil against the seraph's radiance, will now be initiated through a ritual of feeling that employs the body not as a bond of clay or impediment but as a means to heightened perception. Although the seraph has commanded him to open his eyes and see, what he most memorably goes on to "see" are his own internal sensations. The following lines speak of a "mental eye," but they represent nothing visible at all:

> I felt my soul grow godlike, and my spirit
> With supernatural excitation bound
> Within me, and my mental eye grew large
> With such a vast circumference of thought,
> That, in my vanity, I seemed to stand
> Upon the outward verge and bound alone
> Of God's omniscience.   (II.21–27)

The prudish "in my vanity" suggests that even in his Romantic adolescence Tennyson was half a Victorian after all, and the suggestion is strengthened by his later revision of "God's omniscience" into the bet-hedging "full beatitude" of "Timbuctoo" (94). Yet even "vanity" proves to be a trustworthy image of inward sensation: the term suggests with physical precision the concentric expansion, attenuation, and emptying of self often associated with the sort of mystical experience to which Tennyson had been subject since childhood (Brashear 1969, 55–56; Culler 1977, 1–13).

Immediately this new, deeply internal integration of perception— what the seraph will call "inward sense" (III.3)—heightens Tennyson's perception of outward things: "Each failing sense, / As with a momentary flash of light, / Grew thrillingly distinct and keen" (II.27–29). To see thrillingly and keenly is to behold objects in their three-dimensionality, as from the inside out. Tennyson's return to deep sensation has improved his depth perception as well, and the flat tableaux of part I yield to penetrating visions of such elemental substances as "The smallest grain that dappled the dark Earth, / The indistinctest atom in deep air" (II.29–30). The moon, merely a broad circle hatched with lines in part I, now becomes more spherical, with cities, lakes, heights, and depths of her own:

> her silver heights
> Unvisited with dew of vagrant cloud,
> And the unsounded, undescended depth
> Of her black hollows. (II.33–36)

In *The Devil and the Lady* Tennyson played on words as ends in themselves; here, however, gentle puns in "unsounded," "depth," and "hollow" suggest that the prophetic mind can hear a deep hollo while it inspects a hollow depth. As if in response to these cues, the next words of the poem turn to imagery of voice and hearing:

> Nay—the hum of men
> Or other things talking in unknown tongues,
> And notes of busy Life in distant worlds,
> Beat, like a far wave, on my anxious ear. (II.36–39)

Much as sight yielded to sound in the preceding lines, here sound becomes feeling. Tennyson's image of a "far wave" that nevertheless comes near enough to drum upon his ear diminishes at one stroke interplanetary distance, the separation of the senses from each other, and the gap between subject and object.

What remains sublimely unattended to is the relation between self and others, which will furnish matter of incessant concern to Tennyson during the 1830s. But for now, the anxiety of the ear has far less to do with "the hum of men / Or other things"— extraordinary though that enjambed syllepsis certainly is—than with the poet's eager anticipation of the cosmic merger that forms his goal in the following verse paragraph:

> I wondered with deep wonder at myself:
> My mind seemed winged with knowledge and the strength

Of holy musings and immense Ideas,
Even to Infinitude. All sense of Time
And Being and Place was swallowed up and lost
Within a victory of boundless thought.
I was a part of the Unchangeable,
A scintillation of Eternal Mind,
Remixed and burning with its parent fire.
Yea! in that hour I could have fallen down
Before my own strong soul and worshipped it.   (II.40–50)

The first line exemplifies the disarming egotism that in later years was to charm Tennyson's acquaintances in spite of themselves. It also shows how in "Armageddon" wonder at the self and wonder at the universe it beholds are one and the same, as "Time / And Being and Place," the evidences of eye and ear and self-awareness, are borne down in a tide of irresistible feeling. This passage renders not the thinking man's abstraction from experience but the feeling man's absorption in it, and Tennyson's vision is compelling precisely in its fidelity to corporeal sensation. Wings sprout from the back of the mind; a burning, timeless consciousness engorges the differentia of earlier perceptions; and the concluding image of a physical prostration clinches the conviction that the poet's oneness with the universe also involves oneness with his body. No one will deny the current of transcendentalism in Tennyson, but he would not have been ready to respond to Keats as warmly as he did if the tendency toward transcendence had not met in him a countermovement toward the body and the earth. Both poets used the body as an image for the given; and though Tennyson would prove more apt than Keats to regard it as a clog to be kicked off, here he exhibits a quite Keatsian sense of the body as welcome ground. The entire trance is an intensely physical reintroduction to the inevitably given.[7]

The poem might reasonably stop at this climactic juncture; and in a sense it does, since the end of part IV returns to the unheard yet sensed melody of fatality that Tennyson feels here. Meanwhile, between these twin climaxes of sensation he transacts with the seraph some unfinished business in the neglected area of interpersonal relations—business that, by this point, can be nothing but corporate merger. The poet's participation in "God's omniscience" and the fire of "Eternal Mind" enables him at last to look up at the seraph's face and, in a passage suitably combining sight with sound and feeling, to see there what amounts to his own image. The seraph wears "a mournful and ineffable smile, / Which but to look on for a moment filled / My eyes with irresistible sweet tears" (II.55–57). This mournful smile finds its answer in the poet's sweet tears; these tears then overflow by visionary reflex into the seraph's liquid voice, which in turn sounds much the way the poet now presumably looks, "Like a swollen river's gushings" (II.59). This mutual melting of seraph and poet furnishes an emblem of the narcissistic satisfaction attained in the preceding paragraph, and further suggests the congruence of human and supernatural realms, as apprehended by a prophetic consciousness that embraces them both. Such a congruence becomes the theme of the brief part III. There the seraph speaks of "Everlasting God" and "Everlasting Man" as equally "deathless" and prophesies "a day / Of darkness" that is rising on God and man alike. Uncertain and bombastic as these lines are, they arrive at an idea that is central to "Armageddon": All things are moving to a day of doom that no one—not even God, it appears—can alter. As elsewhere in Tennyson's juvenilia, and his later work too, events are mysteriously impelled through passive agents.

A poet who has seen himself as "a part of the Unchangeable" should be committed to expressing the doomsday vision in ways that will honor his sense of the passivity inherent in any action. In describing the seraph, Tennyson first hits upon a trick of style that will enable him to do just that throughout his career. The passage turns on a grammatical confusion between passive and active voices:

> his ambrosial lip
> Was beautifully curved, as in the pride
> And power of his mid Prophecy: his nostril
> Dilated with Expression; half upturned
> The broad beneficence of his clear brow
> Into the smoky sky; his sunlike eyes
> With tenfold glory lit; his mighty arm
> Outstretched described half-circles; small thin flashes
> Of intense lustre followed it.   (III.26–34)

Are the verbs in this passage active or passive? Has the seraph "dilated" his nostril, "upturned" his brow, and "lit" his eyes, or does the syntax imply that some other power has arranged his features for him? The first verb, "was . . . curved," is passive, and seems to govern the verbs that follow as past passive participles in apposition with "curved." But at the end of the passage "described" and "followed" are active verbs, not participles, as the distracting juxtaposition of "Outstretched described" reminds us. We are thus invited retrospectively to see "Dilated," "upturned," and "lit" as active intransitive past tenses. Yet again, the terminal verbs both denote curiously subordinate actions: in "describing" or "following" one imitates what is already there. In brief, this passage blurs the question of responsibility, the very question that an Armageddon battle is supposed to resolve. It induces intimate doubts about the relations of ethos and pathos, activity and passivity, narration and description—doubts that lie at the heart of Tennyson's poetry from *The Devil and the Lady* through "Crossing the Bar." The bulkier thematic mergers of the Eternal Mind with Tennyson's, of the seraph with the poet, and of Everlasting God with Everlasting Man are delicately resumed here in a passage that blends acting with being acted upon or acted through—a tour de force exhibiting "that which is," but begging the question why.

Part IV of "Armageddon" returns to the simpler visual mode of part I in order to purge it once and for all in favor of the mode of feeling, with a considerable reprise of Tennyson's doom music:

> There was a beating in the atmosphere,
> An indefinable pulsation
> Inaudible to outward sense, but felt
> Through the deep heart of every living thing,
> As if the great soul of the Universe
> Heaved with tumultuous throbbings on the vast
> Suspense of some grand issue.   (IV.28–34)

The beating of the solitary heart from part I finds its justification in an inevitable cosmic rhythm that includes every living thing but explains nothing. We may take leave of "Armageddon" by noting that this ontological throb is *the* Tennysonian signature; we find it at or near the end of many of his finest poems, and it also lends redeeming resonance to many poems not so fine. Always, however, it communicates the poet's need to find in the rhythmic evidence of his own heartbeat a means of sympathetic contact with a power beyond anything he could see or hear or touch.

In Tennyson's dominant mood the proper end of poetry itself, and not just the point of poetic endings, was to facilitate such contact. His poetry grew in finesse and range with his growing awareness of all that might keep this contact from taking place; but that it had very early become a habitual imaginative norm appears from the final stanza of another very early piece, "On Sublimity" (1827):

> Blest be the bard, whose willing feet rejoice
>   To tread the emerald green of Fancy's vales,
> Who hears the music of her heavenly voice,
>   And breathes the rapture of her nectared gales!
> Blest be the bard, whom golden Fancy loves,
>   He strays for ever through her blooming bowers,
> Amid the rich profusion of her groves,
>   And wreathes his forehead with her spicy flowers
> Of sunny radiance; but how blest is he
> Who feels the genuine force of high Sublimity!   (101–110)

The bard content to follow Fancy will not greatly care that his perceptions are cloven, as by turns he walks, hears, breathes, smells, and sees all that she has to offer. Such a bard just *may* be blessed, Tennyson's verbs imply, according to his lesser deserts, though he may also stand in need of Tennyson's kindly benediction. But of the blessedness of the bard who is receptive to the sublime Tennyson has no doubt: that bard *is* blessed, for it is he "Who feels the genuine force."

ONE SUMMARY CONSIDERATION arising from the study of Tennyson's juvenilia is that, while a poet's accession to authority may be breathtakingly beautiful, and while for a Romantic aspirant it had better be sublime, it is not, humanly speaking, a very pretty thing to behold. Poetic youth grows cruel in its strength, and other minds do not fare well in its struggle to be born. The quest of the Magus from *The Devil and the Lady* occurs in utter solitude, and the energies it released in Tennyson evidently took him away from the social interest, however rudimentary this may have been, that inhered in his choice of a dramatic form for his first poetic experiment. Tennyson, like his Magus, was venturing away from devils, ladies, and others into his own fastness; and "Armageddon" carried the quest further in the same direction. The split in his loyalties to human relationship and to his own withdrawn selfhood, which had produced the clean generic break between comic and visionary writing in the play, had also taught him something of the cost exacted by the fatal force of his muse: an exclusion of the contingencies of human relatedness. The exultantly naive "Armageddon" suggests that Tennyson was willing to pay that cost, in order to authorize the best poetry that was in him.

In "Armageddon" the cost of exclusion has been absorbed, and all but written off, in the overwhelming reward of a rapture so private that even "visionary" will not do it justice, if by that optical term we grant imaginative validity to anything apart from the self, anything that has not been assimilated to feeling. The conclusive "indefinable pulsation / Inaudible to outward sense, but felt / Through the deep heart of every living thing" is a universal sensation that leaves precious little room for fellow-feeling with the heart of any particular, discretely realized living thing—such as, say, another human being. In accordance with the earlier passage where Tennyson hears, with almost incredible indifference, "the hum of men / Or other things," the indefinable pulsation sunders the poet from others and leaves him instead alone with a sublime otherness. Sympathetic imagination is crowded out by a more technically musical sympathy with the deep or the beyond. If, as an art of language, poetry retains a communicative function that in turn implies a community, the common denominator of the community addressed by Tennyson's earliest poetry approaches the integer one, whether its "oneness" is conceived as the solitude of a detached voice or as the universality of sentient being in the grip of doom.

There is no more emotional compromise or mediation in this poetry than there is middle distance in the landscapes it describes; and the same reasons that bound it most closely to Tennyson's peculiar gifts also made it, as he was aware, unpublishable. His obsession with a sympathy so very primal threatened to become— for want of that transportation between near and far, self and others, on which poetry thrives—a creative dead end. That it did not may plausibly be ascribed to the poet's emergence from the simultaneously empowering and stultifying atmosphere of his black-blooded father's rectory at Somersby into fellowship with the greater world of Cambridge. To a poet as firmly introverted as Tennyson, however, a poet for whom literary experience never lost its ascendancy over the other experiences of his life, the most important challenge Cambridge had to offer was a serious exposure to English Romantic poetry.[8] In the works of Wordsworth, Coleridge, Shelley, and Keats, with their aspirations to a universality based upon the sole self but devoted to exploring avenues out of solipsistic paralysis, Tennyson could read the history of his own writing to date. And he could see that it would not suffice. In one sense, as models these poets showed him that he had not gone far enough for his own spiritual good. In another, more strictly poetic sense, the prior existence of the Romantics' poems rendered his own juvenilia obsolete, as he must have realized with the shock that reverberates through his transformation of "Armageddon" into "Timbuctoo." If at twenty Alfred Tennyson meant, as he told his brother Arthur, "to be famous" (Martin 1980, 22), then he would have to find ways of surpassing those poets, now dead or inactive, who had surpassed him in advance. Thus the Romantics not only brought Tennyson to question his initial detachment from others. Speaking his own language, they were also able to touch him where as a poet he was most vulnerable; and they became, in good measure, the others he now needed to confront.

"Timbuctoo": Blossoming Abysses

Henceforth we shall be concerned with works that Tennyson actually published. Some of them remained private possessions for much of his life (*In Memoriam*, "Tiresias"), and others he tried to confiscate after they were printed (*The Lover's Tale*, "The Hesperides"); but they all went forth at some point with their author's blessing. We might take the occasion of our transition between Tennyson's private and his public writings to emphasize the importance the categories of privacy and publicity hold in his career. There have been few poets so conspicuously successful in publication, as a business matter and as a matter of what is not quite the same thing, cultural prestige; and yet there have been few poets so preoccupied—or dismayed—by the sometimes correlative, sometimes discrepant relation between imaginative and public power. Celebrity naturally influenced Tennyson's sensitivity to this issue, but hardly initiated it: it may indeed have been most acute during the late 1820s, the period that the balance of this chapter will address, when except among his family and a handful of undergraduate admirers the poet had no name at all (Peckham 1970, 8–10). The apparent obsession of Tennyson's first printed works with exposure and protectiveness suggests that there is a publicity in the mind as well as in social fact, and that the two may be reciprocally linked. Poets do not become famous—not on anything like Tennyson's scale in their own lifetime—without imagining and meeting the conditions of their fame; self-fulfilling prophecy, while not a sufficient cause in this matter of luck and labor, surely is a necessary cause. This is one autobiographical allegory it makes sense to read into the mysterious origin of King Arthur, the public self or *turannos* who occupies the center of Tennyson's most extended poem.

In this regard Tennyson's projective imagination of his fame not only antedated but enabled the eventual fame of his imagination. But the relation between inward and outward interests that the publication of his poetry seems time after time to have forced to at least mild crisis—witness his habit of revising in proof, and the anxious circulation of "trial editions" among friends throughout his career—also worked in a counter sense. The public poet could become himself, again like King Arthur, only when socially ratified. Each fresh appearance in print was a fresh submission to the doom of the public. Its disapproval, most starkly figured in "The Lady of Shalott" but not far to seek in other works, meant the death of the public poet as such. Yet too enthusiastic a reception, however pleasant and however desired, portended something almost as disturbing about the public poet's cultural co-optation: it might mean that his crowd-pleasing imagination, having become a euphonic repository of social codes, had ceased to be his own. Tennyson's struggle with this possibility becomes fully manifest, to the reader if not to the poet, in *Maud*, the last (and in some ways least popular) of the published works this book treats. But it haunts such texts along the way as "Ulysses" and "Morte d'Arthur," and it is proleptically, negatively apprehended in the ingrown "Mariana" and "The Poet's Mind." All of which is to say that, like the great popular writers Shakespeare and Dickens, Tennyson fascinated his audience by first convincing them how fascinating he found them to be—even when his fascination took the strategic form of avoidance.

"NOTHING OF MINE after the date of 'Timbuctoo' was imitative," the poet rightly boasted (*Memoir*, I, 46; II, 386), because in "Timbuctoo" he had learned from his Romantic models how to imitate originally.[9] The poem presents a greatly altered version of the pulsating, visionary "Armageddon"; and the best way to appreciate the difference between the two poems is to take their pulses. The pulse of "Timbuctoo" is not the timeless sympathy of the individual heart with the universal soul, as in "Armageddon," but the historically conditioned give and take of myth, as made and remade in cultural transmission. Toward the end of the revised poem the seraph sums up the sensuous intimations of "Armageddon" when he says, "Few there be / So gross of heart who have not felt and known / A higher than they see" (206–208). As in "Armageddon," the seraph has helped Tennyson to transcend the visual, "to feel / My fullness," and "with ravished sense" to hear "the lordly music flowing from / The illimitable years" (210–215). But these last words suggest something new. Tennyson's wisdom of feeling now has a temporal habitation and a name—even as the seraph now names himself:

> I am the Spirit,
> The permeating life which courseth through
> All the intricate and labyrinthine veins
> Of the great vine of *Fable*.   (215–218)

The life that coursed through the poet's own literal, physical veins in "Armageddon" now permeates the metaphorical veins of fable. Tennyson has changed the focus of his poem from the energies of the body, as a fundamental pattern of individual consciousness, to the embodiment of those energies in products of the collective human imagination that creates myths, builds labyrinths, and indeed makes such metaphors as "the great vine of *Fable*." The mythmaking faculty, the mind's ability to give its intuitions concrete and public form, now receives the homage Tennyson earlier paid to the intuitive mind alone.

We can see how explicitly "Timbuctoo" repudiates "Armageddon" if we recall the repudiation of "fabled" tradition with which the earlier poem pushes off: "No fabled Muse / Could breathe into my soul such influence" as might "express / Deeds inexpressible by loftiest rhyme" (I. 20–24; see Day 1983, 65). Like most repudiations of influence and tradition, this gesture is highly traditional. The allusion in its last line to Milton's allusion to Ariosto, "Things unattempted yet in prose or rhyme" (*Paradise Lost*, I.26), affiliates "Armageddon" not just with Milton but with the tradition of eighteenth-century originalism, in which a series of Miltonides crested by Gray and Young had taken aim at the sublime by taking their stand on the inexpressible. Although something like this posture has been taken as the essence of Romanticism, in fact the Romantics' attitudes toward the literary past exhibit much more flexibility than their immediate predecessors'. It is not eighteenth-century originalism but a critically reconstructive, Romantic perspective on tradition that we find Tennyson adopting in "Timbuctoo." Having proudly fabled about himself in "Armageddon," here he bends his pride and fables about fabling instead. Contracting the visionary span and swollen girth of his earlier narcissistic apocalypse, he enters as an equal partner into a lifetime contract with that great benefactor of imagination, the sense of the cultural past, a once and future power that most enriches those who know best how to pay it deference.

Of course, this change of focus and attitude is just the kind of revision that looks designed to please a panel of university examiners who might have been unfriendly to the self-celebration of "Armageddon." Still, Tennyson's revisions in "Timbuctoo" are thorough and searching enough to warrant a belief that he was writing less to please academic judges than to clinch a maturing conviction that the sources of his poetic power were to lie in a confrontation with literary tradition—particularly with the Romantic poetry he had been reading since his arrival at Cambridge.[10] In other words, while Tennyson was writing "Timbuctoo" the truly severe judges at his elbow were Wordsworth, Coleridge, Shelley, and Keats; and in addressing himself to the vicissitudes of fable, the erosion and regeneration of the mind's faith in its own fictions, Tennyson knowingly addressed Romantic themes on the Romantics' ground. Furthermore, in acknowledging that the Romantics had been there before him, Tennyson first encountered the exacerbated dilemma of Victorian Romanticism, whereby a poet's sense of belatedness is compounded by the realization that belatedness itself may already have become a shopworn theme for modern art.

The poet of "Timbuctoo" begins with the mountain prospect

of "Armageddon"; but while visual imagery still predominates, his earlier crisis of perception has now become a crisis of belief. He looks for the fabled pillars of Hercules but finds them "Long time erased from Earth" (13). Likewise Atalantis and Eldorado are "Shadows" to which "Men clung with yearning Hope" in days gone by (20–27), as they clung to "legends quaint and old / Which whilome won the hearts of all on Earth" (16–17). The lacquered diction serves, as in Keats's comparable account of first reading Chapman's Homer, to antique a belief no longer available. Tennyson is disarmingly ready to concede the fictive character of belief: even in the heyday of faith the faithful clung to "Shadows," not substances. In its glory Atalantis was but a "Memory" (21) invested with significance by the faith of its votaries (Bryant 1799, 89–90). Tennyson analyzes this dialectic of fetishistic belief with a protracted simile:

> As when in some great City where the walls
> Shake, and the streets with ghastly faces thronged
> Do utter forth a subterranean voice,
> Among the inner columns far retired
> At midnight, in the lone Acropolis,
> Before the awful Genius of the place
> Kneels the pale Priestess in deep faith, the while
> Above her head the weak lamp dips and winks
> Unto the fearful summoning without:
> Nathless she ever clasps the marble knees,
> Bathes the cold hand with tears, and gazeth on
> Those eyes which wear no light but that wherewith
> Her phantasy informs them.   (28–40)

Half Athens, half Atalantis, this city of no special place or time—first of the poet's many civic images for what the Victorians would soon be calling an age of transition—suffers not an invasion but an insurrection from within. The priestess worships an idol that is long since stone dead ("the marble knees," "the cold hand"), as is the phase of naively receptive faith it stands for. Taking the fall from orthodoxy for granted, Tennyson concerns himself instead with a second-order lapse: the loss of demicroyance. The "ghastly faces thronged" of this cultural revolution are modeled on Milton's "dreadful Faces throng'd" from *Paradise Lost*, XII.644, because "the fearful summoning" of the "subterranean voice" of modernity threatens an expulsion from even the belated, artificial paradise that a religion in retreat has made for itself. For Tennyson the old legends drew all hearts "Toward their brightness, even as flame draws air; / But had their being in the heart of Man / As air is the life of flame" (18–20). His crisis of faith therefore stems less from unworthiness in the demystified object of belief than from atrophy of the will to believe.

This last comparison, between the believing heart and air drawn by the flame it feeds, comes from a simile in Shelley's "Hymn to Intellectual Beauty": "Thou—that to human thought art nourishment, / Like darkness to a dying flame!" (44–45). Shelley's Spirit of Beauty will reappear in "Timbuctoo" as Tennyson's Spirit of Fable, and the recollection of a Romantic precursor suggests a diagnosis of Tennyson's disorder of faith: it is a symptom of the Romantic poet's constitutional incapacity to assimilate anything but what he himself has made. An undeniable symptom of this disorder heads the poem, in the form of a mellifluously Tennysonian epigraph from "Chapman" that no scholar has yet verified: *"Deep in that lion-haunted inland lies / A mystick city, goal of high emprise."* Arthur Hallam, who met Tennyson as a friendly contestant for the 1829 Chancellor's Gold Medal at Cambridge, and who claimed to have originated the theme of Romantic faith with which both their entries approached the set topic of Timbuctoo, wrote a poem far more explicitly derivative of Romantic texts than Tennyson's; its epigraph, typically, comes straight from Wordsworth's "Yarrow Unvisited" (*WH*, 37–40; *LH*, 30, 320; Day 1983, 60). Tennyson, unlike Hallam, has confected a text to put before his poem; this minor invention of a precursor bespeaks a larger Romantic intention to have no other texts before him.[11]

The poem's opening crisis of faith is thus, in Romantic terms, the poet's creative opportunity. The ostensible lament for earlier, happier days is charged with the deferred gratification of a poet who would make the void fruitful on his own.

> Where are ye
> Thrones of the Western wave, fair Islands green?
> Where are your moonlight halls, your cedarn glooms,
> The blossoming abysses of your hills?   (40–43)

"Where are ye?" is Tennyson's version of Wordsworth's "Where is it now?" ("Intimations Ode," 57), Shelley's "Where art thou gone?" ("Hymn," 15), and Keats's "Where are the songs of

Spring?" ("To Autumn," 23).[12] Like his Romantic forebears, Tennyson asks the question in the confidence that he will grieve not, that there is a harmony in autumn, that he has his music too. The old poet's remark about the originality of "Timbuctoo," quoted at the outset of this discussion, registers the memorable experience of self-conscious innovation, within an acknowledged tradition, which he had inscribed into the poem. For what is distinctively Romantic about the confidence of "Timbuctoo" is precisely its engagement with the prior texts of the Romantics, texts that themselves engaged the poetic past with a view to proclaiming the originality of the latecomer.

"Blossoming abysses," in the lines just quoted, offers a resounding image of the paradoxical process of belief Tennyson's long first paragraph has discussed, and also of the Romantic resolve we can read behind his refusal to participate in such a process too quickly. These lines introduce a passage that looks back to a paradise of palpable, liquid light, "Filled with Divine effulgence, circumfused, / Flowing" (49–50). The paragraph manifestly corresponds to the "Armageddon" passage in which "Eve came down," with a reminder of lost paradisal perception; but the Miltonic allusion of that passage has been subsumed by a Romantic allusion, to Coleridge's "Kubla Khan" (Shaw 1976b, 55). Tennyson's "blossoming abysses" suggests the "deep Romantic chasm which slanted / Down the green hill athwart a cedarn cover" in Coleridge's poem (12–13); the allusion comes to a head with the rare form "cedarn," which Coleridge himself learned to use, Ricks points out, from its first appearance in Milton's *Comus*. "Kubla Khan" was a poem multiply indebted to Milton; and as Tennyson must have discovered with dismay, it had already done the post-Miltonic work of rendering visionary dejection—and of rendering dejection visionary—rather more successfully than had part I of "Armageddon." Finding himself preempted by an earlier poetic son of Milton, and perhaps remembering how in the chasm of "Kubla Khan" an abandoned woman wails by moonlight, Tennyson executes a fine recovery and makes of desolation an opening for voice:

> Then I raised
> My voice and cried, "Wide Afric, doth thy Sun
> Lighten, thy hills enfold a City as fair

As those which starred the night o' the elder World?
Or is the rumour of thy Timbuctoo
A dream as frail as those of ancient Time?"   (56–61)

In "Kubla Khan" Coleridge envisioned "an Abyssinian maid" singing of "Mount Abora" (39–41), with an allusion to the false paradise of *Paradise Lost*, IV.280–282: "Where *Abassin* Kings thir issue Guard, / Mount *Amara*, though this by some suppos'd / True Paradise under the *Ethiop* Line." It is worth conjecturing that Tennyson had caught this allusion, and that he was taking the Cambridge Chancellor's set topic of "Timbuctoo" as an occasion for building a visionary city in a blossoming Abyss-inia of his own.

The necessity that the young poet be his own master builder forms a new theme of the seraph's revised message. Instead of asking why Tennyson is not making ready for the battle of Armageddon, the seraph now chides him for musing on "the dreams of old," with their "passing loveliness" and "odours rapt from remote Paradise" (77–80), in lines recalling those that Wordsworth published in 1815 as a "Prospectus" to *The Recluse*:

> Paradise, and groves
> Elysian, Fortunate Fields—like those of old
> Sought in the Atlantic Main—why should they be
> A history only of departed things,
> Or a mere fiction of what never was?   (47–51)

While this passage seems one probable source for the "fair Islands green," "Elysian solitudes," and "Atalantis" that we meet in "Timbuctoo," Tennyson will never find his paradise, early or late, in the terms of Wordsworth's naturalism as a "simple produce of the common day" ("Prospectus," 55). He does, however, borrow Wordsworth's insistence that the poet wean himself from regressive dependence on the past; the visionary city Tennyson goes on to behold will be an ornate "fiction of what never was" before.

On his way to the apparition of that city, Tennyson undergoes a more darkly Wordsworthian rite of passage to poetic maturity. The poet designing to celebrate not his own feelings but the embodiment of feeling in the currency of fable must first weather the fall from sensation into abstraction that Wordsworth commemorated in "Tintern Abbey" and the "Intimations" ode. Lines 113–

157 of "Timbuctoo" replace the apotheosis of sensation we have met in "Armageddon," II.40–50. Yet Tennyson's newly Wordsworthian project of exchanging feelings for ideas, percepts for concepts, turns out disastrously; and he knows it. The new passage he wrote in lines 113–130 is far from satisfactorily clear, but it does establish clearly Tennyson's dissatisfaction with the kind of experience it describes. Visionary sensations of the "Armageddon" type now emit *thoughts*, which tend, unlike the harmonic impulses of sense, to collide and strike each other out. The bizarre Lake District simile Tennyson finds for this process—bizarre in itself, and certainly atypical of his oceanic repertoire—shows that the conversion of feelings into ideas leaves him feeling more than a little stricken:

> as when in some large lake
> From pressure of descendant crags, which lapse
> Disjointed, crumbling from their parent slope
> At slender interval, the level calm
> Is ridged with restless and increasing spheres
> Which break upon each other.   (119–124)

Thought thus begins as a ruin and ends in a confusion of "interpenetrated arc" (129) that baffles the mental eye. In the "Armageddon" passage that this one replaces, the mind given over to sensation can mix and burn "with its parent fire," but here the mind's thoughts, "descendants" of sensation, suffer a primal divorce and crumble "from their parent slope."[13]

With this lapse from perceptual integrity into reflective chaos come doubts about the mind as a reflector, as Tennyson wonders whether "I entwine / The indecision of my present mind / With its past clearness" (135–137). This patently Wordsworthian gambit underscores Tennyson's conscious failure to realize the Wordsworthian mode of creative recollection. A part of Tennyson wanted to share in the melioristic faith that informed Wordsworth's transition from childlike sensation to the philosophical mind—the belief that fired the authentic if programmatic optimism of his contemporary Browning and that was to constitute a tenet of the Victorian orthodoxy for which Tennyson would soon be expected to speak. But his spirit could never lend itself wholly to this progressive belief, least of all when asked to arise from sensation to discursive thought. On the contrary, when Tennyson was most himself he imagined that movement not as an ascent but as a lapse, a betrayal of primal experience and of his genuine gift; and "Timbuctoo" shows that he knew it quite early, before Hallam declared it to the world in a review of the 1830 *Poems* that was to become a classic of Victorian criticism.

In that essay Hallam made the now famous distinction between the Wordsworthian poet of "reflection" and the Tennysonian poet of "sensation." *In Memoriam* repeatedly praises Hallam for being a penetrating reader, and if he was as faithful a critic as he was a friend, he may well have derived his categories of reflection and sensation from an attentive reading of what Tennyson had written by 1830. "Timbuctoo" furnishes the most obvious instance of the distinction of thought from feeling, but a divide between reflective and sensuous poetry fissures all the juvenilia, to the consistent advantage of the latter. For example, while Tennyson ranks among the greatest Romantic exponents of the pathetic fallacy, a predominantly sensuous device for rendering the play between mind and nature (Miles 1942), he is awfully clumsy when he comes to the related projective device of personification, which he evidently admired in Collins and others. The hypostasis of an emotion or ideal into a formal emblem was a process he could not clearly feel. For this reason—and also because his imagination of personal interaction remained peculiarly abstract—Tennyson rarely attempted allegorical personification with any success in fusing its intellectual and sensuous components.

Tennyson was never at home with the abstractions of philosophy (Peltason 1984b); and "Timbuctoo" reaches its nadir with his blunt confession of inability to ride the torrent of experience and yet "muse midway," like a self-consoling Wordsworth or mediating Kubla Khan, "with philosophic calm" (143). Apparently the seraphic Spirit of Fable, a more sly master than his seraphic predecessor from "Armageddon," is ready to let his pupil work through a false start and learn for himself that the proper source of his power as a fabling poet lies in the improvement of sensual enjoyment:

> I play about his heart a thousand ways,
> Visit his eyes with visions, and his ears
> With harmonies of wind and wave and wood,

—Of winds which tell of waters, and of waters
Betraying the close kisses of the wind.   (201–205)

As this cordial intercommunion of the senses should suggest, the
pulsing music of "Armageddon" is about to burst into the revised
poem, though with a difference. The embodiment of feeling in
fable calls for translation of some kind; in "Timbuctoo," however,
the proper medium of translation is not reflective thought but the
poetic image.[14]

Liberation from reflective thought into imaginative sensation
brings its own reward with the disclosure of Timbuctoo, which
is—like Tennyson's later Bagdat, Palace of Art, and Camelot—
the verbal capital of a state of pure image:

Then first within the South methought I saw
A wilderness of spires, and chrystal pile
Of rampart upon rampart, dome on dome,
Illimitable range of battlement
On battlement, and the Imperial height
Of Canopy o'ercanopied.   (158–163)

In "Armageddon" sound mediated between the outwardness of
sight and the inwardness of feeling, but with this vision Tennyson
so arrogates all sound to himself that the only mediating music
we hear is in the verse. Balancing architectural terms on each other
and, more subtly, reshaping their elements of sound ("spires"
comes back transformed in "chrystal pile," as does "Illimitable"
in "battlement"), Tennyson has rebounded from the "wild unrest" (127) of fallen reflection into the aspiring "wilderness of
spires" that build themselves, like living things with their own
principle of organization. The passage recalls the self-begetting
exuberance of language that we found in *The Devil and the Lady*,
but Tennyson has now tamed his verbal energies to the service of
an imaginative power that is more than merely verbal.

Paden (1942, 70) has shown how this Timbuctoo is a city of
the sun that recalls Miltonic visions of paradise. It recalls as well
Tennyson's own earlier "blossoming abysses," paradises once lost
but now regained at the zenith of vision: "wheeling Suns, or Stars,
or semblances / Of either, showering circular abyss / Of radiance" (168–170). In the tradition of metaphysical reflection since
Plato, the distinction between the sun and its "semblance" forms
a crucial trope for the making of fundamental discriminations be-

tween reality and appearance. Tennyson respects that distinction at some of the most poignant moments of his career; but, at the height of the Romantic tradition into which "Timbuctoo" marks Tennyson's initiation, poesy and not the sun must be what Keats had called "A drainless shower / Of light" ("Sleep and Poetry," 235–236). At this height the distinction between what is and what seems simply does not matter, not to an imagination that figures its creative faith with the oxymoron "abyss / Of radiance, " and that figures the conversion of doubt into faith with the return of the "ghastly faces" from line 29, there thronged against belief, but now redeemed as "multitudes of multitudes" (179) who minister around a fiery central throne. Tennyson can now assume the part of his earlier "pale Priestess"—the part of "pale-mouth'd Prophet dreaming" that Keats played before him in the "Ode to Psyche"— because now he ministers to an idol of his own making and not just to some prevenient "Genius of the place" (33). The vision fades as Tennyson staggers and falls beneath its weight; and his fall repays comparison with the climax of "Armageddon," which read: "I could have fallen down / Before my own strong soul and worshipped it." The difference between revering one's own strong soul and being overpowered by a visionary projection from that soul, the difference between worshiping Self and worshiping the goddess Psyche, corresponds to the difference between feeling and fable that Tennyson highlights with his revision of "Armageddon" into "Timbuctoo." In the former text, the visionary numen of the self arose to combat an ominous onslaught of ambiguous signifiers (Ryals 1964, 28); the latter text inverts this procedure, rejecting numinous self-absorption in order to reclaim the omen as a mode of signification within a tradition of secular creativity—religion with a Romantic difference (Dodsworth 1969, 25; Fichter 1973, 404; Starzyk 1978, 31).

This difference forms the topic of the seraph's long final speech. The ministry of Fable is to teach the poet, and through the poet humankind, "to attain / By shadowing forth the Unattainable" (192–193). As Browning's Paracelsus or Tennyson's own King Arthur might read these lines, "attain" would be an intransitive verb, and the vision of "the Unattainable" would serve as an incentive to present work. But these lines also bear a transitive construction that implies a more properly fabulous doctrine: to shadow forth the unattainable is somehow to attain it after all, on the shadowy ground of vision, as Tennyson has attained it in building his Timbuctoo. The seraph explores a related paradox later in announcing, "Lo! I have given *thee* / To understand my presence, and to feel / My fullness" (209–211). To be singled out to "understand" a "presence" is to do what Tennyson left undone in "Armageddon": it is to penetrate the ideal of presence as indeed a myth, albeit a fulfilling one once myth is understood as the representation or cultural rehearsal of what, without representation in some sensuous form, would remain the merely and abstractly "Unattainable." The condition toward which the Spirit of Fable directs Tennyson, then, is both empty and full—an abyss of radiance.

To a poet so conditioned, the seraph's prophetic lamentation over the approach of "keen *Discovery*" (240) may come as the friendliest gesture of all. Readers of intellectual-historical bent have seized on this passage as if it contained the entire point of "Timbuctoo"; in a sense it does, but in order to grasp the point in its subtlety we have to connect it with the complex Romantic argument that has come first. Foreseeing that the Enlightenment spirit of scientific inquest will drain away the splendor of Timbuctoo, his "latest Throne" (236)—something that had already occurred in 1828, when a French expedition reached Timbuctoo and found it a shambles—the seraph leaves the poet alone and darkling, but poised above the distinctively poetic potential that this clearing operation holds forth. Though much is taken from the spirit by scientific and intellectual advance, much abides; according to the logic of elegy that motivates most of Tennyson's best writing, whatever the cutting edge of "keen *Discovery*" may pare away from fable has never really been fable's to begin with (Sherry 1979, 215–216).[15]

Tennyson accordingly ends his disingenuous seraph's lament in an intertextual affirmation of solidarity with the most aggressively elegiac voice in the English poetic tradition. With the seraph's farewell to a proleptically dwindled Timbuctoo, "How changed from this fair City!" (245), Tennyson reaches all the way back to the first words of that archetypal Romantic poet, Milton's Satan:

> If thou beest hee; But O how fall'n! how chang'd
> From him, who in the happy Realms of Light
> Cloth'd with transcendent brightness didst outshine
> Myriads though bright.   (*Paradise Lost*, I.84–87)

The poet of "Timbuctoo" stands with Satan in the abyss he would replenish with his own light. It is a fitting close to a poem that has been, like the inland of its ghostly "Chapman," "lion-haunted" by Romantic poets it deeply respects but refuses to lionize. We might observe in closing how changed is this layered allusiveness from the Miltonic mannerism that makes "Armageddon" so comparatively innocent a text. The change is, of course, that Tennyson has come to "understand" the "presence" of the Romantics. The return to Milton at this stage is in effect an act of generational violence urging Tennyson's claim to be the Romantics' peer in imagining the city that is never built at all, and therefore built forever. Byron's Satanic hero Manfred insisted that "The Tree of Knowledge is not that of Life" (I.i.12)—and neither is the vine of Fable, quite, for Tennyson. But he grows into his own, exceptionally tradition-bred species of Romanticism with an answering realization that the vine of Fable bears what life we have.

Poems by Two Brothers (1827): Moods of Doom

To place "Timbuctoo" against "Armageddon" is to measure the strength of Tennyson's emergent Romanticism, as the poet locates his metier in representative mythmaking and his abode in a darkened present that awaits his light. We may also place "Timbuctoo" against Tennyson's contributions to the *Poems by Two Brothers* he had published with Charles Tennyson two years previously in 1827. Despite an impressive range of formal experimentation, the merest review of their titles will suggest how uniform are the mood and matter of these often dreary pieces. The preponderant topics are death, ruin, and doom, the typical situations devastation and abandonment, and the prevailing emotions regret, remorse, and a victimized exhaustion. These features all point up Tennyson's habitual preference for a belated or postfactual perspective, from which it appears that everything decisive has already taken place. (A minor strain in the 1827 volume, the epigrammatic note heard in "On a Dead Enemy" and "A Contrast," illuminates in a different and more heartening way Tennyson's affair with the conclusive.) Clearly these features manifest the sense of inevitability that informs the more interesting juvenilia the poet left unpublished, and they remind us that a pervasive sense of doom in the poet's mind was in itself no guarantee that he would produce a good poem. They also offer a reminder to the student of poetic influence: although it would be convenient to say that Tennyson's dramatized sense of doom is but a sign of his awareness of poetic belatedness, and although he may indeed have done his most enduring work when he managed to make belatedness in the poem and in the poet coincide, in fact the sense of doom came first.

Paden (1942) and Carr (1950) have ably analyzed under the rubric "the mask of age" what I am calling Tennyson's postfactual stance and sense of doom, and theirs is the account of Tennyson most likely to assist a reader of the 1827 poems. To summarize very briefly Paden's argument as elaborated by Carr: the desires and anxieties of the young poet reappear as the memories and regrets of his usually aged persona. The poet thus escapes confrontation either with the objects of his desire or with impediments to its satisfaction; instead he writes poems that accept the frustration of desire as something irrevocably ordained. He experiences enormous difficulty in imagining action of any kind; and he affirms himself only passively, usually by presiding over the return of his frustrated desire in particularly lush forms of imagery and diction. To this suggestive thesis I draw an ethical corollary. The process Paden and Carr have analyzed might be regarded as an evasion of guilt, an elaborate ruse for protecting not just the poet but anybody else from blame, and thus for insulating the poet against any imperative besides that of acceptance. When Nadir Shah invades Hindustan nothing is to be done about it; Antony and Mithridates proffer their suicide notes without accusing anybody of anything; other speakers deliberately abstain from striking "The Exile's Harp" or wielding "The Old Sword." The voices in these poems are hurt and sorrowful, but never indignant. Other poems that do rise from lamentation to accusation—"The Druid's Prophecies," "Lamentation of the Peruvians," the biblically inspired prophetic pieces—fight doom only with more doom. By invoking the distant vengeance of fortune or time (in "Babylon" even the voice of God sounds like that of the zeitgeist), their speakers assert a prophetic continuum of past and future, in which the historical events that have laid them low and the avenging exaltation that is to come appear uniformly ineluctable. No note arises of anything like righteous protest or culpable villainy; and in this the poems of 1827, and many of the best poems of subsequent volumes too, manifest an abiding kinship with the calm and amoral performances with which Tennyson's career began (Francis 1976, 118–119).

As an illustration of the 1827 "mask of age," consider "I Wander in Darkness and Sorrow." Comprising six stanzas with a slightly varied refrain, the poem is spoken by a solitary who complains of the death of his friends and regrets the days that are no more. A typically fixated composition, this lyric rings its changes on the imagery of an autumnal storm that signifies at once the bleakness of the speaker's circumstances, the violence of his emotions, and the march of the natural process that has brought him to this sorry pass.

> I heed not the blasts that sweep o'er me,
>   I blame not the tempests of night;
> They are not the foes who have banished
>   The visions of youthful delight:
> I hail the wild sound of their raving,
>   Their merciless presence I greet;
> Though the roar of the wind be around me,
>   The leaves of the year at my feet.   (17–24)

"I heed not"; "I blame not." Not much gets heeded in this poem beyond the storms without and within, and nothing whatever gets blamed. The first quatrain hints that the speaker does have "foes" other than blast and tempest, but this is the first and last we hear of them. The next two lines refer to "their" raving and presence, and for a moment we might take it that "they" are those shadowy foes from the past. It soon becomes clear, however, that there is no foe within reach. Instead of grappling with his putative adversaries, the speaker has turned to presences of nature that are both "merciless" and blameless—inimical yet unpunishable—and joins them not in battle but in sympathetic "raving."

If this frail lyric has a plot, it hinges on the speaker's "greeting" of natural flux; for from this point the two-line stanzaic refrains are not declarative or subjunctive in mood, but imperative: "Let the roar of the wind be around me, / The leaves of the year at my feet!" (31–32). In default of any responsible opponent, the speaker enlists his forces with those of tempest and time. The final stanza explicitly acknowledges that his compass of action has been reduced to a performative speech act that can do no more than summon the inevitable. "Like the voice of the owl" (42), he declares,

> So I cry to the storm, whose dark wing
>   Scatters on me the wild-driving sleet—
> *"Let the roar of the wind be around me,*
>   *The fall of the leaves at my feet!"*   (45–48)

The exchange of description for hollow command, of the indicative "It is" for the hortatory imperative "Let it be!" provides an especially bald version of Tennyson's early and pervasive strategy of disguising impotence as empowerment. This speaker's desperate ambition to will the inevitable into being leaves him captive both to his circumstances and to his rhetoric. His "So" is analogical, not logical; the wing of the owl becomes the "dark wing" of the storm with whose "roaring" voice the speaker's blends. Furthermore, the drag of natural decay joins forces with the pull of the refrain; and as so often happens in Tennyson's stanzas, the poetic refrain marks the speaker's refraining from any action other than a speech that justifies inaction. Here the goal of utterance lies in that affiliation with the unquestionable, the mot juste, toward which Tennyson's juvenilia gravitate. Caught in an exile in which the self is the only available antagonist, the most memorable speakers of the 1827 poems assert themselves through self-suppression.

"MIDNIGHT," THE MOST beautifully disturbing lyric from the 1827 volume, seems an exception to this rule. A nearly speakerless still life, this poem confirms Carr's insight that "the more complete is the damming-up of desire, in the moods and situations of these poems, the more certain to rise is a Keatsian lushness of imagery and diction" (51). As happens whenever critical anatomy verges on pathology, we need to beware discounting as mere symptoms the very beauties of imagery and diction for which early Tennyson is to be admired. For among the beauties of "Midnight" is an awareness that its kind of beauty gets produced only on certain conditions, and that the fertility of its eye depends on the occlusion of its "I."

> 'Tis midnight, o'er the dim mere's lonely bosom,
>   Dark, dusky, windy midnight: swift are driven
> The swelling vapours onward: every blossom
>   Bathes its bright petals in the tears of heaven.   (1–4)

By poising his poem at midnight, the horological fulcrum and calendrical threshold, Tennyson prepares us for a poetic balancing act that questions everyday distinctions between creation and perception, activity and passivity, and also narration and description. Little occurs in this poem, but a great deal takes place; and the magic of its busy stasis arises, as usual with Tennyson, from its verbs, which promise action only to cancel themselves out, in a grand vision of nature's dance to the music of fatality. The opening quatrain moves from the perfunctory " 'Tis" to more characteristic enactments of the dialectical or reflexive processes underlying Tennyson's vision of being. The vapors, for instance, "are driven" willy-nilly by some unnamed power but are also "swelling" in their own vigor. With this tension between active and passive voices Tennyson introduces a motif he inventively varies throughout, from the "lengthened sheet of swimming light" (7) through the "gurgling eddies" that "slowly creep, / Blackened by foliage" (15–16) to "the startled doe" that "Leaps from her leafy lair" (34–35). The interplay of active and passive verbals suggests that the generative principle of this text is something like a domino theory of ecological impingement: details enter the poem in response to some prior force, and go on to influence something else in turn.

At the same time, Tennyson's inlaid art respects the particularity of its details by relying on active verbs that are either intransitive or reflexive in force. The broad lake "Lies" (8); the rocks "Rise," and the willows inversely "Hang" (13–14); the wave "Sounds" (18), and before very long the forests "Resound" (33). Each thing "goes itself," to borrow Hopkins's phrase, and while there are no precisely reflexive verbs in "Midnight," the waterfalls do "Salute each other" (29), and the blossom in line 4 that bathes its bright petals is only the first of a series of items doing something to themselves: "the heath-fowl lifts his head" (20), "All nature wears her dun dead covering" (22), and at the close "the swelling river / Winds his broad stream majestic, deep, and slow" (35–36). In their cumulative effect these verbal constructions transform everything's apparently independent action into an act of submission before what it makes poetic if not philosophical sense to call the law of its being.

Moan, quiver, and swell as it may, Tennyson's nature keeps its bounds. What keeps it there? If midnight is the witching hour, where is the power that has dissolved such supernatural witchery into a natural landscape? Tennyson provides a partial answer in the shaping power of "fancy" that the opening of the poem introduces and then quickly withdraws:

> Imperfect, half-seen objects meet the sight,
>   The other half our fancy must portray;
> A wan, dull, lengthened sheet of swimming light
>   Lies the broad lake: the moon conceals her ray,
> Sketched faintly by a pale and lurid gleam
>   Shot through the glimmering clouds: the lovely planet
> Is shrouded in obscurity; the scream
>   Of owl is silenced.   (5–12)

The first two lines, with their canny admission that there is a poet on the scene, a Romantic poet well aware of the reciprocal influence of perception and creation, keep the poem from anonymity and the illusion of objectivity (Peltason 1983b, 339–340). That the poet speaks of *our* fancy reminds us that he is reading a landscape as actively as we are reading a text. This activity of fancy, expressed with the two most transitive verbs in the entire poem ("meet," "must portray"), thus stands revealed in advance as the agency binding Tennysonian nature. In keeping with this principle, the poet's manuscript revisions from T.Nbk. 14 tend to privilege the perceived impressions of objects over their inherent qualities: "voiceless" in line 3 becomes "windy," for instance, and "blue" in line 4 "bright." The rest of the passage just quoted emphasizes the viewer's responsibility for the view, as "Sketched" resumes the painterly metaphor of "portray" to introduce the poem's longest uninterrupted sequence of passive constructions.

"Midnight" thus knowingly incorporates the demystification of its own pathetic fallacies. But the comfort of such knowledge also constitutes a burden, the growing pressure of which was to distill the diffusive emotions of Tennyson's 1827 poems into the concentrated art of *Poems, Chiefly Lyrical* three years later. If fancy bears responsibility for its vision of nature's melancholy, if the "tears of heaven" result from astigmatism in the eye of the beholder, the bondage of nature must be a projection of a like bondage in the poet. The poet, then, is the midnight wizard binding nature in his spell; but this acknowledgment only internalizes the problem of bondage and does not solve it. Although the comparative self-effacement of "Midnight" distinguishes it from the more melodramatic pieces of 1827, its shadowy speaker too wanders in darkness and sorrow, through a landscape that can but mirror his captive isolation.

"Mariana": Flower in the Crusted Plot

The Spirit of Fable in "Timbuctoo" bears a message about fictiveness that in effect takes his seraphic self out of commission and sets the poet up on his own; in accordance with this message, Tennyson recognizes the doom suffusing the landscape of "Midnight" as a product of the poetic fancy that portrays it. The images of "Midnight" are the minutest tendrils of "the great vine of *Fable*" from "Timbuctoo," and when these two poems are considered together they display complementary aspects of Tennyson's Romantic situation. The imagination that recognizes in itself the means of order and value will enjoy visions but will also suffer nightmares. And it will do so without obligation or alibi: its new independence from external causes leaves the Romantic experience, whether of bliss or of pain, singularly exposed.

It is Tennyson's special success in "Mariana," from the 1830 *Poems, Chiefly Lyrical,* to have written a poem accommodating both aspects of his imagination, a poem so simultaneously adequate to Romantic exultation and Romantic dejection that we cannot tell the two conditions apart. Much as "Timbuctoo" incorporated "Armageddon" as a way of correcting it, "Mariana" incorporates a poem capturing the essence of the volume of 1827. I refer to the very minor lyric droned by Mariana herself from the isolation of her moated grange. From the first stanza to the last Mariana harps on one string, with tiny variations, until finally she sounds a particularly intense note that manifests an intention latent throughout:

> She only said, "My life is dreary,
>   He cometh not," she said;
> She said, "I am aweary, aweary,
>   I would that I were dead!"   (9–12)

> Then, said she, "I am very dreary,
>   He will not come," she said;
> She wept, "I am aweary, aweary,
>   O God, that I were dead!"   (81–84)

As in "I Wander in Darkness and Sorrow," a stanzaic speech act derives conclusive vigor from the speaker's willing sacrifice of any satisfaction that might arrive from outside. Mariana's previously unforthcoming lover now *will* not come, she says, and her new claim on the future asks to be read with the same prophetic resonance that closed the 1827 poem. What Mariana means, we may agree with Harold Bloom, is "Let him not come!"; and at the last we realize that this is what she has meant all along (Bloom 1971, 148; 1976, 151). Her refrain reins her in from a contact she scarcely desires, and girdles her more tightly within a moated grange we cannot imagine her ever wanting to leave.

"She only said..." In context and by dint of repetition Mariana's little doom song, like most good poetic refrains, accrues considerable semantic richness: it is *all* she has to say about her solitary plight, it is only what she *says*, and it is only what *she* says. In sum, and in counterpoint to the descriptive stanzas it ends, the refrain underscores a disparity between what takes place within Mariana's grange and what gets mentioned there. Tennyson's third-person narrative leaves us guessing how much more the lady knows than she speaks of; this strategic indeterminacy suggests a Romantic commerce of perception and creation, whereby the deeply satisfying correspondence between Mariana and her surroundings arises from a projection of self onto environment that is so habitual with her as to be unconscious. To imagine a first-person version of "Mariana" is to appreciate the delicacy of this tacit projection. Tennyson will turn to more outspoken, first-person effects with Mariana's spiritual sisters Fatima and Oenone in 1832, as a means of turning his back on the fragile yet formidable power that "Mariana" houses. But Mariana's inarticulateness, important though it may be to her perversely happy housekeeping, keeps her a minor poet and sets off Tennyson's notable advance upon the work of 1827: his ability to write, in the lines preceding each of Mariana's refrains, a poetry of sensation that raises the unconscious projection of feeling to the articulate power of fable.

I argued in the previous chapter that Tennyson took his cue for the superb evocations of the introductory stanza from the participle in his more or less Shakespearean epigraph, "Mariana in the moated grange." He had learned much about the past participle from his reading of Keats and from his own apprentice efforts in "Midnight" and "Timbuctoo." In these opening lines he put that

inert part of speech to work again, in rendering a state of process
without apparent agency or issue:

> With blackest moss the flower-plots
>   Were thickly crusted, one and all:
> The rusted nails fell from the knots
>   That held the pear to the gable-wall.
> The broken sheds looked sad and strange:
>   Unlifted was the clinking latch;
>   Weeded and worn the ancient thatch
> Upon the lonely moated grange.   (1–8)

The entire scene wears Paden's mask of age, which might here be
also called, in Coleridgean or Shelleyan phrase, the film of familiarity. Romantic aesthetics pledged the poet to strip off that
film, but Tennyson here lays on so thickly crusted a coat of age
as to shock us into a refreshed, uncanny perception of the familiar.
The participles enforce the sense that something has been done to
each rusted, broken, worn object in the stanza, even to the "Un-
lifted" latch that clinks for some indiscernible cause. Implying yet
missing the agency behind these changed yet unchanging phenomena, the temporality of Mariana's grange attains a curious
suspension; and the objects that fill its space take on a life of their
own. They become, indeed, the intentional objects of a masked
or overcrusted intention (Sherry 1979, 213); and if we recall
the Kantian association of the "aesthetic" with a purposefulness
without purpose, we should find quite appropriate the literary-
historical linkage between this poem and the Aesthetic movement
in Victorian England. Temporally enveloped by the anonymous
determination of the past and by a future that fails to emerge, the
scenery in "Mariana" exhibits a cumulative permanence that
makes each scenic feature preternaturally vivid. As in "Midnight,"
intransitive verb forms ("fell," "clinking") outline the discrete
spatial particularity of objects, a particularity that Tennyson's syntactically governed lineation further supports, as lines 1–2, 3–4,
and 7–8 form enjambed pairs surrounding the singleton lines 5
and 6.

These discrete details, for all their individual sharpness, conspire
in a common atmosphere. One principle that holds them together,
I have just suggested, is their shared suspension between an absconded cause and an indefinitely awaited interruption. The nearest

thing to an event, the falling of the rusted nails in line 3, seems in context less a completed occurrence than an interminable slide, the verb "fell" less a simple past tense than an imperfect one. A second and more striking principle of descriptive cohesion is the synchronizing force of Tennyson's virtuoso prosody (Peckham 1970, 22–23). Ezra Pound once wrote of Browning, as distinguished from the mass of "Victorian half-wits," that "He does not gum up the sound" (1934, 191); it seems likely that Pound had Tennyson in mind as the prime exemplar of a gummy Victorianism. If so, Pound's comment stands among the most reductive prosodic critiques one poet has ever offered on another; and yet, in its metaphorical terms, Pound's observation is acute. Plainly in "Mariana," but also as a general rule of Tennyson's scenic art, discretely observed details are held together by the power of sound—"fused" was Arthur Hallam's word in reviewing the 1830 poems (*WH*, 191)—here by the "gum" or mucilage of a rare vocalic and consonantal music.

The circular enclosure of the moat and the prevalent hothouse atmosphere might have called for "flower-pots" in line 1; but from the first this hothouse is also out of doors, as the consonantally buttressed *l*'s of "blackest," "flower," and "thickly" invade the expected word to produce "flower-plots."[16] Stressed open vowels are plotted with great uniformity in lines 1–2 and 3–4; even the short *i* in "thickly" could hardly be more hedged with consonants that muffle and broaden its pronunciation (Ostriker 1967, 276). In the spirit of T. S. Eliot's appreciative experiment (1950, 288) of substituting "sang" for "sung" in line 63, if we try replacing "thickly" with, say, "dimly," we hear at once the difference in timbre between the vowels. Likewise, Tennyson's 1862 substitution of "pear" for the original "peach," which he explained on scenic grounds, had less to do with the look of the fruit trees than with the sound of their English names. And while syntax and lineation separate the images in lines 5–8, a subtler force is bringing them together: the consonantal similarity of the rhyming monosyllables "strange," "latch," "thatch," and "grange" grows out of the sound of "broken sheds" that is clinched in "ancient."

These adhesive correspondences represent in language the work of an invisible agency unifying the otherwise disparate attributes of Mariana's phenomenal world (and Tennyson's "phonemenal" one). I have already suggested that this agency is Mariana's consciousness, whether she knows it or not, as she bathes everything around her in the luster of frustration. What is missing from a world in which "He cometh not" is, to put it crudely, *action*; what is present, in abundant recompense, is *passion*, with its original sense of rapturous suffering and with the characteristic sense Tennyson was to give it in his phrase "the Passion of the Past" from "The Ancient Sage" (1885), 219–222: "As if the late and early were but one" (Kissane 1970, 52; Culler 1977, 7). Action lives by deeds in time, but passion lives in a perpetual present by signs, traces, or, in the erotic term that is surely pertinent to Mariana, fetishes. We cannot single out any one object in her environs as Mariana's particular fetish, because she has fetishized everything in the poem. "Old faces glimmered through the doors, / Old footsteps trod the upper floors, / Old voices called her from without" (66–68). Everything speaks to Mariana of something that is gone—we may call it "He," if we like, but we specify it as Shakespeare's Angelo at our peril—and everything speaks with a "wooing" voice that "confounds her sense" (75–77) more deliciously than could any active presence. Passion is her element; and her environment, we might say, is a past passive participle that participates, by synecdoche, in a whole that cannot hope to vie in her affections with its thoroughly fulfilling representation.

"Mariana" is an "atmospheric" poem if ever there was one, and it is because Mariana herself is so vacant that the atmosphere she exudes is so full. She prefers atmosphere to substance; or, to put it another way, the text does, by privileging effects over entities at every opportunity. Thus, when "The broken sheds looked sad and strange," we learn more about their impact than about their actual properties; or when we are told of Mariana that "In sleep she seemed to walk forlorn" (30), we know what her nights are like, even though the language fails to establish whether she is subject to nightmares of restless solitude or is a melancholy-looking somnambulist. At the level of syntax, too, Mariana's preference of atmosphere to substance appears through Tennyson's unrelenting practice of giving descriptive phrases priority over grammatical subjects and terminally positioned main verbs:

> About a stone-cast from the wall
>   A sluice with blackened waters slept,
> And o'er it many, round and small,
>   The clustered marish-mosses crept.   (37–40)

> And ever when the moon was low,
>   And the shrill winds were up and away,
> In the white curtain, to and fro,
>   She saw the gusty shadow sway.   (49–52)

In syntactic duration the effect of the description precedes the described cause, with the same logic we find in Mariana's preposterous affections.

As everything around her bears the traces of absence, so Mariana's time is utterly homogeneous, fixated "Without hope of change" (29) in the timelessness of passion. Whatever happens seems to happen at the wrong time: the cock crows "an hour ere light" (27); Mariana draws back "her casement-curtain" in a parody of revelation revealing nothing, too late for "the flitting of the bats" and too late—or is it too early?—for a glimpse of "the sweet heaven" (15–20). But there is no right time for any of these events either, because her passion has bereft time of meaning. "All day within the dreamy house" (61), it is all one with Mariana: "Her tears fell with the dews at even," but at the same time (and it *is* the same time by the arrested clock of passion) "Her tears fell ere the dews were dried" (13–14). The recurrence of Mariana's refrain, the reappearance of the poplar, and numerous other repetitions suggest the experience of déjà vu, but the poem's real mode is the *toujours vu* of meaningless succession, night following day following night, "the slow clock ticking" (74) but with nothing to measure.

In accordance with the extreme equivalences drawn by Mariana's fantasy consciousness, Tennyson's language begins to behave fantastically. At line 32 morning wakes "About the lonely moated grange," and just a refrain later "About a stone-cast from the wall / A sluice with blackened waters slept." In standard English the word "about" may be used to approximate either location or mensuration, but to use it both ways in identical places in abutting poetic lines, in conjunction with clashing imagery of waking and sleeping, induces vertigo. The "ancient thatch" of the initial stanza lies "Upon the lonely moated grange," yet at the beginning of the third stanza Mariana wakes "Upon the middle of the night" (25), as if in Mariana's prolonged trance space and time were interchangeable. Returning to that extraordinary first stanza, we find another such distemper, or dislocation: "The rusted nails fell from the knots / That held the pear to the gable-wall." It is no easier to tell whether the knots are hempen or wooden than it is to be certain that those nail-less knots are not still holding up the pear by sheer force of habit. The mystery of this image, one of several images of affixing in the poem, is the mystery of Mariana's passionate fixation. Mariana's fix—both her dilemma and her addictive mode of living with it by dwelling on it—resembles that of Tennyson's Romanticism and reflects its ambivalence; for while her situation is so bad that she has made it feel good, the poem furnishes ample grounds for alarm at her, and our, acquiescence in good feelings purchased at such a cost. "In sleep she seemed to walk forlorn," yet even as late as the penultimate stanza the poem can call her home "dreamy" (61), with the sort of lazy approval that adjective has colloquially assumed among us. The creator of her habitat, Mariana has made her bed and must sleep in it, though whether with love or loathing we cannot say.

We can say, however, that Tennyson recognized the achieved ambivalence of "Mariana," and thought sufficiently highly of his achievement to challenge the great master of Romantic ambivalence, Keats, on his own ground in the concluding stanza:

> The sparrow's chirrup on the roof,
>   The slow clock ticking, and the sound
> Which to the wooing wind aloof
>   The poplar made, did all confound
> Her sense; but most she loathed the hour
>   When the thick-moted sunbeam lay
>   Athwart the chambers, and the day
> Was sloping toward his western bower.   (73–80)

John Hollander observes that this stanza is "a travesty of the end of Keats's 'To Autumn,' where light dissolves in darkness and unseen sound" (1975, 683; Bloom 1976, 152). We may observe further that the stanza attempts a point-for-point reversal of Keats's whole poem, recanting several of the leading images in Keats by rehearsing them backward. The stanza begins where "To Autumn" ends, with a "sparrow's chirrup" recalling the "twitter" (33) of Keats's swallows. Reading down in Tennyson and up in Keats, we encounter the sound of the wooing or "light" wind in poplar trees or "river-sallows" (28–29), then the sight of a sun that is "sloping" in Tennyson and in Keats is "soft-dying" and, at the start of the poem, "maturing" (2, 25).

Tennyson's imagery, like that of Keats, implies erotic consummation: "his western bower" might be the goal of Keats's masculine sun, who is "Close bosom-friend" of the ripe season. If we surmise that this hinted consummation is precisely what Mariana most loathes in the sight of the sunbeam, so loathes that it prompts her decisive "He will not come," then we may go on to see what Tennyson's reversal of Keats's poem has omitted: the fertile fruition of the harvest itself. In "To Autumn" Keats blessed the beneficence of a natural process whose ripeness is all, but for the self-fulfilling purposes of Keatsian nature Tennyson substitutes the pointless ticking of a clock. The only fruit in Mariana's world is that "pear," fixed in time and space without reference to blossom or seed, and emblem of the universal arrest that Mariana's passion decrees. Her secret hope to live "without hope of change" (29)—that is, without fear of intrusion—also motivates her will to cheat death by overleaping natural generation and decline altogether. "O God, that I were dead!" (84): she will seize death by the forelock, if that is what it takes in order to rid her consciousness of any power not her own (Lourie 1979, 15–16).

The revision of Keats in this passage holds significance not only for "Mariana" but for Tennyson's entire career. Nothing he ever read moved Tennyson more deeply than Keats's renditions of inevitable process in "To Autumn, " *Hyperion*, and elsewhere. Surprisingly, in conversation Tennyson often denigrated Keats's poetic style while unswervingly praising his genius; on the evidence of the juvenilia, what he admired once he came to read Keats in the late 1820s was an inner ear for the music of fatality Tennyson had been hearing all along. But in this very sense of proximity lies the cause of Tennyson's decisive, sometimes savage revisions of Keats. What Tennyson never could accept was Keats's acceptance of natural process, whether manifested as the frank embrace of sexuality or ultimately as the benevolent welcoming of death. Tennyson's lordly music and deep pulsations joined him not to nature or any mortal presence natural or human, but to a power felt from behind the veil. Although Tennyson, unlike his precursor, lived long enough to secure a comparatively happy Victorian marriage at the comparatively advanced age of forty-one, he never outlived his fear of the fecundity of nature, "from the growths of the tropical forest to the capacity of man to multiply, the torrent of babies" *Memoir*, I, 314). And his assertions about the hope of

immortality, though extraordinary, are for him quite characteristic: "You cannot love a Father who strangled you" (Dyson and
Tennyson 1969, 79); "If it be not true, then no God but a mocking
fiend created us and I'd shake my fist in his almighty face" (Tennyson 1949, 486). Such assertions would also be characteristic of
Mariana, who, to borrow another Tennysonian phrase, has an-
nihilated within herself the "two dreams of Space and Time"
(*Memoir*, I, 171) and has passed into a state of heightened sensation
that is anything but natural.

"Recollections of the Arabian Nights": Withholding Time

A criticism that proceeds on the assumption that good poetry
embodies conflicts and works through resistances, as the best Victorian poetry assuredly does, will have trouble accounting for the
excellence of "Recollections of the Arabian Nights." Insofar as
this poem resists almost nothing in the dreamlike experiences it
describes, or in the Romantic texts it acknowledges, it resists interpretation. To be sure, Tennyson achieves its childlike simplicities
with a preliminary gesture sweeping adult concerns from the field
of vision:

> When the breeze of a joyful dawn blew free
> In the silken sail of infancy,
> The tide of time flowed back with me,
>   The forward-flowing tide of time.   (1–4)

We shall see how adult concerns return to bring the poem to its
close, but the effortlessness with which Tennyson brackets them
here is, for once, not deceptive (Peltason 1983b, 336–337). Both
in the gaiety of its subject and in the felicity of its craft, this is
among the few really happy poems the melancholy Tennyson ever
wrote.

The poet travels back through the tide of time to the Bagdat of
Haroun Alraschid, allegedly from the *Arabian Nights* and Savary's
Letters on Egypt (*PT*, 205), but more importantly from that haunt
of Tennyson's early muse where daytime boundaries thin out into
a charmed space. As in the more troubled "Midnight" and "Mariana," perceptual details retain their edges but also bespeak an
organizing intelligence responsible for their arrangement. That
intelligence is Tennyson's, of course; but again he has chosen to

install a delegate within the text. As the refrain of every stanza reminds us, the dramatized power behind these scenes is not an anxiously fanciful poet or a perversely engranged Mariana but "good Haroun Alraschid." The adjective "good" forms an inseparable part of Haroun's providential identity; coming to the poem from a consideration of the mooted but still active ethical issues "Mariana" raises, we see how questions about Haroun's ethical goodness are repeatedly neutralized in advance by the morally noncommittal adjective "goodly." Morally upright the good Haroun may be, but this poem yields up moral questions in hedonistic celebration of his bounty. Within Tennyson's career, then, its moral neutrality marks "Recollections" as both a nostalgic return and a valediction, against the tide of time, to the holiday mode of his juvenilia.

At the plumb line of each refrain, "Good Haroun Alraschid" occupies a still point toward which each stanza gravitates, and with reference to which the boyish quester assumes what slender identity he possesses. An epiphany of the caliph furnishes the poem with its goal, and also furnishes the poet with his motive: "True Mussulman was I and sworn, / For it was in the golden prime / Of good Haroun Alraschid" (9–11). Prepositions and conjunctions have as much importance in this poem of place and relationship as in "Mariana": here the causal "for" and genitive "of," both heavily recurrent in subsequent stanzas, designate Haroun's logical and economic sponsorship of the poet's journey and all it discloses. Furthermore, Tennyson extensively exploits intransitive and passive verb forms, with effects comparable to those we have found in earlier texts. Again, the difference in "Recollections," and a source of its relaxed joy, is that here for once we and the speaker know the hidden master by his name as well as his works.

The poem is a dream vision, and the fluidities of dream lubricate its formal features. Tennyson's curious eleven-line stanza, for instance, varies its rhyme scheme throughout, with the exception of a single repetition in stanzas 4 and 9—as if to show that even the pattern of fresh stanzaic invention is an obligation that can be thrown off at whim. As it happens, it is in the two formally identical stanzas that the visionary trance ascends to a higher power: in the first the poet enters "another night in night" (37), and in the second he sinks "Entrancèd," "as in sleep" (95–97). But one of the wonderful things about this poem is the way its speaker is perpetually being drawn into something or other, as one inner sanctum yields to another, as it were more inner, sanctum, so that the distinction between sleep and waking, like most of its distinctions, really makes little difference (Sterling 1842, 116). Thus it does not greatly matter that from time to time the poem glides from past to present: we understand that Bagdat is a Timbuctoo or Camelot, always there to be regained in imagination.

Bagdat bears another mark of Tennyson's paradisal places in its openness to synesthesia:

> Still onward; and the clear canal
> Is rounded to as clear a lake.
> From the green rivage many a fall
> Of diamond rillets musical,
> Through little crystal arches low
> Down from the central fountain's flow
> Fallen silver-chiming, seemed to shake
> The sparkling flints beneath the prow.   (45–52)

This artifice of eternity mimics the flow of divided waters through Milton's Eden (*Paradise Lost*, IV.223–263) and also suitably miniaturizes the enjambed flow of the Miltonic pentameter. There is, further, the flow of sense into sense; for the waters fall in "diamond rillets musical" that appeal to both eye and ear, and it is their synesthetically silver chime that seems to shake the visually sparkling waters on the clear surface of the lake. It is as if in Haroun's pleasure dome the senses are temporarily divided, as in Milton's and Spenser's paradises, for the sheer pleasure of reunion. Whereas our readings of "Armageddon" and "Timbuctoo" can suggest reasons why synesthetic pleasures might be particularly significant for Tennyson, this poem's predominant effect of light movement through intricately miniaturized space shows that the perceptual redemption and literary affiliation so arduously sought in those earlier poems have here become faits accomplis.

Tennyson is not a poet widely regarded as funny, but among the pleasures of this text are the gently fanciful jokes it offers to share:

> Dark-blue the deep sphere overhead,
> Distinct with vivid stars inlaid,
> Grew darker from that under-flame:
> So, leaping lightly from the boat,

With silver anchor left afloat,
In marvel whence that glory came
Upon me, as in sleep I sank
In cool soft turf upon the bank,
   Entrancèd with that place and time,
  So worthy of the golden prime
    Of good Haroun Alraschid.   (89–99)

The "silver anchor" has aroused objections, but the fact that Tennyson leaves this prop *afloat* suggests that he is having rather more fun with his mechanical ballet than some readers want to tolerate (Paden 1942, 131). As the floating anchor suggests the traveler's freedom from commonplace worries, so the absurd "So" of the fourth line cuts him loose from the moorings of logic and purpose. He momentarily appears to be in quest of the source of "that glory," the "sudden splendour" of the preceding stanza (81); and though he will find it two stanzas later in the shining "Pavilion of the Caliphat" (114), in the meantime his quest is quite forgotten for the more immediate pleasures of trance. The charm of this poem is that such forgetting does not matter—a point Tennyson reinforces with the subtlest joke in the stanza, the deceptive syntax of the last five lines. By the time the truant quester sinks in sleep at line 95, the participle "leaping" from line 92 seems to have been forgotten, left floating like his anchor and dangling like his broken purpose. But it is we who forget; I, at least, find myself mistaking the syntax at every fresh reading. Tennyson's syntax is, as always, correct. In fact the quester sinks on the bank *as if* in sleep; figuratively but not quite literally "Entrancèd." (The draft in T.Nbk. 18 makes this explicit, but forfeits the joke: "My feet, as in a vision sank.") Of course the difference between waking and sleeping, between literal and figurative meaning, is scarcely at issue in this poem; so we forgive ourselves for our forgetting even as we forgive the quester for his. The entire passage is a triumph of visionary wit that turns syntax against itself to serve the paratactic structures of dream.

THE INTENSE DREAMINESS of Tennyson's early Romanticism yields neither to nightmare nor to wish fulfillment, but poises noncommittally between the two. In "Mariana" this ambivalence wears its fiercest aspect; but, in a vision as wondering and expansive as "Recollections," ambivalence seeks out modes not of ten-

sion but of equivalence. Hence the permeability of Bagdat's formal, temporal, and syntactic barriers. The central stanza establishes
that ordinary conceptual barriers are down, too, in the most stunning tissue of equivalences in the poem:

> Far off, and where the lemon grove
> In closest coverture upsprung,
> The living airs of middle night
> Died round the bulbul as he sung;
> Not he: but something which possessed
> The darkness of the world, delight,
> Life, anguish, death, immortal love,
> Ceasing not, mingled, unrepressed,
>   Apart from place, withholding time,
>   But flattering the golden prime
>   Of good Haroun Alraschid.   (67–77)

The first two lines vibrate with verbal contradictions—"Far off"
yet "closest," "coverture" yet "upsprung"—which anticipate the
more sweeping mixture of contraries later in the stanza. Blending
life with death, and delight with anguish, is a hallmark of the
Tennysonian sublime, most notably at heights of vision from *In
Memoriam*. Here, as often in that later text, the mysteries of Tennysonian merger are compounded with mysteries of syntax. The
pivotal position of "mingled" between the active "Ceasing" and
the passive "unrepressed" leaves it unclear whether "mingled" is
a passive participle or an active intransitive verb, and thus whether
"delight, / Life, anguish, death, immortal love" have been mingled by the "something" of line 71 or mingle on their own.

    Moreover, the catalogue of these commingling abstractions is
itself ambiguous. Are they to be taken in apposition with "The
darkness of the world" as expressions of breathing human passion,
or in apposition with the "something" that possesses and transcends that darkness, as if the intensity of passion were its own
salvation? I find no evidence that these striking ambiguities have
bothered other readers; the reason must be that they serve to
reinforce the stanza's (and poem's) essential message that all things
flow to all. But there are more and less sophisticated ways of
conveying such an easeful Romantic gospel, and Tennyson's way
here is more crafted than it first looks. For while "anguish" and
"delight," "death" and "Life," balance each other, the one item
in the catalogue without a balancing contrary is "immortal love":

a condition in which the distinctions between activity and passivity, possessor and possessed, no longer matter. We are rightly wary of a poet who assaults us with unearned assertions about life, death, and a fistful of other abstractions. But Tennyson's syntax evinces a control that commands respect, as verbals gain ascendancy over nouns to enact in stanzaic time what the hypostatized phrase "immortal love" (here as in the opening line of *In Memoriam*) can in itself only weakly signify.

If I seem to be anticipating the reader's resistance to Tennyson's poem at this point, it is because Tennyson invites it with some outstanding resistance of his own. The bulbul is a Persian nightingale, and the curiously English landscaping of the Bagdat it inhabits should remind us that, some ten years before Tennyson wrote his "Recollections," John Keats heard in an English garden the song of a nightingale that also seemed an "immortal Bird," one "not born for death" ("Ode to a Nightingale," 61). Tennyson's abrupt "Not he" is the only forceful negation in a poem otherwise extraordinarily smooth, and it marks a revision of Keats like the one we have traced at the close of "Mariana." Keats calls his bird "immortal" in a hyperbole that the remainder of his ode belies: the final stanza of Keats's ode returns the nightingale to the status of a natural bird that must, in accordance with the plot of nature, be "buried deep / In the next valley-glades" (77–78), thus intimating the natural poet's destiny to "become a sod" (60). Tennyson's "Not he," when first we read it, looks like a repetition of Keats's "Thou wast not born for death," a sudden repudiation of mortality's seductiveness: the living airs of midnight may have swooned away for a song, but its singer knew better. As the difficult next clause unfolds, however, the arresting "Not he" changes its syntactic reference: the poet takes the song out of the bulbul's mouth and ascribes it to an altogether un-Keatsian transcendent power.[17] Working thus through a false start, Tennyson's syntactically hinged allusion to the "Nightingale" ode recants that naturalist text's return to the local and temporal, by springing upward from the Keatsian hyperbole and seeing the nightingale as the mouthpiece of a force beyond the world, "Apart from place, withholding time." The strange images of partition and withholding, along with the reiterated negatives in "Ceasing not" and "unrepressed," register Tennyson's defensive abstention from the path Keats pursued. No, he says in effect to Keatsian mortalism, the deathless consciousness with which I am in touch does not cease and need not be repressed; in fact it needs to remain "unrepressed" for the sake of my survival and the survival of my poem, which would fall to the ground if you came in.

Tennyson's Romantic hyperbole threatens to shut down a poem that is supposed to be recollecting the *Arabian Nights*. Having arrived at a spot beyond place and time, he has to get back somehow to Haroun Alraschid's golden prime; and he does so only through the interposition of "But"—a disjunction that should have no place in a poem so committed to the indiscriminately additive mode of "And." The poem contains only two instances of "but," both of them in this stanza (71, 76), and the second sews up the textual seam opened by the first. The power that commands "The darkness of the world" cannot quite be identical with the power wielded by good Haroun Alraschid, and Tennyson's "flattering" is a diplomatic mediator between the two powers he here serves. Ricks suggests that the word means "making beautiful" (*PT*, 208), but Tennyson's late-stanza descent from the sublime to the beautiful also neatly implies the sort of courtly compliment ("Good man") that a higher power might graciously pay to an inferior.

Thus patronizing the patron of his Bagdat, Tennyson flatters his poem into seven more stanzas of undiminished beauty. But the double disjunction of "but" has betrayed his awareness of the logical disparity between two different powers: the worldly power of Haroun Alraschid as manifested throughout the text, and the vaguer, greater power from beyond that erupts to sing through the bulbul at the center of all Haroun has made (Peltason 1983b, 339–341). This difference figures larger Tennysonian quarrels between activity and passivity, between poetic making and mystical being, between the poet's impulse toward narrative and his attraction to the stasis of the picturesque. These oppositions remain elusive during the greater part of the poem, since its overall strategy commends the juvenile perspective of a persona blissfully indifferent to logical oppositions. Nevertheless, Tennyson has let them emerge at the poem's midpoint, where his "buts" demarcate a distinctively adult way of knowing; and also at its start, where the distinction between forward and backward tides of time corresponds to the distinction between the adult poet and his boyish persona.

These issues raised at the beginning and middle of the poem

reappear at its end, and bearing them in mind can help us to see that end as more than an arbitrary imposition of upper-case letters. The last two stanzas plot the difference between grown-up poet and boyish persona on the axis of sexual desire. In the first we meet "the Persian girl alone," "Amorous," with "many a dark delicious curl / Flowing beneath her rose-hued zone" (134–140). As adult readers we have been waiting for this seductive portrait since the second stanza, where the boy's vision has penetrated "the costly doors flung open wide, / Gold glittering through lamplight dim, / And broidered sofas on each side" (17–19), there to find no lady adorning those suggestive sofas, but only traces of good Haroun Alraschid. Having passed through similar "doors, / Flung inward over spangled floors" a couple of stanzas back (115–116), the boy now verges at last on what, if he were a few crucial years older, would presumably be the erotic goal of his quest. But he does nothing more than gaze "trancedly" (133) on what remains for him an object: the Persian girl is only a pinup, implicitly labeled by the owner of whose manly golden prime she is "Well worthy" (142).

Here is a ticklish situation, potentially even a ribald jest at the expense of a boy's incapacity to make performance measure up to desire.[18] But to bring off such a jest, Tennyson would have had to render his erotic interest in this amorous and most literary Persian girl with much more conviction. Tennyson fails to make us believe in his puerile desire, I think, because he does not believe in it either. His boyish self loves less the Persian girl than her master, with a desire that comes to fulfillment in the last stanza:

> Six columns, three on either side,
> Pure silver, underpropt a rich
> Throne of the massive ore, from which
> Down-drooped, in many a floating fold,
> Engarlanded and diapered
> With inwrought flowers, a cloth of gold.
> Thereon, his deep eye laughter-stirred
> With merriment of kingly pride,
>   Sole star of all that place and time,
>   I saw him—in his golden prime,
>   THE GOOD HAROUN ALRASCHID.   (144–154)

The voyeuristic quest of the boy's dream vision reaches its goal when he beholds an object of desire that is also a mirror of his satisfied self. A merrily narcissistic eros greets its own image, whose "deep eye laughter-stirred" greets him in return. Contemporary American students stirred to laughter by the "diapered" cloths surrounding Haroun's throne need to learn that the word refers to nothing more than a floral textile pattern, but the spectacularly swaddled figure of Tennyson's infantile caliph makes the error understandable. "The silken sail of infancy" that bears the boy to Bagdat, and the draperies of Haroun Alraschid's cradling throne, are cut from the same cloth: the "kingly pride" and self-delighting solitude of primary narcissism.[19]

"Infancy," as its etymology says, is a condition prior to speech; and the speechless hedonism shared here by Haroun and the boy remind us by contrast that the pleasure dome they inhabit is decreed by language—the language of the adult poet, and before him of Scheherezade, whose fictions in the *Arabian Nights* had served to postpone the pains of a decidedly adult world. One of the most endearing records Arthur Hallam left behind was of his love for "Recollections of the Arabian Nights," his special favorite among *Poems, Chiefly Lyrical*. Noting the sexual dimensions of the poem (the tales of the *Arabian Nights*, he says, "used to make our mouth water for sherbet, since luckily we were too young to think much about Zobeide"), Hallam concluded his appreciation by writing, "And yet there is a latent knowledge, which heightens the pleasure, that to our change from really childish thought we owe the capacities by which we enjoy the recollection" (*WH*, 192–193). Hallam saw that his friend had written a poem of primary narcissism owing its appeal to its suspicion ("latent knowledge") that primary narcissism, like other golden primes, may be itself a myth of pleasure that borrows its gold from the reserves of contemplative adulthood.

"Recollections of the Arabian Nights" is thus more than an imaginative indulgence in regressive wish fulfillment, if only because Tennyson knows so much about the adult character of the wishes his poem fulfills (Peltason 1983b, 341). The elision of mature sexual encounter in stanzas 2 and 13, an evasion of what we call the facts of life, is also an evasion of the fact of death. If the poet can regress to boyhood in such a way as to sidestep sexual generation, then no hungry generations may tread him down. To see that the colossal baby of the final stanza is not born for death is to see how that stanza and the central stanza on the bulbul offer alternate routes to the same goal—or alternate detours around the common human goal of death. We may read an announcement of Tennyson's purpose in the opening lines of the poem, if we consider their allusion to Asia's song from *Prometheus Unbound*:

> We have passed Age's icy caves,
> And Manhood's dark and tossing waves,
> And Youth's smooth ocean, smiling to betray:
>   Beyond the glassy gulphs we flee
>   Of shadow-peopled Infancy,
> Through Death, and Birth, to a diviner day.   (II.vi.98–103)

In later life Tennyson remarked of Asia's song that it "seemed to go up, and burst" (*Memoir*, II, 500); his revision of Shelley here implies a comparable judgment. Tennyson's quester, like Asia, is fleeing backward through time in the enchanted boat of his own soul. But whereas Asia's is a love song celebrating the transforming power of fulfilled sexual mutuality, Tennyson's is an Asia Minor song of himself, which adopts Shelley's erotic mythology and challenges it with a myth of primary narcissism. His mirror confrontation between boy and caliph implies the question Panthea puts to Asia earlier in Shelley's play: "What canst thou see / But thine own fairest shadow imaged there?" (II.i.112–113). Tennyson may be the first of many Victorian revisionists to revise Shelley by slowing him down: Tennyson aims to flee not *beyond* but *into* the glassy, self-reflecting gulfs of infancy and, at least in his "Recollections," to stay there. Deleting, as it were, the last line of the Shelley passage, he stops short before the encounter with "Death," for fear that no birth or diviner day lies beyond it. Tennyson's thirst for immortality was no less strong than Shelley's, but—like most subsequent readers of Shelley, and indeed like a part of Shelley himself—he could not share the Romantic confidence that sexual love would conquer death. On the contrary: sexual love more often seemed to Tennyson likely to invite it, to go up and burst into nothing.

Defense of Poetry, Poetry of Defense

Different as the two poems are in tone, "Recollections of the Arabian Nights" resembles "Mariana" in its rejection of sex and death, its fixation on the past, and its play between the experiences of a dramatized figure and a semidetached poet who knows himself to be more than trivially implicated in those experiences. These texts are the chief glories of the "poetry of sensation" Hallam praised in the 1830 *Poems*, and they give more subtle and concrete embodiment to the principles and dilemmas of Tennyson's Romanticism than we find in any of the more philosophically speculative or programmatically allegorical pieces he published alongside them. It is difficult to read, at least with the full solemnity they often enjoin, the battery of poems Tennyson wrote around this time on the subject of poetry: "The Poet," "The Poet's Mind," "The Mystic," "The Dying Swan," and, flanking the 1830 volume, "To Poesy" (written in 1828) and "The Poet's Song" (published in 1842). These texts are most interesting where they are most typical, in their focus on the poet as an elected figure whose election isolates him both from ordinary mankind and from the sources of his inspiration. There is something mean-spirited about the claim of "The Poet's Mind" and "The Mystic" that nobody understands the message of the excluded, exclusive poet; but we may pardon him when we reflect on the way the poet is estranged from his very message. The central fountain of "The Poet's Mind," which leaps like lightning "With a low melodious thunder," derives "From the brain of the purple mountain / Which stands in the distance yonder"; and even these waters are drawn "from Heaven above" (24–32). It is difficult to know whether the poet's grouchiness arises in his sense of alienation from his power source, or whether he deliberately mystifies that source as a means of coping with an audience whose curiosity he both covets and fears.

"The Poet" charts an equal and opposite distance to that charted in "The Poet's Mind": this time the gap lies between the poetic word and its effect on the world. Tennyson's cluttered personification of "Freedom" (37), wearing a robe labeled "WISDOM" (46) and flourishing the poet's scroll, represents his own embarrassment with the mediations of language, at least when language is conceived as an instrument for affecting a world of readers, rather than creating a self-contained heterocosm:

> Her words did gather thunder as they ran,
>   And as the lightning to the thunder
> Which follows it, riving the spirit of man,
>   Making earth wonder,

> So was their meaning to her words. No sword
>   Of wrath her right arm whirled,
> But one poor poet's scroll, and with *his* word
>   She shook the world.   (49–56)

"Poor poet," indeed, whose bright meaning emits not even the residual glow of Shelley's "fading coal" from the *Defence of Poetry*, but must suffer translation into a medium as different as thunder from lightning (Pipes 1963, 74–76). In 1830 Tennyson could not know Shelley's *Defence*, which went unpublished until ten years later, but he did know Byron's assertion in *Childe Harold's Pilgrimage* that the poet would speak out if he could but concentrate his expansive being "into one word, / And that word were Lightning" (III.xcvii.6–7). Apparently Byron's wish has been partially granted to Tennyson's poet: meaning has condensed itself into a lightning flash. But the instantaneous flash loses its immediacy when the poet has to roll it out in time, into the folds of a scroll or the peals of belated thunder.

"The Poet" rankles most on account of its dishonesty: its abstractly millenarian zeal is not mendacious but is false to Tennyson's instinctual pessimism.[20] His poems on poetry do much better when they leave the lightning to fend for itself and attend to the thunder instead: "Time flowing in the middle of the night, / And all things creeping to a day of doom" ("The Mystic," 39–40); "The last beat of the thunder of God's heart" ("Perdidi Diem," 81). The Spirit of Fable in "Timbuctoo" taught the poet to embody this cosmic impulse not in reflective abstraction but in sensuous symbol; and the finest brief poems of 1830, "A Spirit Haunts the Year's Last Hours" and "The Kraken," bear this lesson out, with powerfully kinesthetic visions of doom that are disturbing in their very equanimity. Here the haunting genius of autumn and the eerie sea beast are presented not as illustrations of ideas but as conveyances for voice, media for the relentless purpose that possessed their creator whenever he was wise enough to let it. As so often when Tennyson trusts his imagination, it rewards him with powerful visions, or auditions, of impotence: the autumnal spirit presides over a decaying exhalation with which he can only sob in sympathy, and the kraken awaits a doom he will witlessly if vociferously fulfill.

In 1830 Tennyson's was not the voice of "The Poet" that shakes the world into action, but the voice that overflows it in the pulsing, eddying song of "The Dying Swan." This most oblique of his early poems on poetry is easily the best, by the time it reaches its magnificent close:

> But anon her awful jubilant voice,
> With a music strange and manifold,
> Flowed forth on a carol free and bold;
> As when a mighty people rejoice
> With shawms, and with cymbals, and harps of gold,
> And the tumult of their acclaim is rolled
> Through the open gates of the city afar,
> To the shepherd who watcheth the evening star.
> And the creeping mosses and clambering weeds,
> And the willow-branches hoar and dank,
> And the wavy swell of the soughing reeds,
> And the wave-worn horns of the echoing bank,
> And the silvery marish-flowers that throng
> The desolate creeks and pools among,
> Were flooded over with eddying song.   (28–42)

The introductory rhetoric of apocalypse—"awful jubilant voice," "free and bold"—recalls that of "The Poet." But this text, by curtailing its claims, succeeds where the other fails. Here Tennyson confines the social and political ambitions of traditional apocalyptic poetry within a simile compounded from the ancient, communally central texts of Homer and the Psalms. This poem also incidentally recalls the much less ancient text of Wordsworth's "The Solitary Reaper," where "the Vale profound / Is overflowing with the sound" of a melancholy feminine voice (7–8), but where the poet's imaginative extension of the song to embrace distant human communities is just what Tennyson here abjures (Stevenson 1980b, 623–625; Peltason 1984a, 88).

Like a lightning rod drawing off the charge of the social apocalypse that Tennyson would not or could not write, this simile modulates from a mighty people through the gates of their city to a marginal shepherd. The succession of images within the simile makes it easy to mistake the period ending line 35 for a comma, and to complete syntactically the implicit imagistic movement from an urban through a pastoral into an unpeopled and at last a lifeless world. This simile, which begins in a human community but points to a transcendence elsewhere, frees Tennyson to enjoy what meant most to him, the revelation of a scene composed of objects bound in the more fundamental community of their natural doom. A melancholy chorus, replete with "horns," that "soughs" and "echoes," Tennyson's thronging nature reproduces in a minor key the joyful tumult immured in his simile. The consolidation of individuals into "a mighty people" is here dispersed, yielding a series of particular details: the creeks and pools, though crowded with flowers, remain "desolate." At the same time, as throughout Tennyson's juvenilia, the discrete particulars of nature are bonded by a music that invests them all, the music of the swan's song as rendered by hypnotic anaphora. In its wave and swell the swan's eddying song partakes of the liquidity of the tidal scene it evokes; a mild pun reinforced by the title further suggests that this eddying song is a dying song: song a-dying, and a song of dying, which simultaneously arises from and sponsors the death of its singer and audience.

We end the poem knowing no more about the audible sound of the fabled swansong than when we began, but we know that its unheard melody communicates a refreshed consciousness of universal doom. The signal exception to the rule of death is humanity, and we must remember that Tennyson purchases his serene conclusion by first preserving all things human within the walls of a simile built to the traditional music of Western culture, whereby psalmists and epic and Romantic poets have made human sense of death. The burden of cultural spokesmanship Tennyson could not yet shoulder, and "The Dying Swan" suggests that he knew it. The fine reserve that rarely deserted him kept Tennyson from attempting this larger task, for which he would not be fit until the death of his best friend had prompted the mortal inquisitions that underlie "Tithonus," "Morte d'Arthur," and *In Memoriam*. This reserve goes far toward explaining why, for the early Tennyson, allegorical poet-figures thrive in exile from human community, and why the pressing and limiting problems of sexuality and mortality lie beyond the pale of his young imagination, and indeed define its boundaries. He was drawn by the doom in things as the subject he was born to enshrine in matchless verse. But he was repelled with equal force by the thought of human mortality—most particularly, and understandably, the thought of his own. Accordingly he wrote about what he knew, and chose for his most memorable human subjects the juvenile quester of "Recollections of the Arabian Nights" and the sublimely defended Mariana, selves who do not confront death but ward it off with every resource at their considerable command.

3

Emergencies: Crises of
Relation in *Poems* (1832)

Y 1830, AS WE have seen, the Romantic poets had taught
Tennyson how the visionary exoticism of "Armageddon"
and "Timbuctoo" might be naturalized for domestic consumption.
He had also learned the Romantic art of making the familiar strange
and new; and from the cultural canon, "the great vine of *Fable*,"
he had bred haunting myths of self-sufficiency that recast his juvenile concerns in more accessibly objective forms. Still, the verses
in *Poems, Chiefly Lyrical* (1830) were indeed chiefly lyrical, insofar
as their lyricism remained the preserve of a Romantic self in proud
or ruinous isolation. In this regard they lagged behind their creator.
Since "Timbuctoo" Tennyson had known that the poetical character becomes itself in relationship, not in isolation; and with considerable allusive finesse he had incorporated his relations with
earlier poets into such lyrics as "Mariana," "Recollections of the
Arabian Nights," and "The Poet's Mind." But this knowledge
had not attained thematic prominence. "Mariana" and "Recollections" would both be quite different poems if the odes of Keats
were not behind them; but they present no figure that stands to
the unattached, otherless consciousnesses of Mariana and the boyish Bagdat quester as Keats stands to Tennyson. Having come out
of himself in 1830 to accept and issue interpoetic challenges, Tennyson had left the figures he imagined behind him in the bower.

By 1832 his characters have begun to catch up with him. The
confrontation of a central self with others—whether sought or
evaded, aborted or achieved—becomes a theme as striking as the
proliferation of subgenres and poetic forms Tennyson devises for

setting his theme forth. Almost all the important poems are either narratives or songs in narrative frames that challenge the prevailing stasis of his earlier writing. There, imaginative energy was invested in maintenance projects, and the whole point of a poem, reductively put, was that nothing might influence the consciousness at its core. In the work of 1832, however, Tennyson imagines minds that undergo the impact of others, experience a self-division that is the prelude to conscious identity, and attempt transactions ranging from the painfully oblique to the daemonically aggressive. The narratives and narrative preambles of 1832 mean that in these poems something actually *happens*, albeit in occluded or stunted ways. Furthermore, for the first time in Tennyson's career the curve of the action these new narratives exhibit—or inhibit—occurs as a function of his imagination of personal relationships.

The Lover's Tale: Narrative of Desire

Just a month before publishing the new *Poems*, Tennyson withdrew, over Arthur Hallam's indignant protest, what was to have been its first and most ambitious piece: a long blank-verse narrative entitled *The Lover's Tale*, on which he had been working since 1827, and which he would finally release, bandaged up with an incongruous sequel, only in 1879—and then only after a pirated edition had forced his hand (Paden 1965). To judge from his notebooks, Tennyson revised this poem more than anything else he ever wrote (possibly excepting sections of "Oenone" and "The Gardener's Daughter"). The way he brooded over it for half a century, suppressing it yet repeatedly reworking its images in manuscript and quarrying them for use in poems he did publish, might justify a biographer of sufficient statistical perversity in calling this the central work of Tennyson's career. Certainly it was not that; with regard to the *Poems* of 1832, though, *The Lover's Tale* has the kind of shadowy yet focal presence that science ascribes to invisible bodies whose existence is inferred from the behavior of the bodies around them. The conspicuous success of the 1832 *Poems* owes so much to the technical and psychological practice its author gained from *The Lover's Tale* that, even if Tennyson had not eventually published the poem, we might be driven to posit something roughly like it, in order to explain his concerns during the early 1830s and the direction of his career thereafter.

Before examining a cluster of celebrated shorter texts of 1832, then, we might consider in general terms the obscure nucleus they initially orbited.[1]

Tennyson kept returning to *The Lover's Tale* because it took up thematically and structurally, and with an analytic rigor too seldom granted him, problems of imaginative relation that lay near the heart of virtually all his subsequent work—problems possessing both emotional and discursive dimensions. This obsessive poem turns (and turns, and turns) upon the insuperable obstacles posed by its narrator-protagonist's confession of his love, whether to his hyperbolically idealized beloved in the narrated past or to his vaguely realized companions in the narrative present. In the central figure, Julian, Tennyson created a man pathologically inept at what we would nowadays call "relating." An emotional cripple and madly digressive storyteller, Julian produces a narrative whose excruciating loveliness is matched only by its sure anatomy of one self's miserable failure to achieve and to express relationship with others. Julian's transfixed horror of bringing himself to "the event" (I.292, III.59, IV.1)—uncannily mirrored in Tennyson's inability either to abandon the poem for good or to manage its narrative to his satisfaction—suggests an imaginative inhibition that is manifest in several of the poems Tennyson did decide to publish in 1832, and that none of them overcomes altogether.[2]

Although of the entire 1832 collection as Tennyson first conceived it *The Lover's Tale* is the roomiest poem, it is the one in which the least takes place. And nothing happens, in this nonstory, because stasis is its very subject: we might indeed call it a narrative about the paralysis of the narrative faculty. What disables narration—what makes Tennyson's poem far less the lover's *tale* than the *lover's* tale—is the doomed strength of the narrator's Romantic desire. The spectacular collapse of *The Lover's Tale* illuminates the subtler problematics of relationship in the 1832 *Poems*, because it confronts most bleakly, and with the greatest analytic explicitness, the most intractable of Romantic obstacles to relation and development: the tendency of desire to displace its object and become an end in itself.

In this sense the poem constitutes an early dead end in Tennyson's career, an initial culmination of his complex and personally charged response to the hopes and dilemmas of Romanticism. As much in the poem reminds us, he first conceived it around the time of his removal from Somersby to Cambridge, where his social circumstances and friendships, on the one hand, and the Romantic poetry he read and wrote at the urging of his new associates, on the other, must have informed each other to a remarkable extent. As a young man exchanging his oppressive family circle for the broader horizon of university life—itself a privileged threshold to the expansive world of early Victorian society—Tennyson seems to have found in the Romantic dialectic of alienation and recovery a set of imaginative terms with which to survey his own position (Buckley 1960, 23; Lourie 1979, 27). At the same time, as a young poet encountering the poets of an older generation with a very direct sense of their creative relevance, he seems to have read his Romantics at Cambridge idiosyncratically. And the way in which he then and there took their influence arguably imparted its bias to Tennyson's Romantic allusiveness for decades to come.

The story a disappointed lover tells his friends about his incapacity to speak out, *The Lover's Tale* manifestly concerns the transition from solitude to communion that occupied Tennyson during his university years, and that was to remain his predominant mode of apprehending the cultural situation of the poet writing under a Romantic dispensation. But while "Timbuctoo" had effected this transition smoothly in the terms of mythic faith and of literary history, the erotic terms of *The Lover's Tale* evidently posed more daunting obstacles. The original preface states that "the lover is supposed to be himself a poet" (*PT*, 300). Despite a long tradition linking poetry and love—the tradition within which Tennyson wrote when he endowed "The Poet" of 1830 with "The love of love" (4)—this work appears to confirm a suspicion that the poet's needs and the lover's are incompatible. "Timbuctoo" asserted the commanding presence of the poet in an abyss, and celebrated his creative, representative power to elicit belief in a world where meaning is fictive to begin with. But in the context of love, as "Mariana" implies, sheer Romantic assertion has a way of turning sour. Among Victorians it was Tennyson's distinction to write, in *The Lover's Tale*, the first love poem that Romantically asks how imagination is connected to desire. He honors this question by pursuing the melancholy answer that a certain kind of imagination—a kind deeply affiliated with the successes of his earlier poetry—demands for its life the sacrifice of love.

The plot of the poem is a simple one. On a spring day in the

bloom of youth Julian and Camilla, cousins reared more or less
as twins, take a mountain walk; and as Julian exults in his unspoken
love for her, Camilla confesses that she has fallen in love with his
best friend. Julian swoons away and, upon awakening to find the
two lovers at his side, resolves to bear his disappointment in silence. Here the long first part of the poem ends; the next two parts
rehearse with briefer intensity the consequences of this self-
suppression, as Julian's solitary wanderings precipitate a series of
extraordinary visions. Although this plot may be easily told, Julian
finds it rough going indeed—as does the reader, whose interest in
the story line is persistently frustrated by Julian's digressions into
self-analysis and, most particularly, by his obsessive dwelling on
scenic descriptions, all of which conspire to extend the scanty plot
over more than a thousand lines. This narrative reluctance doubtless arises in part from Tennyson's inexperience as a storyteller,
but it also serves a maturing artistic purpose. The psychological
and descriptive retardants to the story committed the young poet
to the production of figurative images at a rate rivaling Keats's
comparable apprentice work in *Endymion*. Yet, in Tennyson's
workshop as in Keats's, the sheer labor of craftsmanship meets a
reflective awareness of its human costs; and the conjunction breeds
an arresting variation on a perennial Romantic theme: the addictive
narcissism of erotic idealization.

Julian's narrative inhibition and the proliferation of his imagery are mutually supportive habits, which enable him to
treasure up an emotional wealth that utterance would profane
(I.455–460), and to skim off, as by-products of this untold
emotion, the lavish descriptions that he dispenses like so much
small change. Love is the principal, loveliness the interest, in a
virtually endless substitution of setting for event, imagery for
action, figural representation for literal presence. Dream and
waking, hallucination and perception, past and present, all fall
under the regime of "the inaudible invisible thought" (II.101),
an objectless and therefore insatiable desire. Like one of Chaucer's storytelling pilgrims (or for that matter a suitor from *The
Devil and the Lady*), the teller of *The Lover's Tale* is known exclusively through his profession of love. Yet what he loves, in
his capacity as lover, is love itself, which becomes another
name for the principle of his identity (I.159–165). And Julian's
identity as a lover entails such an interpenetration of the self

and the love it lives by that, at length, it precludes the intrusion of any beloved, any other self at all.[3]

The erotic involution of its central character helps account for other peculiarities of this text. The natural descriptions, while splendid, are uniformly so, thanks to an erotic alchemy that transmutes everything it touches into imagery equally precious, which is to say equally worthless. The impossible locative phrase with which the poem begins—"Here far away"—sets the terms for a topography simultaneously sumptuous and commonplace; and it stations the tale in an imaginative neverland that exists nowhere and always. This spatial homogeneity corresponds with a further narrative tendency to fuse present and past. And this temporal uniformity, in its turn, explains why Julian never comes to the promised rendition of "the event": it is as vain to expect any "event" to affect the Romantic love of love as to expect such love to make room for any flesh and blood epipsyche. A desire as private as Julian's can show no significant advance where it has no goal— no erotic object, spatial landmark, or temporal direction—to advance toward.

Tennyson thus brings a quiet psychological acumen into collaboration with a surprising sophistication in the handling of narrative, to make *The Lover's Tale* a purposefully static study in relational failure. It is a text that deserves higher rank among those early works in which he posited an analogy between crises of literary art and of human identity—an analogy of great importance for a poet as publicly private as Tennyson. If the terminal condition of Julian recalls the helplessness that typifies Tennyson's juvenilia, it also forecasts the principal dilemma of his new *Poems*: the power of doom that once reigned from a distance has by 1832 taken up residence within the self. Desire, the principle of Julian's identity, now provides the means of its own frustration. Character has become a fate that gives this unfinished poem its own brand of desperate closure.

Hence the incongruity of the 1879 sequel, *The Golden Supper*. By the 1870s narrative meant, for Tennyson, idyllic fiction (of the kind analyzed in Chapter 5): a mode of writing to which he turned when, as happened increasingly with the years, he lacked a clear call to write otherwise. Yet he *had* written otherwise in *The Lover's Tale*, in prosecution of riskier aims than the decorous limits of the idyll could compass. To be sure, such characteristics as its narrative

diffusion and descriptive proliferation give *The Lover's Tale* a superficial likeness to the poet's idylls, for which it indeed served as
a turbulent first draft. Perhaps it was this likeness that led Tennyson in 1879 to seek out the shock-absorbing properties idyllic
fiction possesses, in an attempt to mollify the terrible harshness
of his youthful narrative of desire. The attempt fails miserably,
when a suddenly generous Julian restores the long-lost Camilla to
his rival in an improbable triumph of self-denial. Yet it may be
said in the old poet's defense that he rebelled a little at this cozy
ending: at the eleventh hour Julian, unlike his prototype in Boccaccio, exits the poem in frightened retreat from the image of
domestic joy he has made.[4] This last-minute escape, keeping faith
with what is most bitter in Tennyson's Romanticism, frees Julian
to roam, when all is told, in the palace of imagery that the published *Poems* of 1832 also inhabit but endeavor to transcend—
against odds whose steepness this long-suppressed and longer-
neglected poem lets us measure.

"The Lady of Shalott": The Coming of the Curse

Upon Tennyson's removal of *The Lover's Tale* from his 1832
collection, its place at the head of the volume went to a work that
is harder, in several senses of that adjective: more tautly assembled,
more gnomically difficult, and more pessimistic in its outlook on
human relationship and the reciprocation of love. "The Lady of
Shalott" so quickly passed through the hands of the foremost
Victorian iconographers into the public domain—where it still
enjoys a kind of shadow life in the higher pop culture—that its
original foreignness may be overlooked, the extent of its alienation
underestimated. This is the first of a number of popular Tennyson
poems whose very popularity obliges us to estrange ourselves from
them if we wish to recover their original force. But here, at least,
an intransigent poetic formality makes the work of defamiliari-
zation uncommonly easy to undertake. The division of "The Lady
of Shalott" into numbered parts, further subdivided into discrete
stanzas, frames it as an art object; and the invincible rhyme scheme
of alternating quadruple and triple ply, even when it does not
vanquish the poet (as it did in the "waterlily"-"daffodilly"-"water
chilly" triplet from stanza 1 in 1832), insists at every turn that
we acknowledge its artfulness.[5] This narrative poem, like *The*

Lover's Tale, deals principally in description, but its tetrameter
lines renounce the freedom of blank-verse pentameter for a line-
bound, chastened syntax and a simplified diction, which sacrifice
analytic and affective discursiveness for the different subtlety of
symbol. Furthermore, Tennyson entrusts his narrative to an aloof,
neutral scribe of outward events who, psychologically speaking,
handles the central Lady almost as gingerly as he handles the meteoric Lancelot and the other peripheral figures that step once into
the poem and out again. This narrator's very being, the life of his
story, seems a function of his indirection; each of the four parts
shuts down at the moment when description yields to directly
quoted speech.

"The Lady of Shalott" thus presents itself as a Grecian urn in
words, a form for contemplation rather than a lesson for understanding. In this sense it gives as little away as do any of Tennyson's
earliest poems. Yet it tells the story of a Lady who gives everything
away for the sake of contact with someone else—in the very clear
Italian of Tennyson's medieval source, *la Damigella di Scalot morì
per amore di Lancialotto de Lac*—which is something no major figure
in Tennyson has even dreamed of doing thus far. The affecting
generosity of the protagonist thus seems at odds with the stringency both of the unforgiving plot in which she finds herself and
of the rigid verbal structures that convey it. The consistency with
which this large-scale imbalance is reinforced through local ambiguities of phrasing suggests that Tennyson was working at cross-
purposes on an insoluble conflict: a conflict between his drive
toward a new kind of social commitment and his equally strong
residual skepticism about the viability of such commitment in an
unresponsive world (Palmer 1973, 42). Seeking to establish the
grounds of identity in relationship, where all the major poems of
1832 hope to find them, "The Lady of Shalott" clearly narrates
the world's failure to requite the desires of the self. But where the
self is constituted in relationship, this can be only half the story:
this failure also bespeaks an inner failure to identify the world
accurately and embrace its otherness. Far from solving these riddles
of identity and identification, the poem devotes itself to setting
them forth in ways that suggest their irresolution.

THE LADY BEGINS her career in familiar Tennysonian insularity
and enclosure, where "the silent isle imbowers / The Lady of Sha-

lott" (17–18), and where passive, intransitive, or weakly transitive present-tense verbs collaborate with the rhyme scheme to describe a world of repetitive sameness: a world that obeys the natural cycle in its symmetries, or that gravitates without urgency downstream to Camelot, where nature and culture gently cohabit. We recognize this world as that of the earlier Tennyson, but part I marks the new direction of his 1832 poems by raising questions about the Lady's identity in relation to the world that surrounds her. When first named in the second stanza, the Lady seems to be precipitated out of her locale and out of a rhyme scheme that imitates its repetitive natural processes: the phrase "The Lady of Shalott" assumes the place taken by "The island of Shalott" in stanza 1, and the genitive preposition suggests that the Lady is but an exhalation or spirit of the place that names her. Stanza 3, however, introduces complicating questions about this apparently straightforward affiliation:

> By the margin, willow-veiled,
> Slide the heavy barges trailed
> By slow horses; and unhailed
> The shallop flitteth silken-sailed
>   Skimming down to Camelot:
> But who hath seen her wave her hand?
> Or at the casement seen her stand?
> Or is she known in all the land,
>   The Lady of Shalott?   (19–27)

In this poem about the search for relationship, conjunctions are unusually important. Tennyson's "But," like the disjunctions in the similarly fluid world of "Recollections of the Arabian Nights," signals a new turn, a counterthrust corresponding to the upstream drag of the horse-trailed barges earlier in the stanza. The stanza ends with three questions, and the answer to the first two is, presumably, nobody: the Lady who has left the passing shallop unhailed has not been seen waving or standing at her casement either. The initial stanzas' serene overview makes the nonappearance of the Lady up to this point a matter of indifference. The introductory "But," however, along with a shift to interrogation that engages the reader more directly, insinuates a doubt—not as to the Lady's existence, exactly, but as to her identity, the quality and relatedness of her existence. How does it appear to us, or to the Lady, that she fails to appear to others in her world?

The technique is one of insinuation and nothing more; for the third question, with the doubling maneuver that typifies Tennysonian development of all kinds, half retracts the doubt. "Or is she known in all the land?" Like so much else in the poem, this question is ambiguous (Empson 1947, 182). Read in apposition with the preceding questions, it becomes rhetorical: Who has ever heard of this outlandish lady? But read against the first two questions, the third one steals their force by reclaiming, as a genuine alternative to their doubts, the notion intimated earlier that the Lady is a *genius loci*, not to be diminished by specific manifestations but incarnate in the landscape, affirmed "in all the land." Perhaps the turning in this stanza is a false one, perhaps the Lady's identity is secure in its universality, and perhaps the barges as they "slide" are drifting downstream after all, heading home to Camelot along with everything else, and "trailed" or followed by horses that are "slow," like the later "ambling pad" (56), simply because that is the proper pace for the untroubled life over which the Lady presides.

And perhaps not. The fourth stanza reopens the ambiguities of the third by figuring the Lady as a voice:

> Only reapers, reaping early
> In among the bearded barley,
> Hear a song that echoes cheerly
> From the river winding clearly,
> > Down to towered Camelot:
> And by the moon the reaper weary,
> Piling sheaves in uplands airy,
> Listening, whispers, " 'Tis the fairy
> Lady of Shalott."   (28–36)

The reaper's identification of the song as the Lady's confirms that she is indeed known in all the land, and also confirms her status as a fairy, the spirit of her place. At the same time, though, her status in the fairy world jars with the workaday world, as the cheerfulness of her untiring song sets her apart from a world whose work makes men and women "weary." Moreover, that the unseen Lady is known through song (Tennyson's principal figure for poetry in earlier volumes), and that hers is a "song that echoes," should alert us to the multiple echoes of Romantic poetry in this introductory portion of the poem. Part II will identify the Lady clearly as an artist; but first in part I Tennyson takes allusive pains to establish the priority of the context within which her art takes its place, and to imply that art may be at best irrelevant to its context and at worst disabling to the humanity of the person who practices it.

Lionel Stevenson's exploration (1948) of the "high-born maiden" symbol in early Tennyson has prompted readers to approach the Lady of Shalott from the right direction, as a figure of the poet deriving from Shelley's "To a Skylark":

> Like a Poet hidden
>   In the light of thought,
> Singing hymns unbidden,
>   Till the world is wrought
> To sympathy with hopes and fears it heeded not:
>
> Like a high-born maiden
>   In a palace-tower,
> Soothing her love-laden
>   Soul in secret hour,
> With music sweet as love—which overflows her bower. (36–45)

The imagistic parallels between Shelley and Tennyson are manifest, the thematic relationship rather more devious. We have already seen how Tennyson's third stanza introduces a doubt about the Lady's origin and identity, a doubt that recalls Shelley's initiating doubt whether the song of the skylark emanates from a bird or a spirit: "Hail to thee, blithe Spirit! / Bird thou never wert" (1–2). Having chosen to open "The Lady of Shalott" by opening a patently Shelleyan divide between spiritual and natural sources of song, Tennyson adopted with it Shelley's division between rapt singer and listening world. In Shelley's poem the relation between unbidden singer and sympathetic, if at first heedless, audience remains as mysterious as it is potent; the "hidden" poet and high-born maiden, clearly not performing but singing to please themselves "in secret hour," work up their audiences without even trying. Expressive "overflow" neatly equals sympathetic influence, as becomes clearer if we move beyond the similes and recall Shelley's aim to attract and transmit the communicated lightning of the blithe spirit he both hears and invokes: "The world should listen then—as I am listening now" (105).

Given Tennyson's concern in the 1830s with the twin problems of relating the self to others and poetry to a public, what Shelley

called secret sympathy is likely to have struck Tennyson as ap-
pallingly arbitrary coincidence. Where is the good of a poet's
power or a maiden's music if the world, having other work to
do, happens *not* to be wrought to sympathy? What if singer and
auditor come from such different places that communication cannot occur? Here, as often in Romantic tradition, the thematic quest
for origins entails a search for more distant and original precursor
texts: in order to see how Tennyson's images define themselves
against Shelley's, we must retrieve a pair of lyrics by Wordsworth
to which "To a Skylark" was itself a response. "To the Cuckoo"
celebrates the "blithe" song of an unseen bird whose "twofold
shout" or built-in echo first spiritualizes the bird into "a wandering
Voice" (4), like the Lady's voice in Tennyson that echoes cheerly
and winds clearly, and finally etherealizes "the earth we pace" into
"An unsubstantial, faery place" (29–31)—which the environs of
Shalott significantly do not become. The voice of the fairy Lady
of Shalott has just enough in common with that of Wordsworth's
cuckoo to throw into relief what it lacks: it possesses sufficient
charm to spiritualize itself in the ear of its auditor, but it wields
no Wordsworthian or Shelleyan power to make the earth over.
No world is wrought to sympathy here; indeed, as the closing
stanza of the poem shows, the world of Camelot is wrought at
best to sympathy's conventional shadow, pity, in a travesty of
communication that ranks among Tennyson's closest approaches,
anywhere, to unmitigated irony.

Tennyson's allusions in part I prepare for that finale by stressing
the Lady's incapacitating distance from others. The split between
the otherworldliness of the singer and the world through which
her song passes appears in a somewhat different guise if we think
of another Wordsworthian lyric of solitary voice, one to which
we have heard Tennyson allude in "The Dying Swan" of 1830,
"The Solitary Reaper": "O listen! for the Vale profound / Is overflowing with the sound" (7–8). In Wordsworth's figure, voice
flows through a valley to usurp the natural place of water; but
Tennyson's valley is filled by the river first, and the voice of the
Lady can but echo "From the river" as an antiphon or secondary
overtone to the priority of nature. What is more, the collocation
of human labor with the source of the song, the woman "singing
at her work" (27), which provides Wordsworth's lyric both with
its empirical validation and with much of its plangency, is utterly

dispersed in the stanza Tennyson wrote. Those who reap in weariness know the solitude on which Wordsworth insists and which Tennyson queerly deflects into the adverbial "Only reapers." But in binding the grain and piling the sheaves they know, too, a common mortality that connects them to the earth and to each other. The song of the Lady of Shalott, in contrast, remains an airy ditty that may at most relieve work with its alien charm. Tennyson brings this point further home with a "Mariana"-like trick of phrasing toward the close of the fourth stanza, where the reaper is said to work and listen "by the moon." Since the word "by" has occurred in each preceding stanza to specify place (4, 13, 19), the syntactic promotion of the phrase "And by the moon" encourages us for a moment to imagine that the Romantic song of the Lady has transported the reaper into "uplands airy" that lie out of this world—until we understand that the reaper remains bound to a sublunary existence, where the harvest moon means nothing more romantic than an opportunity to extend the workday past sundown.

The Wordsworthian lyrics behind such effects came to Tennyson by way not only of Shelley but also of Keats, most notably through the passage from "Ode to a Nightingale" to which we must recur so often because Tennyson did:

> Perhaps the self-same song that found a path
>   Through the sad heart of Ruth, when, sick for home,
>   She stood in tears amid the alien corn;
>   The same that oft-times hath
>   Charm'd magic casements, opening on the foam
>   Of perilous seas, in faery lands forlorn.   (65–70)

Tennyson appears to have found different attractions in this passage at different points in his career. In the early 1830s he was attracted most, I think, by the arbitrary swiftness of the transition between the natural human affections in the first three lines and their polar opposite, the magical and even daemonic excitement in the last three. It is this opposition, also present in Shelley's bird poem, that Wordsworth's lyrics beautifully aim to elide. But Keats anticipates Tennyson in annulling the Wordsworthian marriage of song to the labors of mortality, as both the immortal nightingale and the arrested Ruth are distinguished from nature's processes and labor's—"the alien corn"—and then as Keats leaps out of nature altogether in the last lines of his stanza. When the nostalgic alienation represented in Ruth leads Keats to imagine an other-worldly home in the "magic," "faery" demesnes of romance, he furnishes not just Tennyson's leading images of casement, harvest, and the pathways of song, but also the opposition between natural and spiritual realms that undergirds this part of "The Lady of Shalott" and forecasts the parts to come.

Tennyson, here as ever, drives a sharper wedge than Keats between the realms of mortality and fairy. Keats's final word "forlorn" will precipitate his descent from the high Romantic vault to the tragic acceptance of mortality. But the height of romance is, for better or for worse, the Lady's native place. She can be half-sick of shadows but never sick for home, since the fairy world of shadows *is* her home. While the poem will take its time in establishing her tower as a prison, the Keatsian conjunction of "casements" with "faery lands forlorn" reanimates the possibility that the Lady's empty or unnoticed casement in stanza 3 may be an early sign of unwelcome solitary confinement. Her casement may let a weirdly dispassionate song out; but it does not bid fair, as at the close of Keats's "Ode to Psyche," "To let the warm Love in."

With this multiplicity of echoes part I risks dwindling into a compendiary footnote to the Romantic iconography of nature and voice, a helplessly secondary text. But then the secondariness of the text takes its point from the secondariness of the Lady, whether she is conceived as the offspring of her place or as an irrelevant grace superadded to a world that could do well enough without her. The secondary status of the Lady takes on a new dimension in part II, where her "magic web with colours gay" (38) imitates what are already "Shadows of the world" as seen "through a mirror clear" (46–48). Though she "weaves by night and day" (37) and thus works as "steadily" as any reaper might (43), her artistic function remains derivative, as the reaper's labor is not. Even in her creative work the Lady merely re-presents or seconds the motions of the natural and social world. Her mirror is so ambiguously positioned, especially by 1842, that it may reflect the objects beyond her casement, or the obverse of her tapestry, or both; in any case, whether receiving her subject at second hand or double-checking her handiwork to ensure its conformity with that subject, the Lady remains in thrall to secondary shadows of reality.

The high mimetic art the Lady practices displays affinities with Tennyson's impassive juvenilia. But it also resembles the objective art of the present narrator, and this reduplication within the text signals the poet's gain in self-awareness. Now that his neutral art is describing a neutral artist, a human subject, Tennyson can make explicit what his juvenilia left us to infer: the high mimetic artist attains objectivity at the high subjective cost of alienation from the world that art labors to mirror. In part II the Lady beholds a series of human figures who are variously bound to each other— "a troop of damsels glad" (55), knights "riding two and two" (61)—or who, if solitary, are bound by their occupations as "abbot," "Shepherd-lad," or "page" (56–58) to the social fabric that the Lady's solitary weaving can but mimic. Furthermore, these human figures are connected to the common life, by what Wordsworth would have called the bonds of the affections. Although such affections in Tennyson get a rather telegraphic treatment restricted to the "surly village-churls" (52) and the "damsels glad," against the reserve of the narrator and the affective anesthesia of the Lady these brief epithets suffice to suggest a spectrum of emotion that the Lady notably lacks.

In 1832 Tennyson wrote, "She lives with little joy or fear"; but he excised the reference to her emotions in 1842 in order to concentrate on the mechanics, or more precisely optics, of her voyeuristic craft. This revision neatly enacts the Lady's own direction of energy away from feeling into the practice of a dispassionate art: "she weaveth steadily, / And little other care hath she" (43–44; similarly, T.Nbk. 16 reads "joy" for "care"). If the central arena of affective life is sexual relationship, there is no dearth of sexual suggestiveness in the procession of images the Lady's mirror presents. Each human figure has a distinct gender; the village-churls pair off with the market girls; or again, the market girls and damsels find male counterparts, from appropriate social classes, in the shepherd-lad and the long-haired page; and the progression in stanza 3 from lad to page to knight so obviously suggests the maturation of a fit consort for the Lady that the narrative departs from description to remark, "She hath no loyal knight and true" (62). But the Lady resists these imagistic overtures for the sake of her art: "But in her web she still delights / To weave the mirror's magic sights" (64–65). One effect of so insistent a rhyme scheme is to isolate lines as independent units of sense, and we might single out the first of these lines as a condensation of the Lady's history to date: in her web she still delights. She repeatedly chooses an art, and an exclusively aesthetic emotion, that fail to move beyond themselves.

This history is about to undergo a dramatic change; but before we can understand the change, we need to investigate the Lady's devotion to an art that is not only secondary but, to judge from part I, less than humanly satisfying. The Lady's reason for this devotion is that she believes herself to be under the compulsion of a most unusual curse:

> She has heard a whisper say,
> A curse is on her if she stay
>   To look down to Camelot.
> She knows not what the curse may be,
> And so she weaveth steadily,
> And little other care hath she,
>   The Lady of Shalott.   (39–45)

I join a number of other critics in finding this curse ambiguous. In the original version "A curse is on her, if she stay / Her weaving," but in the text of 1842 the curse seems to apply equally to the cessation of her art and to its continuance: it obtains whether she stays her weaving and turns to something else, or she stays around and keeps it up. For the present the Lady has adopted the latter alternative, but if the curse is ambiguous so may be the Lady's response to it. The conjunctive "And so" suggests an inner logic in her response, but the double bind of this contradictory curse paralyzes the logic of cause and effect that supports rational choice. Damning her if she does and damning her if she doesn't, the curse in effect undoes itself as a threat in any recognizable sense and becomes instead a condition of the Lady's existence, without regard for any particular course of action she may take.

How much of this does the Lady understand? Does she keep up her weaving simply because she fears the unknown consequences of stopping? Perhaps, but to accept this alternative is to insult the Lady's intelligence by assuming that she has drastically oversimplified the terms of a curse she ought to have made a better effort to comprehend. Or does ignorance of "what the curse may be" free the Lady to go on doing as she likes? This alternative gives her more hermeneutic credit, although in saving her thus from a fairly crude error of interpretation we must implicitly accuse her of an impercipience that is worse. For if the Lady incurs damnation by merely staying in the tower and weaving, then she must be enduring the curse right now. And so she is, if we consider that the curse may in fact be the curse of isolation under which she has been laboring since the beginning of the poem and to which, furthermore, she has submitted—and in the poem's perpetual present tense continues to submit—by her own free choice.

The dignity of choice, however limited, that this reading confers upon the Lady also opens the possibility of change: what she has willingly brought on herself she may, perhaps, willingly throw off. The question of the Lady's will returns us to the pivotal last stanza of part II, which initiates the decisive event of the entire poem:

> But in her web she still delights
> To weave the mirror's magic sights,
> For often through the silent nights
> A funeral, with plumes and lights
>   And music, went to Camelot:
> Or when the moon was overhead,
> Came two young lovers lately wed;
> "I am half sick of shadows," said
>   The Lady of Shalott. (64–72)

In the fifth line the narrative fall into the past tense, while striking, is not quite the clean break that it seems.[6] If we recall the present perfect tense introducing the curse ("She has heard a whisper"), we see that the present tenses of parts I and II correspond to a posture of numbed innocence, which the Lady hitherto has willed and sustained, but here starts to question. This stanza challenges her innocence by presenting the two most powerful agents of temporal experience, death and sex, in the images of a funeral and a recently married couple—which, as images of social ritual, give to the Lady's biological isolation a cultural dimension as well.[7] Either image could serve as an appropriate culmination to the carefully plotted imagery from the preceding stanzas: the progression from lad to page to knight, in particular, conducts the mind with equal plausibility to the wedding bed or to the coffin. What is most remarkable about this stanza is that it treats both possibilities so impartially, offering images of death and of love with an evenhanded "Or" that suggests not an alternative but an equivalence.

To the Lady the two indeed *are* equivalent, in that they represent the twin consummations of the self in the temporal realm of generation, which she has hitherto kept at art's length. The Lady's equation of love with death is borne out by the remainder of the poem, where her commitment to the former earns her the latter with unseemly haste (Peltason 1985b, 158). In order to interpret that commitment, it may be helpful to observe that as the poem recedes into the past tense Tennyson is reaching backward too, to the ruinous but inevitable choices of the child from Wordsworth's "Intimations" ode:

> See, at his feet, some little plan or chart,
> Some fragment from his dream of human life,
> Shaped by himself with newly learned art;
>> A wedding or a festival,
>> A mourning or a funeral
> . . . . .
>> As if his whole vocation
>> Were endless imitation.   (90–107)

This child's vocation is the Lady's as well, as I tried to suggest above in discussing the imitative character of her art; but the Lady enjoys the added dignity, if not exactly the advantage, of knowing what she is about, of choosing her vocation and not simply being summoned by it. In this respect she may be closer to the moral responsibility underlying the ode in which Coleridge answered Wordsworth's with sorrows of his own. In "Dejection," a similar yoking of sex and death crowns a defeated artist's meditation on the relation of imagination to external nature (through pertinent textile imagery): "Ours is her wedding garment, ours her shroud!" (49). The choice of vocations that the Lady begins to reconsider here is a choice between two ways of "imitating nature": the protective but exclusive way of aesthetic mimesis, or the way of the soul that repeats nature's patterns by consciously living them through. Tennyson reverses the Wordsworthian and Coleridgean "natural" sequence of wedding and funeral in order to stress that the Lady's psychological choice of engagement with the world, if freely made, must follow upon her acceptance of mortality. This necessary condition for decisive change, and not the change itself, forms Tennyson's subject at this point; and though the poem never makes it easy to ascertain the Lady's state of mind, the fact that she is now "half sick of shadows" suggests that, before she can heal herself by wounding her art, she will need to fall more than half in love with death.

BY THE END of part II the Lady is as ready for active commitment as, in a psychological vacuum, it is possible for her to be; she now requires someone to be committed to. Enter, then, in rhyming substitution for the "Camelot" he represents, and with the triple heart throb of the most prosodically irregular line of an acutely form-bound poem, "bold Sir Lancelot":

> A bow-shot from her bower-eaves,
> He rode between the barley-sheaves,
> The sun came dazzling through the leaves,
> And flamed upon the brazen greaves
>   Of bold Sir Lancelot.
> A red-cross knight for ever kneeled
> To a lady in his shield,
> That sparkled on the yellow field,
>   Beside remote Shalott.   (73–81)

This is but the first course in a four-stanza feast for the eyes that, if it is not a grievous piece of self-indulgence by a great but un-disciplined descriptive poet, must be read as the cruelest twist in a work not distinguished for its slackness or charity of vision. For just at the point where the Lady needs commitment to some one else, the mirror offers as its last magic sight not a person but a thing—not a thing even but an image, an eidolon so spectacular that no reader of whom I am aware has blamed the Lady for the idolatry into which it fatally seduces her. Tennyson himself, as he read the poem in later life, certainly offered no such condemnation: "The new-born life for something, for some one in the wide world from which she has so long been secluded, takes her out of the region of shadows into that of realities" (*Memoir*, I, 117).[8] This interpretation is incredibly serene, given the destiny that awaits the Lady within a few stanzas; yet its hesitation between "some-thing" and "some one" can focus our attention on those details that make the poem a good deal more knowing than the old poet's cosmetic paraphrase lets on.

The cavalier figure depicted in these stanzas, unlike the chiv-

alrous and fallibly bemused Lancelot we meet at the close of the
poem, is a mirage confected out of bits and trappings, and frosted
by a radiance that is dazzling but entirely reflected (Tobias 1971,
8). The transition between parts II and III strongly suggests a
progression from moonlit shadows to the very sun, which is at
least since Plato the great Western trope for ultimate reality. In
this connection the flaming, glittering, burning light imagery that
dominates Tennyson's blazon is also, and alas, its most meretri-
cious feature. This Apollonian Lancelot is no presence, but pure
representation: a man of mirrors, a signifier as hollow as the song
he sings.

> From the bank and from the river
> He flashed into the crystal mirror,
> "Tirra lirra," by the river
> Sang Sir Lancelot.   (105–108)

The persuasive illusion of full personal presence ("He flashed")
depends upon a three-banked carom shot: the supposedly authentic
light of the real world comes to the Lady only after ricocheting
off the knight's shiny trappings, onto the reflecting surface of the
river, and thence to the mirror she finally reads—an effect strengthened in revision from the manuscript version "He sparkled in the
crystal mirror" (T.Nbk. 16). And the identical rhyme of "river"
with itself, a kind of tirra-lirra reflection in words that is unique
in the poem, calls attention to the way this simulacrum of presence,
while seeming to draw the Lady out of herself, has only driven
her to a further remove from the reality she seeks.[9]

Another, more strictly rhetorical index of deceit is the sudden
cascade of similes. Within fewer than twenty lines (83–99), three
of them burst into a poem that has thus far contained none, relying
instead upon more evocatively symbolic modes of description. In
their specific content all three similes have to do with bright fire,
and their rhetorical prominence shows how mechanically the erotic
furnaces of part III are stoked: being a cipher, Lancelot can be
described only in terms of what he is not. Even irrespective of
their content, the sudden prevalence of similes (the easiest of tropes
to make and to spot) in itself underscores the artificiality of
perception, a favorite Tennysonian theme in which the Lady is
about to be indelibly lessoned. In this connection it may make
sense to refer the similes of part III to the fund of Shelleyan com-

parisons from which Tennyson drew his high-born Lady to begin with. Shelley's outrageous compounding of similes, in "To a Skylark," *Epipsychidion*, and other poems that pressed poetic artifice to the breaking point, formed part of an investigation of convergent epistemological, linguistic, and erotic issues quite as sophisticated as Tennyson's in "The Lady of Shalott." It is important to remember Shelley's sophistication in these matters, if we are to appreciate Tennyson's still early mastery of revisionary allusion here. For one last function of the galactic, fiery, meteoric similes in part III is to set Shelley, as well as the Lady, up for a fall. By associating Shelleyan similes with descriptive deceit, Tennyson makes him out to be a wild-eyed optimist whose apparent knack for coupling anything in the world with anything else reflected a deeper, heartbreaking illusion that at last all perceptions are trustworthy, all minds mutually transparent, all souls benevolently one.

If we ask what makes the Lady, despite her intentions, so liable to be waylaid by this erotic mirage, we come to the kinship between "The Lady of Shalott" and *The Lover's Tale*, with its relentless fixation on the way a lover's imagery can stunt the growth of actual love. The stanzas themselves are curiously fixed, as the fragments describing Lancelot's equipage reach us in no particular order, and as the predominantly intransitive verbs play down all subordinate relationships for the sake of a homogeneous blaze. In Lancelot's shield, with its ever-kneeling knight, the Lady beholds a Keatsian tease, an emblem of perennial, static desire. More important, the shield has the peculiar power of converting everything around it to its own emblematic status. As it sparkles "on the yellow field, / Beside remote Shalott," it flattens vision into two dimensions and transforms what was once ripe golden barley from an agricultural into a heraldic "field," a *champ or*, a uniform scenic background.[10]

As these images suggest, in bold Sir Lancelot the Lady confronts not an alternative to the prison tower of self but evidence of its inescapability. The stanzas devoted to Lancelot enforce Tennyson's conservative pessimism about the Romantic metamorphosis of the self; they imply that we can love only what we have learned to love by having loved it before. If what the Lady has habitually loved in the past is a beautiful irrelevance, that is what will continue to move her, no matter what she resolves to the contrary. This

futile wisdom emerges in the final stanza of part III with an effect
of extraordinary violence:

> She left the web, she left the loom,
> She made three paces through the room,
> She saw the water-lily bloom,
> She saw the helmet and the plume,
>   She looked down to Camelot.
> Out flew the web and floated wide;
> The mirror cracked from side to side;
> "The curse is come upon me," cried
>   The Lady of Shalott.   (109–117)

After over a hundred lines of mainly intransitive description, the
electric series of transitives in the opening lines (not "walked,"
even, but with prosodic reinforcement, "made three paces") registers the strength of the Lady's desire (Boyd 1977, 30). What
Tennyson's comment called her "new-born love" will be pitifully
short-lived, but it is important to feel its intensity here if we are
to avoid sentimentalizing part IV and are to appreciate the revulsion with which the Lady there will turn her energies against
herself. For the present, and only momentarily, the blooming
water-lily betokens the efflorescence of her commitment to generation and to the fertile promise of relationship—and then, in the
next line, the moment shatters as she looks directly out at Lancelot's accoutrements and beyond to Camelot. What this look takes
in we are not told; presumably it is the unlovely environment the
Lady will be entering in part IV, for the very sight is enough to
dismantle the apparatus of her desire, as the web unravels and the
mirror cracks. It is here, with her cry "The curse is come upon
me," that the Lady reads the lesson of *The Lover's Tale*: she has
given her heart to an image nothing in the wide world can rival.

The Lady's curse remains, then, what it was in part II, a voyeuristic isolation from the world; but the poem now asks us to
take the curse more tragically, in the aftermath of the Lady's genuine but doomed attempt to engage the world in spite of her
accursed subjectivity. She confronts not the world, but the impossibility of her confronting the world; and she recognizes her
entrapment in the vicious circle of a desire for illusions of her own
making (Martin 1973). This recognition at last makes sense of the
grim logic of the apparently illogical curse, since the Lady's condition of emotional entrapment obtains whether she sustains her

fantasies by looking in the mirror or shatters them by looking down to Camelot—though she can learn this only by trial and error. The Lady recognizes, too, that the one way to break the vicious circle of desire is to annihilate the self that desires, in other words to die. And that, of course, is what she does in part IV, with a quiet deliberation born of the acceptance of Tennysonian fatality, "Like some bold seër in a trance, / Seeing all his own mischance" (128–129). This, the fourth and last simile in the poem, differs from those of part III by making its comparison not to a starry distraction but to a grave human figure, who beholds his tragic condition and takes responsibility for "all his own mischance." Through the crossing of gender lines in this simile we may glimpse the male poet behind his female persona, while the androgynous gesture also tends to generalize the human plight to any reader: ours is her wedding garment, ours her shroud.

Tennyson's gain in this poem, his advance upon *The Lover's Tale*, resides in the dignity of the Lady's self-knowledge, with her correlative willingness to assume responsibility for her dilemma.[11] Having made her bed, the Lady will lie in it. That bed is a coffin, not a wedding bed; but the Lady retains sufficient awareness of the ironies of her situation to deck herself out as a singularly bridal corpse. Indeed, with her accession to tragic knowledge the Lady takes charge not just of her actions but of the poem's as well. Helpless but no longer quite passive before circumstances, she generates the remaining events of her legend; she also generates a number of its symbolic meanings, with appreciable authorial initiative. She floats downstream "robed in snowy white" (136), an apparition ironically reminiscent of the idly passive, vaguely biblical lilies from part I, and also of the blooming water lily from part III, whose generative promise she has now discarded in acknowledgment of what Yeats might have called her perpetual virginity of soul. Self-conscious irony also informs the Lady's readiness to make of herself what her art and desire have made of the world, an aesthetic image. The same self-loathing that leads her to reject a life that cannot answer to desire—two lives, to be precise, those of the passive aesthete and of the thwarted lover— entitles her to transform herself multiply into art. She dies into sculpturesque opacity; she appropriates a local small craft and makes it the vehicle of her final performance, signed by the artist (126), in an overtly public gesture a world away from the cheerly echoing song of part I. And she accomplishes her exit from life into art by "singing her last song, / The Lady of Shalott" (143–144). I hesitate to take this last line as a title and equate the Lady's carol with Tennyson's poem. Still, the suggestion is there; and whatever the Lady sings, it is a highly reflexive piece in which she herself figures as a vocalist: "Singing in her song she died" (152).

One could argue that the poem ought to end here, once the Lady of Shalott has sung herself to cold, blind death, and once Tennyson has put the traditional device of the self-consuming artifact to the new but apt service of an analysis of Romantic solipsism. The original conclusion, *"this is I, / The Lady of Shalott,"* gave an appropriate finish to the process of the Lady's self-objectification. But this conclusion, while appropriate, was also superfluous, given the Lady's manipulation of emblematic detail in the preceding stanzas. In 1842 Tennyson appears to have decided to have his Lady's abortive quest for reciprocal love end with a parody of reciprocation:

> And they crossed themselves for fear,
>   All the knights at Camelot:
> But Lancelot mused a little space;
> He said, "She has a lovely face;
> God in his mercy lend her grace,
>   The Lady of Shalott."   (166–171)

What the dazzling image of Lancelot was for the Lady, the "gleaming shape" (156) in the Lady's shallop now becomes for Lancelot, though with a bathetic reduction in scope. He beholds in her an object for contemplation, the pretext for a stock response (Cervo 1982, 18). As the Lady's imaginative absorption in the erotic panorama of part III shrinks to "Lancelot mused a little space," so the dismissive courtliness of "She has a lovely face" should remind us that the Lady's fate was to mistake a cliché for a living man. The holy dread of the other knights is surely the more appropriate response to this sublime apparition or prophetic *memento mori*, but in Tennyson's matured view it was the ironically defective response of Lancelot that merited the last word. Lancelot's failure to understand, for which he can hardly be blamed—indeed, nobody is to be blamed for anything in this poem, and that is part of its ghastliness—conclusively underscores the lifelong isolation of the Lady. The poem ends by affirming the incommunicable privacy of her tragic victory over beautiful delusions, the last and loveliest of them all being, perhaps, the belief that the way out of solipsism requires nothing more than the will to love forthrightly, to perceive without mediation, to express sincerely, however mortal the cost.

IN THE SWIFT but full arc of its action "The Lady of Shalott," the first major poem of 1832, offers something like a table of contents for the volume, including as it does both the high comic possibilities of fertility and marriage, and an inevitable fall that yet remembers its abandoned possibilities. Although each of the texts to be treated next is surely more than a gloss on some episode in the Lady's career, it may be helpful in advance to have some idea how all of them expand upon phases in the myth of emergent relationship that generates the most enduring work of the entire 1832 volume and that the Lady's career represents most fully. "The Palace of Art" attempts to rewrite the entire myth in moral terms and to alter its outcome accordingly; a confused and ultimately compromised rescue maneuver, the poem nevertheless has its moments, and even its deficiencies reveal a side of Tennyson with which any appreciation of his work must come to terms. This apologetic poem finds its polar opposite in "The Hesperides," which is not a moral allegory but a hyperaesthetic manifesto carrying us back behind the first two parts of "The Lady of Shalott," back to those daemonic energies of creative inhibition that neither the Lady nor Tennyson would have turned against so vehemently had they not loved them first. "Mariana in the South," an intermediate poem of contrasts and intercessions, presents a soul half-sick of shadows and ready for commitment. "Fatima," although it is the least properly esteemed poem in the group, gives such rein to the momentary rapture of erotic idolatry as to constitute a breakthrough that holds considerable interest for the student of Tennyson's career. With "Fatima" the poet first ventures into a mode of visionary confrontation that will culminate in his great classical dramatic monologues; this mode reaches its first full articulation in the formidable poem of the Lady of Shalott's counteranima, the various and at last tragedy-proof "Oenone."

"The Palace of Art": The Howling for Love

The chief interest of "The Palace of Art" is pathological, though not in the way Tennyson had in mind. The patient soliciting our attention, in this study of the sick soul, is not the aristocratic aesthete languishing in her palace but the aesthetically torn bourgeois poet who created her. Writing in response to R. C. Trench's admonition, "Tennyson, we cannot live in art" (*PT*, 400), the poet embraced the laudable purpose, quite consonant with other interests in the 1832 *Poems*, of letting his art live in the common light by accommodating its vision to that of his public. If this purpose inspired the production in 1832 of such mantelpiece figurines as "The May Queen" and "The Miller's Daughter," it was also to bring admirable results with his more successful idylls of 1842 and most notably with *In Memoriam*, where the bereaved poet's recovery of public concerns would contribute integrally to the therapeutic structure of his poem. But public purpose remains a superficial and at best intermittent motive in "The Palace of Art," and it masks Tennyson's darker purpose: to blinker his despairing vision and cloak its findings in pious moralities. The critical objection prompted by this poem—and by an entire side of Tennyson's art—is not at all to morality in poetry, but on the contrary to a morality that is out of poetry, an extraneous moralism that invades the parable to deform its conclusion.

Tennyson was too honest a writer not to be partially ashamed of this evasion, and accordingly he wrote a poem that is conspicuously of two minds. Numerous doublings within the text faithfully embody a schism within the poet, rather like that which characterizes his allegorical Soul at her moment of crisis:

> When she would think, where'er she turned her sight
> The airy hand confusion wrought,
> Wrote, "Mene, mene," and divided quite
> The kingdom of her thought.   (225–228)

The poem too is "divided quite." First there is the curious escape clause of the final stanza, where the Soul doubles back on her rejection of the palace and asks that it be preserved in case she should choose to return fortified by her religious retreat. Then there is the equally curious disproportion in structure—two parts lavish description (1–212) to one part psychological analysis and moral resolution (213–296)—which has led readers of this architectonically knowing poem to suspect that Tennyson was of the aesthete-devil's party without knowing it.[12] This suspicion is confirmed by the tone of Tennyson's 1832 footnotes, which smuggled canceled descriptive stanzas into the published text along with deprecating or commendatory remarks that are couched in purely aesthetic terms.

Then there is a deeper split in the allegorical conception of the poem, which divides "I" from "my soul" in the first line, yet within four stanzas reapproximates the feminine Soul to the presumably masculine "I" by calling her not a queen but "a quiet king" (14), and thereafter so effaces the "I" (mentioned again only four times in passing) that the Soul's "I" in effect usurps focus. For our purposes the significance of Tennyson's distinction between Self and Soul lies in its failure to accrue significance within the poem. When at last the Soul says, "Make me a cottage in the vale" (291), there exists a real doubt whether she is addressing the "I" that also made the palace, and thus invoking the self's capacity to effect its own salvation, or whether she is surrendering self-sufficiency with a prayer to God, "before whom ever lie bare / The abysmal deeps of Personality" (222–223)—psychological deeps that this poem's allegorical strategy implies but leaves for the most part unexplored. Neither God nor "I" answers the Soul's last request; Tennyson's evasion of the final response repeats a persistent evasion of responsibility, which drains his poem of the moral profundity it wishes to claim.

Perhaps his awareness that a poem thus divided against itself could not stand was what dictated the rather awful lines Tennyson addressed to Trench, "With the Following Poem." We should value these lines less for their explicit instructions on how to read the text than for their implicit confession of Tennyson's dissatisfaction with the text as it stood: if the meaning of "The Palace of Art" were as straightforward as the proem to Trench says, there would be no need of the proem. In this sense the distance between proem and poem is the most graphic discontinuity in a multiply fractured performance. Moreover, "With the Following Poem" is itself divided, and in ways that display the relevance of Tennyson's failure here to his other efforts in 1832. It is good to have the passage "And he that shuts Love out, in turn shall be / Shut out from Love, and on her threshold lie / Howling in outer dark-

ness" (14–16), as a virtually contemporary gloss on the unpublished *Lover's Tale*. But if we ask how this prefatory moral bears
on the poem it precedes, we must answer that it has almost nothing
to do with the moral conclusion the poem draws, and instead a
good deal to do with a refractory psychology of desire, which
contradicts and partially escapes the hygienic labeling in which it
comes wrapped: "A sinful soul" (3), "A glorious Devil" (5). The
Soul poisoned with self-sufficiency at the close does indeed "howl
aloud" (285); she howls there, though, not for love but for ab-
solution from her "sin" (287) and purgation of her "guilt" (296).

    That such moral leverage is pretty cheaply purchased was ob-
served in an incisive contemporary review by John Sterling, a
writer whose Apostolic sympathy with Tennyson let him finger
what was false in "The Palace of Art": "The writer's doctrine
seems to be, that the soul, while by its own energy surrounding
itself with all the most beautiful and expressive images that the
history of mankind has produced, and sympathizing with the
world's best thoughts, is perpetrating some prodigious moral of-
fence for which it is bound to repent in sackcloth and ashes . . . In
all Mr. Tennyson's didactic writing one sees too clearly that, unless
when the Image enchains his heart, the thought has far too little
hold upon him to produce any lively movement of soul" (1842,
121). Sterling deserves credit for having seen the problem so early,
but the credit for seeing it first should go to Tennyson, who
recorded his recognition in the only vigorous moment of his
proem, the lines on love's howling outcast. That lost soul breaks
into the proem to howl for love because love is what the Soul in
the poem should have howled for. Or, to be precise, love is what
the Soul should have *kept* howling for, since if I am right the
authentic pathos of this text hinges on its utterance and instantaneous suppression of the same muffled *cri de coeur* that resounds
throughout the 1832 *Poems*.

    To see how this happens we should turn to the one section of
"The Palace of Art" that requires much beyond the sort of admiring technical appreciation exemplified and solicited by Tennyson's published footnotes of 1832: the knotty final score of
stanzas. Having successfully warded off "the riddle of the painful
earth" (213) for three years, the Soul falls at last into a state of
"sore despair" (224), which arises from "Deep dread and loathing
of her solitude" (229). The riddle of the painful earth, the burden

of the Soul's mystery, is precisely that self-sufficiency will not suffice. The Soul begins, that is, to share the reader's sense of her palace as an elaborated version of Julian's gallery from *The Lover's Tale*, or the towered studio of remote Shalott: another fastness that the Tennysonian self adorns with its own imaginings. The Soul's initial reaction to the realization that she is her own jailer takes the predictable form of denial, as she reasserts the self-defense that has worked so well for three years running:

> "What! is not this my place of strength," she said,
>   "My spacious mansion built for me,
> Whereof the strong foundation-stones were laid
>   Since my first memory?"   (233–236)

The sliding temporality of this stanza can serve as a gauge of the Soul's severe mnemonic repression. The opening lines of the entire poem, after all, gave every reason to think that her existence antedated the construction of her palace; but now she conveniently forgets that fact. To plot the temporal ambiguity schematically: in the fourth line "Since my first memory" ought to mean what a dispassionate reader can still make it mean, "after earlier things I can remember"; to the Soul, though, the phrase means "ever since I can remember." The Soul stands strong by privileging as her "first memory," as the basis of what we might nowadays call the ego's self-image, a protective construction. And, in keeping with this defensive gesture, what began as a "pleasure-house" has at length become a fortress.

If by obvious imagistic affiliations the Soul is another of Tennyson's high-born maidens representing the poet, she stands further revealed here as one of Harold Bloom's strong poets, who reads only herself in the works of others. "I" and not "Soul" built the palace, we may recollect—although the Soul, again, does not. We may also recollect, from the earlier portraits of the poets Milton, Shakespeare, Dante, and Homer (133–140), the repeated stress on a self-sufficiency that mirrors the Soul's own.[13] In crude terms the stanza here quoted showcases the Bloomian sublime by dint of repeating the crucial idea: "my," "me," "strength," "strong." More subtly, as in Bloom's account of poetic anxiety, the Soul as strong poet can celebrate and sing herself only in falling from power (Bloom 1973, 19–22). The context of Tennyson's fable introduces the Soul's assertion of strength as a negative movement, and so does the syntax: "What! is not this my place of strength?" Thus the Soul's bid for autonomy reveals her to be in context after all—a situation that suggests, in turn, the Romantic context in which Tennyson's poem is situated.

The clearest of analogues is probably *Alastor*, where Shelley focused upon the crisis of development at which the mind, once "self-possessed" in its contemplation and modification of "the magnificence and beauty of the external world," suddenly finds that "these objects cease to suffice," and "thirsts for intercourse with an intelligence similar to itself" (Preface). So thirsts the Soul in "The Palace of Art," and the soul more generally in Tennyson's 1832 allegories of relatedness. To be sure, with a typically stringent Victorian reduction Tennyson replaces Shelley's Romantic "objects" in nature with objets d'art, which are already fantasies or "modifications" of the external world; in this sense he is an acute enough reader to follow Shelley's bleak poem rather than Shelley's melioristic preface. But in any case Tennyson's figure of the poetic Soul has at this point developed a complex neurosis that is unmistakably Romantic in its wilderness of successive negations:

> Deep dread and loathing of her solitude
>   Fell on her, from which mood was born
> Scorn of herself; again, from out that mood
>   Laughter at her self-scorn.   (229–232)

This intriguing vacillation, which stops well short of any affirmative commitment (even to irony), suggests that the Soul is just half-sick of shadows. If her malady recalls "The Lady of Shalott," here the familiar symptoms are explored at greater length. Some of the shadows the Soul now encounters are quite literally sickening, as Gothic images of "Uncertain shapes" (238), "white-eyed phantasms" (239), even "corpses three-months-old" (243), erode the ego's carefully maintained place of strength and light with the return of the repressed.

Such decay within drives the Soul out of herself and on a quest for relationship, the futility of which—registered here by an odd narrative recession into the pluperfect—then drives her right back inside:

> Back on herself her serpent pride had curled.
>   "No voice," she shrieked in that lone hall,

"No voice breaks through the stillness of this world:
   One deep, deep silence all!"   (257–260)

This desperate shriek in the void is the howling for love that we
seek in vain at poem's end, and that we rightly expect there because
the stern psychological analysis of egotism that prevails here seems
to leave no alternative. Tennyson has resolved, however, to make
"The Palace of Art" an uplifting work at any cost; and accordingly
a newly moralistic perspective enters to control the despair in the
ensuing stanzas, which represent the Soul as not doomed but
damned: "Inwrapt tenfold in slothful shame" (262) and "all alone
in crime" (272). Agree to dismiss the Soul as a shameful criminal,
the poem seems to propose, concede that her psychological cul-
de-sac is really but a moral perversion, and the way out of the
labyrinth will lie clear to us all. But, as Sterling saw, there is no
justification for this concession, beyond the poet's evident need
to escape the consequences of the fable he has imagined.

Given the evasive drift of this poem, I see no reason why its
final two stanzas could not immediately follow the line last quoted:
"And all alone in crime." The world having failed to respond to
her distress call, the Soul could turn right here to the humble
regimen in which Tennyson wanted to let himself and his readers
believe. Instead, Tennyson ups the ante in four superb stanzas that
momentarily bring the poem back into the Romantic orbit of his
best 1832 work, four stanzas whose heightened vision aggravates
the regrettable effect of the conclusion:

> Shut up as in a crumbling tomb, girt round
>   With blackness as a solid wall,
> Far off she seemed to hear the dully sound
>   Of human footsteps fall.
>
> As in strange lands a traveller walking slow,
>   In doubt and great perplexity,
> A little before moon-rise hears the low
>   Moan of an unknown sea;
>
> And knows not if it be thunder, or a sound
>   Of rocks thrown down, or one deep cry
> Of great wild beasts; then thinketh, "I have found
>   A new land, but I die."
>
> She howled aloud, "I am on fire within.
>   There comes no murmur of reply.

What is it that will take away my sin,
        And save me lest I die?"   (273–288)

The Soul's invocation to the world begins to elicit the reply she
has thought she desires; yet with the last stanza she flatly rejects
its consolation, denying her own senses to boot: "There comes
no murmur of reply."

What has intervened? The answer lies in the extended simile of
the two central stanzas, whose quintessentially Tennysonian imagery invites interpretation as urgently as their punctuational independence resists it. We might begin by noting how many details
within the simile derive from two of the most compelling word
landscapes from the earlier portion of the poem, where a "tract
of sand" and an "iron coast" are depicted in adjoining stanzas (65–
72): the solitary walker, the occluded moon, the sea, the stormy
weather, the rocks, and the deep roar of this late passage are all
first present there. I suggested above that we might take the Soul's
palatial imagery, like comparable imagery in Tennyson's other
poems of this period, as subjective fantasies that both gratify and
imprison the embowered self. The close correspondence between
this late simile and the earlier scenic tableaux means, I think, that
we should take the simile in the same way, as the Soul's conversion
of the "human footsteps" into an image serving needs deeper than
her avowed need for human contact. Each imagined source of the
ominous sound portends a threat to the traveler; and the progression of images—from sea to thunder to avalanche to beasts—
moves in the direction both of increasing palpability and of an
imminent personification that would humanize the source of the
sound.[14]

But just at the threshold on which the human form might appear, love's threshold from the proem, the threat of death inter-
poses to check its apparition. At first the Soul seems to hear a
human reply, the responsive sound of the other; but this response
sounds "dully," with a suggestive graveyard echo or *memento mori*
from "the dull earth's mouldering sod" in line 261. Further, the
"low / Moan of an unknown sea" recalls imagistically and phoni-
cally the recent stanzas (245–252) likening the Soul to "A spot of
dull stagnation" and a landlocked "still salt pool" that, weirdly
personified, "hears all night / The plunging seas" it cannot take
the plunge and join. There the Soul is defined by her alienation

from "onward sloping motions infinite / Making for one sure goal"—an instance of Tennyson's impassive doom music that is likely to soothe some readers and make others' flesh creep. At all events the Soul, by the time the late simile brings this music back, feels less than sure about seeking the "one sure goal" that awaits those who give themselves to life. At this penultimate stage the Soul apparently realizes, as the Lady of Shalott realized, that in recognizing the human other she will be entering a new land of generation and decay that means death to the self. Quite unlike the Lady, however, in her "doubt" or characteristic doubleness of mind the Soul declines the gambit, shores herself in stasis, and refuses any recognition of otherness that might commit her to an acceptance of mortality. She tells herself that she has been exhausted by the world's failure to answer her cry for help, but Tennyson's simile takes us behind this defensive symptom to its cause. So great is her fear of acknowledging the world's mortal riddle that she prefers to play deaf and preclude human contact altogether. With this refusal the Soul arrests her own development and becomes a horribly sublime "great wild beast" herself, howling aloud lest there come some murmur of reply, and blunting the question *who* will save her with the more defensive, less personal *what*.

Here is the properly terminal moment of "The Palace of Art," a solipsistic pitfall that Tennyson had both personal and professional reasons for wishing to fill up with some hope. This authorial psychology, and not any internal logic of his narrative, motivates the vacuous "So" of line 289. But the best hope he could come up with was little more than camouflage, the absurdly pious fiction that the soul might "return with others there" (295). How the Soul's regime of solitary self-mortification might enable her to accept either her own mortality or any love the world might offer, the poem never begins to imagine. It thus leaves us to wonder if humility will give her anything more than the latest frisson, and if her cottage in the vale will not be more like Marie Antoinette's dairy than like anything else (Pitt 1962, 124). The most complimentary claim to be made for this poem is that, like all the best of Tennyson's early work, it can return with others to a renewed recognition of the solipsist's emotional dilemma: the very irrelevance of the solution it embraces shows how desperate the dilemma can become.

"The Hesperides": The Rage for Order

One conclusion to draw from "The Lady of Shalott," and from
the imaginative climax near the flawed close of "The Palace of
Art," is that the once embowered Tennysonian self has by 1832
become self-embowering: the central figure begins in an isolation
that is apparently imposed upon her, but the end of each poem
makes it clear that the Lady and the Soul have also been active
collaborators in their captivity. The preserve of the Tennysonian
self requires continuous effort for its preservation. Although this
effort is initially defensive, it soon acquires an addictive momentum, which the Lady of Shalott can break only at the cost of her
life and which the Soul in her palace never legitimately breaks at
all. On the whole the 1832 *Poems* argues that the habit of self-
preservation is not in the self's best interest—a proposition that is
likelier to earn a reader's respect than are the specific remedial
programs the volume advances.

The curious fact remains, however, that the most enchanting
performance in the volume, the work most fully liberated into
immediate vision, is "The Hesperides," a poem of almost hermetic
perfection, in which the addictive forces of inhibition assume
a mythic form that rests content with its own limited but all-
absorbing satisfactions. While it will not do to claim that all happy
poems resemble Tolstoy's happy families in being the same, this
one, like "Recollections of the Arabian Nights," is best approached
from the standpoint of the form within which it has its perfect
say. But in taking such an approach, we need to remember that
"The Hesperides" is, in context, a revelation of the formidable
power with which the major poems of 1832 all do dubious battle,
the clenched dynamic of suppression that Tennyson's century
tended to dignify as *reserve* and that ours, more homely, calls
shyness.[15]

Lovely yet monstrous, "The Hesperides" approximates that familiar chimera which formalist critics in our century inherited
from the Aesthetes, who were lineal descendants of Tennyson in
his: the pure verbal form, the poem that is music, the poem with
nothing to say.[16] Or, as the daughters of Hesperus themselves put
the matter, with a significant difference: theirs is a poem with
plenty to say but no will to say it—a very active will, on the

contrary, to keep the precious wisdom in its fruits of knowledge "hoarded" (48), "Lest the old wound of the world be healèd" and "the ancient secret revealèd" (69–72). Refusing to speak its wisdom, the song of the Hesperides becomes its own subject, a performative incantation that is largely composed of the sisters' exhortations to themselves to sing it. Tennyson took his epigraph from the Attendant Spirit's epilogue in *Comus*—"Hesperus and his daughters three, / That sing about the golden tree"—and for Tennyson if not for Milton the preposition "about" specifies not just a place but a commonplace, a topos or theme for rhetorical amplification: the tree is what the Hesperides sing *about*. They thus find themselves in their function, and in the mythmaking climate of this poem for them to sing a song about a tree is to bring the tree into being as they form around it.

The manifest danger awaiting a long poem with no subject beyond itself is boredom, but that is a problem Tennyson wards off by making it the Hesperides' problem first. In their antilullaby they sing themselves perpetually awake, and the spur to their daemonic insomnia is precisely the fear lest they, or Hesper, or the watchful dragon, fall asleep (Merriman 1969, 4–5). Anxiety about the cessation of song has often enough spurred clear spirits in Romantic tradition—it feeds even the dim light of the Lady of Shalott—but rarely has it been in so naked and unassisted a way the overt theme of song. Tennyson's Hesperides bind themselves to a project of perpetually fresh invention with a minimum of variables: exhortation on a single theme, description of an unchanging mythic situation in a severely circumscribed environment, and a modest kit of interchangeable metrical parts. But these are enough to let Tennyson weave a text of over a hundred unfaltering lines that rounds to its repetitive coda only, we may suppose, because its impassive auditor Zidonian Hanno is passing out of earshot. And if the text does falter, as I shall suggest it does at one late point, even its faults attest to a rhetorical control that sustains the closest scrutiny.

As a measure of Tennyson's craft we cannot do better than sample the opening lines of the sisters' song:

> The golden apple, the golden apple, the hallowed fruit,
> Guard it well, guard it warily,
> Singing airily,

Standing about the charmèd root.
Round about all is mute,
As the snowfield on the mountain-peaks,
As the sandfield at the mountain-foot.
Crocodiles in briny creeks
Sleep and stir not: all is mute.
If ye sing not, if ye make false measure,
We shall lose eternal pleasure,
Worth eternal want of rest.
Laugh not loudly: watch the treasure
Of the wisdom of the west.   (14–27)

The subtitle "SONG" is scarcely necessary: we are in a realm of sheer incantation. Rhyme, alliteration, and the repetition of such key phrases as "golden apple," "guard it," and "all is mute" form conspicuous devices; these crest a dense and subtle patterning of mainly dimeter phrasal lengths, similar grammatical structures, and like speech sounds within words, to engender remarkable variety within a homogeneous spell. Thus rhyme and meter in "guard it warily" bring forth "Singing airily," whose participial form comes back in "Standing about the charmèd root"—from which line, in turn, "root," "about," and "Standing" are each tapped for the phonemes that compose "Round" at the beginning of the next. A text in which words beget words like this can seem arbitrary; yet Tennyson achieves the opposite effect, his characteristic inevitability, largely by seeing to it that each of his choices is multiply determined. The crocodiles lie in briny creeks not just because zoology proposes that habitat or because alliteration does, but also because the symmetry of "croc-" and "creek" is counterpointed against a regular narrowing of the vowel sounds from the broad opening *o* through the double *i* of "-diles" and "bri-" to a double *e* ("-ny creeks"). Then in the next line the vowels from "Sleep" to "mute" retreat by degrees toward the back of the mouth, the entire couplet exhibiting a symmetry that firmly props up the explicit hypnotic message.

The point of the verbal wizardry thus performed within a virtually closed linguistic system is to keep the singers awake. Tennyson therefore punctuates the formal inevitability of his chant with a series of pinpricks or minor shocks. The Hesperides sustain the patterns they weave just long enough to establish a regularity that they can then disrupt at not quite predictable intervals. This

weaving takes place on a warp and a woof, a binary apparatus
each axis of which has its distinct syntax and prosody, both in
place by the end of the passage just quoted. Metrically the first
four lines fall into two-stress units, chiefly in configurations other
than the trochaic-iambic alternation of stressed with unstressed
syllables; and syntactically these lines form an imperative sentence,
enunciating the vigilance that is to be the burden of the song. But
then, as if to acknowledge something hypnotically counterpro-
ductive in such sustained exhortation, the song modulates through
the transitional line "Round about all is mute" into the indicative
mood, and into the straightforward trochaic-iambic measure that
will furnish the usual accompaniment to that mood throughout
(Ostriker 1967, 275).

A poem as formally inventive as this one is not liable to suffer
reduction to any simple analytic system, but in a general way the
Hesperides' whole song divides along the lines introduced here:
on the one hand into declarative statements in comparatively regular trochaic or iambic measures, and on the other hand into imperative injunctions that more freely accommodate anapestic
substitutions, which quicken the song into wakefulness. In discussing the poem years later with his son, Tennyson underscored
this metrical distinction by the way he accented two of its lines.
The descriptive line 37, "Líquid góld, hóneyswéet, thróugh and
thróugh," is defective trochaic, if we count as unstressed syllables
or musical rests the caesuras marked by the commas, while the
hortatory line 56, "Sing awáy, sing alóud evermóre in the wínd,
without stóp," is, as Tennyson said, anapestic (*PT*, 426–427).
Tennyson's scansions of these apparently quite similar lines sound
arbitrary out of context but make sense as parts of the syntactic-
metrical system that the Hesperides' song develops. Constructions
of the first type, which tend to occur when the sisters are discussing
their circumstances, usually convey either the inevitability of natural process or the binding conditions that circumscribe their singing. Whereas these constructions celebrate the mellowing of the
fruit in repose, the more metrically arresting imperative constructions have to do with its hallowing, a spirited consecration that
calls for preternatural vigilance.

The key to the Hesperides' scheme is the differential way its
two modes keep nudging the mind to attentiveness, and not any
qualities inherent in the modes. The modes themselves are antag-

onistic but ultimately cooperative: natural description offers the sisters a way of obeying their own orders to keep singing; and the purpose of those orders, in turn, is to prolong indefinitely the processes of natural growth that the descriptive passages render. The lines on the crocodiles, for example, would become imperative with the addition of a comma after line 21, and one can easily imagine a recitation that suspends the distinction between statement and command. This same distinction is suspended often in the early Tennysonian bower; one of the hallmarks of the paradisal moment in his later works, too, is a contentment that declines to choose between "that which is" and "Let there be . . . " We may call this a state of contentment with the given only if we recall that in "The Hesperides" the given can never quite be taken for granted, because it is the embowered self's perpetually renewed gift to itself. The merger of indicative and imperative moods may persist only so long as the genuine contrary to both, the subjunctive mood of creative anxiety, stays clearly within earshot.

And so it does. In a series of constructions beginning with "if" or "lest" (there are nine in the first three parts of the song), the Hesperides draw attention to the threatened intrusion of "one from the East" (42). Because it prompts the song that is their identity, this threat would if accomplished mean their undoing. When the sisters' anxieties surface in the first "if" clause of the opening passage (23), Tennyson characteristically reinforces a syntactic difference with a prosodic one. In lines 18–22 a new norm of declarative syntax and iambic-trochaic meter has established itself, but with the "if" clause the poet shakes the prosodic harness afresh: "If ye sing not, if ye make false measure." Of course the measure is false here, since technically neither "not" nor "false" ought to receive the stress both demand; but what is false to the lulling metronome is true to the purposes of the singers, who find eternal pleasure in the "eternal want of rest" (another musical pun?) that enables Hesperian stasis to subsist. Like later references to "number" and the reiterated incantation of "five and three"—which must have less to do with the arcane numerology Tennyson scholars have pursued than with the "numbers" of Tennyson's verse (Stange 1952, 108; Fricke 1970; Fleissner 1973; Gallant 1977)—the false prosodic measure of "false measure" reflects a metapoetic awareness. So complex a self-consciousness, amid so apparently

hypnotic an enchantment, serves to register the Hesperides' sophisticated knowledge that they are singing for their lives.

Was Tennyson singing for his? If my account of the 1832 *Poems*
is accurate, life to the Hesperides was death to him, and he should
have sought routes of escape from the static perfection of their
seductively inhibited chant (Peltason 1984a, 91). The poem offers
two such routes, I think, one lying outside the song, the other
lying through it; and for both the escape vehicle is a technique of
Romantic allusion that brings Tennyson's hermetically sealed text
into relationship with what lies outside. The first way out, the
introductory blank-verse passage devoted to Zidonian Hanno, not
only stands typographically and metrically outside the song
proper, but also consists of an extended image of travel through
"calmèd bays" (4) and departure into "the outer sea" (13).[17] The
Hesperides' song thus emerges as what Hanno hears during a short
digression from a voyage that suggests a greater world elsewhere.
Yet Tennyson's thrifty proem takes a strangely digressive interest
in what Hanno does *not* hear: "neither warbling of the nightingale, / Nor melody o' the Lybian lotusflute" (6–7). Lines like these
on unheard melodies are surely designed to prick up the reader's
ear. Here they mark allusions to the nightingale whose singing
drugged Keats and, further off, to the "symphony and song"
Coleridge gathered in "Kubla Khan" from somewhat different but
equally exotic African and pharmacological sources, the Abyssinian dulcimer in the poem and the opium dream behind it. Since
both these Romantic poems enter paradisal realms, possibly Tennyson means to introduce his reader to a vision of paradise that
vies with theirs, in the mode of "Timbuctoo." It seems likely,
however, that we are also to recall the relapse from paradisal vision
that finally poises both Coleridge's poem and Keats's on the du-
bieties of dream; for the Hesperides' voices come to Hanno "like
the voices in a dream" (12). Do the sisters' voices spell vision or
hallucination? This implicit Romantic question, like the structural
division of the text into proem and song, suggests more ably than
"The Palace of Art" that Tennyson is of two minds, and that the
visionary seductions of the song come with less than his full
endorsement.

The defect of this framing maneuver is that it leaves intact what
it frames, a central song whose fluent enchantment more than

suffices to dispel the prophylaxis of a brief warning. Accordingly, I suggest, Tennyson here supplemented his favorite device of the frame with a more difficult, perhaps impossibly subtle expedient: that of undermining the central song from within, during the long description that constitutes most of part IV. With some two dozen descriptive lines (83–105), punctuated once in the middle by a single imperative (95), this is the place that conforms least well to the shuttling scheme of syntax and prosody outlined above. At this point "The Hesperides" takes a new turn, in other words, and I think it a subversive turn in the direction of Tennyson's Romantic precursors. The poem is evidently a westering song of ripeness, but the volume in which Tennyson published it supplies a context that also makes it appear a portrait of arrested development. Romantic poetry forms an important part of this context, which here certainly includes two great Romantic odes of the west and the season of ripeness, Shelley's "Ode to the West Wind" and Keats's "To Autumn."

Like these odes, Tennyson's incantation takes its stand unapologetically upon an occidental belatedness; and it urges its claim for the west as the place of magic and fertility in the best Romantic fashion, by revising Milton. Tennyson's Hesperian garden grows in a facsimile of the eastward-facing amphitheater that embowers Milton's garden—where, too, golden fruit "Hung amiable, *Hesperian* Fables true" (*Paradise Lost*, IV.250)—but Tennyson's garden has a westward prospect instead: "Till midnoon the cool east light / Is shut out by the round of the tall hillbrow" (97–98). For the Hesperides "All good things are in the west" (96) because the west is all they choose to know; but it is the burden of Tennyson's allusions to Shelley and Keats to show that the Hesperides do not know enough. He suggests the sisters' condition of arrested development by, as it were, arresting the development of the Romantic odes, and drawing upon their imagery in so selective a way as to call attention to what the selection leaves out.

The allusions begin with Shelley:

> Every flower and every fruit the redolent breath
> Of this warm seawind ripeneth,
> Arching the billow in his sleep. (83–85)

Tennyson's sleeping billow has its counterpart in the sleeping Mediterranean personified in the third stanza of Shelley's ode:

"Thou who didst waken from his summer dreams / The blue Mediterranean, where he lay / Lulled by the coil of his chrystalline streams" (29–31). In Tennyson the wind is the accomplice of sleep, perhaps even its agent, "arching" the water bed like a rocking cradle. Shelley's passage, however, describes what is only the eye of an apocalyptic storm; the wind has long since startled the dreamy sea awake. Shelley addresses the wild west wind as a revolutionary destroyer and preserver, but Tennyson's "low west wind, breathing afar," fulfills the latter function only, in its conspiracy with the evening to "Make the apple holy and bright" (90–92). "The world is wasted with fire and sword, / But the apple of gold hangs over the sea" (104–105): the Hesperides' song expressly distinguishes the growth it fosters from the energies of apocalypse, because apocalyptic change and the revelation of secret wisdom are precisely what it aims to prevent.

The autumnal ripeness of Keats's ode might be expected to offer more congenial common ground to such an evolutionary song, and indeed echoes of this ode are more distinctly audible:

> Till midnoon the cool east light
> Is shut out by the round of the tall hillbrow;
> But when the fullfaced sunset yellowly
> Stays on the flowering arch of the bough,
> The luscious fruitage clustereth mellowly,
> Goldenkernelled, goldencored,
> Sunset-ripened above on the tree.   (97–103)

The maturing sun, the mellow ripeness in kernel and core, the lingering warmth, and the heavy reliance on intransitives and passive participles are all Keatsian, as is the resistance to any intrusion of earliness, figured by Keats in his dismissal of "the songs of Spring" and by Tennyson in his exclusion of "The cool east light." But Tennyson's is, as we should predict, the more resistant text, because it will not admit the ultimate lateness of death either, as Keats so movingly does admit it in describing the harvest or listening for the lamb's sacrificial bleat and the mourning of the gnats (Rowlinson 1984, 359–361). The never-ripe apples in Tennyson's garden are never to be plucked, if the Hesperides have any say in the matter; and there are no insects to disturb its stasis with mementos of the ephemeral—or to pollinate its flowers, either, and thus to intrude Keatsian suggestions that the honey of generation entails the bitter sting of death.[18]

We thus come once again upon the twofold elision of sex and death in Tennyson, an evasion of Keatsian change that corresponds to his evasion of the more dramatic changes of Shelleyan revolution. The gorgeously stunted growth of Tennyson's art, when exposed to the light of his more capacious Romantic predecessors, is found wanting—a judgment common enough among readers in our century, but one that here, at least, merits double-checking. For here the hothouse beauties of the inbred Tennysonian imagination, weighed in allusive and prosodic balances, are found wanting by Tennyson himself. I believe that "The Hesperides" is self-parodic at this point, and I stake my claim on the very badness of its art. There is something dreadfully awkward in those tongue-clogging lines on the "fullfaced sunset," and their awkwardness clearly proceeds from a surfeit of Keats—whom, we must remember, Tennyson could imitate far more skillfully, and originally, when he chose to do so. The imitation of Keats here bears all the marks of a second-rate, ersatz reproduction, a monochrome snapshot of "To Autumn." Against the weight and depth of Keats's kinesthetic imagery, which in capturing natural process also moves into the fourth or temporal dimension, Tennyson's seems static and flat. The sun for Keats figures as the "bosom-friend" of the season, but Tennyson's sun is merely "fullfaced," and even this suggested fullness is quickly emptied out by the merely visual "yellowly," an adjective in adverb's clothing. As topics for poetry, especially since Keats, the kernel and core of fruit invite depth perception if anything does, but they are described here solely by their uniform "golden" color. The passage never lets us do more than look at its fruit, which remains oddly "above," tantalizingly out of reach. The imagery, like the verse, is intentionally inhibited at this point, I submit—"gummed up," to recall Pound's phrase—in order to drive home the sterility of the Hesperides' virginal situation and thus enact the souring of Tennysonian isolation.

THIS BOOK ARGUES for the thematic and strategic importance of a highly literate Victorian poet's allusiveness, principally to Romantic poetry; but of course "The Hesperides," like much else in his oeuvre, derives most obviously from classical sources. We might pause, therefore, before proceeding to some decidedly less virginal women from the 1832 *Poems*, to consider how Tennyson's reception of the complex classical myth of the Hesperides illuminates his responsiveness to whatever he read for poetic use. This responsiveness was primarily Romantic, grounded in the dilemmas of the sole self, even when its pretexts lay in the classics or the scriptures.[19] What Tennyson found in a variety of Greek, Latin, and Renaissance English texts on the Hesperides, he read as allegories of the problem with which he most persistently wrestled during the early 1830s: his own simultaneous attraction to and revulsion from a state of perpetual psychic virginity.

The scattered classical tradition ambiguously relates the Hesperides and their garden both to chastity and to fruitfulness. According to the longest thread, which dates from Hesiod's *Theogony* (215ff.), the sisters are not only virginal but virgin-born, Night being their sole parent. Tennyson derives the sisters from a somewhat later parthenogenetic tradition—this one masculine, as commemorated in the Hesperides' very name and in their repeated addresses to "Father Hesper"—a tradition that insulates the sisters against motherhood past or future.[20] The plot thickens, however, when we move from the sisters to their garden. In a chorus from the *Hippolytus* of Euripides (742–751), Phaedra's suicidal defensiveness against the desire she feels for her stepson is figured as a wish to escape to the garden of the Hesperides. But this same chorus then alludes to the garden as the nuptial bower of Zeus and Hera, to whom Gaea, primal earth mother, gave the golden fruit for a pledge of fertility.

It was to this more earthy and fecund side of the Greek tradition that the Roman poets turned—and that Tennyson turns as well, by implication, at the close of his poem. Virgil's Dido in the *Aeneid* (IV.486ff.) follows the *Hippolytus* chorus in associating the Hesperian preserve with an honorable (and in that sense chaste) death. But this association makes dramatic sense precisely because the Hesperides and their fruit also stand for the sexual fulfillment that Dido, like Phaedra, continues to desire. Furthermore, Tennyson would have read in Virgil's sixth eclogue (61) that it is with Hesperian apples that Hippomenes sidetracks the unapproachably chaste Atalanta into marriage; and it is a characteristically carnal version of this story that Ovid has Venus tell Adonis in the *Metamorphoses* (X.640ff.). Ovid's rendition, the *locus classicus* for those golden apples on which Tennyson lays such stress, breathes fresh life into the connection of Hesperian fruit with human fruitfulness.

Tennyson's familiarity with classical literature was, by twentieth-century standards, daunting. Yet in his final years he told his minor Boswell, William Allingham, that "no man can really feel the poetry of any language but his own" (1967, 350). For an ambitious poet writing as late as the nineteenth century, and out of a vernacular tradition as rich as England's, the most important influences were native. Classical poets had invested the Hesperian myth with the contrary energies of chastity and fertility; in the traditions of English poetry Tennyson encountered a similar ambiguity, more pointedly relevant to his own concerns. Spenser's Garden of Adonis in book III of *The Faerie Queene*, with a boost from Herrick's *Hesperides*, might have handed on the Ovidian tradition of Hesperian fertility intact to the nineteenth century, had it not been overshadowed by Milton, the one classic English poet who meant even more to posterity than did Spenser. In *Comus*—a text whose relevance Tennyson's epigraph suggests—Milton had turned Hippomenes' trick around in favor of chastity. With his usual revisionary genius Milton expurgated the myth, finding in the situation of the Hesperides an emblem for continence itself:

> beauty, like the fair Hesperian Tree
> Laden with blooming gold, had need the guard
> Of dragon watch with unenchanted eye,
> To save her blossoms, and defend her fruit
> From the rash hand of bold Incontinence.   (393–397)

A vigilant continence thus became the corrected source from which a chaste but still Spenserian (and Ovidian) fertility might flow with the grace of unfallen nature.

What is likeliest to surprise a reader of Tennyson's enchanting poem who consults this Miltonic passage is the dragon's "unenchanted eye"—a phrase that may well have disturbed Tennyson as he considered how the ethics of *Comus* bore upon his 1832 emergencies. Given his imaginative susceptibility to states of virginal isolation, he would have seen Milton's equation of chastity and demystified vision as itself an egregious mystification. "The Hesperides" shows more tirelessly than any of its companion poems how deeply enchanted with itself the virginal eye can be; what Milton's masque had presented as the enabling condition of growth, and finally of immortality, had become for Tennyson a beautiful but emotionally disabling masquerade, performed in denial of the growth that portends death.

The Hesperides, then, perpetuate a Miltonic sleight throughout their song, enlisting growth and fruition in the service of a magic that is fundamentally at odds with the decline toward death that the natural cycle entails—and that is also entailed in various ways by the classical tradition. (Even the original parthenogenetic account in Hesiod links the Hesperides with the death-dealing Fates as common offspring of their mother Night.) Tennyson must have lent himself to this prestidigitation with mixed motives, knowing that just such evasiveness was his poetic forte, but knowing too that his past successes were antithetical to the poetry of commitment he now wanted to write. Accordingly, he wrote into "The Hesperides" a passage of sham Keats that, allusively evoking the changes of fertility and mortality it omits to describe, faces the myth back, in spite of Milton, toward its fleshy and metamorphic source in Keats's poetic great-grandfather Ovid. This strategy of negative allusion may appear supersubtle; certainly Tennyson was made forcibly aware of its riskiness when reviewers of the 1832 *Poems* attacked this one with virulence, and he withdrew it permanently from his canon. Still, as I shall argue in Chapter 5, tactics of negative allusion were soon to become essential features of Tennyson's practice as a writer of idylls; on this view the very lapses of style for which critics attacked "The Hesperides" mark it as a bracing moment in the poet's career.

"Five links, a golden chain, are we" (65): the image means what it says. The Hesperides do not sing in their chains, they *are* the chains, figures of the self-delighting bondage out of which Tennyson hoped to follow his Hanno from an inner to an outer sea. This seaward movement recalls the inhibited traveler from the final simile of "The Palace of Art," and it also recalls the water voyage of the Lady of Shalott. If we compare the experience behind the Lady's "Singing in her song" to the well preserved innocence of the Hesperides, "Singing airily"—venting an air that weaves a changeless atmosphere—we can measure the distance between their self-delight and her tragic knowledge of its deficiencies. "The Hesperides" is the more limited poem, but then its limitation is its point.

"Mariana in the South": Unweaving the Curse

Tennyson's attempt to resettle the most fixed of his early personae was probably a mistake; but it was an instructive mistake that illustrates the direction in which he wanted his imagination to move in 1832. "Mariana in the South" inevitably gets compared with "Mariana," a poem that makes almost any other feel unaccomplished. The absoluteness of the earlier work, the perfection of what Hallam praised as its "fusion" of inner and outer realities, has caused readers to look in the later work for virtues that it never aims to display. I too mean to compare the two Marianas, but with the explicit understanding that the true sisters of Mariana in the south are the Tennysonian women of 1832 who seek to identify strength with human relationship and not with the defenses of solitude. The new Mariana does not merge with a landscape of the mind; she stands as distinct from her surroundings as from her distant lover. Where the first Mariana was an abandoned woman in both meanings of the term, this one confronts with good sense the plain fact that she has been left behind. She is much more straightforwardly self-conscious than the northern Mariana, who loses herself forever in the shadowy projections of an inchoate desire. Fully aware of her self, of her circumstances, and of the difference between the two, Mariana in the south knows what she *wants* (in the senses of both lack and desire). And what she wants is *out*—to move out of her gorgeous southern prison, and out of herself into commitment with the lover whom her outgoing force of character persuades us she may just win back.

It appears strange to speak so affirmatively of a work whose every stanza ends with Mariana's moaning, night and morn, that she is "forgotten" and "forlorn." But, in addition to the up-tempo prosody of these refrains, we should note that in most instances Mariana is moaning *to* someone, imagining an audience that is, under the circumstances, quite lively, and as various as are the prayers, questions, and even asides that enliven her lament. In half of the eight stanzas she addresses her namesake the Virgin Mary. Mariana's slender interest in virginity makes this address somewhat incongruous, and she herself appears to see as much in changing the tone and mode of her petition as the poem develops. But these little prayers suggest that one way of specifying the difference between the northern and southern Marianas is to invoke the difference between an absolutizing, chilly Protestant iconoclasm and the intercessionary, concretizing Catholic imagination that is at work here. Mariana prays "Before Our Lady" (28), and inhabits a mythically animated, hierarchical universe in which a star can be hailed as "Large Hesper" and the night can rise "Heaven over Heaven" (90–92). Similarly, when this Mariana sees images pass her door in stanzas 6 and 7, they are far more substantial and sociable than their northern counterparts: they stop, look, and let themselves be quoted.

In commenting on the two "Marianas" in a letter of 1831 to W. B. Donne, Arthur Hallam noted that "the essential and distinguishing character of the conception requires in the Southern Mariana a greater lingering on the outward circumstances, and a less palpable transition of the poet into Mariana's feelings, than was the case in the former poem" (*LH*, 401). This letter postdates the "poetry of sensation" review; it also presupposes it, in linking the independence the poet grants to circumstantial details with the poet's independence from the persona he has conceived. It seems generally true that in a Tennyson poem palpability of detail increases in proportion to the poet's imaginative distance from the character through whom he speaks: it is when environment-as-surroundings dissolves into environment-as-ambience—just what happens with image after solid-seeming image from the northern "Mariana"—that we recognize the evanescence of personality and the onset of Tennyson's rapturous, melancholy sublime.

In any case, as Hallam saw, palpability is the distinctive mark of "Mariana in the South," and the firm otherness of the figures in Mariana's southern world corresponds to the chiseled chiaroscuro with which Tennyson stamps the southern landscape. Although heat and light predominate, this landscape is neither fuzzily sun-drenched nor obscured with Lancelot-like glitter, but outstanding for its contrasts. Probably the best illustration of this high relief occurs in the difference between the opening stanza of 1832 and the entirely recast version Tennyson published ten years afterward:

> Behind the barren hill upsprung
>   With pointed rocks against the light,
> The crag sharpshadowed overhung
>   Each glaring creek and inlet bright.
> Far, far, one lightblue ridge was seen

Looming like baseless fairyland;
    Eastward a slip of burning sand,
Dark-rimmed with sea, and bare of green.   (1832)

With one black shadow at its feet,
    The house through all the level shines,
Close-latticed to the brooding heat,
    And silent in its dusty vines:
A faint-blue ridge upon the right,
    An empty river-bed before,
    And shallows on a distant shore,
In glaring sand and inlets bright.   (1842)

In the 1832 version Tennyson all but trumpeted his intention to attain clarity of outline, with "barren," "pointed," and "sharp-shadowed" reinforcing the aggressive "against the light" and the imagistic and acoustic bite of "rocks" and "crag," all within the first three lines. The revised version does the same job in a more efficient and less pugnacious fashion. "With one black shadow at its feet" recalls the opening line of the earlier "Mariana"—"With blackest moss the flower-plots"—only to replace its sickly rhythmic regularity (held over into the prettily alliterative southern stanza of 1832) with a new and dramatic tattoo, whose irregular stress rivets attention upon the operative visual term, "black." What in "Mariana" would have been a bluish ridge faintly descried becomes a ridge toned with chromatic precision as "faint-blue"; as a substitute for the 1832 "lightblue," "faint-blue" also makes the affective coloration more precise by suggesting not lightness of spirit but light-headedness due to oppressive heat—and compounded, perhaps, by the domestic corseting of the "Close-latticed" house. The "empty river-bed" stands for an empty bed of another sort; yet Tennyson arrives at the effect not through his habitual immaterializing magic but through the dry exactitude of physical delineation upon which he would, as an idyllist, soon plume himself. One vague "Tennysonian" line that may feel out of place in the 1842 version is the second; but even here, it could be argued, the image of something shining through "all the level" is justly extrapolated from the visually persuasive renditions of heat-thickened, palpable distance in lines 3, 7, and 8.

Before the poem is long underway we understand that in their clarity of outline these descriptions correspond to what Hallam termed "the distinguishing character of the conception," which corresponds in its turn to the poet's conception of his dramatized character. The southern Mariana's clearly circumscribed identity depends, like the meridian landscaping, on contrast: her sense of herself depends on her sense of what she is not and therefore may be defined against. We first see Mariana when stanza 2 pictures her face within the bounding outline provided by her hair; and in the next stanza Mariana herself has a look at this framed portrait: "And on the liquid mirror glowed / The clear perfection of her face" (31–32). To enunciate the contrast between Tennyson's two abandoned women we need only ask what the 1830 Mariana looked like, or what use a mirror might have served in a house, indeed a terrain, that could do nothing but reflect its mistress. The southern Mariana's look into the glass is thus in itself a distinguishing note of character. What she goes on to do is more distinctive still:

> "Is this the form," she made her moan,
>   "That won his praises night and morn?"
> And "Ah," she said, "but I wake alone,
>   I sleep forgotten, I wake forlorn."   (33–36)

Mariana not only talks to herself about her own image; in the third line she surprises herself in the act, and the word order mirrors the complexity of her surprise: "And 'Ah,' she said, 'but . . . '" In this passage from 1842 Tennyson's technical variation within a refrain of his own devising marks Mariana's changeful psychology, and it also marks a distinct advance upon the relatively simple uses of stanzaic refrain in the poems of 1827 and 1830. The lines here quoted occur within their stanza just where, in earlier stanzas, Mariana has invoked the sympathy of the Virgin Mary. Moving now from passive prayer into analytic soliloquy, Mariana fills the Virgin's place with a realistic, deeply textured self-consciousness, which reflects on the discrepancy between her fantasies and her actual conditions. So it is no surprise that, later in the poem, "Dreaming, she knew it was a dream" (49); the inhabitant of a house underlined twice by "one black shadow" (1, 80) should have little difficulty in seeing her own projected shadows for what they are and distinguishing them from waking life.

Mariana's mirror-gazing, then, while more than a little narcissistic, is less than entirely so; and Tennyson records her saving grasp of the actual by means of Romantic allusion. "The liquid mirror," as Ricks's edition points out, comes from the studied narcissism of Shelley's *Alastor* (462), which may be the premier precursor for the many texts of the early 1830s in which Tennyson's theme was the extrication of the self from its own infatuations.[21] Elsewhere Ricks (1981) mentions this echo of *Alastor* as a figure for allusiveness itself, whereby the poet tempers an expression of timeless loneliness by extending the hand of creative fellowship across the years. Ricks is probably our best scholar of Tennysonian allusion, but here he underplays—or romanticizes, in the bad old sense of that term—the revisionary side of Romantic allusiveness; he overlooks the importance of change both for Mariana and for her maker. Shelley's "liquid mirror" is actually a pool, into which the solitary Poet of *Alastor* gazes late in his irretrievably self-destructive quest: the noun in his phrase is figurative and the adjective literal. With Tennyson the reverse is true: his lady looks into a real mirror and knows it, albeit at the Tennysonian twilight hour when things often start looking wavy. This reversal is noteworthy, especially in a poet usually given to the rendition of adjectival effect rather than objective substance. For Tennyson's reversal of the Shelleyan image signifies both the southern Mariana's hold on a real world and the poet's own break with the Romantic narcissism he had pursued to the extremes of *The Lover's Tale* and the works of 1832 that we have considered thus far.

Tennyson's allusion to Shelley reveals less the interpoetic solidarity of a shared or reflected classic meaning, as Ricks would have it, than a Romantic repudiation or distortion of a specifically Romantic meaning: to wit, the Wordsworthian and Shelleyan surmise that the ardent heart must either die young or else burn to the socket. Furthermore, Tennyson undertakes this allusive distortion for more than merely literary ends: he means to imagine, for the first time in a poem of major ambitions, a self that is ripe for contact with a more than imaginary otherness. Tennyson would have taken a local cue to the erotic implications of the *Alastor* parable from an allusion, just four lines further up in Shelley's text, to the unforgettable "translucent wave" of Sabrina in Milton's *Comus*—a work whose bearing on the virginity of the Tennysonian soul we have already met in "The Hesperides." The ultimate goal of the most important poems Tennyson wrote and revised in the early 1830s is contact with another person, human or divine. But a prerequisite stage, the stage at which this intermediate poem rests, is the establishment of a foothold in some credible externality, exemplified here in Mariana's knowledge that her "liquid mirror" is indeed a mirror, and that "the form" she sees there is not an other but precisely a *form*, her own reflected image.

The next line of the poem, the start of stanza 4, makes it clear how very Romantic Mariana's desolate situation is, and thus how very Tennysonian is her resistance to a certain current of Romantic response to desolation: "Nor bird would sing, nor lamb would bleat" (37). Through the dejection of Keats's fancy-entoiled knight, for whom "no birds sing" in "La Belle Dame sans Merci," we can recognize the precipitating crisis of Wordsworth's "Intimations" ode: "Now, while the birds thus sing a joyous song, / And while the young lambs bound / As to the tabor's sound, / To me alone there came a thought of grief" (19–21, 168–170). Wordsworth's repeated reference to noisy birds and lambs in the ode framed the poet's resolution to arise in independence through the exertions of a deific memory and lift himself by Romantic bootstraps to a more than natural height. And—to tie off what is admittedly a complicated affiliation—with these images Wordsworth was responding in his own right to the seminal invocation to book III of *Paradise Lost*, where Milton had lamented his vanished power to see birds, lambs, or persons ("flocks, or herds, or human face divine") and had called upon the compensatory gift of "Celestial Light" to disclose "things invisible to mortal sight" (40–55). With this strong line of transcendental Romanticism, the very mainstay of Tennyson's early art, "Mariana in the South" decisively breaks. It listens instead for the music of fulfillment and mortalist commitment from Keats's "To Autumn," where redbreasts and swallows sing and "full-grown lambs loud bleat from hilly bourne" (30). Mariana listens, and Mariana fails to hear; but we believe this poem—as we should never believe the northern "Mariana"—when it goes on to ascribe the silence to ecological causes in heat and drought instead of psychological ones. In this sense the faithfully recorded silence is but another evidence of the southern Mariana's hold on the objectively real, which is a part of what we might call this poem's commitment to commitment, even if only as a possibility.

The same instinct for reality permits Mariana to articulate her plight definitively in the penultimate stanza, and then in the last to look beyond the present "day and night" (83) toward an event that the northern Mariana memorably endeavored to deny: "The night comes on that knows not morn, / When I shall cease to be all alone, / To live forgotten, and love forlorn" (94–96). One hesitates to name this event as either the *nox perpetua* of death or the ecstasy of sexual consummation, and one hesitates longer because of the no less ambiguous message delivered by the cryptic "image" of the preceding stanza, "But thou shalt be alone no more" (76). In the poem's reluctance to specify either sex or death as Mariana's place of rest, it remains faithful to a recurrent Tennysonian pattern, and also to the program for change that the poet was working in 1832 to educe from the impassioned fixations of the past—fixations he presumably meant to confront and undo in the first place by returning to Mariana, that memorably fixated figure of his own past poetry. If we recall the way the earlier Mariana perpetuated her solitary desire by rejecting sexual contact and maintaining the absence of the beloved, we understand the events of sex and death to be equivalent in the oncoming night "that knows not morn." And if we recall the way the equivalence of sex and death was accepted at the pivot point of "The Lady of Shalott," we can hear in this lady's prophecy the prelude to a decisive change.

At this point, however, the question a student of Tennyson learns not to ask about the earlier Mariana—Why not just leave and find him?—becomes relevant to this poem and jeopardizes, if not its integrity, its status as more than a document in the history of the Victorian Woman Question. We have it on Hallam's authority that Tennyson intended "Mariana in the South" to be a study in stasis, "the expression of a desolate loneliness." But a woman as resourcefully aware as this Mariana cannot be expected to stay in her desert bower for long. Possibly it was his sense of an imaginative conflict of interest that brought Tennyson to close the poem here, as his persona turns outward from Hesperian self-contemplation in the glass to look on the sweet heaven and thus become at last a Coleridgean emblem of fruitful mutuality: "There all in spaces rosy-bright / Large Hesper glittered on her tears" (89–90; compare "Frost at Midnight," 72–74, and "The Nightingale: A Conversation Poem," 97–105). A suspicion lingers that what Tennyson is really after is the closural force of his habitual music of doom, despite the facts that this has not looked much like a doom poem thus far, and that the force of an inevitable closure is not one to which a resilient persona half sick of shadows should very readily yield. Perhaps the supervention of such gravely composed music—largely, and ominously, composed first in *The Lover's Tale* (Heath MS., fol. 66)—finally suggests as grave a purpose in the poet's conception of this character. His belief in the southern Mariana's clear-sighted readiness seems curbed by a larger fear that the moment she inhabits can be but a moment, after all, one that is condemned to its place within the sadder myth his more ambitious poems were tracing more fully.

"Fatima": Near the Fire

"I *will* possess him or will die" (39): with this line from the sultry last stanza of her love song Fatima tersely states the alternatives entertained by the southern Mariana at the close of hers. There, however, the resemblance between the two women stops. Fatima is anything but the sensible realist of the southern grange; fallen in the opening stanza from her "constant mind" (5), she nonetheless forges an aggressive constancy that is unlike anything we have encountered in Tennyson thus far. It is Fatima, not the Mariana of 1832, who first raises a worthy countersong to the 1830 "Mariana." Her extroverted and apocalyptic fervor aims to match Mariana's insatiable inwardness and to reclaim passion as a drive for relationship, whatever the cost. That this poem fails to match "Mariana" should not surprise us, given the well-formed habits of Tennyson's imagination. But its stridency of tone and formal shakiness are distinctly the faults of a habit-breaking poem. As the expression of an unabashed will to confrontation, "Fatima" is the first work of a kind that Tennyson was to bring to perfection during his next decade—in part by devising extraordinary means of reconciling his habitual, necessitarian rhetoric of acceptance with the unprecedented, volitional rhetoric of confrontation that surfaces here. "Fatima" has been slighted in Tennyson studies, but it exhibits the raw power of a breakthrough; in the following discussion I shall overlook the rawness in order to stress what is new and important about the power.

The opening stanza is mightily confused, because Fatima is. She begins with a threefold invocation to "Love," "might," and the "sun"; the entire poem may be approached as her attempt to bring these three terms into relationship with each other, so as to ascertain her relationship to the passion that both nourishes and consumes her. Throughout the poem Fatima describes her lover, an otherwise unspecified "he" like the swains of the two Marianas, as a sun god; and whether despite his nonappearance or because of it, Fatima's Apollonian lover emerges as a figure with greater mythic authenticity than belongs to the deceptively sunny Lancelot that turns up in "The Lady of Shalott." Furthermore, Fatima's increasingly explicit personification of this deity is accompanied by an increasing confidence in her own power to *know* him, in simultaneously visionary and carnal senses. In other words, the central term Fatima invokes, "withering might," is thematically central too, since her aim is to come into possession of the power she feels here as an external and parching force.

For the present, Fatima is "deaf and blind" (6), not with sensory deprivation but with sensory overload, the excess of light from the "noonday height" (2) and of sound from the "roaring wind" (7). The noisy wind of passion blows in comparable ways throughout the Western poetic tradition, most notably in famous early episodes of Virgil's *Aeneid*, I and IV, and Dante's *Inferno*, V. But Tennyson's overall strategy in this poem, what he for once wants passion to accomplish beyond merely prolonging itself, is best explicated with reference to Romantic weather. The wind that whirls Fatima "like leaves," "parched and withered" (6–7), takes its Romantic rise in Shelley's "Ode to the West Wind," which begins with an image of "pestilence-stricken" leaves propelled by the wind but ends, after the poet's climactic "Be thou me, impetuous one!" with an image of "withered leaves" that may yet fertilize or "quicken a new birth" (5, 62–70). In the first stanza of Tennyson's text the impetuosity of Fatima remains too erratic for any such claim as Shelley's. Yet even her initial confusions in perception and address suggest a passionate reciprocation of which she is not yet aware, a "Be thou me!" in embryo. When she tells the sun how it shudders "when I strain my sight, / Throbbing through all thy heat and light" (3–4), Fatima's primary meaning is that she cannot see straight. But the syntactic ambiguity of "Throbbing" seems designed to make us wonder who is shaking under her visionary strain, the day star, the woman that worships him, or both together.

The poem will end where it has begun, at a high noontide of

passion that makes Fatima's erotic intensity a match for that of
her solar lover, but first three stanzas devoted to night and morning
let her approach this high point by reworking the images of the
first with fresh precision and control. Stanza 2, which Tennyson
interpolated in 1842, is digressive and a little silly; but that is
because it digresses along a road better not taken, a false start in
the course of Fatima's passion. We should take her at her word
when she says that in thirsting for the brooks and showers the
night before, and crushing flowers on her breast and mouth, she
was just wasting her time: "Last night I wasted hateful hours" (8).
Nothing so "tender" (11) as flowers is likely to satisfy Fatima,
whose genuine thirst is not for water but for the fierce purity of
fire. Thus the last two lines tacitly upbraid her by indicating a
truer locus of desire in the region of heat: "I looked athwart the
burning drouth / Of that long desert to the south" (13–14). To
think of the first Mariana, who "glanced athwart the glooming
flats," is to see how Fatima looks not *at* but *to*, and how she can
make the gloom of night take fire from an awaited presence.

   The next stanza, also nocturnal, draws closer to the absent radiance of the beloved through language and memory as means of
representation:

> Last night, when some one spoke his name,
> From my swift blood that went and came
> A thousand little shafts of flame
> Were shivered in my narrow frame.   (15–18)

Not only does Fatima's private, absorbingly physiological reaction
to the name utterly swallow up the social provocation of what
"some one spoke," but within that reaction it is difficult to tell
where stimulus ends and response begins. Where do those shivered
and shivering arrows of flame come from? From inside, Fatima
says, from her own "swift blood." Admittedly the prepositional
syntax here is curious; but the way Fatima's "blood" produces the
shafts that her "frame" then splinters aptly renders the short cir-
cuitry of narcissism that haunts Tennyson's work of this period.
A physical desire that is more than a little stuck on itself finds
plausible mythographic figuration in the myriad arrows of the boy
god Eros. A fully grown archer god nearer to hand than Eros,
however, and closer to the mature concerns of the 1832 *Poems* is
Apollo, in connection with whom "shafts of flame" would also

suggest the rays of the sun. As in stanza 1, here Fatima's apparently hysterical language seems pointedly ambiguous: her vaguenesses of syntax and mythological reference conspire to suggest a "shivering" or splitting of power, so that power may belong jointly to her mighty beloved and to her mighty passion for him.[22]

Having returned to the ambiguously shuddering imagery of the first stanza, Fatima also returns to its invocative mode, but with a difference:

> O Love, O fire! once he drew
> With one long kiss my whole soul through
> My lips, as sunlight drinketh dew.   (19–21)

"O Love, O fire!" The original middle term of power, the "withering might" invoked in stanza 1, has been absorbed in this new, dual invocation, which simultaneously addresses passion and its object—Fatima's "flame," as might be said today. Moreover, her memory of the kiss marks an advance in self-possession, through her willingness to give herself away, her thirst not to drink (as in stanza 2) but to be drunk in quenching the thirst of another. Constrained by her "narrow frame," Fatima gladly suffers an invasion that draws her out of herself and into relationship with her lover, who now approaches with the dawn in the fourth stanza, heralded by another recurrent image from the first, the wind.

Rather than wasting Fatima as it did at the start, the wind of daybreak now confers upon her a Shelleyan prophetic strain:

> Before he mounts the hill, I know
> He cometh quickly: from below
> Sweet gales, as from deep gardens, blow
> Before him, striking on my brow.
> In my dry brain my spirit soon,
> Down-deepening from swoon to swoon,
> Faints like a dazzled morning moon.   (22–28)

It hardly matters whether the sun-lover is rising "quickly" or whether Fatima knows it "quickly," since the informing idea of this symmetrical stanza is that his breath inspires a correspondent breeze in her. His forerunners the "Sweet gales" arise from below, to strike her brow and transmit their energy through her brain to her spirit, which thereupon repeats the vertical movement of the gales in reverse, deepening into obliteration as a sinking moon at daybreak vanishes into the light that illuminates it. Fatima's passionate acquiescence seems complete at this point; and the movement from her earlier withered whirling to this bedazzled swoon—making progress through an intensification of stasis—would have seemed completely satisfying as well, had it appeared a few years earlier in the poet's career. But if in 1832 Tennyson meant to forge a new vision of identity through relationship and confrontation, in its very satisfactoriness this stanza must have constituted a terminal surrender that precluded confrontation, in a manner all too familiar from the passivities of his previous work.

Fatima's dying fall here in stanza 4 is worthy of comparison with Shelley's fall upon the thorns of life at the same spot in his "West Wind" ode; for each is, structurally and argumentatively, a false bottom, a feint through which the prophetic aspirant learns to break into the vigor of an apocalyptic coda. In both poems this prophetic break occurs with considerable violence, but the violence is all the more striking when we find it in the habitually decorous Tennyson. The last two stanzas of "Fatima" are unprecedented in Tennyson's oeuvre as I read it, and they are very nearly without precedent or motive in the poem. There is, nevertheless, a slender thread of transition between stanzas 4 and 5, which we may follow most easily if we attend to another of the Shelleyan echoes with which this poem abounds and note that the "dazzled morning moon" recalls a governing motif from *The Triumph of Life*: the visionary fade-out whereby the spark of individual consciousness is repeatedly, and heartbreakingly, engulfed by indifferent glare. The most memorable of these fade-outs in Shelley's poem occurs when a Circean "Shape all light" tells the hapless figure of Rousseau, "Arise and quench thy thirst," and he obeys her command by drinking from her cup, only to find that "suddenly my brain became as sand" (400–405). Fatima, who has also talked of quenching her thirst, still suffers from a "dry brain" at the close of stanza 4, and this image of burnt-out sterility mars the stanza's closural symmetry. Her lover's sweet gales have come to her "as from deep gardens," but there is no suggestion of an answering fertility in her response. Quite the contrary: by fainting into privacy, Fatima swoons away from relationship with her lover, whom she must come to confront in the final stanzas if she is to emerge from the self-delighting Tennysonian sensorium.

The last stanza of Shelley's "Ode to the West Wind" derives much of its conviction that the poet's fertilizing word may "quicken a new birth" from the way the poem itself is born again, in a metaphoric turn from the passive "Lift me as a wave, a leaf, a cloud" (53) to the cooperatively active "Make me thy lyre" (57). In crossing from the fourth to the fifth stanza of "Fatima," as I have suggested, Tennyson borrows this device of structural regeneration from Shelley. Moreover, he borrows Shelley's transitional image of Aeolian music:

> The wind sounds like a silver wire,
> And from beyond the noon a fire
> Is poured upon the hills, and nigher
> The skies stoop down in their desire;
>   And, isled in sudden seas of light,
>   My heart, pierced through with fierce delight,
>   Bursts into blossom in his sight.   (29–35)

This wind's silver lyre takes its string from the lyre of Shelley, author not only of the "West Wind" ode but of a "Hymn of Apollo." Shelley's "Hymn" stands directly behind Tennyson's personification of the sun in "Fatima," in ways that should remind us that the lyre sounding in the wind is also sacred to Apollo, whose divine attributes are by now indeed indistinguishable from those of Fatima's lover. The "silver" or liquid sound of the wire precipitates the irrigation the previous stanza lacked, as a liquid fire is "poured" upon the hills, after the fashion of "Armageddon" and other early poems. This fire baptism hallows the new birth of Fatima, and of her poem, with the epiphany of the god who comes "from beyond the noon," and who transfigures the world he visits.

Unlike earlier Tennyson texts, though, this one reserves its imagery of liquid light for the blessing of relationship, as may be seen if we compare these lines with a parallel passage from *The Lover's Tale*. On a glorious day when spring "pours" into summer with "sudden deluges of light" (I.309), Julian says to Camilla, "A day for Gods to stoop," to which she replies, "Ay, / And men to soar" (I.298–299). This exchange suggests a convergence of divine and human realms that, in *The Lover's Tale*, ironically portends the nonreciprocation of an incommensurable desire. But Fatima, inebriate of light, can reciprocate the godlike overture with her own fierce rejoinder, a delight that takes her out of her own. No longer crushing "tender flowers" in thwarted passion—the metonymic labyrinth of the northern Mariana's unfulfillable substitutions—in powerful and consistent metaphor Fatima now becomes a flower herself, "pierced through" both with the sudden desire of the lover she feels outside and with a matching desire that germinates and blossoms from within.

A likely Shelleyan source for Fatima's transformation from the fainting lunar reflector of stanza 4 into this strongly creative efflorescence is the song of the Moon from *Prometheus Unbound*, IV: "A spirit from my heart bursts forth" (359); "Green stalks burst forth, and bright flowers grow" (364). But where Shelley gentles his moon's metamorphosis by spreading it across nearly two hundred lines, Tennyson handles it within a single stanza and attains a concentration that is far from gentle. The intensity of his image, stressed to the breaking point with the like sounds of "pierced," "fierce delight," and "Bursts," registers as an epoch in Tennyson's career the imagination of a character's violent emergence from herself—not in the embowered privacy of the Lady of Shalott, to whose muted but glass-shivering violence this passage corresponds, but in the full witness of the other, whom she now sees seeing her in turn: "in his sight."

Fatima's increasing personification of her beloved in his otherness converges with a rapidly burgeoning sense of personal identity, which lets her collect into focused integrity the "constant mind" and "whole soul" she gave up for lost in stanzas 1 and 3.

> My whole soul waiting silently,
> All naked in a sultry sky,
> Droops blinded with his shining eye:
> I *will* possess him or will die.
>> I will grow round him in his place,
>> Grow, live, die looking on his face,
>> Die, dying clasped in his embrace. (36–42)

In its transition from blind and drooping passivity to aggressive command, this stanza recapitulates the entire poem; yet two new notes are to be heard here as well. The first note, consonant with Tennyson's scheme of relationship in the 1832 *Poems*, is the acceptance of death, as a natural consequence of the imagery of growth from stanza 5. "I *will* possess him or will die" begins, perhaps, as an erotic commonplace; but in keeping with her apocalyptic enterprise of going naked, Fatima does not shirk the Tennysonian logic linking commitment to another person with commitment to mortality. Indeed, the sequential "Grow, live, die" puts the logic of the case so matter-of-factly as to engender a suspicion that, while Fatima's acceptance of death remains genuine, it is really but a side issue. The acknowledgment of mortality is a price she willingly pays in order to share an immortalizing passion that she is at last ready to call, with the second new note this stanza introduces, divine. Tennyson's uncharacteristic imposition of italics in line 39 suggests that the strongest drive in Fatima is not toward death but toward a consummate mutuality whereby she and her deified lover will possess each other and stand in each other's place. Earlier Fatima has consistently represented herself as contained in him, like leaves in his wind, like dew evaporated in his light, like an island surrounded in his sea. Now, however, she will embrace his circumference, "grow round him in his place"; and in a sense she is already there as his stellar equal, "All naked in a sultry sky." By asserting a penultimate will to usurp her lover's place and his environing authority, Fatima lays the ground, or clears the erotic air, for that mutuality in love to which equality is a necessary prerequisite, and which she imagines in conclusion by half ceding her usurped power back to him: "in his embrace."

"Be thou me, impetuous one!" Tennyson could not have known that Shelley had written in Euripides' Greek across the manuscript of his "Ode to the West Wind," "In my excellence I being mortal vanquish thee a great god" (Holmes 1975, 502). But before leaving "Fatima" we should observe that in 1832 there was no "Fatima" at all, no title to introduce the poem, only an epigraph from the Greek of Sappho: "That man seems to me to be equal to the gods." The originally published text stood, that is, as a fairly unabashed ode, like Shelley's, on the divinizing poetical character. Tennyson's untitled ode fulfilled a Shelleyan ambition to explore connections between his vocational and his human concerns, between the development of poetic identity and the growth of character through emotional relationship. Of course, Tennyson's imagination was in every way less belligerently political than Shelley's, because more favorably disposed toward the status quo (Fichter 1973, 411–412). It was enough for his Greek allusion to claim, not Shelleyan victory over the divine, but a coexistence that might be the sequel to mutual victory, as later in the beautifully compromising image that seals *The Princess*: "The two-celled heart beating, with one full stroke, / Life" (VII.289–290).

Accordingly, with a characteristic Victorian swerve away from the subjective ode and in the direction of the dramatic monologue, Tennyson added his title in 1842, and his second stanza as well, in an attempt to gain some distance on a risky poem by giving its shrill voice a habitation and a name not the poet's. Nor does the title he added seem casually chosen: Tennyson's wide early reading in orientalism may well have taught him how the Arabic name Fatima was traditionally associated, like the names of Eve and Pandora in Western tradition, with reckless curiosity about a knowledge reserved for divinity and forbidden to humankind.[23] In this connection the new title bore much the same charge as the epigraph it replaced: a charge to transcendent confrontation, which this text could not yet adequately articulate, but which would within only a few years reach consummate expression as the imperative "To follow knowledge like a sinking star, / Beyond the utmost bound of human thought" ("Ulysses," 31–32). Tennyson unleashed in this rough but ready poem a daemonic drive to deify the human by confronting an anthropomorphized divinity, and to "Grow, live, die looking on his face." Although this visionary daemonism would not mature until the publications of the poet's next decade, its explosive strain was already distending the 1832 poem with which we shall conclude, "Oenone."

"Oenone": The Buildup of Sorrow

"Fatima" and "The Lady of Shalott," with their antithetical assessments of the prospects for human relationship, offer a reciprocal critique, which epitomizes the imaginative standoff that generated the 1832 *Poems*, even as it generated the structural divisions within its several texts. From Fatima's standpoint the Lady suffers from emotional anemia, the insufficiency of a desire that has sought a fairy-tale lover and gotten what it asked for. But from the head of the volume the Lady, in turn, sees in "Fatima," with its strikingly comparable stanzaic form, all her own mischance. Her sorrier tale suggests that Fatima's intensity results from a contraction of vision that omits what, in a sense, the stanzas of Fatima's poem omit: those insistent, rhyme-shackled lines on "Camelot," "Lancelot," and "Shalott" that place the project of desire in context, reveal the inadequacy of its object, and doom its course to a tragic relapse into the self.

Poets need not make up their minds about such matters, and it may be well for them not to do so if they want to keep writing (Baum 1948, 175). Tennyson never did, at any rate, in a more than provisional way, though at different times he made different provisions. Certainly he belonged to the melancholy Lady's party at the outset of his career, and also during the later phase that was dominated by his work on *Idylls of the King* (for which he recast the Lady's story in "Lancelot and Elaine"). It is equally certain, however, that he bent his sympathies the other way for the creative phase on which we now verge. I gladly join the consensus that specifies *In Memoriam* as the culmination of Tennyson's poetics of confrontation, but what ended with Hallam's (and Tennyson's) poetic apotheosis in that work began well before the poet received the news of his friend's death in late 1833. As I shall argue in the Introduction to Part II, the death of Hallam accelerated and deepened a development that was already underway in 1832. Although a minor breakthrough certainly takes place in "Fatima," objections like those I have just been attributing to a critical Lady of Shalott carry sufficient weight to make me rest my claim on the more substantial "Oenone."

In a consideration of Tennyson's development—if we remember that a poet's development and achievement do not always coincide—"Oenone" is his most important poem since "Timbuctoo."[24] With that early work Tennyson first tried his precociously skilled hand at Romantic revisionism, and thereby related his poetry to a modern tradition. But the maneuvers of his revisionism for the next several years were markedly conservative defenses against those forces in Romantic poetry that make for confrontation and change. Even as recent a work as "The Lady of Shalott" bent its force toward the acceptance, which is to say the maintenance, of the status quo, the same rich doom toward which Tennyson's juvenilia also tended. "Oenone," however, reconceives relationship itself: not as a mode of patience that accommodates the given, but as an aggressive and apocalyptic mode of creative encounter. This latter mode of relationship occurs in "Fatima"; but "Oenone," more ambitiously, enacts the very moment at which relationship is thus reconceived, as a new lyric kind thrusts up through the narrative husk of the old. For in "Oenone" Tennyson actually composed two texts, a mythic fable and a dramatic crisis lyric. These two texts treat the same subject—the quest for human relationship that in 1832 also represents the quest for poetic identity—in thoroughly different ways, which the poem juxtaposes and invites us to compare. It is as if, when Tennyson approached his current theme in "Oenone," he discovered that in order to do it justice he would first have to engage the question of how that theme ought to be approached. And as the lush but hollow myth of the Judgment of Paris modulates into the lyrical crisis and ecstasy that close the poem, a new direction for Tennyson's writing grows clear as well. In "Oenone" we see him embracing a new intention to face and indict what he has hitherto passively suffered, and to wrest some personal reaction from the power of doom to which his best poetry thus far has been merely, albeit eloquently, responsive.

THE POEM OPENS with a gorgeous landscape that, in establishing a cloven setting for Oenone's speech, also gives a symbolic forecast of its dual structure:

> There lies a vale in Ida, lovelier
> Than all the valleys of Ionian hills.
> The swimming vapour slopes athwart the glen,
> Puts forth an arm, and creeps from pine to pine,
> And loiters, slowly drawn. On either hand
> The lawns and meadow-ledges midway down
> Hang rich in flowers, and far below them roars
> The long brook falling through the cloven ravine
> In cataract after cataract to the sea.
> Behind the valley topmost Gargarus
> Stands up and takes the morning: but in front
> The gorges, opening wide apart, reveal
> Troas and Ilion's columned citadel,
> The crown of Troas. (1–14)

This curtailed blank-verse sonnet is the introduction as Tennyson laboriously, lovingly revised it—through perhaps a dozen variant versions still extant in manuscript (Gaskell 1978; Day 1980)—for the edition of 1842. Although the revision improves in every way upon the preciously mannered original (with its "flowering tendriltwine" and "cedarshadowy valleys"), Tennyson has retained, and emphasized with a "but" in line 11, his original distinction between the intransitively and reflexively rendered valley bower and Troy, the distant arena for civic (and transitive) action into which both the valley and the poem eventually open (Devlin 1978, 141). A reader of "The Lady of Shalott" and "The Hesperides" will recognize in this symbolic distinction familiar conflicts between isolation, beauty, and innocence, on the one hand, and engagement, strife, and knowledge on the other; and the syntactic and imagistic unveiling within the final four lines proves an accurate forecast of the poetic apocalypse to come.

But the rhetorical tricks of hypnotic embowerment—the wholesale verbal iterations, all new in 1842, that run from "vale" and "valleys" through the final hemistich; the subtler phonemic interlock of a line like "The long brook falling through the cloven ravine"—seem more knowingly elaborate than in earlier Tennyson. What this much-revised description knows is, precisely, the defensive use to which such elaboration may be put. It has been objected that Tennyson's descriptions of nature sound too much like Victorian interior decoration; but this outdoor scene, as its vapor is "slowly drawn" (like drapes?) and its lawns and ledges "Hang rich" like a floral tapestry, is so evidently filled with artificial furniture that we may credit Tennyson with having raised the objection long before the anti-Tennysonians did. Where "There lies a vale" with such internal fabrications, we are bound to wonder if the bulk of the description is not a deceptive or lying veil, the primary purpose of which is to conceal the contrary energies of revelation, "opening wide apart," that its final clause intimates.

Tennyson's descriptive beginning serves not only to introduce the title figure but to represent her consciousness as well. At Oenone's entrance in the paragraph immediately following, her set of mind accords to perfection with the mood of the vale and shares its listless tempo. Like the vapor that "loiters, slowly drawn," she is "wandering forlorn" (15). Her hair floats, or seems to; and much as the vapor "slopes" athwart the upholstered mountainside, she is discovered in a languorous pose fit for Regency parlors: "leaning on a fragment twined with vine" (19). Oenone's pose may indeed owe something to the vogue of the parlor "attitude," a fashionable entertainment that, as Culler (1975) has shown, helped prepare the way for Tennyson's later development of the dramatic monologue and monodrama. Part of the importance of "Oenone," in Tennyson's career and in the development of Victorian poetry, is its generic position: standing somewhere between monologue and idyll, it occupies a pivot point commanding the two principal reaches of its author's genius across the next two decades. This tirelessly rewritten poem is, among other things, a laboratory in which we may watch the leading Victorian poet working his way toward both of the major poetic genres we consider distinctively Victorian. Equally significant for Tennyson's future course, and perhaps equally Victorian, is the problem "Oenone" poses in generic integration: the poem falls so dramatically into two dissimilar parts weakly bound by a refrain and a title that it appears, at least in retrospect, to herald the challenges of generic dialogue between idyll and monologue, narration and lyricism, that awaited Tennyson in the decades to come.

Now within the conventions of both genres—within the immediate though ephemeral cultural ambience of the "attitude" and within the venerable literary tradition of the well-wrought Alexandrian idyll that scholars have long identified as one of Tennyson's principal generic sources—such details as Oenone's first pose take on considerable suggestiveness. That she leans on a "fragment," as opposed to the "vine-entwinèd stone" of 1832, hints first at the late ruination she is about to begin lamenting; but it hints, too, through the Romantic dialectic of the fragmentary that we saw triumph amid devastation in "Timbuctoo," at the unfinished business Oenone has yet to conduct. At the same time, or rather a split second after, the fact that this fragment is "twined with vine," ensnared in parasitic modifiers of studied assonantal prettiness, lets us guess that the fragmentary or potential energy of her poem is being kept under cosmetic wraps by an agency that is not to be put by without a struggle. Our surest indication of Oenone's initial distance from struggle of any kind is her pathetic enervation as a speaker, the incapacity of her discourse to break away either from her surroundings or from its own inertial patterns. Thus when she first breaks the thick silence, all she can do is discuss it for six lines and then go on to say repeatedly what we have supposed already, that the static noontide scene images her mood: "My eyes are full of tears, my heart of love, / My heart is breaking, and my eyes are dim, / And I am all aweary of my life" (30–32). Not for the last time in the loitering narrative of the Judgment of Paris that commences here—the first, idyllic portion of the poem proper, which the preceding paragraphs have served to introduce—Oenone seems to be going nowhere. And when the narrative closes at last with a similar blank-verse triplet, its repetitiveness suggests that as far as the title character is concerned no progress has been made at all: "And I was left alone within the bower; / And from that time to this I am alone, / And I shall be alone until I die" (188–190).

At the outset, then, Oenone's invariant, "aweary" lament is the 1830 Mariana's in blank verse. She is installed within an accomplished isolation, in the maintenance of which she herself is a chief accomplice. Oenone's recognition of this complicity, of responsibility for the part she bears, will emerge fully during the more concise and rewarding reprise of her lament with which the poem turns itself over at line 191. But hints of the later emergency are already astir in the second verse paragraph she speaks. For one thing, Oenone compellingly voices, as Mariana does not, a need to be heard and responded to. In asserting this need Oenone starts asserting herself as well, coming into her own as a potentially responsible agent. Oenone's prologue to the Judgment of Paris thus affiliates her outlook not with the northern but with the southern Mariana's:

> O mother Ida, many-fountained Ida,
> Dear mother Ida, harken ere I die.
> Hear me, O Earth, hear me, O Hills, O Caves
> That house the cold crowned snake! O mountain brooks,
> I am the daughter of a River-God,
> Hear me, for I will speak, and build up all
> My sorrow with my song, as yonder walls
> Rose slowly to a music slowly breathed,
> A cloud that gathered shape: for it may be
> That, while I speak of it, a little while
> My heart may wander from its deeper woe.   (33–43)

Like the southern Mariana and Fatima, Oenone is somewhat confused about whom she needs to speak to. By the end of the poem her decisiveness in this matter will betoken the remarkable transformation she has undergone, but for the present the simple fact that she can imagine such a varied audience takes her leagues out of the moated grange. Still, all that lies within Oenone's initial power of address is the ability to speak to her place. As if anticipating the idyll as Tennyson was soon to be practicing it, she invokes only her immediate situation, whether the earth, hills, and caves she can see, or, raising her visionary sights a degree, her parents the mountain and the river—which are also the geological "parents" of the vale that reflects her predicament. Oenone's scattered voice echoes that in the opening paragraphs of *Prometheus Unbound*, where Shelley's self-imprisoned hero invoked in rapid sequence "Earth," "Heaven," "Sun," and "Sea," only to confirm his condition of "No change, no pause, no hope" through repetition of the internally repetitive "Ah me! alas, pain, pain ever, forever!" (I.23–30). Oenone is a wood nymph and not a titan, and the range of her invocatory broadcast is accordingly limited in comparison to that of Prometheus. She nonetheless evinces a baffled ambition like his when her "Hear me, for I will speak" trails off into the painfully bewildered discursiveness of "it may be / That, while I speak of it, a little while / My heart may wander . . ."

In brief, Oenone is far from knowing just what she wants her song to do, just what it might mean to "build up" all her "sorrow." Is this "sorrow" literally her present mood or metonymically its cause, her betrayal by Paris? And whatever "sorrow" means to Oenone, does she propose to enshrine it or cure it? Will her song "build up" a ritual of sorrow—a kind of coping or stress management in which Tennyson's early verse excels—or will it "build up," in a new direction, toward restitution of a more radical kind? These are the alternatives I think the twofold poem "Oenone" was written to explore, as I think they are the alternative responses to loss whose interplay generates Tennyson's most absorbing work from 1833 on; and when the poem pivots from one alternative to the other, Tennyson's career pivots with it. At this preliminary stage, Oenone appears to decide that the end of sorrow's song is to enshrine its cause, since what she proceeds to do is to relate the tale of the Judgment of Paris. Yet her prologue has opened other possibilities for song, possibilities of a divinely inspired, shaping "music" and a "deeper woe," a passion deeper than sorrow, to which she will revert once the excursive tale of Paris has brought her back unchanged to the pretty pass at which she has begun.[25]

Oenone's narrative being a kind of evasive loitering, it is fitting that as a storyteller she should exhibit the evasiveness we associate with Tennysonian narration generally. Even her repeated and in-

ternally echoic litany "Dear mother Ida, harken ere I die," with
its uncanny phonetic link between the earthly mother's name and
the daughter's mortal fate, suggests that Oenone is working language over in order to put meaning off.[26] I am not the first reader—
J. W. Croker had that honor in a contemporary review (1833,
74)—to observe how the three goddesses Hera, Pallas, and
Aphrodite, when they appear naked in the bower, get described
in now embarrassed, now voluptuous ways that deflect attention
from their presence to their surroundings. But this is merely a
notorious symptom of a systemic narrative indisposition: the
mythic frame of Oenone's entire story is similarly embroidered
with the stately dilation of gorgeous syllables that Tennyson offers
as consolation prize whenever a higher vocation is being declined.

A striking example of this repetitive delay occurs within the
next verse paragraphs. In lines 46–51 Paris arises with the dawn
from the waters of "reedy Simois," leading a tame goat up into
the valley where Oenone is awaiting him alone; and then the next
paragraph (53–62) replays the same scene in slightly slowed motion, complete with Oenone's solitude, the accompanying dawn,
a leopard skin in place of the goat, and the cataract's "foam-bow"
in place of the meandering river. Ricks prints manuscript variants
that show what care Tennyson took with the second of these
descriptions (*PT*, 388). But the really curious craftsmanship here
is Oenone's, as she distances herself from the painful narrative
facts by idling over a prolonged and irrelevant introduction—
irrelevant, that is, except insofar as it manifests a narrative sophistication that ought to preempt crudely adverse criticism of the
idyllic mode that Tennyson is advancing here. The technique bears
comparison with what we have seen near the close of "The Hesperides"; only now Tennyson invites his reader to spot, not over-
ripe Keats, but suspiciously slick Tennyson. By having Oenone
overload her story in "Tennysonian" fashion, the poet implies that
the descriptive infatuation to which he himself has earlier been
prone is a beautiful dodge. The evasive Oenone and the Paris who
will choose Aphrodite's gift are "playmates" (16), aesthetes made
for each other. Both his suggestion that she hide from the approaching goddesses where she may "behold them unbeheld, unheard / Hear all" (87–88), and her evident readiness thus to adopt
a voyeur's part, jibe perfectly with her mode of telling a story.

That story, the Judgment of Paris as Tennyson found it rehearsed in a number of classical and neoclassical sources, held particular resonance for him when he approached it in 1832. Readers have tended to idealize the myth into a moral allegory, as if Tennyson were James Beattie, or as if "The Palace of Art" were the key to the 1832 volume; and Tennyson critics have almost unanimously seconded Oenone's preference for Palladian "Self-reverence, self-knowledge, self-control" (142). These tendencies seem peculiar if we consider how corrupt—not just textually but morally corrupt—the story Tennyson inherited actually is. Having been elected the impartial judge of a divine beauty contest, Paris is supposed to declare one of three goddesses "most fair" (71) and to present the winner with a golden apple. As a pun submerged in the recurrent word *fair* reminds us, even a beauty contest should have its ground rules of moral fairness; but nobody in this contest plays fair at all. As the goddesses offer and Paris weighs a series of bribes at best marginally relevant to the ostensible issue of their beauty—a state of affairs to which no one, Oenone included, raises the least objection—the legend becomes not a morality play but a power play, in which even the virtue of Pallas is a bargaining chip like any other.[27] Tennyson's treatment of the Judgment of Paris asks to be read not in moral terms but in the existential terms of power, love, and death, which govern the best of the 1832 poems that surround it, and which return lyrically transmuted in the second part of Oenone's song.

The longer one looks at Hera's offer and that of Pallas, the harder it is to tell them apart. The one promises might and the other right, but might *is* right in an expressly unfair contest like the one Paris has been asked to judge. It makes sense, therefore, that Hera should play into Pallas's hands by extolling power as "wisdom-bred / And throned of wisdom" (121–122), and that Pallas should likewise recant her opening dismissal of "sovereign power" (143) by concluding the eulogy of "right" and "wisdom" (147–148) with references to "endurance," "action," and "perfect freedom" (161–164) that are suspiciously reminiscent of what Hera has promised. Both goddesses, furthermore, tempt Paris with the offer of a god-like life at the upper limits of human potential, and both blur those limits in side-stepping the question of mortality. Queen Hera, indeed, envisions a prosperity lasting "till thy hand / Fail from the sceptre-staff" (123–124), but her politic use of the subjunctive initiates a rhetorical equivocation that will culminate in her vision

of those men of power who "are likest gods, who have attained /
Rest in a happy place" of "undying bliss" (128–130). Pallas, self-
anointed apostle of the "right" though she be, is a more deviously
indirect rhetorician yet. She never mentions death at all; but in
promising Paris that her "vigour, wedded to thy blood, / Shall
strike within thy pulses, like a God's" (158–159), until "the full-
grown will, / Circled through all experiences, pure law, / Com-
measure perfect freedom" (162–164), she manages to offer him
the closural satisfactions of death in a series of absolutes ("full-
grown," "Circled," "all," "pure," "perfect"), which, thanks to
some liberal seasoning with "will" and "freedom," avoids sounding absolutely closed. That the very existence of a quarrel among
the goddesses gives the lie to their pictures of rest, law, and fulfillment as godlike states need not diminish our admiration for the
poem's rhetoric, but it ought to remind us that rhetoric is what
the first two goddesses are dealing out: a verbal subterfuge that,
for all its differences from Oenone's in telling their story, traffics
like hers in suppression of the facts of life and death.

In a fable like this one, when two out of three options are
equivalent—a pair of evil stepsisters, a golden and a silver casket—
we can be sure that the umpire is to choose the third, as Paris does
in preferring Aphrodite's triumphantly pithy offer of "The fairest
and most loving wife in Greece" (183). Gerhard Joseph (1982) has
shown, with reference to Freud's essay on "The Theme of the
Three Caskets," what should be apparent in any case from Tennyson's other poems of 1832: Paris's choice of sexual pleasure, of
human delight over godlike might and right, is also a choice of
mortality. The decision that will convert the fairest and most
loving wife in Greece into Helen of Troy will precipitate the Trojan
War, with its tragic confirmation of human limits and ennoblement of human sacrifices. In choosing Aphrodite's gift Paris makes
the natural choice of the middling-sensual man, and under the
circumstances of the beauty pageant his choice seems fair enough;
we could call it Paris's finest hour, if "Oenone" were sufficiently
his poem to motivate the choice with much more than tirra-lirra
nonchalance. But of course the poem is Oenone's; and of course
she has blinked the critical moment of decision, exercising the
voyeur's privilege of selective viewing: "I shut my sight for fear"
(184). Not her eyes but her very "sight," the site of voyeuristic

consciousness, closes down to leave her where she started, alone and palely loitering.

"AND"—"AND"—"AND"—"Yet, mother Ida, harken ere I die": the additive mode of Tennysonian lamentation over the inevitable, whereby Oenone has been "building up" her sorrow to no issue, is suddenly crossed in line 191 by an antagonistic intention on which not just this poem, but the development of Tennyson's art, swings round to face a new direction. The judgment of Oenone now recapitulates and supersedes the Judgment of Paris, as the more or less objective, idyllic narration of a classical theme yields to the urgently subjective interrogation and redefinition of self that we associate with the rhythms of the Romantic crisis lyric. From this point the pace of "Oenone" picks up so dramatically that it will be best to take up its paragraphs one by one.

Having previously shut her sight, Oenone begins to open it to a new image of herself, as a being empowered to summon and judge with the utmost severity those powers beyond her whose "fairness" she has witnessed and suffered. The process begins with an interrogation of her own image, a heightening of self-consciousness that may remind us again of Oenone's spiritual sister Mariana in the south:

> Yet, mother Ida, harken ere I die.
> Fairest—why fairest wife? am I not fair?
> My love hath told me so a thousand times.
> Methinks I must be fair, for yesterday,
> When I past by, a wild and wanton pard,
> Eyed like the evening star, with playful tail
> Crouched fawning in the weed.   (191–197)

Presumably the nearest mountain ledge would offer Oenone a pool or liquid mirror in which to judge her own beauty, but like the southern Mariana she now understands that beauty acquires its worth in relationship. That, after all, was the meaning of Paris's preference for the human Helen over more godlike bribes. He there affirmed, and Oenone here confirms, something like a "fairness" doctrine in aesthetics, whereby the appreciation of beauty also measures the appreciator. The notion behind this passage is quite Keatsian; and Oenone's psychologically intriguing substitution of the "wanton pard" for the vanished Paris in his leopard skin acquires added significance from Tennyson's multiplex allusion to Keats's description of Lamia, that most wanton, pardlike, fair-eyed, and above all ambiguous heroine of Romantic poetry (*Lamia*, I.42–62). For *Lamia* was the narrative poem in which Keats most clearly declared that a thing of beauty remains a joy—remains at all, for that matter—only so long as its beauty survives in the eye of a beholder whose sympathies redeem it from the status of a mere thing.

The issue of beauty will yield to sublimer issues of power in the rest of the poem, and Oenone begins this transition by calling her earlier self-image into question and by dimly defining as her goal the foundation of a newly constitutive relationship. First her old dalliance with Paris must be summed up and kissed goodbye:

> Most loving is she?
> Ah me, my mountain shepherd, that my arms
> Were wound about thee, and my hot lips prest
> Close, close to thine in that quick-falling dew
> Of fruitful kisses, thick as Autumn rains
> Flash in the pools of whirling Simois.   (197–202)

In its closing simile this nobly sympathetic farewell furnishes Oenone with imaginative grounds for understanding Paris's choice of Helen, if not quite for forgiving it (Kincaid 1974, 223). The virginal "quick-falling dew" passes through the press of fertility in "fruitful kisses" to emerge as something more laden with doom, autumn rainfall eddying away. The intrusion of autumnal imagery is as startling here as in part IV of "The Lady of Shalott." In both poems it signifies the acceptance of mortality; and in following passion thus toward its Tennysonian end in death, Oenone takes a step toward appreciating the significance of Paris's mortalist choice (Sinfield 1976a, 467). In the paragraphs that follow she will find that choice unacceptable, but her rejection of death there becomes all the more striking once we acknowledge her sympathetic grasp of it here.

Of the six verse paragraphs of Oenone's new crisis poem, only the second might be confused with anything we have heard in this or any other work of Tennyson's to date. Here Oenone reads the multiple sense of personal loss registered in the preceding paragraph—her loss of Paris and concomitant loss of self-esteem, her awakened consciousness of the ultimate privation, death—back into the landscape of pines, gorge, and sky, which has served as her evasive haunt earlier in the poem. But the resemblance is only superficial: as a storyteller in the first two hundred lines, Oenone has backed off from her sorrow and endeavored to fill a secret void with natural plenitude; now, by contrast, she describes a defoliated scene that confirms her lyric sense of diminution. Tennyson expands the pointed objection of Ovid's ever-practical Oenone (who complains in *Amores*, V.41–42, that the pines have been felled to make boats for the abduction of her rival Helen) into a rendition of universal disenchantment:

> O mother, hear me yet before I die.
> They came, they cut away my tallest pines,
> My tall dark pines, that plumed the craggy ledge
> High over the blue gorge, and all between
> The snowy peak and snow-white cataract
> Fostered the callow eaglet—from beneath
> Whose thick mysterious boughs in the dark morn
> The panther's roar came muffled, while I sat
> Low in the valley. Never, never more
> Shall lone Oenone see the morning mist
> Sweep through them; never see them overlaid
> With narrow moon-lit slips of silver cloud,
> Between the loud stream and the trembling stars.   (203–215)

From the beginning, as we have seen, the image of pine boughs "overlaid" or draped in mist has represented the veil of a false consolation. Now Oenone disavows such consolation with an explicit undoing of its habitual imagery, with the reiterated force of "never," and with the odd device of referring to herself in the third person. It is as if the "lone Oenone" escorted by her classical epithet, and the naked "I" that is to speak the rest of the poem, represent two distinct beings: one belonging with the vague "they" of the second line, and one aiming to keep quite different company. The "thick mysterious boughs" of the old pines once "muffled" voice; the voice appropriate to Oenone's vision of a demystified bower will sound more clearly. Near the close of Keats's most explicit fable of Romantic recuperation, the "Ode to Psyche," the absence of mythic pines had been a condition for poetic presence of mind, in lines that gloss Oenone's situation nicely: "Where branchèd thoughts, new grown with pleasant pain, / Instead of pines shall murmur in the wind" (52–53). Since Oenone's poem, like Keats's, concerns the arousal of voice, we should note the consistent revision Tennyson made in 1842 by substituting "mother" for "mother Ida" in the opening line of this and each successive verse paragraph. As "mother Ida" yields her place to an unlocalized "mother" whom we may more easily assimilate to the muse, Tennyson's persona proceeds to thin into translucence, and Oenone's project of self-definition to converge with his.

One trouble with the interpretation of the next paragraph, indeed, is how to keep Tennyson out of it. For it is in this extraordinary passage, incorporated in 1842, that Tennyson first dramatically opposes to the given the full strength of angry hatred, with an emotional catharsis toward which the poet's sorrow has, in a sense, been building since the beginning of his career:

> O mother, hear me yet before I die.
> I wish that somewhere in the ruined folds,
> Among the fragments tumbled from the glens,
> Or the dry thickets, I could meet with her
> The Abominable, that uninvited came
> Into the fair Peleïan banquet-hall,
> And cast the golden fruit upon the board,
> And bred this change; that I might speak my mind,
> And tell her to her face how much I hate
> Her presence, hated both of Gods and men.   (216–225)

The despoiled landscape from the preceding paragraph, here resumed in "ruined folds" and "fragments tumbled," gives rise to a new voice that is spoiling for a fight. The "dry thickets" recall the fierce heat of "Fatima," and the daemonic ambition of that poem now feeds Oenone's desire to build up her sorrow by encountering a more original source for it than she has yet imagined: Eris, the goddess of strife who made all the trouble in the first place. Invoking the goddess of strife bespeaks an intention to strive; and as Oenone imagines declaring her hatred of Eris "to her face" she begins to make herself over, like Fatima, into an image divine in its harshness.

The wood nymph who has seen her Paris "judge of Gods" (88), and who at a critical juncture has shut her voyeuristic sight for fear, now aspires to force the moment to its crisis and to seek out a presence that she hates. Oenone's name for this presence, "The Abominable," is as vaguely articulated, at this stage, as her intention to reach it; for by the dialectic of Romantic confrontation here evoked, the clarification of vision and the definition of self are one and the same process. Abomination, like love, is a passion of relationship; and the name "Abominable" demonstrates the interdependence of the abominated object and the power of the hatred that surges against it. Oenone will behold the Abominable by becoming an abomination herself, close kin to Homer's Atè, "she who is only a little thing at the first, but thereafter / grows until she strides on the earth with her head striking heaven" (*Iliad*, IV.442–443, tr. Lattimore).

I do not know what the Abominable is like; but I find it hard to imagine a presence more intense than Oenone's at the end of this poem, for whose visionary fury Tennyson probably meant the interpolated verse paragraph of 1842 to prepare us. Still, if that paragraph does not come on too strong for us, it seems to come too soon for Oenone. The next paragraph relapses from hatred, through personal nostalgia, on beyond the pleasure principle into the ultimate nostalgia, the wish not to be:

> O happy tears, and how unlike to these!
> O happy Heaven, how canst thou see my face?
> O happy earth, how canst thou bear my weight?
> O death, death, death, thou ever-floating cloud,
> There are enough unhappy on this earth,
> Pass by the happy souls, that love to live:
> I pray thee, pass before my light of life,
> And shadow all my soul, that I may die.
> Thou weighest heavy on the heart within,
> Weigh heavy on my eyelids: let me die.   (231–240)

The logical development of the poem would be cleaner if these lines preceded the daemonic outburst they follow, but then their psychological development would be less telling. The backsliding movement here anticipates the hesitant, empirical structure of *In Memoriam*. It also suggests the bearing of this first major classical poem on the greatest of its successors, "Ulysses" and especially "Tithonus," the latter a text whose deceptive longing for death this moment in "Oenone" can prepare us to understand.

Having just announced a new goal of visionary confrontation, Oenone prepares for it here by taking final leave of her old self

and severing the old relationships to heaven and earth, love and
death, which have defined that self. As she does so, she further
takes leave of the repetitive and invocative mode that has characterized earlier parts of her song. Oenone's triple invocation to
the "happy tears" of Paris, the "happy Heaven," and "happy
earth" evinces some understandable confusion—reminiscent of the
initiatory Fatima's—about her nascent emotions. Her tears are
"unlike" those of happy love not because they are sorry but because, as the previous verse paragraph has shown, they express
an angry hatred: a passion whose dangerous charge the old Oenone
is nevertheless still strong enough to want to turn against herself
and disguise as sorrow, through the familiar conversions of Tennysonian melancholy. Yet the unwitting and perhaps unwanted
self-aggrandizement of the next two lines suggests a power that
will not be so easily converted. It is Oenone's eyes that are blinded
with tears, yet like Fatima she ascribes the blindness to heaven as
well; and in modulating toward death by addressing the earth, she
arrogates to herself a more than mortal gravity that makes even
death seem a lightweight, an "ever-floating cloud," curiously represented in the very imagery that has betokened evasiveness since
the beginning. Oenone's invocation of death is unpersuasive, as
critics have said, and it is unpersuasive because Tennyson meant
us to see it as an evasion. To call death soft names, as Keats knew
in the "Ode to a Nightingale," is no way to die—but it may be,
Tennyson suggests here, a way to purge those escapist impulses
that would seduce the self on its way to confrontation.

I have been approaching the last six paragraphs of "Oenone"
as a Romantic crisis lyric. The term is Harold Bloom's; and while
I am confident that Bloom could accommodate each of these six
paragraphs to a stage in his sixfold map of the crisis lyric (1975),
one notion of his seems particularly apt right here: namely, that
the hyperbolic rhetoric typically advanced about two-thirds of the
way through such lyrics also involves the psychic defense of repression. The soothing texture of this profoundly troubled verse paragraph represents Oenone's attempt to neglect her destiny for
higher things, which also appears, as Bloom's model would predict, through an intertextual network that underknits it. I have
already suggested that Oenone's wooing of death owes something
to the "Ode to a Nightingale." If her central repetition of "happy"
further reminds us of the hysteria at the center of Keats's most

explicitly classical ode, the "Ode on a Grecian Urn" ("More happy love! More happy, happy love!"; 25), it should also call to mind how in that poem a bemused spectator is transformed to a sorrowing visionary with "a heart high-sorrowful and cloyed, / A burning forehead and a parching tongue" (29–30)—symptoms that might also describe the fiery prophetess Oenone is about to become in her exclusion from the happy Keatsian field of death. The prophetic vocation, which a part of Oenone still wants to repress, also emerges in a more distant yet distinct allusion, this time to the grand opening aria of Milton's Samson: "O death, death, death, thou ever-floating cloud." We receive here less a semantic reminder than the intimately rhythmic and assonantal echo of a prosodic retard that was already famous in Tennyson's day: "O dark, dark, dark, amid the blaze of noon" (*Samson Agonistes*, 80).[28] Like Samson, Oenone is coming to regard her abandonment as the prelude to a higher relationship. The human destructiveness of this new relationship is something she naturally fears, and she works hard to deny it with her last evasion, the repeated image of a heavy weight in lines 239–240. But these two lines offer a belated and unavailing inversion of the proportions she has authentically measured just six lines before in specifying herself as the heavy one: "O happy earth, how canst thou bear my weight?"

The abandoned Oenone further resembles Samson in her determination to take others with her—if possible, to bring the whole house of Priam, nay Olympus itself, down around her:

> I will not die alone, for fiery thoughts
> Do shape themselves within me, more and more,
> Whereof I catch the issue, as I hear
> Dead sounds at night come from the inmost hills,
> Like footsteps upon wool. I dimly see
> My far-off doubtful purpose, as a mother
> Conjectures of the features of her child
> Ere it is born: her child!—a shudder comes
> Across me: never child be born of me
> Unblest, to vex me with his father's eyes!   (242–251)

Oenone's vindictiveness gathers apocalyptic purpose from a rising tempo of Shelleyan fire images, which will reach its climax in the searing line that ends the poem. For the present, the shape of her "fiery thoughts" is still murky; but whereas the previous verse paragraph has solicited death to "shadow all my soul," now Oenone seeks acuteness above all things. Moreover, her intention to force the issue she would "catch" reverses a crucial image from the close of "The Palace of Art," where the Soul as evening traveler hears "the dully sound / Of human footsteps" but elaborately talks herself into rejecting its overtures. Having taken leave of the secluded panther's "muffled" roar three paragraphs since, now Oenone strains her hearing, actively seeking to break up the interior decoration, strip the woolen carpet from the forest floor, and "catch the issue" of her apocalyptic "thoughts." The sheer daemonism of this "issue" appears in the violence with which she rejects the thought of childbirth, or merely natural issue, in the lines that follow. Tennyson added these lines in 1842, and they match the paragraph he also inserted then on Oenone's abomination of Eris. As Oenone's hatred drives toward its climax, she acquires a leading characteristic of the Abominable, the crone who has "bred this change" and whom she increasingly resembles: the power to be not a breeder of continuity, through love and its "fruitful kisses," but a fomenter of turmoil and change.[29]

The quietly reiterated "I will not die alone" marks Oenone's will to repay the powers that have blasted her and to damn the expense, since she has nothing to lose:

> O mother, hear me yet before I die.
> Hear me, O earth. I will not die alone,
> Lest their shrill happy laughter come to me
> Walking the cold and starless road of Death
> Uncomforted, leaving my ancient love
> With the Greek woman. I will rise and go
> Down into Troy, and ere the stars come forth
> Talk with the wild Cassandra, for she says
> A fire dances before her, and a sound
> Rings ever in her ears of armèd men.
> What this may be I know not, but I know
> That, wheresoe'er I am by night and day,
> All earth and air seem only burning fire.   (252–264)

The cool yet cosmic "Hear me, O earth," the brittle reduction of all the fuss made earlier over "happy" into the distant phrase "their shrill happy laughter," and especially the dwindling of Paris into "my ancient love," an object now as trifling as "the Greek woman," show how far Oenone has come in fewer than thirty lines. Having earlier longed for solitary death, now she repeats "I will not die alone"; having wished happiness on them "who love to live," now she will not hear of it. By this point Paris and Helen signify less in themselves than as tokens in Oenone's private *cause célèbre*: they are but the tools of an affront she aims to redress with new-found dignity. The triviality of Paris and Helen, together with some not at all Tennysonian grammatical contortions, leave "their" in the third line strangely free in its reference, as if to pit Oenone against the world, in the sort of "I-they" paranoia that at least since Rousseau has adjoined the Romantic apotheosis of the self. If this be madness, yet there is method in it—as there is in the classical monologues that were within a few years to be the richest issue of the spiritual crisis broached here. In Oenone's madness there is also a compensatory fellowship, with her final turn in the direction of a prophetic soulmate, "the wild Cassandra." "I will rise and go" twists away from its biblical source, in the Prodigal Son's conversion from autonomy to humility under his father's roof (Luke 15:18), and registers instead Oenone's abandonment of the parental bower of mountain and river, for the sake of the strife she will greet in Cassandra's Troy.[30]

What Oenone and Cassandra will talk about remains a matter for conjecture. Mine is that they will denounce the injustice of the gods, particularly of Apollo, the least fair of them all, who according to tradition was not only the seducer who first maddened Cassandra into prophecy but also Oenone's first lover. In terms of Tennyson's subterranean 1832 mythology of the sun-god lover, "Oenone" thus conflates "Fatima" and "The Lady of Shalott": Oenone's lover was not an illusion, but he deceived her anyway. Ovid treated this amour as a matter of fact glanced at with casual irony: "I am the one," Oenone reminds Paris, "that the famously faithful builder of Troy loved" (*Heroides*, 145: *me fide conspicuus Troiae munitor amavit*). The prudent Tennyson, as one would suppose, presents so scandalous a fact only by implication; but the implication is pretty clear, especially in the version of 1832, where Oenone mistakenly hails Paris as "Apollo" five times at the close of the fifth paragraph (*Letters*, 85–86). Even in the 1842 version Apollo will occur to any reader who hears the Ovidian line echoing through Oenone's comparison of her lamentation to the foundation of Troy: "as yonder walls / Rose slowly to a music slowly breathed, / A cloud that gathered shape" (39–41). Just as Oenone's new voice has discredited that lamentation as a cloudy sham, so now she will join Cassandra in foretelling the devastation of Apollo's nebulous city. The Apollonian connection these two women share discloses a network of classical allusions that is exceptionally rich even for Tennyson.[31] For our purposes here the intertextual web yields Oenone's affiliation with the Cassandra who embodies righteous fury, the same emotional peak Oenone ascends until the astonishing conclusion of her poem.

INHERITING A MYTH that showed the gods to be fallible, in "Oenone" Tennyson made them indictable as well, with an unencumbered spirit's hoarse cry for justice. He won his way to the imagination of an aggressive indignation that, we can see in retrospect, had been smoldering since the beginning (Preyer 1966; Kiernan 1982, 128). I have tried to show how, through the transformation of Oenone's persona, he consciously sharpened his own resentment against the kind of poetry he had hitherto chosen to write, and charted an emotional and rhetorical course for the next phase of his career. But perhaps the clearest indication of Tennyson's breakthrough from grief to grievance in "Oenone" occurs not in its warping of Tennysonian resonances but in its triumphant allusion to the Romantic poem that arguably exerted a wider influence than any other in the Victorian period, Wordsworth's "Intimations" ode. When Oenone says, "but I know / That, wheresoe'er I am by night and day, / All earth and air seem only burning fire," she concludes her poem with the very images with which Wordsworth's had begun:

> Turn wheresoe'er I may,
> By night or day,
> The things which I have seen I now can see no more.   (7–9)

> But yet I know, where'er I go,
> That there hath past away a glory from the earth.   (17–18)

One reason why Wordsworth's conversion of loss into gain haunted the Victorian imagination is that it proposed a congenial model of problem solving, one that located the grounds of the solution in the formulation of the problem. Much as his Victorian successors would find renewed impetus for faith in the condition of doubt itself—witness *In Memoriam*—so Wordsworth in the "Intimations" ode found "Strength in what remains behind" (180), in a divine discontent that linked the "obstinate questionings" (141) he recollected from early childhood with the no less obstinate state in which he wrote the poem. Thus the radiant glory or intimation of immortality Wordsworth sought for himself was already latent in his perception that glory had passed away from the earth.

Tennyson understood as much in his use of an indubitably Wordsworthian phrasing to introduce an image of omnipresent fire, which appears, but only appears, to contradict Wordsworth's insistence that the visionary gleam is gone. Where "All earth and air seem only burning fire," there is plenty of light, maybe even too much, given the redundance of the adjectives. But for Oenone the visionary gleam is *only* burning fire, and she wants more than only that. Like her poet in the 1832 volume in which she first appeared, and I think finally unlike her successors Ulysses and Tithonus, Oenone seeks a companionship beyond what Wordsworth imagined in his ode of strong but solitary joy. Hence the paradox of Tennyson's final allusion: although Oenone ends with a superfluity of what Wordsworth conclusively found in the "Intimations" ode, "a master light of all our seeing" (152), she no less clearly ends with Wordsworth's originating sense that something is missing. Tennyson's finale crystallizes his awareness of the way the ode's Romantic consolation is snatched from the ashes of its elegiac lament—a process the entire bipartite structure of "Oenone" also enacts—while at the same time subversively implying that the resolution to Wordsworth's crisis really does nothing but take it from the top.

The end of "Oenone," then, rebukes Wordsworth for addressing the wrong problem and returns to the Romantic drawing board for a fresh approach to imaginative crisis in terms of relationship with another. Oenone's drive to meet and arraign the powers that be reconceives the Wordsworthian question interpersonally: Where is she, where is he, where are they now? It is this questing drive, and not the quest's object, that is imaged in the fire that consumes Oenone, as we remember it ought to have consumed the reluctant Soul from "The Palace of Art," who cries, "I am on fire within," only to shy away from relationship for reasons of her own (Bloom 1971, 154). Oenone's fire may derive from the "embers" of the "Intimations" ode, where Wordsworth finds "something that doth live" (129–130) in the poet's own mind. But by 1832 Tennyson's doubts about whether that kind of life was worth living compelled him to redefine life as a function of relationship with some *one* that doth live. Under this compulsion Tennyson found a fellow traveler in Shelley, whose "Ode to the West Wind" fanned the Wordsworthian embers into the flame of apocalyptic desire, and whose career-long evocation of an otherness forever on the verge of becoming present resonates behind the final lines of "Oenone" and of "Fatima" alike.[32]

Yet to juxtapose this most incendiary pair from the 1832 *Poems* is to appreciate a relative complexity of tone that lets "Oenone" absorb the kind of charge I began this discussion by supposing the Lady of Shalott might bring against "Fatima." "Oenone" ends in a mode of apocalyptic Romanticism that we can see Tennyson appropriate with evident excitement, but also with a measure of dread that corresponds to his protracted hesitation to lend himself to that mode. Among other things, the telescoping allusion at the close of the poem offers an exposé of the daemonism that lurks just behind Wordsworth's suave appeals to nature and the philosophic mind, and that more manifestly threatens Shelley's millenarian optimism about social betterment with the specter of unreconstructed aggression and the pointless misery of war. For Oenone's metamorphosis from victim to visionary prosecutor is also, as we have seen, the metamorphosis of a wood nymph into an abominable and antinatural crone, the caverned hag we meet sixty years after in the posthumous "Death of Oenone" (1892). Although the *Poems* of 1832 give every indication that Tennyson wanted to find his motive force in love, instead he repeatedly imagined the self-defeating machinations of desire, or else the apotheosis of a passion so fierce that we can call it love only in a fairly restricted sense. It was hatred and not love, Eris and not Eros, that fired Tennyson's first sustained and obstinate quest for confrontation in "Oenone"; and during the months and years following the death of the friend he had loved in Arthur Hallam, the original harshness of Oenone stubbornly remained, tempering his will to believe that all might be made gently well.

Part Two

1833–1855

Introduction to Part Two

*B*ETWEEN THE IDENTICALLY titled *Poems* of 1832 and of 1842 falls the shadow, both for Tennyson and for the literary historian who would reconstruct his poetic biography. For Tennyson the autumn of 1833 brought news of Arthur Henry Hallam's utterly unforeseeable death by cerebral hemorrhage in Vienna at the age of twenty-two. For us to move from acknowledging this decisive event to estimating its consequences in the life of the poet—a maker of very promising poems who aimed to be more than that, to fulfill his father's prophecy and become "the Poet of the Time"—is a naturally difficult job made harder by the poet's having been so assiduously on the job before us.[1] Yet the job solicits our attention, with respect not so much for a hoary legend of Victorian literary history as for the literature in which that legend was first enshrined by Tennyson himself, in the 1842 *Poems* and in much of what he produced later: manifestly in *In Memoriam A. H. H.*; only less so in *Idylls of the King*, whose protagonist does not just happen to bear the name Arthur; and, through variously permeable veils, in *Maud* and a handful of the finest lyrics Tennyson has left us.

It is not merely that Tennyson inaugurated the Hallam legend, or even that the metamorphosis of Hallam from friend to muse inaugurated Tennyson's Victorian eminence. That benign metamorphosis, after all, forms part of the legend. If we go on to consider the fabrication of the legend, we may see how by incorporating blind accident into a meaningful plot Tennyson was also plotting his own career. Not the Hallam legend but the imagi-

nation of the Hallam legend, the creation of a personal myth of
elegiac rescue possessing universal resonance, came to serve Tennyson as a resource from which he could draw, again and again,
those waters of the second birth that seem essential to the consecration of poetic majority in the Romantic tradition. For us it
remains an inaugural fact that in his return to the waters Tennyson
stirred up the evidence before us—raised it to visibility, but mud-
died it too. Conjecture as we may about how close Tennyson and
Hallam really were, what pitches of poignancy and what extra-
poetic forms Tennyson's mourning assumed, we may also seek
significance in the very swirl and blur that Tennyson's multiple
inscription of the record has left behind.

   To see how this may be so, we should briefly rehearse the
bearing of the poet's one supreme friendship upon the already
substantial body of work he had produced before his friend's death.
As the best-loved companion and keenest-sighted critic of the
brilliant, touchy, and laconic Alfred Tennyson, by 1833 Arthur
Hallam had collaborated on the shaping of a set of poetic ideals
that linked personal communion and artistic communication. The
influence of these ideals is perceptible in virtually everything Tennyson wrote from the start of his acquaintance with Hallam at
Cambridge, and it is unmistakable in the substantial portion of
Poems (1832) that was written with Hallam's direct encouragement
and guidance. Given the prominent part that themes of affective
relationship play in the texts of 1832 discussed in Chapter 3, it
seems plausible that by that date Hallam not only stood behind
Tennyson's developing poetic ideals, as their leading contributor,
but actually stood for them, as their representative incarnation in
the poet's mind.

   With the sudden death of Hallam, then, the conventional occasion for elegy—a genre with whose emotional gamut Tennyson
could already boast an expert familiarity—must have leapt out of
convention into horribly blunt fact. In elegy the loss of the beloved
traditionally figures the vulnerability of the elegist and also of his
craft; Hallam's death must have portended for Tennyson, if not
the death of poetry, then the death of the poetry of confrontation
and social responsibility, which with Hallam's encouragement
Tennyson had believed himself called to write (McLuhan 1951,
70). Abruptly the poet found himself at a moment of decision, in
the literal sense of that term as cutoff point; and it was the thin-

spun life of the poet, Tennyson's very career, that now lay on the line. To judge by all outward signs, for a long time the line went nowhere. The literary-historical melodrama of the "ten years' silence," the by now dog-eared legend that the fatal word of Hallam's death sealed the poet's lips for years, is undeniably valid in one important public sense. Having produced in 1827, 1830, and 1832 volumes of poetry that evinced steady, rapid gains in the scope and command of his art, Tennyson published nothing for the next decade beyond very occasional pieces of very occasional verse.

We have known for some time now that this fallow period masked, almost from the first shock of bereavement in October 1833, a germination of extraordinary intensity. By 1842 Tennyson had emerged from ten years' ostensive silence with the fruits of ten years' intensive writing. These included not only the major lyric, dramatic, and idyllic developments of the new 1842 *Poems*, but also a harrowing of his recent poetic past, which entailed large-scale revisions of the principal works from 1832. Beyond all this, Tennyson had gained major purchases on his poetic future, most importantly the core of what would become *In Memoriam* and the seeds of *The Princess*, *Maud*, and even *Idylls of the King*. Indeed, these years of private writing so set the terms of his subsequent career that it requires an effort to recall an obvious fact: during that time, Tennyson had no way of knowing whether he was to have *any* further career to speak of. Poet of retrospection though he was, during his twenties Tennyson enjoyed none of the hind-sighted vantage on his own career from which we perforce regard it now—none, that is, apart from what he could summon up, in the remarkable series of career-molding works to which he devoted himself almost at once.

In this sense the mask of age, the time warp of anticipatory recollection, was never more sorely needed by Tennyson than in the decade following 1833. What had once, however, served him principally as a device for aesthetic disengagement now provided instead a means of establishing continuity: the continuity of relatedness to other people and, more broadly, to the community for whose traditions the poet hoped to speak; and, prerequisite to this Hallam-sanctioned hope, the poet's continuity with his own past self, as the ground upon which he might imagine a future. The achievements of the ten years' silence bear at every turn marks of the creative anxiety Tennyson bore in working self-doubt slowly over and up into art. Not the least impressive feature of this outwardly shiftless but dialectically rich decade of brooding was the poet's resolve to shape a vocation, plot a career, figure himself into a literary history that was continuous without being closed.

For these reasons, despite the likelihood that recently released manuscripts will bring more of this crucial decade's chiefly private utterance into the public light, I predict that the ten years' silence will keep its hold on the literary-historical imagination, both as a reminder of Tennyson's own fears and as a trope for the uncertainty to which his active response to those fears permanently sentences our efforts to reconstruct this most important period of his literary life. We shall continue to need some such term in order to register the cloud that Tennyson's decade of germination has spread across any attempt to outline his development too neatly in terms of formal and generic innovation or spiritual breakthrough. We need to live with a blotted outline if we are to appreciate not only how extraordinary was the creative activity of Tennyson's late twenties and early thirties but—what was itself a part of that creative activity—how the decade figured in his evolving sense of vocation. Tennyson was as careful an architect of his career as of his texts; a tireless rephraser of lines and reorganizer of poems in sequences, like Wordsworth before him and Yeats after, he knew it was himself that he remade in his revisions.[2] So we should note a certain careerism, as well as truth-in-advertising, behind the memorandum he appended to the first volume of the 1842 set: "The second division of this volume was published in the winter of 1832. Some of the poems have been considerably altered" (see *Letters*, 130; *Memoir*, I, 198). Considerably altered, too, we are invited to surmise, was the man who had made and then remade them: we stare, with eagle eyes, upon the birth of a legend.

Yet the wholesale changes Tennyson introduced in the republished 1832 poems make it paradoxically harder, not easier, to specify what the inner alteration undergone during ten years of silence consisted in. While discussing these poems in the previous chapter I duly noted a number of 1842 revisions, but I finessed the question whether those revisions amount to a fresh imaginative departure that suggests some coherent picture of change across the intervening decade. Now is the time to submit that this finesse is rather the poet's than the critic's. In each instance Tennyson's "considerable" alteration is considerate as well, considerate of his already remarkable accomplishments of 1832. Even where he effects a radical twist in the fable, as at the close of "The Lady of Shalott," the change is radical in the sense that it returns to his text's imaginative roots and draws out implications that are at once latent within it and consonant with the concerns we find in the new poems of volume 2. The alterations Tennyson diffidently asked his 1842 reader to note thus represent an argument for continuity within a poetic career whose thematic and technical accomplishments were not arrested but confirmed, even accelerated, by the loss of the friend who had once witnessed it at closest hand.

This argument takes on extra force when we recall the way Tennyson's career through 1832 advanced by means of allusive, often self-allusive, repudiations. "Armageddon" took a Romantic stand against biblical and Miltonic orthodoxy; "Timbuctoo" then reflected Tennyson's reaction to this belated, and belatedly diagnosed, case of his own naive Romanticism. In 1830 "Mariana" incorporated the plaintive voice of the poems of 1827, but in a more cannily alienated fashion. "The Lady of Shalott," "Oenone," and other works of 1832 then proceeded to unseat the embowered self, by setting it into a defining social or mythic context and, most effectively, by unsettling it from within, remodeling or even disfiguring the bower and projecting the once placid self into a new range of emotion and flexibility of address. Tennyson's career through 1832, then, bears out a thermodynamic theorem of literary history. Inspired and ambitious poets blow hot and cold; progressive action in their careers involves an equal and opposite reaction to selected features of the literary past, which as they apprehend it certainly includes their own prior works.

The first thing to observe about the *Poems* of 1842, as a work not just in literary history but of it, is that very nearly half its contents, almost all the poems in volume 1, are reissued from the collections of 1830 and 1832. The next thing to observe, if necessary with a light prod from Tennyson's endnote, is that among this group the poems of 1832 received far more revision than did those of 1830, and revision of a different kind. The earliest pieces reappear intact or tuned up by replacement of such small parts as the poet found worn out, or rusty with the lexical antiquarianism that had appealed to him a dozen years before. The 1832 poems, in contrast, had whole sections added or cut, with an aggressiveness that bespeaks a qualitatively different authorial care (Fuller 1976). On the evidence of these revisions we may say that Tennyson cared *for* the 1830 poems but cared *about* those of 1832. He took care of the former the way a connoisseur might, or a repairman (*LTJ*, 271). With the latter, though, he took a proprietor's real pains—better yet, a parent's, since Tennyson's major thrust in correcting these texts was to mature them, by counterpointing them against his juvenilia and by making them grow more responsive to the Romantic tradition from which they came.

These strikingly different patterns of revision within the first 1842 volume all but propound a thesis in literary autobiography. During the ten years' silence Tennyson so distanced from himself the stable texts of 1830, and so engaged the still moving texts of 1832, as to establish the great divide in his literary life as having fallen in or before 1832—well before the great personal loss that had assaulted him the next year, and that a number of his most striking new poems dramatized (Saintsbury 1923, III, 186). In discussing the poems of 1832 I have tried to show how this plot for Tennyson's career makes sense: his leading theme of confrontation, and especially his severe dynamic of intertextual repudiation, had engendered in 1832 a pronounced liminal consciousness. The fact that Hallam had crossed the absolute threshold of death played into this liminal consciousness but did not determine it. The revisions Tennyson made for the 1842 edition sharpened the edge of "Oenone" and other works, to be sure, but they could do so only because the edge was there to begin with. In the following chapters I shall suggest how the new poems of the ten years' silence, for all their impressive variety and even mutual divergence of approach, also bear out the anticipations of 1832 in designedly continuous fashion. Here I want to stress that by 1842 Tennyson himself had come to view his evolving career in comparable terms. He returned to the 1832 poems, and made that return part of his long-delayed return before the public eye, because he had there first broached concerns that might keep him an active writer—because, indeed, he had there begun to explore psychic mythologies that had now, with an awful suddenness, come to provide means of discovering what it might mean to remain an active writer, or indeed remain active at all (Green 1951, 683–684; Fredeman 1972, 368).

To sum up: the continuity we discern across Tennyson's decade of silence is in large part a willed effect of the poetic imagination, trained no longer merely on individual texts, but now also on texts in their grouped configuration, on the book as text, and thereby on the shaping—inextricably private and public, driven and opportunistic—of the poet's career.[3] Yet, at the same time, the creative effort underlying that effect was possible for Tennyson only because he had been training for it unawares in his work since 1830. Furthermore, the artful contrivance of continuity across the two volumes of 1842 meshes with topics recurrently treated in the poems themselves: dialectical themes of continuity and change do much at the level of content to weld those volumes into the single work Tennyson called *Poems*. And if we note the book-level enjambment of contents resulting from the placement of a cluster of new but otherwise negligible poems at the close of volume 1, we may guess that the overall effect of career continuity in 1842 meant more to Tennyson than did several of the actual poems that conduced to it. His new *Poems* was not merely an anthology of works to date or a friendship's garland; it was a book of life, and in its advance and accomplishment it strongly rivals *In Memoriam* and *Maud* as the book of a lifetime.

SPECULATIONS OF THIS type open the possibility of a quite different approach to the ten years' silence. One might choose to call Tennyson's careerist orchestration of continuity by another name, like psychologically mandated forgery. Healing a rift in his writing life may have seemed to Tennyson a substitute gratification answering his boundless need to repair an irreparable personal breach, the same need to which the weaving therapies of many 1842 texts, but particularly of his work-in-progress *In Memoriam*, bear eloquently equivocal witness. According to such a psycho-biographical approach the life of the poet, while decidedly second best, would have seemed to Tennyson better than nothing. By ensuring the faithful preservation of his own memory through the vocation Hallam had urged him to pursue, Tennyson would be declaring fidelity to Hallam's memory as well, in a partial but by no means contemptible way. Besides—to run this line of explanation into the ground—in the desperation of an inconsolable grief Tennyson had every reason to prize whatever relations to the living past he could lay hold of; and he found the continuance of his creative writing no less valid, if ultimately no less unavailing, than any other form of therapeutic relationship.

Still, to prize is not just to find but also to appropriate; to prize any past as Tennyson did his years with Hallam is not just to make much of the past but also to make it over. And it is the making-over that counts: Tennyson's refashionings of the actual past, and then of the textual past, reward attention in their own right. Admittedly, a subtle pathological inquiry, which moves from the artfulness of the work to the defensive watchfulness of the worker, can come close to exhausting the abiding but limited interest of many of the poems of 1827 and even 1830. But the creatively neurotic constructions we meet in the Tennyson of 1842, while still legible as symptoms of a psychic need, assume a beauty and an import that make a strictly psychobiographical approach to the ten years' silence and its sequel look not irreverent but irrelevant, simply off the mark.

Here it seems that the literary biographer and the historical biographer proper, since they take interpretive aim at such different marks, must part company. Both may agree that the central problem of Tennyson's career, the problem the poet planted at its center, is what he made of Hallam's death. But the ultimate interpretive task of a historical biographer being to reimagine from the facts a person's life, and of a literary biographer to rehearse the life of imagination as a historical fact itself preeminent, the two are bound to place different constructions on this problem. Alfred Tennyson's biographer will stress the unquiet heart's perennial bewilderment amid a natural and cultural world afflicted by lack; will point to artistic achievement, political and religious orthodoxy, and social prestige as welcome though inadequate means of patching over pain; and will emerge with the sad tale of an essentially pathetic heroism. The literary biographer or critical historian of Tennyson's art will, with gaudier aims, put the heroism before the pathos; will ask what, if not the inspiriting splendor of genius, makes poets' careers worth attending to; and will subordinate the life to the creative achievement, in the conviction that this was what the poet himself did, precisely in so far as he *was* the poet.

This difference in approach is too sharply abstract, of course, to apply without qualification to the study of any poet's career. Certainly historical and literary-critical interests both inform our best accounts of Tennyson, as they should. But, where one might have hoped for a natural affinity between them, in practice these two interpretive approaches tend to cohabit without equality; indeed, they seldom seem even on speaking terms. Having discussed this situation more fully at the beginning of the book, I recur to it now because the divergence between testamentary or textual interests on the one hand, and documentary or contextual interests on the other, impinges particularly hard on the study of Tennyson's middle years—for the compelling reason that the major work of those years anticipates just such a divergence. As I shall argue at length in the following chapters, an ambivalent fascination with the mutual antagonism, or dependence, between creative agency and contextual determination typifies the great series of Tennyson's publications between 1842 and 1855. If works as various as the 1842 *Poems*, *The Princess*, *In Memoriam*, and *Maud* share a common theme, it is the fluctuating, reciprocally definitive relation between circumstance and volition, history and originality, opportunity and genius.

The Introduction to Part I addressed some of the ways in which this Tennysonian conflict between essentialist and conditionalist values is reproduced in much twentieth-century Tennysonian scholarship. We might now illustrate a specific crux from Tennyson's own writing, set it as a text for our putative historical and literary biographers, and predict their behavior. For an exemplary text with pronounced chronological as well as tropological features, one that exemplifies too the central problem of what Tennyson made of Hallam's death, we may as well leap at once to the vexed zenith of that making in *In Memoriam*, section xcv:

> So word by word, and line by line,
>   The dead man touched me from the past,
>   And all at once it seemed at last
> [His] The living soul was flashed on mine,
>
> And mine in [his] this was wound, and whirled
>   About empyreal heights of thought,
>   And came on that which is, and caught
> The deep pulsations of the world,

Aeonian music measuring out
      The steps of Time—the shocks of Chance—
      The blows of Death. At length my trance
Was cancelled, stricken through with doubt.   (33–44)

I have bracketed the pronouns that in the original edition bound Tennyson's epiphanic moment to the living memory of the man he had loved. The deletion of these words in 1872 by a poet apparently stricken through with orthodox scruples, decades after the fact, ought to exasperate the biographical mind historically wedded to that which was. Tennyson seems to betray both Hallam's memory and his own, both the individuality of the man his poem purports to memorialize and the veracity of his own powers of recall, which must have been more trustworthy in 1850, when he was closer in time to the experience these stanzas describe (Rosenberg 1959, 234; Bishop 1962; Hinchcliffe 1983, 257). The historian of Tennyson's imagination, however, should rejoice to find in this 1872 revision a retroactive and exemplary confirmation of the imaginative, the representative power that had made Tennyson a poet before he ever knew Arthur Hallam and that kept him a poet after his friend was dead (Shatto 1978; Buckler 1980, 180–181; Mason 1981). The habitation of that power had been in 1827, was in 1872, and would be until the end not that which was, but (as the passage says) "that which is": the Aeonian "this," the creative and recreative present (Wordsworth 1981, 215; Joseph 1983, 61). If this be orthodoxy and upon the poet proved, it is the orthodoxy of that Romantic error or Protestant iconoclasm without which this poet never writ—and without whose idealizing capacity to preserve the essence of the beloved, as opposed to the mere accidents of personality, no labor of poetic love ever bore it out even to the edge of doom.[4]

   This claim sounds exegetically heady, yet I think it historically plausible as well. Without question a major supplier and guide of the poet's mind, Hallam influenced Tennyson during undeniably formative years. Still, within a relationship so close that we should be ashamed not to call it, as Tennyson did, love, the personal influence was certainly reciprocal, and certainly too rich for satisfactory charting by either of the two men then or by us now (*LH*, 31). But influence has cultural as well as individual dimensions; and we may consider that Tennyson influenced Hallam—in a sense other than the biographical or personal, yet no less significantly historical—through the mythmaking energy of his loving idealization. By 1833, to resume a point made earlier, Hallam had helped to shape the poet's ideals, and had also come to represent those ideals in the poet's own mind. Insofar as Tennyson thus assimilated Hallam to a poetic ideal before his death, he performed an uncommonly gifted man's version of what we can all nevertheless recognize as a common office of tenderness, even a lover's generous error. But insofar as Tennyson assimilated Hallam to a poetic ideal after his death, and in the best writing of which he was capable, he changed him for all practical purposes from a historical into a representative man.

Here the authentic poetic power comes into play, and with it a danger lest this episode of literary history reduce to just another incarnation of that great giant with a single idea, the Romantic imagination. We may evade this ahistorical temptation by remembering that poetic idealization, truly gigantic though it be, is an *act*: a drama, a history, a story, which unfolds—and in any past instance once unfolded—in time. Tennyson's idealization of Arthur Hallam bears a date, an illegible but indispensable one. Although we cannot specify its hour or even year, we do know that the process was well underway before Hallam's death and that it took on thereafter a new burden and a newly independent impetus. Once Hallam's help had vanished forever, Tennyson was left to shape his career's ideals alone; and a great part of his solitary shaping was so to idealize his former helpmate as to disentangle the ideal from the man and set it free (Schulman 1983, 641).

This, or something quite like it, is the project Tennyson overtly plotted in *In Memoriam*; but, as I hope that the chapters to follow will show, this project commenced in powerfully occluded fashion almost as soon as he heard of Hallam's death. From the fall of 1833 Tennyson drove himself with redoubled intensity past Hallam as idealized representative and sought contact, however tenuous, with the weird power that Hallam had come to represent. At a fairly early stage in this quest Tennyson came to regard the power Hallam represented as identical with the power of representation itself, or in other words with the poetic imagination as it reads or writes, "keen through wordy snares to track / Suggestion to her inmost cell" (*In Memoriam*, xcv. 31–32). This act of identification was, on one hand, a projective cast into the future Tennyson desperately needed to imagine; and the balance of his

career shows that there is a sense in which he clung to this line
(on Hallam, on himself and his art) for life. On the other hand,
there was something profoundly regressive about Tennyson's
drive back beyond Hallam toward a faceless power closer than
friendship, nearer than hands and feet. Even as Tennyson was
laying down new lines for a career, he was also rehearsing the
steps of the "keen *Discovery*" of imaginative gain in empirical loss,
which had marked his response to the Romantics in "Timbuctoo";
in so doing, he was comforting himself with a welcome reprise
of a familiar elegiac motif. The death of Hallam thus brought on
a nostalgic surprise, the bittersweet sense of homecoming that
makes a Romantic poet. It is a token of Tennyson's greatness that
he did not rest here, but pressed on to the sort of uncanny find
that a Romantic poet makes. For, at the heart of his quest, Tennyson came to the surmise that the power he sought through
Hallam worked in collusion with the power of fatality, the very
force with which he had been uneasily seeking relationship all
along (Shaw 1971, 102).

This delayed discovery or uncanny recognition of his own earliest inspiration is, I think, what our set text from *In Memoriam*
proves to be all about, especially once we regard the text as having
been set in motion over forty years of Tennyson's second thoughts.
Those stanzas give us, in a revisionary nutshell, first the maneuver
disentangling the ideal from the accidental: the movement from
"The dead man" to "The living soul." And with this movement,
from the field of death to what we must conclude was in Tennyson's considered judgment the ground of life, comes the emergence of the Aeonian doom music that accompanied his career far
more faithfully than the mortal Hallam could ever do. For our
purposes the revision of these stanzas means that Hallam's death
and the ten years' silence did not change Tennyson's voice but
established his vocation; that the poet's career was confirmed anew
in whatever he afterward wrote, revised, or republished; that this
confirmation is not just plausible but is legible in Tennyson's texts
and deserves attention in any full interpretation of those texts.
Placing this crux within the poet's career yields an ampler reading
than either a strictly biographical or a strictly literary-critical approach can provide. When we read with an awareness of the career
shaped by the texts and their revisions, the texts themselves shift
shape in unanticipated yet conformable ways; the poet's history

and the intensely compressed stories that are his poems become mutually informative.

I hesitate to prophesy that the disciplinary needs and concerns of history and of literary criticism will ever merge in mystic compromise. Still, I am reluctant to believe such a merger impossible in theory and am confident that glimpses of it illuminate good exegetical practice all the time. Tennyson and Hallam appear to have shared for a time a like confidence, with their Romantic belief in a poetry of sensation that might "shake the world," bringing back into contemporary life a unity of being and community of purpose that intellectual, political, and industrial currents threatened to dissipate indefinitely. This desired union between daily life and the vitality of imagination Tennyson never effected, either in his poems or in his public. He may, in truth, never have desired it wholeheartedly; the suppressed *Lover's Tale* and the major texts of 1832 suggest that he had given over this Romantic hope, in its extreme form, by the end of that year. Thus, while Tennyson reprinted the Apostolic manifesto "The Poet" in the edition of 1842, he counterbalanced it by giving the authority of final say to "The Poet's Song," a new and intensely privatistic self-presentation in which the poet's first act is to leave town for good and sit "down in a lonely place" (5).

Certainly in 1842 Tennyson could not fuse Romantic, bardic vision and "the sense that handles daily life" ("Walking to the Mail," 16). But he did not altogether abandon the project either. Instead he took the different tack of veering between extremes, playing the eternity of imagination and the dailiness of contingency against one another in mutually corrective ways. This tacking operation appears most plainly at the level of the book: a glance at the table of contents for volume 2 shows how Tennyson interspersed the strong vocal presences of his lyrics and dramatic monologues with the more equable and socially diffused voices of his idylls. A similar zigzag also stitches the individual poems; although the lyric and the idyllic impulses pull different texts along strangely different diagonals, it is the cooperation of those often antagonistic impulses that fashions Tennyson's most distinctive poetry from 1842 until the end.

The balance of this book will trace, through extended readings of exemplary texts, the generic constitution of Tennyson's career: first his double invention, across the ten years' silence, of the lyrical dramatic monologue and of the domestic idyll, which became his chief vehicles for the rendition of experience as defined respectively in psychological and in contextual terms (Chapters 4 and 5); and then, with another ten years' publication, his longer experiments in combining these reciprocally definitive genres and the subjective and objective modes they represented (Chapter 6). Critical hindsight inevitably detects some anticipation of these constituent modes even in Tennyson's earliest work; but there is no denying the maturation suddenly begun around the time of Hallam's death, yet remarkably sustained over the next two decades. In 1833 a searing subjective desire and a fine situational tact quickly germinated—together, and with explosive, interactive force—and very soon ramified across the generic spectrum from love song to epic. These impulses, established in print and identified with distinct poetic kinds by the collection of 1842, Tennyson variously cross-bred in his next several publications. And the rest is history: institutionalized with *In Memoriam* and the laureateship in 1850, the results of Tennyson's generic innovation were canonized shortly thereafter in imperial marble.

My account of the career halts at 1855 because, at least by the very high standard of creative development set during the preceding decades, the career halts then too. The last text I consider, *Maud*, is among other things an uncanny prophecy of that arrest, as if a statue were to break its repose and explain with the utmost animation what has obliged it to forswear movement. But we should recall that what sometimes seems static or mechanically self-confirmatory in the work of Tennyson's later years had its start in a moving and unpredictable personal crisis. The binary genres the poet came to manipulate with expert aplomb first came to him as alternative, often jarringly contradictory means of piecing together a poetic life, in the aftermath of the catastrophe that had ripped his and Hallam's Romantic ideal of psychosocial integration right down the middle. That inaugural catastrophe the legend of Hallam still commemorates for us precisely because it did the same for the poet himself, repeatedly reopening the wound, between self and world, from and of which his best writing sings.

4

In Extremis: Margins of the Self in the Classical Dramatic Monologues

ENNYSON INVENTED THE modern dramatic monologue in 1833, several years before Drowning, with "St Simeon Stylites." I have argued elsewhere (1984) that this poem illustrates with particular clarity the polemic against naive Romantic lyricism that would be conducted, implicitly or explicitly, by the important line of Victorian and modernist dramatic monologues it inaugurated. "St. Simeon Stylites" establishes a generic norm by pitting a strong-willed speaking subject against his constituent environment, in such a way as to humble the Romantic arrogance of the lyrically Romantic claim to autonomy. In the pedestal-sitting anchorite Simeon, Tennyson seizes on a more or less historical figure who, in his quest for sublime sainthood, has abjured the world as completely as possible; and Tennyson has him unwittingly demonstrate that, since to speak in the world is to be shaped by the world, his metaphysical position is if anything less tenable than his physical one. The business of articulation reveals that the self-presence St. Simeon wishes to sustain relies upon, and therefore repeatedly collapses into, a rhetorical fabric of self-representations; the lyrical drive of his monologue only furnishes the impetus for its own overthrow. The result of Tennyson's ironic strategies of contextualization is not, however, pure demolition. While exploding the essentialist fiction of the integrity of the soul, this first and in some ways fullest of Tennyson's dramatic monologues installs the modern self in the soul's place, at the transactional site where the insistence of desire meets the discipline of the world.

This funny, moving, and historically significant poem deserves to be better known, both for its own merits and for the sake of its author's reputation as at least co-originator of a leading modern genre. Yet its comparative neglect may owe less to Browning's eclipsing brilliance than to the spectacularly aberrant uses Tennyson found for the dramatic monologue almost as soon as he had written this nearly perfect prototype. The poet's work in the genre after "St. Simeon Stylites," and after Hallam's death, adopted another tonality altogether. He in effect relyricized the genre, retaining the constitutive dialectic of self and context but turning it inside out. To speak a dramatic monologue is normally to declare oneself in context and under the regime of circumstance, but the three extraordinary instances taken up in this chapter run the contextualizing devices of the genre in reverse. Tiresias, Ulysses, and Tithonus quest after an absconded power that is at once closer to home psychically, and more alien to the historically contingent self, than anything in the natural or cultural environment— this despite the normative presupposition of the dramatic monologue that environment, broadly understood, is what conditions and indeed authorizes speech in the first place. If Tennyson's classical monologues feel unusually like lyrics, that is because each of them reconstitutes, at a helically giddy remove from the usual grounds of lyric, an antithetical self or newborn soul, which the poet's sublime artistry keeps just within the utmost bound of human thought. Elaborately disentangling themselves from context, the speakers of these poems emerge as principles of nearly naked aggression, identities matched only in the highest, most daemonic texts of the Romantic tradition.

"Tiresias": In Context and Out

"Tiresias," "Ulysses," and "Tithonus," while budding from a common stem, came to fruition at remarkably different rates: they were first published, respectively, in 1885, 1842, and 1860. Any sequential discussion of these texts, therefore, will appear arbitrary; but there are good reasons for putting "Tiresias" first. The earliest pertinent manuscript passage, an eight-line fragment of soliloquy to which we shall turn in a moment, fits Tiresias rather better than Ulysses and Tithonus. More important, the relative emphases on self and on context in "Tiresias"—whether in the

manuscripts surviving from the 1830s or in the version Tennyson
finished half a century later—display in the clearest way the poet's
methods and aims in developing the lyrical subgenre of the dramatic monologue that constitutes the larger subject of this chapter.
In proportion and design "Tiresias" comes closest of the three to
the generic norm for the dramatic monologue, because it gives
the most room to its mythic speaker's socially emplotted situation.
And yet the attention Tiresias pays to public affairs, extensive
though it be, is so patently valedictory, and so serenely self-serv-
ing, that he belongs not with the befuddled St. Simeon Stylites
but with the daemonic Ulysses and Tithonus. Tiresias's civic address to the young patriot Menoeceus, which occupies most of
the early manuscript fragments, manifestly renders his final dues
to a sightless body, and a thankless body politic, of which he has
had enough. And the published version of 1885 encases this kernel
of already antisocial intention with lyric paragraphs venting the
immortal longings of a prophet in quest of the honors awaiting
him elsewhere. It is the gradual accumulation of this thirst for
otherness, across the years as across the published text, that gives
"Tiresias" such an important place as a transitional dramatic monologue. The generic ingredients of definitive context and free desire are measured out in "Tiresias" with a precision that feels
deliberate—partly, no doubt, because by 1885 the poet could look
back over his major work and see the pattern so clearly, but partly
too because the fragments written down fifty years before disclosed so much of the pattern already.

The ground of the pattern, the core of Tennyson's classical
monologues, appears in a notebook fragment that may date from
as early as 1832. I quote it in full:

> I wish I were as in the days of old,
> Ere my smooth cheek darkened with youthful down,
> While yet the blessed daylight made itself
> Ruddy within the eaves of sight, before
> I looked upon divinity unveiled
> And wisdom naked—when my mind was set
> To follow knowlege [*sic*] like a sinking star
> Beyond the utmost bound of human thought.   (T.Nbk. 15)

This yearning to travel back to a primal, even auroral consciousness anticipates all three of the great classical monologists: Tiresias,

who lost the blessed daylight after looking upon divinity unveiled; Ulysses, two of whose unforgettable lines are lifted from the last two here; and Tithonus, whose daily erotic initiation by the ruddy dawn goddess has at length prompted a quest, beyond nostalgia, for a state anterior to his own birth. Indeed, this passage so strongly anticipates the famous monologues that it is easy to overlook another possibility: that Tennyson wrote it with no dramatic speaker in mind at all. From a poet versed in the odes of high Romanticism these lines might well come as pure lament over a primal seeing that has been undone by maturation, shadowed first by the coming of a beard or "youthful down" and then, not very elliptically, by the beholding of a primal scene. We might take the voice here to be no monologist's but Tennyson's own, speaking with the quintessentially elegiac lyricism of one who moved once through a world appareled in celestial light ("blessed daylight") but who has since darkened down into manhood and the common day, there to behold only the bare truth of "divinity unveiled" (Mermin 1983, 24).[1]

Furthermore, like the opening movement of a first-person crisis lyric, this passage introduces something of a sad perplexity as to the relation between the Romantic fall with which it starts and the Romantic drive with which it concludes. This perplexity presents itself in a grammatical riddle: What is the temporal status of the "when" clause that the dash of line 6 sets off from the rest? "When" may be read in apposition with "Ere," "While," and "before" as referring to a prelapsarian reservoir of boundless desire to follow knowledge—a pursuit that the sudden access of naked wisdom has brought to a halt (Goslee 1976, 158). Alternatively, the "when" clause may refer to results, to what has happened since that epiphanic instant when "I looked," when the speaker's mind was irrevocably set upon its quest down, out, and beyond (Joseph 1972). Tennyson's eight-line fragment thus laments an ambiguous catastrophe and yearns for it knows not what. Equally unsteady in its reference to the past and in its purchase on the future, the passage demonstrates the interdependence of two questions that will haunt the classical monologues to come, and that will provide their chief means of approach to the problem of identity: What happened to me? And where do I go from here? Given the structure and function of Tennyson's passion of the past, we might say that his way of settling the latter question—always, even for this gorgeously retrograde poet, the one that matters—was to address the former. He conferred upon his inchoate yearning a shape and an object by giving to its precipitating catastrophe a local habitation and giving to its speaker a name; in short, he converted a lyric impulse into a dramatic monologue.

That conversion may have been underway, of course, by the time Tennyson wrote these lines down. Even in 1832 he was accustomed to using mouthpieces; he more than likely did have a dramatic speaker in mind, and it may well have been Tiresias from the start.[2] But much as this eight-line speaker needs a firmer sense of context if he is to make his dilemma intelligible, even to himself, so we need more context than this fragment provides if we are to make a confident identification of genre. Like any utterance, the passage is potentially dramatic, but it cannot yet be called a dramatic monologue: although it occurs clearly and plangently in time, it lacks a situation and a history. It is the stuff of which dramatic monologues are made—particularly Tennyson's, because its irresolution as to origins and aims sets the terms within which the classical monologists frame their resolves and thus make themselves clear. We need not approach this fascinating scrap of notebook verse as a lyric in order to agree that the dramatic monologues Tennyson drew from it also drew toward it; that the textual origin of "Tiresias," "Ulysses," and "Tithonus" also constitutes their common goal; that the contextualizing devices we find in these dramatic monologues, unlike "St. Simeon Stylites" and most of Browning's, are not ends in themselves but byways of the soul, detours serving lyric ends.

When Tennyson rewrote this passage for the beginning of the 1885 "Tiresias," the grammatically ambiguous pursuit of a "sinking star" had long since fallen to the lot of a certain Ithacan mariner. But the poet found an equivalent ambiguity, and one more suitable to the pedestrian soothsayer whom a surprise sight had permanently blessed and cursed with prophetic vision, in the image of an *ambush*:

> I wish I were as in the years of old,
> While yet the blessèd daylight made itself
> Ruddy through both the roofs of sight, and woke
> These eyes, now dull, but then so keen to seek
> The meanings ambushed under all they saw,

The flight of birds, the flame of sacrifice,
What omens may foreshadow fate to man
And woman, and the secret of the Gods.   (1–8)

"Ambushed"—which here means both "waylaid" and "laid
away," "surprised" and "ready to surprise"—seems a perfect term
for the dialectic of encounter that plays throughout Tennyson's
classical monologues. As a keen-eyed quester, the young Tiresias
sought out a kind of meaning that might find him in return,
electing him as recipient of a divine secret. "Ambushed" thus
suggests a fit object for priestly nostalgia, a hermeneutic paradise
of reciprocal recognition. But by also suggesting the sinister intention without which no paradise would be complete, the recip-
rocating hermeneutic of "ambush" darkens into ambivalence,
especially with Tiresias's later description of his fatal encounter
with Pallas Athena amid the "shadow" and "bush" of "a secret
olive-glade" (35, 38). When we know how Tiresias's quest for
meaning has cost him both the ability to read nature with human
eyes and the power to be heard by human ears, the tonality of a
phrase like "then so keen to seek" becomes a problem. Does the
wish of Tiresias to go back to "the years of old" indicate a desire
to affirm the past, or to correct it by contriving somehow to know
less about the world and to see more of it? Tiresias longs for more
meaning—but does he long for or against the kind of preternatural
meaning he already possesses?

These are in essence the questions raised by the eight lines from
the Trinity notebook, where it seems Tennyson found them un-
answerable. The occurrence, later in the same notebook, of dis-
jointed but recognizable drafts of what became the address to
Menoeceus (roughly lines 83–144 in the 1885 text) suggests that
the poet puzzled out these Romantic questions by recasting them
in another form, a form suggested to him by the configurations
of classical myth. His principal source for "Tiresias" was *The
Phoenician Women* of Euripides, one of the numerous Athenian
tragedies that used the legends of Thebes to underscore a conflict
between familial and civic responsibilities. As with the Sophoclean
tragedies of Oedipus and Antigone, the formulation of this conflict
is the special province of Tiresias, here in the blunt choice he offers
Menoeceus's father Creon: "to save your city or to save your son"
(*Phoenician Women*, 952, tr. Wyckoff). The classic dilemma staking

private against public interest Tennyson subsumes within a more drastic, and Romantic, dilemma staking self against world. The monologue's repeated address to Menoeceus as "my son" stations the prophet where the actual father Creon stands in Euripides: at the place of a decision that in either text troubles the eager patriot-martyr less than it does his older counselors. This distillation of the Greek dramatis personae into the English dramatic monologue exerted upon Tiresias's options an extreme compression, which wrested the myth into alignment with the Romantic terms we have already found in Tennyson's initial notebook fragment. Those terms so stress the divide between the isolated self, and whatever might frustrate or gratify it, that the claims of family and of city are fused. "Tiresias," in effect, pronounces the Euripidean moral choice between those claims to be no choice at all.

The choice of Tennyson's Tiresias lies, instead, between courting the world's validation and imagining other grounds for validity altogether. Seeing the myth in these terms should let us improve our earlier formulation of the Romantic question that underlay this and Tennyson's other classical monologues. Tiresias longs for more meaning. But meaning on whose terms? Does he covet the significance of fame, a meaning that society alone can award and history alone can confirm? Or does he want the ambush of still bigger game, a meaning that entails divination of and by "the secret of the Gods"? Does he aspire to the status of a culture hero or of a prophet whose honors, by definition, lie elsewhere? Whether or not these questions capture the direction Tennyson's meditations on the figure of Tiresias took in the 1830s, they manifestly direct the plot of the dramatic monologue he was finally to compose. For this lavishly orchestrated poem builds to two quite different outbursts of voice, which correspond to the two Tennysonian voices: the one that merges with fate and the one that resists it. By the end Tiresias has declared his preference for prophetic alienation over cultural merger, although it takes most of a longish poem for him to make up his mind, and although he closes with a hint of bet hedging that compromises his character and marks his as a transitional monologue.

The poem is superficially complicated but ultimately clarified by the presence of Menoeceus, who slips rather suddenly into the text after the solo murmur of the first eight lines and then leaves for good before the finale of the last twenty. This earnest and pliable auditor serves revelatory purposes of a different kind from those he would serve had Browning taken up this situation. There more would be made than Tennyson makes of the striking rhetorical occasion—which is, after all, that of persuading a man in the prime of life to kill himself. But here we have to do with the kind of writing Yeats recognized as not rhetoric but poetry, the kind made out of the quarrel with oneself. Menoeceus, as auditor and as representative of the polis he is ready to die for, plays the part of context in this dramatic monologue; and his function curiously resembles the function assumed by the conventions of that still callow genre in ministering to Tennyson's urgent need for subjective assertion. It is Menoeceus's lot to fall under the spell of a speaker for whom context is no obstacle but rather a convenience, raw material to try questions on, eventually a foil with which to distinguish oneself. Nowhere during lines 9–159 is Menoeceus felt as a presence to be reckoned with, either through implied interruption or through any Browningesque forestalling maneuver on Tiresias's part (Mermin 1983, 24). Hence, the poem sounds the same when it is a monologue as when it is a soliloquy. Tiresias, like Ulysses and Tithonus, has nothing to hide—or almost nothing—but devotes himself instead to the unfolding of his own resolve, which is hidden from him until he articulates it, and in the articulation of which Menoeceus chiefly serves to mark a corner turned.

At the midpoint of this symmetrical text, after Tiresias has concluded the story of his past and before he turns to consider the future, he takes stock of his present condition in terms that make explicit the dilemma that is ambushed under everything he says. He has been granted "The power of prophesying—but to me / No power" (56–57), because it exerts "no power on Fate" (62). This collision between the self's prerogative and its doom has opened the space of a typically Tennysonian sorrow, a space that Tiresias tries to imagine as a public arena:

> This power hath worked no good to aught that lives,
> And these blind hands were useless in their wars.
> O therefore that the unfulfilled desire,
> The grief for ever born from griefs to be,
> The boundless yearning of the Prophet's heart—
> Could *that* stand forth, and like a statue, reared
> To some great citizen, win all praise from all

Who past it, saying, "That was he!"
                              In vain!
Virtue must shape itself in deed, and those
Whom weakness or necessity have cramped
Within themselves, immerging, each, his urn
In his own well, draw solace as he may.   (76–87)

The possession of an indubitable power, which is yet "to me /
No power," insinuates that question of identity with which major
dramatic monologists have always to contend. To St. Simeon
Stylites's primal, generically definitive query "What am I?" (124)
Tiresias's rousing "That was he!" is certainly one answer, an answer rather like Simeon's in its instinct for the statuesque. The
passage figures both the desire for public approval and, as the
prerequisite to such approval, the desire to attain a pillar-of-state
integrity that might fulfill "unfulfilled desire" and bind "boundless
yearning." As Tiresias starts to recognize here, however, these
desires to halt desire are "vain," not just because they are self-
regarding (seldom a demerit for a Victorian monologist) but because they are internally contradictory: what is boundless cannot
obey limits. Indeed, the passage shows that what is boundless can
scarcely be talked about at all—something the laureate of "The
Higher Pantheism" (1869) and "The Ancient Sage" (1885) would
eventually take grim pleasure in propounding as a mystic thesis,
but that Tennyson in the 1830s was taking too seriously as a
problem of imaginative discourse to treat thematically. First a
"desire," then a "grief," then a "yearning," and most eloquently—
in the referential humiliation of so well versed a speaker—a *"that"*
beyond denomination, the power Tiresias dreams of being known
by is itself unknowable. It shares, in this regard, the properties of
the divine vision that provoked its onset and that has long since
assumed for him (as for his poet) the attributes of an interior
paramour: "Behind this darkness, I behold her still, / Beyond all
work of those who carve the stone, / Beyond all dreams of Godlike womanhood, / Ineffable beauty" (51–54).

Tiresias's contradictory wish to express the ineffable in himself
conducts him to a choice of greatnesses. At stake is the question
whether he means to pledge allegiance to the greatness of citizen-
ship, which is the greatness of having been ("That was he!"), or
to the ineffable desire that is great in him and whose province lies,
however sadly, in the future, born as it is "from griefs to be."

The paragraph break within line 83 gives Tiresias's answer, though
in a muted form that will emerge more fully as the poem proceeds:
the prophet's heart in him is too strong to suffer limitation. "Virtue
must shape itself in deed," and that shaping or reduction to form
is indeed the problem. As Euripides' Tiresias had put it, waiving
questions of executive method, "Others must deal with action. I
must speak" (*Phoenician Women*, 928). Tiresias is not yet proud of
his prophetic strength, and for now he even regards it defensively
as a "weakness." His civil defenses, however, begin to erode pretty
quickly, with the retreat from "weakness" to "necessity," and
thence to the image of the "well," which evokes Romantic metaphors for the self as a boundless source, metaphors that receive
yet further confirmation in Tiresias's audibly Romantic challenge
to himself to "draw solace as he may." By the close of this critical
passage Tiresias has reclaimed the prophetic initiative from patriotic "virtue" and has shaped himself a different project con-
forming to a more elementary idea of "virtue" as unharnessed
power. From this point onward, Tiresias will discriminate his own
aims from public works that are for others; and he will disengage
and isolate the prophetic self by rendering unto context the things
that are context's—all residual sympathy for Menoeceus and his
kind, our shared human kind, included.

  This isolating activity appears in miniature as Tiresias approaches his first rhetorical climax, the proleptic integration of the
martyr Menoeceus into monumental history. Of patriots he says
at first,

>   Their names,
>   Graven on memorial columns, are a song
>   Heard in the future; few, but more than wall
>   And rampart, their examples reach a hand
>   Far through all years, and everywhere they meet
>   And kindle generous purpose, and the strength
>   To mould it into action pure as theirs.   (119–125)

The "memorial columns" remind us of the candidacy for civic
honors from which Tiresias has withdrawn his name in the earlier
passage, and this parallel thus revives the contrast between the
narrowing of Menoeceus's options and the enlargement of his
own. Much as Tiresias's earlier "weakness" has masked prophetic
strength, here the "strength" he offers Menoeceus is contingent

upon the young man's undoing. Furthermore—in a metaphorical illustration of the way character in Tennyson's dramatic monologues develops along an axis of clarification instead of change—Tiresias gradually appropriates such architectural props as "columns," "Wall," and "rampart" for his own design, which is so to identify the marmoreal suicide Menoeceus with the commemorative city Thebes as to heighten Tiresias's contrast with them both.[3] In the lines above, Tiresias's presentation of the choice of patriotism sounds a little too much like his own choice of an alien vision. When he says that the patriot, more than wall or rampart, casts his influence *far* through *all* years, and *everywhere*, the redundant diction of excess encroaches upon the rhetoric of the "boundless" that the prophet has earlier claimed for himself. His paragraph comes more suitably to rest with the idea that patriotism must know bounds and "mould" purpose "into action"—a resumption of the earlier dictum "Virtue must shape itself in deed"—which gives Tiresias both the start of the extraordinary passage to come and a key to its magniloquent course.

Beginning again in a new paragraph, Tiresias reiterates the difference between patriot and prophet, with an intention that governs all that is to follow:

> Fairer thy fate than mine, if life's best end
> Be to end well! and thou refusing this,
> Unvenerable will thy memory be
> While men shall move the lips: but if thou dare—
> Thou, one of these, the race of Cadmus—then
> No stone is fitted in yon marble girth
> Whose echo shall not tongue thy glorious doom,
> Nor in this pavement but shall ring thy name
> To every hoof that clangs it, and the springs
> Of Dircê laving yonder battle-plain,
> Heard from the roofs by night, will murmur thee
> To thine own Thebes, while Thebes through thee shall stand
> Firm-based with all her Gods.   (126–138)

Tiresias first congratulates Menoeceus on the foregone decision "to end well," but he brackets the merits of ending well in a punning conditional clause that leaves a prophet free to seek other "ends" for life and conditions instituting other scales of value. There follows an oddly veiled threat outlining the consequences if Menoeceus fails to act. The oblique contrapositive phrasing of this appeal to the power of infamy as a public constraint on individual action makes the appeal unmenacing, ineffectually pro forma; and it is precisely this rhetorical indifference, this lack of menace to Menoeceus or to Tiresias either, that constitutes one of the permanently frightening things about the poem. Should Menoeceus refuse to sacrifice himself—that is, should he behave like Tiresias—his name will be not accursed but just "Unvenerable," and not forever but only "While men shall move the lips." In the psychological terms that would count in a Browningesque "Tiresias," the menace is light, because Menoeceus does not need to be scared into virtue in any case, and more importantly because Tiresias here anticipates history's verdict upon himself. That verdict, whether of condemnation or neglect, is the worst that history can muster. And yet what is horrible about this passage is how lenient, even inconsequential, Tiresias plainly feels history's most stringent verdict to be.

"While men shall move the lips," no longer than that. The phrasing here, which harkens back to similar austerities in "The Palace of Art" and "Armageddon," reveals more bluntly than anything thus far in the poem Tiresias's enormous detachment from human affairs. It is as if to make the choice of Tiresias, refusing "this" for the sake of what at the moment of decision we examined earlier he could only call *"that,"* is to regard humankind as automata, programs to be shaped in deed and molded into action: a race, in short, composed of the likes of Menoeceus. The powerful passage that ensues complements this automation of the human by animating the inorganic into chillingly depopulated activity. From Tiresias's forecast it appears that men will not be moving the lips for any great time to come. Rather, the power of civic speech will be usurped by those entities to which civic virtue would sacrifice the self: municipal edifices, ancestral waters, and the tutelary gods. Accept the patriot's ends, the passage implies, trade the living self for the verdict of fame, and you become the spirit of a perennial but purposeless necropolis, where the roofs have ears and the pavements have tongues—and only, indeed, for you—but where no self, no person whatever, remains.

FROM THE VANTAGE purchased here we can look back to scattered passages that portend Tiresias's radical isolation in ways not evident to him as he speaks. One such portent is a grammatical schism between forms of the pronouns "I" and "they" that tends to leave the latter in a limbo without specific antecedents. He inveighs against

> their unbelief, who heard
> And heard not, when I spake of famine, plague,
> Shrine-shattering earthquake, fire, flood, thunderbolt,
> And angers of the Gods for evil done
> And expiation lacked—no power on Fate,
> Theirs, or mine own! (58–63)

Even across four lines filled with possible antecedents natural and divine, we know well enough to whom "Theirs" in the last line refers, thanks to the prophetic invective setting the exasperated speaker against an inattentive crowd. His grammar knows better than Tiresias does how thoroughly his world is polarized already: "their" fate splits off from "mine own" a little too sharply for us to find Tiresias's wish for civic praise quite credible. As it happens, that wish includes a more dramatic version of the same grammatical gesture: "This power hath worked no good to aught that lives, / And these blind hands were useless in their wars." The reference to the Theban wars is clear, although the referent of "their" is not: it could mean "all" (73–74), "kings," "cities" (70), "states" (69), "multitude" (65), or "crowd" (63), which are all more or less synonymous in Tiresias's lexicon anyhow. Without as yet weighing the consequences of his doing so, Tiresias lumps all social otherness together—and sets it apart from the socially useless power that is his. More disturbing, he lumps with it what is, after all, the closest antecedent for "their": his own "blind hands." In sharp contrast to the prophetic kinesthesia of "Armageddon," Tiresias's very body seems to him instinctively alien: violences of trope and grammar here conspire to eloign the visionary prophet from the natural man, who has warred thus far in struggles irrelevant to the purposes the poem will proceed to imagine.

Indeed, it is when Tiresias turns to imagine war-torn Thebes that his voice first manifests a positively daemonic exuberance, in a passage dating from the 1830s:

> Menoeceus, thou hast eyes, and I can hear
> Too plainly what full tides of onset sap
> Our seven high gates, and what a weight of war

Rides on those ringing axles! jingle of bits,
Shouts, arrows, tramp of the hornfooted horse
That grind the glebe to powder! Stony showers
Of that ear-stunning hail of Arês crash
Along the sounding walls. Above, below,
Shock after shock, the song-built towers and gates
Reel, bruised and butted with the shuddering
War-thunder of iron rams.   (88–98)

These militant lines indulge a vicarious jubilation that ill suits their
speaker's avowed role as peacemaker (Goslee 1976, 160). Their
scarcely veiled glee is inappropriate rhetorically, as well, because
it does much to disable in advance Tiresias's appeal to pathos, the
human "murmur void of joy" (99) with which he goes on to move
Menoeceus. If we are to understand the delight Tiresias takes in
imagining this scene, we need to ask what it substitutes for, or in
other words what force behind this description is moving Tiresias
himself.

He describes a rhythmically percussive scene, in which the violence of attack meets a matching resistance in the city's forti-
fications. The "hail of Arês" stuns the ear, but the walls are
"sounding" too, and are thus still *sound*—as befits the "song-built"
city of Thebes, to whose constructive energies Tennyson's ringing
passage gives their due even in undertaking its demolition. As the
iron rams thunder at the threshold they have not yet crossed, as
the "full tides" of war are full only with "onset," the violence
Tiresias hears at the Theban gates is powerfully preliminary; and
here lies a key to the prophet's inappropriately bracing rhetoric.
The linked sounds of beasts (butting rams, hornfooted horses) and
of vehicles straining in readiness (axles, bits) accompany each of
Tennyson's major classical monologists; and for each of them these
sounds figure an apocalyptic transition, which lies outside his
poem but for which his poem is an imaginative girding. In "Tiresias" the two sounds converge in the "tramp of the hornfooted
horse" that are both beasts and conveyors of men; and the Virgilian
provenance of this image deepens its significance. Virgil's Sibyl
in book VI of the *Aeneid* describes Salmoneus as "a madman who
would mime the tempests and / inimitable thunder with the
clang / of bronze and with the tramp of horn-foot horses": *demens,
qui nimbos et non imitabile fulmen / aere et cornipedum pulsu simularet
equorum* (590–591, tr. Mandelbaum). Tennyson liked to cite this

passage for its "descriptive beauty and fine sound" (*Memoir*, II, 13); but, as is often the case with Tennyson's touchstones of formal excellence, the passage deserves thematic consideration as well. It constitutes, after all, a showcase of imitative onomatopoeia in which imitation is the explicit theme: Salmoneus has failed to mimic Jove, but the passage invites us to agree that Virgil's words and rhythms have mimed the *non imitabile fulmen* rather better.[4]

What Virgil wrote for his prophetess the Sibyl to speak, like Tennyson's description of "song-built" Thebes, celebrates the godlike power of poetic sound. Tennyson's Tiresias joins the celebration by reading the noises of warfare—"their wars"—in his own prophetic terms, as figurations of the onset of the divine. In the violence of his desire Tiresias evokes a violent god, like St. Simeon Stylites at his most daemonic: "Now, now, his footsteps smite the threshold stairs / Of life" (188–89). He would reclaim from its mistaken entanglement with history his Romantically prophetic vocation, which is in part the power to take the rumble of civic crisis as auditory evidence of a sublime individual encounter, appointed for some time soon and at some place out of this world.

Under the aspect of this desired divination the central rhetoric of the poem, Tiresias's advice to Menoeceus, appears in its true colors as a preliminary *askesis*, a ritual sloughing of the merely human, which frees the prophetic self to articulate the heroic mergers of the poem's last paragraph:

> He will achieve his greatness.
>   But for me,
> I would that I were gathered to my rest,
> And mingled with the famous kings of old,
> On whom about their ocean-islets flash
> The faces of the Gods—the wise man's word,
> Here trampled by the populace underfoot,
> There crowned with worship—and these eyes will find
> The men I knew, and watch the chariot whirl
> About the goal again, and hunters race
> The shadowy lion, and the warrior-kings,
> In height and prowess more than human, strive
> Again for glory, while the golden lyre
> Is ever sounding in heroic ears
> Heroic hymns, and every way the vales

Wind, clouded with the grateful incense-fume
Of those who mix all odour to the Gods
On one far height in one far-shining fire.   (161–177)

The retirement Tiresias predicts for himself, far from a surcease,
is semantically hyperactive. "Rest," in the second line, punningly
suggests both the saving remnant of identity that is left after this
monologue's purgations and the support of the new, heroic context that Tiresias's spirit gathers around its undestroyed core. In
the next line "mingled" hovers between active and passive voices,
as verbs of merger typically do in a Tennysonian paradise, to
suggest the interdependence of imagination and what it imagines.
In the domain of the "more than human," the hitherto exclusive
pronoun "their" becomes inclusive and assigns the blessed isles
both to the superhuman kings of old and to the gods. Likewise
Tiresias's own kingly possession, "the wise man's word," is
"crowned with worship," in a paradisal ambiguity that directs
worship with equal plausibility toward the gods and toward the
wise man himself.

Tiresias appears at last to have imagined his way back to the
superflux of recognition he began the monologue by confusedly
desiring. For the last half-dozen lines of the poem all time, place,
and personality not worthy of the gods dissolve in a fluent syntax,
in a vocabulary of boundless totality—"ever sounding," "every
way," "all odour," "one far-shining fire"—and, supremely, in the
effortless transmemberment of sound that welds the golden lyre's
glorying and the winding of the clouded vales (like hunting horns?)
into a single Orphic process. In shedding the empirical self, Tiresias
finally summons a context that matches his ultimate desire: not
human affection, as Tennyson's revision of "The men I loved" in
line 168 to the Ulyssean phrase "The men I knew" confirms
(T.Nbk. 32), but the boundless prophetic yearning to join the
gods as an equal. In this transcendence of the dramatic circumstances of monologue, Tennyson renders the fulfillment of his
prophet's deepest wish, in a rich lyricism that would rank as a
triumph of imagination from any poet, much less a poet in his
seventies.

But was it too rich? Tennyson, true to form, had his doubts.
When he published "Tiresias" in 1885 he enclosed it within a
sturdy verse epistle to his old friend and confrere Edward Fitz-

Gerald. The news of FitzGerald's death had, by a touching coincidence, reached Tennyson while he was at work on the epistle
and had then, by a sure tact, been incorporated into it. The occasion, and the epistolary middle style, offered Tennyson a vantage
from which to improvise some self-criticism apropos of the monologue he had finally brought to so stately a finish:

> "One height and one far-shining fire"
>   And while I fancied that my friend
> For this brief idyll would require
>   A less diffuse and opulent end,
> And would defend his judgment well,
>   If I should deem it over nice—
> The tolling of his funeral bell
>   Broke on my Pagan Paradise.   (57–64)

"Diffuse and opulent": How would Tennyson, rolled back to his
sole self, have defended against FitzGerald's his own judgment in
bringing "Tiresias" to such an end? The charge of diffuseness I
think he would have accepted, by converting it into an accurate
description of what a pagan paradise ought to be: its dynamic
harmonies should effect a sharing of power among heroes and
gods, which the former have continually to earn through striving
with the latter, and in which the daemonic poet-prophet takes part
through the imagination of "hymns" that may claim "heroic"
status themselves. In response, though, to the imputed charge of
opulence—of a poetic ostentation at once stylistic and spiritual—
I think Tennyson would have mounted a different, generic defense,
of the sort Browning often used. In emphasizing that "Tiresias"
remains, its lyricism notwithstanding, a dramatic monologue, he
could have cited one or two late passages where the showiness of
his text masks a poverty of spirit that the poet acknowledges,
although his speaker does not.

   In the final paragraph Tiresias's contempt for "the populace,"
and his needless gloss that the actors in this visionary scene are
"more than human," remind us that the prophet remains himself
a shade too human to escape entirely from voyeurism into vision.
The old context clings, tarnishing his spirit and marking him as
a residually dramatic speaker trapped in the history from which
he would struggle free. The persistence of an autobiographical
impulse in Tiresias stands out especially some dozen lines further

up in the text, with what looks like a Freudian slip in his peroration
to Menoeceus:

> thou art wise enough,
> Though young, to love thy wiser, blunt the curse
> Of Pallas, hear, and though I speak the truth
> Believe I speak it.   (148–151)

Blunt *whose* curse? It is Ares, not Pallas, that Menoeceus aims to
placate; but his aims are not Tiresias's aims, nor are Tiresias's aims
at this point consonant with the heroic grandeur he would devote
himself to imagining. Menoeceus's business is to appease Ares, to
"quench / The red God's anger" (152–153), while Tiresias seeks
not appeasement but a joining of issue with the gods on their own
grounds. Both purposes, however, are here displaced by three
lines that betray Tiresias's residual itch to correct the biographical
record and thus to aggrandize just the wrong self: the self that
lives in the world and dies there, and that survives, if at all, only
in history and on the world's terms.[5]

Now the world's terms are those that make for human interest
in character and that the dramatic monologue generically tends to
privilege. Here, for a penultimate moment, "Tiresias" highlights
human finitude and makes uniquely, poignantly credible an appeal
to human affections: "love thy wiser." Tiresias sounds for an
instant like a man who is afraid to die and is all the more afraid
for his having led a futile life.[6] If we return from this passage to
the final clauses of the poem and their Keatsian imagery of "winding" and "clouded" vales—"bowery," even, in H.Nbk. 46, fol.
4—we may suspect that the opulent finish of "Tiresias" represents
a very human endeavor to diffuse the threat of death. In this
connection the final lines of this monologue bear comparison with
those of "Oenone," where the winding vales veiled an apocalyptic
will that at last made "All earth and air seem only burning fire."
For Tiresias it is not the fires but the vales that are everywhere,
accompanied by a holy smoke screen that, together with the stress
on "far" in the last line, separates him from the pure energy that
he seeks and that neither selfishness nor selflessness seems adequately to characterize. This current in "Tiresias" permits us to
place its speaker as a human self, if we like, and to type the poem
as a dramatic monologue. At the same time we should remember
that this current is but a countercurrent: the overwhelming thrust

of the poem, and of Tennyson's work in the monologue form during the 1830s, points toward a quite different human, and generic, condition. But of this thrust no close reader of the tighter, surer-handed, and scarier "Ulysses" or "Tithonus" is likely to need reminding.

"Ulysses": At the Prophet Margin

Although "Ulysses" embraces designs continuous with those of "Tiresias," it works its work in well under half the time and calls accordingly for more meticulous unpacking. The comparative swiftness of this, the one classical monologue that Tennyson wrote out more or less at a stroke (his manuscript specifies October 20, 1833), results in part from the dispatch with which its speaker handles the questions of cultural and familial relationship that so exercise Tiresias. With great brevity but considerable fairness of mind, Ulysses thus puts context in its place:

> This is my son, mine own Telemachus,
> To whom I leave the sceptre and the isle—
> Well-loved of me, discerning to fulfil
> This labour, by slow prudence to make mild
> A rugged people, and through soft degrees
> Subdue them to the useful and the good.
> Most blameless is he, centred in the sphere
> Of common duties, decent not to fail
> In offices of tenderness, and pay
> Meet adoration to my household gods,
> When I am gone. He works his work, I mine.   (33–43)

To this point "Ulysses" has been so private, so soliloquizing a monologue that the presence of Telemachus indicated here ought to feel more intrusive than it does. Recall, for comparison, the shocking conclusion to "Tintern Abbey," where Wordsworth emerges from apparently solitary meditation to address his by-standing sister. An important difference between these two famous poems of growing up or old, a difference that may explain the comparative serenity of the passage just quoted, is that in Tennyson's the youthful delegate, unlike Wordsworth's Dorothy, inherits the offices of responsible maturity, while the speaker keeps the wild eyes for himself. The Wordsworthian interest in a filial continuity that naturalizes imagination forms a sharp contrast to

Ulysses' generational sundering and the antithetical project it feeds: a secession from generation itself, a valediction to the genealogies of natural and cultural history alike.

We know from Tennyson's manuscripts that this ostensibly intrusive moment in the finished text also happens to be an insertion within the poem as first written. It thus furnishes another instance of the delayed contextualization that is habitual with this poet and that becomes especially interesting in his experiments with the dramatic monologue. For Ulysses' (and Tennyson's) belated acknowledgment of the generic conditions of the dramatic monologue, in this verse paragraph, is principally a repudiation of those conditions; and as such it provides a handy recapitulation of the lonelier, murkier, yet thoroughly consonant manuscript sections from which it rises here into public light. In a dramatic monologue of the variety to which Browning has accustomed us, or indeed in almost any other Tennyson poem, this backing and filling operation would serve as a trace of character and would mark our point of entry into the text. Such a nod as Ulysses' to the circumstances out of which he speaks would provide a means of grasping his three-dimensional, contextual fullness. But here it is not so: in this smoothest of interpolations nothing knots up. Ulysses' nod to circumstances so simply bids them farewell, and Tennyson's backing into context is so effortless a bowing out of it, that what these lines of potentially dramatic revelation most reveal is their speaker's dismissive way of taking context quite for granted. Tennyson's interpolation of the lines on Telemachus thus interrupts the original manuscript only to confirm it—a dramatic exception proving a lyrical rule.

To be sure, some readers have found in this passage the key to a moralistic debunking. Particularly in recent decades, when critical sympathy with and judgment of dramatic monologists have been dispensed and registered to the dram, readers of conviction have found in Ulysses' casual abandonment of his responsibilities an unforgivable malfeasance (Chiasson 1954; Smith 1963). But what on earth is wrong with what Ulysses says in the lines quoted above? To me they appear far less a sinister dereliction of duty than a deftly left-handed compliment to Telemachus's abilities in a sphere of action that Ulysses esteems rapidly yet thoroughly— esteems, indeed, with a rhetorical thrift that exemplifies the administrative virtues of discernment, prudence, and decorum he is commending in his son (Marshall 1963; Buckler 1980, 172). Centered in his sphere, Telemachus remains an unmoved mover, an heir to his father's legendary propriety as well as to his property, who in the inherited offices of kingship and priestcraft will know just what to make of his father's example (how "to fulfil / This labour") and will know, too, just what practical weight to give his father's incipient station among the ancestral "household gods."

Ulysses can pronounce this admiring if businesslike encomium because, like Tiresias but to an even greater extent, he feels himself to be so far removed from its values. What Tiresias discovers only after lengthy preliminaries to his valediction ("He will achieve his greatness. But for me . . . ") Ulysses articulates in a dozen lines. Furthermore, Ulysses' graceful blessing leaves no taste of the bitter and self-interested repudiation that underlies Tiresias's ensphering of Menoeceus in his Theban civic center. As Ulysses takes historical context for granted, so "Ulysses," we might say with an eye on Tennyson's career, takes "Tiresias" for granted. This formulation is less anachronistic than the publication dates make it look, since the part of "Tiresias" that exercised Tennyson during the 1830s was precisely the central address to Menoeceus, with the prophet's arduous disengagement from social concerns.

"Ulysses" takes the struggles of "Tiresias" for granted because in "Ulysses" Tennyson undertakes struggles of a different order of elusiveness. The problem is no longer how to define an adequate context for the alienated self but how to regard context, any context, to begin with. Tiresias's goal of imaginative removal from the prophet's place of dishonor and into another country is here superseded by Ulysses' desire for "that untravelled world" (20), "a newer world" (57) beyond imagination. Ulysses seeks a perennial extravagance that, in consuming all contexts, also consumes the self, and that in the process radically dismantles the speaking subject of the monologue, as it were, from the inside. According to Tennyson's own gloss, which postdates the poem considerably, "Ulysses" even more than *In Memoriam* rendered his "feeling about the need of going forward" (*PT*, 560). This phrase is often quoted but seldom read closely: it refers not to progress, nor to that rather different thing a need for progress, but instead to a feeling about such a need. The phrasing is bizarre yet trustworthy: we might, after all, describe much of Tennyson's best work through 1832 as the expression of a feeling about a need. But whereas the predominant feelings there arise from needs occluded or denied, the emotional mode of "Ulysses" has more to do with its speaker's feeling for, or feeling his way toward, he knows not what: "something more" (27), "something ere the end" (51). "Ulysses" is, in other words, not only an experimental monologue for its poet but an extraordinarily tentative utterance for its speaker, one that critics have rightly distinguished for the discrepancy between its manifestly strenuous meaning and the pervasive fuzziness of its tone (Robson 1957, 155–159; Brie 1959).

Another look at the lines on Telemachus may help us both to understand this discrepancy and to suspend the moralism that has sometimes interfered with efforts to interpret it. Those polished lines exhibit one internal rhetorical wrinkle, which significantly recurs: Ulysses' tendency to define his son's virtues by negation (Pettigrew 1963, 40; Findlay 1981, 146). "Most blameless is he," "decent not to fail": when a speaker begins using such convoluted language about someone else, he is also reflecting upon himself. Ulysses' theme here is Telemachus's *decency*, or in the etymologically allied term we now prefer his *decorum*, the striking of an ethical bull's-eye between the extremes of excess and defect that systematic Greek thought loved to illustrate in the Homeric heroes (and in none more than Odysseus of the many counsels). As a "blameless" man, the "decent" Telemachus refrains from excess, quite unsurprisingly according to the ethical system Tennyson's imagery here invokes. What is surprising is the double negative whereby Telemachus is said to refrain as well from the defect, to lack the lack, "not to fail." Ulysses derives his son's virtues by subtraction; and since the opening books of the *Odyssey* present Telemachus as a junior Ulysses, we may presume that Ulysses derives these filial virtues by subtraction from characteristics of his own—which, we may then infer, overflow the common measure.

Even this carefully measured eulogy of decorum, then, by implication presents a Ulysses characterized by excess, a Telemachus and then some. Tennyson's double-jointed phrase thus represents once again his habit of turning to Romantic ends what he found in the classics. His Romantic Ulysses aims not to hit the classic target but to find a target worth aiming at. Extra-vagant, ec-centric, in-decent so as not to fail in desire, Ulysses seeks to articulate a destination in the pursuit of which he will not have to yield; he seeks to identify which way may be forward, given that "forward" is where he needs to go. What the direction of this extravagance may be, Ulysses undertakes his monologue in order to learn.

AT THE OUTSET Ulysses knows little more than that he is in a world he is not of. Nothing matches, nothing fits or is fitting. Hence the sullen improprieties of his opening snarl, which even upon multiple readings retains its shock value for a reader bearing Homer's tale in mind, or even Dante's episode.

> It little profits that an idle king,
> By this still hearth, among these barren crags,
> Matched with an agèd wife, I mete and dole
> Unequal laws unto a savage race,
> That hoard, and sleep, and feed, and know not me.   (1–5)

"Profits," "idle," "barren," "Matched," "mete," "dole," "Unequal," "hoard"—such economic imagery suits an old man's summing up. But the outstanding feature of Ulysses' tally sheet is that the quantities fail to tally. The books are out of balance; and the ensuing disequilibrium between self and context accounts for Ulysses' oddest turns of phrase. "Unequal laws" just possibly refers, as Ricks says it does, to the primitive state of Ithacan jurisprudence in the heroic age (*PT*, 561). Yet the natural aristocrat we meet in Tennyson's Ulysses, as in Homer's, seems most unlikely to sponsor a Reform Bill for the benefit of a nation he consistently treats en masse and with condescension: in this regard there is little to choose between "a savage race" and his later, more politic formulation "A rugged people."

The inequality of which Ulysses complains far more likely has to do with a Tiresian disparity between that uncomprehending bloc and himself.[7] In dispensing justice to a race who are not his equals, as in being matched with an aged wife who can, he evidently believes, be no match for him, Ulysses suffers a daily pettiness that diminishes him and that he figures in the dulling repetitions "mete and dole," "hoard, and sleep, and feed." This threat of diminution, furthermore, reveals the logic behind his otherwise disjunctive completion of the indignant litany of verbs in the last line: "and know not me." The phrasing recalls the thinly draped pride of election that underlies the poem called "The Mys-

tic" that Tennyson published three years before writing this one:
"How could ye know him? Ye were yet within / The narrower
circle; he had wellnigh reached / The last"; "Ye knew him not"
(41–43, 2). In one early manuscript of "Ulysses" the verbal parallel
to "The Mystic" was even closer: "That hoard, and sleep, and
feed, and know me not." In revising "Ulysses" Tennyson pointedly suspended the first-person pronoun at the outer edge of utterance; but whereas in the pontificating "Mystic" such personal
outrance was unequivocally circumferential, drawing its sure
power from the embrace of Tennysonian doom, Ulysses' opening
place feels more marginal, his tone more edgy.

Ulysses' prideful sense of marginality, encapsulated in the ambivalent later assertion "I am become a name" (11), emerges at
the outset through grammatical contextualization. Forestalled for
two and a half lines by what looks like a third-person clause about
an idle king, the "I" of the opening sentence remains governed
by the impersonal construction "It little profits" and matched by
verbs it can contemn but cannot disown (Findlay 1981, 141). By
the close of the passage the speaking self is presented as a residuum
defined by its inaccessibility to genealogical, marital or social context: a "me" not recognizable by any outward show, an unknown
quantity for which the imaginative algebra of the poem will work
out a solution. Like the unfathomably older and more daemonized
Tithonus, Ulysses pushes off into monologue by discarding his
current role and positing a "me" about which he himself knows
as yet nothing beyond an existential predication. To follow that
knowledge is the aim of the poem. Its method develops through
an initial dissatisfaction with contexts present and past, as inadequate to the self; then leads on to the imagination of an agonistic
or participatory relation to context, a relation whose equal law
may do justice to the self; and culminates in a transfiguration of
context, which discounts and finally effaces the self in favor of a
Romantic desire, no less relentless than circumstantial fate, that
cancels altogether the work of knowing and being known. For
now, however, Ulysses seeks to know his hidden self by denying
the one with which circumstances present him; and the result of
his initial survey reduces to the message encoded, perhaps fortuitously but only perhaps, in the homonymy produced by Tennyson's manuscript reordering of the last three words of the
paragraph: *No, not me.*

As the second paragraph modulates from negation to guarded and choppy assertion about the self, Ulysses reenlists context, under the capacious name "Life," less as a force to be known by than as something to be discerned and measured against:

> I cannot rest from travel: I will drink
> Life to the lees: all times I have enjoyed
> Greatly, have suffered greatly, both with those
> That loved me, and alone; on shore, and when
> Through scudding drifts the rainy Hyades
> Vext the dim sea. (6–11)

Probably the first thing to observe about these lines is the peculiar persistence of their enjambment, which formally flouts the balance one would have thought mandated by the anaphora and antithesis of the syntax: a pair of short parallel clauses in the first person, then the same first-person subject with two complementary predicates, which are expanded in turn by two similarly complementary pairs of adverbial modifiers. Tennyson's lineation and his syntax are dismayingly out of phase; and even without the evidence of the Harvard manuscript, which gives instead of lines 6–9 merely the line "Much have I suffered both on shore and when . . . ," any reader accustomed to earlier Tennyson will feel the disjunctiveness of the published version as a deliberate jolt (Ostriker 1964, 283–284).

This studied imbalance, together with verb tenses that leap, out of kilter, from present to future to past, works to neutralize the symmetrical antitheses into which Ulysses endeavors to sort his life. The difference between "enjoying" and "suffering," for example, counts for less than the alleged greatness of either condition. It also counts for less than the subtle note of passivity in the verb "enjoyed"—as opposed to "performed," say, or "achieved," verbs of action that would be more obviously complementary to "suffered" and more responsive to Ulysses' apparent will to be up and doing. The shared passivity of the verbs Tennyson chose suggests, behind Ulysses' restless urge to travel, a life of strenuous, eventful, yet ultimately disengaged tourism, bearing out the conspicuous consumption implicit in Ulysses' intention to toss off the wine of life. Again, there is something scandalous about Ulysses' division of his life into those experiences shared "with those / That loved me" and those undergone "alone," as if the sole function of others has been supplying love. But the scandal here seems minor in comparison to his syntactic presumption, worthy of Julian in *The Lover's Tale*, that the company of those that love him has been, all told, equivalent to solitude (Leggett 1970, 153). The turbulence of the entire passage directs us to Ulysses' sense of experience as a disposable commodity, perhaps a stimulating aliment but at last a means to an as yet undiscerned end. We may specify this end as self-knowledge, if we like, on the strength of the first verse paragraph. But thus far in the second, Ulysses' inventory of the past has affirmed little beyond the marginality of a self whose dismissal of an entire realm of human definition, the social sphere, appears most tellingly in his conception of that sphere as no less marginal to himself: not "at home" or "on land," but "on shore"—the place where in Keats's sonnet "When I Have Fears" the social values love and fame to nothingness do sink.

It is revealing that in the last of these lines the prosody and syntax come back into more satisfactory alignment: "Through scudding drifts the rainy Hyades / Vext the dim sea." Here at last a subject and a predicate fall into conventional place, and yet in their mythic and metaphoric reference these are the wildest lines we have met to this point in the poem. By way of assimilation, it helps a bit to know that the scudding drifts come from Horace, the rainy stars from Virgil, and the vexed, dim sea from Shelley (though a modern reader may think first of Yeats's Shelleyan reveries on Oisin and Fergus). Clearly these lines render a poet's weather, not a navigator's; and in their ensemble they render not just any poet's weather but Tennyson's, whose manuscript suggests that he wrote these lines first, then backed up to lengthen and roughen the approach. As the prosody and syntax of this passage at length slide together, so the dramatic speaker Ulysses merges in lyric epiphany with the poet, imagining an empowered scene that mingles vexation with remoteness, menace with allure. Ulysses' retrospect has brought forth a grace note that is unmotivated by his overt intention to measure out his life in a general equilibration, and that constitutes the nearest thing in the poem thus far to an affirmation of his definitive desires. "All times," all personal relations, all environments gather for the hungry-hearted Ulysses into one great event, the draught of life that, as his somewhat vacant repetition of "greatly" suggests, has not been great enough. If the versification gratifies, it does so because Ulysses is temporarily gratified by the imagination of a wild otherness answering to his unarticulated depths.

The prosody of "Ulysses" is never again quite so irregular as in this passage. But the poem repeatedly homes in, as it does here, upon versions of the dim great deep—Tennyson's favorite image for his poetic origin and goal, for his creativity and for his fate—as the one ground on which Ulysses finds poise. In this sense the next half-dozen lines repeat the movement of the half-dozen we have just considered:

> I am become a name;
> For always roaming with a hungry heart
> Much have I seen and known; cities of men
> And manners, climates, councils, governments,
> Myself not least, but honoured of them all;
> And drunk delight of battle with my peers,
> Far on the ringing plains of windy Troy.   (11–17)

Lines 16–17, like lines 10–11, seem an afterthought with at best tenuous grammatical connection to the main clause; but their having the last word is right, since they too image the drift of Ulysses' thoughts. From "rainy Hyades" to "windy Troy," from "scudding drifts" to "ringing plains": Ulysses appears to have traced his itinerary backward through the world of the *Odyssey* to that of the *Iliad*. Tonally, though, he has merely come home again, thanks partly to verbal echoes of the earlier line on the Hyades but thanks more to the uncanny placement of that most Tennysonian word "far." Neither adverb, quite, nor adjective, the word suggests both Ulysses' distance now from the Trojan theater of war and the enlargement of life's scope he remembers it as having offered then.

"Far," like the word "dim" earlier, makes the diffuse scene it describes more intimately present to consciousness than any of the more conceptually plausible references of the preceding lines (Rosenberg 1974, 308). There Ulysses has resumed the fruitless attempt, from which the siren song of the Hyades had momentarily enticed him, to know himself after the fashion of the dramatic monologue proper: in quantitative terms, through a kind of summing up and drawing of ratios. The "Much" he has seen and known boils down to little enough. The jingle of "men / And manners" takes each of its terms a step away from referentiality

toward mere sound; "councils" and "governments" seem identical; and if these curiosities do not suffice, the impatient, time-
keeping insertion of "climates" into Ulysses' catalogue of the social
and political achievements of mankind gives the game away. It is
far from clear what Ulysses means to say he is "not least" of,
technically, or what the precise antecedent of "them" might be.
But the point of his carelessness is that he does not, at bottom,
care to take his measure by such human tempers or climatic tem-
peratures as "theirs." Framed by his "hungry heart" and "drunk
delight," Ulysses' survey of the objects he has seen and known
can but make him, in turn, an object of knowledge, a cipher, "a
name."

The seen and known, and the self they are able to define, pale
into insignificance beside what Ulysses has neither seen nor known
but manifestly has *felt*, where vision and cognition fail, on the dim
sea and the ringing plains. Both those remote locales derive their
paradoxical intimacy from the replacement of visual by tactile
stimuli, evoking that close language the body speaks when pressing back against what confronts and thus defines it. We recognize
here the redeemed body language of "Armageddon," a poem
whose fortunate fall into the mediations of "Timbuctoo" marked
Tennyson's embarcation on the studious reworking of traditional
materials that "Ulysses" splendidly exemplifies. But now Tennyson's persona draws sustenance not from the vine of fable, a
nurturing seraph-pedagogue, or even visionary "cities of men,"
but from the imagination of a conflict that tasks potential to the
limit: "battle with my peers." We do not know whether these
"peers" represent the best of men or something more than men—
the *Iliad*'s godlike warriors or the warring gods themselves—or
whether they have fought on the side of Ulysses or against him:
"battle with" can carry either meaning. The passage leaves these
questions undecided in order to stress a newly contentious mode
of self-awareness. What matters here is not comparative quantity
("greatly," "much," "not least") or bestowed identity ("a name,"
"honoured") but an opposition that is truest friendship, that sets
the boundaries of the self in flux and at risk, and that declares the
self at any moment to be "peer" or equal to what it strives with.

By lines 16–17, in short, Ulysses has formulated the "feeling
about the need of going forward" in the terms of "Fatima" and
"Oenone," Tennyson's most progressive poems of relationship

from the volume of 1832. But the agonistic theater of Troy lies as surely behind Ulysses as it lies ahead of Oenone, and in what ensues he and his poet break quite new ground. In the next lines, the most resonant and difficult of the poem, Ulysses proceeds to fix into a proposition what he has just imagined, and then to recoil into a rider or escape clause that changes the entire direction of his monologue. The passage demands a slow reading and deserves a patient exegesis:

> I am a part of all that I have met;
> Yet all experience is an arch wherethrough
> Gleams that untravelled world, whose margin fades
> For ever and for ever when I move. (18–21)

Ulysses is "a part" of experience because the contour of the self, as he conceives it at this point, results from the mutable balance of inner and outer pressures upon each other, as with the fluid dynamics of storm and sea that attracted him to the image of the Hyades.[8] This new image of participation corrects what was lop-sided in Ulysses' earlier intention to drink life in and thus make it a part of him: the intervening memory of having drunk "delight of battle" has focused his truculence and led him to regard context as a setting for definitive contest. Moreover, Ulysses' participatory image confidently dispenses with the anxious self-aggrandizement of the Virgilian line to which Tennyson here alludes, Aeneas's proem to the last days of Troy, "of which I was a great part" (*Aeneid*, II.6: *quorum pars magna fui*).

One can imagine a stoically Keatsian poem ending with this recognition of experience as give and take—elaborated, perhaps, in another image of oceanic inevitability that might send Ulysses forth upon the waters, where death waits to absorb him into full participation with the empirical world. Tennyson was perennially attracted by such an accommodation to experience; and he expressed the attraction memorably in such lyrics as "To J. S." (1832) and "Move Eastward, Happy Earth" (1842), both written around the time of "Ulysses."[9] A comparably stately resignation was to constitute a stopping point for *In Memoriam* at section lvii, where it appears that for a time Tennyson thought his elegy should conclude. We need to remember this stoic appeal if we are to retrieve the abruptness of the "Yet" that introduces the deservedly celebrated image of lines 19–21. Here Ulysses abjures the roles of participant and of voyeur alike for one we would now call, awkwardly enough, that of participant-observer. "Experience" as Ulysses uses the term here displays its old etymological kinship with *experiment*: it conveys much of the tentativeness that pervades the essay called "Experience" written by Emerson a few years after the publication of "Ulysses" and that *expérience* still retains as the French word for laboratory testing.[10] For, according to Ulysses' stunning image, "experience" offers not fulfillment but significance, the hint of a purpose beyond itself, a provision of surplus meaning that no event can compass. No neutral recorder can transcribe it, either, since the receding margin emits its supplemental gleam only when activated by the questing energy of the investigator, whose mobile focus defines its circumference: an ever fading threshold of inextinguishable excitation. Whatever Tennyson knew of classical architecture, the peculiar image of the arch may owe less to (anachronistic) Roman engineering than to a good Greek lexicon: the "arch," through which Ulysses glimpses the inaccessible, marks all experience as an *arche* or first point, a forever preliminary stage in an archaeology that seeks origins not in history but on the edge of a perpetual present. In defining himself as a quester upon that limit, Ulysses discovers that only a part of him—a dispensable part—is part of all that he has met. He reserves another part, the unknown "me" from line 5, to match "that untravelled world" he has forever just begun to know.

Tennyson cannot have meant "margin" in the economic sense we bring to it today; yet the constitution of a surplus reserve of imaginative or semiotic capital, in this rapidly famous poem of experience, just may have influenced the later Victorian economists who coined our use of the term. In any case, the visionary gleam with which Ulysses here invests his future lives in a space of prophecy—we might call it a prophet margin—which he shares with Tiresias, to whom Tennyson originally gave the lines on the superhuman pursuit of knowledge toward which this verse paragraph is moving. Tiresias ascends into prophecy, in the manuscript draft of his monologue that is roughly contemporaneous with "Ulysses," by claiming for himself a perennially residual kind of "virtue," which refuses to "shape itself in deed" or to be molded into "action." Ulysses' image of the arch, with its premium on the initiative of the mobile, actively knowing subject, denies this Tiresian distinction between experience and action; and it does so not in order to bridge the split between self and context, but in order to hurl the two yet further apart. We appreciate anew the extremity of this dramatic monologue—and of Tennyson's experimentation with the relations between self and context that are constitutive of the genre—when we see how Ulysses' prophet margin, more dizzying than that of Tiresias, is produced by a withdrawal of the "me" not just from deeds but from experience itself: a withdrawal that perhaps only a poem devoted to a hero of action like Ulysses could make convincing. One could argue, further, that the structures of reciprocation in the "diffuse and opulent" paradise with which "Tiresias" closes correspond to the ideal of empirical participation Ulysses here rejects. Thus the poem Tennyson finished in 1885 took as its resting place an accommodation that had given "Ulysses" the point of departure for its startling second wind.

In the lines that follow, Ulysses consolidates the difficult gains that have been made with such breathtaking ease in the three just discussed. The vituperative note of the marginal man from the first verse paragraph returns as Ulysses metes out the consequences of his newly prophetic empiricism. The gleam of an interminable initiation casts into the shadows, or onto the junk pile, the self-sufficiency of experience:

> How dull it is to pause, to make an end,
> To rust unburnished, not to shine in use!
> As though to breathe were life. Life piled on life
> Were all too little, and of one to me
> Little remains.   (22–26)

Ulysses discards any perception that would "make an end" in itself, any experience that, being accepted as its own justification, becomes a cul-de-sac instead of an arch. "Shine in use," accordingly, points not to a utilitarian calculus but to a gospel of work quite Carlylean in its consecrated instrumentality. What makes the reflected "shine," after all, is the inaccessible light source three lines up, the visionary gleam at the margin of things that gives the prophetic self its edge. Or, to return to an economic discourse, this time in terms that were very much in the air of early Victorian capitalism: what shines on the margin "in use," with a usurious sparkle, is an ever unspent and therefore ever accumulating interest.[11]

Ulysses' polemical language here bears comparison with that of the opening verse paragraph; and one explanation for its brusqueness may be that, whereas there Ulysses was repudiating Ithacan contexts, here Tennyson through Ulysses is repudiating Romantic ones. "How dull it is": we think of "Dejection," where Coleridge's sobbing draft and the stagnant pain it represents are both described as "dull" (6, 20), and where the poet seeks remedy in a joy he figures as an emphatically inner light: "from the soul itself must issue forth / A light, a glory, a fair luminous cloud / Enveloping the earth" (53–55). In Tennyson's text, though, the light is not here but over there, in a world beyond envelopment. Furthermore, the most bitter phrase of the entire monologue, the fragmentary "As though to breathe were life," entails a rejection of the naturalist Romantic myth equating literal respiration and spiritual inspiration.

This myth, with its easy commerce of inner and outer realms, lies at the heart of "Dejection" and any number of Romantic works besides. For Tennyson's purposes it probably appeared most conveniently in a passage from Byron's *Childe Harold*: "I live not in myself, but I become / Portion of that around me" (III.lxxii.1–2). Ricks adduces this passage as a source for Ulysses' earlier naturalist line "I am a part of all that I have met" (*PT*, 563). There already, by displacing context from the Byronic present onto history—onto what Ulysses *has met*—Tennyson suggests some detachment from a Romantic credo that he acknowledges as appealing, but nevertheless so situates in his text as to declare it a creed outworn. The great lines on "experience" then disavow any such naturalist creed, both in what they say and in the incomparable slowness with which they say it. Taking up, as Arnold observed with fitting exaggeration, "nearly as much time as a whole book of the *Iliad*," these lines when read aloud so exhaust the breath as to bring home the limitations of any merely respiratory or Aeolian conception of "life."[12] Tennyson's disavowal is heightened in what follows by the way the three-piled repetition of "life" makes a cipher of the word; by the way the alliterative linkage to "little," itself repeated, diminishes to virtually nothing the appeal of natural experience and with it the part of Ulysses that belongs to all that he has met; and by the way syntax cuts against prosody, as at the top of the paragraph, but now to mark the distance Ulysses has come from the countings and recountings that he there thought might amount to a life.

The passage that brings this remarkable verse paragraph to a close further deepens Ulysses' rejection of experience. And, as it does so, it further complicates Tennyson's affiliation with a Romanticism that could never have engaged him as it did had it been a mere celebration of the natural present.

> Little remains: but every hour is saved
> From that eternal silence, something more,
> A bringer of new things; and vile it were
> For some three suns to store and hoard myself,
> And this gray spirit yearning in desire
> To follow knowledge like a sinking star,
> Beyond the utmost bound of human thought.   (26–32)

The first line, if read in isolation, concerns the redemption of time, which in good Romantic fashion has by this point overtaken self-knowledge as the principal concern of the poem. "Every hour is saved" for Ulysses, which is to say that his hitherto evacuated experience is made meaningful once more, by the positing of the prophet margin, the hope for the spirit not as breath but as abiding difference. To grasp the meaning that underwrites this subliminal hope, we need to reinstate the second clause in its proper syntax: "Every hour [there] is saved . . . a bringer of new things." Even with this syntactic map in mind, however, we encounter further problems of reference: What is being saved every hour from what? Is the "saving" an adventurer's rescue mission or the banked reserve of a farsighted investment? What is that inscrutable "eternal silence"—a vault from which capital savings may be realized, or a menace prompting a timely save?

If we bear in mind Tennyson's accumulation of Romantic allusions in preceding passages, we may begin by noting that the burden of the mystery, "that eternal silence," is a holdover from the crucial ninth section of Wordsworth's "Intimations" ode. That text is especially germane to Tennyson's purpose in "Ulysses," since there for once Wordsworth explicitly forswears the "simple creed" of unmediated participation in experience. The entire passage leading up to the phrase Tennyson borrowed is worth quoting:

O joy! that in our embers
Is something that doth live,
That nature yet remembers
What was so fugitive!
The thought of our past years in me doth breed
Perpetual benediction: not indeed
For that which is most worthy to be blest;
Delight and liberty, the simple creed
Of Childhood, whether busy or at rest,
With new-fledged hope still fluttering in his breast:—
Not for these I raise
The song of thanks and praise;
But for those obstinate questionings
Of sense and outward things,
Fallings from us, vanishings;
Blank misgivings of a Creature
Moving about in worlds not realised,
High instincts before which our mortal Nature
Did tremble like a guilty Thing surprised:
But for those first affections,
Those shadowy recollections,
Which, be they what they may,
Are yet the fountain light of all our day,
Are yet a master light of all our seeing;
Uphold us, cherish, and have power to make
Our noisy years seem moments in the being
Of the eternal Silence.   (129–155)

The shadowy yet masterful light of the visionary gleam, "something that doth live" in the embers of a still but unextinguished hearth, puts sense and outward things into question, or into a prophetic context of "worlds not realised." "That eternal silence" in "Ulysses," parallel in its deictic gesture to "that untravelled world" seven lines above it, is also interpoetically *that* "eternal Silence," Wordsworth's, which in the daemonic passage just quoted eclipses natural joys and tunes human history down and out to the level of low cosmic noise. The Wordsworthian dialectic of loss and gain, whereby "Fallings from us, vanishings," have an antithetical power to "Uphold us" through what they disclose about the creative powers of the mind, can clarify the analogous relation in Tennyson between the margin that fades forever and the bringing of new things with every hour.[13]

A no less Wordsworthian effect occurs in the double flotation of Tennyson's crucial phrase for gain, "something more." Grammatically it goes uncompleted by any available "than" construction; like Wordsworth's "something far more deeply interfused" in "Tintern Abbey" (76), it implies an infinite ratio, a comparison beyond compare. Syntactically, too, "something more" is clearly a phrase in apposition; yet in apposition with what? The phrase hovers between the apparent opposites of "that eternal silence" and "A bringer of new things," so as to suggest the perpetuity, whether of eternity or of novelty, that they share. The opposition between the two senses of "eternal silence" as threat and as resource—or of "saved / From" as "defended against" and as "eked out of"—thus dissolves for Ulysses' purposes, which at this stage of the poem are continuous with Tennyson's, which are in their turn continuous with Wordsworth's in the ode on immortality. For all three what is at stake is the arched rainbow's pledge of "something more": the promise that the desire of the upleaping, unquiet, hungry heart will not fall away. And for all three, to this end, a perpetual loss serves to spur a perpetual compensatory creation.

Tennyson's "feeling about the need of going forward," then, answers very closely to Wordsworth's "We will grieve not, rather find / Strength in what remains behind" ("Intimations," 179–180). So close, indeed, are the correspondences of argument and image between Tennyson's text and Wordsworth's that we ought to ask what, if any, fresh creation compensates Tennyson in his indebtedness as a later Romantic poet. Interpoetic comparison may seem more than usually odious at this moment in "Ulysses," which proposes a valediction to all specific comparisons whatsoever. Yet the verbal echo urges the comparison upon us, and I suspect it does so with Tennyson's blessing. For while the difference that emerges between Wordsworth's and Tennyson's crisis poems is one of degree rather than kind, it is also one in which Tennyson occupies the more extreme, the more marginal, and the more prophetically empowered position. If we consider the way each poem takes up the Romantic problem of where power is located, we discover—to the discomfiture of Victorian compromise but consistently with the widening gyres of Romantic revisionism—that it is the "I" of "Ulysses" that makes the greater sacrifice and aspires to the greater transcendence of context.

Wordsworth's strength abides "in what remains behind," in a residual surplus within the compass of the self. But if Ulysses were to employ such a phrase as "what remains behind," it would indicate something quite different: what remains behind the veil, what winks at the recessive margin he can never grasp. When he actually does repeat after Wordsworth, it is with the difference that he is *out* of what Wordsworth is *in*. The indwelling ontology of Wordsworth's phrase "in the being / Of the eternal Silence" is precisely what Ulysses does without, as he points across the hermeneutic horizon (Tennyson pointing with him across the textual margins) to that eternal silence, whose other ness is indistinguishable from the promise it holds for him, and whose intimacy is all the stronger for the distance its intimations travel.[14]

The same distinction emerges between Wordsworthian immanence and Tennysonian alienation if we compare the "something far more deeply interfused," which in "Tintern Abbey" plants the egotistical sublime in the natural mind of man, to the spare and purely outward-bound "something more" that Tennyson finds will do instead. "Interfused," "in the being," "in what remains behind": such are the rhetorical signs of an inwardness with which Wordsworth was endowed and which overflowed from him to apparel the common earth "in celestial light." This confident and godlike immanence Tennyson very rarely shared; though he could write about it with appreciation, and with envy, he almost always did so from the perspective of an outsider (House 1955, 125). Here we may recollect that where Wordsworth wrote a lyrical ode, Tennyson wrote a dramatic monologue. But even within the more detached genre Tennyson chose, the great outsider Ulysses deploys a language of inwardness in ways that stress his own outrageousness. Ulysses reserves his Wordsworthian rhetoric of immanence for Telemachus, the very different character whom he will go on to discuss in order to define himself: "centred in the sphere / Of common duties." Ulysses too is under an arch and ringed with a margin, yet he never represents himself *in* any such circumstantially spatial sphere as centers his son. Rather, he represents himself in time and in process, desirous "to shine in use," "yearning in desire," and at last "strong in will" (69)—which is to say, borrowing pertinent terms from Yeats, Ulysses conceives of himself as a man who is in love and loves what vanishes through arches and scudding drifts.

Let me now venture a paraphrase of the passage on the "eternal silence" that will respond to the cluster of questions I raised about it earlier. Every hour is redeemed for the self, and every hour the self is saved from the living death of engulfment by the given, through vigilant awareness of certain ineffable options abiding on the far edge of the experience that signifies them; the self is saved from an incapacitating doom by the insatiable curiosity which that doom feeds. Any paraphrase has its dangers, but a major problem with mine is its reliance on the category of the self, which the passage on the "eternal silence" increasingly disregards. The passage owes much of the stateliness with which it fully unfolds to its impersonality, as it factors out the self that loomed so large at the start:

> vile it were
> For some three suns to store and hoard myself,
> And this gray spirit yearning in desire
> To follow knowledge like a sinking star,
> Beyond the utmost bound of human thought. (28–32)

Apparently Ulysses, for all his initial devotion to the knowledge and salvation of the self, discovers that in order to save the self on his own terms he must lose it on any others. Saving the self as ardent spirit requires spending the self as historically constituted psyche.

This principle, which lies behind Tennyson's most enduring dramatic monologues, merits restatement from the perspective of what we know about the manuscript provenance of the last two lines in the "Tiresias" fragment. To lyricize his dramatic monologue fully, the poet found it necessary to analyze the character of his monologist. And this analysis took him back beyond personality to a drive that was prior to ethical or persona-shaping purpose. That drive, even in the manuscript fragment that first gave it expression, hovered between nostalgia and the need of going forward. "I wish I were as in the days of old": the manuscript line merely joins two clichés; yet, when backlit by the pyrotechnics of the classical monologues, both clichés leap into strange, reciprocally definitive relief. Thanks to a favorite Tennysonian coincidence of verbal mood, "I were" conflates a present subjunctive with a ghostly preterite indicative, breeding a hypothetical future out of a mythologized past. May-be and has-been thus engender might-have-been, this poet's characteristic mood of ideal regret. Likewise "the days of old," a commonplace that denotes its apparent opposite (the days of youth), carries paradoxical connotations of a primal future or a crepuscular beginning (Ricks 1972, 124; Bloom 1975, 159). As the memory of a desire thus shades into the desire of a memory, the self that was and the self that would be divide between them the self that is.

The psychic vanishing act that thus played beneath Tennyson's earlier, lyrical fragment manifestly surfaces midway through "Ulysses," as the monologue reaches a pitch of self-assertion that in effect undoes the self. Hence the insertion, at just this point, of the manuscript lines on the sinking star. Hence, too, a related phenomenon: as the verse paragraph winds up, the first-person pronoun "myself" occurs only as a thing, a vile empirical body, the storing and hoarding of which is the last impediment to a daemonic supersession of the human. Despite Tennyson's insistence, more than fifty years after the writing of these lines, that "spirit," like "myself," is the object of the infinitives "store" and "hoard" (*PT*, 564), it is difficult not to take the lines governed by "yearning" as an absolute construction that grammatically enforces the absoluteness of Ulysses' desire. But in either construction what matters is the difference between the two terms "myself" and "this gray spirit" (Kincaid 1974, 230). The disproportionately great investment in the latter term constitutes a declaration of poetic priorities, as with the comparably unbalanced passage on the rainy Hyades earlier. "Myself," a term of identity to whose air of possessiveness Tennyson here imparts a special charge, is discarded in favor of "this gray spirit," a dispossessed principle of desire whose presence, or this-ness, acquires meaning in its reference to "that untravelled world" and "that eternal silence" toward which it yearns.[15]

THE ENTIRE PARAGRAPH we have been considering articulates a Romantic religion, a structure of transcendence without a grounding dogma. Tennyson's version, like those of the Romantics before him, secularizes the patterns of earlier Christian psychology—a process he evidently could carry out with a freer hand through pagan speakers than through a Christian like St. Simeon Stylites. Christian paradigms haunt the lines in which Ulysses gives fullest rein to what Tiresias calls "The boundless yearning of the prophet's heart." The salvific aspect of the prophet margin already has appeared in the saving "something more"; "A bringer of new things" has an evangelical aura about it; and the reference to "some three suns" fulfills the subliminal gospel with resonances of Easter. This last reference, with its gratuitously specific enumeration, takes final leave of Ulysses' will to quantify experience; it also suggests the greatest Christian image of redemption, the Resurrection: a spiritual bursting of natural bonds that confirms Ulysses' Romantic drive to sacrifice the self for the spirit's sake.

So it is that when Ulysses turns to Telemachus in the paragraph that follows, he speaks proleptically as pure spirit, in the words of the Spirit of God that moved in Genesis on the face of the waters and in the gospels over the river Jordan at the baptism of Jesus. "This is my beloved son, in whom I am well pleased" (Matthew 3:17); "This is my son, mine own Telemachus, / To whom I leave the sceptre and the isle— / Well-loved of me." The language and imagery of possession, pronounced in the archaism of the third line and strengthened by Tennyson's manuscript revision of "my child" to "mine own" in the first, measures the grandeur of Ulysses' prophetic spirit by the largess of his bequest. He divests himself not just of the scepter but of love for his son, "love" being here, as distinct from the earlier "desire," a storing and hoarding of what, while it is precious to the self, perplexes and retards the spirit. Ulysses' mention of "my household gods," near the close of this paragraph, reveals both an awareness of his incipient status as a culture hero and tutelary presence—"become a name" to his very family—and a serene acceptance of the incongruity of any domestication of his wildness. We may call Ulysses' energy *unheimlich*, if we follow Freud's German, because it pledges him to a home elsewhere; but the English *uncanny*, with its root notion of "kenning" or knowing, is more appropriate. This extraordinary dramatic monologue dwells on the issue of knowledge (5, 13, 31) because its strength of will—not quite the same thing as strength of character—arises through a systematic unknowing of the empirical world. Ulysses forepardons his diminishment to a household word because he understands its human necessity, and understands it the more fully because he is so far out of the picture of fulfilled kingship that he has painted, in part, as a means of escaping it. In this sense Ulysses' perfect acknowledgment of the sphere of common duties, the finality of his valedictory understanding, is also the start of his unknowing.

The text has become so uncanny by this point that Ulysses' economic language, with a foretaste of Tithonus's way of talking about life and death, means the opposite of what it says: henceforth its assertions of ownership disown whatever they name. "My household gods" means "those relics that pertain to that impertinence and clog to the spirit named Myself." "He works his work, I mine": from one perspective this eerily chiming sentence is centered in the sphere of a common tautology, since the work one works is of course one's own. But from a perspective that considers the self-canceling character of Ulysses' "work" as he has defined it in the preceding paragraph, the last words—"I mine"—are dispossessed, abysmally free of reference. Ulysses' work is "to shine in use" by moving after a gleam or following a sinking star beyond the limits of the human self that can properly say "mine." The bottom line of this paragraph, as Tennyson revised it from his first manuscript reading, thus furnishes another instance of subliminally suggestive lineation: "When I am gone. He works his work, I mine." The task that defines the "I" of "Ulysses" from this point, through an ordeal of desire that refines the empirical away, is the task of being gone.[16]

And precisely that is the final paragraph's affair. In a narrative, the disappearance of Ulysses would be an event in the world of the fiction; it had been one already, though indeed of a shadowy sort, through the prophecy of Tiresias in book XI of the *Odyssey* and through the tale the damned soul of Ulisse tells in canto XXVI of the *Inferno*. But in a dramatic monologue, especially one written so rigorously under the dispensation of Tennyson's Romantic lyricism, such a narratable event remains on the far side of utterance. The disappearance of Ulysses constitutes the goal of his speech in a double sense: it is a physical event for which his words prepare rhetorically; but what the words actually bring to pass, as a psychological and linguistic event, is the effacement of the speaking subject, the replacement of "Ulysses" as a man's name by "Ulysses" as a text. Readers' shrewd doubts as to whether Ulysses intends to leave at all, whether his resolve to push off does not look suspiciously like Mariana's or the Lotos-Eaters' resolve to stay put, attest I think to the predominance of the second, per-

formative goal over the first, rhetorical one. Ulysses' appearance
of listlessness manifests his selflessness, his radical reduction of the
once contextualized, active self to "a feeling about the need of
going forward": a will so pure that no event, no actual going
forward, can either violate or confirm it.

After forty-odd lines of generalization, reminiscence, and esti-
mation of his own character and his son's, at the beginning of the
last paragraph Ulysses finally turns outward to describe the immediate setting: "There lies the port; the vessel puffs her sail: /
There gloom the dark broad seas" (44–45). The description depends on a personification that grows stronger with each image:
once the vessel puffs her sail and the seas are said to "gloom" or
scowl, even "lies" suggests in retrospect not just location but
repose. At the same time, intransitive and reflexive verbs counter
the personification, so that the description, though not literal, feels
objectively neutral. Of course the wind and not the vessel puffs
the sail, but that fact leads us to the point of Ulysses' scenic imagination. These things are simply working their work, like Telemachus or Ulysses himself; and if in their conjunction of vehicular
and animal imagery they also seem ominous with ambushed meanings, that is because their work works through them as instruments
of a purpose from beyond.

This alien purpose behind nature is ultimately indistinguishable, in "Ulysses" and in Tennyson at large, from the alienated
spirit's purposeful pursuit of the visionary gleam. The blind drive
behind the controlling ego, which earlier movements of the monologue have identified, here usurps voice and unsettles character
altogether:

> My mariners,
> Souls that have toiled, and wrought, and thought with me—
> That ever with a frolic welcome took
> The thunder and the sunshine, and opposed
> Free hearts, free foreheads—you and I are old;
> Old age hath yet his honour and his toil;
> Death closes all: but something ere the end,
> Some work of noble note, may yet be done,
> Not unbecoming men that strove with Gods. (45–53)

This, the first instance of direct address in one of the best known
dramatic monologues in the language, comes so late—in the poem,
in the tradition of writing about many-minded Ulysses, and in

the life of Ulysses as Tennyson thence inherited it—that it ought
to give us pause. Our thinking about the dramatic monologue as
a genre has tended to prize audience above all other components
of context. Yet what kind of audience is convoked here? Homer's
Odysseus now and then exhorts his mariners during their wanderings, though he alone lives to return; and in Dante's truncated
version of the story Ulisse persuades his crew to set course not
for Ithaca but for the *mondo sanza gente*, the unpeopled world
(Robbins 1973, 186). For Tennyson's Ulysses, though, Ithaca to
all intents *is* the unpeopled world. The sublime disregard for other
people this hero has manifested from the first is now reflected in
his poet, who in resurrecting a crew, or perhaps creating one out
of nothing, takes stunningly bland leave of one of his deepest
traditions (Ward 1974, 314–315). It is a very disconcerting moment, in a poet generally punctilious as to fact and reverent of the
broadly "factual" aspect of traditional fictions, and it sent his commentator son into a nosedive. "The comrades he addresses are of
the same heroic mould as his old comrades"; "Perhaps the *Odyssey*
has not been strictly adhered to, and some of the old comrades
may be left" (*PT*, 560). Perhaps? If some old comrades, why not
all? Why not the great Achilles?

The generically definitive moment in this dramatic monologue,
the moment of direct address at which audience-as-context ought
to enfold the lyric voice into history, is also its cleanest break with
literary history, its moment of sheerest invention. Ulysses needs
to draft a crew, of course, if he is to sail; but at this stage, in this
poem about quite other needs, such considerations profit little. It
will take us nearer to the truth to suppose that Ulysses needs to
draft an audience if he is to go on speaking, and to suppose further
that, since he has gotten along so well thus far without one, he
and his poet are now attempting something new. The goal of this
poem, as of "Tiresias" and of "Tithonus" in their different ways,
is the imagination of a new context: here, a context that will feed
but will not satiate its speaker's heart. Conversely, the pathos of
this poem, as Ulysses in his Romantic grandeur never acknowledges, is that no given context, nothing we or the poem would
call "the world," "life," or "experience," will measure up to desire
(Kincaid 1974, 231). As we have seen, this realization entails a
rejection of context, duly and nobly performed in the interpolated
lines on Telemachus, a rejection that in turn entails the dissolution

of the contextually constituted, historical self. But since this same self is by generic imperative the subject of the dramatic monologue, Tennyson here encounters the unique problem of contriving language for a vanishing, finally a vanished, self. This problem he met, I suggest, by inverting the conventions of the genre. The simultaneously appropriative and disowning address of Ulysses to "My mariners" provides a particularly rich instance of the sort of linguistic dispossession we have considered above (Duncan 1959, 22–23; Ryals 1962, 234; Mermin 1983, 30–31). Whoever these free-floating signifiers may be, "My mariners" belong to Ulysses at the cost of a repudiation of the rich legend that has made him "a name," a heroic personage in the traveled world's terms. A Ulysses who has not won his way home alone is not the great Ulysses whom we knew. Likewise, and more disturbingly, a Ulysses who in the parallel passage ten lines later can address "my friends" is no longer even the great Ulysses whom we thought we knew from the high scorn in this very poem's first paragraph.

For either mariners or friends to be "mine" at this late stage, then, is for the continuous, identifiable "me" to cease to be, and to yield instead to a spiritualizing drive whose invocations in effect call up kindred spirits from the vasty deep. Hence the incantatory movement beneath Tennyson's wonderfully supple blank verse, where arithmetical mensuration yields to the measures of ritual chant: the triplet of port, vessel, and seas, followed by the three verbs "toiled, and wrought, and thought"; the pairings of "thunder" and "sunshine," "welcome" and "opposed," "free hearts, free foreheads." I call attention to the lyrical properties of the verse here—its status as song—because at the semantic level much in the poem's final movement constitutes a ritualization or musical rehearsal of the figures of thought we have analyzed already from its second paragraph. As in lines 1–18, the poem now moves again from present contexts through a summing-up of past achievements, to dwell on a naturalist mode of definitive resistance to circumstances: "a frolic welcome" that, being identical with the free soul's opposition to those same circumstances, seems identical too with Ulysses' earlier, paradoxical "delight of battle with my peers."

This is as far as the passage quoted above goes. Its latter phrases are devoted to a brand of last-ditch decorum that holds the line against the degradations of mortality and oblivion, the side of natural life that never evokes in Tennyson a frolic welcome or anything like it. "Not unbecoming men" may be diction appropriate to the ambitions of mariners whose tangle with Circe has taught them the risks of un-becoming or ceasing to be men, and it sketches out a program slightly preferable to the status of having "become a name." But in the main this bizarre diction, recalling as it does the double-negative constructions appropriate to Telemachus, articulates a hope that Ulysses and crew will be "decent not to fail"—a hope that asks all too little by way of conclusion to a poem about the need of going forward. Hence the recapitulation and corrective extension of these ten lines in the passage that immediately ensues:

> The lights begin to twinkle from the rocks:
> The long day wanes: the slow moon climbs: the deep
> Moans round with many voices. Come, my friends,
> 'Tis not too late to seek a newer world.
> Push off, and sitting well in order smite
> The sounding furrows.   (54–59)

As at the opening of the paragraph, the natural environment gradually, intransitively comes to a life that culminates in the crying of supernatural spirit to spirit. This powerful invitation to communion receives further support, in a negative way, from the adjacent fellowship of the mariners, and in particular from the toastmasterly "my friends." As before, the mariners are ranged in opposition to the elements ranged against them, only now more symmetrically. "Sitting well in order": the mariners in rows, ready to row, mirror the "sounding furrows," even as Tennyson's wording echoes the picture it paints. The mariners now seem less ranged than arranged and thereby seem diminished from the frolic welcomers of ten lines back: a part of all that they will smite, they now serve to set their captain apart from engagement with nature and human society alike.

This separation reopens the prophet margin, which the free-floating comparative "a newer world" has heralded and which a positive rhetoric of excess is about to confirm:

> for my purpose holds
> To sail beyond the sunset, and the baths
> Of all the western stars, until I die.
> It may be that the gulfs will wash us down:

> It may be we shall touch the Happy Isles,
> And see the great Achilles, whom we knew.   (59–64)

The first clause administers last rites, in this most lyrical of monologues, to the first-person singular. The deceased is "I," the executioner-executor "my purpose," the means of death a superflux of Romantic desire for what, lying "beyond the sunset" (and not dwelling, as in Wordsworth's "Tintern Abbey," 79, in "the light of setting suns"), emancipates the questing will from the historically constituted self. Only at this point does the poem say "us" and "we"—pronouns tactfully skirted while Ulysses' "I" is on the scene—and while these pronouns are by definition inclusive, it is very hard to know just what or whom they include, and with what sense of address.[17] Should the first-person plural be construed as meaning "you and I" (as at line 49), or as meaning "they and I" or "it and I"? If it is the royal pronoun of a now unsceptered and truly idle king, over what domain does it assert sovereignty? Does "Ulysses" end in rhetorical declamation with a view to persuasion, or in simple declaration beyond such needs? What remains beyond deconstruction in this text, the measured pageantry of its language, has at length so reconceived context—an impossible audience and an attitude less toward circumstances than beyond them—as to exhibit a paradoxical Romantic decorum that verges on stupefying indifference. Maybe death by water, maybe the Happy Isles and Achilles to boot—and maybe not: the thirst for "that untravelled world" grows so strong that these draughts of life's best vintage are contemplated quite evenhandedly.

So is the calculus of profit and loss, in the appropriately economic finale to a poem that has begun with a discussion of "little profits":

> Though much is taken, much abides; and though
> We are not now that strength which in old days
> Moved earth and heaven; that which we are, we are;
> One equal temper of heroic hearts,
> Made weak by time and fate, but strong in will
> To strive, to seek, to find, and not to yield.   (65–70)

Romantic desire is a great homogenizer of what it feeds upon, mere nostalgia included. One "much" is as good as another; the strength that once "Moved earth and heaven"—whether that hyperbolical phrase signifies the sack of Troy (Tennyson's early manuscripts here read "Swathed Troy with flame"; see *PT*, 566), or whether it embraces any human, titanic, or divine act one might care to mention—that strength, and its loss since the old days, matter only if earth and heaven do. And by this point in this poem they simply do not. Its ultimate indifference to time and place appears most clearly in Tennyson's audacious allusive reach: back through the Coleridgean "I AM," the act of creative perception whereby the Romantic monad or "finite mind" of *Biographia Literaria* had declared itself; back further through the Satanic assertiveness of "What matter where, if I be still the same?" (*Paradise Lost*, I.256; see Wordsworth 1981, 216); to the scriptural sources of the Protestantism that had underwritten Romantic religion and its underminings of established authority: "And God said unto Moses, I AM THAT I AM" (Exodus 3:14).

"That which we are, we are" effects a revision of the Protestant and Romantic tradition consistent with the disabling of the self in "Ulysses." This revision points not to autonomous godhead, or to the Satanic resistance that is its shadow, but instead to a deferred merger with the "newer world," that untraveled world, a perpetually emergent context that the will does not build up but seeks out. "One equal temper of heroic hearts," the curious serenity of the otherworldly Romantic quest envisioned here, can afford to give all to "time and fate" that time and fate can take; to let given contexts, the older world of history, nay the dramatic monologue genre itself, do their worst. For what remains after this blithely deducted concession to human weakness is, precisely, the prophet margin: the strength of a will that transcends the self in the service of what exceeds experience, what has power on time and fate and what, in saying "we," the voice of "Ulysses" finally joins.

This deep passage moans round with many voices, as the surrender of Ulysses' self to his antithetically questing will enters into harmonic or contrapuntal relation with a host of texts: to Ricks's citations from Homer, Dante, and Arthur Hallam (*PT*, 565) can be added those passages at which we have just glanced in Wordsworth, Coleridge, Milton, and the Bible. In taking leave of "Ulysses" we should attend to one more allusion, this time to Shelley—the most devoutly oppositional voice in the Romantic tradition out of which Tennyson wrote with redoubled intensity in the aftermath of his best friend's sudden death. Tennyson persistently linked "Ulysses" to *In Memoriam* because this experimental dramatic monologue was, among other things, his first accomplished elegy for Hallam. As one young poet's classically inspired elegy for another, then, "Ulysses" would invite comparison to *Adonais* even without its substantive and rhythmic parallels to Shelley's ocean-going close:

> Why linger, why turn back, why shrink, my Heart?
> Thy hopes are gone before; from all things here
> They have departed; thou shouldst now depart!
> A light is passed from the revolving year,
> And man, and woman; and what still is dear
> Attracts to crush, repels to make thee wither.
> The soft sky smiles,—the low wind whispers near:
> 'Tis Adonais calls! oh, hasten thither,
> No more let Life divide what Death can join together. (469–477)

For Ulysses, too, Telemachean man, Penelopean woman, and the revolving year ("Life piled on life") shed all too little light in comparison to the visionary gleam that awakens antithetical options. It is in the seventh and eighth lines of Shelley's stanza that these options stir into personified life and voice; and it is these lines whose syntax and rhythm anticipate Tennyson's lines 55–56: "The long day wanes: the slow moon climbs: the deep / Moans round with many voices."

Tennyson's quester verges on a course his Romantic precursor appears to have charted; and yet, as we often find in Victorian appropriations of Shelley, the passage Tennyson worked out makes Shelley's sound hasty in both its matter and its manner. First, a comparison of these very differently paced passages should make us hesitate at the place where Shelley accelerates: at the leap with which Shelley identifies and names the presence his personifications of a smiling, whispering nature have intuited. This piercing recognition, which no lover of *Adonais* would want changed, is one that no lover of the Cambridge Shelleyan named Arthur Hallam, who was responsible for the first English edition of *Adonais*, could have failed to read carefully either (*LH*, 293; Kennedy 1977, 363–365). Tennyson's management of pathetic fallacy in *In Memoriam* would show what appeal a preternatural yet personal call like that of Adonais came to hold for him. There, however, he would finally, consistently turn that appeal down, finding Hallam neither in nature nor beyond it, but in a mode of commemoration that furnished his elegy with its origin, goal, and title. A similar rejection of quick answers structures the revision of Shelley here in "Ulysses." 'Tis great Achilles calls? No; what gets heard in "Ulysses" is a plurivocal, impersonal deep that echoes, if any Shelley text, the "many-voicèd vale" that dizzies the poet's mind near the start of "Mont Blanc" (13). The voice beyond Ulysses' bespeaks not an apocalyptic familiar but a brooding and diffusive strangeness, an unidentified multitude corresponding to the "we" that is about to assume the poem, disband the self, and dissipate the self's old anxieties as to time, place, and destination.

Such anxieties can be movingly incorporated into *Adonais*, even at its most daemonic, because for Shelley the pressure of mortality concentrates the liminal self: "oh, hasten thither"; "I am borne darkly, fearfully afar" (492). But for Tennyson, the deliberateness of whose rhythms resists the thrust of Shelley's even where it recalls them most clearly, there is time enough: "'Tis not too late." Where is the Shelleyan rush (the hurry or the thrill) when that which is, is; when that which we are, we are; and when the will beyond the self is a fact like moonrise and mortality—a fact no stronger, perhaps, than earth and heaven, time and fate, but no whit weaker? The moaning round of many voices muffles all punctual alarms. In the otherworldly ambience of this evidently therapeutic poem, the prophetic feeling about the need of going forward supplants the personal feeling—at the least a knot of love, grief, anger, and fear—that was prompted by Hallam's death and attended Tennyson during the curative work of composition. Shelley's admonitions not to "linger," "turn back," or "shrink" before the coming sea change are delivered to his "Heart," and they bespeak a split between mind and heart, or soul and self, that, because of its treatment in earlier portions of "Ulysses," no longer signifies by the time of its selfless close. Nor does it signify whether captain and crew, if that is who "we are," will or will not embark (Altieri 1978, 294). Why should so equal a temper of heroic hearts, equal to anything because incorruptibly tempered by the bottomless surplus at the prophet margin, not linger? Among these barren crags and twinkling rocks what fruit of event, and to what empirical sustenance, can the self-consuming hunger of this monologue imaginably yield?

"Tithonus": None Other Than a God

The compositional history of "Tithonus," the relative obscurity of its mythological provenance, and the very ultimacy of its utterance have left it in the shadow of the more confidently written and published "Ulysses." But the tendency of Romantic revisionism to exalt second efforts should make the relation between these two master texts more fruitfully problematic. The later monologue is in every way a vindication of second thoughts. A petition for the redress of grievances the petitioner long ago brought upon himself, "Tithonus" represents a change of mind that itself becomes subject to change in the course of its articulation. Furthermore, the shape in which Tennyson first published the poem in 1860 constitutes, as I shall suggest in passing, a brilliant and pointed revision of the already impressive manuscript he had entitled "Tithon" in 1833. Finally, the poem seconds Tennyson's other classical monologues of the 1830s by bringing their sometimes ragged initiatives to a fulfillment one wants to call flawless. In its crisis and resolution "Tithonus" so intensifies the drive behind "Tiresias" and "Ulysses," yet so subdues that drive in its tonality and manner of address, that there is small wonder the poet had second thoughts about just where to lodge it in his career, writing "1833" on the 1860 proof sheet and then deleting the date.

It was Tennyson who first forged the canonical yet dangling link between this dramatic monologue and "Ulysses," when he said of "Tithonus," "It was originally a pendent to the Ulysses in my former volumes" (*Memoir*, I, 549). This image of the "pendent," which governs a good deal of the commentary the poem has attracted in our century, is worth puzzling over. The image probably reflects, for one thing, the poet's awareness of his text as unaccountably "pending," across the ten years' silence and then for two additional decades after those "former volumes" were published in 1842. It also suggests that Tennyson regarded "Tithonus" as a sort of appendix—or dependent younger relation—to the glamorous forerunner that he did not scruple to call "*the* Ulysses." Against this hierarchy, however, we may adduce from the *Oxford English Dictionary* a rarer yet still available meaning of "pendent" as simply "companion-piece": in the antithetical senses retained by its stout Saxon synonym "hanger" today, a "pendent" can be both something that hangs and what something else hangs from. I like to think that this sense of mutuality was what Tennyson had in mind and that he wanted to suggest what is certainly the case: that the two monologues help to interpret each other. Their genesis and composition in 1833 were very likely interwoven; and for a student of Tennyson's career they seem interdependent as well, the questing appetite of "Ulysses" and the gravity of "Tithonus" being mutually informative and corrective.

Yet, with consequences that have not been altogether fortunate for our understanding of either text, "Ulysses" went out uncompanioned in 1842. Although it stood on its own very well, it may have done so for reasons beyond the poet's expectation or control. Tennyson's monologue based on an antique hero so happened to meet the burgeoning ethos of the first industrialized society that its onward, outward, and upward mobility was inevitably coopted, even capitalized on, by the ideologues of Victorian modernity, and after a fashion that the poem's own rhetoric can best describe: "Ulysses" became a godly household word, meetly adored by generations of mentors and dutifully memorized by the generations of pupils they subdued to the useful and the good.[18] For all its antipathy to "experience," the poem spoke directly enough to the experience of Tennyson's contemporaries. It captured the imagination of an era, which is to say that the era captured it—misread it, to be sure, but at any rate domesticated it to the conventions of the strenuous bourgeois ethic that was working up an empire. The cultural afterlife of "Ulysses" in its reception and assimilation by Victorian readers, which has imparted both positive and negative biases to twentieth-century appreciations of the poem, might have been different had it enjoyed from the first the benefit of its pendent. The downbeat "Tithonus" might have served as a counterweight retarding the hasty Victorian valorization, and also preempting the consequent modern dismissal, of Ulysses' ethic of strive-and-seek-and-find.

As it is, the surprising conspiracy of "Ulysses" with the zeitgeist has impeded our understanding not only of that poem but of "Tithonus" as well (Hughes 1979, 87). Although we now rightly read the two monologues in conjunction, we tend to specify their relationship in too strictly complementary a way: the higher the transport of "Ulysses," the more ponderous the ballast of "Tithonus." We have thus failed to see how similar are their arguments and how "Tithonus" may be less a complement than a dangerous supplement, an audacious sequel that pursues the arc traced in "Ulysses" far enough to circle back and undermine its grounds. Rhetorically "Ulysses" points the restless way up and out, and "Tithonus" the way down to easeful surcease. But at the daemonic pitch that Tennyson's classical monologues share, the way up and the way down are much the same. If, in view of Tennyson's reverence for the deep, we should expect the way down to be more authentically the method of the sublime, the poem we are about to examine will not disappoint us. Each monologue contains much of the other's energy, as each puts experience to the acid test of an oblivion that dissolves the self as initially given and known. Finally, neither Ulysses nor Tithonus yearns for an action in the world or for a recognizably human interaction with another self; nor, I would argue against most readings of "Tithonus," does either monologist yearn for death, except insofar as "death" figures a threshold that both desire to cross.

In the simplest analysis we probably read "Tithonus" as a "pendent" text because it opens with one of the most heavily freighted passages in English literature:

> The woods decay, the woods decay and fall,
> The vapours weep their burthen to the ground,
> Man comes and tills the field and lies beneath,
> And after many a summer dies the swan. (1–4)

Imagistic parallels, verbal repetitions, and cumulative syntax all bring round the one idea of nature's wheeling sameness, in four end-stopped yet sweetly varied lines of what certainly sounds like a *planctus Naturae* in the spirit of *Poems by Two Brothers*: an autumnal lamentation over the evanescence of things. The very next lines will reverse this impression; but, before considering that reversal, we should note how the subdued artistry of this nearly rhyming quatrain counters the passivity of the physical processes it describes. Tennyson's substitutions of "burthen" for the less musically airy "substance" in line 2 of "Tithon," and of the implicitly tuneful "swan" for the earlier "rose" in line 4, underscore his vocal virtuosity in what we recognize as a traditional elegiac mode. Further, the 1864 revision of the original first line, "Ay me! ay me! the woods decay and fall," establishes the literariness of the opening in more specific and interesting ways. As Ricks

points out (*PT*, 1114), it alludes to "The Simplon Pass," one of
the few excerpts from *The Prelude* that Wordsworth released during his lifetime (*LTJ*, 27). When it appeared in 1845 "The Simplon
Pass," with its immeasurable height and interminable lapse of
"woods decaying, never to be decayed," must have reminded
Tennyson of the endless decay of his own mythical monologist
from the "Tithon" of 1833. Wordsworth's example probably confirmed Tennyson in the uses of poetic repetition as a means of
playing mutability against permanence (Dodsworth 1969, 9, 16;
Conrad 1982, 529). It may have schooled him, too, in the wisdom
of incorporating such repetition into externally descriptive passages ("The woods decay, the woods decay") rather than self-
expressive ones: "Ay me! ay me!" makes an inauspicious beginning
for a speaker bent, as Tithonus surely is, upon decisive change.

Apart from these matters, I think that Tennyson seized upon a
feature of "The Simplon Pass" that makes it virtually unique in
Wordsworth's career-long treatment of natural phenomena: a
strongly emblematic and thus transcendental reading of nature that
splits empirical details off, as signifiers, from the presence they
signify.

> Tumult and peace, the darkness and the light—
> Were all like workings of one mind, the features
> Of the same face, blossoms upon one tree;
> Characters of the great Apocalypse,
> The types and symbols of Eternity,
> Of first, and last, and midst, and without end.
>
> (*Prelude*, VI.635–640)

This hermeneutic vision of nature as a text compacted of characters, types, and symbols, so alien to the studied homeliness of
Wordsworth, seems appropriate instead to the alienation we find
in Tennyson, whose Ulysses would have understood "The Simplon Pass" very well and approved it heartily as an advance upon
the immanence of power dwelt upon in the "Intimations" ode.
Indeed, had this aspect of Wordsworthian vision been accessible
to Tennyson when he wrote "Ulysses," his poem would have
forfeited much of its revisionary space.

The fact that Tennyson could afford this allusion in "Tithonus"
brings us to an important difference between his two greatest
classical monologues. Although Tithonus would have understood

as well as Ulysses the discrepancy opened in "The Simplon Pass" between nature and meaning, he would have endorsed it less enthusiastically. In other words, Tennyson's initial allusion creates a strong presumption that "Tithonus" will not probe the gap between phenomenal experience and transcendent purpose, but will depart thence into concerns even more extravagant. Much as "Ulysses" takes "Tiresias" for granted, so "Tithonus" presumes "Ulysses." The later monologue begins, after all, where the earlier one aspires to go, beyond the bounds of mortality and in exclusion from "the kindly race of men" (29; see Kincaid 1974, 232). And its speaker, unhappy though in heaven, so articulates his dissatisfaction with immortality as to distill, not a death wish that would make his monologue complementary to "Ulysses," but a refining discipline of desire that spurns both the natural contexts that Ulysses also spurns and, beyond these, the preternatural contexts that Ulysses can but eagerly foresee. The poem as thus described sounds impossible, but then the myth of Tithonus, involving Aurora's gift of immortality without perpetual youth, does too. It was Tennyson's great achievement to find in this myth both a modern parable of Romantic desire and a means of "pendency" to ancient tradition that let him humanize the impossible, by basing it first in a recognizably domestic dramatic scene (Shaw 1976b, 275; Wiseman 1978, 215), and then pushing off from the failure of that drama into an uncharted lyricism.

As the monologue gets underway and moves from panorama to drama, what has sounded like a lamentation over nature is upended in line 5, with the intrusive self-identification of a speaker who is anything but natural. Once Tithonus comes into focus as a character, the compelling voice of lines 1–4 appears, in retrospect, to have been yearning after the state of natural affairs it at first seemed to lament:

> Me only cruel immortality
> Consumes: I wither slowly in thine arms,
> Here at the quiet limit of the world,
> A white-haired shadow roaming like a dream
> The ever-silent spaces of the East,
> Far-folded mists, and gleaming halls of morn. (5–10)

"Me only": here is the syntax of victimage, inverted with a vengeance that promotes the victim into arresting singularity. Only this speaking self stands apart from the natural process he has described, and among immortals only he knows his immortality as an affliction. This prominent "Me," unlike the less continent Tithon of 1833, with his purely pathetic and tautological "Ay me!" *(I-me),* makes his entrance through an assertion of relationship to a personified other he calls "cruel immortality." The pathetic fallacy in that personifying adjective "cruel"—unlike the neutral term "fatal" from the "Tithon" manuscript—is recuperative and not just passive. The Hardyesque distinction between fatality and cruelty, which is one of the things that distinguish the classical monologues from the bulk of Tennyson's works, creates in the else-cosmic environment of these opening lines an ethical pocket, a space for character.

In this connection the hyperclassicized syntax of lines 5–6 serves the Romantic end of asserting reciprocity between object and subject, beholding and becoming—as we may see by asking whether the adjective "cruel" modifies "immortality," "Me," or both somehow at once. That Tithonus finds the condition of his immortality cruel his monologue will establish beyond question; yet "Me only cruel" makes sense too as a phrasal unit that reflects Tennyson's furiously projective speaker: a man victimized and alienated, yet also resistant and even vindictive. If we review the preceding lines we note that their single departure from literal language, "The vapours weep their burthen to the ground," has figured the power of voice in plangent relationship. If the burden of the vapors can be a chorus as well as a shower, then the very ground they weep to may be charmed into sympathetic audience. Hearing and being heard are certainly the avenues of relationship that matter most to Tithonus; and it is the power of lamentation, which is also the power of imagining sympathetic fellowship against the merely lamentable, that provides both his initial occasion for voice and the provocation that keeps him speaking to the end. Through a protracted meditation on the bounds and the prerogatives of this Tennysonian power, as against that red herring a mere natural death, Tithonus will forswear his relationship with given contexts, in the hope that he may encounter an answerable presence.

Despite its abstractness, "cruel immortality" is the nearest thing to an answerable presence that this opening paragraph presents. The other immortality on the scene is Aurora, the goddess of the dawn, whose affectionate nature we incline to presume but who is in fact introduced and rendered throughout with painstaking neutrality. Never once named in a monologue that addresses her throughout—commentators cannot decide whether to name her Aurora in Latin or Eos in Greek—she appears in odd, piecemeal fashion. Tithonus's reference to "thine arms" is only the first in a series of bodily synecdoches that recur with consistently impersonalizing, ultimately automating effect. The arms are simply there, like a space or a season: whether they mean support or confinement, Aurora's arms are from Tithonus's perspective the medium he withers in. And since they are conspicuously withered "slowly in" (and not, say, "slow into"), the sense of withering as a fading or pining away suggests at the outset some aversion in Tithonus to Aurora and what she represents: natural context and process, secular place and time. The Tennysonian monologue's presiding *genius loci* or Lady of Situations, Aurora embodies the stunning arbitrariness of conditions in general, to which the final four lines of this verse paragraph give wonderful expression and from which "Tithonus" as a whole attempts to formulate terms of release.

If ever a dramatic monologist has spoken from the limits, it is Tithonus. But his station "at the quiet limit of the world," amid "ever-silent spaces," sets him at a boundary that persistent sensory deprivation makes peculiarly, eerily impalpable. The logically if not grammatically dangling participial construction of "roaming" sets Tithonus free to stay where he is, in a prison without walls; withering in the circuit of Aurora's arms and roaming at large through her spaces and halls appear to be equivalent conditions of aimless confinement. "Far," as we have seen, is a strange enough word in "Ulysses"; "Far-folded" here is stranger still. The mind's eye readily pictures mists as "far," and the mind's skin gladly imagines them as "folded"; but "Far-folded mists" seems to enfold even the blur of misty distance from clear sight, while the "far" in this highly Romantic compound epithet estranges the pleasures of touch as well. This hazy realm Tithonus roams "like a dream"; the simile applies equally to the skyscape and to its inmate, who amid such vagaries regards himself as "A white-haired shadow," a bright cipher whose cloudiness matches his environs. Ulysses' simile "like a sinking star" discloses a similar ambiguity, whereby the pursuit of starry knowledge entails an astral projection on the part of the knower (Baum 1948, 300; Halio 1961, 393; Leggett 1970, 152). The verbal parallels between Tennyson's two roaming monologists suggest that Tithonus, too, is incipiently on the move, attempting to transform his withering into a whither-ing, and seeking directions out of Aurora's dreamily ambient space and cyclical time.

In order to awaken from place into direction, Tithonus needs to drive a vector across such Aurorean circles. Tennyson's extensive revision of the second verse paragraph of "Tithon" serves this need by dropping into the past a narrative line that puts Tithonus's immortal present into the mythical equivalent of a historical context. The original Tithon at this point again repeated "Ay me! ay me!" and moved though an abstract analysis of his predicament to a request for release (11–19). The section Tennyson newly wrote replaces this synchronic analysis with a strongly colored history that, in stepping out of the dramatic present, makes a step toward the imagination of change:

> Alas! for this gray shadow, once a man—
> So glorious in his beauty and thy choice,
> Who madest him thy chosen, that he seemed
> To his great heart none other than a God!
> I asked thee, "Give me immortality."
> Then didst thou grant mine asking with a smile,
> Like wealthy men who care not how they give.
> But thy strong Hours indignant worked their wills,
> And beat me down and marred and wasted me,
> And though they could not end me, left me maimed
> To dwell in presence of immortal youth,
> Immortal age beside immortal youth,
> And all I was, in ashes. (11–23)

Where the first paragraph dwelt on inevitable and impersonal process, the emphasis here falls upon decision and difference, as Tithonus envisages options that awaken the poem from its consumptive and pointless initial dissolve. Whether or not an immortally aging man still counts as a man at all, Tithonus is at least an immortal who remembers being a man—a man, moreover, who in comparing himself to "a God," ages ago, affirmed the difference he wished to negate. Tithonus emplots the past by recalling a series of unique events impelled by acts of will: Aurora's doubly stressed "choice" to love him, his asking, and then her granting, the boon of immortality.

As Tithonus wills personal causality and its attendant ethical pressures into his life story, he also introduces the sort of dramatically rhetorical opportunity that Tennyson's other classical monologues slight. "Thy choice, / Who madest him thy chosen" is designed to hurt, as is the nasty comparison of Aurora to "wealthy men who care not." The injuries these lines aim to inflict are, despite the superhuman *donnée* of the myth, as double-edged as in any domestic quarrel; and they lay bare not just Aurora's divine idiocy but, with keener irony, the pettiness of Tithonus himself. The man who was once "So glorious" and magnanimously "great" of heart can wheedle and sting, it appears, with the worst of us—and the irony with which he now spits those adjectives out owns as much. Tithonus, in other words, is willing to share responsibility for his catastrophe, as the price of bringing responsibility into his cloudily overdetermined world. Similarly, in lines 18–20 he is willing to suffer again in memory the onslaught of time and accept the degradation of his bodily decrepitude, if by acknowledging these indignities he can keep indignation a viable response. "Tithon" had imagined the hours as embowering allies, ready "to wind me in their arms" and "lap me deep within the lonely west" (25–27); but in revision Tennyson substituted for their embracing presence a bracing hostility. The stronger the wills of the personified "Hours indignant," and the weaker Tithonus's physical constitution, the stronger the ethical charter of his resistance. Such is the logic of pathetic fallacy in this monologue, which will discard pathos at the last, but only after giving the emotional complexities of the dramatic situation their due.

The final phrase of the passage, "And all I was, in ashes," forecasts the imminent collapse of this dramatic relationship by rendering the extreme pulverization of whatever give-and-take these unlikely lovers may once have enjoyed. "All" may be the object of the preposition "beside" in the preceding line or of the verb "left" two lines above that; Tithonus's phrase thus may describe either Aurora or himself. This ambiguous grammatical pendent projects the devastation of an ageless past onto the wasteland of an immortal present: whether Tithonus turns in memory to the immortal youth he once enjoyed or turns to Aurora as the daily representative of that condition, all is ashen. But because his his-

torical retrospect has let him explain his present condition instead
of passively describing it, from the ashes of relationship he can
snatch the spark of an ethical resolve. Although linear time has
left all Tithonus was in ashes, it has also left him a self, "me
maimed," that arises from the participial intercourse of memory
and perception, past and present. "Me maimed," like the "me"
not known in "Ulysses," is a far cry from Tithon's "Ay me!" and
it suggests a more resourceful identity than the patient "Me only"
of the first verse paragraph. The victimized, past-participial self
that sighs its stasis through much of Tennyson's earlier poetry is
girding here instead to cry for justice; in this sense the first two
dozen lines of "Tithonus" recapitulate the breakthrough that had
taken up over two hundred in "Oenone." But, Tithonus's speech
being not half over yet, he may go on to raise a question that
Oenone's sheer will-to-confrontation elides: Justice on what
ground and before what tribunal?

Tithonus's first recourse is to Aurora, who necessarily fails him.
His dawning realization of the necessity of her failure—which is
also the failure of the necessity she embodies—furnishes both the
subject of the next several verse paragraphs and the pretext for
the fresh departure with which the monologue will close. But
even here, as Tithonus begins to plead before Aurora, he can barely
bring himself to believe the plea worth making:

> Can thy love,
> Thy beauty, make amends, though even now,
> Close over us, the silver star, thy guide,
> Shines in those tremulous eyes that fill with tears
> To hear me? Let me go: take back thy gift.   (23–27)

All the amends that Aurora can make, at this or any other point,
are here pledged in the deflection of purpose into beauty, which
characterizes a principal mode of the Tennysonian imagination
and which overcomes Tithonus despite himself in the halting
march of his syntax toward aesthetic surrender. What begins as a
direct request stammers into lush descriptiveness that relaxes from
the original aim: "though," in the second line, is less a semantic
disjunction than the sign of a shift between incompatible discourses. This victory of "beauty" over "amends" follows with
imaginative rightness from the autobiographical sketch of the preceding lines, because it is a relapse that repeats—for the last time

in the poem—the succumbing to process that is the story of Tithonus's life to date. Aurora gives to misery all she has, a tear;
and whether her eyes are "tremulous" with a fluttering of lids or
so weepy that they distort perception, in either case what Tithonus
beholds in Aurora obscures the responsibility of vision he has
attained in earlier lines. The actual petition for deliverance, therefore, when it belatedly arrives seems curiously pro forma, painfully
blunt in view of the pathos that precedes it—and thus again dramatic, more psychological than logical in import.

With the last four lines of the paragraph, however, Tithonus
appears to have given up on Aurora altogether, as he addresses to
himself a question that not even a more verbally responsive goddess than Aurora could answer:

> Why should a man desire in any way
> To vary from the kindly race of men,
> Or pass beyond the goal of ordinance
> Where all should pause, as is most meet for all?   (28–31)

I differ from most critics in finding this something other than a
rhetorical question. Since "vary" and "pass beyond" here mean
the same thing, the redundant phrasing, taken together with the
peculiar hesitation of "pause" where one expects "stop," suggests
that Tennyson himself found the question not rhetorical but un-
answerable. And well he might: that most of us men and women—
and poets in the Romantic tradition probably more than most—
do desire distinction from the kindly race, and do aspire beyond
set limits, is a definitive paradox of our culture, which the Tithonus
myth presents for unusually direct contemplation. It is a paradox
this same myth raises very near the wellhead of Western literature,
when at the opening of book V of the *Odyssey* an allusion to
Tithonus and the dawn goddess (1–2, also 125) introduces the
choice of Odysseus to leave the blissful obscurity of immortal
Kalypso's isle for the heroic distinction that immortalizing poems
are made on. The venerable connection between Tithonus and
Odysseus is not, even in Homer, one of simple complementarity,
whereby the one represents the other's road not taken. Their association becomes more complex and interesting once we conceive
Odysseus's choice as a preference of adventurous desire over routine: "the nymph had ceased to please" (*Odyssey*, V.155, tr. Fitzgerald). "Ulysses" gives every reason to believe that Tennyson

conceived Odysseus's choice in this way. But where desire in
"Ulysses" is a given, the one constant term in a repeatedly collapsing calculus of experience and possibility, in "Tithonus" Tennyson lifts his erotic inquest to higher ground. Tithonus, casting
a cold eye on desire, ventures to ask a question that never occurs
to Ulysses: Why?

The propositional point of the second verse paragraph of "Tithonus," its speaker's demand for release from Aurora and her
world, is flanked on either side by questions highly pertinent to
Tennyson's investigation of desire. These questions are weak and
strong, rhetorical and open, versions of each other. Will divine
love and beauty, the richest gratifications of desire that human
imagination has shaped, suffice? Since they manifestly will not,
then to what end is desire insatiable? Why should a man desire in
any way? Answers to questions such as these are found in sacred
texts more commonly than in poetic ones, and we should certainly
not expect to find them in the work of the accomplished doubter
who had written *The Lover's Tale* and "The Lady of Shalott" a
few years before drafting "Tithon" and who returned to finish
"Tithonus" at the close of the decade that had witnessed the publication of *In Memoriam* and *Maud*. But if we credit Tennyson with
having broached such questions in this monologue, we shall better
understand how it follows upon "Ulysses" and the poems of 1832
than if we take the question of desire as settled in advance, by
presuming that all Tithonus wants is to be dead.

We shall also better appreciate Tennyson's dramatization of partial answers in the paragraphs that follow. In the first of these
Tithonus returns from narrative and argumentation to a newly
quarrelsome kind of description:

> A soft air fans the cloud apart; there comes
> A glimpse of that dark world where I was born.
> Once more the old mysterious glimmer steals
> From thy pure brows, and from thy shoulders pure,
> And bosom beating with a heart renewed.
> Thy cheek begins to redden through the gloom,
> Thy sweet eyes brighten slowly close to mine,
> Ere yet they blind the stars, and the wild team
> Which love thee, yearning for thy yoke, arise,
> And shake the darkness from their loosened manes,
> And beat the twilight into flakes of fire.   (32–42)

Coming on the heels of the agonized questions of the preceding paragraph, the first line teases with a revelation. The parting cloud reveals, however, merely an obscure intimation of the mortality from which Tithonus remains barred. If the passage recalls the optics of the "Intimations" ode, which plays "celestial light" (4) and "clouds of glory" (64) against the worldly darkening of vision, it does so only to put Tithonus doubly in the wrong, on the bright side of the Wordsworthian lens, where he can claim neither a splendid immortality nor the spiritual balms reserved for benighted mortals. Pinnacled at the celestial light source yet standing on his own shadow, amid alien glory Tithonus glimpses a homely darkness that confirms his separation from the kindly race of men.

The rest of the paragraph confirms Tithonus's analogous separation from the unkindly race of gods, with another revelation, this one as brilliantly positive in its crescendo of light as the first is privative. The odd verbal chime of "the old mysterious glimmer" with "glimpse" a line above suggests that in their very opposition the two revelations of this paragraph have something in common. The superb sexiness of Aurora's gradual awakening needs no elucidation from the critic, yet we should not let it blind us to the way Tithonus's description of it also resists it, especially during the last four lines. The clause "Ere yet they blind the stars" (revised from "As when they blind the stars" in T.Nbk. 20, fol. 3) pulls Tithonus from stepwise description of Aurora's arousal into anticipation of its foreknown, disastrous sequel. The responsive arousal—not of Tithonus but of "the wild team / Which love thee"—is I think less a reticent Victorian sublimation of male sexuality (Greene 1980, 297), and less an impotent old lover's vicarious substitution of wish for deed, than it is Tithonus's willful fall out of love with the process he is describing (Donahue 1949, 403). The impersonal relative pronoun "which" makes the lusty and virile team with their "loosened manes" functional parts of a cosmic light-organ that appears emphatically as an enslaving mechanism of desire: a mechanism that drives not just the horses, "yearning for thy yoke," but their driver Aurora as well. "Thy yoke" is a sign both of the team's obedience to the goddess and of the goddess's obedience in turn to a force behind the yoke of light her own shoulders have worn five lines before. The beating of the horses' hooves joins Aurora's "bosom beating with a heart renewed," to own the very pulse of the machine in which all are caught. All, that is, but Tithonus. His descriptive language declines a dance that, being the celestial and perpetually early counterpart of the autumnal woods' earthbound and perpetually late decay and fall, takes part in the same old story.

The "old mysterious glimmer" that steals from Aurora steals her from the realm of responsibility and responsiveness, and delivers her over to blind natural necessity instead. While the glimmer is "old" in part because Tithonus has beheld it countless times, it is also old in that Tennyson has stolen it from two searching Romantic confrontations of primary natural process with antithetical imaginative life: the "Intimations" ode and its most captious descendant, Shelley's *Triumph of Life*. Tennyson's "glimpse" and "glimmer" inevitably recall Wordsworth's "visionary gleam," an abiding, transcendent memory countering the else-irresistible pull that "Life" and "her equipage" (105) exert upon the soul fading into the light of common day. But for Tithonus, the intimate *par excellence* of immortality, the visionary gleam he sleeps with has become equivalent to common day, just the daily cue to a handsomely executed fade-in. If we think back to the importance of the untraveled world's marginal gleam, as the object that validates desire in "Ulysses," we can see how "Tithonus" questions that validation. Tithonus does not dwell on the "untraveled world" as Ulysses does, for the excellent reason that he dwells in it already.

In this respect Tennyson's greatest monologue approaches the inset narrative of Rousseau in *The Triumph of Life*, the last and most embittered of the many responses to Wordsworth's ode that Shelley wrote. There a robot charioteer trammels or tramples all who yield to life through desire, and the maimed figure of Rousseau, desire's sorry apostle, narrates his enslavement by a ravishing female figure:

> A Shape all light, which with one hand did fling
> Dew on the earth, as if she were the dawn,
> And the invisible rain did ever sing
>
> A silver music on the mossy lawn.   (352–355)

While Tennyson's myth makes literal what is only a hypothesis in Shelley's—the shape all light with which Tithonus tangles actually *is* the dawn—numerous parallels suggest that both spectral shapes are *belles dames sans merci*. Moreover, the conjunction in

Shelley of a luminous figure with vocal vapors, raining their burden to the ground, supports our surmise that the distinction between natural and divine realms in "Tithonus" has been but a preliminary step toward their reconciliation. Like the visionary dreamer of Shelley's poem, Tithonus yearns to see around the blind yearning for the yoke and to reground desire in a substrate that, underlying the mechanism of mortality and immortality alike, may be answerable for it.

Certainly the Aurora this third verse paragraph describes is no such respondent. Her change is, rather, an action eloquent of her divine irresponsibility, her incapacity to make any amends beyond "pure" responsiveness to the mystery, at once celestial and sexual, that works through her. Tithonus's arrival at this conclusion is important enough for Tennyson to give it a paragraph in itself:

> Lo! ever thus thou growest beautiful
> In silence, then before thine answer given
> Departest, and thy tears are on my cheek.   (43–45)

Nothing has happened with Aurora's transformation but what was to happen. The tears that earlier filled her eyes have fallen, and if we read those tears as the dews of daybreak, following W. David Shaw's suggestion that the radiant goddess is herself a vast pathetic fallacy (1976b, 42), then we understand that such natural dews are the only dues a goddess of nature can ever pay. Like the vapors, Aurora can but weep her burden and then leave the burden of further proof to Tithonus, whose "Lo!" reasserts the mere visuality of Aurorean silence.

Tithonus proceeds at once in a second tight paragraph to complete the proof, and to draw the lesson of Aurora's display by returning to his difference from the gods:

> Why wilt thou ever scare me with thy tears,
> And make me tremble lest a saying learnt,
> In days far-off, on that dark earth, be true?
> "The Gods themselves cannot recall their gifts."   (46–49)

The final line, part apposition and part answer to the lines that precede it, quotes not a divine "saying" but, significantly, a human one, recalled from long ago "on that dark earth," the home of needy speech. What scares Tithonus most about Aurora's tears—and in retrospect about the "smile" with which eons ago she conferred the gift of immortality—is her speechlessness. She exemplifies the mindless gods who, in the grip of fate and beyond the reach of language, cannot change their minds because they cannot learn, and cannot learn because theirs is a power that cannot be re-minded. As in the first act of *Prometheus Unbound*, where in order to unsay his curse Shelley's hero must suffer its repetition, "recall" here means both "revoke" and "remember." In the second verse paragraph Tithonus's recollection of Aurora's gift affirmed the power of mind over present circumstances, which Aurora as goddess of space and time represents. Recalling now, at the prompting of the juggernaut of daybreak, that the gods themselves cannot recall their gifts the way a man can, Tithonus reaffirms mind and the uniqueness of the moment in linear time, against the repetitive patterns of fatality—albeit at the cost of accepting as irrevocable that past-participial given, Aurora's devastating original "gift."

The quoted answer of line 49 is both the poem's moment of simplest pathos and its major pivot. Henceforth "Tithonus" ceases to exhibit, as it has exhibited to this point more consistently than any of its Tennysonian "pendents," the characteristics of a full-dress dramatic monologue, in which the mutually responsive relation of speaker and auditor shapes speech. Because Aurora cannot bend from her daily trajectory or bestow anything but the gift of an immortal presence, the flexible give-and-take of the dramatic monologue cannot be sustained. It must, indeed, be dismissed as a delusion that, while it lasts, turns and turns again the key to her heavenly prison. From this point Aurora as an auditor ceases to matter; perhaps she has departed the scene by line 45 and perhaps not, but her presence or absence has little to do with the remaining concerns of this poem. For while Aurora ceases to matter as an auditor, she commences to signify as the vehicle of a doom that works through her; and it is through her that Tithonus aims, in the two remaining paragraphs, to attune his utterance to the power she expresses. What has been a comparatively well-defined petition to a goddess that she perform a practical task now becomes a more lyrical prayer, which speaks to known divinity in order to find the unknown motive that divinity bodies forth.

"AY ME! AY me!" (50): in altering the poem Tennyson reserved this purest of laments for the point at which it is hardest won,

Tithonus's recognition that the consequences of his past choices must be lived through, not undone. But this cry marks the end of pathos in this monologist, who embarks at once upon a fresh encounter with the past, and now with a knowing survivor's aims. Tithonus plays back the daily metamorphosis of Aurora—a revised version, as it were, of the spectacle he has just described on the spot—this time under the surveillance of a memory eager to ambush meanings rather than to record phenomena:

> with what another heart
> In days far-off, and with what other eyes
> I used to watch—if I be he that watched—
> The lucid outline forming round thee; saw
> The dim curls kindle into sunny rings;
> Changed with thy mystic change, and felt my blood
> Glow with the glow that slowly crimsoned all
> Thy presence and thy portals, while I lay,
> Mouth, forehead, eyelids, growing dewy-warm
> With kisses balmier than half-opening buds
> Of April. (50–60)

As with the earlier metamorphic description of Aurora, the eroticism of this rival passage speaks for itself; yet the interest now lies in what does not speak for itself but rather speaks through the senses to the adverting mind. The Wordsworthian scruple introduced at the outset as to the continuity between Tithonus's past and present selves prepares for his careful discrimination between the phenomenon and the omen, between the merely luminous and the numinous. Tithonus's acceptance of the "mystic change" that has disjoined him forever from his mortal past now prompts him to search Aurora's pageantry for marks of decision that may prove to be evidences of an election beyond Aurora's. Hence his emphases upon her "lucid outline," the aura that lingers in her name; upon "the glow" that is not her own but suffuses her from elsewhere; and upon her "portals," which in alliterative antithesis to her "presence"—an effect Tennyson achieved in revision—suggest the means of egress from her splendid prison-house.

It is unclear whether the primal scene here recalled precedes or follows Aurora's gift of immortality. The corresponding passage in "Tithon" refers to "my mortal frame / Molten in thine immortal" (46–47), and the phrase "In days far-off" repeats verbatim Tithonus's memory of mortality three lines above; at the same time, however, Tithonus's memory of changing with Aurora's change and glowing with her glow suggests an immortalizing fellowship with essence. Tennyson leaves the distinction between mortal and immortal pasts vague—clouds it, indeed, when revising his draft—so as to highlight the difference between either of these pasts and Tithonus's active quest to wrest from memory a fugitive, mystic hint. Having fatally yielded to the fulfillments of Aurora's eternal presence, Tithonus now so re-presents that surrender as to obtain a purchase on the liminal: "portals," "half-opening buds." He thus situates himself at Ulysses' prophet margin of experience, but raised to a higher power.

Tithonus's recollection is strongest in the last four lines of the paragraph, where the once "quiet limit of the world" becomes, in this most soundproof of monologues, a passageway for voice. Tithonus recalls how he

> could hear the lips that kissed
> Whispering I knew not what of wild and sweet,
> Like that strange song I heard Apollo sing,
> While Ilion like a mist rose into towers.   (60–63)

The parallel passage of sublimated phallicism in the third verse paragraph climaxed in obliteration, in a "blinding" and "beating" that linked Aurora's cosmic processes, and the male desire she prompted and contained, with the slow assault of the strong hours (Sinfield 1976a, 470–471). The imagery here, in sharp contrast, is creative, through its association with the erection of Troy (not, as earlier, with its downfall in "flakes of fire" through the machination of the horse) and above all with the prophetic medium of voice. "The wild team" were wild with an enslaving desire Tithonus knows all too well, but the divine glossolalia that issues from Aurora in something "wild and sweet" is semantically wild and is sweet with the breath of an unapprehended inspiration. The gradual departure of the passage from second-person pronouns (not "thy lips" but "the lips that kissed") further enacts Tithonus's transformation of Aurora from a person to a persona, the mask of an alien power. The tempo of the entire paragraph quickens the dim into the concrete, as crescent images of sight, touch, and smell gather into an outburst of voice that whispers and then sings of what transcends the concrete, being its motive force.

Tithonus thus recalls Aurora's gifts, as the goddess herself cannot do, in order not to revoke but to read them. Rather than a synecdoche for an enfolding presence, the lips that whisper as they kiss become the instrument of an extravagant promise. Tithonus so scans the text of memory as to apprehend Aurora's celestial body not according to the participatory and unitary mode of symbol, but according to the different and spiritual mode of allegory. The music of the mnemonic text, while it is "wild," has the uncannily "strange," homely "sweetness" of forgotten options freshly recognized; for what Tithonus chiefly remembers here is his own alien origin or antithetical nature. As Ricks points out, Tennyson would have read in Jacob Bryant's exuberant *A New System; or, An Analysis of Antient Mythology* (1807) that the name and myth of Tithonus derive linguistically from "Amonian" etymological radicals that, as Bryant combines them, denote a tower built upon earthworks and consecrated to the sun.[19] The empowered song of the prophetic sun god Apollo may earn its place, in the bizarre though beautiful transition with which this verse paragraph ends, as Tithonus's privileged memory of his own hieratic beginning.

Rather than figuring either his natural birth as a man or his immortalization through Aurora's gift, the strange song may stand as a mistlike or screening memory of another birth, by inspiration and the word, that converts being into meaning—as in the book of Genesis that man of earth Adam, himself awakened by the breath of God, first named whatever lived within his world in an original tongue long since lost. The loss of that tongue, we recall from the Genesis tradition that Bryant privileged, came with the erection of another tower upon earth, when men aspired at Babel to transgress the goal of ordinance where all should pause. Later in his *New System* Bryant writes of Babel much as he does of the Tithonus myth, and says that the confusion of tongues "did not consist in an utter change of language" but "was a labial failure; an alteration in the mode of speech. It may be called the prevarication of the lip" (IV, 59–60). Tithonus's memory of Aurora's babble, "the lips that kissed / Whispering I knew not what," thus takes him back, via Tennyson's memory of the scriptural Babel, to a partial "labial failure" through which he can overhear the music of his own genesis, Apollo's strange and creative song.

Each of these associations is speculative, of course; but in their ensemble they suggest the recollection of a scattered origin, which belated language cannot name, but which the purged ear can still apprehend as music, the song that lingers in the measures of the prophet's or poet's inspired speech.[20] The last lines of this verse paragraph reveal an additional logic, and a source nearer home, if we view them as a recapitulation of the movement in Keats's "Ode to Psyche" from the initial "tender eye-dawn of aurorean love" (20) to the affirmatively penultimate dressing, amid a "wide quietness," of a holy fane with "casement ope at night / To let the warm Love in" (58, 66–67). We know from "The Lady of Shalott" and other poems how consistent a role Keats's ode played in Tennyson's attempts to elaborate myths of emergent connection with others. But with "Tithonus" and other dramatic incarnations of the "pale-mouthed prophet dreaming" (35, 49), Tennyson made it his aim to dramatize emergencies of human disconnection, as the preliminaries to transcendent encounter. The way extends here not toward warm love but away from it and toward the cold liminality of the paragraph to come.

Tithonus's review of his life with Aurora has reminded him that beneath his fatally limited request for immortality there ran a broader quest for confirmation of his own light, the nimbus of "glory" that he wore when a man but in the folly of youth sold short: "So glorious in his beauty and thy choice, / Who madest him thy chosen, that he seemed / To his great heart none other than a God!" We caught earlier the ironic tone of this exclamation; with Tithonus's recognition of the limitations of godhead, we can better grasp the significance into which its irony opens (Hughes 1979, 86). None other than a God—and no more than that! From the first, Tithonus has sought not the immortality but the intimation, the strange familiar whisper and not the daily kiss. The pagan pathos of his having requested eternal life but not eternal youth thus becomes—by way of the idolater's Christian sin of mistaking an image of renewal for the renewing spirit—the Romantic error of reading the signifier for the signified, the light of common day for the light that never was, the gleaming halls of morn for the mystical and mistlike city built to music and therefore never built at all. What stirs most deeply, then, in the penultimate verse paragraph is Tithonus's recognition that in surrendering to desire he forgot what that desire meant and thereby betrayed his nature.

The final verse paragraph expresses his will to forget that lethal

forgetting and turn desire against itself. The close of this monologue owes its aplomb to the chastity with which it pursues this
negative aim, to the exclusion of any posited alternative:

> Yet hold me not for ever in thine East:
> How can my nature longer mix with thine?
> Coldly thy rosy shadows bathe me, cold
> Are all thy lights, and cold my wrinkled feet
> Upon thy glimmering thresholds, when the steam
> Floats up from those dim fields about the homes
> Of happy men that have the power to die,
> And grassy barrows of the happier dead.
> Release me, and restore me to the ground;
> Thou seëst all things, thou wilt see my grave:
> Thou wilt renew thy beauty morn by morn;
> I earth in earth forget these empty courts,
> And thee returning on thy silver wheels. (64–76)

Where the pleasure principle is so thoroughly depressed as in this
passage of superb anhedonia, our culture tends to infer the ascendancy of a death instinct. Given Tithonus's talk of the power
to die, the happy dead, the grave and the rest, it is not surprising
that most readers of these magnificent lines have found in them
the alleged Tennysonian death wish writ large. But it is important
to distinguish between the desire to die and the dying of desire,
especially in a speaker whom we accept as immortal in accepting
his myth and who, moreover, has himself accepted immortality
for keeps at line 49. If we read this paragraph as a renewal, necessarily futile, of Tithonus's petition for cancellation of his life
sentence, then the poem becomes a tape loop doomed to pointless
reenactment, on argumentative and emotional planes, of the silver
whirling of Aurora's natural cycle (Ricks 1972, 134; Mermin 1983,
32). Read as a death wish, the poem becomes the pathetically
oblivious mantra of a divine despair, the consumptive and tautological *Ay me! I-me!* of pity for a self that aims to forget not less
than everything, its own recent mnemonic gains included, and
that takes death's total oblivion—as it has taken death's defining
opposite, unconditional immortality—as a desirable end in itself.[21]

Against such a reading I contend, first, that it traduces the integrity of the poem by trivializing the continuity between this
paragraph and its predecessors. In broader terms, such a reading
slights the dialectic of memory and repression in Tennyson, who

was a good forgetter but a purposeful one; and it mistakes the Tennysonian spirit's imagination of relationship *with* doom for a simply terminal submission *to* it. The closing paragraph of "Tithonus" seems to me Tennyson's highest chant of release into power, a psalm addressed through the visible instrument of power, Aurora of the silver wheels, to a hidden god the passage gnostically respects by abstaining from all positive assertion and thus keeping it hidden.[22] As the monologue thus far has made clear, Tithonus once limited his conception of godhead to mere immortality, and for that disastrous failure has been condemned to live within the limits of just what he asked for. His having thus been doomed to survival on perpetually diminishing returns explains the strict and cold method of the *via negativa* on which he now embarks (Shaw 1976b, 284).

"Yet hold me not for ever in thine East": Aurora's East, the place of merely natural and repetitive beginnings, is not early enough for Tithonus's easterly quest after an origin that will answer to his "nature"—a term the next line leaves undefined save by contradistinction to what in Aurora, for all her divinity, is all too natural. The colors, brights and darks of Aurora's light show leave Tithonus sexually "cold" because they cannot imaginatively move one who is moving upon "glimmering thresholds," at the solitary prophet margin where what spoke through Aurora called to his glory from the first. At that liminal vantage Tithonus solicits from without a further recognition that lies, as ever with Tennyson, somewhere outside the confines of the text. If we like, it lies after the end of the monologue, where Tithonus, in the unTennysonian whimsy of the legend, will crack his chrysalis and emerge as a grasshopper, to play perhaps on the grassy barrows of the happy dead. More important, it lies beyond what words can adequately name, the word "immortality" among them. For Tennyson's ends the readiness is all, a readiness entailing a preliminary purgation of the impedimenta of desire.

From the glimmering thresholds Tithonus peers into the abyss, which in the phrase of Shelley's Demogorgon cannot vomit forth the secrets of its imageless, deep truth (*Prometheus Unbound*, II.v.114–116)—but which is, for that very reason, the matrix of tropes. The trope that comes to Tithonus in his hard-won reluctance to inflect and deform the intimations of the deep is death, the Atropic trope to end all tropes. Death comes to Tithonus as a figure for the unknown; more specifically, "the power to die" is Tithonus's figure for the lyrical monologist's work of unknowing. The way Tithonus works his work links him again with Tennyson's Ulysses, in whose monologue the evenhanded contemplation of opposite yet equivalent destinies functions much the way Tithonus's cool forecast of his own, literally impossible death does here (Bloom 1976, 159–160). The former arrests us more with an outlandish rhetoric, the latter with imagery of an *unheimlich* homecoming; but both abandon the desires of the conditioned self, for the sake of a transcendent meeting. Within the narrow and intense spectrum of Tennyson's prophet margin, it is Tithonus who occupies the outer belt, because it is he who, least reckoning the cost, gives the most away. "Release me, and restore me to the ground": in a daemonic identification of ends with beginnings, Tithonus fulfills the project of the germinal "Tiresias" manuscript "I wish I were as in the days of old"—by voicing nostalgia for a home that not even the cosmos can house.

The release for which Tithonus makes this last petition is not a withering away from the circumstances that enfold him but an escape into relationship with the unknown principle that encompasses those circumstances in its greater turn. The "ground" to which he seeks restoration, and from which he seeks a more than natural renewal, is the ground to which all of Tennyson's most characteristic creations move; and among those creations "Tithonus" enjoys unsurpassed distinction in finding the poetic means of transcendence in natural imagery itself. Or, to put the matter in terms of the poet's uneasy affiliation with his closest precursor Keats, in the high requiem of "Tithonus" Tennyson so transumes Keats's pagan naturalism as to make his speaker's prayer to cease and become a sod into an affirmation that he is not born for death. Tithonus stands so far out of nature that he can use its silent beauty as a vehicle for the sublime tenor to which his own accomplished voice calls. In turn, this imagined stance enables the poet to mute the stridencies of "Tiresias" and "Ulysses" and to meet—for once without compromise—his final criterion, the authority of the beautiful.

Once Tithonus figuratively represents as a natural death the sublime destiny he cannot name literally without risk of reduction, he can co-opt the cycles of nature that have hemmed in the immortality he once slavishly desired. This is one reason why the closing lines of the monologue are uniformly end-stopped and exhibit internal repetition to an exceptional degree: Tithonus now reads all of nature the way he has just learned to read the nature goddess Aurora, as a system that is closed because it is enclosed by the mystery to which humankind sacrifices ("when the steam / Floats up") and to which he has already sacrificed what amounts to life piled on life. From this perspective, death stands for an immortality beyond the gods'. 'Tis life, not death, for which he pants, as the not-quite-suicidal speaker of "The Two Voices" puts it (line 397); but a dizzying process of elimination has taught Tithonus that a carol of death is the surest vehicle in which to convey that aspiration. If we follow the cycling tendency of the close of "Tithonus" back to its beginning, we can restore to the opening lament its proper, prophetic import. The burden the vapors there weep to the ground figures the burden of the mystery to which Tithonus now prays to be rejoined: Let "all things"—as things—pass away, and let the bodily self go with them to "my grave," the grave of the "me," the death-in-life of perishing mortal desire (Lourie 1979, 27).

To compare the status of desire in "Tithonus" and "Ulysses" is to see again Tennyson's extraordinary penchant for outstripping himself. Ulysses' contempt for the vile bodily self, and his desire to spend the self in a deed that the very strength of his unearthly desire nonetheless invalidated in advance, left his monologue curiously unresolved, straining at the sheet yet indefinitely in port. By contrast, the serenity of "Tithonus" is a function of its readiness to countenance the storing and hoarding of whatever can be stored and hoarded: to restore to the earth "me maimed," the desiring bodily self, as a means of releasing a spiritual presence that is not to be put by. This doom of the self finds a fine reprise with the last two lines, respectively the most sublime and beautiful in the poem: "I earth in earth forget these empty courts, / And thee returning on thy silver wheels." If the fine afterthought of the second line defies exegesis, the first line, with which an early draft of the poem concluded, no less courts it.

The best way to appreciate the generic peculiarity of this superb finale is to ask the standard questions about identity and circumstance that arise with any dramatic monologue. First, who is speaking? Tithonus, of course; but by this point what has "Tithonus," as speaker or as text, become? Better yet, what does "Tithonus" become in the address of these extraordinary lines? Does the impossible appositive "I earth in earth" name a willfully negligent agent forgetting on purpose, or a bodily self consumed with that which it was nourished by? Any answer to this question of identity entails further questions as to time. When is this forgetting supposed to occur? The line asks to be read on its own as a present-tense formation: either as a proleptic purchase on a purely negative futurity or as a performative valediction, which isolates the disembodied spirit more vertiginously still. The very enumeration of the things this "I" forgets, however, would appear to make of them, not things now forgotten, but things to be forgotten later in death; it thus would lead us to read the verb as a future formation dependent on the preceding line, "Thou wilt renew thy beauty morn by morn."[23] Yet then, if we equate Tithonus's forgetting with his death, should the verb tense not be the future perfect "I shall have forgotten"? Either a present or a future construction of the verb "forget" returns us to the paradox of body and will we have already met in construing "I earth in earth." Finally, just where are these forgotten, or forgettable, "empty courts"? If present to the "I," as the deictic "these" insists, then they cannot be "empty," because the "I" must be there within them—not to mention the "thee" who is addressed as returning to fill them in the simultaneous hail and farewell of the final line.

In both its predicate and its subject, therefore, this passage enacts grammatically the paradoxes of self and context out of which the dramatic monologue as a modern poetic genre arises. We encounter at the close of "Tithonus" the vanishing act of an "I" that is both a corpse and a will strong enough to evacuate itself from any context, through an anticipatory forgetting that unsettles the home grounds of time and place, to restore instead the ever marginal, glimmering grounds of prophecy: a presence neither given nor predictable, and imaginable only in negative terms as absence. "That which we are, we are," Ulysses concluded, having stripped the self of defining context and thereby of singularity. The comparable eclipse of the self in "Tithonus," where even desire is annulled, teeters on the verge of a more abysmally gnostic formulation: That which I am, I was not to be and shall not have been; for I am not that I am.

So scandalous a poise cries out for naturalization of some kind; and since the poem bids defiance throughout to the naturalist and at last to the logician too, the best home for Tithonus's dizzying last stand may be in the literary history from which it comes. As Tennyson's most finely articulated and even-tempered rehearsal of the Romantic ego's transcendental creed, the end of this poem deserves a place beside such statements as Wordsworth's "By our own spirits are we deified" ("Resolution and Independence," 47), Keats's "I will be thy priest, and build a fane / In some untrodden region of my mind" ("Ode to Psyche," 50–51), or the arch conclusion to Shelley's "Mont Blanc": "And what were thou, and earth, and stars, and sea, / If to the human mind's imaginings / Silence and solitude were vacancy?" (142–144). But to juxtapose these works to Tennyson's is to note again the reticence, the negativity, of "Tithonus." Whether out of reverence for the mystery with which Tennyson sought to commune, whether from antipathy to the explicit philosophical grounding of Romanticism (ground he regards as too thin to trust), whether in reaction to the tendency of Romanticism to up the ante of assertion by raising its demands—and each of these motives very likely played its part—Tennyson stopped short of calling the power intimated by his dramatic monologists self-deifying spirit, the human mind, the imagination, or anything else. It is the final achievement of "Tithonus" to call it, precisely, nothing.

THE CLASSICAL MONOLOGUES that date from the 1830s are Tennyson's greater Romantic odes. When we ask, pursuing the increasingly vaporous character of the dramatic address in these poems as we have taken them up, just whom or what they are odes to, our answer will be: to nothing that can be named without an ostentation that impoverishes; to a mystery that Tennyson's speakers at their best do not invoke but rather evoke, through imagistic rites of passage and preeminently through the incantatory craft of voice itself, as it arouses and composes the spirit bent upon the rhythms of its end. This end subsumes the ends of society, of experience in the world, and even, if we can conceive it at thought's utmost bound, of desire. If we can think at all under so extreme a dispensation, it is texts like "Tiresias," "Ulysses," and "Tithonus" that enable us to do so.

But then why should we do so? If we inquire into the uses of such extreme thought, we are bound to return to the biographical scene where for poets, as for those who follow their careers, thinking and living jostle, and to ask what good the writing of these poems did their author in his personal bereavement and in the creative aftermath we call the ten years' silence. Tennyson's major works of 1832 had been preoccupied with relationship: the severest had narrated its failures, the most urgent had demanded it at all costs, and the happiest had managed to loosen the casement of the absolute self and let the warm love in. During the next year Tennyson began fumbling toward poetic forms that not only thematized relationship but also embodied, in their structural conception, a dialogical poetics corresponding to this leading theme. The first, quickly matured, but admirably sound fruit of this formal experimentation was Tennyson's prototype for the modern dramatic monologue, "St. Simeon Stylites." This poem furthered the quest for relationship in an ironic mode, which invited readers to share the grotesque spectacle of a soul who confirms his worldliness more deeply the harder he strives to deny it. In view of this quite continuous development across several formative years, and of the markedly different turn taken by Tennyson's later dramatic monologues, it is impossible to dismiss as coincidental the facts that "St. Simeon Stylites" is the poet's one monologue in the fully ironic mode and that it is the one monologue he had substantially written before learning of Arthur Hallam's death.

The generic change in Tennyson's monologues was not only a formal matter but also an index of the most decisive change of heart—we could say with little exaggeration the one decisive change of heart—his long career was to witness. From all available evidence it seems that the absence of Hallam made the opening of the self's casement less an admission of warm love than a traumatic wound. The birthright of poetic isolation that perennially pressed Tennyson's art into shape had altered its character radically with Hallam's death. Where once the exclusiveness of the self had threatened to shut it out from a universe of love, now the self risked bleeding to death and losing its identity to a universe gone ashen, mechanical, and cold. An awful solitude remained the emergency for Tennyson, as emergence into relationship remained its resolution. But to view as urgent therapies the rhetorical tactics of his classical monologues is to see how dramatically the grounds of relationship, and with them the status of the self that relationship defines, came to shift as the poet found himself in a world of death and absence.

The portion of "Tiresias" he wrote in late 1833 beat a blind retreat from such a world, and decades elapsed before he returned to the manuscript with the complementary vision of a better world. "Ulysses" expressed much the same defensive impulse; but by expressing its rejection of experience as desire for the untraveled world, even at the cost of dissolving the self past recognition, it made that bitter rejection more palatable—manifestly to readers, but also to the poet himself, whose substitution of an affirmatively projected future for a rejected present was arguably what let him finish and publish this monologue while still dissatisfied with its companions. Finally in "Tithonus" Tennyson demystified both the revulsion of "Tiresias" and the desire of "Ulysses," by imagining a speaker so impossibly yet persuasively abstracted from the given world of death that he could read it with favor, as an immense sign of the life beyond personality that had always been the poet's deepest faith and supremely generative fiction.

Although the quick cauteries of "Tiresias" and "Ulysses" had sealed off the severest wound Tennyson would ever receive and had transumed nostalgic yearning into the need of going forward on the crest of unfulfilled desire, "Tithonus" gave voice to Tennyson's equally strong and assuredly more characteristic need of going backward. Memory matters so much in "Tithonus" because there Tennyson is remembering his own vocation, as the measurer of a doom in which he is implicated, together with everything that lives, and to which he can therefore claim an abiding relationship that death may represent but may not alter. This overarching relationship puts Tennyson back in touch with the world, as my discussion of the domestic idylls of 1842 will show more fully, by imparting to the world the melancholy tinge of evanescence we associate with the adjective "Tennysonian." Remembering the object of desire in "Tithonus," we have seen, involves re-membering the beloved's person as the signifier of a disembodied doom that is both a motive and a destiny. And the fate of Aurora in Tithonus's powerful reminiscence represents the fate of Arthur Hallam in Tennyson's. What Tennyson had loved in Hallam became, through the writing of "Ulysses" and "Tithonus" as of *In Memoriam* and *Maud*, what he had loved *about* Hallam; the halo of affectionate regard merges with the visionary gleam that gilds perception in the Romantic texts to which Hallam had introduced him.

The instance of Tennyson thus brings into alignment two senses of the "Romantic desire" our culture still so largely lives by; and it justifies our habitual use of that term to denote both the vivid stuff of our pulpiest dreams and the psychic motor whereby we attempt, in either clinical or conversational fashion, to understand how we live. The nexus of art and life in Tennyson's poetic response to the death of Hallam lets us see Romantic desire at once as the core of our love affairs and as the pulse of the artistic movements with which our culture has been seeking salvation, high and low, for nearly two centuries. With the maturation of Tennyson's poetry Romantic desire becomes not an end in itself but a means of intuiting the end, of giving to the void a last kiss that makes it live, a means of reestablishing contact, through the remembered touch of a vanished hand, with the tranquilizing and inclusive power upon whose flood and toward whose purposes Tennyson's mysteriously piloted craft drifts.

The dramatic monologues of the 1830s are the most irresistibly furious rapids through which Tennyson's career passed. As we leave them for the more equable levels of the 1842 idylls, we might note how, for all their fury, the dramatic monologues too paid tribute to the current of Victorian events. Tennyson's relentless movement toward the sublimation of desire paradoxically let him bring the often frightening acrobatics of a high Romantic daemonism into line with the needs and beliefs of his more orthodox Christian contemporaries. The abstraction of an eternal soul from an increasingly anatomized body, and the extrapolation of a compensatory heaven from an ever more secular earth, became during Tennyson's lifetime the principal polemical concerns of a Victorian religious establishment that was under siege from any number of scientific and economic quarters. As the established church broadened its base in response to these pressures, its edges thinned into those of much Victorian secular literature. The adaptive symbiosis of the canonical church with the rising poet's canon, which both parties sought and which the award of the laureateship in 1850 ratified, was as thorough and immediately successful as with the work of any of his contemporaries (*LTJ*, 225–226). Whether in the end this practical merger of secular and ecclesiastical canonicity has more importantly supported or sapped the bases of religious authority is a moot question, to the further investigation of which the rapprochement we are now witnessing between literary criticism and the hermeneutics of religious studies should give fresh impetus. For the present we live, in any case, with the consequences of a merger between secular and sacred writing that conditions much of what we do in literary practice, criticism and theory—conditions it most, perhaps, when we assert the disciplinary purity of our enterprise.

Insofar as we read the departures of Tennyson's monologues from dramatic situation into agonistic lyricism as conversions of rhetoric into prayer—and that is finally how I have meant to read them here—we join hands across a century and more with such an eminently common reader as Queen Victoria, who regarded *In Memoriam* as something very like a sacred book. That we and she, for all our manifest differences, should in this sense read alike attests to the existence of a considerable common ground sustaining modern culture. The enduring trust in literature we share with that bourgeois empress attests, finally, to an unslaked cultural thirst for restoration to "the ground," in Tithonus's uncanny sense of original life. Tennyson's poetry-reading sovereign, the sovereign New Critical reader, the symbolist in soulful reverie, the modernist poet of reality on the open road to the contagious hospital, the poststructuralist exploding fictions into textuality, all have sought improved relations with an inaugural ordering power—call it God, or nature, or language—that authenticates their methods and indeed their ways of life. This common search binds us together as surely as the disparity among the various grounds of belief we seek rives us intraculturally. And it is this search, Tennyson's ground swell and deepest theme across the years, that makes him a central figure of the modern tradition. He was manifestly the central poet of Victorian England; and if we conceive the modern period broadly as running from the middle of the eighteenth century to the present, in chronological terms he stands more nearly at its center than any English poet of comparable standing save the ever-eccentric Browning. And yet, like Browning, Tennyson may be more central to our tradition at the imaginative extremes of his *sui generis* dramatic monologues than in the more topically hedged works he devoted to the immediate concerns of contemporary readers.

Within the distinct limits of his gifts Tennyson is large and contains multitudes: multitudes not of characters, as with Browning, but of readers his tonality speaks for. Tennyson gains this amplitude and this centrality by virtue of the same capacious receptivity that let him house the contradictions of the modern temper, which had surfaced most memorably in poetry with the sensibilities of the Romantics a generation before. Somehow Tennyson managed to contain the two spirits that have meant most to English poets of the later nineteenth and twentieth centuries: the naturalist quietude of the medical student who became, in Keats, our preeminent poet of earth, astride a wild surmise yet with both feet on mortal ground; and the utopian skepticism of the revolutionary who became, in Shelley, our indispensable poetic spur and our scorner of all given grounds whatsoever. The spirits of both found not just a lodging but a home in Tennyson. Often enough it was a broken home, to be sure; the marvel is not that it should be thus, but that these antithetical spirits, the fugue of whose voices has woven so much of the lasting poetry written in English since their early deaths, could ever be brought to speak as one. Yet for evidence of this uncanny unison we have but to turn again to the closing lines of "Tithonus." The concord of those lines will tell us, as well as anything written since, where we have been and where we are now.

5

In England: Arts of the
Joiner in the Domestic Idylls

ENNYSON'S OEUVRE FROM the volumes of 1842 onward
strikes a balance between the outrageous procedures of
his classical dramatic monologues and the domesticating tactics of
the blank-verse poems he called English idylls. Where the monologues exercise a private aspiration to annihilate the two fictions
of space and time, in the idylls Tennyson advances a poetry of
absorption into the here and now. Where the classical inspiration
of the former affiliates them, as poets' poems, with a fabulous and
above all literary tradition, the latter—while no less classically
inspired—present themselves as responses to current events, and
mirror contemporary mores in scenes and situations immediately
recognizable by a widening public (Shaw 1973, 67). In Tennyson's
hands the dramatic monologue was a new form in which to pursue
a venerable bardic calling; the idyll, by contrast, was an antique
form that lent itself, with only minor adaptations, to a genteel
depiction of modern life in the middle style (Peckham 1962, 292).
Often enough political in their overt pronouncements, and even
more so in the implications of their imagery, Tennyson's idylls
are always politic in their courtship of the contemporary reader
and in their eagerness to find grounds for compromise between
lyricism and daily living, between a high Romantic vocation and
the more tender offices of laureateship. In writing the idylls Tennyson exchanges the demanding arias of the monologue for
English airs; and the discontinuous leaps that impel the one genre
yield in the other to the arts of the joiner, who so smooths his
transitions and rounds his tales as to merge his own concerns with

his readers', and to show how those concerns emerge from a common life.

For a fine sample of this common life rendered in common style, consider the opening dialogue of "Walking to the Mail," composed during the late 1830s:

> *John* I'm glad I walked. How fresh the meadows look
> Above the river, and, but a month ago,
> The whole hill-side was redder than a fox.
> Is yon plantation where this byway joins
> The turnpike?
> *James* Yes.
> *John* And when does this come by?
> *James* The mail? At one o'clock.
> *John* What is it now?
> *James* A quarter to.
> *John* Whose house is that I see?
> No, not the County Member's with the vane:
> Up higher with the yew-tree by it, and half
> A score of gables.
> *James* That? Sir Edward Head's:
> But he's abroad: the place is to be sold.
> *John* Oh, his. He was not broken.
> *James* No, sir, he,
> Vexed with a morbid devil in his blood
> That veiled the world with jaundice, hid his face
> From all men, and commercing with himself,
> He lost the sense that handles daily life—
> That keeps us all in order more or less—
> And sick of home went overseas for change. (1–18)

This pair of more or less interchangeable speakers clearly talk each other's language, and their exchange earns its subdued vindication of life's ordered dailiness by a series of minor breakdowns in communication, followed by quick and tactful saves that keep the conversation alive. "This"?—"The mail"; "No, not the County Member's"; "That? Sir Edward Head's"; "He was not broken"?—"No, sir." Tennyson's ear for the near misses and readjustments of understanding on which chat thrives is quite wonderful and, to a reader who knows the poet only from anthologies, quite unexpected. Here Tennyson attends less to individual voices than to the unspoken conditions that let voices signify within a communal context. These conditions are represented in a formal way by the accommodation of the speaking voice to the pentameter measure in which all Tennyson's best work in the idyll is framed (Drew 1964, 557; Rosenmeyer 1969, 14, 92). In another, negative way the conditions of idyllic speech are represented by the larger topic toward which the small talk of this modern eclogue gravitates. Sir Edward Head, placed by his title and name, by his home's high eminence and its emblematic Wordsworthian yew, stands for a denial of relationship that is the domestic idylls' road not taken, just as surely as it is the emigrant way of Tennyson's estranged speakers in the classical dramatic monologues.

The conversational rapport established between John and James relies on a shared allegiance to common grounds of order that bespeak Tennyson's broad conservatism, especially in public and political affairs. James, "A Tory to the quick" (73), acts as principal spokesman for the conservative viewpoint, and each of the three stories he tells illustrates a belief in the fixity of human nature. The tenant Jocky Dawes's inability to shake off his household ghost; the souring of Sir Edward's wife, "the daughter of a cottager, / Out of her sphere," to "what she is: a nature never kind" (51–54); James's own cruelty in his student days to a neighboring "flayflint" and his hapless sow—all reinforce the same assumptions about the reciprocal support of natural and cultural imperatives. This idyll abounds in animal images (ten species in a hundred lines), which in the aggregate bear out a view of human relations conflating instinct with an acculturation that is second nature to humankind as social animals. Similarly, James speaks of society in terms of the body politic, and speaks of current social history as merely a recurrent case of the ills that flesh is heir to:

> but, sir, you know
> That these two parties still divide the world—
> Of those that want, and those that have: and still
> The same old sore breaks out from age to age
> With much the same result.   (68–72)

This stabilizing vision of change is essential to Tennyson's idyllic order. It anchors the give-and-take of the eclogue by situating the middle-class John and James between the crudely classed, imaginatively untouchable social extremes above and below them. The reactionary Sir Edward and the Chartist insurgent he has fled, lacking any common ground for discourse, must resort instead to pike, shudder, and outcry, the crude signs of their mutual exile. In marked contrast, John's and James's sense of their station between such divisive parties, and of themselves as reasonable men who neither have too little nor want too much, enables them to accept "the world" as a set of shared assumptions that lets them keep talking even as they disagree: "But, sir, you know . . . "

The extremities of the body politic as these speakers agree to conceive them, the aristocratic metonym Head and "the raw mechanic's bloody thumbs" (67), stake out the mediate space of the idyll as a distinctly bourgeois form. Whenever Tennyson works in the form, he does at least tacitly what he does fairly explicitly here: he impounds social extremes beyond the pale of a sympathetic understanding and acknowledges them only by representing them as unknowable. Where they appear violent, whether as provocateurs or as reactionaries, they appear so because they violate the common sense that steadies idyllic compromise: "Well—after all— / What know we of the secret of a man? / His nerves were wrong. What ails us, who are sound?" (93–95). Sir Edward's sociopathic loss of the common sense that handles daily life is at once a neurological and a cultural disorder; and James and John draw their diagnostic confidence from a larger faith that the tide of time is flowing forward with them and their class. It is "this bill that past, / And fear of change at home" (59–60), John reports, with reference to the Reform Bill of 1832, that has driven Sir Edward out of the evolving bourgeois social compact (*Letters*, 69). Not so John and James; on the contrary: "But put your best foot forward, or I fear / That we shall miss the mail" (101–102). The dependable mobility of the mail coach represents for Tennyson's bourgeois swains a familiar way of life. The exchange of correspondence and the intelligence of current events that the mail promises to bring—versions of the gossip and news that have constituted this eclogue—prompt scant anxiety lest such genial conversationalists fail to meet the mail as duly as they have met each other on common ground throughout.[1]

Despite its uniquely dialogical form, then, "Walking to the Mail" is a remarkably consistent text, where moments of imbalance or contradiction between the speakers serve as correctives keeping their dialogue on course, and where larger alternatives to their shared psychosocial vision (aristocracy, Chartism) serve as markers outlining and consolidating the common property that makes their dialogue possible. Like Tennyson's other domestic idylls, this one admits contradictions to its homogeneity of outlook only in order to digest them; and the noncommittal poise with which it regards troublesome current issues plays into a system of checks and balances that contains the troubles it ventilates. Tennyson wrote such poems in the hope of the broadest public acceptance, and in that hope he bent his talents to the articulation of an acceptable world. In its contemporary social aspect, the project of the idylls committed Tennyson to endorsing the assumptions he shared with readers of the middle class, while withholding sponsorship of any one special interest within the ideological spectrum that class included.[2]

At the same time, Tennyson's idyllic project committed him to the most inviting formal closures he could contrive, as means of securing the aesthetic illusion of a world, an agreeable poetic microcosm. The joint result of the thematic and formal commitments of these poems emerges most clearly in their final lines, where we can locate a variety of attempts to make poetic closure as ideologically inclusive as possible. "Walking to the Mail" makes its attempt with what looks like a throwaway:

> But put your best foot forward, or I fear
> That we shall miss the mail: and here it comes
> With five at top: as quaint a four-in-hand
> As you shall see—three pyebalds and a roan.   (101–104)

The understated tone here engages in understatement of a deeper kind: a virtual declaration of assumptions that have underlain the whole idyll, and that indeed have made it whole. The passage rewinds and sets both speakers in step with their times, and it places those times under such handy management—even the census tallies, as the four horses plus driver equal the passengers, "five at top"—that any grander voice of complaint or approbation would seem intemperate and out of place.

Had Tennyson undertaken a more pointedly contemporary vehicle for his idyll and written, say, a "Walking to the Train," the evocation of an iron horse instead of piebalds and a roan would have required for the mimesis of its technology a more technically magniloquent close. As it happens, we find such a close in a slightly later idyll, "The Golden Year," not published until 1846 but written as early as 1839. Here another James, this one older, gruffer, and decidedly Carlylean, explodes the utopian airs of his young interlocutors with the hard-nosed assertion that, "in an age, when every hour / Must sweat her sixty minutes to the death" (67–68), the mythic golden age is now or never: "unto him who works, and feels he works, / This same grand year is ever at the doors" (72–73). James's words seem authoritative but in fact are only penultimate, since the last word comes from on high:

> He spoke; and, high above, I heard them blast
> The steep slate-quarry, and the great echo flap
> And buffet round the hills, from bluff to bluff.   (74–76)

The last word on work proves to be that of work itself, or rather of work as taken up into the familiar air of Tennyson's atmospheric melodizing. This conclusion is curiously noncommittal: it seems to confirm what James has just said about the dignity and the limiting conditions of labor, but it also seems to swallow up all talk, James's included, in a mystery that is not without menace. Stranger yet, the menace too is baffled by the ingratiations of superb onomatopoeia, which diffuses, de-fuses, and thus contains the threat of apocalyptic rupture within the tacit assurance of a style. The poet's tone is equal to the detonations of the engineer, and for a reason: they both register the transindividual doom that is, beyond all revolution, industrial culture (McLuhan 1959, 88; Rosenmeyer 1969, 17–18; Culler 1977, 114).

Tennyson could hardly have produced credible renditions of nineteenth-century English life without some success in rendering so distinctive and conspicuous a feature of the modern scene as technology. And indeed, a case can be made that he put machinery into verse as skillfully as any poet of the industrial era before or since.[3] Typically Tennyson, like Dickens, treats machines as animated yet inscrutable beings, mutant crosses between griffin and daemon. His engines, packet boats, and locomotives are varying species of an epic "machinery" that has been scaled down to idyllic gauge: at once technically servile and imaginatively predominant, they stand in impassive—and thus all the more impressive—attendance upon the human affairs they dwarf (Pitt 1962, 198). The point of Tennyson's forays into the industrial sublime is always to find a position, and a measure of verse, that will enable a domestic reception of industrial products as sheer phenomena (Hunt 1973,

194; Pattison 1979, 139). What he does not attempt, with the slate quarrying at the close of "The Golden Year" or with any other manifestation of modern technology, is to restore the technological product to its source in human invention; for to do so would be to raise issues of social initiative and responsibility that could not but divide the readership Tennyson wanted to conquer en masse. The Tennysonian idyll intends a reader who seeks impressions and consumes effects. Thus the blast enters "The Golden Year" as what "I heard," and as made by "them"; and its echoing report among the untroubled hills becomes a model for the reception of sound effects no polemical or explanatory position can corner. Tennyson's well-tempered outburst, a voice without a message, is designed to render, at a very high level of inclusiveness, unflappable music for a worried class on the make (Bayley 1980, 46).[4]

Reversing the countercurrent of his dramatic monologues, Tennyson the idyllist thus swathes narrative or polemical purpose in the folds of a textured description of the physical world, which brings individuals together at last on common ground: the ground at once of their shared corporeality and of their shared perspective on the things that matter most and will outlast them all. "Audley Court" (1842) shows with especial clarity how Tennyson resolves individual differences, or at least finesses them, in the lingua franca of the image. The poem tells how two friends rendezvous for a picnic, one of them a "farmer's son" and the other a man of independent means "having wherewithal" (74–75), but both scions of a newly emergent, partially leisured class. They discuss, among other things, "The four-field system, and the price of grain; / And struck upon the corn-laws, where we split, / And came again together on the king" (33–35). The king's touch always heals dissension in Tennyson's idylls, but here the truly sovereign power appears in the culminating lines, a fusion of natural and cultural details to form one pure image of gladness:

> but ere the night we rose
> And sauntered home beneath a moon, that, just
> In crescent, dimly rained about the leaf
> Twilights of airy silver, till we reached
> The limit of the hills; and as we sank
> From rock to rock upon the glooming quay,
> The town was hushed beneath us: lower down
> The bay was oily calm; the harbour-buoy,

> Sole star of phosphorescence in the calm,
> With one green sparkle ever and anon
> Dipt by itself, and we were glad at heart. (78–88)

Much of the secret contentment of this passage lies in syntactic and imagistic hints of a disturbance it nevertheless keeps well contained. "But ere the night we rose" murmurs of an urgency that "sauntered" then levels out; "The limit of the hills," "the glooming quay," the "hushed" town and "oily calm" bay arouse an expectancy that is curiously alleviated by the ease of the descent (through the text as through the landscape) in which each image marks a downward stage: from hills to graded rocks, to quay and town, to sea level, and at last to the grace note of the buoy freely dipping "by itself," a visible sign of unconstrained acquiescence amid the blessed silence.

Moon, gloom, rocks, harbor, twinkling light: we have met them all together before, in the passage from the close of "Ulysses" to which these lines form Tennyson's complementary idyllic undersong. To rise, to sink, to eye and thus to yield: at this settled margin all trace of the numinous is effaced, as is all distinction between natural and civic realms, between experience and desire, between the needs of self and of others—the kinds of distinction, in sum, on which a poem like "Ulysses" depends, with its uncanny and anything but communal "we." If there be prophecy abroad in this poem of deliberately diminished expectations, it concerns the gentlest and most welcome of imagined deaths: an acceptance of the natural and culturally specific gravity whereby the idyllic "we" gathers collective identity, through the unquestioning absorption of the bodily eye whose projected image winks back in final reassurance from the cradling harbor.

No deep moans round with many voices here. As surely as Tennyson's monologues voice a compelling extravagance, his idylls whisper a descriptive persuasion that the surface is enough. In the idylls the linearity of purpose—whether we look to the definition of its characters or to its narrative thrust—gets subordinated to the lineaments of scenery and absorbed into the mediate space of the public image. Tennyson's creation of public images in the idyllic mode involved his own public image as well, in the twentieth-century sense of that term, which attaches to Tennyson, the celebrity laureate, more justly than to any other poet in the language. If the greatest passages of the dramatic monologues were summits of soul-making (or, in their extremity, abysses of soul-unmaking), the idylls were methodically career-making works; and since each of these routes helps to define the other, an adequate account of Tennyson's creative life should map both of them in their divergence and intersection.

Before turning to the three leading idylls of 1842, we might remark in this connection that the generic contrast between monologues and idylls has an analogue in compositional history. If we oppose to the protracted revision and delayed release of "Tithonus" and "Tiresias" Tennyson's steady production of poems in the idyllic mode from the 1842 volumes on through his final decade, we may regard his career as the overlapping of two sometimes contradictory projects. The one was a lifelong and often submerged quest for communion with an unresponsive yet indubitable destiny, a quest that proceeded according to the now imperative, now listless mood of the spirit; the other was a professional program executed in the writer's workshop and delivered on schedule for publication.[5] The one, an idiosyncratic and heretical elaboration of hybrid lyrical modes, was published only erratically and, as it were, incidentally; the other exhibited an orthodox poet's progress from pastoral seclusion through georgic engagement toward epic scope and spokesmanship. At chief nodal points of Tennyson's career, in *The Princess, In Memoriam, Maud,* and *Idylls of the King,* these two projects converged, with inevitably mixed results; indeed, the problem of creative stamina often presented itself to Tennyson as the problem of finding a subject for poetry that would let the two concur. But in the *Poems* of 1842 the emphasis lay upon individual and mutually divergent texts. This chapter chooses for extended discussion the three very different idylls that came first in volume 2 of *Poems,* the volume in which Tennyson introduced his readers to the new work of his ten most fertile years. I privilege these three idylls in part because Tennyson did, and in part because they exhibit the range of ambition—generic ambition for the poet as craftsman, social ambition for the poet as spokesman—that Tennyson would be exploring further in the decades to come.

"The Gardener's Daughter": The Painted Shell

Whether or not Tennyson believed that *idyll* derived from the Greek *eidyllion* and meant "little picture," his idyllic practice locates itself so squarely in the tradition of the picturesque that it is fitting to begin with the poem of 1833–34 he called "The Gardener's Daughter; Or, The Pictures." The subtitle refers primarily to portraits that the unnamed narrator and his friend Eustace have painted of their respective sweethearts. But it might equally describe the poem's chief fare, the narrator's lovingly delineated memories of the bygone days when he first saw, courted, and won Rose, the gardener's daughter, whose likeness in words occurs at what Tennyson called "the central picture" (*PT*, 508), and the unveiling of whose portrait brings the poem to its conclusion. Like *The Lover's Tale*, "The Lady of Shalott," and "The Palace of Art," this poem is an album of verbal sketches; but unlike those 1832 texts, in which a gallery of images becomes an isolation booth, this one is relentlessly unruffled in its manner, aggressively "idyllic" in the now primary sense which that adjective first assumed in Victorian times (Hunt 1973, 182).

Tennyson would appear to have written "The Gardener's Daughter" as an earthly and amorous paradise that echoes his earlier texts in order to block their infernal direction. Significantly, he managed to do so only by keeping its narrator nameless, virtually featureless, and all but invisible either as a storyteller or as a principal in the bland story he tells. Indeed, all the characters here are filmy, transparent to each other as well as to the dumbfounded reader; and their foursquare love story is one long wish fulfillment, a holiday of hopes well met. Good storytelling and compelling character construction are evidently lost arts in Tennyson's idyllic paradise. But his studied banality in these areas serves to foreground descriptive word painting, which is anything but dull in "The Gardener's Daughter" and the idylls it introduces (Bayley 1980, 347).

The text is a tissue of equivalencies that repeatedly couples terms so as to prize the relationships between terms over any term in itself. These relationships frequently reduce to the simplest relationship of all, the pure identity of one term with another; and when they do not, they tend to harmony, complementarity, and balance (Rosenmeyer 1969, 47)—all forms of relationship that bear out the regime of a benevolent eros: "some law that holds in love" (9). The very opening line elides the difference between past and present—"This morning is the morning of the day / When I and Eustace from the city went" (1–2)—and this elision becomes the germ from which most of the other equivalencies of the text are generated (Hunt 1973, 191).[6] If time is a wheel and "this morning"

is the beginning of the past, then whole regions of recent history
may be factored out of the poem's mimesis of contemporary England. An industrially "humming" city and the bucolic garden of
a landed estate, for example, will lie within easy cultural and
geographic reach of each other, under the sway of "The windy
clanging of the minster clock" (35, 38); and gardeners' daughters
may mingle freely with a class of young townsmen who enjoy at
least sufficient leisure to study painting, spin out theories of art,
and engage in philosophical banter. If the morning of the narrative
present thus interpenetrates with the narrated past, then other
categorical boundaries are likely to give too: those between art
and nature, imagination and actuality, for example, or between
landscape and state of mind, place and person, or person and
person.[7]

At every opportunity Tennyson marries details to their opposites or complements. The opening passage continues with an
elaborate equilibration:

> I and he,
> Brothers in Art; a friendship so complete
> Portioned in halves between us, that we grew
> The fable of the city where we dwelt.   (3–6)

Cantabrigian in its biographical origins, this fabled city is manifestly Philadelphian in spirit, thanks largely to effects of redundancy that Tennyson contrived in reworking his early drafts
(T.Nbk. 15, fol. 13v). Not just brotherhood but friendship too,
and friendship portioned, and portioned in halves, and in halves
between them to boot: one begins to see double. Yet this is merely
the first of a series of systematic doublings. As the friends become
a "fable" or piece of communal art, so they turn their sweethearts
into works of art—and not, it seems, so that tensions between art
and life may be explored (as in Browning's coeval poem about an
unveiled portrait, "My Last Duchess"), but for the sake of the
idyllist's formal pleasures, "A certain miracle of symmetry, / A
miniature of loveliness" (11–12). After such introductions it is no
surprise when, a hundred lines later, having accompanied the narrator and Eustace to "a meadow slanting to the North," before
long we are told as if by narrative reflex that "The garden stretches
southward" (107, 114). What looks like scattered detail, the raw
stuff of realist mimesis, in fact enters this text by virtue of its part

in a pattern (Rannie 1912, 93; Rosenmeyer 1969, 47). The symmetry that holds here for direction holds elsewhere for locality ("Not wholly in the busy world, nor quite / Beyond it, blooms the garden that I love"; 33–34) and for the dynamics of personal relations: "neither self-possessed / Nor startled, but betwixt this mood and that, / Divided in a graceful quiet" (151–153). At the core of the text such symmetry provides the crowning touch for the central picture of Rose herself: "Half light, half shade, / She stood" (139–140). Tennyson's idyllic heaven makes room for little else *but* marriage; we are in the grip of a matchmaker gone wild (Nash 1972, 421).

The pervasive symmetry of this poem raises a suspicion that its obsessive mediations may be, like obsessions generally, remediations of some sort. What imbalance within the narrator requires these repeated affirmations of equilibrium? What purpose is the mechanical coupling device behind this text designed to serve? Since the pairings of "The Gardener's Daughter" are often explicitly ascribed to "the Master, Love, / A more ideal Artist he than all" (168–169; see also 24–28, 102–104), we might plausibly look for a slave to whom the master may be dialectically linked. And if we scan this highly conventional idyll, as our culture instructs us to do, for evidences of love's conventional antagonist death, we find our search rewarded at the conclusion, where the narrator's unveiling of the portrait precipitates a revelation that its subject, the gardener's daughter, is no more:

> Behold her there,
> As I beheld her ere she knew my heart,
> My first, last love; the idol of my youth,
> The darling of my manhood, and, alas!
> Now the most blessèd memory of mine age.   (269–273)

Tennyson's melodramatic finale obliges a reassessment of the entire poem in view of the pathos here displayed. "Alas!" betokens an irremediable loss; in a text where wording has manifestly gained ascendancy over referentiality, we have even more warrant than usual for pursuing the hint of Tennysonian wordplay and observing that "Alas!" arises in the text to mark the passing of a lass.

With this conclusion the idyll justifies itself, falling into place in terms that may suggest an overall approach to Tennyson's work in the picturesque mode. The network of internal correspondences in the idyllic narrative constitutes a text woven across an absence, a beautiful illusion designed to lie against a void. Hence the habitual shuttling between past and present tenses, as forecast in the opening line; and hence the habitual stop-and-start of the plot, most neatly elaborated in the isochronic "we went" of lines 3, 32, 74, and 106, all of them attempts to get beyond the same point in the story. Hence, too, the most puzzling passage of all, the narrator's one digression not into the picturesque but into a reflection on storytelling and its uses:

> Shall I cease here? Is this enough to say
> That my desire, like all strongest hopes,
> By its own energy fulfilled itself,
> Merged in completion? Would you learn at full
> How passion rose through circumstantial grades
> Beyond all grades developed? and indeed
> I had not stayed so long to tell you all,
> But while I mused came Memory with sad eyes,
> Holding the folded annals of my youth;
> And while I mused, Love with knit brows went by,
> And with a flying finger swept my lips,
> And spake, "Be wise: not easily forgiven
> Are those, who setting wide the doors that bar
> The secret bridal-chambers of the heart,
> Let in the day." Here, then, my words have end.   (231–245)

Since the narrator's words do not "have end" here but go on for another thirty lines, the point of the passage lies elsewhere, in its conversion of a question about where the story should end into a different question about the end of storytelling: Why should this story be told at all, and why in this fashion? The narrator's ambiguous explanation, "I had not stayed so long to tell you all"—whether "stayed" refers to his lingering over every minute circumstance of his courtship or to his postponing a full disclosure of its sequel—acknowledges that his narrative is governed by a holding pattern. The personifications of Memory as "Holding the folded annals of my youth" and of "Love with knit brows" suggest that the function of narrative in this idyll, much as in *The Lover's Tale*, is not to unfold objective events but to enfold their pathetic import against profanation. The story ends with the disclosure of a death; but the end of idyllic storytelling—less exposition than benign imposture—is to defend against this disclosure. The benevolent despotism of love's manifold couplings throughout the text, then, arises in reaction to the sullen counterforce of death that runs beneath the text, only to emerge at its bottom line.

In "The Gardener's Daughter," as so often in Tennyson, death is the mother of the picturesque. When we return to the poem's chief sources of interest, its descriptive set pieces, we find that they betray the mortal ancestry of the picturesque mode; they tell the truth that lies behind the artist's will to stay the losses of time. The poetic centerpiece, the picture of Rose, presents a study in chiaroscuro that flickers into an emblematic contest between life and death:

> For up the porch there grew an Eastern rose,
> That, flowering high, the last night's gale had caught,
> And blown across the walk. One arm aloft—
> Gowned in pure white, that fitted to the shape—
> Holding the bush, to fix it back, she stood,
> A single stream of all her soft brown hair
> Poured on one side: the shadow of the flowers
> Stole all the golden gloss, and, wavering
> Lovingly lower, trembled on her waist—
> Ah, happy shade—and still went wavering down,
> But, ere it touched a foot, that might have danced
> The greensward into greener circles, dipt,
> And mixed with shadows of the common ground!
> But the full day dwelt on her brows, and sunned
> Her violet eyes, and all her Hebe bloom,
> And doubled his own warmth against her lips,
> And on the bounteous wave of such a breast
> As never pencil drew. Half light, half shade,
> She stood, a sight to make an old man young.   (122–140)

Time's tempest having "blown" the rose, the gardener's daughter is discovered, clothed in virginal if somewhat seductively tailored white ("closefitted" in T.Nbk. 15), trying "to fix it back"; and the attempt of this fair daughter of earth to repair a minor ravage gathers additional force with our recognition that what is at stake for Rose is an emblem of herself. The bodily description that follows extends its emblematic defloration into a miniature narrative: "Lovingly" tender but undeterred, the amorous shadow "Stole all the golden gloss," "and still went wavering down."

If we recall the play of light and shadow over Aphrodite's figure in "Oenone," and recall from that poem the significance of Paris's mortalist choice of sexuality and death, we shall see whither tends this descriptive descent toward "shadows of the common ground!" We shall also appreciate the excitement behind the exclamation point and, with the "But" that immediately follows, the narrator's instant sublimation of that excitement, in a resolve to dwell on the bright side of the picture alone. This Rose is no goddess whose steps (again as in "Oenone") break the ground into blossom, but a living, which is to say a mortal, woman.[8] And it is precisely her mortality that creates her appeal. That is why her foot "might have danced / The greensward into greener circles," but in fact does not. Rather, the cooperating rivalry of eros and death, of which she is an embodiment and a reminder to the mortal who pictures her, makes her live with the different power to elicit a definitively human response: "Half light, half shade, / She stood, a sight to make an old man young." The narrator's apostrophic turn at the precise midpoint of the piece—"Ah, happy shade"—departs from the standard middle style of the idyll to register, through the pleasures of the voyeur, his own implication in the mix of desire and death that shadows his vision of Rose and makes it deeply please.

Tennyson's half-apologetic comment on this passage shows that he was proud of it: "The centre of the poem, that passage describing the girl, must be full and rich. The poem is so, to a fault, especially the descriptions of nature, for the lover is an artist, but, this being so, the central picture must hold its place."[9] Part of the poet's satisfaction emerges in the comparison between his own craft and the painter's: "such a breast / As never pencil drew." With this comparison Tennyson engages one of the principal classicizing conventions of his idyllic writing: *ekphrasis*, whereby an object of visual art is put into language. While we do not learn until the final lines of the poem that the description of Rose is a kind of *ekphrasis* (the narrator's translation into words of what he has already done in paint), we might well guess it from the elaborate play between image and narration that gives the description its life. A certain sisterly rivalry between the visual and verbal arts has typified ekphrastic poetry since Homer—and nowhere more insistently than in the Alexandrian tradition to which Tennyson's work in the idyll owes its most obvious debt.[10] Some such rivalry figures into the competition between pictorial space and descriptive time that inspires this passage and all the best of Tennyson's idyllic miniatures. Indeed, we might take the subtitle of this poem, "The Pictures," as an invitation to compare the painter's melodramatic apocalypse with the more subtly phased disclosures that are the prerogative of the descriptive poet. Pictures, we say, can narrate stories; Tennyson's idylls are very often stories that narrate pictures, both by stringing individual descriptions in diachronic series and by imparting to the individual descriptions a strong narrative direction.[11]

The description of Rose, a case in point, is extraordinarily rich in verbs, which first point out of pictured stasis into a layered past ("there grew," "had caught, / And blown," "Gowned") and an intended future ("to fix it back"), and which then animate the scene in the lines that follow. The hair is "Poured" in a temporal stream; the shadows steal, waver, and tremble into the slow motion of a Tennysonian cataract, until the temporal conjunction "ere" clinches the triumph of poetic time over pictorial space. In the additive symmetries of the last half-dozen lines, with their redundant doubling of the sun's warmth upon Rose's lips and breast—an effect achieved in revision (H.Nbk. 12, fols. 2–3)—the narrator attempts to still this moving picture, only to give all back to time once more with the tidal image of "the bounteous wave." Tennyson's artist-lover thus aims, like the woman he is describing, to arrest time, "to fix it back"; yet the aim these lovers share dissolves into the ground of their common entrapment in the web of time, sex, and death that sustains all of Tennyson's work in the idyll. The rose never is fixed back; Rose surrenders it instead, as a mute earnest of the conjugal bond that is to be spoken only later but that is drawn up here already, in descriptive writing, as the bond of mortality. In that surrender both principals are caught: she tongue-tied (156), he both speechless and rooted to the spot "statue-like" (158), their individual voices disappear in the voice of the older narrator who, now knowing the whole story, "stays so long to tell you all" through the oblique, plot-delaying yet truth-telling eloquence of a spoken picture.

The central picture is "full and rich," as Tennyson said, heavy with the inarticulate knowledge of doom that, mingling love and death in the profoundest of earthly marriages, dwells in the body of the idyllic text. As a principle of description, the oxymoronic marriage of love and death radiates from the portrait of the gardener's daughter to tinge the garden, the pastoral approaches to it, and even the busy world of the city; the several descriptive layers pick up the color scheme of the portrait and reinforce its constellation of symbols. Ricks's observation that "It is the garden, not the girl, that fires the poem" (1972, 100) records a valuable perception that Rose herself does not count for much.[12] But then neither does the garden: both the *locus amoenus* of this poem and its inmate matter because of the mix of vitality with fatality that they equivalently shadow forth.

Much as the gale has "caught" the emblematic rose, so the eloquent image of Rose has "rapt" its beholder (141), who as he lingers until nightfall amid the garden to take it in finds himself absorbed in turn by the mortal temporality it represents. The garden is both a common English place and a literary common-place: as "the gardener's daughter," Rose descends from Adam and Eve, and "that Eden where she dwelt" (187) becomes a topos that teaches the narrator his place in fallen time. This lesson recurs throughout the text in its praise of gentle process, the blessing of gradual time that is a cardinal feature of the Tennysonian idyll. From its first description the garden is associated with time's passage as specifically keyed to rituals of death and love, the "sound of funeral or of marriage bells; / And, sitting muffled in dark leaves, you hear / The windy clanging of the minster clock" (36–38). In "The Lady of Shalott," whose scenery of bower, stream, and city "The Gardener's Daughter" resumes (48–51), the conjunction of wedding and funeral took on the starkest possible aspect and reinforced the tragic divorce of country from town. Here, however, all is smoothed into idyllic equivalence like the "sliding season."

Upon returning from the garden to his city home the narrator spends a night of insomniac bliss, tranced to wakefulness by "The heavy clocks knolling the drowsy hours. / The drowsy hours, dispensers of all good, / O'er the mute city stole with folded wings" (180–182). When these angelic hours mature into personified months the effect is much the same:

> The daughters of the year,
> One after one, through that still garden passed;
> Each garlanded with her peculiar flower
> Danced into light, and died into the shade;
> And each in passing touched with some new grace

Or seemed to touch her, so that day by day,
Like one that never can be wholly known,
Her beauty grew.   (195–202)

The narrator insists on the processionality of time ("One after one," "day by day") in order to enjoy its lingering benediction; and what he most enjoys in this pageant of daughterhood, as the images of light, shade, and death remind us, is their perpetuation of the vision of mortal beauty that was originally revealed in his first long glimpse of the gardener's daughter as *virgo intacta*, yet "touched" by time.

In a later passage, as Rose and the narrator prepare to confess their love, the bells from the cathedral towers return: "from them clashed / The bells; we listened; with the time we played" (215–216). If the specific context of courtship and the momentary violence of "clashed" recall time's winged chariot and the linkage of sex with death in the *carpe diem* tradition, a passage like this one must give us pause. Yet its serene eros is entirely characteristic: the Tennysonian idyll, the locus of the poet's very best erotic writing, habitually neutralizes the urgency of persuasion and reverses the traditional attitude of literary lovers to time. Tennysonian lovers do not seize the day but are seized by it; cultivating the supreme seductiveness of quiet acceptance, they do not make passes but instead are made lovers by their submission to time in its irresistible passage (Conrad 1982, 529).

What is most remarkable about the blessing of time in this idyll, when it is compared either with the *carpe diem* tradition of classical poetry or with the more brazen Romantic tradition of lying against natural time altogether, is its utter elision of worry. The attitude of acceptance that frees the idyll from anxiety about time also appears to offer the idyllist an escape from a closely related malady, anxiety about poetic influence. Consider first the example of a passage quoted above: "sitting muffled in dark leaves, you hear / The windy clanging of the minster clock" (37–38). The narrator here receives the admonitions of death and time with his customary placidity, but no less customary is Tennyson's idyllic manner of receiving, and assimilating, its admonitory images from very different moments of Keats's "Ode to a Nightingale." In Keats an "embalmèd darkness," replete with "fast fading violets, covered up in leaves" (43–47), is the condition from which a word with

the force of "a bell / To toll me back" (71–72) awakens a conviction of solitary identity. Tennyson, however, hammers these an-
tipathetic images into sonorous sympathy with the music of
natural process. In this way his text achieves what we might think
of as an allusive version of the idyllic picturesque: an equivalence
with (and of) antecedent poetic images, which corresponds both
to the poem's obsessive benediction of the equable course of time
and to the larger structural and thematic equivalences informing
its narrative procedures.

A comparable effect occurs, again with allusive reference to
Keats's ode, some ten descriptive lines further on:

> The fields between
> Are dewy-fresh, browsed by deep-uddered kine,
> And all about the large lime feathers low,
> The lime a summer home of murmurous wings.   (44–47)

Keats, foreseeing from his ode's vernal perspective "The coming
musk-rose, full of dewy wine, / The murmurous haunt of flies on
summer eves" (49–50), imagines nature's yet-unborn ephemera,
the flies of summer, as already dead, and thus makes the place of
mortal voice a "haunt" (Pattison 1979, 162). The Tennysonian
idyll, with its contrary design to domesticate and unify voice, can
afford no place to such dark prophecy. Tennyson's "lime," therefore, while it seems to be precipitated by the reverberant consonance of the passage it echoes from the "Nightingale" ode,
transforms the Keatsian "haunt" into a "home." Through manipulation of the verbal surface, Tennyson contrives from discrepant Romantic materials a structure whose murmurous
homogeneity plays an essential role in the idyllic picturesque.

Just as essential, though, to the idyllic effect is the eeriness that
hovers in this description and many others like it. Our sense that
the glossy scene of fields, kine, lime, and wings promotes sheerly
linguistic over mimetic interests contributes to this effect. And
our awareness not of the things described, but of the coordinating
voice that describes them, returns us to the poem as *written* and
thereby to the problem of idyllic allusion. As the belated Tennyson
well knew, Romantic poesis is never the construction of a new
home from the ground up but always in part the occupation of
an echoing haunt. If the descriptions we have just examined lie
against the complexity of Keats's ode in the sense that they coun-

tervail it, they rely no less on that complexity as an otherness they exclude yet also are defined by. What attracts the narrator of "The Gardener's Daughter" to dally with scene after descriptive scene is an unspoken sense that "the garden that I love," and with it everything in the native landscape the garden centrally organizes, bespeaks the vision of mortality that his first vision of Rose has indelibly engraved. Just as this unspoken conviction suffuses the narrative and makes of its digressions revelations, so at the intertextual level the suppressed content of its allusions remains an evicted yet unexorcised ghost behind the scenery.

WE VERGE HERE upon a theory of idyllic allusiveness, which at least in Tennyson's case may be distinguished with some sharpness from the allusiveness of his major lyrics and dramatic monologues. All allusion is inherently selective and entails a dialectic of acceptance and exclusion; but where a poem like "Ulysses" wields its allusions as tools in an interpoetic argument that engages the prior text so as to adjust or refute or exceed it, allusiveness in the idyll presents itself as an exclusively formal affair that takes prior texts not to task but to bits. As an idyllist Tennyson assimilates an impressive variety of textual details from the past, but he does so by ignoring their original contexts and reassembling them in a mosaic that by design excludes any dissonance of sound, image, or mood (Rosenmeyer 1969, 53, 104; Nash 1972, 324; Pattison 1979, 20). Willfully blinkered in its anthological collage of images from earlier poems and selectively tone-deaf in its orchestration of their isolated echoes, idyllic allusion declines to acknowledge the otherness, the historical particularity, of its literary resources and treats them instead as atomized particles to be reworked on the terms strictly of formal craft (Peltason 1984a, 90).

Yet the study of allusion, which deals not in resemblances but in echoes and regards poetic craft not as an effected product but as an efficient scheme of production, perforce introduces into our reading just the diachronic dimension that the idyll's glossy patina is designed to repel. Through the loophole of allusion the picturesque text, which on its surface appears to resist exegesis on any but formal terms, and which rewards formal exegesis handsomely, can be read as a sign of the exclusions that produce it. The voices silenced by idyllic allusion constitute an abiding textual unconscious that—whether or not we postulate a corresponding psy-

chological unconscious in the narrator—infuses the superficial
beauties of the idyll with truths that furrow its surface and so-
phisticate its appeal. Tennyson's idyllic allusiveness, then, is not
simply but perversely naive. It is a device, furthermore, quite in
keeping with the deliberate naiveté of a learned idyllist who, in
his devotion to surface semblances, knew very well what he was
doing and how he was bringing a venerable minor tradition up
to date.

From its inception among the later classical poets the idyll was
a self-consciously belated genre. Seeking perfection at a time when
grandeur no longer seemed to lie within a modern writer's scope,
the idyllists of Alexandria dwelt on lesser episodes from saga and
heroic poetry; and they condensed and refigured the rhetorical
devices of the epic in the interest of a heightened precision of form,
an interest that has always served artistic latecomers (in English
poetry Jonson, Pope, Pound as well as Tennyson) as a prominent
compensation for shortage of matter. The pastoral mode in which
the Alexandrians chose to write acknowledged their vast distance
from the culture-founding epic texts to which their idylls methodically paid homage. At the same time, these classical idyllists'
interweaving of epic allusions with the urbanities of some pretty
courtly rustics shows that the green cabinet of the idyll was intended from the first to contain and further civilize the grander
energies of the literary past; to discipline the barbarity of epic while
capturing, in little, some measure of its power and importance.
We might say that this relation of idyll to epic, like the relation
of the descriptions in "The Gardener's Daughter" to the narrative
they occlude yet illustrate, gets resumed in the relation of any one
of its idyllic allusions to the more capacious prior text to which
it alludes, and whose force it aims to borrow through the peculiar
but consistent expedient of burying it.

While the idyllist's subliming art makes all disagreeables evap-
orate, the clouds engendered by that making persist to disturb its
precarious concords. This process probably appears most clearly
in "The Gardener's Daughter" when the narrator and Eustace
come upon that preeminent poetic topos, a chorus of birdsong:

> The steer forgot to graze,
> And, where the hedge-row cuts the pathway, stood,
> Leaning his horns into the neighbour field,

> And lowing to his fellows. From the woods
> Came voices of the well-contented doves.
> The lark could scarce get out his notes for joy,
> But shook his song together as he neared
> His happy home, the ground. To left and right,
> The cuckoo told his name to all the hills;
> The mellow ouzel fluted in the elm;
> The redcap whistled; and the nightingale
> Sang loud, as though he were the bird of day.   (84–95)

This parliament of fowls inspires in Eustace a question that establishes the bearing of the passage on Tennyson's poetics in general and on the designs of the idyll in particular: "Think you they sing / Like poets, from the vanity of song? / Or have they any sense of why they sing?" (98–100). Does the song of the birds, like the idyll it miniaturizes, display the "vanity" of pure form, or has it a content, "any sense"? Eustace's genteel advocacy of a formalist poetics seems instantly suspect, by reason of its very explicitness in the mouth of a painter with his own axe to grind. The narrator's somewhat indirect reply that the birds sing only from "love," which is "cause enough for praise" (104), seems little better—except insofar as it alerts us to the operation of the pathetic fallacy and leads us to exchange the question why birds sing for the question why men, especially these young men, so enjoy hearing them.

Birdsong is a mindless reflex, or at least a reflex not accessible to our minds; so in seeking to understand a text that repeatedly reads into the voices of birds "contentment," "joy," and "happiness," we need to look for a more humanly reflective content. We can find this content in the passage's systematic echoing of a flock of Romantic texts that take the hearing of birds as an occasion for the pitting of erotic and creative rapture against pensive human mortality. The vocal doves come to Tennyson from the opening stanzas of Wordsworth's "Resolution and Independence" (most apparently so in H.Nbk. 12 and Heath MS., where they are "self-contented"); the lark is Shelley's in "To a Skylark," by way of Wordsworth's later sonnet of the same name; and the echoing cuckoo is again Wordsworthian, from "To the Cuckoo," the bird poem that probably prompted Shelley's in the first place. The phrase "The redcap whistled" recalls—as Tennyson seems to have intended in substituting it for "The starling chittered" in his manuscript—Keats's whistling redbreast from the final stanza of "To Autumn." Finally, the inevitable nightingale descends from conversation poems by Coleridge and, of course, Keats's ode. Even the line on the melodious ouzel, which features a species not in the Romantic aviary and which has rightly caught critical ears as distinctively Tennysonian in its melody, owes something to that romantic comedy *A Midsummer Night's Dream*, where a translated Nick Bottom lows to his absconded fellows a ditty of birdsong beginning, "The woozel cock so black of hue" (III.i.112) and later with his colleague Flute performs a tragical interlude of young love and death.[13]

I adduce these sources summarily because that is what Tennyson does, shaking half a dozen Romantic songs together in an echoing text that simplifies each source through a radical truncation of what fails to suit the prevailing mood (Buckler 1980, 136). Loss, grief, despondency and madness form part, arguably the better part, of the Romantic poems I have named; but the purpose of this idyll is to dispel all such vapors in joyful unison. These lines offer a strained display of the partiality of idyllic allusion, and the strain shows at moments when the poetry buckles up as if in spite of itself. First, the passage images its own censorship in the oddly hapless happiness of the lark, who can "get out" his song, get it produced in the text, only by exchanging Romantic exaltation for domesticity and submitting to the demands of the choral ensemble: "The lark could scarce get out his notes for joy, / But shook his song together as he neared / His happy home, the ground." "But," the sign of disjunction, in Tennyson's idylls nearly always reveals some inner contradiction of the generic norm. Here the word splits the condition of "joy" from "the happy home" that by rights ought to be its synonym, with a violence further represented in the verb "shook": a surprisingly direct suggestion of the compulsion that tacitly supports the effects of idyll and that we properly acknowledge whenever we speak of its author's formal "mastery." More surprising still, of course, is the special guest appearance of the nightingale, flushed from his usual habitat in time and pressed into day service. Under such circumstances we may imagine that "the nightingale / Sang loud" in understandable alarm at somebody's tampering with the poetic-biological clock.[14]

Tennyson's denaturing of the Romantic nightingale and lark suggests that in order to be naturalized into the idyllic mode, in order to be "idyllized," prior texts must be idealized—but only incompletely, so that odd notes in the chorus, symptomatically constituting a textual return of the repressed, may serve as minor keys to the idyll's bland deceptions. The imperfectly suppressed content of the Romantic sources echoed in these lines provides much of the contentment they offer to their readers—whether aware of specific source texts or not—and especially to Eustace and the narrator as they innocently read the scene to begin with. The pain of the lover's loss and the artist's anxiety of belatedness have no place in the consciousness of these two young men; the same tacit, well-hedged communality makes such things unthinkable as makes their minds mutually transparent: "Lightly he laughed, as one that read my thought" (105). Nevertheless, what has no place in the superficies of idyll remains a subtextual support that is crucial to the idyllic effect. Written off in advance and consigned elsewhere, the painful events and feelings that the idyll works over form the basis of its sophisticated enjoyment.

The craft of the idyll, then, rides on a network of suppressions. Its narrative terminates in the disclosure of a grief that may be seen to have darkened its graceful symmetries and roseate insistences all along, and indeed to have motivated them. The temporality of its descriptions undercuts the patent attempt to fix the past into picturesque snapshots; likewise, its rendition of the course of time as one melodic accord relies on a discordant awareness of loss and death. In its allusive practice, too, the idyll's studied ignorance of the antecedent works that it plunders functions as a mode of repression, converting pretexts into subtexts that produce symptomatic disturbances in the poetic surface. T. S. Eliot's dictum that "Tennyson's surface is intimate with his depths" (295) has particular application to the idyllic mode, for it is just this conspiracy between a superficial articulation and an unspoken latency that gives "The Gardener's Daughter" and its successors their surprising power. As a class they represent a superb artificer's most manifestly artificial achievements, precious to the eye and fragile to the touch. Tap these hollow pieces, though, hold these painted shells to the ear, and they resound with the suggestive, "full and rich" force of what they do not say (Peltason 1984a, 92).

Here, in just this reverberating space between surface and depths, lies a clue to the idylls' mimesis of contemporary life, both for their immediate audience and for us, who perforce read Ten-

nyson's texts as colored by the history of their reception. The
domestic idylls so manifestly take up into pleasing artifice details
from contemporary English life during the early decades of the
nineteenth century that we cannot help seeing as the products of
artifice what the surface and temper of the idyll present as the
most natural things in the world (Pitt 1962, 133). What we encounter throughout the teeming descriptions of this idyllic romance is not nature but, *pace* Polixenes, a nature that art makes;
the "nature" itself is culture. The majority of Tennyson's growing
readership were surely content to take his cosmetic nature at face
value, and his steady production of idylls across the decades suggests that he was content to let them continue to do so. But more
enlightened readers very quickly understood how he had fashioned
the classical idyll into a self-consciously modern poetic form. Thus
in the fourth chapter of Elizabeth Gaskell's *Cranford*, the stoutly
admirable but old-fashioned yeoman Thomas Holbrook catechizes
Mary Smith apropos of a line from "The Gardener's Daughter"
that he admires but does not fully understand:

> "Now, what colour are ash-buds in March?"
> Is the man going mad? thought I. He is very like Don Quixote.
> "What colour are they, I say?" repeated he, vehemently.
> "I am sure I don't know, sir," said I, with the meekness of
> ignorance.
> "I knew you didn't. No more did I—an old fool that I am!—till
> this young man comes and tells me. Black as ash-buds in March.
> And I've lived all my life in the country; more shame for me not
> to know. Black: they are jet-black, madam." And he went off again,
> swinging along to the music of some rhyme he had got hold of.[15]

Holbrook gets hold of a rhyme and prizes a line for its botanical
exactitude, as if the descriptive power of the poet were merely a
function of accurate transcription from nature (Nash 1975, 338).
But Holbrook's enthusiasm seems misplaced, in view of the way
he misquotes the line he refers to and disregards its context. As
we can see by comparing "More black than ashbuds in the front
of March" (28) with Holbrook's portable field-guide version,
"Black as ash-buds in March," in Tennyson the blackness of ash
buds plays into a highly wrought metaphorical comparison between the face in a painting and the face of a season, neither of
course actually a face at all. Furthermore, if the buds of ash trees
are indeed "jet-black," as Holbrook says, then Tennyson's hy-

perbolic comparative "More black" calls into question the very
powers of observation Holbrook means to praise. And if its rhetorical context denatures the line, its syntactic place does so even
more explicitly, for Tennyson's narrator is asserting at this point
that the beauty of the portrait Eustace has painted proceeds not
from accurate observation of the subject but from its erotic
idealization.[16]

In thus mistaking effects of artifice for natural facts, Holbrook's
response represents a common reading that still has proponents
today but that there is good reason to believe Gaskell, herself no
mean idyllist, did not share. For *Cranford*, with its gentle but
searching anatomy of a society on the outskirts of industrial transition, furnishes grounds for putting into a historical context Holbrook's neglect of a poetic one. Holbrook mistakes culture for
nature because his position as a yeoman, a freeholding farmer of
an independent yet vanishing English class, commits him to belief
in an organic, unmediated relation to an uncontaminated "natural"
order. Besides, having in his youth courted Matty Jenkyns but
lost her to the demands of a societal decorum that *Cranford* shows
to be outmoded, Holbrook is predisposed to read the story "The
Gardener's Daughter" tells as a triumph of unadulterated feeling,
a story that fulfills his own balked desires and confirms his sense
of their natural fitness. Holbrook's fond misprision of the line on
the ash buds thus finds a place in a consistent and historically
situated reading of "The Gardener's Daughter": a reading that
Tennyson's narrator encourages (he being, we may suppose,
roughly Holbrook's contemporary) but that Tennyson's text,
along with Gaskell's acute response, should make us question.

A THOROUGH QUESTIONING of the "natural" premises of this idyll
should also prompt us to reassess the poem's equilibration between
the master forces of love and death. The pearls of beauty and
wisdom this poem comprises are manifestly of the cultured sort,
and as cultural artifacts they disclose an implicit politics. This
politics structures, among other things, the relationship between
the central pair of lovers—precisely the sort of relationship that
Victorian poets and novelists took such pains to insulate, in various
forms of the domestic idyll, against erosion by the environing
currents of social life. In Tennyson, as perhaps in all the best
Victorian writers, this implicit politics of personal relations appears

most strikingly at those moments we recognize as "sentimental," for it is there that the conventions of feeling are least subject to examination and can exert their influence most openly.[17] Near the climax of the story, the narrator attends the wedding of Eustace to Juliet; and having heard Eustace's "deep 'I will,' / Breathed, like the covenant of a God" (203–204), he goes on to find Rose in the garden and to stage there an exchange of vows that is less institutional than the wedding he has left but no whit less conventional. Indeed, this private ceremony yields the poem's most sentimental passage:

> Then, in that time and place, I spoke to her,
> Requiring, though I knew it was mine own,
> Yet for the pleasure that I took to hear,
> Requiring at her hand the greatest gift,
> A woman's heart, the heart of her I loved;
> And in that time and place she answered me,
> And in the compass of three little words,
> More musical than ever came in one,
> The silver fragments of a broken voice,
> Made me most happy, faltering, "I am thine."   (221–230)

As with her earlier gift of the rose, Rose gives herself by declaring herself already given. Her faltering curiously undermines the resolute promise of the last voice we have heard quoted, Eustace's deep "I will," by delving to that which is, an authority deeper than the performative will. "I am thine"—as opposed, say, to "Yes"—is an utterance that makes the narrator "most happy" because, as the one speech of Rose's his narrative incorporates, it aligns her feelings both referentially and musically with the "compass" of the temporal process to which she has belonged since his first glimpse of her.

So, at any rate, runs the narrator's account of his bliss; within that account, however, we may read another story. "I am thine": Rose's confession of love asserts not her pure being but her being possessed, and she submits not to a neutrally temporal process but to a process that is already cultural, instinct as much with sexual politics as with biological drive. However we respond at the vantage of a century and a half to Rose's faltering reply to her lover's reiterated "requirings"—the compulsive sentimentality of the scene will strike most modern readers as unsavory and some as downright offensive—the point is that she responds with "A woman's heart," which of course denotes not a bodily organ but a structure of feeling dictated by social definitions of a woman's place in a man's world, whether as gardener's daughter or as painter's beloved. We learn almost nothing of Rose's personal feelings at this or indeed at any other moment; the narrator instead consistently represents her as an icon of womanhood, a fair daughter of Eve fostered in the demiparadise of an idealized English here and now. But even this slender knowledge of Rose's place suffices to plant her in history: her status not just as Woman but as the flower of English femininity makes her perfect meekness a historical phenomenon comprehensible in terms of gender and class politics. As an Englishwoman of the early nineteenth century her surrender to the inevitable is, inevitably, surrender to male dominion; in faltering toward her foregone conclusion "I am thine," Rose submits to "the pleasure" of a man (Pattison 1979, 70).

At the same time, lest we overplay an idyllic melodrama of victimage and villainy, it is important to observe that the narrator, in taking pleasure "at her hand," submits as well to the role his culture prescribes for a man. The emphasis in this apparently spontaneous yet highly ritualized mutual confession lies less on what the narrator demands of Rose than on what the scene, here a sheerly cultural scene stripped of the idyll's usual nature imagery, demands of them both. That is why the narrator "requires" Rose's confession, "though I knew it was mine own." Her confession is also his; and the words she speaks for them both are strictly speaking superfluous, since they are predicated by the logic of the historical script: "Then, in that time and place, I spoke to her"; "And in that time and place she answered me."[18] The narrator, prototypically naive idyllist that he is, apprehends in formal, "musical" terms a pleasure that the reader can comprehend as on one level natural or cosmic, in the manner of Holbrook—lovers' shared submission to a natural, temporal order that is bigger than the both of them—and on another level historical, by virtue of its place in a political ordinance so fundamental that it goes unsaid.

Cultural context surrounds the couple with a force like nature's, and its unresisted victory exacts a tributary note of capitulation that represents them both but that the Victorian scene assigns, naturally, to the woman's part: "silver fragments of a broken voice." That the man's part, too, required a broken voice, despite prevailing Victorian norms of muscular and capable masculinity,

is an insight Tennyson spent some of his best energies making
artistically accessible. His series of early girl poems from "Mariana" to "Oenone" had provided one means of approach to an
androgynous ideal; others were to be provided later with the role
reversals of *The Princess* and the barely controlled hysteria of the
male speaker in *Maud*, during recitations of which Tennyson's
own voice would frequently break down.[19]

In the more modestly decorous "Gardener's Daughter" our
manly narrator maintains a stiff upper lip, but does so through a
process of suppression that various narrative, descriptive, and allusive breakdowns reveal behind the idyll's genteel composure.
For one last, historically specific illustration of the breaks this text
papers over, consider the narrative conclusion:

> Might I not tell
> Of difference, reconcilement, pledges given,
> And vows, where there was never need of vows,
> And kisses, where the heart on one wild leap
> Hung tranced from all pulsation, as above
> The heavens between their fairy fleeces pale
> Sowed all their mystic gulfs with fleeting stars;
> Or while the balmy glooming, crescent-lit,
> Spread the light haze along the river-shores,
> And in the hollows; or as once we met
> Unheedful, though beneath a whispering rain
> Night slid down one long stream of sighing wind,
> And in her bosom bore the baby, Sleep.   (251–263)

What events does this passage describe? Or, to take the hint of its
initial hemistich: What events does this passage so describe as to
avoid narrating them? We cannot be certain, but the topic of sexual
passion invites the imagination down an awfully methodical prim-
rose path. From stupendous, heart-stopping kisses the passage
leaps to a celestial insemination where the heavens "Sowed all
their mystic gulfs with fleeting stars"; this sublime and arguably
sublimated image then appears more gently veiled in the spreading
of "the light haze" into earthly "hollows"; at last a disturbingly
"Unheedful" rendezvous issues syntactically, if not causally, in a
sliding sigh that bears "the baby, Sleep" (Sinfield 1976a, 467;
Timko 1978, 4).[20] To be sure, this baby is a poetical conceit, but
the preceding images may make us wonder whether the text has
not thus conceived a figurative baby because Rose conceived a

human one first. Once we entertain this possibility, the idyllic suppression of social context assumes its most sinister aspect: the introductory "pledges given, / And vows, where there was never need of vows" lose the merely formal look of grace notes and become instead instruments of a seduction plot, the social implications of which summon back with fresh urgency the suppressed historical context of the idyll. If the fruits of the lovers' trysts included an "unheedful" pregnancy, then public and not private "vows" were just what Rose did need (Croker 1833, 72; Ford 1977, 43).

It is important to tread lightly here: I do not advance a scenario of infatuation, seduction, pregnancy, abandonment, and early death (in childbirth?), as if these constitute the real but intolerable truth Tennyson's narrator confesses out of an obscure guilt. I do, however, point to the narrative occlusion of just those social facts about which this passage incites curiosity.[11] According to the facts the narrator makes available, the course of true love never ran smoother than during the hours he spent with Rose. But the subliminal suggestiveness with which those facts are reported lets us see once again how the blessing of idyllic time serves to sanction the extraordinary intercourse of a gardener's daughter with a prosperous young bourgeois. The neutral surface of the poem does all it can to make us forget a political circumstance it is worth the effort of remembering: Rose and the narrator represent the two social classes and walks of life—based, respectively, on "Murmurous" rural agriculture and "humming" urban industrialization—whose emergent antagonism lay at the heart of English social awareness circa 1832.

Tennyson began work on this first English idyll in the year of the first Reform Bill, and both the poetic and the parliamentary text may be regarded as structures of compromise directed at the containment of a national conflict to which the poet, an unacknowledged legislator with indubitably national ambitions, was beginning to address himself. ("Might I not tell / Of difference, reconcilement, pledges given?") Tennyson's maiden idyll addressed the simmering passions of a national life by reconciling differences under the chaperonage of a cosmic process, which achieves its power to oversee historically constituted conflicts by simply overlooking those facts of the story that might count as matters of historical fact as well (Bayley 1978, 247). But that elegant idyllic negligence, for all its intricacy of surface texture, becomes transparent to an analysis of its historical content; the same dialectic whereby the narrative, descriptive, and allusive artifices of this text reveal what they suppress also produces a surprising historical pertinence.

Such pertinence would have surprised no one more than Tennyson himself.[22] His career-long uncertainty as to the ultimate sources and effects of his gift—secrets one sometimes suspects he hid from himself in order to keep writing—makes the ever-shaky identification of poetic meaning with poet's intention in his case more than usually problematic. Still, since form so manifestly has the upper hand in the text of "The Gardener's Daughter," we may suppose that form was uppermost in the compositional process as well. From extant manuscripts and other relevant records it appears that Tennyson approached this first idyll as an exercise principally in technique; most of his draft revisions concern problems of harmony, integration, and concision. In this the poet resembles his narrator: the most important compositional function of the artist who tells the story of the gardener's daughter may have been to let Tennyson relax the referential obligations of too strictly contemporary a mimesis and to enfranchise the formal imagination instead (Rosenmeyer 1969, 192).

Yet the very purity of the poet's technical focus would seem to have had thematic consequences, not only for this idyll but for the many that followed. Tennyson's habitual sense of form as an achieved reconciliation of opposites—a sense apparently instinctive with him and surely reinforced by his association with the young Coleridgeans at Cambridge—required for its satisfaction plots that led from conflict to resolution. The story in a Tennysonian idyll can celebrate reunion, a marriage of minds if not an actual marriage in the classic comic mode ("Audley Court"); or it can give rein to that strongly pathetic species of tragic vision that ends in a good death ("Enoch Arden") or its inward equivalent, resigned acceptance of a hard but irresistible order of things ("Edwin Morris"). Or it can offer a bittersweet medley of both sorts of plot. "The Gardener's Daughter" incorporates, as a good generic prototype should, more than a hint of both; and its obsessive will to reconcile everything it touches makes clear what is the essential generic requirement: the idyll must round its story to as full a closure as possible and must tuck loose ends well out of sight.

A prerequisite to this formal resolution was, of course, some antecedent conflict; and Tennyson's decision to write idylls that rendered modern life led him to seek his subjects in topics of contemporary debate (Hunt 1973, 181). The 1842 idylls and, a few years later, "The Golden Year" center on the struggle for control over England's future between bourgeois industrial interests and the landed aristocracy; *The Princess* grafts upon this issue the Victorian Woman Question; "Enoch Arden" and *Idylls of the King* deal in different ways with the privileges and sorrows of empire. There is no denying that Tennyson wrote about such subjects because as a Victorian man he was involved with them in historical as well as emotional ways; but he also, and I think primarily, chose such subjects because they gave him conflicts of general public interest that he could resolve in the therapies of verse. In assessing Tennyson's handling of contemporary issues, if we are not to be disappointed for the wrong reasons, we need to remember the priority of formal to thematic considerations in the poet's own approach. Tennyson did not succeed in working central conflicts of the Victorian era through to resolutions that will withstand a rigorous twentieth-century analysis. Of course not: Tennyson the idyllist never works contemporary conflicts through to resolution but always works them over into an art that, "topical" in a double sense, converts current issues into smooth surfaces (Culler 1977, 128; Sedgwick 1985).

That the "actual," historically contextualized story of the gardener's daughter goes untold in "The Gardener's Daughter" is a small but noteworthy fact of literary history, a significant introductory episode in the story of Tennyson's endeavors in contemporary mimesis, a story deserving a prominent place in the history of the Victorian imagination that we are slowly learning to write, and that we shall write the more adequately for focusing on the means of imaginative representation rather than on some alleged (and more often than not prematurely hypostatized) object of representation. The pronounced formal emphasis of the idyll, and the relation between its formalism and its latent but quite visible politics, make this genre an excellent training ground for a criticism that aspires to be at once literary and historical. Few of us would call ourselves Victorian in makeup or outlook; yet we are now far enough from Victorian conventions to confess that we stand with one foot planted in an ideology that is in some way Victorian, and that often serves as the home base from which we step out into our several modernities. This situation is not the dilemma but the privilege of Victorian studies today: our mingled complicity and disaffection with the values of the Tennysonian idyll provides our special charter for understanding how the idyll works. It requires for the perfection of its microcosmic miniatures the subordination of all voices—those of individual character, of literary history, and of contemporary history—to a picturesque vision that, through such subordination, presents itself as authoritative and ultimate.

Transmuting contradictions to complements where he can, excluding them as heterogeneous where he cannot, Tennyson the idyllist presents as mirrors of the mighty world what are in effect patterned responses to the demands of a form—a form that must have held great allure for a poet so fond of finish, yet also so skeptical in intellectual matters. Committing himself to the rendition of an actuality he knew he was far from comprehending, with an audacity commensurate to his bewilderment Tennyson gathered his formidable resources about him, made a heterocosmic realm, and reigned, in the sovereignty of style and with that alien majesty his public found most congenial. Tennyson was so scrupulously attentive to the demands of technique that the historical subject matter his idylls technically subordinated may be said to have had its way with him. The domestic idyll came to Tennyson an imperious genre; thanks to the way his formal preoccupations conspired with his ambitions to become a national poet, it left his hands an imperialist genre. In that sense, all this master's idylls were idylls of the king.

"Dora": Sacrifice to the Idyll

One comes with a shock from the baroque stylishness of "The Gardener's Daughter" to the severity of "Dora," the next English idyll Tennyson was to complete to his satisfaction (Shannon 1952, 62). Whereas the former describes as much and narrates as little as it can, the latter does just the reverse. As if in flight from ornament, "Dora" binds the picturesque muse to a strict narrative regimen that, by the poet's own account, cost him more than usual pains to follow (*Memoir*, I, 196). The results, nevertheless, are remarkably successful on their own and also valuable in proving Tennyson's characteristic opulence an effect deliberately sought and not an unbreakable habit. The relative emphases given to action and ambience, direction and digression, could hardly be more complementary than they are in "The Gardener's Daughter" and "Dora." Indeed, the two poems seem so methodically antithetical that a doubt arises whether idyllic wealth and idyllic thrift may not be but two perspectives on the same picture of human options and limits.

In order to grasp the underlying similarities that make both poems Tennysonian idylls, consider how "Dora" differs from the idyllic prototype. The most obvious difference is style. A line like "A labourer's daughter, Mary Morrison" (38) displays a pedestrian prosiness quite alien to the indulgent stroll of "The Gardener's Daughter."[23] Where the style of the earlier idyll luxuriates in a meandering that becomes the principal object of interpretation, the unpretentious style of its successor clearly carries different instructions. The use of verbal repetition in the lines that open the two poems underscores this distinction: "This morning is the morning of the day / When I and Eustace from the city went"; "With farmer Allan at the farm abode / William and Dora." In "The Gardener's Daughter" the overlay of narrative and narrated "mornings" alerts us to the manipulative presence of the teller, but in "Dora" we move at once into circumstantial character relationships deemed sufficiently important to warrant the flat-footed iteration of "farmer" and "farm."

In contrast to the mobile bourgeois we meet in the earlier idyll, from the start farmer Allan is put in his place, and his son William and niece Dora are first known as relations by their standing with him there. Though as a freeholder Allan owns the land, the position of ownership exerts an abiding claim on him as well, which in one sense constitutes the point of the tale. The apparent redundancy of "at the farm," instead of some specification of a particular place or time, has the further effect of removing the tale from individual to general reference. Just as "farmer Allan" (unlike, say, the proper name "Allan Farmer") sets the idyll's general property relations, so "the farm" is a rural topos, a generic term establishing the traditional proprieties of parable or fable. Unlike the present-tense "Gardener's Daughter," "Dora" is not only cast in the past tense, with the comforts and constraints Tennyson vested in the pastness of the past; it also explicitly presents itself as old-fashioned. That line on Mary Morrison is so bald because, in such an old-fashioned tale, Mary's status as a laborer's daughter provides the one characterizing fact, the one line on her place, that we need to know her by.

"Dora" comes to us, then, in a narrative, as opposed to a narrator's, style. Narratorial self-presentation yields to the strait and narrow story itself, which eschews alike scene painting, physical description of its characters, and rendition of their inner lives, subordinating all to plot. The biblical flavor to which readers of "Dora" since Carlyle have responded arises in part from Tennyson's extraordinary stringency with adjectival and adverbial forms (*Memoir*, I, 217; Buckley 1960, 80; Fredeman 1972, 369). The descriptive modifiers that were this poet's stock in trade usually set off persons and objects so as to endow them with an independent interest—a feature of Tennyson's art that the sparseness of this text lets us appreciate. Here such independence from the plot, whether in characters or descriptions, would jar both ethically and aesthetically. Manifestly biblical in its valorization of self-sacrifice against the law of personal will, of mutual forgiveness against patriarchal right, and of a meekness that inherits the earth, "Dora" is no less biblical in the spare simplicity of its telling.

These moral and formal features are more than a matter of happy coincidence. "Dora" is that rare thing in the work of Tennyson, a poem that endorses action, though not without the duly acknowledged imposition of a surcharge. In accordance with what seems a Tennysonian law of conservation, the ascendancy of action is purchased by taxing character into submission (Mackail 1926, 221–222). Dora's capacity to initiate a plot of familial reunion and carry it through attests, albeit in strictly qualified fashion, to the efficacy of human deeds and to the ability of characters to act decisively upon one another. Both are matters of common testimony in world literature, but they occur as seldom in the Tennysonian corpus as does this idyll's lean style. Restricting itself to the recounting of actions, the narrative economy of "Dora" treats even speech as a species of action. Despite a high proportion of dialogue, the characters speak not to reveal themselves but to advance the plot; their language of statement and persuasion is as forthright as that of the narrative. Even the one interior monologue, Dora's curt "It cannot be: my uncle's mind will change!" (45), reports not deliberation but resolution; and in brief compass it forecasts the larger subsequent action. If the characters in this antique-seeming fable strike us as less than fully realized, that is because they are not modern, not self-conscious characters; and they are not self-conscious because they have, properly speaking, no selves to reflect upon. Rather, they have and declare positions: knowing their places, they so speak and act as to remind one another what those places are, with the shared aim of preserving the familial hierarchy that is this idyll's major principle of order (Preyer 1966, 336; Kissane 1970, 93). Tennyson's strongly directed and descriptively stingy narrative keeps his characters agents in a family romance that wholly defines them.

The operation of this old-fashioned storytelling—we might call it "Doric"—is conveniently schematized in the recurrence of the phrase "for the sake of." Versions of this phrase, like other key terms ("hard," "broken," "meek") appear often enough in "Dora" to accumulate some of the formulaic authority we attribute to ancient texts, and the old English word *sake*, associated with ideas of guilt, moral claim, and primitive justice generally, contributes to the archaic effect. But beyond this, the sequence in which characters act, or exhort others to act, "for" or "for the sake of" someone else provides a synopsis of the idyllic action and conveys much of its ethos. Having quarreled long ago with his brother, farmer Allan informs his own son William that "for his sake I bred / His daughter Dora" (17–18). An old family rift has thus found healing restitution in an action performed for the sake of the forsaken one; and the pattern here established shapes the entire plot. Allan instructs William to marry Dora—"take her for your wife" (18)—and explains that "in my time a father's word was law, / And so it shall be now for me" (25–26). William, however, refuses to live by the old law and marry for his father's sake, and the "harsh ways" he soon adopts toward Dora repeat in the younger generation the "hard words" of the old fraternal rupture (16, 33). This pattern is fulfilled with William's consequent estrangement from the family, his hasty wedding with Mary Morrison, and, after a hard and foreshortened space of married life and the birth of a son, William's untimely and isolated death.

On the heels of this latest forsaking, the meek Dora goes into action and performs her work of atonement. As she tells Mary,

> it was all through me
> This evil came on William at the first.

> But Mary, for the sake of him that's gone,
> And for your sake, the woman that he chose,
> And for this orphan, I am come to you.   (58–62)

Dora arranges to take the child of William and Mary to the fields, where Allan may see him "And bless him for the sake of him that's gone" (68). The formula Dora here repeats in her address to Mary will return verbatim in her petition to Allan: "Do with me as you will, but take the child, / And bless him for the sake of him that's gone!" (91–92). Although Allan consents to adopt his grandchild, he resists Dora's maneuvering ("I see it is a trick"; 93) and reinvokes a patriarch's right:

> You knew my word was law, and yet you dared
> To slight it. Well—for I will take the boy;
> But go you hence, and never see me more.   (96–98)

Allan's anomalous "for"—an idiomatic detail that stands out from the chaste diction of this text—may be shorthand for the dialectic of forsaking and compensatory for-saking that is by this stage well in place. Still, according to the covenant Allan embodies, the price of adopting his grandson for his son's sake is a fresh forsaking of his adopted daughter Dora, which now in turn elicits from Mary a new initiative on Dora's behalf. In the last scene of the poem Mary returns with Dora to Allan's farm and proposes that the new arrangement be canceled:

> O Father!—if you let me call you so—
> I never came a-begging for myself,
> Or William, or this child; but now I come
> For Dora: take her back; she loves you well.   (137–140)

Mary's proposal to exchange the child again for Dora, buttressed by her remembrance of William's deathbed blessing of his father, finally suffices to break the old man's will and with it the old law of retribution: "all at once the old man burst in sobs" (155), "And all the man was broken with remorse" (161); and a new order of mutual forgiveness is ratified in kisses.

Thanks largely to the discipline of its style, "Dora" is a more genuinely moving story than my précis makes it out to be. Certainly its staying power across the years exceeds that of Tennyson's source, Mary Russell Mitford's first-person vignette "Dora Creswell" from *Our Village* (1825), a text as prettily cluttered as "Dora" is direct, and in its way more like "The Gardener's Daughter" than "Dora." There nevertheless remains something coldly calculated about Tennyson's idyll; and it is the quality of its exercise in abstraction, a structural corollary to the Doric style, that a skeleton summary like the one offered above can illuminate.[24] Dora's four-stage journey around the family, reiterated in the multiple transfer of her little cousin, smacks of an economic exchange, a circulation of goods that sits uneasily with the distribution of quite different "goods"—affection and mercy as springs of conduct—that Dora effects within the family. Dora's name means "gift"; and though she is both generous in herself and the cause of generosity in others, the idyll's conclusive ethos of loving forgiveness is soured by a disjunctive note in its final lines: "as years / Went forward, Mary took another mate: / But Dora lived unmarried till her death" (165–167). Superfluous to the fable in one sense, in another this footnote registers a tough honesty. Dora is taken in at last by the broken family she has reunited, but then she has been taken in by them all along, adopted yet in the same stroke adapted to their needs, which have provided her unique means of definition.

This fate is less a psychological than a narrative phenomenon. In another author's hands the connection between ethical affect and economic fact would have prompted some reflection on the consequences, for Dora's own marital prospects, of her restoring a male heir to the fold. But "Dora" takes no more interest in characters' inner life, or in that life-beyond-plot regularly conveyed by Victorian novels, than any of Tennyson's idylls do: its heroine is kept a spinster not by her own choice, nor by the system of primogeniture, but by the economy of idyllic action. The closure of the tale, its satisfactory solution of the calculus of forsaking, forecloses Dora's future. Having once played out her role as orphaned interloper and go-between, Dora finds her narrative options exhausted and herself installed permanently as an unattached angel in the house. A pattern of feminine self-sacrifice, she becomes herself only by living up to her name and giving her self away to her relations. The final line thus justifies simultaneously the formal organization of the poem and its morality. A blessing to her family, Dora becomes as well a sacrifice to the idyll.[25]

In this regard Dora's lot is not unique but typical. The plot takes ascendancy over the other characters too, each of whom ends up in the place dictated by mutually reinforcing familial and narrative structures. Mary finally matters, in the patriarchal terms that count, as a consort for men and a vessel for heirs: hence the propriety of her eventually attracting "another mate"—and, perhaps, of the masculine surname "Morrison," which Tennyson gave her in place of the gender-free "Hay" she had enjoyed in Mitford. Of course the subservience of such women as Dora and Mary obeys conventions that are at once literary and cultural. But, with a consistency that earns respect for Tennyson's idyllic vision of doom, male principals no less than female fall under the idyll's totalizing dominion. The grandson functions, like Dora, primarily as a token in the pattern of exchanges that articulates the family system; and when the boy does exhibit a will of his own, it plays into that system. Upon being transferred from Dora's into Allan's hands, the child "cried aloud / And struggled hard" (99–100), confirming a family resemblance to his hard-willed sires. Shortly thereafter, over the shoulders of Mary and Dora we see grandfather and grandson reconciled over an icon of lineage so firmly described by this generally nondescriptive text that one critic calls it "a sacred object" (Hair 1981, 52):

> they peeped, and saw
> The boy set up betwixt his grandsire's knees,
> Who thrust him in the hollows of his arm,
> And clapt him on the hands and on the cheeks,
> Like one that loved him: and the lad stretched out
> And babbled for the golden seal, that hung
> From Allan's watch, and sparkled by the fire.   (127–133)

Note again the ubiquitous particle "for." The boy not only reaches a hand through time to catch his own far-off interest, but in babbling *for* "the golden seal" he learns the dialect of his tribe. This vignette furnishes a nearly mythic instance of the various speakings-for that motivate the story, since all the family members who speak for others find themselves already spoken for, by the family relationships in the name of which they speak. The heir is known by the heirloom, and the golden seal proleptically seals the plot. If the pictorial perspective that opens here also marks Allan as an heir in his own place, we can see Allan's imminent peripety: a conversion from forsaking to forgiving, which affirms his deepest values and supersedes autonomous selfhood by appointed familial role. Not "my word" but "a Father's word" is ultimately law, the binding logos of idyllic completion. In the playing out of its self-contained logic, the plot gives a retroactive blessing to Dora's minimal intervention: "It cannot be: my uncle's mind will change" turns out to have been the murmur of a niece who has always "felt her uncle's will in all" (5) and who, in her meek adoration of the household gods, has known Allan's mind better than Allan has known it himself.

The subordination of character to plot pattern in "Dora," which gives one of the clearest indications of the deterministic psychology that runs unresisted through Tennyson's work in the idyll, also informs the few, carefully measured excursions the poem permits itself into descriptive verse. It is no accident that in the passage we have just examined the instrument of reconciliation, the golden seal, hangs from a watch, a machine emblematic of lineage and the authority of time. Likewise the only other scenic description, in its repetitive design, reinforces the subjection of individual wills to larger patterns. If the verbal genre-painting of grandsire and heir by the hearth constitutes the epiphany of this domestic idyll, here is its picturesque heart:

> So saying, he took the boy that cried aloud
> And struggled hard. The wreath of flowers fell
> At Dora's feet. She bowed upon her hands,
> And the boy's cry came to her from the field,
> More and more distant. She bowed down her head,
> Remembering the day when first she came,
> And all the things that had been. She bowed down
> And wept in secret; and the reapers reaped,
> And the sun fell, and all the land was dark.   (99–107)

This, we need to remind ourselves, represents Dora's moment of triumph as engineer of her family's reunion; yet its ambitious plangency cannot be mistaken. When Tennyson pulls out the stops of any style, even the Doric, we may surmise that his subject has made contact with the familiar ground of the inevitable. Here the inevitable takes poetic shape in a verbal iteration that mirrors the recurrence of a family's self-perpetuating destiny. The progressively reductive insistence on Dora's posture of abasement in the third, fifth, and seventh lines gradually transforms a physical response into an existential image.[26]

Dora's position at the edge of the harvest becomes, by dint of repetition, a virtual statement of her marginal position within the kindred systems of family and narrative. Her humiliation falls naturally into place with the many other fallings shadowed in this passage—the wreath of flowers, the child's voice in its dying fall, Dora's tears, the reaped grain, the sun itself—and her place seems no less inevitable than theirs. To be sure, we get a rare glimpse of Dora's inner life with her memory of "the day when first she came, / And all the things that had been"; yet in its summary totality even this mental event enforces a sense of personal history as fated. We do not know whether Dora weeps from sorrow, from gratitude, or from both (Spedding 1843, 146; Hunt 1973, 194). The idyllic interest lies rather in the depiction of a pattern that it is futile to resist, and that includes Dora's relations as well as herself. The cries of her little cousin in Allan's arms remind her of her own arrival at the farm as an orphaned girl. However she may have cried on that occasion, she now cries "in secret" because she now recognizes the futility of protest against a common doom. Tennyson leaves her recognition unspoken in order to represent it in the more eloquent mode of the speaking picture, transforming his heroine into a falling body that knows the idyllic law of universal gravitation too well to oppose it.[27]

This forceful pictorial rendition of a generational pattern not only repeats (in three lines verbatim) the scene of the day before when Dora failed to catch Allan's eye (69–77); it also repeats a number of Tennyson's favorite images from the odes of Keats. The harvest scene recalls "To Autumn": Dora's placement with the child "upon a mound / That was unsown, where many poppies grew" (70–71) recalls the drowsy Keatsian incense of sacrifice and mercy, where Autumn is "Drowsed with the fume of poppies" and the reaper's hook "Spares the next swath and all its twinèd flowers" (17–18). It also recalls, as the condition of such mercy, the Keatsian stance of acceptance. As in "Tears, Idle Tears" from *The Princess*, the imagination of happy harvest fields entails an embrace of "all the things that had been," and exacts tears—idyll tears—in tribute to the irrevocable days that are no more.

For a Keatsian analogue to those tears Tennyson reached back through the clouds and mists of "To Autumn" to what may well have been, in interpoetic terms, the generative image behind the entire idyll, the picture of Ruth from the "Ode to a Nightingale." Keats's allusion to Ruth occurs in a context that plays continuity against individual alienation: the poet fancies that the universal song of the nightingale once "found a path / Through the sad heart of Ruth, when, sick for home, / She stood in tears amid the alien corn" (75–77). Dora, too, is sick for home, and with a complex nostalgia that reanimates the dialectic of familiarity and acceptance that is latent in Keats. Dora's trespass and Allan's sentence of banishment have suddenly made her home ground into alien property. Yet the meaning of her homesickness is not that Dora can't go home again, owing to an economy she could not evade even if she wanted to; rather, the root of her nostalgia is the idyllic constraint that she can't go anywhere *but* home. Like Ruth in the Bible, Dora is not sick with longing for home but sick over the staying power of an adoptive home she cannot forsake: "And Ruth said, Entreat me not to leave thee, or to return from following after thee: for whither thou goest, I will go; and where thou lodgest, I will lodge; thy people shall be my people, and thy God my God" (Ruth 1:16). Dora does not stand with Ruth in tears but bows down in ritual obeisance to the overarching power that stands in this idyll where the "immortal Bird" did in Keats's ode: the power of a family structure that no hungry generation can tread down—not Allan's, nor William's, nor the struggling child's. Curiously, the echoing voice of Keats's bird enters Tennyson's passage as the cry of the child. Dora hears his voice coming "from the field, / More and more distant," much as the suddenly elegiac note of a demystified bird's farewell came to Keats: "Thy plaintive anthem fades / Past the near meadows" (85–86). The more distant the cry, for both poets, the greater its intimate pathos in the sad heart that is, as Keats's ode suggested, its real corridor of power anyway.

IDYLLIC ALLUSIVENESS, I proposed earlier, involves acceptance rather than revisionism, and aims more to understand prior texts than to overcome them. The central picture of "Dora" bears this distinction out: Tennyson evokes Keats in order to come to an understanding that enriches our reading of the idyll and the odes alike. His text under-stands Keats's, defers to them, so as to grasp anew their Romantic dialectic of alienation and homing. In return, the passages Tennyson evokes form an idyllic subtext that, as in "The Gardener's Daughter," undergirds the narrative surface and fills its vacancies. In this regard Tennyson's allusive tact shows to advantage when we compare "Dora" to its source in Mitford. "Dora Creswell" is a prose idyll explicitly built upon the same "picture of rural life" (86) that stands at the center of Tennyson's poem—Dora and the boy in the harvest field—and its setting owes so much to the odes of Keats that one suspects it was this intertextual dimension that first attracted the poet's attention. Mitford's picture of autumn features "the whole earth teeming with fruitfulness, and the bright autumn sun careering overhead"; "The air is gay with bees and butterflies; the robin twitters from amongst the ripening hazel-nuts" (85). This catalogue, because it neglects the semantic burden of mortality that the same details assume in Keats, builds to no issue. There is a similar failure to engage the import of details in Mitford's picture of Dora "twisting a rustic wreath of enamelled corn-flowers, brilliant poppies, snow-white lily-bines, and light fragile hare-bells, mingled with tufts of the richest wheat-ears" (86). Like her own Dora decorating the boy's hat, Mitford seeks only an effect of fetching profusion; and, in contrast to the idyllic profusion of detail in "The Gardener's Daughter," her text gives no play to the elegiac undertones of the anthological garland as we find it in the poetic tradition of the "Nightingale" ode, Milton's "Lycidas," or Spenser's *Shepheards Calender.*

To be sure, Mitford writes thus with an express purpose: arousing direct sympathy for her characters. Having conceded the literariness of her scene and its power to evoke "memories of 'Dis and Proserpine,'" "of the lovely Lavinia of our own poet, and of that finest pastoral of the world, the far lovelier Ruth," Mitford immediately goes on: "But these fanciful associations soon vanished before the real sympathy excited by the actors of the scene, both of whom were known to me, and both objects of a sincere and lively interest" (86). Tennyson's narrative approaches the actors of the scene as "objects" in quite another sense; he aims to excite sympathy less with individuals than with the contextualizing scene and scenario into which they play. He refracts action through the literary mediations of a strongly marked style and of a controlled allusiveness that fosters "lively interest" by means of, and not despite, "fanciful associations" with the imaginative past. Where Mitford's youthful pair "were known" to her personally, as individuals, Tennyson is more careful of the type; and his characters are known to us because we have already read so much that bears upon their story in biblical and Romantic traditions. Mitford's idyll ends with Dora's tears of joy at the success of her scheme; but the tears of Tennyson's Dora, and later of Allan, pay tribute to the forces of determining circumstance.[28]

The literary links between "Dora" and earlier texts, then, form part of the larger chain whereby this idyll binds present to past and straitens human options. It is this interlocking system of constraints, I think, that most tellingly approximates "Dora" to biblical narrative. The terse narrative manner of the Bible, as Auerbach (1953) has shown, represents the actors in a universal history as *hintergründig*, "fraught with background" (12). Auerbach's term is not spatial in its reference but, like the Tennysonian picturesque properly understood, temporal. Abraham and other biblical figures are "fraught with their own biographical past" (17), a past that embraces the history of the Jewish people as molded, individually and collectively, by God's choice to confront them throughout time with terrible and exemplary choices in their turn. Now the idyll is a structuralist genre that, stressing patterns and conventions over origins, has no place for theophany or for moral confrontation at anything approaching the pitch of the sublime. This is no less true for the biblical idyll of Ruth, whose theological pronouncements remain at the level of God-bless-you, than it is for the urbane pastoral idylls of Theocritus. Nonetheless, "Dora" presents characters that are as fully *hintergründig* as any biblical personage; and the fact that Tennyson's characters move upon a background that is in effect God-less only narrows their options the more. In the abeyance of a deity that, ruling secular time, may always disrupt its regularity, Tennyson's idyllic characters tread a pattern of inescapable routine. Thus the biblical Ruth, even at her level of subsistence gleaning, seems a far freer agent than Dora. Here is Ruth before her kinsman and benefactor Boaz: "Then she fell on her face, and bowed herself to the ground, and said unto him, Why have I found grace in thine eyes, that thou shouldest take knowledge of me, seeing I am a stranger?" (Ruth 2:11). Against this voluble and open wonder, set the mute abasement of Dora upon the margin of her family circle: "She bowed down / And wept in secret; and the reapers reaped, / And the sun fell, and all the land was dark." The background that freights "Dora" is, in a sense, this darkened land: a field without choices; a ground of determinate being; "the farm" of the first paragraph and the "one house" of the last; the "abode" (1, 164) of an environing domestic economy whereby the past dwells on into the present to become its way of life.

I have discussed "The Gardener's Daughter" in Eliot's terms of "surface" and "depth"; my recourse to Auerbach's "foreground" and "background" to account for "Dora" acknowledges a related phenomenon of Tennyson's idyllic art. Both poems present sweet images of human action that must be read through to bitter ends, which then produce, in conjunction with the ever-present sweetness, the sharp seasoning that has made Tennyson's narrative poetry last and to which I suspect his most enthusiastic readers have always responded, even without knowing it. We read *through* Tennyson's idylls in the primary sense enforced by poetry's temporality; such little pictures as the narrative portrait of Rose, or the barely animated image of Dora bowing ever closer to the ground, tell of time's passage and of the logic that binds and structures moments. We can also conceive this reading-through spatially, if we privilege a hermeneutic of penetration that moves the mind past foregrounds and surfaces in order to confront distances and depths. But the far depth or background in which idyllic interpretation finds its object should itself be understood in relation to time. Auerbach's "background" is confessedly a trope for a process of temporal development; and Eliot's "depths," whether we think of them as reserves of the creative unconscious or as a historically constituted cluster of fundamental assumptions, bring us back to the authority Tennyson vests in the passion of the past.

Because this passional authority endangers the active self that handles daily life—and thus endangers Tennyson's ambition in the idylls to install lifelike contemporaneity within a vivid and popular poetry—both "The Gardener's Daughter" and "Dora" set up defenses against it. The rhetorical prestidigitation of "The Gardener's Daughter" is a sustained attempt to distract the eye and so glut it on beauty that the ear attuned to doom may slumber for a space (Bagehot 1864, 348–349); "Dora" makes its appeal to the heart and proposes the display of human affections as the idyll's proper field. Although these defenses are as different as the idylls that erect them, they have certain features in common. Each relies on the mediation of ordered relationships, which take precedence over the individuals—larks or crops, gardeners' daughters or farmers' grandsons—that their structures define. The overdetermination of structure that thus shields the idyll against its content finds different means in different texts: in "The Gardener's Daughter," the enumeration of balanced details that are referentially superfluous; in "Dora," quite otherwise, the persistence of behavior patterns across the generations. But a systemic feature of either text is the ease with which one term, image, or person replaces another without alteration to the abiding order. The frequency with which such substitutions occur makes it hard to find any particular substitute very gratifying; and that may be because the entire superficies of idyllic relationship is one massive substitute itself. The defenses that stand against doom in Tennyson's idylls also, curiously, stand for it. The fine weave of relationship that the idyll now describes, and now narrates, served Tennyson both as a hedge against the greater calling his monologues and lyrics were concurrently pursuing and, in its seamless perfection, as an image for the ultimate relationship which that calling had promised since the beginning of his career.

Such double duty returns us to the collusion between Tennysonian surface and depth; and it helps explain why the mediating familial and institutional structures that might have given Tennyson's characters a theater for significant action, and protected them from the paralyzing grip of fate, turned into their fated prisons instead. In turning away from his most private poems' obsession with the ultimate, through the structures of the idyll Tennyson attempted to preserve a public arena. But while he succeeded in formulating an impressively flexible middle style, the preservation of a middle distance lay beyond him. Witness the polarization of effect among the domestic idylls' little pictures: on one hand the close-up, with its tendency to absorption in the exquisitely trivial; on the other hand the dissolve of specific perception into the neutral sentiment of being—an absorption of a very different order, which Tennyson's pageantry of the concrete seems designed to keep at bay, but which the even-tempered idyllic surface reflects and reinforces in spite of that manifest design.

We might historicize this phenomenon by approaching it more philosophically: the peculiar successes of Tennyson's idyllic poetry proceed from his failure to find means of transportation between facts and meanings. During Tennyson's era it became an increasingly widespread practice to regard facts, not as self-evident portions of a common knowledge, but as scientific data requiring a specialist interpretation that threatened to confiscate their meaning from the public domain. Probably this circumstance more than any gave the poet's exactitude of description its importance in the opinion of his contemporaries. For, while data proliferated as never before, a coherent global picture accommodating science to more traditional concerns appeared to be in accelerating recession from human grasp. Lacking grounds of mediation, the fact and the meaning pulled apart: as belief in a fact lost touch with belief in its significance, the superfetation of fact came into conflict with an unsatisfied demand for explanation (Millhauser 1971; Joseph 1972, 315). The result of this conflict, as we now know only too well, was less a genuine Victorian compromise than a truce, a tacit demarcation of spheres of influence, as the separate realms of fact and of meaning became increasingly exclusive and self-sufficient. What Tennyson's art teaches about this familiar crisis of modern culture is how, in terms of the schism between science and culture, each isolated sphere resembled the other—at least to the neutral, estranged eye that the Tennysonian idyll consistently projects and trains (Carr 1950, 64). It is this likeness in opposition that the structure of the idylls we have been analyzing beautifully mirrors, showing an apprehensive yet grateful age the very form and pressure of movements whose tremors had long been underfoot but were in Tennyson's day first being acknowledged by the reading public at large.

Within the Victorian climate of semantic rarefaction, it remained possible to posit a great, if greatly flawed, redeemer in the category of character. The ascendancy of fiction, biography, and autobiography in the nineteenth century shows it; so, in poetry, does the challenging instance of Browning. The economies of the observed and observing self let Browning build in the dramatic monologue a precarious but credible halfway house for the modern temper; for it was precisely the tension between phenomena and meanings that underpropped Browning's gallery of high-strung speakers caught between reach and grasp. Not so with Tennyson. His instinct for an older-fashioned perfection—the extremity of purpose that drives all Tennyson's most typical writings toward the condition of ultimata—so wedded characters in the idylls to their circumstances as to seal their common fate. The same uncompromising instinct led, in Tennyson's dramatic monologues, to a divorce of personality from experience, which in the final analysis bound the self not to circumstance but to circumference, the dim but sure abode of motive power. That is why we know the monologists of Tennyson by their flight from the mediations of relationship, but the characters of his idylls by their relations; indeed, "Dora" treats them first and last *as* relations, in the familial sense.

The imagination of Tennyson declined to traffic in the negotiations of the Browningesque self. That mobile center would not hold. Nor would a stable center materialize either, as Tennyson had known since "Timbuctoo." The orthodoxy of permanence was gone, save as a patient elegist might reconstruct its image from centrifugal fragments, or as a visionary chronicler might discern it in the already immaterial realm of a backward-looking mythology. So it was that the displacement of the center—at once the passing of the self and the fracture of the institutional hub of a perennially absent, once and future culture—furnished Tennyson with the great myth of his career: the Arthurian allegory of sense at war with soul that found its first major embodiment in the archetypally English idyll to which we turn next.

"Morte d'Arthur": The Transmission of Epic

Because the mythological character and epic intention of "Morte d'Arthur" set it apart from the English idylls we have considered thus far, Tennyson's choice to class it among them may occasion some surprise. His contemporaries quickly and persistently expressed reservations about reviving the matter of Arthur, in this poem and in the lifelong serial project it initiated, *Idylls of the King*: the modern temper seemed to require from its poets images of itself, not an overworn and irrelevant chivalry.[29] Furthermore, the poet's own anticipation of the charge of irrelevance is clear from the apologetics of "The Epic," the protective frame in which he dressed "Morte d'Arthur" for publication several years after first drafting the central myth in 1833–34. Within this framing poem, in the course of some Apostolic *conversazione* on leading topics of the day (Culver 1982, 51–52)—"Geology and schism," "the general decay of faith" (16–18)—the poetic alias Everard Hall diffidently asks, "Why should any man / Remodel models?" (37–38). The poet's question, though it arises in self-depreciation, bears on the whole of Tennyson's revisionist practice; and it leads here to the very heart of his epic ambition to rewrite the story of Arthur.

What relations obtain between "models" and "modernity," in the Victorian era, that might enable an epic mode?

"The Epic" offers answers only of a testimonial sort. Francis Allen's having rescued the fragmentary manuscript of the "Morte" implies that the poem possesses, beyond its verbal riches "as a sugar-plum" (43) and the "modern touches" that "Redeemed it from the charge of nothingness" (278–279), a redemptive value worth snatching from oblivion; and the nameless speaker's concluding dream of "King Arthur, like a modern gentleman" (294) constitutes a somewhat clumsy visionary stand against the general decay of faith. Hall, Allen, the speaker, and parson Holmes represent varieties of contemporary witness to the staying power of Arthurian myth, which corroborate Tennyson's hopes for epic and illustrate the faith in communal reception upon which those hopes are founded. But these invented contemporaries' affirmative responses, within "The Epic," remain inert assertions because they are unargued, ungrounded in a narrative of reception that might give them explanatory force. The way between the modern interrogation of models on one side of Tennyson's frame and the answering affirmation on the other lies through the narrative "Morte" itself, a text whose subtle and multiple concerns with transportation, mediation, and tradition make it its own best defense, an argument at once in, on, and for a Victorian epic mode. For the subject of "Morte d'Arthur" is cultural transmission, the handing on or handing over of a communal ideal whose very essence is communication.

In order to grasp both the novelty of this poem and its continuity with the epic, we should consider the role that cultural transmission had come to play in the epic tradition Tennyson inherited. In a sense the function of any epic is cultural transmission, the consolidation and teaching of a tradition of values through a story epitomizing the culture for which it speaks. In Western literature at least since Virgil, such cultural transmission has been not only an epic function but expressly an epic subject: Western epics tend to educate their audiences, in part, by thematizing education itself. The comparatively self-sufficient Homeric epics may carry their instruction in their structure alone; but for Virgil and his major successors the transmission of a cultural story becomes an indivisible part of the story they tell. Aeneas shoulders, in his father Anchises, both the burden of his past and the guide to his posterity, a prophetic shade to whom he turns to learn the future that the Roman poet and reader recognize as the past conditioning their present state. Dante's Virgil takes Anchises' place, in *The Divine Comedy*, as the ancestral transmitter of a culture loyally pursued and then as loyally transcended, under a Catholic dispensation the Roman poet has imperfectly foretold. In the English tradition, Spenser's intermittently Arthurian *Faerie Queene* and the epic Milton wrote instead of an Arthuriad, *Paradise Lost*, periodically draw themselves together around explicit scenes of instruction, which draw liberally on the biblical or the British past as means of teaching Christian and gentle readers where they have come from and thus who they are to be. And for Wordsworth, at the start of Tennyson's century, the scene of instruction becomes the basic compositional unit: in *The Excursion* and *The Prelude* local anecdote, natural history, and individual perception converge in spots of time from which the poet induces subtly graduated narratives of personal and cultural development, so recreating the exemplary poetic self as to create the taste by which the Romantic epic is to be enjoyed.

The increasing explicitness with which Western epics make historical reconstruction a method of instruction, fashioning the past in order to fashion their audiences, attests to two kinds of historical pressure that have special relevance to Tennyson's situation. First, there is the pressure of cultural disintegration, already perceptible behind the imperial propaganda of the *Aeneid* and unmistakable in the epic solitudes of Milton and Wordsworth, which in making communal consensus ever more fragile, made cultural commemoration an ever more binding obligation on the epic poet. Working in uneasy tandem with this historical pressure and the anxiety of audience it induced was a second, literary-historical pressure, the accumulating imperative to originality, with its attendant anxiety of influence—in no genre more stringent than in the ambitious epic, and at no previous time more urgent than during the nineteenth century. It is to the confluence of these pressures that we point in describing Virgil and his descendants as the authors of *secondary* epic. The poets of lasting epic inspiration have been those who manage to address cultural fragmentation and epic belatedness in the same breath, who most closely identify their artistic strategies and their ethical precepts, and who thus supplant antiquated codes of heroic conduct and antique modes of conducting epic poems in a single act: a work that imagines grounds, at once historical and literary-historical, for a fresh cultural cohesion.

As the "faint Homeric echoes" ("The Epic," 39) of such creatively secondary reflection grew ever fainter, it became incumbent upon the poet to listen all the harder. And as the recollection of an authentically directive epic voice became an increasingly difficult poetic task, its accomplishment became a good in itself, indeed something of a heroic virtue. It is this virtue that Tennyson celebrates, with wholly modern uniqueness of focus, in "Morte d'Arthur" (Goodman 1954, 202–203; Laury 1959, 403; Preyer 1976, 101). Tennyson approaches Arthurian legend in the 1830s by adopting the remarkable and drastic expedient of conceiving his theme in perennial recession from the present, and then making that recession his theme (Kincaid 1977, 241). Instead of transmitting a culturally originative tale, he tells of a culturally originative transmission. He commences to write *Idylls of the King* at the close of the story, the winter midnight that ends knightly deeds, but that also ushers in the sunrise of the new year and with it the beginning of fabulation about knightly deeds. He takes the epic plunge *in finales res* and dips into the creative matrix from which the matter of Arthur takes its rise, conceived not as historical event but as traditional story. Tennyson's expanded version of this poem in the completed idylls took the title "The Passing of Arthur"— a title that beautifully identifies the moment at which a history passes into a tradition, the moment at which Arthur's passing away becomes the occasion of his being passed along as a perennially recreated cultural possession, the once and future king. But Tennyson's original title carries, as its intertextual freight, much the same implication: the death of King Arthur, which constitutes the fundamental "action" of the poem, is the birth of the "Morte d'Arthur," as it is the birth of the Arthurian miscellany which Malory set down, and to which centuries of tradition in their wisdom have given that oddly appropriate name. Tennyson's title follows Malory, and so does his text, in its narrative outline and even, where possible, in its wording; the death of Arthur being the birth of the author, Tennyson finds his secondary epic authority in high fidelity to the avowedly legendary character of what he means to transmit to modern readers. That is why, in the modernizing frame of "The Epic," Tennyson has picked from the domestic holocaust of a hypothetical twelve-book epic the one scrap needful, the coded key from which the whole story—any story that aspires to integrity in his late day—can be mapped out once again.

If, in the Virgilian tradition of secondary epic, the poet self-consciously reflects his revisionist aesthetics in his modern ethics, and vice versa, then we might call Tennyson's epic effort *tertiary*. With great concentration in "Morte d'Arthur" and more diffusely in the ensuing *Idylls*, Tennyson writes epic by raising it to the higher if more desperate power we also find in Browning's *The Ring and the Book*. The capacity to revoice a silent, mainly antiquarian text through a reinvention of its latent mythology—the power of "remodeling models"—becomes in effect the poem's prevailing ethic. The traditional epic ideal of transmitting a culture yields at last, in the Victorian epic, to an ideal of culture *as* transmission. "Not a having and a resting, but a growing and a becoming" was Matthew Arnold's formulation of such an ideal of culture (1965, 92); and to juxtapose this Victorian dynamism to Wordsworth's title for the autobiographical epic we know as *The Prelude*—"The Growth of a Poet's Mind"—is to glimpse abiding Romantic embers within the more elaborately banked fires of the Victorian epics. While Browning exults in the obscurity of the foreign tale his epic resuscitates, and Tennyson observes a decorous reverence for the capitally British matter of Arthur, the recreative work that plays past into present furnishes both poets with an epic value that exceeds whatever values might be taken to inhere in the stories themselves.

The obvious and steep costs such an attitude entails—the emaciation of narrative interest as such, the precipitancy of a many-storied culture that is always a-building on a shrinking ground—are not much more obvious to us, I think, than they were to the Victorian poets. Browning's persistent teasing of the British public with the play of fancy and fact attests to these costs; so do Tennyson's multiple narrative mediations ("The Coming of Arthur," "The Holy Grail") and his last-ditch attempts to impose on the allegorical drift of the *Idylls* moralistic, interpretively inert specifications of a struggle between "true" and "false" ("Geraint and Enid," 4) or of "Sense at war with Soul" ("To the Queen," 37). The doom of Romanticism and its sequel, the profusion of realist fictions of the social self in the novel, sentenced Victorian epic poems to the cognate tasks of teaching English readers that they had a tradition—even if that meant trumping one up, in Tennyson's pre–Pre-Raphaelite medievalism and Browning's Higher Critical yet still evangelical Christianity—and of inducing a current English awareness of how a tradition *comes to pass*. The poet's need of a myth to write, and the public's need of a myth to live by, conspired to produce Victorian epics whose values center in the making, breaking, and dissemination of myth itself (Rosenberg 1973, 142).

In Tennyson's case the die was cast with "Morte d'Arthur," a stylistic template on which further *Idylls* were to be modeled. The textured style of the "Morte" precipitates its own spectacular emblem in the jeweled hilt of the sword Excalibur, on the right disposal of which the poem turns. Tennyson gets his epic handle on the matter of Arthur through this elegiac episode; and, by the logic of elegy that informs *Idylls of the King* as much as anything in Tennyson's oeuvre, the idyllic pattern this episode initiates is one that a poet, or a culture, may hold by only in giving it away.[30] The artifactual, all but palpable weight of the "Morte" recalls the preponderance of pattern in other English idylls, where an overall strategy of containment darkens each local cadence of an inevitable form. But "Morte d'Arthur" does more than that: it presents its traditional content as a pattern of pattern making, a recipe for the gift of a literary heritage, which is to say of a humane transmission, which is to say of a culture. In this sense it represents not just another idyll but the archetypal one, the one Tennyson published at the head of "English Idyls" in 1842 and at the end of *Idylls of the King* in 1885 because it prefigured, and retroactively validated, the evolving myth of consensus to which his work in the public form of the idyll aspired to give shape.

THE POEM OPENS WITH the "hollow oes and aes, / Deep-chested music," promised by its frame ("The Epic," 50–51), in as handsome and efficient a piece of narrative setting as Tennyson was ever to compose:

> So all day long the noise of battle rolled
> Among the mountains by the winter sea;
> Until King Arthur's table, man by man,
> Had fallen in Lyonnesse about their Lord,
> King Arthur: then, because his wound was deep,
> The bold Sir Bedivere uplifted him,

Sir Bedivere, the last of all his knights,
And bore him to a chapel nigh the field,
A broken chancel with a broken cross,
That stood on a dark strait of barren land.
On one side lay the Ocean, and on one
Lay a great water, and the moon was full. (1–12)

For Tennyson, to set a story is to set it up in imagery and theme as well as place. Although Arthur is mortally wounded, he is "uplifted" too, by a survivor, in a forecast of the governing dialectic of the poem and of its larger epic aspiration. In the aftermath of so final a battle, the chapel with its broken cross offers not socially sanctioned asylum but natural shelter; and although the only shrift or uplift awaiting the two warriors there will be what they carry in themselves, the halfway situation of the ruined holy house and the curiously expectant tranquility of the scene outside it suggest that what they carry in themselves will suffice. The physical intermediacy of the opening scene has an intertextual analogue in the opening word "So," which quickly situates this text in its tradition whether we read the word as a conjunction or as an adverb. If the former ("therefore"), it assumes the consequential force of a Greek particle, a diacritical hallmark of the classical epic. If the latter ("thus"), it allusively tells us how the noise of battle rolled; it rolled like the rhythmic periods of Malory's prose, or like the long epic line extending back from Milton to Homer.

The passage certainly accumulates a sonorous roll of its own, through aggressive alliteration and through a verbal iteration that varies the position of a repeated word or sound within or across poetic lines ("King Arthur," "chapel . . . broken chancel . . . broken cross," "On one side . . . and on one"). This verbal recycling derives within the English tradition from the example of Milton, who uses it primarily as a sophisticated elegiac keening ("For *Lycidas* is dead, dead ere his prime, / Young *Lycidas*"; 8–9), which both registers loss and proleptically whets the edge of the elegiac crisis in promise of an abundant return: "Weep no more, woeful Shepherds, weep no more" (165). This Miltonic turn of style survives through the Romantic period in the understated accumulations of Wordsworth's "Tintern Abbey" and (with special relevance to the project of "Morte d'Arthur") in the sculptural aplomb of Keats's epic fragment *Hyperion*, the first verse paragraph of which anticipates the repetitive stationing devices used by Tennyson in setting the "Morte." In one sense Tennyson's recourse to a self-returning elegiac style, here as in the early portions of the epic-bound "Oenone," signals a first stage of bereavement that the poem will undertake to transcend. But in another sense, because the transcendence Tennyson reserves for his Arthur is—even more than in the surprisingly non-Christian Malory—a mode of secular commemoration, Tennyson's register of grief also serves as an already redemptive registration of heroic names and places lost once to history but reborn in legend now again.

Arthur's first words refer to just this matter of consequence: "The sequel of today unsolders all / The goodliest fellowship of famous knights / Whereof this world holds record" (14–16). Regarding "today" as the "sequel" or result of a determining past, the model king laments not his own wound but the dissolution of the Round Table, his projected public image. This keynote sounds a theme that occurs throughout the ensuing dialogue: the king regrets foremost the loss of further "talk of knightly deeds" (19), and his consolation comes from thinking ahead to "wheresoever I am sung or told / In aftertime" (34–35). While yet alive, King Arthur already leads the afterlife of heroic legend; and the overriding concern of his last moments is to lead what remains of his life to its foreordained conclusion, to oversee the making of his myth and seal the present as a worthy gift to posterity. In accordance with the epic-making force of the poem's initial "So," Arthur aims to shape his catastrophe in conformity with a model of tragic heroism, projecting "today" as inevitable "sequel" into the tomorrow of *legenda*, matters to be read.

Today's unsoldering will enable tomorrow's recollection, the binding energy that gathers collective identity through myth. That is why the "Morte" presents the dissolution of the Round Table as a special, confirming instance of its solidarity. The knights are "fallen in Lyonnesse about their Lord" because he is the theme of their valor, what they have fought *about*. And as he is the occasion of their fall, they are likewise the occasion of his: when Arthur asserts, "I perish by this people which I made" (22), he asserts his place not only nearby the battlefield but also within the ritual of the dying god, who stands or falls by the reciprocal making and unmaking of his culture. Like Tennyson's Ulysses, Arthur is become a name; yet he welcomes such becoming and quests for nothing but to be centered in the sphere of common duties, set down as a cultural treasure in the tables of the communal round. There is no clearer indication of the complementary difference between Tennyson's dramatic monologues and idylls than the fact that during the same critical months he drafted both "Ulysses" and "Morte d'Arthur," almost equally impressive poems that depart from human shores in radically divergent directions.

If the "Morte" is slightly the weaker poem, its weakness proceeds from that of the antagonist against whom its central figure achieves definition. Where Ulysses has in Telemachus a worthy example to strive with, Arthur has only the weak reed Sir Bedivere. Clearly Bedivere enters the poem (reft of the additional help of his brother Sir Lucan from Malory's account) in order to provide a resistance that will clarify Arthur's singularity of mind. But a pretty passive resister he is: his first speech (40–44) amounts to saying that he really shouldn't leave the wounded king alone but will anyhow; and if the dim-witted vacillation with which he twice fails to do Arthur's will, only to be scared into ultimate compliance, escapes bathos, it does so principally through the brilliant distractions of Tennyson's descriptive style. We shall see in a moment how the lesser patternings of this style play into a larger design that weighs and finally discredits the fitness for epic purposes of at least one species of idyllic description, and how Bedivere executes a crucial role within this larger design. But for the present Bedivere remains what the opening paragraph has made of him, a supporting character. In generic terms he is the kind of character that a domestic idyll ought to display, a plot convenience who is most himself when standing, like Dora or Rose, as the centerpiece of a landscape. He comes into his own as an idyllic character once he stops speaking:

> So saying, from the ruined shrine he stept
> And in the moon athwart the place of tombs,
> Where lay the mighty bones of ancient men,
> Old knights, and over them the sea-wind sang
> Shrill, chill, with flakes of foam. He, stepping down
> By zig-zag paths, and juts of pointed rock,
> Came on the shining levels of the lake.   (45–51)

From the second to the fifth line the syntax appears to forget Bedivere altogether: we await the verb that would make of these lines a second independent clause, but none emerges. What emerges instead is the scene, with its ambience of wasted grandeur, and what we hear is not Bedivere's tonal mood but the wind's. Because the verb governing these lines remains "stept," Bedivere remains frozen in the space of his step, a knight petrified not by fear—what *does* he feel?—but by a purely statuesque fellowship with the imperturbable dead, whose "mighty" company he will properly join, as an actor on the same scene, only much later in the poem. Even after the narrative snaps back to attention with the self-prompt "He, stepping down," the action inheres not at all in the actor but in the zigzags and juts of a terrain that upstages the actor. Ricks's observation that "There is a rupture between the deepest moods within the poem and any moods felt by its human figures" (1972, 137) seems open to bathymetric challenge in Arthur's case; but for Bedivere it certainly holds true, as it holds true for the human figures generally in Tennyson's idylls, where character comes, willy-nilly, under an atmospheric regime.

Still, "Morte d'Arthur" is a peculiarly self-conscious instance of idyll, a trial epyllion forecasting more complex epic options; and its lay figure Bedivere enjoys the special distinction of not only inhabiting an idyll but also, as it were, learning to read one, in the highly wrought imagery of the brand Excalibur. I have suggested already that Excalibur may be regarded as an intratextual emblem of the "Morte," and that in the ways the sword gets handled we may find the poet imagining ways of wielding the Arthurian corpus. Tennyson's preferred term for Excalibur is not "sword" but "brand"—a revision in line 27 of the earliest manuscript records this preference (T. Nbk. 17)—because a "brand" is a sign, the meaning of which depends in part on the attitude of its user. Bedivere's three trips to the lakeshore constitute an essay in the hazards and opportunities that the idyllic mode discloses for a poetry of epic scope, a narrative proof of what Tennyson's Arthuriad might lapse or rise into, and thus of what an idyll of the king ought to be.

The reading of Excalibur that emerges from Bedivere's first solitary encounter is suspiciously reminiscent of the way such readers as Mrs. Gaskell's Holbrook responded to "The Gardener's Daughter." Bedivere is simply fascinated:

> For all the haft twinkled with diamond sparks,
> Myriads of topaz-lights, and jacinth-work

> Of subtlest jewellery. He gazed so long
> That both his eyes were dazzled, as he stood,
> This way and that dividing the swift mind,
> In act to throw: but at the last it seemed
> Better to leave Excalibur concealed
> There in the many-knotted waterflags,
> That whistled stiff and dry about the marge.   (56–64)

For the second time in a dozen lines Bedivere is paralytically absorbed in the scene of his commissioned act—suspended "In act to throw"—but whereas earlier he stepped forth as a picturesque subject among the tombs, now his gaze is that of a minimal subjectivity caught, for the protracted twinkling of an eye, in the grip of his own reductively picturesque apprehension. The ability to "draw" Excalibur, the sword in the stone, plays a memorable part in Arthurian legend; but Bedivere can only draw the stones in the sword, after the fashion of an amateur draftsman or idyllic colorist, intrigued by surface effects as ends in themselves (Kincaid 1977, 244). Hence the idyllic cover-up of his leaving Excalibur "concealed": his vision of the sword requires a suppression of its history and of the mission for which it has been entrusted to him, the once and future dimensions of its meaning. Hence, too, his inability to convert vision into meaningful speech. When Arthur asks what he has seen or heard, Bedivere leaves his sightseeing untold and answers merely, "I heard the ripple washing in the reeds, / And the wild water lapping on the crag" (70–71)—an imagist or Idiot Boy haiku of mere flux, rendering a pointless temporality that corresponds to his entrapment in the visual present.

It is not a lie, exactly, that Bedivere here tells; the blank little couplet speaks truly of his phenomenological absorption, and its omissions transparently suggest that his mission has gone unperformed. Yet Arthur instantly and indignantly treats it as one: "Thou hast betrayed thy nature and thy name, / Not rendering true answer, as beseemed / Thy fëalty, nor like a noble knight" (73–75). Arthur's outburst contains two surprises: he chastises Bedivere's word, not his deed, and he accuses Bedivere not of high treason to the king but of self-betrayal. Apparently for Arthur the word fully implies the deed, as the "name" the "nature," and the assumption of a role as knight or king implies a full system of obligations. Arthur espouses, that is, the sovereign view that the conventions of language and of society are not arbitrary but absolute: his kingship is founded on an assumption of the inherence of meaning in speech and of duty in relationship. "For surer sign had followed" (76): if not, then Bedivere can be no noble knight and Arthur never king. We might observe of the conflict between Tennyson's two principals that Arthur's performative absolutism and Bedivere's dazzled phenomenology are strong and weak versions, respectively, of the guiding principle behind the Tennysonian idyll. Both characters—unlike Ulysses or Tithonus—fuse ends with means and facts with meanings; but where Bedivere does so by collapsing import into surface, prizing the sword for its own sake as an object, and offering lip service for fealty, Arthur in his extremity requires a world instinct with meaning, a world where every thing is a sign conducting to other signs, whose ultimate linkage among "new men, strange faces, other minds" (238) makes the world one.

Of these two views only Arthur's might sustain an epic poem, a verbal image of the mighty world that possesses microcosmic unity; and it is Tennyson's project in the "Morte" to make Arthur's view prevail over Bedivere's shadowy illusionism, which threatens to split a work composed of idylls into heterocosmic components whose sum fails to produce the larger whole of epic. Understanding the exchanges between Arthur and Bedivere in these terms can help us appreciate what was at stake for Tennyson as he approached the matter of Arthur, and why he engaged and resisted Bedivere's frailty as staunchly as he did. For the passivity of Bedivere represents a danger that beset Tennyson throughout the writing of his epic, and that the finished *Idylls of the King* by no means escape altogether. The vertigo of the surface with which each sight of Excalibur afflicts Bedivere, "the giddy pleasure of the eyes" (128), is precisely the malady that "Morte d'Arthur" aims to cast off. Tennyson found in Malory's account a personal, writer's allegory no less important—or poignant, in view of the mixed results he achieved in later *Idylls*—than the biographical reminiscences of the late Arthur Hallam that the poem inevitably evokes. It tells us much about Tennyson's scrutiny of his own proclivities during the ten years' silence that he took from Malory what is patently an archetypal episode—the disciple's anguished denial of his stricken master—and centered it on the temptations of a purely descriptive poetic phenomenology.

Tennyson did not need to escape this tempting mode because it was in itself escapist; it was not. When he yielded his spirit to it wholly, as in *The Lover's Tale* and "The Gardener's Daughter," the full draught of cowslip wine brought to Tennyson, like Keats before him, soberer truths than meet the idyllic eye. He turned so sharply on the muse of the visual trance in "Morte d'Arthur" because he knew such an enchanting muse could not sing epic. Narrative arrest formed part of the problem; worse yet was the tendency of Tennyson's accretive descriptions to load every rift with ore, until sensory overload turned descriptive euphony into static interference and thus failed in its goal of transmission. An Arthuriad written on Bediverean principles, even if it got out of narrative low gear, would so cherish each detail of its telling as to degenerate from epic into chronicle, or into that bogey of ambitious nineteenth-century poetry, the long poem merely made up of independent shorter ones. Bringing its "myriads of topaz-lights" to the surface and leaving no room for the receptive work of the adverting mind, such a work would in effect "leave Excalibur concealed / There in the many-knotted waterflags" of its text. If Excalibur was to be not a sword but Arthur's brand, a "surer sign" transmitted to the nation, the jeweled hilt would have to be let go.

Bedivere's continuing resistance to just this imperative of transmissive release gives substance to his second failure to carry out Arthur's mission. While the king's charge now spurs Bedivere into speech, he remains "fixed in thought" (84) and fixated upon the brand as an object. "A precious thing," he calls it, "one worthy note" (89). Although the difference between the first phrase and the second marks an important difference between Bedivere's first and second refusals to follow instructions—now Excalibur not only *is*, for Bedivere, but *means* something—the new note of signification remains wedded to the thing itself, "Which might have pleased the eyes of many men" (91). Bedivere now proposes to retain Excalibur as an icon, a physical signifier that will outlast his generation and remain, in the truth of its beauty, a friend to man. If Keats's "Ode on a Grecian Urn" underlies this questioning speech, the allusive point is that Bedivere looks the wrong way through Keats's telescope, simplemindedly asserting the priority of the art object over the creative mediations of language (Bagehot 1859, 184).

Without the object, Bedivere reasons, "What record, or what relic of my lord / Should be to aftertime, but empty breath / And rumours of a doubt?" (98–100). He intends this as a rhetorical question; but if we recall Arthur's faith in the "aftertime" in which his exploits with Excalibur are to be "sung or told," the question becomes double-edged. What record of Arthur will persist to aftertime, beyond breath and doubtful rumor, even though the sword be kept? What will the material object matter without the explanatory mediations of the word? As Bedivere fancies a future exhibition of the sword, he himself cannot help supplying the exhibit with a caption:

> Some one might show it at a joust of arms,
> Saying, "King Arthur's sword, Excalibur,
> Wrought by the lonely maiden of the Lake.
> Nine years she wrought it, sitting in the deeps
> Upon the hidden bases of the hills."
> So might some old man speak in the aftertime.   (102–107)

These lines, easily Bedivere's best in all the *Idylls*, endow Excalibur with a temporal and genetic mystery that tips the scales of idyllic *ekphrasis* in favor of language and story, as against reliquary veneration. Bedivere's ostensible icon reposes on a myth of origins that only narrative can convey. Finely replenishing "empty breath"—as he will do in "The Passing of Arthur," where he is "no more than a voice" (3)—Bedivere unwittingly champions the medium of communication he professes to mistrust.[31]

But, for the present, Bedivere's sole resource is to lay the sword away for posterity. He has gathered enough from Arthur's first rebuke to regard Excalibur as a sign and not just a precious thing, but its significance remains bound to its physical presence. In holding by the precious hilt as the only way of holding off change and loss, Bedivere commits the idolater's sin of forgetting that even idols, as physical objects, must submit to the universal doom. So he idolizes the sword, even as he idyllizes his reasons for doing so: "I heard the water lapping on the crag, / And the long ripple washing in the reeds" (116–117). In its new context Bedivere's slightly altered haiku bespeaks not the *epoche* of a dazed phenomenologist, but a curator's impulse to stem the sapping tides of epochs to come.

It is the epical, not the epochal, that concerns Arthur, and his stinging second rejoinder both rebukes Bedivere's idolatry and reasserts the different authority of epic:

> Ah, miserable and unkind, untrue,
> Unknightly, traitor-hearted! Woe is me!
> Authority forgets a dying king,
> Laid widowed of the power in his eye
> That bowed the will. I see thee what thou art.   (119–123)

Bedivere is "miserable" because susceptible to the miser-y of hoarding and not transmitting his trust, and "unkind" precisely because "untrue, / Unknightly," false to the duty authorized by his oath and thus false to his true identity as defined by the Arthurian ideal. Bedivere has bungled his role in relation to the king, which is his role in the great story Arthur is dying to transmit. In cleaving to Excalibur instead of the king, the "unkind" Bedivere has made a genre mistake: he has acted like a character in the wrong kind of plot, prized a prop over the properties of character that subserve larger actions, and sent the poem into a melodramatic or farcical tailspin. Bedivere's proper business is the translation of Arthur, the bearing of his liege across the threshold between history and myth. But here the destined *traduttore* turns *traditore*, a "traitor-hearted" knight who, in Arthur's accumulating indictment, would "betray me for the precious hilt, / Either from lust of gold, or like a girl / Valuing the giddy pleasure of the eyes" (126–128). Bedivere's visual absorption and lust of possession amount to a preemptive bid to stop the transmission of epic. Such a bid threatens to convert Bedivere from the actor of a role transcending selfhood—an epic functionary, in the high sense of the term—into a blocking agent, a sight-gagger: "I see thee what thou art."

Bedivere's misprision of his epic charge threatens, further, to convert Arthur from the conductor of his catastrophe into its helpless victim, a figure of unredeemed pathos: "Woe is me! / Authority forgets a dying king." These lines bring us to the epic crux of the "Morte": Arthur fears to lose not his life but his life story, which "Authority"—the tradition of *auctoritas* running from Geoffrey of Monmouth and Malory to Tennyson and beyond—will forget, unless Arthur can summon the authority to move Bedivere hence now, and to make "the power in his eye" prevail over the "pleasure of the eyes." In the earliest draft from T.Nbk. 17 the verb in line 121 is not "forgets" but "deserts," which makes

locally easier but finally thinner sense. "Forgets," as a verb normally taking a personal subject, subliminally attaches itself to the
"dying king," to suggest that for Arthur to forget his authority
will be for him to be forgotten by the tradition in which he seeks
commemoration. The difficulty of the passage as revised proceeds
from Tennyson's difficulty in conceiving the motive power of epic
as emotive without being simply pathetic. Heavy sexist artillery
in Arthur's speech ("widowed," "like a girl") attests to the poet's
need to distinguish this, of all characters, from the passive, typically feminine personae in his earlier work; the one conspicuous
self-allusion at line 132 ("I will arise and slay thee") recalls Oenone,
to be sure, but Oenone at her least "feminine," her most biblically
and patriarchally inspired. If we feel sorry for Arthur, if he merely
wheedles Bedivere into personal sympathy rather than eliciting
knightly submission to an exigent role, then the poem will forfeit
its epic command and relapse into well-worn melancholia. Arthur
must not move the heart but bow the will, by virtue of his own
will to die into traditional stature, if he is to effect and not just
affect his posterity. That a king's authority, dying or living, resides
in his subjects' faith is a grounding theme of the *Idylls*; the singularity of "Morte d'Arthur" as an essay in epic is that it makes
this theme the very stuff of its narrative, and extends its application
to the writing and reception of the narrative itself.

Arthur's crucial appeal to Bedivere takes effect, then, in the
name of the story they both inhabit. The king succeeds by his
power to invoke an epic succession; his story goes on both in order
that we may read it and—where cyclical epic meets hermeneutic
circle—because we are reading it. Leaping at last to his allotted
task, Bedivere

> clutched the sword,
> And strongly wheeled and threw it. The great brand
> Made lightnings in the splendour of the moon,
> And flashing round and round, and whirled in an arch,
> Shot like a streamer of the northern morn,
> Seen where the moving isles of winter shock
> By night, with noises of the northern sea.
> So flashed and fell the brand Excalibur:
> But ere he dipt the surface, rose an arm
> Clothed in white samite, mystic, wonderful,

And caught him by the hilt, and brandished him
Three times, and drew him under in the mere.   (135–146)

Nothing so becomes the passage of Excalibur through Arthurian
legend as this wonderful departure. The transmission of the great
brand from historical and human hands into fantastic and mythic
ones is a spectacularly cinematic event, whose dynamism subsumes the ocular dazzle of idyll in a temporal chorus of purpose,
motion, and sound. This chorus climaxes with the first epic simile
of the poem: Tennyson has strategically saved the most notable
of epic devices for this moment of liminal transfer, so as to locate
the origin of his epic vision in an empirical loss that, as in "Timbuctoo," requires cultural recuperation. The matter of Arthur gets
underway for good by giving away the material icon at its core;
the sword becomes "the brand Excalibur" once it is "brandished"
as a sign in the hand of legend. The translation of an iconic object
into a subject for storytelling transforms the brand doubly into a
"character": as a sign whose only home is now a narrative text,
Excalibur also becomes a sort of romance personage, a "he" and
not the "it" Bedivere has cherished for so long.

The "arch" described by Excalibur's passage from the natural
man's into the supernatural Lady's keeping, from historical into
literary custody, constitutes the keystone of this arch-*Idyll* (Gray
1980, 11). Coming first in the genetic design and last in the narrative execution, the passage may have had a comparable function
in Tennyson's projection and completion of *Idylls of the King*.
Much of its splendor, and of its thematic suggestiveness for Tennyson's eventual epic, inheres in the disposition of active and passive verbals. "Made" and "flashing" are clearly active forms, as
"Seen" is clearly passive; but what of "whirled" and "Shot"?
Mimetically these ambiguous verbals poise the sword at the apex
of its trajectory—an effect the epic simile reinforces—but, in addition, the grammatical blur at this focal point bears on the ethics
of epic transmission as Tennyson conceives it. Recall that the
flinging of Excalibur is the narrative sequel of Bedivere's abandoning his will to Arthur's, and that in turn Arthur's thrice-
repeated appeal to Bedivere has been made not on personal grounds
but in the name of the story they are both living out. Both Bedivere's act and the speech act of Arthur witness to the imperative

epic action that surrounds them as its exponents; and the active-passive arch of the discarded sword, which is both an object and a person, conforms to that overarching epic doom and to the fatality of the characters who abandon themselves, as selves, in order to figure in it.

The last will of "Morte d'Arthur," its testamentary authority, belongs to the story itself, rather than to Arthur, to Bedivere, or even—so Tennyson contrives the matter—to the epic narrator. For the actual passage of Excalibur occurs somewhere beyond the ken of its human accessories, none of whom beholds the event as an eyewitness (Rosenberg 1973, 142). Bedivere, enlarged in scope yet still true to character, shuts his eyes before letting go the hilt: "Sir King, I closed mine eyelids," he reports, "But when I looked again, behold an arm" (152, 158). Bedivere has missed precisely the transmissive passage that matters most in Tennyson's epic account. Arthur trusts Bedivere's hearsay report implicitly, since it confirms his expectation of the miraculous. (He even trusts it proleptically, as soon as he reads in Bedivere's face the delayed reflex of the earlier "power in his eye": "Now see I by thine eyes that this is done"; 149.) Arthur's willingness to see by his knight's eyes is fully justified by the knight's uncanny report, which repeats verbatim the description of the arm we have read some dozen lines above in the narrative proper: "Clothed in white samite, mystic, wonderful, / That caught him by the hilt, and brandished him / Three times, and drew him under in the mere" (159–161).

The narration of a spectacular miracle thus brings forth a little miracle of narration. The coincidence between lines 159–161 and 144–146 is so close that we must wonder whose words they are. Historical common sense, bolstered by the convention that an epic is a tradition or handing down, tells us that the words are Bedivere's and that his speech to Arthur initiates a faithful communication passing through Malory, whom Tennyson follows here quite closely, and culminating in the present text.[32] But such common sense then makes nonsense of Excalibur's aerial transit, which Bedivere has just disclaimed seeing and which must therefore constitute a departure from the documentary source. (The problem arises with even greater force in "The Passing of Arthur," a text that includes Bedivere's disclaimer yet explicitly represents itself as his story.) If, however, we adopt the epic poet or muse as our source, we must wonder at Bedivere's clairvoyant divination of the very phrasing to which the text of aftertime will resort—and at Arthur's clairvoyance as well, since the words of the identical lines 144 and 159 are "originally" his: "an arm / Rose up from out the bosom of the lake, / Clothed in white samite, mystic, wonderful" (29–31).

Tennyson contrives a stunning narrative overlay that resumes Bedivere's earlier, idyllically visual syncope in a finer, epic tone. The bearing of its paradoxes upon the central question of cultural transmission becomes apparent when we remember, first, that the event in question is a literal reception, the mysterious grasping of the released hilt; and, second, that the hand that draws Excalibur under—the hand of the Lady of the Lake—is the same that drew Excalibur up to begin with. If that reception be a deception, it is the great deep feint of faith in which all successful narration originates and ends, and by which we are willingly taken in whenever we take in Arthur's story or any other. In the dispensation of the Victorian epic as Tennyson forecasts it here, the mystic end of Excalibur merges with the mystique of acculturation. The brand returns to the matrix of its once and future fashioning, resoldering mythic transmission and reception in a continuous epic process that bonds hero with poet with reader, and that—for once, triumphantly—identifies the wild power of Tennysonian doom with the imaginative productions of time, the inevitable mastery of this human tale. "Behold an arm": the bold Sir Bedivere ascends to the authority of command—both imperative and performative— on the strength of his releasing what he once thought was all he had to hold by. Henceforth Bedivere moves in order with his king and takes us with him, in order that the transmissive reception of an epic matter be fulfilled.

THE REMAINING HUNDRED lines or so of the "Morte" comprise a twofold recapitulation of the essential action of epic transfer— the transportation of Arthur to the lakeshore and his departure for Avilion on the dusky barge—together with a final exchange between Bedivere and Arthur, which expounds the elegiac logic behind Tennyson's epic theme. The largely repetitive structure of the narrative from this point (Palmer 1973, 48–49) derives in some measure from Malory, whose Arthurian book habitually renders multiple, homologous versions of a basic action. And this very fidelity of Tennyson's "Morte d'Arthur" to Malory's forms part of its message about cultural transmission, even as the higher frequency of heroic similes in the last movement of the poem underlines Tennyson's intention to assimilate an insular prose romance into the extended international family of the epic tradition.

Arthur initiates the subsequent action by ordering Bedivere to carry him to the margin of the lake, but the immediately ensuing passage freezes action once again in a pictorial moment:

> So saying, from the pavement he half rose,
> Slowly, with pain, reclining on his arm,
> And looking wistfully with wide blue eyes
> As in a picture. Him Sir Bedivere
> Remorsefully regarded through his tears,
> And would have spoken, but he found not words.   (167–172)

This wordless and compassionate mutual gaze recalls both Bedivere's habit of idyllic arrest and Arthur's temptation to pathetic despair ("Woe is me!") over the betrayal to which that habit has led. The passage thus conflates two earlier obstacles to epic progress, as if to suggest by its narrative inertia the necessity of the second effort, which secondary epic often requires of its belated heroes. Indeed, this next section of the "Morte" is the secondary character Bedivere's *aristeia*, for the primary protagonist Arthur is now the worse afflicted of the two. "Looking wistfully with wide blue eyes / As in a picture," Arthur becomes what he beholds: he looks like a wistful figure in a picture because a picture is what he seems to be wistfully looking into, as the isolation enforced by his imminent death makes everything he sees a fait accompli. Arthur thus is caught in a snapshot that emphasizes the pathetic or human-interest angle of his dying. If that dying is to be an epic passing and not just an idyllic rest, then the initiative must pass to Bedivere, who rises splendidly, on the spur of remorse, to his finest hour. Bedivere finds "not words," but the impetus for an action about which words may be written, in the energy of guilt— an emotion whose obvious relevance to Tennyson's guilt as a survivor of his own Arthur should not blind us to the way its complex of fidelity and belatedness might bear on the composition of a modern epic.

During the paragraph that follows this *tableau vivant*, it is hard not to share Tennyson's exhilaration at imagining a circumstance in which something can actually be done for a helpless Arthur;

but it is important to see how the belated Bedivere stands in for Tennyson the latecoming epic poet as well as Tennyson the man. To the disabled king, "Like one that feels a nightmare on his bed" (177), history has become a nightmare, from which only the activity of his former dependent can awaken him into the higher reality of legend. In shouldering the king, then, Bedivere takes on a kind of independence: not independence from the king's story, but rather the independence the king's story can confer with the free acceptance of its duties: Bedivere's cue for action now comes from within (Preyer 1966, 347; Boyd 1977, 28). Thus Arthur's superfluous imperative, "Quick, quick! / I fear it is too late" (179–180), merely seconds the remorse whereby Bedivere's "own thought drove him, like a goad" (185).

Bedivere traverses the same landscape we have seen him sleep-walk before (45–51), yet now his own action organizes the scene. No longer statically "Clouded with his own conceit" (110) but "Clothed with his breath" (182), he is inspired to and by an epic deed that will fill the otherwise "empty breath" of posterity. "He heard the deep behind him, and a cry / Before" (184–185): the route of Bedivere and Arthur through an increasingly resonant and vocal landscape brings them out of physical place and into mythic time, within hail of their destiny. Furthermore, as Tennyson tones the narrative with "faint Homeric echoes" of a conventionally epic style, so Bedivere's activity calls forth from the landscape echoes answering to his newly purposeful thought:

> Dry clashed his harness in the icy caves
> And barren chasms, and all to left and right
> The bare black cliff clanged round him, as he based
> His feet on juts of slippery crag that rang
> Sharp-smitten with the dint of armèd heels—
> And on a sudden, lo! the level lake,
> And the long glories of the winter moon. (186–192)

To compare the descents here and in lines 45–51 is to gauge the difference between idyllic description and epic narration. Persistent enjambment enacts Bedivere's drive; rhythmic counterpointing underscores the obstacles that oppose him; and bravura patterns of alliteration and assonance—note the interlinear staircasing effect with "clashed," "chasms," "clanged," and "crag"—ring with the sense of difficulty met and, finally, overcome in the congratulation of the ending couplet (Rosenberg 1973, 97). During this last knightly deed Bedivere does hard work, in sharp and refreshing contrast to the repeated "lightness" of his earlier locomotion; and the reward for his effort arrives in the way he animates the landscape instead of its automatizing him.

The two best reasons for the rewarding difficulty of this passage are also the simplest, and both speak to the question of epic. For one thing, Bedivere now sustains the weight of two bodies, his own and Arthur's. Carrying the matter of Arthur, in the most physical sense, he figuratively bears a Virgilian burden of the past toward an imminent epic release that aggrandizes the bearer, "Larger than human on the frozen hills" (183), worthy at length of the ancient and mighty-boned dead he merely bypassed before. Beyond this extra freight, Bedivere's epic burden is aggravated by the lateness of the hour: having made war all day and run errands all night, Bedivere ought to be suffering the last stages of a fatigue correlative to the exhaustion of the epic line. Yet Tennyson, who was genius of nothing if not the recuperation of belatedness, ends the passage in celebration of the beauties peculiar to so extreme an hour, composing from a dead calm and a declining moon an idyll that he redeems into epic grandeur with a Virgilian *mirabile visu*: "And on a sudden, lo! the level lake, / And the long glories of the winter moon."[33]

Bedivere's heroic portage of his king retraces the movement from static, idyllic lamentation to epic redemption that we have already seen in the Excalibur episode. The arrival of the funeral barge with the three queens initiates the transmission motif a third and final time, now in terms avowedly larger than life and stiff with ritual state. It is only at this stage, once the scene has been set for the reception of the matter of Arthur, that the note of lamentation this text has suppressed for so long gets full vent:

> and from them rose
> A cry that shivered to the tingling stars,
> And, as it were one voice, an agony
> Of lamentation, like a wind, that shrills
> All night in a waste land, where no one comes,
> Or hath come, since the making of the world.   (198–203)

No one who recalls the date of composition of the "Morte d'Arthur" will deny this passionate moment its bearing on the life of

Alfred Tennyson. A transfiguring outburst of pure pain, the cry of the three queens has its only rival in "Achilles over the Trench," the splendid fragment of earth-shaking grief for a friend's death that Tennyson was to translate from the eighteenth book of the *Iliad* two decades later. Whatever biographically motivated rage and sorrow Tennyson had to express, on either occasion, he chose to mediate through the epic tradition, transfiguring his life's greatest visible grief by figuring it into a narrative that might contain and direct it.

It seems particularly significant that this most nakedly stricken reaction to Arthur's loss issues from those who have come in order to receive him. The supernatural voice arising here to pang even "the tingling stars" is the voice not of loss but of reception, and its aesthetic power has much to do with the aesthetic of epic reception that the "Morte" as a whole concerns. The cry of the queens represents in fuller diapason the "cry / Before" that Bedivere has heard a dozen lines above; and the ambiguous temporality of that poetically upthrust word "Before," which situates the cry in Bedivere's future, yet also in the deep past that has preceded him, becomes active again: Arthur's departure to his doom constitutes a return to his beginnings.[34]

The keening of the queens voices their kenning, their recognition of the king; and as we recognize a wider tracing of the concentric pattern of return we have already seen in the arch of Excalibur, we recognize further that Arthur's passage on the dusky barge is to be the ground of a perennial remaking: the restoration of Arthur to his legendary home means that his proper home is in culturally restorative legend. The tongueless, superhuman or infantile cry of the queens, like deepest grief, or like the alien wind of Tennyson's denaturing simile, exceeds understanding: it sounds, the simile weirdly says, like a sound no one can ever have heard, "where no one comes, / Or hath come, since the making of the world." Although that sound antedates the making of meaning in one sense, in another it is the condition, the founding occasion, of such making. The human, linguistic project of understanding may note, score, and thus contain the panic senselessness of such a cry—indeed, must contain it, if a culture is to thrive in its recurrent rebirth from those energies that, because they matter most, cause greatest pain. Out of such agonies survivors' worlds, and the culture-founding epics that survivors write and read as global images, are made, shivered, and made again.

The sense of communal survivorship is made most firmly, "Morte d'Arthur" repeatedly suggests, when it is founded in a text. The word made flesh in Tennyson's Christlike Arthur—the blameless king for whom, throughout the *Idylls* to come, "Man's word is God in man"—achieves its final power when the flesh is made word and restored to the place of human making. We all but see this final transformation of the king, from a body into a textual corpus, once the queens have received him "and chafed his hands, / And called him by his name" (209–210). His brow "Striped with dark blood," his face "white / And colourless" (212–213), his armor "dashed with drops / Of onset" (215–216), Arthur seems a document inked with the signs of his undoing:

> the light and lustrous curls—
> That made his forehead like a rising sun
> High from the daïs-throne—were parched with dust;
> Or, clotted into points and hanging loose,
> Mixed with the knightly growth that fringed his lips.
> So like a shattered column lay the King.   (216–221)

The youthful page who has ascended to kingship alters before our eyes to a page legibly graven, a parchment "clotted into points." From rising man to tangled text to shattered column—a conventional type of ruin, but here also a ruin of columnar type, a broken font? In any case, the elegiac translation of Arthur from person to exemplum, from individual to typical form, answers to larger aims of the "Morte." Even the image of disappearance that ends the poem highlights Arthur's textuality, as Tennyson brings the "Morte" to a full stop by providing a virtually typographical image of one: "the hull / Looked one black dot against the verge of dawn" (270–271). The translation of Arthur from a king to a text makes of his passing not a death but a "mort," in the sense of that old hunting term still current among the Victorians: a death note, a summons to the commemorative survivorship of those who, "Revolving many memories" (270), live on to transmit Arthur's now literary remains.

The last dialogue between knight and king brings the principal argument of the poem into final focus. Having surrendered Arthur to the three queens, Bedivere suffers a bout of separation anxiety and reverts to lamenting the king's lost presence in persistently visual terms: "Where shall I hide my forehead and my eyes? / For now I see the true old times are dead"; "now the whole ROUND TABLE is dissolved / Which was an image of the mighty world" (228–235). Bedivere fears equally the loss of iconic light from this visible image, as "the days darken round," and the supervention of other sights that will supplant it, "new men, strange faces" (237–238). Such fear of dispossession is the unexorcised shadow of Bedivere's idyllic hoarding; yet Bedivere's language extends, as before, a more consoling promise than he knows. For of "the true old times" now passing away Bedivere strangely asserts, "Such times have been not since the light that led / The holy Elders with the gift of myrrh" (232–233). The parallel between Arthurian and Christian story, barely submerged throughout the poem, here surfaces unmistakably; but the curious tense of the verb "have been" suggests that Tennyson wants to put this parallel to a so phisticated modern use. If Bedivere, who has just declared the true old times dead, were to say, "Such times *had* not been" since Christ's, he would be affirming their pastness and thus their specific historicity. But when he says instead that they *have* not been, he cancels their historicity and installs them instead in the realm of story, as a graft upon what "Timbuctoo" called at an analogous moment "the great vine of *Fable*."

Tennyson's poem thus recalls contemporary developments in the Higher Criticism, which supplemented its demolition of the historical veracity of Christian scripture by shifting the grounds of belief away from scripture as factual record to the history of scriptural reception among the community that canonized and transmitted it (Shaffer 1975). Bedivere becomes, by accidental grace, a Higher Critic of Arthurian legend, both a last citizen and a first witnessing guide to the Camelot that is never built at all and therefore built forever. It is precisely because the icon is shattered, because the whole Round Table is dissolved, that Bedivere may surround himself amid darkening, evil days with new men, strange faces, other minds: the fit audience though few of Protestant epic tradition. The last of Arthur's knights, he will "go forth companionless"; yet he will be accompanied by a tale capable of attracting that saving remnant who, in the still darker days of the nineteenth century, may form the nucleus of a recreative culture. "Such times have been not"—save as a tradition of communal telling makes them again modern, such times as, *mutatis mutandis,* the old books sing: "So all day long the noise of battle rolled."

Arthur's final speech offers Bedivere comfort and challenge at once, through the continuity that undergirds a tradition of recovered loss. He speaks first, and least cogently, of the zeitgeist:

> The old order changeth, yielding place to new,
> And God fulfils Himself in many ways,
> Lest one good custom should corrupt the world.   (240–242)

I find these often-quoted lines about as consoling as the speech of Oceanus that they condense from Keats's *Hyperion* (II.173–243), and I suspect that the Tennyson of "Morte d'Arthur" did too. Planned obsolescence never took deep root in Tennyson's imagination, though he tried to foster the idea during the 1830s in some of the first-written sections of *In Memoriam* and in the political quatrain lyrics ("Love Thou Thy Land" and others) that came with them. Tennyson presents epic transmission as a species of cultural evolution requiring conscious accomplishment, not a blind manifestation of social weather. Not even Arthur seems to put much stock in such a model of mindless change:

> Comfort thyself: what comfort is in me?
> I have lived my life, and that which I have done
> May He within Himself make pure! but thou,
> If thou shouldst never see my face again,
> Pray for my soul. More things are wrought by prayer
> Than this world dreams of. Wherefore, let thy voice
> Rise like a fountain for me night and day.
> For what are men better than sheep or goats
> That nourish a blind life within the brain,
> If, knowing God, they lift not hands of prayer
> Both for themselves and those that call them friend?
> For so the whole round earth is every way
> Bound by gold chains about the feet of God.   (243–255)

Arthur understands that in committing himself to God, as to the legendary queens, he also makes a commitment to cultural aftertime. The disappearance of his "face" or visible presence is the condition for the perseverance of his "soul" as an enduring influence among his successors; and the medium of this succession is language, in its work of representing what is absent. "More things are wrought by prayer / Than this world dreams of": work for the spirit in words, prayer is the definitively human analogue to the craft whereby the Lady of the Lake "wrought" Excalibur.

And the work of prayer is binding. The "voice" that Arthur charges to "Rise like a fountain for me night and day" will take the departed king's place and make him a commonplace in cultural memory (Landow 1974, 424). That prayerful voice will bind past and future moments each to each: Tennyson's conflation of the Wordsworthian "night and day" of visionary deprivation from the "Intimations" ode with its commemorative "fountain-light of all our day" (8, 155) enacts a characteristic revision stressing cultural over natural piety. The overflowing vocal fountain of prayer will, finally, work elegiac self-interest up beyond the mere gregariousness of "sheep or goats" into the nourishment of a human culture. Through the antiphony of past and future, self and others, a people recalling Arthur's story will invoke him to speak to them in turn and "call them friend." "The whole ROUND TABLE is dissolved" in order that its circuit may increase through the good faith that keeps its word and voices "the whole round" again, in canon: "For so the whole round earth is every way / Bound by gold chains about the feet of God."

THAT THIS LAST image is a reverend commonplace, especially common in the epic tradition—Ricks refers us to Homer, Spenser, and Milton among others (*PT*, 596)—makes a corollary point about genre. The epic poet's will to integrate his work, in an intrinsic or formal point of view, has become by Tennyson's time, and with a redoubled urgency we do not find even in the nostalgic humanism of Renaissance epic, a will to affirm diachronic integrity as well. Solidarity with the past has become an indispensable foundation for the building of a modern epic, and the amplitude of the nineteenth-century poet's backward reach engenders within the epic text a mirror image in the hearkening of his hero—Tennyson's Arthur, Browning's Pope—toward the future. We have seen from "The Gardener's Daughter" and "Dora" how fully the Tennysonian idyll displays the arts of the joiner; and much in the pace and deliberate glamor of "Morte d'Arthur" affiliates it with those poems. But where we may regard the other English idylls as Tennyson's attempts to join his public where they stand, giving them on their own short terms the poetic commodity they want, the "Morte" represents his ambition to legislate for them and join them to the authoritative past that he believes to be modern culture's longest-term need.

All three texts are idylls, but they evince very different kinds of poetic responsibility toward the public—kinds of responsibility that correspond to the literary kinds to which each of the three idylls belongs. If "The Gardener's Daughter" is an experiment with bourgeois pastoral, and "Dora" a more disciplined exercise in georgic, one of the ways in which "Morte d'Arthur" scales the traditional epic summit is by standing on their shoulders and then kicking them away. Bedivere's infatuation with work of the surface, after the fashion of "The Gardener's Daughter," represents Tennyson's version of the pastoral stopping place that has threatened to waylay poets en route to epic since Virgil's time at least. More subtly, a comparison between the different ways in which roles are fulfilled in "Dora" and the "Morte" reveals fine but crucial distinctions between georgic labor and the work that is epic: between the taking of an order and the making of one, between the passive acquiescence that diminishes actor and action alike and the conscious welcome that ennobles both. "Morte d'Arthur" is so stately a poem because its epic pretension, however imperfectly that pretension was to be realized at length in *Idylls of the King*, bespeaks not a consumer's cunning or a craftsman's know-how but a statesman's conscience. Its largest significance inheres in its wager that a private need—a man's personal bereavement, an epic aspirant's contest with the mighty dead—might fulfill itself in a communally representative creation.

Tennyson won this wager handsomely; and the cultural reasons for his success may give us appropriate pause, on the threshold of a chapter that will address his three most culturally engaged major works. "Morte d'Arthur," like *Idylls of the King*, is a profoundly conservative poem. For all its mythology of progress, and the globality of its mythmaking ambition, the poem gains its victories on thoroughly elitist grounds, where "King Arthur, like a modern gentleman," would be quite at home. "The whole round earth" bound in the fellowship of fervent voice proves, upon inspection of the social and ideological content of the poet's Arthurian fable, to be bounded by fairly insular poles: at one pole a moribund aristocratic ideal of ordered fealty, at the other a parvenu (and to Tennyson's imagination a diminished) bourgeois ideal of expansive change and communication. These poles also represent the chief constituents of his readership, as of the mixed, but far from open, ruling class in which his birth and education had installed him. Tennyson's public wager in "Morte d'Arthur" succeeded, we might say, because in transmitting the mythology he had received from an antique culture he found means of pitching it right to the class that he knew contained the majority of his readers.

I see little point in making Tennyson's success the basis for an ideological rather than a literary critique. In this chapter I have tried, on the contrary, to develop means of bringing the two sorts of criticism closer together, in the belief that their conjunction can enlarge the range—and the sympathy—of each. Before writing Tennyson off as the mellifluous ideologue of the constituency from which and to which he wrote, it is well to treat the size and diversity of that constituency with a healthy respect, and to ask what other poet has reached in his own lifetime so great a number or so broad a spectrum of readers. Still, and by virtue of Tennyson's very achievement, the question of ideology persists: the bases of his exceptionally wide appeal were, of necessity, culturally specific to a high degree—as no hermeneutic of tradition and reception, such as has informed my discussion of "Morte d'Arthur," can afford to forget. What seemed most nearly universal in Tennyson's work to a Mr. Holbrook, or a William Allingham, or an F. T. Palgrave, were some of the very features that now strike us as most parochial. Such is the doom of culture, when viewed under the aspect of history. As we move now to Tennyson's most culturally engaged writings, that doom will be among our leading themes, even as Tennyson found it becoming his.

6

Pyrrhic Victorian: The Incorporated Imagination in *The Princess*, *In Memoriam*, and *Maud*

THE PUBLICATION OF the 1842 *Poems* put Tennyson clearly on the map, but it was far from clear what turning he should take next. His double-volume collection marked an itinerary along two tracks that appeared mutually divergent, even mutually exclusive. On one hand lay the public thoroughfare of contemporary mimesis paved by the narrative domestic idylls; on the other rose the craggy, marginal way of "Ulysses" and "Break, Break, Break," where lyrical intensity verged on the suprasensual. These forking routes need not have constituted an insoluble dilemma: the midcareer choices of Browning and Yeats, for example, show that a poet may work out his destiny through the flexible medium of the collection, where an arrangement of shorter poems in different genres gathers into a whole book that exceeds the sum of its parts. Tennyson's 1842 *Poems* represented such a collection; and to a taste formed by the study of such major successors as Yeats and Hardy, Frost and Stevens, it may indeed figure as the best of all his productions. He would continue to present himself in this format, publishing new collections and revised selections of shorter verse regularly from the 1860s through the year of his death. All these volumes would exploit, with varying degrees of success and with a gradual steepening of generic antagonism, versions of the juxtaposition of poetic kinds he had established as his own by 1842.[1]

In the meantime, however, during the prime years of his poetic majority Tennyson evidently was working from a need to do more. The evidence lies in the publication record of the later 1840s and 1850s: *The Princess* (1847), *In Memoriam* (1850), *Maud* (1855), and at decade's end a definitive down payment on his epic estate, the four-book *Idylls of the King* (1859). The last title points beyond the scope of this study; but the first three alone, severally and in the aggregate, suggest that self-collection in the anthological mode of 1842 was no longer enough. Driven by congruent thirsts for inward stability and outward standing, Tennyson was encouraged by a generally friendly public reception in 1842; he was also challenged by a sense, classically inspired and Romantically confirmed, of the shape a major poet's career ought to assume; and—not the least spur to this poet's ambition—he was attracted by the opportunities for a technical experimentation in which all these pressures might meet for formal resolution.[2] After 1842, therefore, Tennyson began to collect himself, not anthologically, but for a qualitatively new effort. He repeatedly devoted his mature talents to the perfection of the book-length poem: a work that might be extensive yet coherent, encyclopedic yet whole (Shannon 1952, 82–83, 92).

If perfection was Tennyson's goal, none of the three large poems completed during his thirties and forties attains it, though *In Memoriam*, it is argued, comes close. That each work involves its exponents in difficulties and its proponents in apologetics is a cardinal fact of Tennyson studies. At the same time, as the best studies have recognized, the first uneasy critic of these works was their maker, who not only registered dissatisfaction with each text after the fact, but set the seal of his uneasiness on each as he wrote, making an anxious wrinkle of self-reflection part of their texture. The fictive poet of *The Princess* calls his transcript of an experiment in group narration "a strange diagonal" that "maybe pleased neither myself nor them" (Conclusion, 27–28). Throughout *In Memoriam* versions of the topic question "What words are these have fallen from me?" (xvi.1) recur as a writer's analogues to the metaphysical scruples of that doubt-stricken testament. Even the less contemplative *Maud*, in which the latent contradictions far outweigh the explicit, gives regular checks to its speaker's eagerness for commitment: "What! am I raging alone?" "My dream? do I dream of bliss?" (I.i.53, xix.686).

The vein of self-consciousness that runs through these long poems does more various work than the mere registration of analogies among thematic, formal, and careerist concerns. There is every reason to believe, for instance, that the scrupulous hesitancies of these texts express Tennyson's own uncertainties about the range of social and intellectual matters they address; nor does Tennyson's credit necessarily totter under the consideration that the timely expression of an honest doubt was among the surest rhetorical means of carrying conviction home to a Victorian audience. Still, the analogy between poet's and poems' concerns is worth pursuing, for the insight it can yield into one signal feature that these very different essays in the long poem share. In *The Princess, In Memoriam,* and *Maud* Tennyson composed three strikingly composite works: works that in their structural segmentation, their common thematic insistence on the collapse and reincorporation of the self, and their habitual reference to dramatic versions of their own genesis and sustenance as texts, call attention to questions that the long poem especially, but usually just implicitly, poses. Are its episodic units fitly joined? Is it over now? Are its personages consistent with themselves and with their environment? Does that environment represent a credible world? Are the constituent genres of the work aptly chosen and mutually consonant?

That such questions of plot, character, circumstance, and genre arise within the works themselves, directly and persistently, is remarkable in the long view of poetic tradition, but less so within the compass of the nineteenth century. The great line stretching from Homer to Pope, the line that had given cachet to the achievement of the long poem, is not a tradition conspicuously self-conscious, at least not in Tennyson's manner, about what the long poem as such might signify. If *Troilus and Criseyde* and *The Faerie Queene* now look to us occasionally like monuments of creative angst, that is because we have learned to read them through Romantic lenses. The requisite collusion of the reader in the production of the long poem, which undoubtedly formed part of Tennyson's strategy, stands as a nineteenth-century invention. This is so whether we look to Wordsworth's incorporation of the "Friend" as ideal readerly colleague in *The Prelude,* to Byron's duelist challenges to the reader of *Don Juan,* or in Tennyson's decades to the way Browning prods and complots with the reader of *Sordello* or *The Flight of the Duchess.* Within the Romantic tradition circa 1850, then, when Tennyson conducts in-house diagnoses of the health of his long poems he is following a convention that hovers somewhere between avant-garde and old-guard status.

A fact of greater Romantic interest about Tennyson's midcareer experiments is that for each of them the questions of plot, character, circumstances, and genre turn out to be versions of one another. In his choice of themes and techniques that might enable an extended, comprehensive, and topical work, Tennyson's Romantic situation led him, inevitably, to the practice of what might be termed *Bildungspoesie*: the verse narrative of a central figure's progress from self-division and cultural alienation, through stages of therapeutic encounter, to a hard-won goal of inner and outer reconciliation. Such a pattern, prevalent in nineteenth-century verse narrative from Blake and Wordsworth on, offered a special advantage to a poet in Tennyson's situation. For it made the questions attendant upon the composition of the long poem each other's solutions. Where the essential action was the protagonist's developing a sense of self in the world, consistency of character equaled coherence of plot, and the conclusive affirmation of the rehabilitated self was at the same time the circumstantial validation of the world. If *The Princess* is the least successful of the three works to be considered here, its relative failure hangs in part on inadequate assimilation to this Romantic model. The focal split between the Princess and the Prince as rival protagonists, and especially the incompletely realized narrative machinery, impede the Romantic identification of character with action and expose the final resolution to charges of force or fraud, domination or imposture—charges that *In Memoriam* and *Maud* must face as well, but that their monodramatic format lets them absorb in more interesting and moving fashion.

Tennyson's term for the pattern of *Bildungspoesie*, in a discarded alternative title for *In Memoriam*, was "the way of the soul." This phrase nicely captures the coincidence of a direction with a method, which constituted much of the pattern's appeal to a poet who by the 1840s was particularly concerned with the attitudinal ramifications of genre. A strong but flexible teleology guided the poet's deliberations as to the genres his new long poems might comprise. At its upper, structural reach as archetypal myth, genre furnishes a shape for the whole: Tennyson left Shakespearean and Dantesque keys to the comic structure of *The Princess* and *In Memoriam*, respectively, and he called the darker *Maud* a miniature *Hamlet* (*Memoir*, I, 396; Ray 1968, 43). Furthermore, at the microlevel of tone and implication, local generic choices (love lyric, pastoral, mockheroic, and so on) serve as cues to the various stances in which protagonists conduct transactions with the world of ideas, of natural and social facts, of other selves: cues, as it were, to the way the soul takes its way, in a sequence of liberal changes broadening to a presaged goal. It is this latter, more particular set of generic options that I shall stress here, in part because larger issues of genre have been capably treated elsewhere, but principally because the local interplay of genres lets us grasp Tennyson's long poems as elaborations of a dialectic that his earlier work had established, and that imparts to his most ambitious works their curious blend of complacency and anomie.

For Tennyson by the 1840s genre had become the attitudinal index par excellence, the literary sign of an emotional and perceptual posturing that reduces to two contrary kinds: lyrical dismissal, which exhausts the world of social contexts and literary pretexts for the sake of unmediated commerce between self and cosmos; and idyllic acceptance, which accommodates the given world within an artifice that concedes the fictiveness of the self, as a construct authorized by its place in history. How these antithetical attitudes might meet became the ground issue, inextricably personal and artistic, of Tennyson's long poems; and the issue was joined on the field of genre. Generic overviews based on the large mythic structures of these works can deliver only a limited and uniform report: the idyll wins, in a laureate hat trick, three to nothing. Princess Ida comes down and caves in, the poet of *In Memoriam* will not shut him from his kind, and the speaker in *Maud* awakes to the better mind and feels with his native land. That is what the integrative pattern of *Bildungspoesie* means for these poems; but it is hardly what Tennyson meant them for, if we attend to the how as well as the whither in "the way of the soul."

The plot of these works was largely a matter of convenience, offering a relatively uncontroversial form of architectonic stability within which Tennyson could weave the traceries of manner for whose sake we read them today—whether we are students of Victorian manners or of a great mannerist technician in poetry. Furthermore, Tennyson's methodical miscellany of genres constitutes a counterplot challenging the overall narrative action. Readers who wish that Ida had not caved in, who feel the solitary doubt of *In Memoriam* superior to its collective faith, and who are sure that the speaker in *Maud* makes a better madman than an enlisted man, are responding to the generic infighting that makes these works live. Read closely, the extended poems of Tennyson's middle years are not the idyllic shutouts they seem from a distance, but densely knotted ties, exquisite draws between the idyllic and lyric impulses that divided his work of 1842. For Tennyson's narratives of triumphant cultural integration suffer constant erosion from the reflection that such integration is purchased at the high cost of their protagonists' Romantic integrity—a reflection not extrinsic to these ambitious texts but insubordinately solicited within them by the poet who remained, even as laureate, a Pyrrhic Victorian. The household jar within these works by no means disintegrates their larger architecture: the narrative frames Tennyson imposed on all three were built to last. Rather, it creates a more intensely charged, second-level continuity, which will be served less well by critical overview than by the sort of selective close-up or underview that is practiced in the following discussions. I offer such a close-up here in the hope that it can bring these disparate works together, can bring us nearer to grasping Tennyson's career whole, and can refresh our appreciation of the integrity of an artist who persisted in regarding the conventions of his art as the human consequences they are.

The Princess: Muffled Like the Fates

The Princess, everyone agrees, is a problem poem; and as with *The Winter's Tale*, the problem play cited in its Prologue, the difficulties here center on the adjustment of genres and calibration of tones. It addresses a very touchy subject, the relation between the sexes in contemporary culture, with degrees of tact that range from a broadly conventional plot resolution, where boy and girl get each other for good, to a finicky narrative apparatus that diffuses authorial responsibility for the plot as thoroughly as possible. A textbook Victorian compromise, the poem avoids taking a position on a hotly debated issue by taking up any number of positions, letting reciprocally ventilated views cool each other off, and leaving affairs pretty much where they stood. If *The Princess*, consid-

ered polemically, has the diplomatic and anonymous air of a committee report, that is probably what Tennyson wished. His newspaper verses of the early 1850s show him capable of savage
partisanship when stirred; but neither the rallying of Victorian
feminism nor the patriarchal status quo was a sufficient stimulus
to commitment here.

Indeed, the Woman Question seems to have attracted Tennyson
as an occasion not for ideological but for stylistic mediation, a
sounding board for tonal effects (Elton 1924, 24, 50; Killham 1958).
The Princess is primarily a tone poem, both a book of charming
lyrics and an almost clinically disengaged exercise in the modu-
lation of voice across an extended narrative and topical field. The
work declares its experimental character in advance, and with
appropriate undergraduate indecorum, as a "tale from mouth to
mouth" (Prologue, 188; Stevenson 1974, 24); and the idea of a
round-robin narrative counts for more than any actual use Tennyson puts it to. His decision not to retain the thumbnail sketches
he wrote of each contributing narrator (*PT*, 1768–69) was a wise
one, for the poem's feint at collective storytelling places less emphasis on a Browningesque or Chaucerian clash of particular perspectives than on the art of the collector, the scribal poet who
undertakes "to bind the scattered scheme of seven / Together in
one sheaf" (Conclusion, 8–9). If the seven narrators turn out to
be indistinguishable, that is because they speak each other's language, like James and John from "Walking to the Mail," in the
broadly cultural sense that they share a set of social as well as
literary assumptions. The narrative circulates among these young
collegians so smoothly because not only everything about it, but
everything about them and their circle, is so conventional (Bergonzi 1969, 49; Eagleton 1978, 102–103; Sedgwick 1985, 127–130).

This framing circumstance gives extra resonance to the internal
thematic of Ida's rebellion against convention and eventual reab-
sorption within it, as we shall discover. It also means, though,
that we can make our discoveries only by abandoning the usual
interest in character and plot, and by getting interested instead in
the descriptive and attitudinal traits—matters of narrative tone—
that our otherwise boring entertainers hold in common. This may
be one reason why the best readers of *The Princess* have been British
critics (Elton, Ricks, Bayley, Eagleton) attuned to the local color
of its rhetoric and to the finesse of a style that, especially given so

implausible a parable, constantly implies a social world structured by subtleties of manner. The ease with which, after the first edition of 1847, Tennyson could incorporate references to the Continental revolutions of 1848 suggests that this medley is ideological through and through; the distinctive critical challenge lies in the linkage between its ideology of compromise and its meddling tonal ways.

We might appropriately seek examples of the subtlety of narrative tone in passages that depend on a dialectic between violence and containment. Such passages occur everywhere in the text, partly because they are natural outcroppings of Tennyson's fundamental contest between idyllic and lyric modes—his idyllic strategies being always strategies of containment, while his lyrics bespeak a discontent that yearns against all bounds—and partly because violence is so central a concern in the plot itself. Everyone in the story, including Princess Ida, regards her foundation of a women's university as a violent break with convention. The intrusion of the Prince and his cronies patently represents an answering act of violation, the revenge of the establishment: "So was their sanctuary violated" (VII.1). And the ensuing battle and aftermath, though they lead to benign reconciliation between the patriarchal and feminist camps, make it quite clear that the women's cause is the weaker only insofar as might makes right. Even the comic resolution is drawn up in blood; and while the Prince's benedictory image of "The two-celled heart beating, with one full stroke, / Life" (VII.288–289) does much to sublimate the cruder narrative facts, the menace of force pervades Ida's ordeal, as indeed it pervades Tennyson's handling of the story at large, where something suspiciously like bad faith keeps surfacing at the level of mere description.[3]

Consider, for example, the coded table of contents the narrator smuggles into the Prologue under descriptive cover:

> And me that morning Walter showed the house,
> Greek, set with busts: from vases in the hall
> Flowers of all heavens, and lovelier than their names,
> Grew side by side; and on the pavement lay
> Carved stones of the Abbey-ruin in the park,
> Huge Ammonites, and the first bones of Time;
> And on the tables every clime and age
> Jumbled together; celts and calumets,
> Claymore and snowshoe, toys in lava, fans

Of sandal, amber, ancient rosaries,
Laborious orient ivory sphere in sphere,
The cursed Malayan crease, and battle-clubs
From the isles of palm: and higher on the walls,
Betwixt the monstrous horns of elk and deer,
His own forefathers' arms and armour hung.   (10–24)

This encyclopedia of "every clime and age" attests to the inclusive ambition of Tennyson's long poem in obvious ways. Less immediately apparent is the way the superfluous remark about flowers "lovelier than their names" suggests the role played by linguistic flowers of rhetoric, in giving order to the potentially violent jumble of potentially violent things the passage proceeds to name. "Celts and calumets" are hatchets and peace pipes, primitive instruments of war and concord brought together as much by alliterative as by semantic affinity; and when both affinities converge in "Claymore" at the head of the next line one thinks less of a broadsword than of its exotic yet phonetically domesticated Gaelic name. The rich medley of consonants and vowels across the next two and a half lines typifies the "laborious" poet's will to harmonize his congeries and to minimize eruptive effects, making of all "toys in lava" (Dietrich 1976, 186). "The cursed Malayan crease" is musically graced in its poetic setting, as are the "monstrous horns," becoming demonstrations of the virtue of "arms and armour" sustaining ancestral Vivian-place and the whole show it sponsors. If "battle-clubs / From the isles of palm" at last sound downright convivial, that is because Tennyson has spared no pains in establishing a rhythm of fear and reassurance, which predisposes his reader to accept the advantages of that pattern in the sequel (Buckler 1980, 137).

The pattern recurs a page later, in the phenomenal paragraph describing the imperial bread and circuses of the people's institute. This Victorian Penshurst is a Crystal Palace without the walls, charming the people from "the neighbouring borough" (5) within a private park whose enclosure was, presumably, one historical cause for their ancestors' forced migration from countryside to city. And the secret of the charm is another presumed cause of this industrially mandated resettlement, the magic exhibition of technological advance, beautifully adapted to Tennyson's miniaturizing techniques:

round the lake
A little clock-work steamer paddling plied

> And shook the lilies: perched about the knolls
> A dozen angry models jetted steam:
> A petty railway ran: a fire-balloon
> Rose gem-like up before the dusky groves
> And dropt a fairy parachute and past:
> And there through twenty posts of telegraph
> They flashed a saucy message to and fro
> Between the mimic stations.   (70–79)

The steamer shakes only lilies; the fire-balloon is but a "gem-like" and "fairy" thing after all; even the railway, so often an awesome icon of the Victorian religion of progress, is here "petty." We get the saucy message, as later when Lilia's feminist protest is muffled in diminutive descriptions: "She tapt her tiny silken-sandaled foot" (149); "Daintily she shrieked" (173). The idyllized steam engine embodies, in nineteenth-century terms, the controlled release of pent-up force in work: an image, and an ethos, linking Tennyson with his imperial forebear Virgil. As "The patient leaders of their Institute" teach the people "with facts" (58–59) that look more and more like propagandistic special effects—C.MS. Add. 6345, fol. 2, has "Amused" instead of "Taught"—so the people learn from their "angry models" the virtues of continence. "All the sloping pasture murmured," not with disaffection but "With happy faces and with holiday" (55–56), the idyllic buzz of a rare day's leave (Pitt 1962, 158; Killham 1973, 166–167).

The idyllic dispersal of the narrator's attention across a field of equivalent details is internally structured by a consistent pattern of menace and reconciliation:

>   somewhat lower down
> A man with knobs and wires and vials fired
> A cannon: Echo answered in her sleep
> From hollow fields: and here were telescopes
> For azure views; and there a group of girls
> In circle waited, whom the electric shock
> Dislinked with shrieks and laughter.   (64–70)

The momentarily threatening cannon makes a harmless panoramic conquest of echoing fields, leading on to coolly telescopic "azure views": its technological "knobs and wires and vials" become as delightfully mysterious as the mythological personification of Echo their operation provokes. Likewise the occult force of electricity, handsomely harnessed into sound by the deft verb "Dis-linked," arouses "shrieks" and then "laughter," in that order, which gives in brief the whole order of the day. If the imagery and syntax in this passage recall "Kubla Khan"—with its hollow depths, stone-dancing artificial fountain, and balanced vistas of "here" and "there"—such a reminiscence befits Tennyson's open-air pleasure dome, where violent energies are held in check by the mutually reinforcing authorities of heaven, a great lord, and a master poet.

"STRANGE WAS THE sight to me" (54), the narrator confesses; and we may read into his adjective the neutralizing pattern of stunned apprehensiveness, instantly allayed by the conventional and fa-miliar, which his narrative all but obsessively repeats. In H.Nbk. 24, fol. 6v, Tennyson inserted in a corresponding line the phrase "a pleasant sight," a change that suggests a revealing indecisiveness in the paramount matter of tone. His decision to stay with "strange," which the late description of the whole poem as a "strange diagonal" and the subsequently interpolated passages on the Prince's "weird seizures" confirm, represents a tonal preference that, whether we find it rich or just vague, is certainly character-istic. We have been looking at passages from the Prologue where idyllic strategies predominate, and where what they predominate over is a violent insurgency that belongs to Tennyson's most lyric moods. Such writing served the mature poet as a constant exercise in self-control, and the pursuit of its discipline across his subse-quent career entailed a no less constant acknowledgment of the lyric energies it designed to suppress. That is one reason why passages like these recur not just in the Prologue and Conclusion but throughout the narrative proper. There the fabulous story line exposes in slower motion the collusion of prevailing social codes with Tennyson's idyllic artifice, which by substituting linguistic structures for social ones masks the force whereby those codes prevail.

The most overtly institutional form violence takes in *The Princess* is military. Tennyson manages warfare here as he does in the occasional "Charge of the Light Brigade" and the mythic *Idylls of the King*: by transforming the sacrifices of war into musical offer-ings. In *The Princess*, especially, he correlates this aestheticization of violence with a gender-specific approach to the instincts. At

once a male duty for Tennyson and a male preserve, war elicits
what a man, as a man, truly feels; and in this text of good feelings,
Tennyson takes pains to suggest the satisfactions of such authenticity without engaging its risks. Bizarre results ensue, as in canto
V when Ida's ludicrously bellicose brother Arac enters with such
military fanfare that even the nice Prince finds himself stirred: "I
that prated peace," he says, "when first I heard / War-music, felt
the blind wildbeast of force, / Whose home is in the sinews of a
man, / Stir in me as to strike" (V.255–258). Lines like these, in a
work centrally concerned with marriage and written by a poet
who would notify a friend after his own wedding, "I have not
beaten her yet" (*Letters*, 328), lead down a strange diagonal linking
marital and martial ritual. Wherever brute force may end, in human terms it begins at "home"—in the sinews of a man, yes, but
also in the habits of domestic culture, where those sinews are bred
(Sedgwick 1985, 123). That is why, in this tame passage, the
"wildbeast of force" ends where it has begun, in the artificial or
acculturated condition of music:

> other thoughts than Peace
> Burnt in us, when we saw the embattled squares,
> And squadrons of the Prince, trampling the flowers
> With clamour: for among them rose a cry
> As if to greet the king; they made a halt;
> The horses yelled; they clashed their arms; the drum
> Beat; merrily-blowing shrilled the martial fife;
> And in the blast and bray of the long horn
> And serpent-throated bugle, undulated
> The banner: anon to meet us lightly pranced
> Three captains out; nor ever had I seen
> Such thews of men. (V.235–246)

The "blind wildbeast," amply represented here by trampling, yell-
ing horses and a horn that brays, modulates through the "serpent-
throated bugle" into a study in fluent form. The serpentine prosodic gamble of "undulated" enacts the sort of synesthetic diver-
sion that, by the 1840s, Tennyson could create in his sleep; and
at the close the three lightly prancing captains figure as broken
stallions, unprecedented men indeed. From brute force to animal
spirits: so the gilt edge of idyllic sublimation cuts great energies
to measure.[4]

Instinct in the toils of culture: this is Tennyson's theme in *The*

Princess, and for his male principal it unfolds straightforwardly because all the forces stack up in mutual reinforcement, the ideologically blind as well as the idyllically visible. It is otherwise, though, with the title character, for whom the recognition and containment of violence take forms both more obvious and more indirect.[5] Ida's separatist feminism constitutes a radical break with the ways of her father and brother; yet maintaining the countercultural establishment she has founded commits her to rhetorical tactics of control mirroring theirs—like Milton's Satan, whose forensic situation Tennyson repeatedly has Ida's recall. Furthermore, events compel her to recognize the dependency of her regime on the sufferance of the male armed forces that environ it. This humiliating recognition has the effect of driving Ida's initially epic, outward-bound energies back upon herself. We can observe this process most clearly in the recognition scene that climaxes canto IV (on which the poet worked especially hard in the Cambridge manuscript). A messenger delivers to Ida in public forum the written ultimata of the leagued fathers, and she reads

> till over brow
> And cheek and bosom brake the wrathful bloom
> As of some fire against a stormy cloud,
> When the wild peasant rights himself, the rick
> Flames, and his anger reddens in the heavens.   (IV.363–367)

The insurrectionary image of the wild peasant righting himself has historical roots in Tennyson's own university days: he had joined a bucket brigade against Cambridgeshire rick burnings during the agricultural uprisings of 1830. But what is the referential force of the image here? At first it appears a trope for the righteous indignation of the champion of women's rights—"For anger most it seemed" (368)—but as the passage unfolds, Ida seems to acknowledge her helplessness and to crush that stormy anger back within her clouded self:

> while now her breast,
> Beaten with some great passion at her heart,
> Palpitated, her hand shook, and we heard
> In the dead hush the papers that she held
> Rustle: at once the lost lamb at her feet
> Sent out a bitter bleating for its dam;
> The plaintive cry jarred on her ire; she crushed

> The scrolls together, made a sudden turn
> As if to speak, but, utterance failing her,
> She whirled them on to me, as who should say
> "Read," and I read. (IV.368–378)

"Palpitating" and "shaking" between the contradictory imperatives of the right she believes in and the might she confronts—
confronts perhaps most forcibly in the "bitter" appeal of the child
she has adopted (Sedgwick 1985, 123)—Ida seems at length a type
of the recanting radical, the once wild peasant who now "rights
himself" by abandoning the error of his ways and falling back into
line with public rectitude. "Utterance failing her," Ida cedes her
right of speech to what the fathers have written, in an ominous
silence that signals the opening of an inner, lyrical space of defeated
melancholy, and portends the tearful inarticulateness that will be
her chief means of expression once the final canto seals her fate.

This repressive introversion is a gesture that the style of *The
Princess* tirelessly rehearses. It was important enough, or appealing
enough, for Tennyson to write it out again as a plot event later
in the same canto, this time making explicit use of the civilizing
resources of idyll. Having read the missives Ida has cast before
him, the Prince launches a long-windedly wooing apology, which
ends with an apt, if tactless, appeal to the letter of recommendation
he holds from her father:

>   On one knee
> Kneeling, I gave it, which she caught, and dashed
> Unopened at her feet: a tide of fierce
> Invective seemed to wait behind her lips,
> As waits a river level with the dam
> Ready to burst and flood the world with foam:
> And so she would have spoken, but there rose
> A hubbub in the court of half the maids
> Gathered together: from the illumined hall
> Long lanes of splendour slanted o'er a press
> Of snowy shoulders, thick as herded ewes,
> And rainbow robes, and gems and gemlike eyes,
> And gold and golden heads; they to and fro
> Fluctuated, as flowers in storm, some red, some pale,
> All open-mouthed, all gazing to the light,
> Some crying there was an army in the land,
> And some that men were in the very walls,
> And some they cared not; till a clamour grew

> As of a new-world Babel, woman-built,
> And worse-confounded: high above them stood
> The placid marble Muses, looking peace.   (IV.448–468)

Again Ida is arrested at the level of pregnant pause, her speech frustrated by the preemptive force of an idyllic description that, if it does not take her breath away, has at least filched her tropes. The flood tide of Ida's invective, the "river level with the dam," fails to arise because "there rose / A hubbub" instead, a turbulent press that falls into "Long lanes of splendour" and "fluctuates" because that is what a river contained at flood level would do.[6]

This descriptive passage presents an extraordinary mix of concessions to the pleasure principle and to the reality principle: the former, because it caters to cultural ideals of feminine loveliness (snowy shoulders, gemlike eyes, open mouths); the latter, because it represents the effect such ideals have in foredooming the kind of radical reform Ida has sought. If we try beholding this idyllic scene through Ida's eyes—and she is the only character in Tennyson's fable for whom such an exercise of sympathy has much point—its vision of pretty, helpless femininity is a pretty hopeless vision as well. Her flock are "thick as herded ewes," impervious to her teachings when push comes to shove and the herd instinct of deep acculturation prevails. The cry "that men were in the very walls" voices Ida's own growing realization that her university has been built from the ground up on men's terrain, and the fluctuation of the multitude writes large the palpitation of the breast that this realization induced when it first dawned on her at line 369. Under the aegis of the placid Muses, expressing the idyllic peace of insuperable convention, the entire description reduces protest to a least common denominator, a "level with the dam"— for the pun here compare line 373 quoted above—the ewe's-eye view of women bred to wifedom, motherhood, and defenselessness.

In the face of such knowledge Ida is not quite speechless, but what she goes on to say reflects its introversive pressure. Her speech is now introduced with a new simile, which figures her not in an image of fluent power but in a peculiarly baleful image of its opposite:

> Fixt like a beacon-tower above the waves
> Of tempest, when the crimson-rolling eye

Glares ruin, and the wild birds on the light
Dash themselves dead.   (IV.472–475)

The lighthouse often serves in Romantic tradition as an ambivalent
emblem of self-sufficiency and solitary vastation, but its destruc-
tive potential is nowhere more cruelly emphasized than when Tennyson uses it here to preface the desperate measures that are now
Ida's sole recourse. Her fury has nowhere to turn but inward,
either against herself or—what amounts to much the same thing—
against the gender with whose cause she has identified herself.
First comes a wounded retreat to the bastion of self:

On me, me, me, the storm first breaks: *I* dare
All these male thunderbolts: what is it ye fear?
Peace! there are those to avenge us and they come:
If not,—myself were like enough, O girls,
To unfurl the maiden banner of our rights,
And clad in iron burst the ranks of war,
Or, falling, protomartyr of our cause,
Die.   (IV.478–485)

From "me, me, me" to "protomartyr," the Princess compasses
the trajectory of a Satanic logic that binds self-assertion to self-
destruction, in despite of an intractable world. A submerged ana-
grammatical logic is at work here, too, as "Ida" becomes a principle of pure defiance ("*I* dare") that can but foresee, with Oenone,
Ulysses, and Tithonus, the extinction of the self ("Die"). The
dreadful, subversive apostrophe "O girls" manifests the bathetic
inconsistency of such speech: again as in "Oenone" and the classical
monologues, Ida's stance can hardly coexist with the fiction of a
sympathetic audience. Accordingly her rhetoric alters its tone and
its object. She proceeds to unleash the "tide of fierce / Invective,"
which she originally prepared for the male assailants, upon her
herded female sympathizers instead, "dismissed in shame to live
/ No wiser than their mothers, household stuff, / Live chattels"
(IV.492–494)—a savage race, in short, that hoard and sleep and
feed, "To tramp, to scream, to burnish, and to scour, / For ever
slaves at home and fools abroad" (IV.499–500).

THIS EPISODE FROM the middle of *The Princess* exhibits to advantage the way Tennyson's generic medley deploys the reciprocal
determinations of idyllic and lyric modes, as means of letting self

and context take each other's measure. A self-willed exile since
the beginning, utopian authoress of "awful odes" and "rhymes /
And dismal lyrics, prophesying change" (I.137–141), Ida finds
herself—somewhat like her poet by the 1840s—in idyllic and conventional culture after all. In recoil from this discovery, she executes a sharp inward turn, which undercuts both her mission and
her identity, but which in so doing creates the space of a peculiarly
selfless, haunted lyricism. This reactive or compensatory lyricism,
which it is tempting to call simply Victorian lyricism, comes to
expression within the blank-verse narrative mainly in nonverbal
ways: as silence, or in the many sighs of the final cantos. But
Tennyson gave this private yet impersonal mood a voice of its
own, with the three great unattributed lyrics that he embedded in
the narrative, and that have understandably won a wider fame
than anything else in the poem: "Tears, Idle Tears," "Now Sleeps
the Crimson Petal," and "Come Down, O Maid." These lyrics
play into Tennyson's experimentation with generic counterpoint
in *The Princess*, as do the lighter-weight intercalary lyrics sung by
the women at Vivian-place while the narrative duty passes from
man to man. But the special quality that has perennially drawn
anthologists to the three imbedded lyrics arises from the way each
of them, with an inclusiveness that is highly concentrated and
above all things sad, articulates the dialectic of will and surrender
infusing the narrative they inhabit.

All three are poems of the puzzled will, chants invoking some
impersonal power that floods up from unfathomable psychic
depths to engulf the conscious self, whose terminal awareness of
inundation coincides with the epiphany of the irresistible power.
This virtually ritual movement of anagnorisis, versions of which
structure such poems as "Mariana," "The Kraken," "Break,
Break, Break," and the classical monologues, is given most nakedly in "Tears, Idle Tears," probably the greatest of the *Princess*
songs and certainly the one that has received the most illuminating
critical analysis. From the best readings a consensus emerges that
"Tears, Idle Tears" provides a symbolic meditation on the paradoxical presence of absence within the memory. This quasidivine
presence is apostrophized in the last line as "Death in Life" (IV.40);
it was later variously glossed by the poet as "the sense of the
abiding in the transient," "the yearning that young people occasionally experience for that which seems to have passed away from

them for ever," "the passion of the past," and a "mystic, *dämonisch* feeling" (*PT*, 784–785; *Memoir*, I, 253). Sense, yearning, passion, feeling: Tennyson's comments point to an indwelling mood, a state of mind occasionally experienced by anyone but belonging to no one, independent of personal control. If we follow Peltason's insight that the subject of this poem is not "thinking of the days that are no more" (25) but rather thinking about thinking about those days (1984b, 53), and if we ask further who this thinking subject is, we can situate the lyric purity of this song within the larger designs of *The Princess*.

"Tears, Idle Tears" expresses a universal dispossession, a common loss. At the same time, its language enacts a particular loss, the disappearance of the individual subject. This ego loss takes place remarkably early in the poem, as early as the second line if we scan the text for instances of the first person singular, more gradually if we judge by such signs as the communal "we" and "our" that appear in stanza 2 but not thereafter. A subtler index of the self-effacing design lies in Tennyson's syntax. The poem contains only two declarative clauses, both in the first stanza: the speaker knows not "what they mean" (21), but idle tears "Rise in the heart, and gather to the eyes" (23). "The," as opposed to "my," already effects a certain depersonalization, which the dangling verbals "looking" and "thinking" in lines 24–25 underscore: it is as if the eyes and heart are doing these things, not the speaker. From this point on, the poem consists of grammatical fragments loosely dependent upon the already loosely dependent—or impersonally absolute—phrase "thinking of the days that are no more," to which the subsequent stanzas are bound far more by analogical resemblance and by the expansive music of refrain than by the directly willed logic of grammar.

Thus "Tennyson's Weeper," as Cleanth Brooks (1944) has called the speaker in a discussion that epitomizes the shortcomings of persona poetics, scarcely exists at all.[7] The effect of this text's rapid and consistent expunging of the willing "I" is to discourage interest in the speaking subject and to enhance subjectivity itself in its place, which is the place of extreme and decontextualized lyricism toward which we have seen Tennyson's classical monologues tend. The progression of imagery across the poem also tends to this effect. The opening stanza glances at one actual context, "In looking on the happy Autumn-fields" (24); but this is only a glance, and it is obliterated by what follows. The parallel phrasing of the next line, "And thinking of the days that are no more," introduces a mental and mnemonic representation of absence, which usurps the visual present, and around which all the succeeding images of the poem orbit. In stanzas 2 and 3 these images are intermediary and increasingly liminal: sails bearing the objects of love and loss rise above and sink beneath "the verge" (29); "dying ears" hear "half-awakened birds" (31–32); and in the light of dawn "The casement slowly grows a glimmering square," in the crescent yet unstable vision of "dying eyes" (33–34). The oxymoronic balance of approach and recession throughout these stanzas convincingly renders not a specific set of memories but the very experience of remembering, of an *Erinnerung* that drives inward to bring memories "up from the underworld" (27), "from the depth of some divine despair" (22). The reiterated adjective "sad," in contradistinction to "happy" from stanza 1, sets the interior experience of recollection off from external nature, while the uncanny "fresh" and "strange" sustain the "mystic, *dämonisch* feeling" that also dictates Tennyson's rhetoric of the supernatural in "underworld" and "divine despair."

The locus of the supernatural, for Tennyson as for most of his contemporaries, lay beyond the pale of death, and this is the direction the final stanza takes. Suggestions of death in the first three stanzas, from autumn fields, through the subsidence of all we love below the verge, to dying ears and eyes, accumulate to drive the poem across the threshold of mortality at the start of the fourth: "Dear as remembered kisses after death" (36). The ghoulishness of this line is if anything intensified by its resemblance to an only slightly less strange moment in "Break, Break, Break," when the speaker yearns to feel and hear the imperceptible and inaudible: "But O for the touch of a vanished hand, / And the sound of a voice that is still!" (11–12). If "Tears, Idle Tears" here invites us to think not just of a mourner's fantasies but of a corpse's too, it does so not in pursuit of kinkiness but in order to prompt a reckoning of the costs incurred in dwelling on the represented absence of a past we unthinkingly call "dear." The cost of dwelling in memory's abode, "the abiding in the transient," is not less than everything, natural and social, that might stand in objective relation to the mind.

The power of "hopeless fancy" to feign impossibly sweet, impossibly alien kisses takes up into the mind the theurgy of "divine despair," identifying imagination and desperation as mutually inciting phases of a vicious circle both deep with primal desire and "wild with all regret" (39). Shortening phrasal periods hurry this eddying stanza to the implosive, paradoxical epiphany "O Death in Life," which we should read both as an exultant celebration of power and as a recognition of that power's indifference to the human. Both an apostrophe that merges "I" with "thou" and a last, distancing maneuver that knows and names the power of alienation in its otherness, these four words hail the hidden god in its proper seat by finding it at home, within the despairing self it masters (Spitzer 1950, 194). Their cry preempts every coming loss, including death itself, but at the "dear" cost of acknowledging the insignificance of anxiety beside the deep grief they lament: grief over the first loss of all, the loss of primary narcissism, of free and purposeful selfhood (Carr 1950, 50; Joseph 1983, 61). In its apostrophic identification of, and with, the divinity that shapes its ends, the final line breaks the prevailing syntactic and analogical patterns of the poem. Yet pattern has the final say: the line goes on to fulfill the formal stanzaic contract, with its reassertion of the inaccessible yet inevitable "days that are no more," a full stop beyond exclamatory triumph or protest.

"Tears, Idle Tears" is thus a Romantic divinization of the re-membering, imagining mind in its own place, but with the Tennysonian stipulation that this place is no man's land. As I have tried to show, the poem makes this stipulation in a number of ways, the plainest practical consequence of which may be the impression formed by many readers that this blank-verse lyric is written in rhyme (Hough 1951, 187–188). Stanzaic form, phrasal refrain, lineation, and internal musicality all contribute to this effect, but the most telling contribution is probably semantic: the poem gradually unfolds an inner state whose relentlessly sealed privacy constitutes an emotional and intellectual equivalent to the formal seal that rhyme can impose in making a lyric its own space (Homans 1979, 696). But, apart from its inner coherence, Tennyson also took pains to find the poem a space of its own in Romantic tradition. "The happy Autumn-fields" capitalizes on Keats's scene for one of the most movingly impersonal meditations on time and death anywhere in poetry.[8] Yet the point at which Tennyson cuts into "To Autumn" is the point at which Keats is most personal and self-referential: "Where are the songs of Spring? Ay, where are they? / Think not of them, thou hast thy music too" (23–24). This is the one imperative in Keats's ode, the one overtly dramatized act of will; and it is an imperative Tennyson explicitly disobeys. "In looking on the happy Autumn-fields, / And thinking of the days that are no more," Tennyson's lyric pointedly rejects the Keatsian injunction to stay within the present, in order to depart into the realm of pure subjectivity and find at its heart an impersonality that rivals Keats's.

As usual in Tennyson's appropriations of Keats, the break with a mortalist, natural vision is clean and decisive. The intertextual relation is (again, as usual) more intricate with Wordsworth's most prominent poem of mnemonic introspection, "Tintern Abbey." Tennyson not only specified Tintern Abbey in a note to the Eversley edition as the place of origin for "Tears, Idle Tears"—"This song came to me on the yellowing autumn-tide at Tintern Abbey, full for me of its bygone memories"—but a comment he made elsewhere praised Wordsworth's climactic lines for delivering precisely the effect claimed for his own poem in the Eversley note. About the "sense sublime / Of something far more deeply interfused," Tennyson had this to say: "It is almost the grandest in the English language, giving the sense of the abiding in the transient" (*Memoir*, II, 288; I, 253). *Almost* the grandest expression of this sense in English, but not quite—or no longer, since the publication of "Tears, Idle Tears"? Whether or not Tennyson's ranks as the grander song, what aggrandizes it is the extent of the comparative loss that it is prepared to take (in this regard like "Ulysses," a poem also indebted to Wordsworth). "Tintern Abbey" dwells on the irrecoverable past as a means of recuperating a future for the self, blessed by a power whose dwelling is the light of setting suns yet is also "in the mind of man." Tennyson is more ready to quench that light of nature and the language of the sense, and to abide solely in the mind of man, with "the abiding in the transient" and, if need be, with a futureless, "hopeless fancy."

From Tennyson's mystic, *dämonisch* perspective "Tintern Abbey" had too nearly gone, like "To Autumn," the way of natural religion. Witness the odd status of analogy in "Tears, Idle Tears": the similes seek to illustrate inner with outer events, yet such phrases as "So sad, so strange" also point beyond analogical comparison in a colloquial gesture, familiar to us all, of utter despair over language's illustrative power. Moreover, whereas according to the Romantic universalism or egotistical sublimity of "Tintern Abbey," "the mind of man" stands or falls with the mind of Dorothy Wordsworth's older brother at a particular place and time, Tennyson's poem is far less personal. Discounting the Wordsworthian version of memory as the core of individual identity, it portrays memory as a force disrupting identity instead. Thus, where Wordsworth supplies full particulars as to date and place of composition, Tennyson composes his 1884 note under evident revisionary pressure to move away from the particular scene of writing. In his manuscript (now at Lincoln) "Written at Tintern Abbey" first becomes "Made at Tintern Abbey" and finally takes the form quoted above, "This song came to me . . ." (*Letters*, 201; Knowles 1893, 168; Butler 1911, 48). The poet as artificer yields to the poet as *sacer vates*, in a late recapitulation of the dispossessive action of his most knowingly Romantic lyrics.

MOVING FROM ROMANTIC contexts to the immediate context of *The Princess*, we may note that "Tears, Idle Tears" elicits from Ida only a defensive scorn. This lyric devised by a male narrator and placed in the mouth of an unnamed minstrel "maid" (IV.19) stakes out a no man's land that is no woman's either, as Ida understands in rejecting its sirenic, "haunting" message as "So sweet a voice and vague, fatal to men" (IV.46). Only in the course of this canto will Ida begin to exchange her activist utopianism for the displaced Tennysonian lyricism that awaits her at the narrative close. In the final canto Ida's uneasy submission to the powers that be receives its most eloquent expression when she reads, within earshot of the convalescent Prince, but in the lyrically authenticating belief that she is alone, two songs from "A volume of the Poets of her land" (VII.159–160). The songs are of course remarkable in themselves; but so is the whole episode, not least for its implication that a poetry anthology is the proper hornbook for Ida to spell her new self by. Immensely cultured in other respects, Ida is now acquiring culture in a more painful and intimate sense, as she lessons herself in the conventional women's roles that circumstances have forced upon her after all.

No reader would hesitate to declare either of the poems Ida reads in canto VII lyrics. But Tennyson's generic project in *The Princess* makes them lyrics of special kind: both poems work hand in hand with the tactics of idyll—he actually calls the second "a small / Sweet Idyl" (VII.175–176)—to extend the dominion of culture within the general domain of feeling and the particular province of intimate sexual relations (Priestley 1973, 83). Both of the poems Ida reads are persuasions to love, patently addressed by male speakers to female auditors; that she reads them in the presence of a male auditor reinforces Tennyson's programmatic theme that men and women need to appreciate and practice one another's virtues. In another sense, though, this reinforcement is a pressure exerted pretty exclusively by men upon women. It is the ministering Princess, not the gallantly wounded Prince, who must internalize the perspective of the other sex by reciting its words; even by a sheer line count, Ida's recitation greatly outweighs what she says on her own during the rest of canto VII, where her burden is a stupefying sense of histrionic irreality: "a Queen of farce" (228); "I seem / A mockery to my own self" (316–317). The act of reading makes Ida impersonate at once the persuasive masculine self that speaks and the acquiescent feminine self that pliably listens, in a division of attention replicating the division between the past Ida and the Princess, nay Queen Mother, that she is to be.

This division between active and passive roles is also replicated in the lyrics themselves. The carpe diem tradition that underlies "Now Sleeps the Crimson Petal" posits a rhetorical situation in which lover persuades beloved to abdicate one kind of responsibility—the preservation of her chastity—by making that abdication seem a way of taking charge; in becoming his no longer coy mistress, the lover argues or at least implies, she will become mistress of her own destiny. Tennyson's deliciously narcotic version bends this carpe diem tradition in significant ways. First, the lover's appeal is extraordinarily languid: while his message plainly transpires through the words that frame each stanza, "Now . . . me," the case could hardly be more gently put (Ricks 1972, 201). Furthermore, the relation between declarative and imperative moods in this seductive poem sets up a hypnotic suggestion: yielding to his blandishments will simply be an acknowledgment of the way things are. The lyric rebuts no objections, because in the seamless mode of "And" and "So" it never raises any; such issues as purity and responsibility cede place to an atmosphere of pure responsiveness. In order to grasp the ethical dimensions of this poem, we have to step outside it and consider the situation of Princess Ida as she reads; and when we do so, we find the poem urging in especially limpid tones precisely the stance of acceptance that is being imposed on her by the narrative at large (Fletcher 1979, 91). The social imperative, which figures prominently in the *carpe diem* tradition as the prohibitive injunction to chastity and self-possession in daughters and wives, is replaced here by its opposite, the prescriptive injunction to oblivious fecundity in mates and mothers.

This lyric of surrender is extremely prolific in several species of verbal design that typify earlier paradises of pure response in Tennyson. The form he adapted from the Persian *ghazal* mandates phrasal and rhythmic repetition, which he enriches with analogical and conjunctive links that bind the stanzaic units into a continuous whole. All but two of the verbs are active intransitive forms, and those two—the silent meteor "leaves / A shining furrow" (169–170), and the lily "folds . . . all her sweetness up" (171)—are virtually reflexive, conveying with the rest a self-delighting cession of the will to the circumambient moment. What may be unprecedented even for Tennyson is the extent to which "Now Sleeps the Crimson Petal" seems to generate itself out of the sounds of its leading verb, in an extreme variant of practices we have met before (Assad 1963, 72). In stanza 1 the clustered consonants of "sleeps" come back reshuffled in "palace," redoubled in the larger phrase "cypress in the palace walk," and again, *p* softening to *f*, in "winks the gold fin" and "The fire-fly wakens." In subsequent stanzas of this actively passive lyric, with only minor adjustments and displacements every verb appears a phonemic permutation of "sleeps": "droops," "glimmers"; "lies open"; "slides," "leaves"; "folds" (the sounds spread out again in "all her sweetness up"), "slips" (yet again, "bosom of the lake"), and at the last "be lost." The mere repetition of sound counts for much in such enchantment as this poem performs, but Tennyson's phonemes function beyond this as sememes, units of sense. The slow dance of sibilants, liquids, labials, fricatives—shop terms that sound positively sensuous in the vicinity of this text—accumulates a meaning of drowsy compliance that each instance communicates afresh. Never has a shooting star had less power to startle than Tennyson's silent sliding meteor, thanks to its participation in this pattern of sound. The pattern is so gentle, yet so insistent, that it may finally evoke

in the reader allied words—lips, slope, lapse, pillows, pulse, bliss—
words it never has to mention in order to enlist their suggestiveness.

Probably only an age as sexually reticent as the Victorian could
have produced a poem of so nearly salacious a purity. Ricks (1972,
202) expresses many a reader's curiosity about what bodily organ
is really involved when the line "And all thy heart lies open unto
me" directly follows an allusion to the amour of Danaë and Zeus
(167–168), and similar doubts arise about the referential force of
the "shining furrow" and the double slip into the bosom at the
close. And yet these are not scandalous images, at least not in the
way one might expect. To raise the possibility of scandal is to try
to think what is just unthinkable within the socially controlled
confines of this text, whose verbal daring is secured by the institutional authority all around it. "Now Sleeps the Crimson Petal"
no more concerns a liaison or tryst than "The Gardener's Daughter" does. Unsettling though the thought may be to modern readers, this lyric concerns marriage. It is indeed a woman's *heart* that
is at stake here, her socially encoded affective life; and the real
scandal of the piece is that it takes its institutional context so
serenely for granted. Marriage is certainly what this poem means
to Ida, and the seductive invitation "Be lost in me" speaks with
the authority of her culture.

The folded sweetness of this lyric contains a summons to Ida
to assume her assigned familial and societal place. Its lyricism
insists on a phenomenological moment ("Now") that nevertheless
belongs to history, just as the lyric itself belongs to an enveloping
narrative. Its persuasive rhetorical power arises from the assumption that selflessness is what the self most deeply craves—an assumption most tellingly validated by the apparent independence
of its recombinant language from any willing intelligence (Groom
1939, 111). The power of this lyric is also its limitation, however,
for Ida's socialization will be complete only when her anony-
mously dictated role comes to her as one that she has actively
chosen. The next and last lyric in *The Princess* accordingly argues
for what "Now Sleeps the Crimson Petal" merely assumes.
"Come Down, O Maid" offers Ida a choice, or at least the highly
effective charade of one, as it contrasts the pleasures of sublime
isolation with those of cultural membership. The thrice repeated
opposition between mountain and valley figures the heroine's

identity conflict: she may remain Ida, a mountain-christened maid (Tennyson composed the poem near the Jungfrau); or she may become a cultural fixture, a pillar of the hearth: the Princess. The whole surrounding narrative of social containment exposes the illusory character of this option; but it is important that the option be presented: important to Ida for the sake of psychological ver-isimilitude, and important to Tennyson as a climactic occasion for raising the deeper concerns behind his artificial fable.

"Come Down, O Maid" is the most densely nested text in all *The Princess*, coming to the reader by a seven-times-sifted media-tion: from the singing shepherd via the published poet of Ida's land via Ida's recitation via the Prince's eavesdropping via the Vivian-place narrator of canto VII via his friend the diagonal scribe via Tennyson. This concocted chain of textual transmission would be of little moment were it not obtruded on our notice by the conspicuous parenthesis in the second line: "(the shepherd sang)" (VII.178). This apparently needless attribution gives to Tennyson's poem something of the flavor of "Morte d'Arthur," eliciting a hermeneutics not of suspicion but of belief. Far from undermining the reliability of the text, it enhances the fidelity of the text as a register of cultural suppositions shared among a number of minds. On this firm basis the poem can make its pitch in the guise of an exceptionally even-handed case for the two modes of life—and of writing—around which all Tennyson's work in the long poem is organized. As its first words show, "Come Down, O Maid" is a piece of advocacy, but the strength of its case comes from its appearance of fairness to each of the chief modes of Tennyson's Romanticism: the *Allegro* and *Penseroso* modes the Romantics in-herited from Milton; or, in the generation before Tennyson's, the spheric speed of Shelley and the earthly bower-building of Keats. This lyric takes its stand with "L'Allegro" and with Keats, as does the larger poem of which it is a part; but it qualifies this stand with an abiding awareness of what it stands against (Ricks 1972, 203).

Within *The Princess* it is the task of "Come Down, O Maid" to make a virtue of cultural necessity; and it performs this task by making the acceptance of social duty a pleasure—not a pleasure relative to pain, but a pleasure greater than the pleasure it freely grants to its opposite, the evasion of social duty in Romantic exaltation of self:

> Come down, O maid, from yonder mountain height:
> What pleasure lives in height (the shepherd sang)
> In height and cold, the splendour of the hills?
> But cease to move so near the Heavens, and cease
> To glide a sunbeam by the blasted Pine,
> To sit a star upon the sparkling spire.   (VII.177–182)

"But" is a cardinal word in this poem of choice: in the fourth line it concedes the possibility of an affirmative answer to the ostensibly rhetorical question it follows. "The splendour of the hills" does please, as the ensuing lines on the sunbeam and the star allow; but even so, the shepherd contends, such pleasures are not worth what the valley has to offer. Alliterative wealth almost always serves Tennyson as an index of pleasure; but there are different denominations of pleasure in the verbal counting house, and the choice is clear between the brittle crispness of "To sit a star upon the sparkling spire" (a line Empson 1984 calls ugly) and what follows it: "And come, for Love is of the valley, come, / For Love is of the valley, come thou down / And find him" (183–185). Only the caduceus magic that wraps identical phrases in varying positions around a strict metrical core preserves these bold lines from collapse into a stammering hum (Gunter 1967, 104). But that magic beautifully suffices to make the valley seem, against all imagistic evidence, the more various and challenging place. The occupations of the heights are fabulous, yet they are also intransitively pointless. I take it that the maid does not "glide a sunbeam" the way one might a model airplane, but rather becomes that gliding sunbeam, as she becomes a sitting star in the next line. The descent to the valley, as urged by the shepherd, and as against the *Excelsior!* vision of Romanticism, has the appealing transitive force of a mission: to find one's calling in love.

Hence, during the next lines, the association of the personified Love with Keatsian images of unison in agricultural work, and, most originally, with the threshold state that is the antisocial salvation of Tennyson's outward and upward questers in the classical monologues. In this "Sweet Idyl" the liminal stage is not a transcendent subjectivity but rather "the happy threshold" (185) of companionship, a companionship played off against the colder-shouldered society of the heights. Love is not to be found

> With Death and Morning on the silver horns,
> Nor wilt thou snare him in the white ravine,

> Nor find him dropt upon the firths of ice,
> That huddling slant in furrow-cloven falls
> To roll the torrent out of dusky doors. (VII. 189–193)

These beautiful lines do the important argumentative work of socializing the mountain solitudes, and thus of eroding the opposition between individual aloofness and collective breadth. For if Death and Morning make a couple, however odd, and if the glacial firths huddle together in cooperative enterprise, then the maid's choice lies not between life in context and its opposite but between two already contexted situations, between hard and soft attitudes toward relationship. The thread of continuity between these two options is the falling stream, whose enjambed gravitational lapse now draws the argument toward its conclusion. The maid still prosecutes an active quest for love, but it appears that this quest will be most capably achieved if she yields to the downward drift. So in the next line "But follow," which sounds resolutely disjunctive, has a latent hypnotic sense. Only yield; do but that, and you will succeed beyond all premeditation—like the Prince, whom "a Voice" in the descending north wind has told, "Follow, follow, thou shalt win" (I.98–99), or like Shelley's Asia, whose descent to the seat of love begins with the dream message "Follow, follow" (*Prometheus Unbound*, II.i.141–162).

Following the stream, the maid will join a social "dance" (194) that leaves behind it the minimal society of shared solitude, where "Lean-headed Eagles yelp alone" (196). She will

> leave
> The monstrous ledges there to slope, and spill
> Their thousand wreaths of dangling water-smoke,
> That like a broken purpose waste in air:
> So waste not thou; but come. (VII. 196–200)

The broken cataract suspends the continuous descent of the river, in order to create a space for the will that actively yields. This space Tennyson figures in the brilliant simile "like a broken purpose," which comes to the reading Ida as no trope at all but the literal truth of her situation, and which thus smuggles into the lyric, at its very moment of choice, a hitherto suppressed consciousness that the choice has already been taken. The descent to human love is inevitable, yet it is also unfulfilling if not chosen;

thus the poem, which intends nothing other than to break the chaste purpose of the maid it addresses, contrives to make the breaking of that purpose a vindication of her own free choice.[9] To the same end, the next images are instinct with purpose: unlike the wasting, "dangling water-smoke," the vestal fumes of "azure pillars of the hearth / Arise" to a goal, "to thee" (201–202); unlike the pointless yelping of the eagles, the children's and shepherd's voices are appealing precisely because they are making a personal appeal.

   The ground of this beseeching, the purpose this poem ultimately invites its maid and reader to pursue, is self-annihilation: the choice of love and death made by the Lady of Shalott, by Paris in "Oen-one," and by Guinevere and Lancelot in *Idylls of the King* (see "Balin and Balan," 235–275). The Tennysonian plunging of in-dividuality into a larger choral whole finds one of its loveliest and most fatal formulations in the concluding lines of "Come Down, O Maid":

> sweet is every sound,
> Sweeter thy voice, but every sound is sweet;
> Myriads of rivulets hurrying through the lawn,
> The moan of doves in immemorial elms,
> And murmuring of innumerable bees.   (VII.203–207)

The second of these lines, which might seem an afterthought, occurs intact in Tennyson's early drafts as an integral enactment of the entire argument: the melting maiden will most become herself—a Hermione and not a Niobe—through incorporation, when a larger unison swallows her up. This incorporation is nei-ther natural nor cultural alone, but both together; and the marriage of nature with culture supplies much of the famous strangeness in the last three lines. A lawn is not a prairie or heath; it is people that plant elms, raise doves, and keep bees; and if the nearby "hearth" brings dovecotes and beehives to mind, we see that Ten-nyson has selected as images of cultured nature the most sociable of species.

   No one reads these lines without marveling at their studied euphony, but study need not stop there. The most conspicuously musical words, "Myriads," "immemorial," and "innumerable," all denote the fainting presence of the subjectivity their music is busy drowning. The mind gets lost in the attempt to measure innumerable myriads, and surrenders instead to the measure of doom whereby every sound is sweet insofar as every sound is sad. Love does not care to walk with Death and Morning, because there is no need to mount the silver horns; love hurries, moans, and murmurs with death instead, in a mellifluous Keatsian undersong that sobers sweetness into muffled demur. "Come Down, O Maid," a pastoral tracing of the cultural gravity behind *falling in love*, culminates in one of Tennyson's finest encounters with Arcadian death. With the final line, as with its trial run in "The Gardener's Daughter," the recollection of Keats's "murmurous haunt of flies on summer eves," and bees that "think warm days will never cease, / For summer has o'erbrimm'd their clammy cells" ("To Autumn," 10–11), evokes an undercurrent woe that runs too deep for utterance, too smooth for insurgent protest, but too broad for neglect.

"So she low-toned" (VII.208): the once eagle-like Ida (III.90) ends her reading in the accents of a mourning dove, and what she mourns is both the proleptic loss of her virgin sufficiency and her hold on an independent, critical stance toward the culture that possesses her. This minor overtone arises most poignantly in the phrase "immemorial elms," with its implication that even the disenfranchised memory can remember that it has forgotten something. That inaccessible yet not entirely repressed residuum, engorged as meaning in the text yet emitted as sound, has a political dimension, in Ida's own frequently voiced conviction that the structures of cultural domination, made and sustained by man and woman alike, are susceptible to human reform. Immemorial elms derive their impressiveness as tokens of ancestral power not only from the witness they bear to generations of stability, but more effectively from the oblivion they can inspire of their cultural roots, of the violence and oppression that have inaugurated and maintained the power they represent.[10] The muffled violence of this entrenched power appears in terms of the explicit theme of *The Princess*, sexual politics, with the Prince's report of Ida's late confession: "something wild within her breast, / A greater than all knowledge, beat her down" (VII.222–223). Like the male "blind wildbeast of force" the Prince has earlier found within himself, the no less inbred feminine counterpart that here vanquishes Ida owes its "wildness" to its home in the political unconscious—the cultural circumstance, at once intimate and public, that neither Prince nor Princess can remember to see.[11]

Tennyson remembers this circumstance, though, and on balance he approves it. As in the contented Prologue "The broad ambrosial aisles of lofty lime / Made noise with bees and breeze from end to end" (87–88), so on the final page of the Conclusion the shout of a grateful people deflects vaguely Jacobin birds of omen, making "The long line of the approaching rookery swerve / From the elms" (97–98). And yet when comparable bees, trees, and birds find their way into "Come Down, O Maid," the gesture of idyllic acceptance becomes more complex. Marital and social bonds are accepted, but not the acceptance itself, not quite. In "Tears, Idle Tears" Tennyson's drive into subjectivity overpowers an empirical self whose protest against the evanescence of the present—"O Death in Life"—is ontologically but not poetically vain. In "Come Down, O Maid," likewise, the idyllic pressure of the cultural present extracts, from the self it incorporates, a volatile spirit, a free memory of loss. The two lyrics thus converge from opposite directions on what is less a resolution than a charge: the tension from which Tennyson's greatest writing springs, in *The Princess* and in the long poems that follow it.

In Memoriam A. H. H.: Transient Form

The student of *In Memoriam* confronts the claims of three impressive narratives: the story of its composition and revision, from 1833 well into the laureate decades; the progressive, therapeutic structure of the eventual text itself; and the history of its reception as a cultural heirloom, across a century of response and exegesis. The central, textual narrative will concern us most here, but we can at least glance at the others by noting a certain homology among all three. The private composition, published form, and cultural uses of *In Memoriam* share a common drift: starting from the assertion of a social claim, each withdraws into a subjective realm of analysis and refinement, and at length each, "Remerging in the general Soul" (xlvii.4), articulates a heightened consciousness of the reciprocal, historically conditioned impingement of self and society.

The poem was the first of Tennyson's enormous popular successes; the coincidence of its publication with the year of his accession to the laureateship is more than a coincidence, and it continued to be read with enthusiasm and reverence throughout his life. When reaction against all things Victorian set in during the early decades of this century, like the rest of Tennyson's oeuvre the composite *In Memoriam* underwent a scrutiny aimed at winnowing its lyrical essence from its accidental cultural excrescences. More recent appraisals have endeavored to heal the resultant split between the private and the public *In Memoriam* by amalgamating the practices of close reading and intellectual historiography, in an effort to see the poem at once steadily and in history. Study of the numerous extant manuscripts has determined with some precision the stages through which the poem passed during two decades of gestation. This editorial scholarship, culminating in the recent edition by Shatto and Shaw, suggests an intriguing correspondence between the history of the poem's reception and the order in which Tennyson produced the kinds of lyric that make it up.

The earliest sections Tennyson wrote, well before he knew that "sections" they were, display a firmly social orientation. Heart-stricken yet comparatively untroubled in address, they eschew lamentation and self-anatomy, in favor of the institutional, ritual supports of Christmas (xxviii, xxx), the funeral service (xviii), and the gospel story of Lazarus (xxxi-xxxii), or in favor of placid welcome to the ship (ix, xvii) and to a sympathizing friend (lxxxv). The sociably idyllic tone of these stabilizing overtures of 1833 Tennyson radically inflected across the ten years' silence, adding lyrics that articulate something diametrically opposite: the despair and ecstasy of an intensely subjective experience. Two variant yet generally conformable notebooks now at Trinity and Lincoln—both dated 1842, the latter incorporating most of the former and extending it substantially—represent the earliest recognizable versions of *In Memoriam*. What elicits the recognition is what the two notebooks have in common, above and beyond several dozen poems: namely, the counterpoint of idyllic objectivity against lyrical subjectivity that we have seen informing both the *Poems* of 1842 and *The Princess*. *In Memoriam* became a work, and not merely a stanza for the discipline of occasional meditation, once the interplay of its genres became an organizing principle; and the majority of the sections Tennyson added after drafting the Trinity and Lincoln notebooks owed their existence to the place they filled

in a conscious design. Many of them are either "pendents" like
sections xxxix, lix, and cxix, which smooth over or correct their
wilder predecessors ii, iii, and vii; or else they are orthodox idyl-
lizations like the Prologue and sections viii, xcvii, cvi, and cxvi,
which bespeak a recovered faith in social good, and in good as
socially defined by the Broad Church ideology that the completed
poem underwrites. The double process of aesthetic and cultural
integration whereby Tennyson adjusted his poems into "sections"—"weaving them," as he said with noteworthy syllepsis,
"into a whole, or for publication" (*PT*, 859)—thus describes a
pattern in which early and late idyllic elegies envelop a private,
lyrical note. In this sense the poetic ontogeny of *In Memoriam* pre-
capitulates its philology, forecasting the history of its reception
and interpretation.

All this may be only another way of saying that the poet shaped
his published work with appreciable fidelity to its compositional
history, and that the work since publication has had exceptional
success in creating the taste and the terms by which it is to be
enjoyed and understood. Still, noting the mutually reinforcing
patterns of composition, text, and reception may keep criticism
of *In Memoriam* from falling redundantly into line and rehearsing,
yet again, the poem's explicit, evolutionary ideology of conflict
resolution. It is not that the plot of *In Memoriam* is a poor thing,
as Eliot said its faith was (1950, 294); its narrative course aims to
be and demonstrably still is therapeutic. Psychological or intellectual-historical focus on the plot does, however, have a way of
impoverishing criticism and reducing it to the small change of
cliché. The poem itself trades in clichés, at great and local levels.
But it does so most actively when it sets up an exchange between
the worn tokens of stock response and freshly minted reactions
to its precipitating occasions; and the changes it rings by striking
the one against the other are the secret both of its initial success
and of its continuing currency. The poem becomes most energetic
at moments that juxtapose the conflicting moods, and dialectical
poetic modes, that arguably led Tennyson to write it in the first
place, and that unquestionably let his writing go on (Shaw 1976a,
53; Bruns 1978, 248; Rosenblum 1980, 124; Armstrong 1982, 192).
For it is the poet's indecisive flight to and from the world, his
alternation between cultivating and suppressing an alienated self,
that impels the poem—ultimately, to be sure, toward a resolution

that identifies self with world, but en route into discoveries about the relation between self and world that anticipate this resolution in subversive ways.

We might take the progressive ethos of the poem on its own terms, had Tennyson not made that very ethos a stumbling block at the threshold. The Prologue invokes the "Strong Son of God, immortal Love" (1), as sponsor of a melioristic faith "That mind and soul, according well, / May make one music as before, / But vaster" (27–29). Since a "vaster" monotony is hardly preferable to a lesser, one of the things we mean when marveling over the prosodic inventiveness of *In Memoriam* is that this text of one stanza somehow, thankfully, escapes the tonal equivalent of its faith in the "one music." Its most reliable route of escape from monotony is the one that doubles back, the palinode; and the late insertion of the Prologue, dated "1849," enabled Tennyson to make such a retraction his first narrative move. For when the implied tale of three years' therapeutic mourning begins in section i, precisely the expansionist faith of the Prologue is put in question: "I held it truth," the poet says, once upon a time, "That men may rise on stepping-stones / Of their dead selves to higher things" (1–4). This contradiction between the opening of *In Memoriam* and of its narrative proper, which remains a sharp one even to seasoned readers, deflects focus from the dogmatic substance of faith onto its means and makes the concern of the poem less its faith in progress than its progress in faith. Instead of stepping upward in communal aspiration, the poet insists on the authenticity of private experience, preferring "To dance with death, to beat the ground" (12) in an isolation intensified by his embrace of poignantly personified abstractions of love, grief, death, and time. As elsewhere in Tennyson's lyricism, the repudiation of a communal context (here, an explicit ideology) precedes a rarefied private communing, which strives to keep some core of identity intact.

The mode of phantasmic address persists in the opening movements as a symptom of fixated bereavement and as a tacit acknowledgment that, even at its extreme of withdrawal, the self knows itself through imagining its relatedness. The poet addresses a series of nonhuman others that cannot talk back: a "Yew" that is pointedly not a responsive "you" (ii); his own "Sorrow" (iii) and "heart" (iv); Hallam's "Dark house" (vii); and then at greater length, across the second division of the poem (ix–xvii), the "Fair

ship" bearing Hallam's body. In section xvii "Thou comest, much
wept for" (1) derives its pathos from our realization that it addresses not Hallam but the ship, the vehicle of a corpse that is
itself a vehicle empty of its tenor, the vanished life. The early
sections figure Hallam's absence though repeated images of clasp-
ing, grasping, and embracing what is emphatically not Hallam,
and through a habit of vagrant invocation to a series of substitutes
for the confidant who will not hear or answer. At the same time,
the very inconstancy of the poet's address works in tandem with
the segmented structure of the poem to render a consciousness
precariously poised above moods less indulged than entertained
and assessed. The poet's deep self, like the loved one, is only
elusively or allusively present, withholding full investment in any
one posture of grief.

   The tenuous disconnectedness of the speaking self forms the
topic of section v, the first of numerous metalyrical reflections on
the act of writing and its relation to the inexpressible.

> I sometimes hold it half a sin
>   To put in words the grief I feel;
>   For words, like Nature, half reveal
> And half conceal the Soul within.   (v.1–4)

A study in equivocation, this stanza raises more questions than it
answers. Language can but "half reveal / And half conceal" the
inner truth of the soul, "that large grief" that words "enfold"
(11); and the poet accounts this partiality "half a sin"—or at least
half the time he does. But which half is the sin, the exposure or
the disguise, the publicity or the privacy? And what is the status
of "sin," an affair of single conscience or a socially negotiated
consensus? Tennyson here engages two antithetical conventions
governing much Victorian literature of self-expression: the confessional expectation of full disclosure flanks the apologetic decorum
of reticence, and he produces the lyricism of *In Memoriam* in the
theater of their conflict.

   This highly personal lyric turns out to center on public issues
after all: the poet mediates his relation to his public through reflecting on the mediations of language as a communal structure
(Pitt 1962, 59). Tennyson serves notice that there are limits to the
reliability of his language; and this very notice confirms him as a
trustworthy confessant, drawing (through the inexpressibility to-

pos) on the soul-saving reserve of what he cannot say. The strange, deft simile "like Nature" makes what is called by Wordsworth the "sad incompetence of human speech" (*Prelude*, VI.593), and by Tennyson here "The sad mechanic exercise" (7), the most natural thing in the fallen world. For nature is no less subject than grief to the mediations of language and consciousness (Shaw 1971, 93; Peltason 1984a). The mediacy of nature forms a constant theme in Tennyson's poetry, one he has sounded just two lyrics ago in the accents of Sorrow: "all the phantom, Nature, stands / With all the music in her tone / A hollow echo of my own" (iii.9–11). If words—words like "Nature"—leave essential truth expressed "in outline and no more" (12), that inevitable fact need not aggrieve. It may instead become the basis for a central project of *In Memoriam*: investigating the linguistic and literary conventions through which the mind works in accommodating that other inevitable fact, natural death. That such limiting yet enabling conventions of language are also social conventions is beautifully captured in the final stanza: "In words, like weeds, I'll wrap me o'er, / Like coarsest clothes" (9–10). Having initially likened words to "Nature," the poet concludes with an analogy to "clothes," the most basic of human artifacts made from natural materials; and the medial simile "like weeds," by pointing both to growths in nature and to ritual tokens of mourning, wraps in a single phrase a complex of Victorian ideas about the creative operation of a human collectivity (Armstrong 1982, 183; Peltason 1985a, 43).

The social and collective necessity discovered in section v impels Tennyson into the idyllic mode of its successor, which devotes itself to stereotyped vignettes that it also subtly interrogates. First, and for the first time in the poem, the words of others enter by quotation: " 'Other friends remain,' " " 'Loss is common to the race' " (1–2). The words are "commonplace" (3), everyone's and no one's. What is special is the reaction they provoke in the poet:

> That loss is common would not make
> My own less bitter, rather more:
> Too common! Never morning wore
> To evening, but some heart did break.　　　(vi.5–8)

The poet here treads one of the lines that make his idyllic writing fine. On one side lies the poetic death of banality—"Too common!"—while on the other lies the threat of elevating the self

above life's follies and its comforts too. The universality of loss
"would not" console the poet; yet evidently it does, as he modulates through the tonally neutral statement that closes this stanza
into the patently sentimental vignettes that follow. He apostro-
phizes in series a father, a mother, and a girlfriend yet "unconscious" (25) of their several losses; yet he redeems the heavily
sentimental irony by including among these cheap vignettes that
of his own futile situation as he awaited Hallam's return from
abroad. Not the least pang of mourning is the one inspired by
awareness of its potential triviality, and *In Memoriam* makes a
handsome gesture of humility in this, its first reduction of the
poet's grief to the lingua franca of idyll (Rackin 1966, 226–228;
Kissane 1970, 78).

The next idyllic section, viii, which concludes the first of Tennyson's proposed structural divisions, was written late; and, with
the architectonic effect Tennyson's late additions often sought, it
pursues the dialectic of idyllic and lyrical conventions to a subtle
early climax. Section viii, like section vi, sketches a domestic analogy: now the poet compares himself to a disappointed suitor who
calls on his mistress only to find her "gone and far from home"
(4). While this homely occasion borrows some force from section
vii ("Dark house"), it remains pretty pat—as it is meant to do, in
order to set up the breakthrough that occurs at its midpoint:

> He saddens, all the magic light
>   Dies off at once from bower and hall,
>   And all the place is dark, and all
> The chambers emptied of delight:
>
> So find I every pleasant spot
>   In which we two were wont to meet,
>   The field, the chamber and the street,
> For all is dark where thou art not.   (viii. 5–12)

This last line is the one and only apostrophe to the deceased Hallam
that will occur during the first four hundred lines of Tennyson's
elegy. "All is dark where thou art not": here, one wants to say,
is what *In Memoriam* wants to say at last. But the very banality of
the context ushering this flat apostrophe in ("all the magic light,"
"every pleasant spot")—indeed, the whole labor of the preceding
sections—has been to establish that what the mourner wants to

say is only part of what *In Memoriam* wants to say. As the therapy of bereavement depends on resituating the bereaved in the context of life, so the lyric cry requires its place amid the dailiness of "The field, the chamber and the street." The very contrast, figured in the contrast between Tennyson's leading genres, forms the essence of grief; or, better still, at such junctures the poem discovers that grief is not an essence but a condition, an existential crossing repeatedly encountered afresh. The poetical corollary to this discovery is an injunction to create original effects by crossing one utterly stereotypical genre upon another—a corollary Tennyson draws in the remaining stanzas, where the conventional lover finds by his mistress's home a flower, "Which once she fostered up with care" (16), and which the poet likens to "this poor flower of poesy" (19). As friend and critic Hallam advised Tennyson that writing a poetry of sensation was the way to fulfill the poet's social calling; the effect of this poem about a social call is so to convey the sensation of grief as to keep faith with its admixture of the trivial.

A similar effect clinches the tour de force of section xi:

> Calm on the seas, and silver sleep,
>   And waves that sway themselves in rest,
>   And dead calm in that noble breast
> Which heaves but with the heaving deep.   (xi.17–20)

The tranquilizing incantation of "Calm" throughout this section finds its ultimate refrain in the horrible, literalizing resuscitation of two dead metaphors from the common tongue, "dead calm" and "heaving deep." As the protracted analogy between outer and inner calm issues in such clichés as "silver sleep" and "that noble breast," this text discovers the barrenness of the pathetic fallacy (Armstrong 1982, 188–189). The field of Romantic originality, the poet's cultivation of the hitherto unapprehended relations of things in the analogical mode, yields little, while his predictably dead diction blossoms into sudden life. The succeeding section xii reaches the same conclusion from a different angle. Departing from the given scene and the middle style, the poet likens himself to an imaginary and very literary bird: "Lo, as a dove when up she springs" (1). But the "wild pulsation" (4) of this fanciful upsurge stops before long in the impasse of a holding pattern: the poet-dove is brought to "linger weeping on the marge,"

> And saying; "Comes he thus, my friend?
>   Is this the end of all my care?"
>   And circle moaning in the air:
> "Is this the end? Is this the end?"
>
> And forward dart again, and play
>   About the prow, and back return
>   To where the body sits, and learn
> That I have been an hour away.   (xii. 13–20)

The thrice quoted question "Is this the end?" suggests the futility
not only of Hallam's aborted purpose and his mourner's, but also
of the unitary poetic mode in which this lyric has begun. Only
with the return of fancy to "the body," to context and the claims
of the given, does Tennyson reimplicate his writing in a dialectic
that, keeping the experience of grief alive, keeps his text from
coming to a premature "end." And the return to "where the body
sits," in its weird conflation of Tennyson's motionless body with
Hallam's, subjoins to the claim of context the claim of death: what
context gives it also takes away.

Is it true, though, that keeping the poem going provides a reliable means of maintaining contact with the experience of grief?
Section v implies this question; and the next metalyric, xvi, raises
it again, by returning to ponder the relationship between grieving
and writing. Reviewing his expressions of "calm despair and wild
unrest" (2) from sections xi and xv, the poet wonders how such
antinomies can coexist as "tenants of a single breast" (3) and
whether the sorrow of the "deep self," the "Soul within" and
"large grief" of section v, is inaccessible or just delirious, the
unmoved mover of his words or the superficial sum of their effects.
Does sorrow

>   only seem to take
>   The touch of change in calm or storm;
>   But knows no more of transient form
> In her deep self, than some dead lake
>
> That holds the shadow of a lark
>   Hung in the shadow of a heaven?   (xvi. 5–10)

If so, then the "deep self" preserves its profundity at the cost of
doubly trivializing the poem. An untouchably deep self will be "dead"
to the world and immune to all therapies. Moreover, if the poem is
thus pursuing an impossible goal, then the "transient form" of its

generic mix is an evanescent surface phenomenon going nowhere.

An alternative question, in the lines that follow, depicts the self as but the surface field of its symptoms. There seems little to choose between the two pointless conditions of manic fixation and delirious error; yet the option to which Tennyson gave the provisional sort of last word the structure of *In Memoriam* can confer has the stronger, because the less final, claim:

> Or has the shock, so harshly given,
> Confused me like the unhappy bark
>
> That strikes by night a craggy shelf,
>   And staggers blindly ere she sink?
>   And stunned me from my power to think
> And all my knowledge of myself;
>
> And made me that delirious man
>   Whose fancy fuses old and new,
>   And flashes into false and true,
> And mingles all without a plan?   (xvi.11–20)

The inspired oddity of these stanzas arises from their imagistic relation with the earlier "dead lake." An immobile reality principle, the "craggy shelf," still resides in the depths, but now the self takes its origin not down there in repose but in the dismaying intimacy of surface with depth, and in the peril of conflict: "Has the shock . . . made me?" This trope for the self as an event rather than an entity, by ceding more to the world, can expect more in return. The world and the self precipitated against it may react upon each other once more, in unforeseen, gradual or sudden ways. Tennyson's second thought also holds language accountable, as his first cannot: the "fancy" that "fuses," "flashes" and "mingles" contraries may lack a plan, but it is going someplace, if not single-breastedly sincere then a double-hulled survivor; and the "transient form" that is its modus vivendi at least figures as a vehicular construct yet afloat.

The image of the "unhappy bark" occurs within a sequence devoted to the ship restoring Hallam's body from alien soil to "his native land" (xviii.4). The placement of xvi within this sequence prefigures Tennyson's large wager that committing the alienated self to an accountable language means committing the self to the cultural world that language occupies and shapes. This discursive world is multiform, like *In Memoriam* itself; indeed, one of the daunting things about the poem is the variety of discursive forms it engages, especially within the span running between the ship lyrics and the structural center of the poem, sections lvii-lviii. These discursive forms range in kind from the purely poetic conventions of pastoral (xxii-xxiii) to the quarterly reviewer's croak (xxi, xxxvii, xlviii), and from pious or heterodox meditations on the afterlife (xl-xlvii) to the evolutionary theories of materialist science (xxxv, l, liv-lvi). Tennyson's ability to assimilate so much proceeds partly from his own gift and partly from a gift entailed on him by Victorian culture: namely, its habit of viewing every issue from the complementary, mutually definitive perspectives of the individual and of some larger entity—class, church, species, party—to which the individual belongs (Johnson 1958). When we see that this Victorian bifocalism constitutes the very dialectic of private and public that informs all the work of Tennyson's middle years, we begin to understand how *In Memoriam* can take such a disparity of topical materials in stride.

" 'I' is not always the author speaking of himself, but the voice of the human race speaking through him" (*Memoir*, I, 305). Tennyson's conception of "the human race" tends to give short shrift to "those wild eyes that watch the wave / In roarings round the coral reef" (xxxvi.15–16), but then the ethnocentrism of *In Memoriam* is precisely the point. The poet's incorporation of a range of Victorian issues makes his work a monument to the culture he monumentalizes, in part, through his failure to see around it. Instead he sees through it, or within it, alternately asking what the leading issues of his culture may mean for him and how his words may play into its embracing discourse. As the best topical studies have shown (Sendry 1967; Millhauser 1971; Appleman 1974), whatever discourses Tennyson essays he assays too—not by standing apart to establish a balance, but from the inside and with his own thumb unavoidably on the scale—within the opposition of private and public consequences that was the prime analytic reflex of the Victorian mind.

Thus, while the next three dozen sections of *In Memoriam* sustain the generic and attitudinal interference its opening has established, they seek more broadly to heal an initially alienated grief by generalizing it, in dialectically opposed, philosophical and sociological, modes of generalization. First, the poet targets universal or timeless themes of individual incorporation into a larger being—the relation of human to natural life, the fate of the soul after death—and he typically guides this aim by reference to ancient, stable texts: pastoral tradition, scripture, the book of nature. But, as the Victorians' experience with scriptural and geological strata made them see so forcefully, even the timeless must be apprehended in time, which is to say in the historical, apprehensive moment of modern discourse. This is why Tennyson follows his homages to Christian faith and ritual in sections xxviii-xxxiii with syncretically agnostic speculations on the afterlife in xl-xlvii, and why he recasts the Arcadian naturalism of sections xxii-xxiv with the hammer and bellows of a stern geology in liv-lvi. In each instance he exchanges an old belonging for a new, a mythically universal reassurance for a historically specific dubiety that binds his condition to that of his contemporaries.

This exchange turns on two kinds of assertion, each instinct with Victorian doubt, that have been present since the beginning of the poem. The first points beyond the utmost bound of human thought to the unspoken and unknowable: "He told it not; or something sealed / The lips of that Evangelist" (xxxi.15–16); "What hope of answer, or redress? / Behind the veil, behind the veil" (lvi.27–28). This mystic assurance, which corresponds to the ontology of the "deep self" from section xvi, corresponds as well to the rhetoric of silence whereby Victorian writers voiced their nostalgia for a vanished faith. But a constant companion of such mystic assertion is the dramatic assertiveness of the "unhappy bark," which inheres not in silence but in speech (Fichter 1973, 417). Our sense of the poet's individuality in *In Memoriam* becomes sharpest when his voice doubles back on the conventions it has been playing into: "And was the day of my delight / As pure and perfect as I say?" (xxiv.1–2); " 'So careful of the type?' but no" (lvi.1). While both kinds of assertion tend to isolate the self—from the haven of traditional consolations, even from the merely local governance of self-consistency—both also conspire to produce the peculiar brand of solidarity-in-isolation that makes *In Memoriam* a landmark of Victorian culture.

The orchestration of these conventions as means of convening a public represents a major achievement in itself, and in section lvii Tennyson pauses to ask himself and his reader whether it may not be enough:

> Peace; come away: the song of woe
>   Is after all an earthly song:
>   Peace; come away: we do him wrong
> To sing so wildly: let us go.
>
> Come; let us go: your cheeks are pale;
>   But half my life I leave behind:
>   Methinks my friend is richly shrined;
> But I shall pass; my work will fail.   (lvii.1–8)

Given the crisis of address that beset earlier sections, the inclusion of the reader's sorrow with the poet's ("your cheeks are pale") marks an important, potentially terminal stage in the work of consolidation. The poet bids farewell to the mourning that has shrined his dead friend and greets a living friend instead. Coming and going, valediction and greeting, blend in a stoic resolution that takes appropriately repetitive leave of a woe that will yield nothing but its own iteration in "earthly song." The loyalty, the pride, the poise of these verses would make a fine conclusion to an imaginable *In Memoriam*; and yet something in the tone of the first two lines disturbs their closural gesture with a doubt that "earthly song" may not suffice. This doubt the last two stanzas write large in their allusion to a celebrated closure in Keats:

> Yet in these ears, till hearing dies,
>   One set slow bell will seem to toll
>   The passing of the sweetest soul
> That ever looked with human eyes.
>
> I hear it now, and o'er and o'er,
>   Eternal greetings to the dead;
>   And "Ave, Ave, Ave," said,
> "Adieu, adieu" for evermore.   (lvii.9–16)

The very bell is like a word—Catullus's "Ave" or Keats's "Adieu"—that tolls Tennyson back, from the classical or Romantically pagan stance of acceptance, to his own higher calling: to raise a song that will be more than earthly. The supervention of Keats's "Adieu, adieu" ("Ode to a Nightingale," 75) upon the expected Catullan "Vale" (*PT*, 913) signals the Victorian poet's unfinished business with a supernatural longing his secular culture had by no means abandoned. From this midpoint Tennyson will prolong his testament, with the aim of transforming plaintive anthem or earthly song into more godly speech, words committed *à-Dieu*—and dedicated, by the end, to "That God, which ever lives and loves" (Epilogue, 141), as the highest idealization of the poet's culture (Eagleton 1978, 106).

That this renewed Romantic ambition to amplify elegy into modern theodicy has a strong public dimension emerges in section lviii. This, the first section in all of *In Memoriam* cast entirely in the past tense, completes the valedictory pivot begun in section lvii and contains an explicit promise of higher things to come:

> The high Muse answered: "Wherefore grieve
> Thy brethren with a fruitless tear?
> Abide a little longer here,
> And thou shalt take a nobler leave."   (lviii.9–12)

Noblesse oblige: though it seems severe to judge the first half of the poem ignoble, the source of such a judgment clearly lies in Tennyson's view of the poet's social obligation to soothe the cares and lift the thoughts of his contemporaries. And here lurks a paradox, which the conjunction of social and ethical codes in the word "nobler" crystallizes. The ennobling of *In Memoriam*, the calling of the "high Muse" of Romanticism, must draw on inward sources; yet the motive for this elevation is felt as a public duty to the poet's "brethren." The elegiac conversion of the poem will entail connecting the silent, "deep self" to the self that speaks and reacts with the world. The "here" in which the high muse invites the poet to linger is the presence of the text, the scene of the writing he has talked in section lvii about leaving behind; and the rapprochement the poem goes on to seek with the vanished presence of Hallam will be a massive figuration of the poet's own reconciliation of private brooding with public display.

ON ITS WAY to the climax of this reconciliation in section xcv, the poem dramatizes the rift it hopes to heal by setting the generic poles of lyrical subjectivity and idyllic objectivity as far apart as possible. The dozen sections that follow lviii veer widely between the two genres: on one hand lyrics of introspection and dream (lix, lxvii–lxxi), on the other idylls of social sentiment (lx–lxvi). This design serves more than a formal need. The stakes have gone up since section lviii, and Tennyson knows he is handling more risky and fugitive psychic material: the dream sequence of lxvii–

lxxi, in particular, engages an undisciplined consciousness the poet has suppressed since section iv ("To Sleep I give my powers away"). Our clearest measure of the danger the high muse solicits is the idyllic freight with which Tennyson now ballasts his exploratory lyricism. For the idylls of lx-lxvi consistently, and without precedent in *In Memoriam*, engage the heavily charged topic of social class. The poet is likened to "some poor girl whose heart is set / On one whose rank exceeds her own" (lx. 3–4), and Hallam to "some divinely gifted man, / Whose life in low estate began" (lxiv. 2–3). It is as if the more fully the poet plumbs the deep self, the stronger the contemporaneity of the social countermeasures he requires. At length issues of social standing invade the sphere of dream itself: in section lxix the poet dreams about his own civic status; and in section lxx the way to fantasize about Hallam, to see his "features right" (1), is to see them in hierarchical and pacifying relation to a social vision of chaotic masses, "crowds that stream from yawning doors, / And shoals of puckered faces" (9–10).

Taking "a nobler leave" and regarding Hallam as "a soul of nobler tone" (lx. 1) evidently involve a reckoning, at some level, with the social content of "nobility." Nobility for a poet further involves the issue of fame, and involves in addition a certain lordliness toward the social eminence that poetic fame implies. Accordingly, as Tennyson addresses the topic of fame in the next grouping of poems (lxxiii-lxxvii), he both airs and deprecates his own ambition: "I care not in these fading days / To raise a cry that lasts not long" (lxxv. 9–10). What is most interesting about this haughty scorn is its collusion with the familiar rhetoric of silence that aggrandizes the deep self:

> O hollow wraith of dying fame,
>   Fade wholly, while the soul exults,
>   And self-infolds the large results
> Of force that would have forged a name. (lxxiii. 9–12)

In section v half-revealing, half-concealing words enfolded "the Soul within"; now the soul—at once Hallam's and Tennyson's—"self-infolds" the power of the unspoken, and exults in its freedom from the forgeries language imposes. In lyrical hauteur no passage of *In Memoriam* exceeds this one, which nonetheless, and fittingly, arises in the explicitly social context of a meditation on fame. Moreover, the exaltation of noble silence itself participates in a topic of contemporary social discourse: the prominent Victorian debate, conducted in Arnold's *Culture and Anarchy* and practically any Victorian novel one lights upon, concerning "The grand old name of gentleman, / Defamed by every charlatan, / And soiled with all ignoble use" (cxi.22–24). In the fame sequence the aristocracy of Tennyson's pose is apparent, most so in its assumption that genuine aristocracy of spirit needs no definition or apology: "I leave thy praises unexpressed"; "So here shall silence guard thy fame" (lxxv.1, 17). Nobility is what goes without saying; and in the ethical and social turmoil of Victorian culture, where the definitions of nobility, like its patents, are up for grabs, silence seems its best defense.

In withdrawing into an aristocratic preserve of silence, Tennyson still speaks the highly contemporary language of his own mobile class. But he speaks only for half of it—albeit the half with a controlling interest in his imagination—and registers only its retrograde, conservative motion. Accordingly the ensuing sections, which turn to the business of commemorating Arthur Hallam as he was in his own time and place, pick up the progressive momentum of Tennyson's other, industrial and entrepreneurial constituency, by speaking the language of finance and manufacture. In section xvi the imperturbable ontology of the deep self portended a kind of death, until the stagnation of "some dead lake" was broken by the image of the impaired but still venturing "bark"; so now in sections lxxx-lxxxiv Tennyson exchanges the living death of noble silence for the burgeoning recovery of capital. The first of these sections makes this exchange most efficiently, fancying how the sudden death of Tennyson might have affected Hallam had matters fallen out otherwise:

> I make a picture in the brain;
>   I hear the sentence that he speaks;
>   He bears the burthen of the weeks
> But turns his burthen into gain.
>
> His credit thus shall set me free;
>   And, influence-rich to soothe and save,
>   Unused example from the grave
> Reach out dead hands to comfort me.   (lxxx.9–16)

"Credit," "rich," "save" are economic terms figuring the therapeutic magic of *In Memoriam*—which in the broadest terms converts the debt burden of "loss" into "gain"—as a miracle of
emotional capitalism. The "Unused" example of Hallam accrues
as interest to the poet's account; even the image of the "dead
hands" matures the bond despaired of in section i, where the poet
asked how to "find in loss a gain to match" and how to "stretch
a hand through time to catch / The far-off interest of tears"
(6–8).

The language of capital, forecast in section i but absent since
that beginning, now returns in force as the rhetoric of Victorian
power, which Tennyson's long poem requires in order to accredit
the subjectivity of its longing. Sections lxxxi and lxxxii work the
same associative vein, and consolidate Tennyson's capitalist and
aristocratic constituencies, by grafting images of financial growth
onto an agricultural base. In section lxxxi the poet checks a complaint that Hallam's premature death has blighted the "hope of
richer store" (5), with the reflection that the dues of love, though
paid early, have been paid in full: "My sudden frost was sudden
gain" (10). Likewise the next section affirms that, although death
has borne "The use of virtue out of earth," a "transplanted human
worth / Will bloom to profit, otherwhere" (lxxxii. 10–12). And
when section lxxxiv presents a full-dress portrait of Hallam as the
culture hero he might have become, Tennyson's idyllic projection
is exceptionally rich in the diction of wealth and sway: "prosperous
labour," "golden hills," "bounteous hours," and, in a triumph of
inclusiveness, "lavish mission richly wrought, / Leaving great
legacies of thought" (25–35).

I have suggested that Tennyson's rhetoric of cultural power
functions dialectically to guide and validate the Romantic project
of self-cultivation that begins afresh with section lviii and continues
to sections xcv and beyond. During this portion of the poem
frequent correspondences and juxtapositions of idyllic with lyric
modes do much to further the high muse's task of integrating a
private with a social consolation—as much, perhaps, as may be
done without taking that task up as an explicit subject. Still, the
task of making the psychic depths accountable requires explication
in speech, as Tennyson acknowledges in one of the economic
sections we have just been considering:

> For this alone on Death I wreak
> The wrath that garners in my heart;
> He put our lives so far apart
> We cannot hear each other speak. (lxxxii.13–16)

If the husbandry of "wrath," a new emotion in this most melancholic poem, recalls the lyrical accumulations of "Oenone" and the classical monologues, we should also note a limiting difference. Wrath arises here as a "garnering," a hoard that builds within the heart, for which the classical monologists' expense of spirit is not possible. The deep self, "the unquiet heart" of section v, still yearns for an answerable speech—something that ranting to "Death" can no more provide now than in the earliest sections of the poem. In this socially responsible text, unlike "Tiresias" and its successors, answerable speech will hinge not on the imagination of an otherworldly context but on an appropriation of the historically real.

The deep self finds its speech when contact with Hallam occurs in section xcv, a climactic episode that owes part of its conviction to the delicate preparations made in sections xc-xciv. These first sustained invocations to Hallam, remarkable for the quietness of their apostrophes, compose the spirit gently rather than nobly. As the initial demand, "Come, beauteous in thine after form" (xci.15), abates with the realization "I shall not see thee" (xciii.1), the mourner's natural craving for visual presence—and, with it, the poet's craving for objectivity—are stilled and redirected in anticipation of a manifestation more essential, "Spirit to Spirit, Ghost to Ghost" (xciii.8). Realizing Hallam's presence will mean realizing empirical limits to a subjectivity always subject to constitutional and historically contingent mediation. Indeed, one of the most persuasive features of these preliminary sections is their status less as spiritual than as spiritualist exercises. Almost as private as the dream lyrics earlier, these meditations nonetheless knowingly take part in a larger social debate, their psychological hunger and rationalist skepticism covering the ground of faith and doubt that marked the discourse of Victorian spiritualism (*LTJ*, 277; Reed 1975, 452–459).

The same delicate balance of private and public motifs informs section xcv, a greater Romantic lyric that turns on the lived experience of a dead man's touch and succeeds through the tact with which it keeps that supernatural occurrence in touch with the particularity of its occasion. Visionary at its Romantic center, the poem is anecdotal in its Victorian frame. It thus recapitulates the envelopment of lyric altitude by idyllic breadth that characterizes the composition of *In Memoriam* at large, and that on global and local levels stresses the contingent, even accidental character of the lyric moment—which Tennyson's lyricism, left to itself, tends to essentialize. A poem expressly concerning the relation of ultimate meaning to human time, section xcv epitomizes the conflict of genres that made Tennyson's maturity so fruitful (Bruns 1978, 250). Its socially embedded past-tense narrative, a rarity in *In Memoriam*, strongly affiliates it with the idyll. But its subject matter resists such an affiliation; so, more subtly, does the defensive artificiality of its structure. Regarded formally, the confessional section xcv may be the most obsessively designed text in the entire work, falling into four divisions of four stanzas, each in turn four-lined and four-footed.

Such hyperdetermination of lyric form troubles the idyllist's posture of easy retrospection; yet it also directs attention to a concern that both the raconteur of this poem and its lyric craftsman hold in common: the mediating function of language. And this concern is crucial to any reading of section xcv, a text that turns, thrice, on the role of language as mediator: between Hallam's occult presence and Tennyson, between a Romantically animate nature and Tennyson, and between Tennyson and the reader. The emphasis this major poet's principal text of spiritualist witness places on "wordy snares," the "matter-moulded forms of speech" (31, 46), lets us know how much stronger the poet in Tennyson was than the mystic, or indeed than any of his other masks. For the medium enabling the spiritualist experience this poem narrates is no psychic third party, but the medium of language itself.

Having dissolved the eerily stable genre scene of the opening stanzas and put out the lights of social companionship, Tennyson seeks a deeper intimacy in reading Hallam's old letters by lights of his own:

> A hunger seized my heart; I read
> Of that glad year which once had been,
> In those fallen leaves which kept their green,
> The noble letters of the dead:

> And strangely on the silence broke
>   The silent-speaking words, and strange
>   Was love's dumb cry defying change
> To test his worth; and strangely spoke
>
> The faith, the vigour, bold to dwell
>   On doubts that drive the coward back,
>   And keen through wordy snares to track
> Suggestion to her inmost cell.   (xcv.21–32)

The high muse in section lviii promised "a nobler leave," which the poet now finds in the "fallen leaves" of "noble letters" that extend an uncanny welcome, the strange recognition of a "love," a "vigour," a "worth," that are indistinguishable either as Hallam's or as Tennyson's, admirably lucid in their verbal operations yet obscure in their personal origins. The "faith" that binds writer and reader proceeds from the inner "hunger" of the heart and leads back to the "inmost cell" of suggestion, traversing a circuit of intimation that gives the alienated, deep self currency at last. The confusion of persons here anticipates, and may indeed have precipitated, the revisionary confusion of Hallam with transcendent power in the succeeding stanzas (discussed in the Introduction to Part II above). The poet's diffident syntactic ambiguity represents, of course, the fusion of deceased and bereaved, of lover and beloved, for which his poem has yearned since the start. But it is highly significant that this fusion should be figured as a reading experience. To the Victorian or modern reader's question as to what such an occult encounter is like, the text offers—for once, and all tributary ambiguities notwithstanding—an unequivocal answer. It is like the hermeneutic fusion of differing horizons that occurs in any historical act of understanding. It is like what you are doing now.

Tennyson's awareness of the historicity of understanding conditions the visionary climax of xcv, not just its exegetical preamble:

> And mine in this was wound, and whirled
>   About empyreal heights of thought,
>   And came on that which is, and caught
> The deep pulsations of the world,
>
> Aeonian music measuring out
>   The steps of Time—the shocks of Chance—

> The blows of Death. At length my trance
> Was cancelled, stricken through with doubt.
>
> Vague words! but ah, how hard to frame
>   In matter-moulded forms of speech,
>   Or even for intellect to reach
> Through memory that which I became.   (xcv. 37–48)

"That which is," the transcendental analogue of the deep self, has its being in the movement of time, as the deep self has just been seen to have its being in the movement of language (Welch 1976, 202). Hence its existence as a measured audition or serial sensation; hence, too, the inevitable subsidence of the poet's vision into natural time. This subsidence is less a lapse than a fortunate fall into the verbal mediation that, "word by word, and line by line" (33), uplifted the poet to begin with. The close parallel between "came on that which is" and "that which I became" confirms the historicity even of Tennyson's transcendent apprehension of history: it not only took place but took time, and at length it came to an end (Griffiths 1983, 73; Peltason 1985a, 40). And the parallel wording transmits to the invigorated reader of "matter-moulded forms of speech" a challenge parallel to the "wordy snares" that the poet has negotiated, to find Hallam negotiating them too.

As the late twilight of evening yields to the "doubtful dusk" (49) of earliest morning, the poet reconstitutes, in place of the fellowship of "others" singing "old songs" (13, 17), a new community and a new word, made out of the airs of nature and on the ground of an experience that has embraced the natural rhythms of time, chance, and death:

> And sucked from out the distant gloom
>   A breeze began to tremble o'er
>   The large leaves of the sycamore,
> And fluctuate all the still perfume,
>
> And gathering freshlier overhead,
>   Rocked the full-foliaged elms, and swung
>   The heavy-folded rose, and flung
> The lilies to and fro, and said
>
> "The dawn, the dawn," and died away;
>   And East and West, without a breath,
>   Mixt their dim lights, like life and death,
> To broaden into boundless day.   (xcv. 53–64)

The first of the three epiphanies in section xcv, the personal recognition of Hallam's undying presence, takes its course in language; the second takes its origin there and ascends to a cosmic pulsation the poet despairs of putting in any but vague words. Now the third epiphany arises in a natural repetition of that ineffable rhythm, only to issue in language once again: " 'The dawn, the dawn.' " Tennyson's great gift for suspending action between transitive and intransitive forms never served him better than in the penultimate stanza, where elms, roses, and lilies appear to rock, swing, and fling themselves as natural embodiments of "that which is," with a momentum that makes "The dawn, the dawn" seem to say itself as well. But the verbs are indeed transitive: just as earlier stanzas have established "that which is" as a process, no less measured and directed than the dawn, so now the environing syntax subordinates all that undulant agitation of the natural scene to the directive force of the breeze beyond it: Tennyson's understated version of the major Romantic trope for creative inspiration.

As the belated pathos of an abandoned man's reading a dead man's remains has heralded a revelation of the originating force that informs creative understanding, so now the mixture of early and late, "East and West," "life and death," figures the perseverance of poetic power from the altitudes of vision into broadening day. The simile "like life and death," so offhandedly illustrating a physical with a metaphysical perception, may seem a poetically illegitimate kind of thematic contraband (Mason 1972, 176). But if, in this poem about the benefit of the doubt, we trust the literality of Tennyson's account, we shall appreciate its proper stress not on some metaphysical meaning but on the historical circumstances in which any meaning—exegetical, transcendental, autobiographical—actually occurs. The matter-of-fact voice in the wind, which could hardly say anything more commonsensical than it does, brings to the bedazzled poet a dawning realization of where he is in time. To his bemused surprise, he finds himself literally at daybreak, and the literality of this fact matters at least as much as the metaphorical associations of unconditioned earliness that "The dawn" as a poetic image also brings with it (Foakes 1958, 116; Wordsworth 1981, 218). Indeed, if we pursue those associations along their allusive dimension, we find in the literality of Tennyson's dawn an advantage on Wordsworth's elegiac recoveries in the "Intimations" ode. In a connotative reversal of the Wordsworthian relation of dawn and day, which also turns inside out Wordsworth's gnostic intimations of immortality, "the faith, the vigour" Tennyson's poem has disclosed imparts no revelation, no broken clouds of glory. Instead it imparts a confidence: the light of common day need not entail a loss, in angst-making fashion, if it has subsumed the loss, as Tennyson always excelled at doing, in advance.

IN *In Memoriam* the poet's dedication in the light of common day recommits him to the common wealth of his culture, and the remainder of the poem is primarily devoted to reproducing various forms of fellow feeling in public discourse. Sections immediately following xcv take pains to insert its private daring into a succession of Victorian pieties: scripture (xcvi), gender and marriage conventions (xcvii), the nostalgias awakened by the moving of a household (c–cv). The more personally reflective among these pieces likewise tend toward a social, even festive vision. The most highly regarded of these is the dream of ciii, with Hallam's invitation to embark; but in the no less impressive section xcviii a comparable cordiality informs Tennyson's attitude toward Vienna, "That City" of ill omen, which the poetic description virtually forgives for Hallam's death (6, 21–32). Indeed, in the sections after xcv closure is most often secured through imagery of fellowship and embrace: "They know me not, but mourn with me" (xcix.20); "our memory fades / From all the circle of the hills" (ci.23–24); "They mix in one another's arms / To one pure image of regret" (cii.23–24). Each of these passages takes its subject and its tone from the activity of mourning; yet by this point the familiar impulses of grief, without seeking overtly ritual consolation, reach as by instinct for social images that are Tennyson's secular equivalents for ritual.

"To scale the heaven's highest height, / Or dive below the wells of Death" (cviii.7–8) has been for Tennyson, as the substandard musicality of these lines in its own way proposes, to indulge a "barren faith" because a solitary one. But solitude, never an unproblematic concept in *In Memoriam*, receives a characteristic complication before the poem is out:

> What find I in the highest place,
>   But mine own phantom chanting hymns?

> And on the depths of death there swims
> The reflex of a human face.
>
> I'll rather take what fruit may be
>   Of sorrow under human skies:
>   'Tis held that sorrow makes us wise,
> Whatever wisdom sleep with thee.   (cviii.9–16)

Here Tennyson articulates a central Romantic humanism that discloses, like Melancholy in Keats's temple of Delight, a central Victorian allegiance to the poet's cultural situation. It is not just that imagination, looking high and low for consolation, finds only projections and reflections of itself (Shaw 1976a, 61). In order to console a mourner, comfort must come in the mourner's own terms; and the mourner's "own" terms are those his context makes available.

"Chanting hymns," even chanting in solitude and even hymns to oneself, means participation in a collective confession, here the confession of a Romantic faith. The "reflex" of a generalized "human face" greets the poet with a reminder that, even at its most impulsive, his profoundest meditation on the most solemn of subjects is what Victorian physiology was already calling a "reflex action": here, a social behavior whose promptings lie in the cultural script. The poet therefore chooses what he cannot help choosing, the acculturated condition that lurks in the highest place and on the depths of his Romantic humanism. With considerable sophistication, as he has done throughout his career he wills the inevitable, taking what fruit of sorrow may be under human skies because he not only will not but *cannot* eat his heart alone—as his resort to the cliché about eating one's heart implied to begin with. The most poignant poetic fruit of this willed acceptance is the poet's return in the final two lines from Romantic originality to a reproduction of the collective commonplace, " 'Tis held that sorrow makes us wise," which is reproduced again, in another twist of the sad mechanic exercise, in section cxiii.

The balance of *In Memoriam* represents the commemorative, affirmative labor of the poet consciously incorporated—or, to use the British term, "limited"—by his culture. Writing "under human skies," inspired by what he finds sustaining in the discursive atmosphere of his day, Tennyson continues to play subjective and spiritualist against objective and materialist modes; but henceforward he shuttles between well-established Victorian stops. Sections cix–cxiv praise Hallam alternately for his social promise and for such intrinsic virtues as make up a cultural ideal. When in sections cxv–cxvii the poet returns from these eulogistic duties to consider his own position, he pointedly conducts his analogical commerce with nature under the regime of a culturally sanctioned supernaturalism. In section cxvi it is not entirely regret that spices the freshness of spring:

> Not all: the songs, the stirring air,
>   The life re-orient out of dust,
>   Cry through the sense to hearten trust
> In that which made the world so fair.   (cxvi.5–8)

As so often, Tennyson has contrived a diction that does equal justice to the physical sensations of springtime and to something beyond, which cries "through the sense" from a suprasensual origin. If the second and fourth lines do not refer, strictly speaking, to the Resurrection and the Creation, Tennyson was well aware that they would be taken in a Christian sense by most of his readers. And this awareness forms part of his point: if technically the lines describe nothing but a creative mind's joyful perception of the season of rebirth, by this highly acculturated juncture that perception may as well be made available, as it were, in Christian translation. Since on high the poet has found his own phantom chanting hymns, he may as well chant his public song or "stirring air" in the dialect of the tribe (Kincaid 1975, 111).

Likewise, following the discovery of section xcv that the victor hours are to be conquered only in time, which is to say in Victorian contemporaneity, the poet figures time's progressive returns in a reprise of the Victorian imagery of profit and industry. He tells the "days and hours" in section cxvii that their "work" (1) is to defer a cumulative gratification, so that "out of distance might ensue / Desire of nearness doubly sweet" (5–6), and "Delight a hundredfold accrue" (8) as the clock ticks off emotional profits with "every kiss of toothèd wheels" (11). In the next section "all this work of Time" (1) moves suavely through Victorian astronomy and geology to its culmination in that master technology of the Industrial Revolution, steel manufacture. "Life is not as idle ore,"

> But iron dug from central gloom,
>   And heated hot with burning fears,

And dipt in baths of hissing tears,
And battered with the shocks of doom

To shape and use. Arise and fly
    The reeling Faun, the sensual feast;
    Move upward, working out the beast,
And let the ape and tiger die.   (cxviii.20–28)

The life of mankind in cultural time is not a passive process of animal instinct, bodily death, and the fears and griefs that natural loss naturally prompts, but a willful process of industry, in which the poet's work of mourning and of writing participates as well. "I see in part / That all, as in some piece of art, / Is toil coöperant to an end" (cxxviii.22–24). The existence of labor cooperatives in the early nineteenth century lends the adjective "coöperant" a social force: the poet's work sees "in part" what will become wholly visible to a collective eye in the fullness of time.

But the progressive, technocultural Eden that Tennyson wants to celebrate harbors a serpent: the unexorcised spirit of reductive materialism that haunted sections liv–lvi. As the images of the "reeling Faun" and the lesser animals from section cxviii suggest, the poet achieves his rhetorical triumph there by pitting the productive results of technology against the findings of evolutionary science, dividing these common descendants of the Enlightenment against each other as representatives respectively of soul and sense. Even at this late stage of the poem, in other words, Tennyson is reproducing its fundamental conflict between subjective desire and the objective ordinance of its context; only now he locates the schism not in the self's cultural alienation but right within Victorian culture. It is this opposition—value versus fact, morality versus ontology—that provides the subject of the rest of the poem, and its terms arise from the two discourses in which the Victorian contest of the two cultures was most visibly carried out: the religious and the scientific. The anguished question of section lv, "Are God and Nature then at strife?" (5), comes back at the close of *In Memoriam* as a question about the compatibility of two cultural codes. While the rolling final sentence of the Epilogue will do all that poetic rhetoric can to merge the discourses of science and religion (Rosenberg 1959, 236), in the meantime the discovery of an intracultural friction produces some of Tennyson's most chafed writing.

Having taken his stand on Victorian culture, he finds the ground shaking under his feet, and the orthodox affirmation he wants feels as nakedly subjective as anything that has come before it:

> I trust I have not wasted breath:
>   I think we are not wholly brain,
>   Magnetic mockeries; not in vain,
> Like Paul with beasts, I fought with Death;
>
> Not only cunning casts in clay:
>   Let Science prove we are, and then
>   What matters Science unto men,
> At least to me? I would not stay.
>
> Let him, the wiser man who springs
>   Hereafter, up from childhood shape
>   His action like the greater ape,
> But I was *born* to other things.   (cxx)

The conundrum of *thinking* one's way past the brain finds an equally bitter corollary in Tennyson's fear of "Magnetic mockeries" and "cunning casts in clay"—technological bugbears that sit in uneasy proximity to the affirmative "shape and use" he has made of technology just two sections back in cxviii.[12] Embracing the technological power behind industrial culture, the poet has laid a viper to his bosom; and he recoils into an awkward repudiation of the cultural spokesmanship his poem has manifestly sought: "What matters Science unto men, / At least to me?" That "At least" shrivels the scope of the poem and arrests its public drift. The italicization of *born* in 1872 epitomized the aging poet's post-Darwinian emphasis on the divide between physical and spiritual generation, yet redoubled emphasis on the word hardly solved the rhetorical problem it originally posed. The birth on which Tennyson insists is but a sleep and a forgetting, whereby he suppresses half of what his culture has to tell him in order to hear the other half, the weakening voice of the faith he reckons its more precious legacy. The raw violence of such suppression, which must have greatly pained this poet of compromise and inclusiveness, left its scars in the subjective schismatics of many later sections: "For though my lips may breathe adieu, / I cannot think the thing farewell" (cxxiii.11–12); "And all is well, though faith and form / Be sundered in the night of fear" (cxxvii.1–2); "Behold, I dream a dream of good, / And mingle all the world with thee" (cxxix. 11–12).

   Probably the finest of such despairing lyrical assertions arrives in section cxxiv, where Tennyson confronts his cultural contradiction head on, and hammers a late but credible synthesis out of the resources of his Romantic maturity. Finding signs of the divine neither in natural phenomena ("I found Him not in world or sun"; 5) nor in the intellectual polemics of high culture ("the petty cobwebs we have spun"; 8), the poet counters the abyss of unbelief with the testimony of the sole self:

> A warmth within the breast would melt
>   The freezing reason's colder part,
>   And like a man in wrath the heart
> Stood up and answered "I have felt."
>
> No, like a child in doubt and fear:
>   But that blind clamour made me wise;
>   Then was I as a child that cries,
> But, crying, knows his father near;
>
> And what I am beheld again
>   What is, and no man understands;
>   And out of darkness came the hands
> That reach through nature, moulding men.   (cxxiv. 13–24)

The sole self here is not altogether simple or altogether alone. The voice that cries "believe no more" (10) puts the poet in ambivalent touch with his doubt-racked culture, and the voice with which he answers it is one that his culture puts in him. The spontaneous language of the poet's heart is a quoted speech, " 'I have felt' "; and what it quotes in the face of loss is arguably the comparable testimony of his favorite passage from "Tintern Abbey":

>   And I have felt
> A presence that disturbs me with the joy
> Of elevated thoughts; a sense sublime
> Of something far more deeply interfused,
> Whose dwelling is the light of setting suns,
> And the round ocean and the living air,
> And the blue sky, and in the mind of man.   (93–99)

As we have seen before, Tennyson finds strength in what remains behind, in what Wordsworth's language may prove to say once a portion of Wordsworth's meaning is deducted. Tennyson affirms not a natural piety toward "world or sun" (5), but rather a primal need like Coleridge's (whether in the homiletic works or in "Dejection," with its screaming child). In "Tintern Abbey" Wordsworth cuts his juvenile losses in order to assert the gains of the maturing self; Tennyson, instead, cuts the self back, in order to keep an elemental hunger alive (Donoghue 1968, 101; Peltason 1985a, 153). Pulling up short at Wordsworth's subliming enjambment, Tennyson declines to say *what* he has felt; but the immediate and allusive contexts let us know that it is less a "presence" than the desire for one. The voice that cries "believe no more" finds its rejoinder in no language but an infant's cry that, "crying, knows his father near." The poet says, "That blind clamour made me wise," because the cry calls out the presence, in a voice whose demand validates the fideist hypothesis it has advanced: "A voice as unto him that hears" (cxxxi.6).

Tennyson abases the needy self from the thinking man's status (Wordsworth's "elevated thoughts") to the feeling child's, in such a way as to raise its demand. He thus augments its satisfaction, too, from what a sustaining presence readily provides to what a comforting father can more greatly promise. As the wish is father to the deed of faith, in the evangelical strain of the Broad Church tradition, so Tennyson's uncomprehending yet reassured child is father to the faithful man, whom the hands of "what no man understands" reach, grasp, and mold. "What is," "that which is" from section xcv, is now "beheld again," working from beyond nature yet also "through nature," in a labor of love that has its generic analogue in Tennyson's adroit recuperation of cultural context through the mediations of this powerfully distilled family idyll. Finding a common denominator in the clamoring child that abides within the self and possesses the minimal but sufficient power to name its need, Tennyson can move from the summary alienation of the opening stanza to a conclusion that joins him to "men" in general—if not to "the human race," then to as much of it as any historically situated poet may hope to speak for.

Section cxxiv thus recapitulates the doom of Romanticism in Tennyson's masterpiece, and indeed in his career. The poet's alienation finds itself in context as he abandons Romantic eminence for Victorian breadth; yet in this very cultural incorporation the poet continues to rely on the Romantic assertion of individual experience—which by midcentury was part of the Victorian cultural inheritance—as an indispensable means of saving his culture from itself (Ball 1968, 175–178). As the poem approaches its close, Tennyson's terms for the culturally salvific power Romanticism represented are carefully eclectic: "What is, and no man understands," "Love" (cxxvi), "living will" (cxxxi). This eclecticism is important as a gesture toward the poet's broadening audience, but so is his final choice to repose in the term that still meant most in the compromised theology of the Broad Church:

> That friend of mine who lives in God,
>
> That God, which ever lives and loves,
>   One God, one law, one element,
>   And one far-off divine event,
> To which the whole creation moves.   (Epilogue, 140–144)

To say that Hallam "lives in God" when he dwells *in memoria*, in the poet's living recollection, in one sense identifies God with the poet's own mind (Kincaid 1975, 87). In another sense, though, it acknowledges that the poet's mind is not Romantically his own, except as mediated through the words and meanings—like "God"—which his culture produces; he can find himself only by writing *in memoriam* and working toward a cultural commemoration publicly shared. In consigning Hallam to God, Tennyson makes a final, reparative offer of his mourning upon the cleft altar of Victorian culture. Tennyson's God is a "law," the inner wisdom of all science; an "element," immanent and ambient, that inspires and conditions all effort; and, strangely yet typically, a "divine event": both a trusted outcome history moves toward and the movement of history itself, to whose prompting and accompaniment the whole laboring dance of culture moves. Such a death as Arthur Hallam's, for such a poet as Tennyson, crystallizes the ultimate horror of history, the fact that we are in it. Yet the horror of history is also its only hope: the hope that cries in doubt and fear, and that without this cry would not be hope at all (Bruns 1978, 260; Nash 1975, 349; Kozicki 1979, 80). Whether human history ascends to "noble type" (Epilogue, 138) or "the great Aeon sinks in blood" (cxxvii.16), it rises or falls to "Aeonian music," the tempo of the time. With the close of *In Memoriam* Tennyson's transient form clinches its maturing conviction that the soul makes what way it can only in culture, marching to the beat of what *Maud* will confirm as the only drummer there is.

Maud: The Doom of Culture

Tennyson was understandably apologetic about the *The Princess*, and even about the faith of *In Memoriam* he had twinges of bad conscience. Things are dramatically different with *Maud*. This third panel in the triptych of Tennyson's middle years stayed with him like nothing else he ever wrote, and it invariably stirred his most truculently protective instincts. Tennyson was nettled more by what was harsh in the mixed reviews *Maud* received than by any of the voluminous criticism his career called forth. Although his habitual choice of this text for after-dinner recitation may have had a compensatory motive, there must have been more than a wish for compensation behind the obsessiveness with which he flourished *Maud* as a test for all comers. The note of obsession remains audible in the bravura performance of "Come into the garden, Maud" that he chanted into a microphone during his very last years, and no fresh reading of its headlong measures will fail to find it in the written text either (Elton 1924, 34; Stokes 1964). Tennyson had little cause to worry about *Maud*'s being, like *In Memoriam*, "too hopeful" (Knowles 1893, 182)—those who disapprove the conclusion, one suspects, are reprehending its grim despair as much as anything else—and he evidently felt that this poem, unlike *The Princess*, was more than "only a medley" (*Memoir*, II, 70–71). Nor did he ever offer much by way of an interpretation. Public recitation, instead, became his defense of poetry; what was required was not to reason why, but to read *Maud* straight through, ideally in polite mixed company.

The poet's insatiable demand for social ratification of this work suggests that he, like the rest of us, found it impossible to endorse *Maud* wholeheartedly. Furthermore, the uniquely social dimension of this text's after-history bears directly on its procedures and themes. For *Maud* is indeed more than a medley: at once love story and social critique, an imperialist tract riddled with anatomies of a sociopathic yet also sociogenic madness, it represents the most complete fusion of private with public codes anywhere in Tennyson. The poem makes the laureate's principal contribution to the Condition of England question, by representing that condition and the condition of its deranged hero as utterly congruent and as reciprocally determined, in a dizzying weave of "cause" with "consequence" (I.x.374) that raises Tennyson's habitual confusion of active and passive moods to a rare analytic instrumentality.[13] *Maud* begins at the point of cultural cooptation at which *The Princess* and *In Memoriam* end; and there, despite the narrative movement of its plot of young love, death, and recovery, it fundamentally stays. The marvel of this "monodrama" of over a thousand lines is that its brooding on the interpenetration of personal incitement and social enticement escapes tedium. Somehow in its unfolding *Maud* manages to deepen and broaden at once, simultaneously to intensify its psychological inquest and to expand its cultural reach, without acceding either to smugness or to the subtler relief of indignation. It elaborates a tragically disabling vision of doom, and it remains a radical, perennially disturbing document.

The composition of the poem began, like so much else in the work of Tennyson's maturity, in 1833–34. The stanzaic fragment "Oh! That 'Twere Possible," which found a place eventually in part II of *Maud*, epitomizes the exploratory work of the ten years' silence, with its tension between impulses of inward and outward reference. The opening stanza hearkens back to the English undefiled of "Westron Wind," an anonymous lyric that for centuries has spurred readers to imagine a narrative context for its pure pathos. *Maud* was written in order to provide its lyric germ with such a context, but the original lyric both does and does not lend itself to narrative explanation. While it suggests that the speaker's "true love" (3) is dead to him, the poem leaves unanswered the question of what happened. It interests itself instead in the mood of frustration that an acknowledged impossibility imposes, and its interest for us lies in the scenic juxtapositions whereby Tennyson rendered this mood. For the alternating stanzas of "Oh! That 'Twere Possible" play conventional images of a rural past against something quite new in the canon of English poetry: hypnotically surreal imagery of a desolate urban present. Tennyson was aware of the novelty of this imagery, if we may judge from the way he capitalizes on it in T.Nbk. 21. Already in the first draft the bereaved lover is stealing "Through the hubbub of the market" (42), "Through all that crowd, confused and loud" (45); and decades before his successor J. Alfred Prufrock, he loathes "the squares and streets, / And the faces that one meets" (58–59). These stray early images of the modern city Tennyson systematically expands in the Trinity notebook, inserting new stanzas on "the leagues of lights, / And the roaring of the wheels" (21–22), "the yellow-vapours" (37) and "drifts of lurid smoke / On the misty river-tide" (40–41).[14] These revisions show the poet installing a traditional expression of erotic grief within a markedly modern context, and generalizing that grief into a malaise whose cultural specificity, at the level of imagery, widens its appeal beyond the power of narrative explanation.

Tennyson's only significant publication during the ten years' silence—picked out in 1837 (as was the nugatory "St. Agnes' Eve" in 1836) from an array of unpublished manuscripts that few poets can ever have matched—"Oh! That 'Twere Possible" at first seems an odd choice for that honor. But if we reflect that this poem uniquely combines a traditional passion with an unprecedented contemporaneity, we may see it as an unerring choice: a dispatch from the field, a telegraphic progress report on the directions in which Tennyson's explorations of genre were leading him. That progress culminates in *Maud*, and it is fitting that this experimental lyric should have found its home there; for what was a lyric germ in "Oh! That 'Twere Possible" becomes in *Maud* the rampant virus of modern life, "the blighting influence," as the poet later named it, "of a recklessly speculative age" (*PT*, 1039). The major analytic innovation of *Maud* is its measured and diffusive contamination, by imagery drawn from economic and political life, of a series of lyrical passions that run the Tennysonian gamut from fury to ecstasy to resignation. We could think of the poet's practice here as a kind of inoculation by the jaundiced eye, if only the poem had the strength, or the naiveté, to imagine a cure. But in this text, where the hero at last donates his body and his intellect in military service to the very interests that have crippled him, the cure *is* the disease. The virulent poem Tennyson wrote has force to resist both the antidote of patriotic sublimation, which his own later glosses would prescribe, and the antibody of liberal and humanitarian criticism, which *Maud* has provoked since the year of its publication (Killham 1973, 172).

Before inspecting the text, we might first consider the implications of its genre for the eddying dialectic of its public and private motives. The poem was subtitled *A Monodrama* only in 1875, with a term Tennyson borrowed from reviewers trying to label the *sui generis* production he himself had first issued simply as *Maud*, after toying with a title that despaired of generic classification: *Maud, or the Madness* (*Memoir*, I, 402). The new term appealed to the poet as a match for the generic innovation of his favorite brainchild: "No other poem (a monotone with plenty of change and no weariness) has been made into a drama where successive phases of passion in one person take the place of successive persons" (Ray 1968, 43). Tennyson's career began with drama in *The Devil and the Lady*, and his sad late attempts to write a stageworthy play let us see in retrospect how important the drama remained to him as a genre affording direct contact with the public. Monodrama offered a version of such contact, as A. Dwight Culler (1975) has shown in tracing its descent from the parlor "attitudes" in vogue around the turn of the nineteenth century: intimate performances for select audiences of much the same kind that Emily Tennyson would convene for her husband's readings half a century later.

A failure at drama, Tennyson nonetheless could succeed at monodrama because of just the generic difference his comment on *Maud* emphasizes. In a monodrama he could circumvent his constitutional weakness at imagining other minds and concentrate instead on his forte, the depiction of fixed moods or "phases of passion." Tennyson makes these moods public in two ways. In accordance with the use to which he puts cliché in *The Princess* and *In Memoriam*, he keeps the moods stereotypically standard, as in the Regency "attitude" or the Victorian melodrama. Beyond this, and in sharp contrast to his early mood pieces, Tennyson consistently renders his hero's phases of passion as reactions to stock situations drawn from contemporary life. Thus, while on one hand this monodrama parts company with the social interaction that Tennyson the failed dramatist appears to have craved in vain, on the other hand it repeatedly represents its solitary central consciousness as instinct with a largely unacknowledged social content. The highly individualist generic form of monodrama appears to counteract the poet's unmistakable intention to indict the social consequences of laissez-faire values (Spatz 1974, 506); yet the form as he deploys it carries his indictment into the very stronghold of individualism, planting conspicuous social codes within the supposed confessional sincerity of the lyrically speaking, lyrically overheard self.

It is never easy to know how much awareness of the social weave of his rhetoric to attribute to Tennyson's hero. The pervasive ambiguity of this issue is one of the features that distinguish the monodrama from the dramatic monologue, where undecidability on this scale would soon burst the generic limits of tolerance. In dramatic monologues we require to know more firmly whether and when speakers know what they are talking about; *Maud* very often leaves this question wide open, so as to open its discourse, and its version of the self, as fully as possible to the influence of the "recklessly speculative age" that not only blights but largely constitutes it. Clearly Tennyson's hero is a rather recklessly speculative type himself when it comes to social analysis, as appears from his vision of peace in a "Mammonite" culture (I.i.45) as nothing less than an undeclared civil war of each with all. No class struggle here, because no class consciousness; and therefore no witting solidarity, either, to focus the hero's blurry maledictions. He adopts the pose of a nostalgically anarchic satirist, sharpening on one social object after another the tools of an unsteady Romantic irony that implicates him as well: "Sooner or later I too may passively take the print / Of the golden age—why not? I have neither hope nor trust" (I.i.29–30). In referring to "the golden age," the hero yokes idealized and mythical with modern and economic associations, in a satirical counterpoint that chastizes the present with the standard of the past. Within the economic sphere the hero may also be consciously playing the old and forthright order of "gold" against the more dubious "printed" currency he will have to "take" as a citizen in a modern economy. This much is sturdy fulmination of a recognizable sort. How are we to take it, though, when the scion of a fallen family, manifestly feeling bilked of his inheritance, complains that he has no "trust"? The term implies a relation between his legal and his metaphysical situation, which the plot insists we entertain later on: if he marries Maud he will be recouping his family's fortune with justice (and with interest). But this same relation, if apparent to the hero himself, would place his disinterested absorption by the salvific power of love in a peculiar light indeed.

We cannot know with any precision, in this entirely representative passage, how much the hero knows whereof he speaks; and our bafflement arises from Tennyson's monodramatic rendition of the modern self as lunatic, tidally swayed by a cycle of passional phases that fall, in turn, under the influence of the age. When the hero recalls how, upon his father's bankruptcy, "the wind like a broken worldling wailed, / And the flying gold of the ruined woodlands drove through the air" (I.i.11–12), we may assume that the economically pathetic fallacy lies within his control. But is a similar assumption justified when this inhabitant of a world where "only the ledger lives" (35) describes the scene of his father's suicide as a deranged accountant's entry in the red, where "The red-ribbed ledges drip with a silent horror of blood" (3)? Jonathan Wordsworth (1974) and others have noted the sexuality of this primal scene, but the overdetermination of imagery here and throughout *Maud* seems to call for not just a Freudian but also a social psychology, an account of manic boom and depressive bust (Basler 1944; Priestley 1973, 115; Spatz 1974). To take another example, there is bitter wit in the hero's charges that "a company forges the wine" (36) and that "chalk and alum and plaster are sold to the poor for bread, / And the spirit of murder works in the very means of life" (39–40). In conflating the adulteration of subsistence staples with that of the sacramental elements of eternal life, the hero scores his point with prophetic keenness. Yet when he turns closer to home, in a related image, and approaches the lyrical sphere of personal feelings, his language starts veering out of control and into a social orbit: "Maud with her sweet purse-mouth when my father dangled the grapes" (71). Pursed lips are sweet, but so are purses, especially in a context that includes the bankrupt father. The hero cannot intend such economic associations, yet he cannot avoid them either—least of all, it seems, in passages that touch on the most private parts of his life.

Given this pattern of obsessive return, it is no wonder that he has such difficulty imposing upon his inventory of social and personal ills the explanatory pattern of cause and effect. "Villainy somewhere! whose? One says, we are villains all" (I.i.17). Like Hamlet, to whom Tennyson liked to compare him, the hero of *Maud* wants the comfort of clearly assigned virtue and blame. But this desire is inhibited, first by a Hamlet-like sense of complicity in what he attacks, and more generally by a Dickensian vision of universal implication in an unbeatable system: "We are puppets,

Man in his pride, and Beauty fair in her flower; / Do we move ourselves, or are moved by an unseen hand at a game / That pushes us off from the board, and others ever succeed?" (I.iv.126–128). If others ever succeed where we lose, their success is not their doing but that of the invisible hand; worse yet, those who "succeed" figure not as recipients of success but merely as later victims in a blind succession. In sum, the galloping exposition with which *Maud* opens dismantles responsibility and suspends a baffled passion in its place—thus articulating Tennyson's familiar vision of doom, but now with a degree of mimetic realism and cultural specificity that is without parallel in his work.

The hero seeks anesthetic refuge from this condition of passive suffering in the "passionless peace" of an Epicurean "philosopher's life" (I.iv.150–151). Yet his philosophy falters when it comes to explaining his alienation in causal terms: "Do we move ourselves, or are moved?" The explanations the hero produces contradict each other. At times he seems to himself the victim of his history and environment,

> Living alone in an empty house,
> Here half-hid in the gleaming wood,
> Where I hear the dead at midday moan,
> And the shrieking rush of the wainscot mouse,
> And my own sad name in corners cried,
> When the shiver of dancing leaves is thrown
> About its echoing chambers wide,
> Till a morbid-hate and horror have grown
> Of a world in which I have hardly mixt.   (I.vi.257–265)

These circumstances, the hero says, have made him what he is; yet if Mariana were to account for herself in this way, as she could with virtually no change of imagery, we should rightly suspect that the conditioning circumstances were fantastic projections from a self less acted upon than active. And indeed, when a few sections later a preaching pacifist has come into town, the hero reverses his behaviorist position and insists on its moral opposite, the purity of inward discipline:

> This huckster put down war! can he tell
> Whether war be a cause or a consequence?
> Put down the passions that make earth Hell!

Down with ambition, avarice, pride,
Jealousy, down! cut off from the mind
The bitter springs of anger and fear;
Down too, down at your own fireside,
With the evil tongue and the evil ear,
For each is at war with mankind.   (I.x.373–381)

To compare these two passages is to see how the hero gains in
rhetorical control when he lifts his sights from pathetic to ethical
discourse, and from personal to public affairs. Although this effect
bears out the homely truth that preaching is easier than self-
understanding, Tennyson is after bigger game in *Maud*. The chias-
tic relation between these two passages—private moods arise from
circumstances, whereas the public arena evokes an individualistic
morality—illustrates the crossing of social upon personal issues
that is the poet's larger theme. Not just the "huckster" but the
hero too confuses cause with consequence, in a repeatedly frustrated attempt to grasp, from within, the monodramatic dialectic
in which he lives and speaks.

The form of monodrama, as a kind of lyrical narration, lends
itself particularly well to Tennyson's rendition of the problematic
social and individual reciprocity of cause with consequence. Monodrama is a narrative form in which, within the phenomenology
of reading, consequences always precede causes. *Maud* thus situates
its hero reactively, his phases of passion having been prompted
by some action anterior to the text, usually a social encounter. His
speech, which is to say his whole poetic existence, is in this fundamental sense, and with great cumulative force, a product of his
social environment. As we read we learn to ask not what he will
do next, but what will have happened to him in the interim. *Maud*
thus is a poem not only written backward but inevitably read
backward as well, from moment to moment, despite the forward
thrust of its plot. This monodramatic retrospection kinks up the
chain of cause and effect by compelling us to gather the story by
extrapolation from what the hero tells us. Especially given so
suspiciously erratic a narrator, this technique emphasizes the arbitrary and inferential nature of the causal linkage involved in
understanding any narrative; it lands us, therefore, in uncertainties
akin to those that beset the nonplussed hero himself.[15]

It is in representing the pivotal deed, the hero's fatal duel with

Maud's brother, that Tennyson exploits the narrative resources of monodrama most brilliantly and makes the question of causality most strikingly problematic:

> "The fault was mine, the fault was mine"—
> Why am I sitting here so stunned and still,
> Plucking the harmless wild-flower on the hill?—
> It is this guilty hand!—
> And there rises ever a passionate cry
> From underneath in the darkening land—
> What is it, that has been done?   (II.i.1–7)

This last question is a version of the one Tennyson's monodrama provokes in its reader throughout, and its passive wording is precisely right. The hero's implication—something uncomprehended has taken its unstoppable course—faithfully reproduces the bewilderment that has suffused his vision since the start. Without dodging responsibility ("It is this guilty hand!"), his narrative of the duel depicts both antagonists as caught up in roles that their high passion assumes by social reflex: roles ordained by "the Christless code" of honor (II.i.26), dated by 1855 but still very much in force, which marshals the vindictive energies of their caste (Reed 1975, 142–155). The doom, and the guilt, that the hero thus shares with his victim are brilliantly presented with the opening line, which is both the most naked admission of responsibility in all of *Maud* and the most resistant to personal attribution. "The fault was mine"; but the words are whose? They repeat what the brother has said, yet obviously they tell the hero's truth too. However the *beau geste* of Maud's brother was intended, his unimpeachably terminal confession is the noble, Christless code's last cunning article, one that will rivet the hero for life to a fugitive and inexpiable guilt. " 'The fault was mine,' he whispered, 'fly!' " (II.i.30). Although winning the duel, the hero has lost by the rules of every code he might stand by: the dictates of human decency, true lovers' faith, the biblical commandment—even, now that Maud's brother has upstaged him forever, the standard of honor underlying this most lethal of aristocratic field sports. And yet the hero has played the game: having done wrong, he cannot say where he has *gone* wrong, because he is finally victimized by the confluence of incompatible cultural imperatives.

In a sense this terrible confluence is just bad luck. Luck is the prosaic underside of the doom Tennyson's poetry envisions ("the shocks of Chance," says section xcv of *In Memoriam*, not "Change"); but it is a side he rarely risks exhibiting so nearly as in *Maud*, his chief foray into the province of realist fiction. If the poem escapes the charge of plot contrivance, it does so principally through the very excess of that contrivance. For while from one perspective the monodrama suspends the connection of cause with effect that binds together more traditional narratives (like Tennyson's idylls), from another it furnishes a surplus of explanations. The hero has not one but every reason to quarrel with Maud's brother, to flee the scene of the duel, to take leave of his senses, to enlist at last in the war effort. This causal overload imparts to the poem much of its driven fatalism; to ask motivational questions about any of its main events is to be stormed by a rush of eligible answers—passional, economic, political, clinical—none of them especially convincing, by reason of their very multiplicity and cooperation. It is this interlock of motives, the whole self-reinforcing, self-perpetuating ideological complex, that Tennyson has taken up in *Maud*; and as the poet pursues its strategy across the phases of passion, the poem raises the etiological stakes from happenstance, through the charisma of personal good or bad fortune, toward an inescapable cultural bondage.

THE OPERATION OF a cultural complex, and not just an Oedipal one (Weiner 1966), is nowhere stronger or more poignant than where Tennyson's contemporaries would least have expected to find it: in the hero's love affair with Maud. The erotic sphere notoriously served the Victorians as a stay against the allied forces of selfishness and impersonality that a society founded on the cash nexus had unleashed. The hero of *Maud* certainly regards love in this way, as did his poet when commenting that the hero is "raised to a pure and holy love which elevates his whole nature" (*PT*, 1039); and most criticism has followed suit. It is a demerit of essentially psychological approaches to *Maud* that they split its personal from its social analysis, instead of viewing the two synoptically (Spatz 1974, 507). Already in the domestic idylls Tennyson had told conventional stories of individual and familial love that implied, within their erotic and gender conventions, the weighty authority of larger social conventions that were their ground. With *The Princess* and *In Memoriam* we have seen him allowing more and more explicit weight to social conventions governing the experience and expression of love. In *Maud* the integration of lyric love and its public conditions is as complete as the poet was ever to make it. When we consider the widespread ideological resistance of Victorian culture to any desecration of its Romantic erotic ideal—a resistance to which Tennyson's comment on "a pure and holy love" shows him also subject—we may surmise that this was the feature of his scandalous poem that aroused the profoundest indignation, as it was also his hardest-won triumph (Sedgwick 1985, 119).

The social analysis of love begins where the love story does, as the hero fatally overhears Maud singing by the manorial cedar "an air that is known to me" (I.v.164). In this poem that ends with a decision to enlist, it matters of course that Maud's is "a martial song" (166); but it equally matters that her song is a traditional one, a ballad the hero recognizes at once. Because Maud has not invented the song but found it in the aristocratic past, the hero can deflect his spontaneous devotion from Maud herself onto the nobility that speaks through her: to "adore / Not her, who is neither courtly nor kind, / Not her, not her, but a voice" (187–189).[16] If we compare this passage to Tennyson's lines on the singing bulbul from "Recollections of the Arabian Nights"—"Not he: but something which possessed / The darkness of the world"— we glimpse in little the thoroughness with which in *Maud* the poet has devoted his usual rhetoric of impersonal transcendence to hegemonic conditions of culture. From the beginning the hero loves courtliness, not Maud; and the imagery of stars, flowers, and especially gems in which he consistently represents her, like the singularity of her voice here, points to an imaginative and erotic elitism that is not merely figurative but refers to the constellation of rank and wealth that determines the place of these lovers in the Victorian world.

In view of the events this incident precipitates, it is an awful coincidence for both lovers that he should hear her singing just this song at just this point. And yet, in their time and place, what else *should* she sing, and how else *should* he react? This decisive first link in a concatenated plot is already decided before it begins, an entirely natural consequence flowing from who the two principals are, which is to say, from where they are in society and history. A reader who means to condemn the hero in part III for joining troops who "have proved we have hearts in a cause, we are noble still" (III.vi.55) will have to read the judgment backward to this moment of apparently innocuous lyricism, where a song of noble men "in battle array, / Ready in heart" (I.v.169–170), stirs the hero's heart so readily because the codes of nobility are what his heart is ready for (Byatt 1969, 81; Drew 1973, 136). The hero's peroration declares the Crimean War "a cause"; and though his part in it seems less a cause than an irresistible consequence, his declaration rings true. The cause that is "noble still" remains the same cause that has determined the love whose aftermath his soldiering may bring to terminal resolution.

As the love story advances, Maud appears to her lover not a person intrinsically worthy, nor an object of desire, but a sign whose worth arises from the place she holds in a social system. The concept of intrinsic personal worth, so central to nineteenth-century literature, is one that this poem severely questions. Even physical beauty, the most inalienably personal of possessions, exists in Maud only as it appears to her socially conditioned beholder. Here is one of the very few glimpses of Maud's person that the poem offers:

> I kissed her slender hand,
>   She took the kiss sedately;
> Maud is not seventeen,
>   But she is tall and stately.   (I.xii.424–427)

Readers have not been kind to this stanza, taking offense at the patronizing decorum of its courtship and its rhyme. But the stiffness of the lovemaking, and of the language that describes it, makes an important point: Maud's beauty *is* her decorum, her school-finished poise a cultural accomplishment for which the semipublic "stately" is just *le mot juste*. Here is a young woman bred to receive a courtly kiss as her due; and the hero's patronizing approval of her breeding includes his awareness that, at seventeen or a little older, she will be able to raise him to her estate as a landed paterfamilias. Not her, not her, but a poise, a prize, a place.

The hero's metaphor of choice in describing Maud is the gem or pearl (I.iii.95, v.175, x.352, xviii.640), with its obvious connotations of wealth. More often, though, he describes her metonymically instead, in tropes focused on the associations that make her such a catch (Fletcher 1979, 86). This metonymic displacement, from Maud's proper self to her properties, often leads the hero to dwell on the other men in her life, who are always described in greater detail than Maud herself, for the simple reason that their opinions, doings, and prospects are of greater account. The "dandy-despot" brother (I.vi.231), the "snowy-banded, dilettante, / Delicate-handed priest" (I.viii.310–311), the "padded shape" and "waxen face" of the new suitor he calls "little King Charley snarling" (I.x.358–359, I.xii.441), fix upon the hero's imagination with the fascination of a social taboo; the trappings of their power represent what, for all his philosophy, he cannot help coveting. He finds a warrant for his courtship in a dream memory of "two men," his father and Maud's, plotting their children's future together, their voices spectrally empowered by dream but also by a patriarchal convention that is nowhere and everywhere, "Somewhere, talking of me; / 'Well, if it prove a girl, my boy / Will have plenty: so let it be' " (I.vii.297–300). Even in rare moments of speculation about Maud's mind, the hero assumes that her marriage choice—the one culturally crucial exercise of a Victorian lady's will—must turn on her estimate of a husband's prospective standing in a gentleman's world: "She would not do herself this great wrong, / To take a wanton dissolute boy / For a man and leader of men" (I.x.386–388).

Metonymy is the rhetorical mode of nineteenth-century realism; and since the real, the Tennysonian that-which-is, appears in *Maud* as the ideological ordinance of culture, it makes perfect sense that his hero's nervous love should crackle at every synapse with the rhetoric of power. The climactic sections of part I take as their subject the empowerment of love; and it is here, in the realm of erotic fantasy, that Tennyson's experimental interfusion of private with public discourse becomes most acute.

> O beautiful creature, what am I
> That I dare to look her way;
> Think that I may hold dominion sweet,
> Lord of the pulse that is lord of her breast,
> And dream of her beauty with tender dread,
> From the delicate Arab arch of her feet
> To the grace that, bright and light as the crest
> Of a peacock, sits on her shining head,
> And she knows it not: O, if she knew it,
> To know her beauty might half undo it.

I know it the one bright thing to save
My yet young life in the wilds of Time.   (I.xvi.546–557)

A King Arthur of desire, the hero seeks salvation from "the wilds of Time" in the establishment of just the masculine "dominion" that, in his time, the ideology of gender prescribes. Maud must not "know her beauty," because that is her lover's prerogative. It is he who will *own* it when confessing his love ("For I must tell her"; I.xvi.569), while her part is confined to the giving, keeping, or breaking of "her word" (561–565), yes or no, when man proposes—a version of the passivity, the mere responsiveness to social mandates, from which the hero means to carve himself an escape by asserting the claims of male dominion.

The exotic images the hero imports for Maud's beauty (the "Arab arch," the curiously male peacock's crest) suggest that his fantasies of erotic dominion are imperial fantasies as well, and the next section bears this suggestion out very fully indeed. Section xvii, though it has not fared well with critics, seems to me one of Tennyson's tours de force, a chaste imagination of erotic triumph to which images of global hegemony come as if unbidden:

> Go not, happy day,
>   From the shining fields,
> Go not, happy day,
>   Till the maiden yields.
> Rosy is the West,
>   Rosy is the South,
> Roses are her cheeks,
>   And a rose her mouth
> When the happy Yes
>   Falters from her lips,
> Pass and blush the news
>   Over glowing ships;
> Over blowing seas,
>   Over seas at rest,
> Pass the happy news,
>   Blush it through the West;
> Till the red man dance
>   By his red cedar-tree,
> And the red man's babe
>   Leap, beyond the sea.
> Blush from West to East,

> Blush from East to West,
> Till the West is East,
>   Blush it through the West.
> Rosy is the West,
> Rosy is the South,
> Roses are her cheeks,
> And a rose her mouth.   (I.xvii)

This lyric, originally written for *The Princess* and certainly consistent with the interest that text exhibits in issues of gender and culture, is no less at home in *Maud*. The imagery repeated in its final quatrain emphasizes its place in a larger literary context as well: the tradition of poetic comparison between women and roses. Poems in this tradition usually explore through simile and metaphor the connection between beauty and mortality, and thus impinge on the *carpe diem* poem, a favorite genre Tennyson here revises once again with a supremely languorous seductiveness. This version of the rose poem elides the traditional, universalizing issue of mortality, or rather replaces it by giving the comparison of woman and rose a pronounced cultural bias. The effect of cultural specificity comes in part from the context that the monodrama has accumulated by this point: the initial rhyme of "fields" with "yields" directs us not to the generalized "happy Autumn-fields" of "Tears, Idle Tears," but to Maud's real estate, whose rich yield her surrender to the hero will be conveying with her person.

Even apart from the monodramatic narrative, the form and images of this poem speak eloquently to the relation between erotic and cultural power, and about both in relation to language. The lines fall into natural quatrain stanzas (as in sections vii and xii), but here the poet has fused his quatrains into a formal continuity that mirrors the seamlessness of a global vision. The most remarkable fusion occurs at the end of the eighth line, which Tennyson consistently left unpunctuated, I think in order to stress a crucial point about the rhetorical power of his hero's metaphor-making in the rose poem tradition.[17] "Rosy," describing the west and south, is either a straight adjective or a buried simile; "Roses are her cheeks" crosses the rhetorical line into metaphor, but metaphor of a weakly conventional sort that suggests rather too many literary girls with roses in their cheeks (Shaw 1976b, 179). The empowered metaphor of this quatrain is the last, "And a rose her mouth"—an image that would be wonderfully erotic even in the naturalistic context that the rose poem tradition suggests, but that the unusual punctuation shows to be simply irresistible from the vantage of Tennyson's acculturated hero. For Maud's mouth can not only kiss but speak, and thus can bear the news of a surrender whose import is hyperbolically global because the cultural freight behind it is literally global. Love makes the world go round, for Tennyson's hero, as and because the British empire does. That is why the hero breaks through into original metaphor at the point at which eros and culture form one "dominion sweet." Maud's mouth is a rose when it assents to the authority of patriarchal empire, which her faltering blush of submissive pride also confirms, and which the succeeding images of the westering course of commerce ("glowing ships") and of colonial bliss and fecundity ("the red man's babe") expand upon, until a young man's fancy and the first flush of sexual conquest have utterly merged with the Victorian Englishman's proudest boast: that upon his empire—rosy red on any good Victorian map of the world—the sun never sets.

If the shadow of mortality from the rose poem tradition falls across this text, it does so not as in the idyll of Rose, the gardener's daughter, but after the fashion of "Come Down, O Maid," to signal the death of unconditioned subjectivity, the preemption of lyrical by imperial wealth, the cultural doom of romantic—and Romantic—desire. We can catch this fatal shadow best by comparison to Wordsworth's ode on a germane topic, "Intimations of Immortality." In Wordsworth "the Babe leaps up on his Mother's arm" (49) as a culminating figure of communal joy, which the poet joins only after a singular admonition from "a Tree, of many, one" (51) has exiled him to a state of solitary *thought*; from this state, in turn, a visionary memory that sees "the Children sport upon the shore" (166) effects partial restoration, again only "in thought" (171). Precisely the thoughtlessness of section xvii has provoked adverse critical comment; yet it is only its thoughtlessness, its uncritical absorption in a phase of passion, that makes possible its success as an ecstatic lyrical essay in the cultural sublime. The single tree and the leaping babe, which are opposed images for Wordsworth, come back joined in Tennyson's lyric by the rhythm of an imperialist ethnic mythology. With his red babe leaping by his red cedar tree, the red man dances to the rhythm of the white man's burden. Such primitivism locates primal sympathy not in the philosophic mind but in the greater deep of unconscious acculturation, where custom lies upon the self with a weight deep indeed as life.

Insofar as the erotic was the sphere into which Victorian culture most notably domesticated the Romantic ideology of the autonomous self, and insofar as *Maud* deconstructs the self into its cultural constituents, it is appropriately when Tennyson is dwelling on romantic love that he draws most conspicuously on Romantic texts—and draws on them, moreover, as parts of the culture within which he is writing. We have just seen how a revisionist allusion to Wordsworth's ode sharpens the cultural argument of section xvii. Its greater successor, section xviii ("I have led her home"), goes beyond allusion, taking Keats's "Ode to a Nightingale" as a central argumentative and imagistic model. The parallels between Tennyson's eight-stanza meditative lyric and Keats's are striking: high Miltonic syntax and purity of diction, the embalmed darkness of a fragrant setting, starlight playing through verdurous glooms, the opposition of human imagination to misery, a flirtation with death and then a rejection (itself rejected) of mortality, a valedictory bell. Yet all these parallels set off an essential difference, itself different in kind from Tennyson's frequent earlier revisions of this ode. "Ode to a Nightingale" turns on a dialectical relation between imagination and nature, or between the imagining self and its own mortality. But for Tennyson neither term of the Keatsian dialectic is simple or stable. He has presented each as subject to mediation by the linguistic structures of consciousness since very early in his career; and when he has alluded to the "Nightingale" ode he has always done so with an eye, or an ear, for some transcendent ground that subsumes both the created world and the creative mind that confronts it. In *Maud* this transcendent ground stands revealed, with unique force, as *culture*, in its contemporary Victorian incarnation; and this revelation lets Tennyson rewrite Keats's ode with remarkable fidelity to its images and even to their sequence, but with an altogether original purpose that conduces on occasion to poetic effects more Keatsian than those we find in Keats.

The note of section xviii is acceptance, which if not finally Keats's note is certainly the note Tennyson heard when he read Keats. The hero's blissful calm proceeds from his having found, after hundreds of lines of alienation and nostalgia, "the promised good" (I.xviii.604), a rightful place that justifies the world around him. "I have led her home": whatever has or has not happened this day among the wildflowers by his home, it is now the hero's conviction that Maud's home, within whose grounds he reposes as he speaks, will be his; and that "long-wished-for end" (603) provides the social substrate for the sense of erotic arrival—coming rather than consummation—which the poem also lavishly elaborates: "Maud made my Maud by that long loving kiss" (656). Keats's gift for recreating the natural world of generation and death, and finding it good, takes in Tennyson's lyric the form of an acceptance of the cultural world. For both poets a full acceptance entails recognition of what is not easily accepted; but where for Keats the obstacles are such natural facts as pain, illness, and death ("Nightingale," 23–30), for Tennyson they inhere in cultural interpretations of nature, "A sad astrology, the boundless plan" that brands "His nothingness into man" (634–638). The hero, who "would die / To save from some slight shame one simple girl" (642–643), seeks an easeful death that is not Keats's blank mortality but an act in a script indited by nineteenth-century chivalry, which he not only would die for but also will kill for soon enough.

The hero's acceptance of love's "madness" and his gallant death wish both illustrate his acquiescence in a cultural role, as the interpolated seventh stanza, based on the seventh stanza of the "Nightingale" ode, makes clear:

> Not die; but live a life of truest breath,
> And teach true love to fight with mortal wrongs.
> O, why should Love, like men in drinking-songs,
> Spice his fair banquet with the dust of death?
> Make answer, Maud my bliss,
> Maud made my Maud by that long loving kiss,
> Life of my life, wilt thou not answer this?
> "The dusky strand of Death inwoven here
> With dear Love's tie, makes Love himself more dear."

(I.xviii.651–659)

Dying means living the life of a culture hero, which Tennyson risks spoiling his poem by describing in the virtuous bromides of these first two lines. But the stanza executes a handsome recovery in what follows, which complicates its verbal magic with a suggestion that it is the verbal magic of culturally canonical texts that largely inspires the hero's moral reform. "Like men in drinking-songs": we would do the "Ode to a Nightingale" no disservice in calling it the finest-toned drinking song in the canon, and the ode receives something like that compliment here from Keats's great port-loving successor. Tennyson finds his way to a meditation on the Keatsian themes of love and death through meditating on the tradition of which the "Nightingale" ode forms a part, and the quoted answer at which the stanza arrives feels like what the Keats of "When I Have Fears," "Why Did I Laugh?" and "Bright Star" meant but never came out and said.[18]

Just as in its entirety *Maud* treats the Romantic mythology of imaginative immortality as a dusky strand in the fabric of a cultural hegemony, so section xviii welcomes the influence of "Ode to a Nightingale" by presenting that influence as part of a cultural tradition. Tennyson at once confirms the ode's Romantic assertion of imaginative priority to natural facts of love and death, and diminishes the saliency of this particular text against the vast tapestry of culture with which it is entangled. When stanza 8 begins, "Is that enchanted moan only the swell / Of the long waves that roll in yonder bay?" (660–661), we cannot know whether "that enchanted moan" is the sound of the sea or the delicious Keatsian phrasing of the preceding lines. Keats is made one with nature: the Romantic perspective of the "sole self," which Keats's incantation over charmed casements and fairy lands forlorn helped produce, has been incorporated by midcentury into the structures of mediation that make the sea audible to Victorian ears in this particular way. Tennyson's allusiveness, in other words, undoes the opposition between self and context on which Keats's dialectic depended. The hero continues to figure, in his own eyes, as a sole self, but this very self-perception bespeaks the institutionalization of Romanticism that contributes to making him what he is.

This is why the Keatsian tolling bell prompts in Tennyson's hero no anxiety whatsoever: "And hark the clock within, the silver knell / Of twelve sweet hours that past in bridal white, / And died to live, long as my pulses play" (662–664). "No more so all forlorn" (630), he enjoys for the moment the entire idyllic security of a Victorian man whose love, whose ambition, and whose literary experience all converge in "the promised good," the behavior-reinforcing reward. Finally this satisfaction is intimately and expansively physical; no poem is more sensuous than the "Nightingale" ode, but Tennyson has written one here that is more *corporeal*, in representation of his no longer disaffected hero's bliss-ful merger with the body cultural and politic. Hence the fulfilling bodily imagery that governs the opening and closing stanzas on the "blood" (601), the "heart" (608), and the "pulses" that swell to cosmic dimension: "Beat, happy stars, timing with things below, / Beat with my heart more blest than heart can tell" (679–680).

To be sure, the idyllic residue of "some dark undercurrent woe" (681) remains to draw the hero back to unsolved problems that the monodramatic narrative holds in store. But when his joy re-vives in the final love lyric, the hero's body language dances once again to the music of the time, in the appropriately specific form of a Victorian polka: "And the soul of the rose went into my blood, / As the music clashed in the hall" (I.xxii.882–883). This pulse resurges most powerfully in the lines that close part I:

> She is coming, my own, my sweet;
>   Were it ever so airy a tread,
> My heart would hear her and beat,
>   Were it earth in an earthy bed;
> My dust would hear her and beat,
>   Had I lain for a century dead;
> Would start and tremble under her feet,
>   And blossom in purple and red.   (I.xxii.916–923)

Well over a century has passed since Tennyson wrote these lines of prophetic rapture, and it is no accident that their reputation has risen and fallen, and now rises again, with a sympathy for Vic-torian tastes. There may be no firmer testimony of Tennyson's intention to explore in *Maud* the pervasiveness of cultural deter-minants for behavior and feeling than the fact that in this last, climactic expression of love's ecstasy, from the most personally invested of all his major works, this prosodic adept chose to stake so much on the specifically contemporary beat of a popular fad.

FROM THE START of part II, the cultural determinants are dra-matically realigned against the hero they have capriciously sup-ported at the end of part I. The ensuing dissonance makes the abandoned hero, "so stunned and still" (II.i.2), begin seeing dou-ble. Maud, now irrecoverably lost, becomes a "ghastly Wraith" (II.i.32), a "hard mechanic ghost" (II.ii.82) that the hero explains as "a lying trick of the brain" (II.i.37), or "a juggle born of the brain" (II.ii.90). He is blaming the victim, of course, in the neu- rophysiological terms of his day (Colley 1983, 125, 166). But his ambidexter images of the lie and the juggle point beyond a psy- chology of self-division to the schism in society that furnishes the germinally twinned imagery of "Oh! That 'Twere Possible." In this long-deferred lyric (now section iv), images of the mutually alien city and country, the "woodland echo" (II.iv.178) and the market "hubbub" (II.iv.208), may meet only in the hero's mind, which is now more plainly than ever a crossroads of contradictory memories and impressions.

The mad scene of section v carries this tendency to its extreme. Tennyson piqued himself on having drafted the mad scene in twenty minutes, and it is in this most spontaneous poetry that the unreflective mind most forcefully reflects its social victimization. Insanity is a topic, like love, that summons up the deepest pri- vacies, and Tennyson calls upon it in part II in order to practice a sociopathology similar to that whereby he has earlier dissected "the cruel madness of love" (I.iv.156). In describing his passion earlier in the conventional terms of "madness," the hero was sur- rendering to the beat of his culture; so he must do again now in succumbing to madness itself: "And the hoofs of the horses beat, beat, / The hoofs of the horses beat, / Beat into my scalp and my brain" (II.v.246–248). The rhythms have changed since part I, but it is still the drum of culture that sounds the inevitable tattoo.

The mad hero's *idée fixe*—that he has died but wants proper burial—affords Tennyson occasions to sustain the urban imagery of the preceding section in a vividly necropolitan mode, and also to venture a reprise of the overt social satire that has been blunted by the coming of love in part I. Churchman, lord, statesman, physician all come under the lash (II.v.266–274), principally for sins of linguistic deviancy. "There is none that does his work, not one" (264); and what fills the space of this unperformed work is language, "chatter," "blabbing," and most significantly "idiot gabble" (257, 274, 279). Etymologically *idiocy* is privacy, and what the hero censures as "idiot gabble" is a cross between autism and bad breeding. The maddening thing about the dead men's chatter, from the hero's standpoint, is its violation of the Victorian de- corum that segregates public from private spheres. Tennyson has practiced just this violation since the beginning of *Maud*, as a poetic means of confounding a cardinal Victorian prejudice; but now that the hero shares the poet's secret, it is driving him out of his mind. In its methodical madness section v constitutes the hero's new and crippling consciousness of a breakdown between public and private discourses—a breakdown that unleashes a semiotic bedlam from which he seeks protection. Although he defensively calls the chorus of voices mere "babble" (284), what assails him is rather an excess than a dearth of meaning, an overload of confessional secrets he wants neither to hear nor to have heard by anyone else:

> For I never whispered a private affair
> Within the hearing of cat or mouse,
> No, not to myself in the closet alone,
> But I heard it shouted at once from the top of the house;
> Everything came to be known.
> Who told *him* we were there? (II v 285–290)

What is the intolerably open secret from which the hero wants burial? The abortive tryst with Maud to which he suddenly recurs has long since suffered its most devastating exposure; yet it offers a clue, for what was exposed in the exposure of his "private affair" with Maud was the notion of privacy itself. The hero's debacle has exacted his recognition of the inevitably corporate nature of language (Schulman 1983, 645); and this recognition "Is enough to drive one mad" (II.v.258), into an insanity that is also the poem's most comprehensively public gesture. The subjectively incoherent perspectives of the madman regroup themselves at the level of cultural analysis into an irresistible phalanx that serves Tennyson as the monodramatic equivalent of a tragically fatal objectivity. "Prophet, curse me the blabbing lip, / And curse me the British vermin, the rat" (295–296): simultaneously "prophet" and "vermin"—accuser, criminal, and judge in one breath, as the condensed syntax suggests—the hero can but perpetuate the discourse that entraps him if he is to speak at all.

Placing social invective against the "Wretchedest age, since Time began" (259) in the mouth of a madman serves the poet laureate, of course, as a means of self-defense—a man would have to be crazy to talk about England like that (Stange 1973, 478; Thesing 1977, 20)—but it also defends the reader against a too immediate disclosure of a too intimate vision of the pervasive force of culture. The hero requires defense from this vision as well, of

course; and since he lacks the dramatic distance available to poet
and reader, he pleads insanity. Even this asylum gives no real
refuge, however, and he knows it:

> O me, why have they not buried me deep enough?
> Is it kind to have made me a grave so rough,
> Me, that was never a quiet sleeper?
> Maybe still I am but half-dead;
> Then I cannot be wholly dumb;
> I will cry to the steps above my head
> And somebody, surely, some kind heart will come
> To bury me, bury me
> Deeper, ever so little deeper.   (II.v.334–342)

As death represents acculturation in part I, here half-death represents an acculturation tantalizingly unconsummated. The hero
"cannot be wholly dumb" until he becomes wholly deaf to the
incongruity of the ubiquitous yet personal idiot gabble that circulates around and within him. He cries out for a burial so full,
a cultural immersion so total, that he will no longer know that
engulfing rite for what it is. More than anything else, the hero
wants to lose a mind he wishes, or suspects, he has never properly
possessed. This goal he may achieve only by ceasing to be—or,
barring literal suicide, by ceasing to be piercingly aware, as he
now is for the only time in the poem, of culture as an otherness
that he has internalized, in the tangled nest of public properties
that constitutes his private self.

These equivalent modes of oblivion, either of which the hero
would prefer to his current torment, come together in the prospect
of military self-sacrifice he accepts in part III. Unable to "bury
myself in myself" (I.i.75), whether through the cool reason of a
philosopher's life or through the irrational escapes of a lunatic's,
the hero says at last, "I have felt with my native land, I am one
with my kind, / I embrace the purpose of God, and the doom
assigned" (III.vi.58–59). With the natural images of "my native
land" and "my kind," the politicization of any ostensibly natural
substrate below culture is complete; and with the invocation of
"the purpose of God" and its Tennysonian synonym "the doom
assigned," supernatural options for transcending culture are terminally politicized as well. In answer to the pathetic final prayer
of part II, the merciful ground of culture has opened to swallow
the hero up, and he has fallen into the bliss of the state.

Culture never did betray the heart that loved her, not when she is loved as by Tennyson's hero, with "the unselfishness born of a great passion" (*PT*, 1039). But great passion is greatly blind, and in awaking to "the better mind" (III.vi.56) the hero has deadened himself to a mass of inconsistencies—something we have watched him do throughout the poem, to be sure, but not yet on this scale or with this urgency of implicit appeal to the reader's conscience. At earlier phases of his passion our hero would have been torn, at some level of awareness, between his claims of sympathy with his "kind" and his zealously bloody intention to go to war; and between his dedication to the business interests behind modern warfare and his hatred of the "wrongs and shames" (III.vi.40) of the commercial *Pax Victoriana*. He is not thus torn now; now his cultural entombment can weather the most Orwellian of contradictions. The abiding horror of part III arises when the hero's defection into lobotomized jingoism leaves us to take up the ethical slack, without a clue to imagining a credible alternative course of events. The hero's unacknowledged contradictions remain, to sear the critical conscience that would free itself of patriotic heroics without falling into step with some other cultural or countercultural troop.

" 'Maud': I leave before the sad part" (*LTJ*, 82): Emily Tennyson's discreet exit is understandable but unavailing. We crave excuse from the cultural vision of *Maud*, but such excuse comes hard once we recognize that its hero has satisfied precisely this craving, in one fell swoop of moral abdication. We may imagine its poet feeding such a craving, too, in repeatedly indulged yet never quite fulfilling debauches of vicarious abandonment to full acculturation, as he subjected circle after circle of empire's best and brightest to readings of a poem that held up their shared eminence to such unforgiving scrutiny (Robson 1957, 159–163). "Only once, as it seems to me, (at the close of 'Maud')," wrote an American culture pilgrim who had undergone the Tennysonian rite, "has he struck the note of irrepressible emotion, and appeared to say the thing that must be said at the moment, at any cost" (James 1875, 176). What struck young Henry James about the close of *Maud* was the reckless extremity of its contemporary commitment: a unique fusion of Tennyson's antinomian, lyrical intensity with the cultural absorption and finish that always seem so smooth in his idylls of the hearth or of the king (Shaw 1976b,

189–190). *Maud* is an achievement of lethal force, one that Tennyson himself seems not to have understood very well and that his career never repeated (Wordsworth 1974, 361). But then he had no cause to repeat this published experiment, because he was able to repeat it in public all the time. The experiment was never over: *Maud* remained a rhapsode's work-in-progress at each of those command performances for captive audiences that nobody (Emily Tennyson included) seems to have rationally willed but that nobody (Alfred Tennyson included) seems to have been able to escape. Those evenings at Farringford or London or Aldworth cannot appear more quintessentially Victorian to us than they must have felt to their participants, who, if they wondered what they were doing there and minded the poem with even the least attentiveness, must have received some deeply disquieting answers. Well may the cultural vision of *Maud* sting us still.

Afterword

AT THE BEGINNING of this book I considered the twentieth-century reaction against Tennyson in exclusively literary terms. In fact it was something more than that, a broadly modern and not just a modernist phenomenon; and it deserves a parting glance in the light of questions that have arisen, especially during the last two chapters, about the cultural situation of Tennyson's poetry. For Tennyson's status crumbled among modernist coteries just as the empire of Victorian values was falling in ashes around the larger generation to which those coteries belonged. In the aftermath of World War I, when the first generation to come of age in our century underwent sudden and permanent disenchantment with the legacy of the nineteenth, their indignant scorn sprang from a widely shared sense of betrayal at the hands of the Victorian cultural tradition, which the late poet laureate appeared to epitomize. It seemed in particular that the glamorous Tennysonian rendition of a hopelessly outdated martial ideal, in works like *Maud* and *Idylls of the King*, had seduced the best of them into the nightmare of the Great War.

Such scapegoating seems grossly unfair, especially when we consider how the disastrous career of the hero in *Maud* prophesies that of the doomed generation of 1914. World War I was not, of course, Alfred Tennyson's fault. Yet with some effort we can imagine what our cultural forebears meant in saying that it was, and the effort is worth making for his sake as well as theirs. For if we take the imaginative leap back across our century into the outrage of a generation betrayed, we find ourselves imagining something else besides. Sympathetic understanding of a generational disappointment so large and bitter requires us to posit, as its ground, a commensurate expectation. In this case that expectation concerns the importance of poetry; and it constitutes a compliment, both to Tennyson and to literature, that from our standpoint looks nothing short of extravagant. Here, for once, a poet ranked among the *acknowledged* legislators of mankind. The wholesale revulsion that set in against Victoria's laureate, and against the culture he represented in the popular mind, attests to the depth, breadth, and immediacy of the influence once wielded through Tennyson, for better or worse, by the art of poetry itself. With its thoroughgoing rejection of the "poetic"—that is, of Tennysonian melodiousness and rhetoric—postwar culture in effect bestowed on poetry, for the first and probably last time in modern experience, the immense compliment of taking it seriously.

The sort of backhanded tribute that postwar culture paid, through Tennyson, to high literature is reserved in our decades for writings deemed pornographic or sacrilegious, libelous or seditious. Our moment, that is, confers the honor of its outrage upon paraliterary genres, the formulation of whose rules falls not to poets or academic humanists but to acknowledged legislators of the usual kind, whose cultural power and prestige nobody doubts. Knowing more than the generation of the Great War—knowing principally, indeed, what they and their successors from World War II have taught us—we can now dismiss with a smile their holy rage for demystifying the heritage of Tennyson. But the kind of knowledge that lets us rule the postwar case against Tennyson out of literary court, arguments unheard, is not purchased without loss of power to ourselves, or without dishonor to literature. In the conviction that these are losses indeed, I end this book with an open question that is prompted by my abiding concerns with the manifold fatalism of Tennyson's poetry and with the phenomenon of his poetic career. Granted that Tennyson was not responsible for World War I, what might his sense of doom and his superb poetic logic of the foregone conclusion have to do with the new "last battle in the west," what every journalist now means by "Armageddon," the prospect of World War III?

Tennyson failed his readers, with *Maud* and practically every other poem he wrote, when he came to imagine alternatives to that which is. But this failure, I propose, also constitutes his imagination's radical strength and its enduring value as a challenge to the social and political imagination. When Tennyson's vision of doom takes on the cultural aspect it wears in *Maud*, its seamless concatenation of cause and consequence gives the lie to the kind of temporizing reform that his less deeply felt poetry more cautiously endorses. If we still turn to poetry, and I think we do, for what Wordsworth calls "the breath and finer spirit of all knowledge," and Shelley "the creative faculty to imagine that which we know," we find in Tennyson a fascinated apprehension of that knowledge we have learned to name science or technology, presented with a poetic technique that is the match of such knowledge, and perhaps its not too distant cousin. He offers exhibit after exhibit of freshly sensed data about a world of physical detail, and beyond this he evinces remarkable power to feel his way into the nerve and reach of the best theories about the universe that were available in the decades during which his mind matured. We find much science in Tennyson, then, but pathetically little support or direction for the practical knowledge—call it resolve—that grasps the world in order to understand it and change it as well.

And yet, beyond its science and its capitulation to the known, Tennyson's poetry communicates something further and potentially more affirmative, which he calls wisdom and which I can only call the sense of comprehensiveness. Its content is the imagination of a knowledge more global than theory and more wholly sensuous than factual detail, stretched to the immensity of the sublime, and drenched in the determinism of the tragic, which were his imaginative and ethical elements. At the level of imaginary action in the poems Tennyson wrote, the usual result of such systemic wisdom is an impassive or a sorrowing quiescence. But this baffled and diffusive kind of knowledge can also enlarge the practical resolve it seems to starve. The Tennysonian measure of doom can fix and revolve, within the mind that actively contemplates, an ever fugitive knowledge that, as we cope with what we take the destiny of our time to be and work to shape it, partial measures will avail next to nothing. How a poetry or spaciously imagined knowledge of Tennyson's kind may affect our resolve for reform—or, in our doom-shadowed age, for survival—remains to be seen. But if that resolve should wither in frustration, Tennyson's grandly minor music will seem its inevitable accompaniment.

Notes
Works Cited
Index

Notes

Introduction to Part I

1. The bibliographical surveys in Killham 1960 and Francis 1980a conveniently serve to mark two watersheds in the history of recent Tennyson criticism. See also Madden 1973 and, on *In Memoriam*, Sendry 1980.

1. The Measure of Doom

1. See Ricks 1972 on the poet's "extraordinary powers over situation and mood, played against a known outcome" (275), and on his fondness for quoting or alluding to his own earlier poems in later ones (298–312). The teleological cast of Tennyson's compositional practice seems especially appropriate to a poet who, with rare exceptions (*Maud*, II.v; "The Holy Grail"), composed in his head slowly and revised extensively, and who, on losing his manuscripts, could retrieve from memory whole volumes for publication (Gillett 1977).

2. See Korg 1958, 11. What Korg calls the "pattern of fatality" need not disable all narrative, of course; at least since the *Iliad* the fulfillment of a preordained destiny has made for satisfactory plots (McLuhan 1951, 93). That such a model—it may be *the* classical model—usually evokes in Tennyson not just satisfaction but also defeat is a measure of his reluctant but undeniable Romanticism. Even when the plot of fate remains benign and overtakes his characters in wish-fulfilling ways, his verse expresses a counterwish that character had retained a more properly Romantic ascendancy over circumstance.

3. In 1831, long before anyone had heard of the Symbolist movement, Hallam praised Tennyson for his "vivid, picturesque delineation of objects, and the peculiar skill with which he holds all of them fused, to borrow a metaphor from science, in a medium of strong emotion" (*WH*, 191); and in 1835 Mill identified Tennyson's "power of creating scenery in keeping with some state of human feeling; so fitted to it as to be the embodied symbol of it" (86). On

Tennyson and the Symbolists, see McLuhan 1951; Baker 1967, 48–53; Sinfield 1971, 201–210; Shaw 1976b, 62; Altieri 1978.

4. See Brashear 1969, 28; Shaw 1976b, 49. In the indictment with which Faulkner closes chapter 13 of *Light in August* (1932), Reverend Hightower turns from the window shortly after "the first dark" to escape into his dog-eared copy of Tennyson. Faulkner's hypnotic syntax, atmospheric richness, and ambivalent response to cultural decadence place him among Tennyson's uneasy American heirs; hence, perhaps, the arresting bitterness of Faulkner's attack, and the accuracy with which he sets it at a quintessentially Tennysonian hour (Bidney 1985).

5. In *Memoir*, II, 149, the poet remembers weirdly *feeling*, through a wall, the beating of a clock he could not hear. See also *Memoir*, II, 401: "What will people come to in a hundred years? Do you think they will give up all religious forms and go and sit in silence in the Churches listening to the organs?"

6. Against Tennyson's sager formalist pronouncements, it is helpful to set this bit of self-depreciation: "I don't think that since Shakespeare there has been such a master of the English language as I. To be sure, I've got nothing to say" (Martin 1980, 317–318).

7. Compare the nexus of psychological with verbal mood in other celebrated poems: "Life piled on life / Were all too little" ("Ulysses," 24–25), "I would that I were dead!" ("Mariana"), "such / A friendship as had mastered Time" (*In Memoriam*, lxxxv.63–64).

8. *Memoir*, I, 268, 381. On the historical particulars, see Chambers 1903, 228; Martin 1980, 381; McGann 1982.

9. Compare the phrase "bowery loneliness" in line 9 of "Milton: Alcaics" (1863), one of Tennyson's "attempts at classic metres in quantity" (*PT*, 1154) and thus close kin to the metrically experimental "To Virgil." When not just impressionistic, critical comparisons between Virgil and Tennyson tend to address either the poets' parallel historical situations as melancholy apologists for empire (Killham 1973, 178) or else their formal similarities as polishers of memorable verses (Shaw 1976b, 33–38). A more satisfactorily comparative account of Virgil and Tennyson might investigate the relations between imperial content and formal mastery, with a further view to each poet's place in literary history as a self-consciously belated author working in secondary, superbly *literary* modes.

2. Keen Discoveries

1. See Groom 1939, 98: "Tennyson attained a characteristic style early in his career and he never lost it; in language, at least, the child was father of the man." Emerson's journal for 1849–50 observes, of the "japanning" or verbal varnish with which "Tennyson supplied defects," "It seems an indemnity to the Briton for his precocious maturity" (1975, 194). See also Kenner 1973, 380–384.

2. Culler 1977, 9–12, extrapolates a conclusion from hints in the unfinished script. Even if one joins him in imagining a fifth-act triumph of poetry and love,

it seems significant that Tennyson left his play in the grip of powers less evidently benign.

3. On frustration in early Tennyson, compare Paden 1942, 58–64; Carr 1950, 63; Brashear 1969, 67. Brashear contends that Tennyson very early embraced as his theme despair and not frustration; but the subtler thesis of Paden and Carr suggests that, while despair may have been the theme the poet aimed to choose, frustration was the theme that chose him.

4. In "O Bosky Brook," an unpublished ode Tennyson began around the time of his play, the reflection of moonlight in water gleams "With such a lustrous chord of solemn sheen, / That the heart vibrates with desire to pace / The palpitating track of buoyant rays" (67–69); the "chord" is both a path of light and a sounding string. Further explicit evidence of an early interest in synesthesia occurs in a manuscript draft of a dialogue poem from T.Nbk. 20, which answers the question why the scents of flowers recall music. "within the brain or soul itself / There is a common ground or marriage bond / Of all the senses, whence they sometimes are / Consonant chords that shiver to one note" (see *PT*, 453).

5. Further speculation on the young poet's interest in such fatal empowerment might lead back to his earliest surviving production, a translation into heroic couplets from Claudian's *De Raptu Proserpinae*. The passage exhibits remarkable similarities to the narrative of the Magus: its war-in-heaven contest over primeval rights comprises much lurid emotion and din; but its principal energies are spent in self-suppression, the sum total of the action being that Pluto decides to drop his brother a line. Both Tennyson's original narrative and his Claudian translation turn on curiously overwrought yet inert actions of containment, and thus both are little allegories of the formal problems likely to be uppermost in the young poet's mind. See Tucker 1983 for extended discussion of the Claudian translation and of another very early piece, "The Coach of Death."

6. Compare "To Poesy," written in 1828, with its millenarian hope "that these expectant eyes / Shall drink the fulness of thy victory, / For thou art all unconscious of thy Might"; and the yet earlier ode "Perdidi Diem," which represents the music of the spheres as potable light: "The latest energies of light they drink: / The latest fiat of Divine Art, / Our Planets, slumbering in their swiftness, hear / The last beat of the thunder of God's heart."

7. See *Memoir*, II, 521: "Milton beats everyone in the material sublime." These last two words, however, may have come to Tennyson from Milton's chief rival in this Romantic contest: see Keats's "Epistle to J. H. Reynolds, Esq.," 69.

8. The test case for this assertion is the death of Arthur Hallam in 1833, which according to standard accounts of Tennyson's development marks the intrusion of actual life into the secluded and above all literary bowers of the poet's youth, the decisive victory of reality over imagination. But this victory had been won already in the *Poems* of 1832, written with Hallam's encouragement and under the influence of the Romantics, who had shown Tennyson how the conflict of literary imagination with modern life might itself become a subject

for poetry, and to whose works Hallam among others had introduced him. On the biographical conjunction of Cambridge with Romanticism, see Allen 1978, 36, 45–51; Lourie 1979, 25. On the pronounced literariness of the poet's appropriation of his dead friend, see the Introduction to Part II.

9. See also *Memoir*, II, 386, and Arnold's judgment that "Timbuctoo" contained the germ of Tennyson's future powers (Collins 1901, xv); also Buckler 1980, 29.

10. For biographical evidence that Tennyson began reading Wordsworth, Coleridge, Shelley, and Keats at Cambridge see *Memoir*, I, 36, 256; Tennyson 1949, 34; Kennedy 1978; and Allen 1978. But of course the best evidence is what we find in comparing the poetry Tennyson wrote at college to what he had written at home under the sole Romantic influence of Byron, whom he subsequently repudiated as an adolescent infatuation. A note in the old poet's hand at Lincoln reads: "My Schwärmerei for Byron entirely ceased when I was about 18 & I don't think I have ever opened him since."

11. Another Romantic precursor this "Chapman" masks may be Wordsworth in "Peter Bell," 96–100: "I know the secrets of a land / Where human foot did never stray; / Fair is that land as evening skies, / And cool, though in the depth it lies / Of burning Africa."

12. Versions of the same question virtually constitute another of Tennyson's earliest publications, "A Fragment," printed in *The Germ* one year after "Timbuctoo": "Where is the Giant of the Sun" (1); "where, / Mysterious Egypt, are thine obelisks?" (11–12); "where thy monuments?" (19). As in "Timbuctoo," Tennyson sounds the theme of cultural loss through Romantic allusion, here to a passage in Keats's *Hyperion* that sounds the theme of loss resisted: "Where was he, when the Giant of the Sun / Stood bright, amid the sorrow of his peers?" (III.29–30). A note on this apparently anomalous fragment may be the place to plead for a fuller study of Tennyson's relationship to the Higher Criticism. A study of this kind, building on Hungerford 1941, Paden 1942, and Shaffer 1975, and assessing the poet's earliest intellectual influences, should elucidate Tennyson's consistent recourse to the charmingly preposterous hypotheses of Faber and Bryant; his fascination with a sun-god myth that unites works as diverse as "Oenone," "Tithonus," and "The Coming of Arthur"; his orientalism; his thinking about the historical dimensions of religious faith; even his generic interest in the relation between idyllic and epic forms.

13. Compare Coleridge's image in the preface to "Kubla Khan," where after the interruption of the man from Porlock, the poet's vision "had passed away like the images on the surface of a stream into which a stone has been cast, but, alas! without the after restoration of the latter! 'Then all the charm / Is broken—all that phantom-world so fair / Vanishes, and a thousand circlets spread, / And each misshapes the other.' "

14. One of the finest formulations of the reciprocal relation of thought to sensation in Tennyson comes from a text on which he had begun work by the time of "Timbuctoo," *The Lover's Tale*: "Alway the invisible inaudible thought, / Artificer and subject, lord and slave, / Shaped by the audible and visible, / Moulded the audible and visible" (II.101–104).

15. Butler 1911, 44, transcribes his wife's journal account of a conversation

with the poet during his last year: "He also thought the supposed identifications of topography absurd, and preferred to believe that Homer's descriptions were entirely imaginary. When I said I thought that a disappointing view, he called me 'a wretched localiser.' 'They try to localise me too.' "

16. Bloom 1976, 147–149, reads "Mariana" against the one substantial Romantic flower-*pot* poem, Keats's *Isabella; or the Pot of Basil*.

17. Compare "The Ancient Sage," 21–22: "What power but the bird's could make / The music in the bird?"

18. Chambers 1903, 230, shows how fully Tennyson derives such details as the porch, the sofas, and the laughing caliph from the end of the 236th of the *Arabian Nights* ("Noureddin and the Fair Persian"; see Killham 1958, 180–182). But in the tale the youth and his Persian girl are the same age; the consistency of Tennyson's borrowings makes this signal departure the more striking. The Keatsian word "rillets" in line 48 likewise chastely departs from its probable source in *Endymion*, II.943–945: "O that her shining hair was in the sun, / And I distilling from it thence to run / In amorous rillets down her shrinking form!"

19. Babies find their way into Tennyson's poetry, most palpably in *The Princess*, as symbols triggering the reflex sentiments of the adults around them. But the poet was also fascinated—attracted and repelled—by infants' unacculturated subjectivity. In a copy of *Poems* (1842) now at Trinity, Edward FitzGerald recorded Tennyson's reactions to his own newborn son: "I am afraid of him; Babies have a Grandeur, which Children lose—their Look of Awe and Wonder. This morning he lay half an hour *worshiping the Bed-post*, on which the Sunlight flickered" (154–155). See *The Lover's Tale*, IV.307–312; "De Profundis" (1880); and *In Memoriam*, xlv, liv, and cxxiv.

20. Observe what becomes of its key Shelleyan trope of universal dissemination by the time of "The Flower" (1864), a tight-fisted little fable about originality and property : "Most can raise the flowers now, / For all have got the seed" (19–20).

3. *Emergencies*

1. Tucker 1982 grounds in a close reading of the text the conclusions summarized here. Short 1967 reviews earlier scholarship, establishes the imaginative divide between the original three parts and *The Golden Supper*, and explodes the idea that Boccaccio was the important precursor Tennyson later claimed. Briney 1973 offers pertinent discussions of desire in Shelley (26–44) and of Tennyson's sophistication in the use of dreams (113–127).

2. A further parallel between the narrative reluctances of the fictive and of the actual poet emerges with a version in T.Nbk. 18, fols. 27v–29v, which skips from I.541 to I.631 and thus leaves unwritten the crisis of Camilla's confession, "the event" upon which the entire story turns.

3. As Walt Whitman—who liked to call the laureate "the boss" (Nicolson 1923, 210)—observed of Tennyson's love poetry, "It goes screaming and weeping after the facts of the universe, in their calm beauty and equanimity, to note the occurrence of itself" (Daiches 1961, 217). See also Bloom 1976, 147.

4. In the fourth tale of the tenth day of the *Decameron*, Julian's counterpart lives on in Bologna happily ever after with the couple he has nobly reunited.

5. See *LH*, 702, for William Jerdan's culinary parody, the orthography of its last line often unwittingly reproduced in undergraduate essays: "The yellow-leaved piccalilly / The greensheathed pepper chili / Tremble (pen me aught more silly!) / Round about Shallot."

6. The poet's comment on "The Lord of Burleigh" (1842), 63–64, suggests that his association of melancholy with the passion of the past may have had an instinctive grammatical analogue: "The mood changes from happiness to unhappiness, and the present tense changes to the past" (*PT*, 604).

7. Tennyson's use of the topos conjoining sex and death is distinguished by its insistently cultural dimension. See the discussions below of "Oenone" and "The Gardener's Daughter"; see also part III of *The Lover's Tale* and the twelfth stanza of "Forlorn" (1889; written 1854?): "Black with bridal favours mixt! / Bridal bells with tolling" (69–70).

8. The authenticity of this often quoted comment, which has sponsored a range of upbeat interpretations (Packer 1964; Shannon 1981), has recently come under fire. Tobias 1971, 8, casts doubt on the entire attribution, arguing that Hallam Tennyson reprinted as his father's something that Canon Ainger had written for an anthology of *Tennyson for the Younger*, where in any case the comment seems most at home.

9. Stein 1981, 293–294, reproduces Holman Hunt's illustration to the poem and points out that Lancelot is "seen at a distance, in a landscape without shadow . . . a blank rather than pure."

10. Malory describes Lancelot's shield as "all of sable, and a quene crowned in the myddis of sylver, and a knyght clene armed knelynge afore her" (1971, 502); Tennyson may have changed the colors with the barley fields of part I in mind.

11. On the "idyllically" or "tragically" amoral vision of this poem—allegorical though not didactic—see Hill 1968, 424; Pattison 1979, 49–50; on tragedy in Tennyson, see Kozicki 1966, 15–20; Brashear 1969.

12. The best known judgment is probably that in Leavis 1932: "The explicit moral of this poem is that withdrawal will not do; but when he comes to the moral Tennyson's art breaks down: the poetry belongs to the palace" (16; but see Sendry 1966). Some Victorian readers responded similarly: for Hallam's reservations see *LH*, 576, 607; for analysis of Rossetti's illustrations to the poem, see Meisel 1977, 340. Finally there is the ambiguity of the poet's later comment— on the poem as "the embodiment of my own belief that the Godlike life is with man and for man" (*Memoir*, I, 118)—with which the Soul at her most sinful hour might exultantly agree.

13. The stanza on Homer is particularly interesting: "A million wrinkles carved his skin" (138) both amplifies and trivializes Keats's epithet "deep-brow'd Homer" ("On First Looking into Chapman's Homer," 6), and thus forecasts the picturesquely superficial procedures that will typify Tennyson's practice as an idyllist.

14. More or less animal voices frequently accompany the onset of prophetic vision in Tennyson: see "Oenone," 245–246; "Tiresias," 88–98; "Tithonus," 39–

42. In his old age, as an increasingly rigid transcendentalism split body and soul asunder, the poet developed an animus against the animal, as in "By an Evolutionist" (1889), where the ascending visionary declares—like the Soul in 1832, with perceptible relief—"I hear no yelp of the beast" (19).

15. *Diffidence* is John Bayley's name for it, in the best recent exposition (1981) of the perennial dialectic of private and public in Tennyson's writing. Bayley's term suggests nicely the conjunction of circumstances that enabled an affective skeptic like Tennyson, a poet constitutionally diffident or distrustful of entire reaches of emotion, to speak for his age's crisis of faith.

16. Obeisance to the pure form of this poem, its mystery that defies analysis, has been made by almost every commentator, especially with the advent of the New Criticism: see Bush 1937, 200; Eliot 1950, 288; Green 1951, 668; Stange 1952; Buckley 1960, 47; Smith 1964, 122. The Hesperides themselves, however, insist that they are the guardians of a *wisdom*; and the formal techniques they employ have enough resemblance to those of brainwashing to let us guess that what they serve is the conservative ideology of formalism itself.

17. Tennyson strengthened the linearity of Hanno's course in revising line 2 to its present reading from the manuscript version that had him "wandering about" Soloë (T.Nbk. 23, fol. 24v; also Allen MS., fol. 26).

18. Tennyson would have encountered in Faber the neoplatonic association of bees with generation, which is presented in Porphyry's commentary on the Cave of the Nymphs in the *Odyssey*, XII. Paden 1942, 156–157, finds this text in the mythic background of "The Lady of Shalott"; it also may inform Tennyson's most complete and eerie version of the nymph's descent, "Come Down, O Maid."

19. Far ampler attention has been paid to Tennyson's classical than to his Romantic allusions: see Collins 1901; Mustard 1904; Turner 1976; Pattison 1979. Such scholarship is indispensable; but whatever textual sources poets engage, their allusiveness—their apprehension and use of all prior texts, however ancient—will be specific to their time. Poets of different eras allude not only to different texts but also to the same texts in different ways, ways that they moreover share with their contemporaries; and in Tennyson's era the reigning allusive manner was incurably Romantic (see Chandler 1982).

20. Relations between the Tennysonian defenses of autoerotic virginity and verbal overdetermination are explored in Rowlinson's excellent essay (1984); see also Ostriker 1967, 277; Dodsworth 1969. In "Hendecasyllabics" (1863), the poem itself is personified as a sort of fourth daughter of Hesperus, a "half coquette-like / Maiden" (20–21): "Hard, hard, hard is it, only not to tumble, / So fantastical is the dainty metre" (13–14). A similar verbal defensiveness recurs in Tennyson's correspondence: see *Letters*, 77.

21. Paradoxically *Alastor*, that anatomy of incapacity for human relationship, was a favorite among the Cambridge Apostles with whom Tennyson formed such lasting relationships—perhaps because it appealed to their shared elitism (Jamieson 1952, 407–413; Allen 1978, 1, 81). Hallam harbored the peculiar conviction that "Timbuctoo" was "modeled upon the Alastor" (*LH*, 326). See the fine discussion in Lourie 1979, 6–11, 16–22.

22. Perhaps the best context for the fire imagery here, in "Oenone," and

elsewhere in Tennyson is to be found in *Memoir*, I, 326–327: "One of the traditional and unwritten sayings of Christ which oftenest came home to him was, 'He that is near Me is near the fire.' "

23. In chapter 9 of *Father and Son* (1907), Edmund Gosse alludes to a Fatima from the *Arabian Nights* who is literally abandoned and shut up in a tower. On the general subject of the poet's orientalism, see Paden 1942, 127–132.

24. Much as, in retrospect, Tennyson dated his poetic majority from "Timbuctoo," so he insisted in a note to the 1885 edition now at Lincoln, "The form of 'Oenone' and the 'Lotos Eaters' is not borrowed from any classical or modern poem, as some have suggested. The treatment of both subjects is, as far as I know, original" (54). See Ostriker 1967, 281; Saintsbury 1923, III, 184.

25. For Romantic resonances confirming the epic potential in this exceptionally mythological passage, compare Keats's *Hyperion*, I.202–212, where "slow-breath'd melodies" attend the advent of an all but fallen sun god.

26. Edward FitzGerald noted in his copy of *Poems* now at Trinity, "Francis Edgeworth could not away with this jingle. Ida—I die" (119). Another coincidence worth noting is the jingling palindrome of Oenone's own name as sounded in English.

27. See Shannon 1977, 698. In a version of line 150 in T.Nbk. 26, Pallas acknowledges what is going on, disingenuously but still perhaps a bit too nakedly for comfort: "I bribe not choice with gifts."

28. Tennyson's first surviving letter, written at age twelve, quotes the opening soliloquy from *Samson Agonistes* and singles out this line as particularly beautiful (*Letters*, 2).

29. Hair 1981 finds at the close of Oenone's song an "unreasoning passion which marks the disintegration of her personality" (74); but of course one person's "disintegration" is another's "reorganization." This distinction matters because something closer to psychic disintegration concludes the even more extreme "Ulysses" and "Tithonus."

30. Visionary and military strife—and in that order. The newly prophetic mode into which "Oenone" marks Tennyson's fiery baptism employs the political figuratively rather than referentially (Pattison 1979, 53). As Buckler (1980, 97) and Sinfield (1977, 33) point out, Oenone ends her poem in the grip of a visionary wisdom but in ignorance of the historically specific knowledge that Cassandra possesses: like Yeats's Leda, Oenone embodies a truth but does not know it. This characteristic gravitation from concrete historicity toward gnostic apocalypse has important generic consequences for Tennyson's later work in the long poem and the epic. The Judgment of Paris was traditionally a theme marking a poet's progress from pastoral to heroic genres (Hair 73); the swerve away from the literalist pole of prophetic vision that marks "Oenone" anticipates Tennyson's generalizing, allegorical approach to his epic materials in *Idylls of the King*. Note, in this regard, that the poet drew scenery for "Oenone" from the Pyrenees landscapes that he had visited with Hallam during the summer of 1830, after the debacle of their abortive apostolic mission to assist the revolutionary Torrijos (DeMott 1962; Allen 1978, 119).

31. Ricks (*PT*, 396) cites the parallel between the lines on "The Abominable" and Apollo's imprecations against the Furies in Aeschylus' *Eumenides*, 644. We

might find prophesied in Tennyson's emergent dramatic monologue a miniature anti-*Oresteia*, as Oenone and Cassandra prepare to arraign the Olympians on charges of Apollonian illusion. In this connection Brashear 1969 demonstrates a Nietzschean conflict of Apollonian illusion with Dionysian impulse throughout Tennyson's career. Oenone's very name in Greek suggests the Dionysian element (*Oinone / oinos*); and Tennyson introduces her leaning on a "fragment twined with vine." But beyond this etymological link lies a surer literary bond in Tennyson's reading of Virgil: Oenone's powerful lines 253–256 derive from the dreams maddening Dido in *Aeneid*, IV.465–468 (Bush 1937, 206), a text that also supplies allusions to Aeschylus's Orestes and to the madness of Pentheus as brought on in Euripides' *Bacchae* by Dionysus himself.

32. One contemporary admirer who responded to the poem's movement toward transcendence ("etherisity") was Poe, who wrote that "Oenone exalts the soul not into passion, but into a conception of pure beauty, which in its elevation—its calm and intense rapture—has in it a foreshadowing of the future and spiritual life" (Joseph 1973, 424).

Introduction to Part II

1. "The life of the poet": I mean the phrase in Lawrence Lipking's sense. Some of Lipking's most arbitrary criteria for the "book of new life" (1981, 17–18) he finds Dante, Blake, and Yeats writing at midcareer have a surprising pertinence to the careerist *Poems* of 1842. Tennyson attained the Christological age of thirty-three in the year of its publication, and its mixture of lyric and idyllic modes loosely corresponds to the amalgam of poetry and prose Lipking finds characteristic of such a book.

2. The egotism that emerges in Tennyson's scattered comments on individual works and lines had a careerist dimension as well (see *Letters*, 83–85). Among the papers at Lincoln is an undated sheet that copies in the poet's later hand, apparently from some biographical notice, such laudatory phrases as "the well-known Maud" and "His latest work The Idylls of the King, which many consider his greatest." Observe that the texts cited come from the second half of his career: not even as laureate would Tennyson rest on his laurels.

3. The poet's own comment on this process occurs in *In Memoriam*, lxxxv.49–56:

> And so my passion hath not swerved
>   To works of weakness, but I find
>   An image comforting the mind,
> And in my grief a strength reserved.
>
> Likewise the imaginative woe,
>   That loved to handle spiritual strife,
>   Diffused the shock through all my life,
> But in the present broke the blow.

4. Compare the revision in line 4 of "In the Valley of Cauteretz" (1864), which originally read "I walked with Arthur Hallam" (*PT*, 1123). Although Tennyson often complained about the inaccuracy of the internal dating in this

autobiographical poem—"two and thirty years" should have been "one and thirty"—no word of his is recorded about the more startling excision of his beloved's name from the published text. Possibly he felt, once *In Memoriam* had become public property, that the name would be superfluous. Tennyson would later take advantage of his and Hallam's unique celebrity to commingle private experience and public knowledge in the final line of "Vastness" (1885), where the reader's identification of "him" as the unnamed Hallam is sublimely, and correctly, presumed, even as the whole consolatory argument of *In Memoriam* serves as collateral for the old poet's else-desperate credit: "Peace, let it be! for I loved him, and love him for ever: the dead are not dead but alive." (See also Emily Tennyson's *Letters*, 330–331.)

4. In Extremis

1. Here, for comparison, is another fragment from a different Trinity notebook (T.Nbk. 22, fol. 5), which occurs sandwiched between drafts of "St. Simeon Stylites" and "Ulysses," and has marked affinities with both texts, as with "Tiresias":

> What did it profit me that once in Heaven
> I walked, a Seraph among Seraphim,
> In shadowing incense-woods that showered down
> Fountains of flowering fire?—or that I flew
> Drenching my plumes in fragrant sprays, which made
> Those all-hued arcs that span the beautiful
> Cataracts thro' inexplorable ravines
> Rolling melodious thunders mingled with
> Far Hallelujahs from the hills, where o'er me
> The untrembling splendours of almighty God
> Smote those vast cliffs with crowns of towers? or that
> In place of cloud on every topmost peak
> Shot round a sleepless sphere of flame that changed
> To colours such as are not known to thee?

Context, which is the problem with which this voice seems to be wrestling, is also our problem as we seek to classify its speech generically.

2. Tennyson's interest in experimenting not just with dramatic persona but with grammatical person appears in H.Nbk. 4, fol. 41, which gives a first-person version of the final lines from "Sir Launcelot and Queen Guinevere," a narrative fragment published in the third person in 1842.

3. This distancing maneuver emerges, in little, with Tennyson's manuscript revision of "this marble girth" to "yon marble girth" in line 131 (T.Nbk. 32).

4. Perhaps this imitative Virgil passage imitates a literary model as well, in Tennyson's main source *The Phoenician Women*, 1174–86: Zeus's smiting of the mocker Capaneus may have brought the more familiar passage from the *Aeneid* back to Tennyson's mind.

5. Compare the version of lines 81–83 in Harvard Loose Paper 251, where the prophet wishes that his boundless yearning might "Stand forth, & like a

silent statue, placed / High on the pedestal, collect all praise / Till contemplation made us Gods!'' This vision of the self as a public object of contemplation, rather than a privately contemplative subject, is antithetical to the divinatory thrust at the close.

6. Goslee 1976, 162 finds a pertinent timidity in lines 29–37, which show that Tiresias has abandoned the higher quest even before the occasion of his blinding.

7. Compare "Whispers," an unpublished contemporary lyric that immediately precedes "Ulysses" in the Heath MS., on "A hint of somewhat unexprest" (8); "So were my tale misunderstood" (16).

8. For a different reading see Bloom 1976, 159: "When Tennyson's quester says: 'I am a part of all that I have met' he means 'I understand only myself, and so everything I have met I have made out of myself, and I have become all things by transforming myself into them.' " Apt as this line of approach unquestionably is, it jumps the gun by a few lines, and thus slights the uncanny later consequences, for the very "self" on which Bloom lays stress, of what he rightly identifies as Ulysses' larger project "not to know, not to understand" (160).

9. In fact Tennyson had written but not published a sonnet of empiricist joy a year or more earlier in "Life" (*PT*, 296), which anticipates a major image from "Ulysses": "Would I could pile fresh life on life, and dull / The sharp desire of knowledge still with knowing" (5–6). The fact that "Ulysses" explicitly scraps just the kind of vital pileup this sonnet seeks shows again the "thermodynamic" relation, in Tennyson's career, between going forward and pushing off.

10. It is hard to discriminate Emerson's ambivalence about Tennyson from his ambivalence about all things English; but by 1858 he was expressing strong admiration for "Ulysses"—probably because its impatience with context echoed his own (1978, 202).

11. A note in FitzGerald's copy of the 1842 *Poems* (now at Trinity) explains, "This was the Poem which, as might perhaps be expected, Carlyle liked best in the Book" (II, 91); and Tennyson's annotation to the edition of 1884 (at Lincoln) records, in what sounds like Tiresias's image for the prophet margin, that "Carlyle wrote to me when he had read Ulysses that he felt within him a fountain of unwept tears" (95). For the economic connotations of "use" in line 23 compare Horace's *nisi temperato / splendeat usu*: "there is no lustre to silver concealed / in the greedy ground, Sallustius Crispus, / you foe to metal unless it shine / from rational use" (*Odes*, II.2.1–4, tr. Shepherd).

12. *On Translating Homer* (1861; in 1960, 147). Arnold not only exaggerates the effect but misquotes the text, evidently from memory: "That untravelled world, whose distance fades / For ever and for ever, as we gaze." The difference between Arnold's "we" here, and Tennyson's by the end of "Ulysses," epitomizes the difference between culture and anarchy, between imaginative reason and prophetic imagination.

13. This Wordsworth passage seems to have led Tennyson back on more than one occasion to *Hamlet*. "That untravelled world, whose margin fades" points through the Wordsworthian "eternal silence" to "The undiscovered country, from whose bourne / No traveller returns" (*Hamlet*, III.i.79–80); and the phrase "like a guilty thing" passes verbatim from *Hamlet*, I.i.148, through the

"Intimations" ode to *In Memoriam*, vii.7. The coincidence is striking, as is the triple configuration, in each Tennyson passage, of the relations between fathers and sons, poetic precursors and successors, and spiritual and natural realms.

14. In his later years Tennyson remarked to W. F. Rawnsley of "Lancelot and Elaine," 444–450, "When I wrote that I was thinking of myself and Wordsworth" (1925, 23). Lancelot speaks:

> Me you call great: mine is the firmer seat,
> The truer lance: but there is many a youth
> Now crescent, who will come to all I am
> And overcome it; and in me there dwells
> No greatness, save it be some far-off touch
> Of greatness to know well I am not great:
> There is the man.

It is, as Rawnsley says, a generous tribute. Note, however, the characteristic technical pride—what successor ever does unseat Lancelot?—and the relation, as in "Ulysses," between center and margin, "in me" and "some far-off touch."

15. The first reading of line 30, altered in the Heath MS., gives "this old heart yet yearning in desire." As with his revision of the close of "Tiresias" half a century later, Tennyson moves away from human and bodily affection into its spiritual sublimation.

16. In T.Nbk. 22, line 43 reads, after some tinkering, "He works his work, I mine. All this is just." Tennyson's final version exchanges the Tiresian need of justification for the more prophetic undertaking of exodus. The line thus answers W. J. Fox's adjuration, in a review of the 1832 volume, that Tennyson "ascertain his mission and work his work" (Shannon 1952, 56)—though the answer "Ulysses" proposes may not be what the progressive Fox had in mind.

17. H.Nbk. 16, fol. 11v, shows Tennyson at close grips with problems of grammatical person: line 59 is altered to its present reading from "for I purpose now," line 61 from "until we die." On Tennyson's early use of the first-person singular, see Peltason 1983a. For a syntactical parallel with lines 59–61, see Tennyson's favorite passage from *Cymbeline*, the play he asked to read on his own deathbed: "Hang there like fruit, my soul, / Till the tree die!" (V.v.263–264).

18. "They use me as a lesson book at schools, and they will call me 'that horrible Tennyson!' " (*Memoir*, I, 16). As evidence of the global voyaging of "Ulysses" through Anglo-American culture, consider that the Scott Antarctic Memorial is engraved with the poem's final line, and that in April 1968 Robert Kennedy quoted its peroration when speaking in Cleveland on the occasion of the assassination of Martin Luther King, Jr. (Tapsall 1968, 2–3). On the cultural content of "Ulysses," see Robbins 1973, 192, and Storch's excellent article (1971).

19. Bryant 1807, II, 127–139; IV, 59–67. On the "Amonian" primal tongue, see Hungerford 1941, 20–22. T.Nbk. 15, fols. 20–19v (leaves adjoining the leaf containing the eight-line "Tiresias" lyric discussed at the start of this chapter) bear a drawing of a tower upon a hill. Tennyson liked to adorn his notebooks with architectural sketches, and the tower was a favorite doodle; another pertinent example occurs opposite "The Palace of Art," 233–236 ("Is not this my place of strength?") in a copy of *Poems* (1832) in which Tennyson entered some of his

1842 revisions. For more reliable evidence of the poet's interest in Bryant's sun towers as they may bear on "Tithonus," see *The Princess*, III.324–327 ("the crownèd towers / Built to the Sun"), on which Hallam Tennyson's note in the 1884 edition at Lincoln comments: "of Troy."

20. Tennyson's poetic norm for the paradisal yearning behind these lines is incantation, which in his hands is purest when it verges on nonreferential music or babble. See the early "Ilion, Ilion" (1828?)—a poem whose subject is as germane to this moment of "Tithonus" as is its repeated petition "When wilt thou be melody born?" See also Tobin 1976 on Horace's *Odes*, I.7.25–31, where the sun god Apollo has extended the Ulyssean promise of a newer world (*tellure nova*).

21. Even critics who take Tithonus's death wish figuratively, as a humanist affirmation of some kind, still tend to read the figure in naturalist and thus mortalist terms: Shaw (1976b, 89–97) and Peltason (1984b, 68–71) do so most persuasively. But the way to the affirmation of this poem—and of the subgenre it brings to perfection—lies through a more strenuous sense of the transcendental light it casts on such terms as "humanity" (Kissane 1970, 136; Wiseman 1978, 215) and "self-identity" (Starzyk 1978, 22).

22. Inside the front cover of T.Nbk. 32, which includes versions of "Tithonus" and other classical monologues, Hallam Tennyson penciled this sentence: "The name that can be named is not the enduring and unchanging name." (See also *Memoir*, I, 311; II, 90.) To think of the Ancient Sage crooning "the Nameless" and of the opening of "Armageddon" is both to apprehend the continuity of Tennyson's career as an agnostic religious poet and to appreciate the Romantic triumph of "Tithonus": an allegorical ode to transcendence, without a transcendental signified.

23. The words "will forget" are written in Hallam Tennyson's hand next to the underlined "forget" in the annotated 1884 collection now at Lincoln; but the authority of the gloss is uncertain, and in any case it serves more to highlight the textual crux than to resolve it.

5. In England

1. Tennyson's most powerful means of establishing this common ground are not thematic but verbal. Note, for instance, how the most threatening image of the poem, the Chartist "raw mechanic's bloody thumbs," comes back liberalized in John's concluding plea for tolerance: "this raw fool the world, / Which charts us all in its coarse blacks or whites, / As ruthless as a baby with a worm" (96–98).

2. Kiernan 1982, 129: "Tennyson could never be the confident spokesman of any class, with a clearly focused political outlook." Yet Tennyson's entire success, ideologically speaking, lay in his genius for responding to the typically *un*focused outlook of the Victorian bourgeoisie.

3. Tennyson's techniques for rendering technology poetic have received surprisingly little attention, and that principally of a condemnatory kind. Mill, who sought in poetry a special range of emotional effects that decidedly excluded

the mechanical, denounced Tennyson's practices in 1842 in a letter to Sterling (quoted in Shaw 1973, 70). See also Millhauser 1971, 10.

4. See the wonderfully illustrative diary entry in *LTJ* for October 13, 1854. The context is the Crimean conflict that will figure in *Maud* the next year: "A moment of great excitement came when we saw flags flying and heard guns firing but it proved that the flags were only in honour of a Coast guard wedding. He read to Mr. de Vere & a party from Swainston 'The Golden Year,' 'Edwin Morris,' 'Audley Court,' and 'The Gardener's Daughter' " (39).

5. To an even more productive poet, Browning, Tennyson once confided that during the summer of 1833 he had written "basketfuls of such poems" as "The Gardener's Daughter" (Tennyson 1949, 143). It is to this side of Tennyson's craft that Emerson responded in 1848, calling his poetry "as legitimate a fruit of the veneering or cabinetmaker style of English culture, as the Dinnertable" (1973, 352), and that Pound alluded in dubbing it "verbal patisserie" (1954, 290). See also Baum 1948, 236–237; Francis 1980a, 8; Mason 1981, 158.

6. Compare with this contrived temporal overlay the more prosaic opening in H.Nbk. 22, fol. 1, "The morning brings another to my mind."

7. These compromises may mark Tennyson's as the first modern suburban imagination. See Chesterton 1913, 161, on the poet as a "suburban Virgil," and Creese 1977 on the development of the Victorian suburb. Tennyson's word for *suburb* in this poem is *garden*; and though the socioeconomic indeterminacy of the actual setting he keeps lovingly describing makes it difficult to know just what kind of a gardener Rose's father may be, at least since the Alexandrian origin of the idyll the garden has been conceived as an extension of city culture (Rosenmeyer 1969, 195).

8. On the cosmic-mythic impulse of idyll, brought down from Callimachus's *Aetia* through "oriental" idyllists of the eighteenth century to Wordsworth and Coleridge, see McLuhan 1959, 91; Pattison 1979, 34; Shaffer 1975, 96; and especially Hair 1981. Traces of such mythopoeia are more clearly marked in working manuscripts of "The Gardener's Daughter" than in the published text.

9. To judge from the manuscripts, Tennyson could not leave this passage alone. See FitzGerald's comment on the flyleaf of his copy of *Poems* (1842) now at Trinity: "The MS. page of the 'Gardener's Daughter' is one of many versions of a Passage which gave the Poet some Trouble when he was bringing out the Volume in which they occur. This took part in Spedding's Chambers at 60 Lincoln's Inn Fields, in the fore-part of 1842." T.Nbk. 17, fol. 37v, includes from an unadopted preamble this apology: "But if in speaking I should lapse into / An overfullness, or too much translate / My colours into language bear with me."

10. See Tennyson's comments on Theocritus in *Memoir*, II, 495; also Turner 1976, 81.

11. For pictorial (and cinematic) approaches to Tennyson's art, see McLuhan 1959, 81–83; Devlin 1978; Joseph 1978, 425. Whiting 1964, 15–16 provides accounts of the Victorian paintings inspired by "The Gardener's Daughter." On *ekphrasis*, see Spitzer 1962, 72; Krieger 1967, 105–128; Steiner 1982, 41; see also "Enoch Arden," 762: "things seen are mightier than things heard."

12. Elizabeth Barrett Browning found these priorities unforgivable in a letter

of September 1847 to Mary Russell Mitford: "His gardener's daughter, for instance, is just a rose; and 'a Rose' one might beg all poets to observe, is as precisely sensual, as fricasseed chicken, or even boiled beef & carrots" (1983, III, 220; see also II, 119).

13. Bottom's song is quoted in the poet's hand at this point in the annotated 1884 edition at Lincoln, with the following comment: "I am a poet if I had never written but this line. 'The merry blackbird sang among the trees' would seem quite as good a line to 9/10ths of all Englishmen & women."

14. Birdwatchers aver that, although nightingales are now virtually never heard in England, when they do sing they sing at what hour they please; in this fact, as in the untraditional yet scientific gendering of his male songbird, Tennyson is as usual correct. Yet even in the 1830s the nightingale was already rare in England, more frequently a literary than an empirical phenomenon. See Emily Tennyson's letter of May 7, 1835, to Ellen Hallam: "Once on a time indeed a solitary one came to Lincoln & trilled for some time in a poor man's garden. Of course, crowds came to hear, and see it"—such crowds, she goes on, that the poor gardener shot the bird (*LH*, 423–424).

15. On literary relations between Tennyson and Gaskell, see Killham 1958, 277; Ford 1977, 43. For a nonfictional counterpart to Mr. Holbrook, consider (of all people) the duke of Argyll, who associated this poem with the solitary hunting trips of his youth (Pattison 1979, 162).

16. It is hard to know whether one's sense of Tennyson's powers of observation should be shaken or confirmed by the fact that T.Nbk. 15 puts the ash buds in the front of *May*.

17. See McGann 1982, 230. For contemporary witness to the power of the sentimental, hear George Brimley's 1855 rapture over the love poems of 1832 and 1842: "Mr. Tennyson's glory is to have portrayed passion with a feminine purity; to have spiritualized the voluptuousness of the senses and the imagination by a manly reverence for a woman's worth" (Houghton 1951, 379). Sterling analyzed this Tennysonian effect early and well: "All skill of labour, all intellectual purpose, [are] kept behind the sweet and fervid impulse of the heart. Thus, all that we call affection, imagination, intellect, melts out as one long happy sigh into union with the visibly beautiful" (1842, 125).

18. Compare *The Lover's Tale*, I.541: "To centre in this place and time"—terms which, in that text, come to mean nowhere and never. The early drafts of "The Gardener's Daughter" resemble *The Lover's Tale* more than anything else in Tennyson; the increasing idyllization of his many manuscript revisions shows the poet writing his way out of the impasse the earlier poem represented.

19. The narrator's no less idealized relationship with the perfect Eustace exemplifies the strong current of Tennyson's imaginative homophilia, which arises most prominently in *In Memoriam*, and with which Tennyson studies have yet to come fully to grips (Ricks 1972, 215–220). Although Tennyson's sensitivity to male beauty was acute, homosexual topics seldom occur in his poetry for their own sake. Instead they mediate the trajectory of desire: between a heterosexual norm and a narcissistic ground in "Recollections of the Arabian Nights" or *The Lover's Tale*; in "The Gardener's Daughter" or *Maud* between individuality and

the overwhelmingly masculine seats of power in Victorian culture (Sedgwick 1985).

20. An unadopted passage from T.Nbk. 17 leaves less to the imagination:

> she resigned
> Her bosom to the transport of mine arms;
> Or trembled without speaking when the storm
> Of my first welcome, pouring kiss on kiss
> Incessantly, like flashes of soft light,
> Melted from lip to lip & from my heart
> Sank fused in her's then growing one with mine.

Compare the epithalamion in the final section of *In Memoriam*, 117–124, where the outburst of moonlight figures marital consummation.

21. See Killham 1973, 156; Fletcher 1979, 87–88. The Trinity manuscripts abound with extensions of the plot into a world of social detail that Tennyson clearly chose to omit: the death of an uncle (T.Nbk. 17, fols. 45v–46v), visits to Rose in disguise (T.Nbk. 17, fols. 37v–38), her churchgoing (T.Nbk. 26, fol. 19v), the narrator's attendance at an aristocratic wedding (T.Nbk, 17, fol. 49), news of a victory at sea (T.Nbk. 26, fol. 21). In T.Nbk. 26, fol. 16, the narrator and Rose have produced a surviving son, "The living symbol of two hearts made one."

22. Among the annotations to the 1884 edition at Lincoln is a note, in Hallam Tennyson's hand, to "Locksley Hall," 47 ("As the husband is, the wife is: thou art mated with a clown"): "Nothing to do with rank, as some critics suggest, but a simple statement." The comment is defensive but not necessarily disingenuous. Tennyson often seems simply not to have known how fully his idyllic work embodied the social life of Victorian culture; it is precisely such ignorance that makes this work so revealing ideologically.

23. The line also comes perilously close to that burlesque of the Wordsworthian plain-style pentameter, "A Mr. Wilkinson, a clergyman." In FitzGerald's copy of *Poems* (1842) he writes beside "Dora": "I remember AT's saying he remembered the time when he could see nothing in 'Michael,' which he now read with Admiration: though he thought Wordsworth often clumsy and diffuse." See also *Memoir*, II, 70, 505. For contemporary comparisons to Wordsworth, see Sterling 1842, 124–125; Bagehot 1864; Arnold 1960, 206–207 (on whom see also Tillotson 1953; Timko 1974; and Laird 1976). *LTJ*, 285, 286, 297, records Tennyson's reading "Michael," "The Brothers," and "The Old Cumberland Beggar."

24. See Culler 1977, 116. See also *Memoir*, I, 210 for Tennyson's remarks on the "gift of a hard pathos" that he prized in Crabbe.

25. Victorian illustrators were alive to this idyllic subordination of the heroine. C. Lucy's *The Reconciliation of Dora* (1852) has Dora hiding her face while Mary makes her supplication to Allan; and in A. H. Burr's *Dora* (1863), according to the *Athenaeum* reviewer, it is Mary and not Dora who makes for striking portraiture (Whiting 1964, 36).

26. As Hair reads this scene, Dora's appearance amid the harvest "associates her with something vital," which "goes beyond the domestic affections to a

more elemental fertility" (1981, 53); see also Johnston 1978, 73, 91, on parallels to the Persephone myth. Although this idyll of the hearth does make a Victorian vestal of its plain heroine, it also registers this transformation as a loss of individual identity. With the glassy-eyed veracity that typifies the Tennysonian idyll, the poem presents Dora as a nun to its own symbolism.

27. A similar suggestion of familial hegemony arises with the ambiguity of the opening clause from this passage. Either "he" (Allan) or "the boy" may be the subject who "struggled hard"; and in the timeless scheme of idyllic generation they are the same man.

28. A note to "Dora" in the 1884 edition at Lincoln explains that "Miss Mitford's story is cheerful in tone. This is sad; & it is the same landscape, one in sunshine, the other in shadow." This "shadow" is the shade that Tennyson's awareness of tradition typically casts across his voicing of primal sympathies.

29. Culler 1977, 223, quotes Tennyson's vehement denial in 1859 that he had an epic in mind: "I should be crazed to attempt such a thing in the heart of the 19th century." "The Epic" of 1842 and the twelve-book format that *Idylls of the King* assumed by 1885 throw suspicion on this disclaimer, but the worry it expresses forms part of the emotional texture both of "Morte d'Arthur" and of the *Idylls*.

30. Contemporary reviewers caught something of this intention. Horne sees that "the idea of the death, or fading away of Fairy-land, allegorically conveyed . . . is apparently the main basis of the design, and probably original" (1844, 156). For Sterling this sort of allegorizing is a road the poet has failed to take: "The poet might perhaps have made the loss of the magic sword, the death of Arthur, and dissolution of the Round Table, a symbol for the departure from earth of the whole old Gothic world, with its half-pagan, all-poetic faith" (1842, 120).

31. See Joseph 1968, 142. The draft in T.Nbk. 17 is accompanied by several drawings of fists, one of them grasping a stick: the poet's pictorial illustration of his text thus mirrors his character's invention of a verbal tag for his relic.

32. The double-columned collation of Tennyson with Malory in Staines 1982, 164–174, demonstrates nicely that what Bedivere sees is what Malory has written, while the unwitnessed magic of the simile is Tennyson's own.

33. Wilkinson 1969 calls attention to an aptly imperial echo here: the line recalls Dryden's translation of *Aeneid*, I.22 (*tantae molis erat Romanam condere gentem*): "And the long glories of imperial Rome."

34. Compare the ambiguous use of "before" in "Balin and Balan," 278–280, where Balin staves off his realization of Guinevere's adultery with Lancelot by internalizing its shame: "My father hath begotten me in his wrath. / I suffer from the things before me, know, / Learn nothing." See Homans 1979, 696, on the situation of the *Idylls* "between two inevitabilities," and for a tragic reading counterbalancing mine.

6. Pyrrhic Victorian

1. "I knew I must make my mark by shortness" (Tennyson, in Knowles 1893, 173). It is important to remember that the poet at midcareer regarded as

a failure his one earlier effort at the long poem, *The Lover's Tale*. On the published collections, see Pattison 1979, 64ff.; Francis 1980b, 189–214.

2. James Spedding, "who succeeded Hallam as Tennyson's literary adviser" (Shannon 1952, 196), put the challenge very clearly in his thoughtful review of the 1842 *Poems*. "What is to be expected of him hereafter . . . is something that will make all he has yet produced appear only like preliminary essays and experiments" (140). "He has not yet ventured upon a subject large enough" (141); he requires "a subject large enough to take the entire impress of his mind, and energy persevering enough to work it faithfully out as one whole" (152).

3. See Preyer (1958, 244) and Buckler (1980, 41) on the way this text takes revenge on itself. The enforced-marriage theme stirred deep-seated ambivalence in Tennyson; see Reed 1975, 109, and, for biographical context, Rader 1963.

4. See Hollander 1975, 677, on synesthesia; also the comment of Poe: "he seems to see with his ear" (Joseph 1973, 419).

5. The sexual politics of the poem are discussed most incisively by Eagleton 1978 and by Sedgwick 1985. See also Millett 1969, 76–79; McGann 1982, 227.

6. VI.58–74 gives another sustained fluvial description of a crowd of women, but by that point a diminished Ida is going with the flow: "The lovely, lordly creature floated on" (73).

7. There can be no more appropriate indication of the nondramatic or impersonal character of this lyric, given its setting in *The Princess*, than the sexual indeterminacy of its speaker, whom most twentieth-century critics have regarded as a man but nineteenth-century painters unanimously depicted as a woman (Whiting 1964, 27).

8. See *Letters*, 65, for Edward Tennyson's Keatsian sonnet on a similar subject, a poem whose vulnerability to the influence of Keats sets off his brother's revisionism to advantage.

9. The rightness of "broken" emerges from comparison with other adjectives the poet tried first in C.MS. Add. 6345. The simile reads "failing purpose" in fol. 100v, then "idle purpose" in fols. 101 and 101*, then "failing" again in fol. 102. "Idle" and "failing" may make sweeter music than "broken"; but they both elide the question of violent agency on which the rougher "broken" insists, to the enrichment of the text.

10. Howitt 1838 provides contemporary testimony: "When we wander through the pleached alleys, and by the time-stained fountains of these old gardens, perished years indeed seem to come back again to us. In the centre of some vast avenue of majestic elms or limes, sweeping their boughs to the ground, 'the dial-stone aged and green' arrests our attention, and points, not to the present, but to the past" (I, 102).

11. Such political considerations raise a final question about the title of this work. *The Princess* seems less apt than others the poet entertained: *The New University*, *The University of Women* (PT, 741). Was it an allusion to Machiavelli's political classic?

12. *In Memoriam* struck FitzGerald, who wished it unwritten, as if evolved from a poetry machine (Mays 1965, 42). Tennyson's image of the "sad mechanic exercise" (v.7) suggests that he shared something of this feeling, which he may in turn have invested in the repeated mechanical images of cxx.

13. The private side of the monodrama came to Tennyson first, in such lyrics as "Oh! That 'Twere Possible" and "Go Not, Happy Day"; and in the manuscripts it is the elaboration of social detail that gives him the most evident trouble. Issues of causality pertinent to *Maud* are treated, with primary reference to *Idylls of the King*, in Kincaid 1975, 154, 182; and Culler 1977, 239.

14. Chapter 9 of Charles Kingsley's *Alton Locke* (1850) begins with a paragraph suggesting that Kingsley had felt the new effects in Tennyson's experimental lyric: "the roar of wheels, the ceaseless stream of pale, hard faces... beneath a lurid, crushing sky of smoke and mist." Two pages later Alton, himself a proletarian poet, devotes a paragraph to praising Tennyson for "the altogether democratic tendency of his poems... his handling of the trivial every-day sights and sounds of nature"; here, however, he clearly has the domestic idyllist in mind. See Tennyson's extemporized metaphor of the city, as recorded in FitzGerald's copy of *Poems* (1842) at Trinity: "One Day with AT in St. Paul's—1842. 'Merely as an enclosed Space in a huge City this is very fine.' And when we got out into the 'central roar'—'This is the Mind: that, a mood of it' " (135).

15. See Priestley 1973, 107–108; Sinfield 1976a, 476, 478, Robert James Mann, the first systematic expositor of *Maud*, found it necessary to stress this feature of the text: "The object of the poet is evidently not to picture these individuals as they are, but to describe them as they appear to the irritable and morose nature to which they are hostile personalities... It must never be forgotten that it is not the poet, but the chief person of the action, who paints them" (1856, 25–26). Mann was defending his friend against malicious misprision, but he was also pointing to generic features that puzzled readers because they were new.

16. Compare I.xvi.549, "Lord of the pulse that is lord of her breast," with an earlier version in T.Nbk. 36: "Lord of the pulses that move her breast." The more interesting revised line plays down the biological in favor of what Sedgwick calls the hero's "homosocial" desire: to lord it over the lord by obtaining the lady.

17. In T.Nbk. 36, fol. 23 there is a period after "mouth" (though none after "yields" four lines above). Evidently the unusual punctuation came to Tennyson late; it occurs in every published edition I have consulted. Compare with Tennyson's lyric Keats's *Hyperion*, III.14–22, where a rosy glow passes in the opposite direction, from the rose itself through "the clouds of even and of morn" to culminate in the erotic: "let the maid / Blush keenly, as with some warm kiss surpris'd."

18. This passage came into existence in one of the most interesting of the Trinity manuscripts. At this point T.Nbk. 36, fol. 27 moves directly from line 650 to a version of line 660 ("I scarce can think this music but the swell... "), which is altered to its final reading on a third try. The curious second version—"What threefold meaning echoes from... "—suggests that Tennyson was hearing a reverberant music whose source troubled him. Stanza 7 (which H.Nbk. 30, fols. 3–4, likewise lack) is first written out on the facing fol. 26v. It is tempting to believe that at this point Tennyson realized his indebtedness to Keats's ode and capitalized upon the debt—"Not die" corresponding to "Thou wast not born for death," and the "drinking-songs" allusion acknowledging, at a higher level,

the complexity of the intertextual weave. The writing of stanza 7 then let Tennyson make sense of the "music" that had mystified him before. That music was Keats's enchanted moan: the stanza from the "Nightingale" ode that Tennyson was uncannily hearing because to that point he had left it out of his unwitting, brilliant imitation.

Works Cited

Abercrombie, Lascelles. 1931. *Revaluations: Studies in Biography*. Oxford: Oxford University Press.

Adams, Michael C. C. 1979. "Tennyson's Crimean War Poetry: A Cross-Cultural Approach." *Journal of the History of Ideas* 40: 405–422.

Allen, Peter. 1978. *The Cambridge Apostles: The Early Years*. Cambridge: Cambridge University Press.

Allingham, William. 1967. *William Allingham's Diary*. Fontwell, Sussex: Centaur Press.

Altieri, Charles. 1978. "Arnold and Tennyson: The Plight of Victorian Lyricism." *Criticism* 20: 281–306.

Anderson, Warren D. 1967. "Types of the Classical in Arnold, Tennyson, and Browning." In *Victorian Essays: A Symposium*, ed. Warren D. Anderson and Thomas D. Clareson, pp. 60–70. Oberlin: Kent State University Press.

Appleman, Philip. 1974. "The Dread Factor: Eliot, Tennyson, and the Shaping of Science." *Columbia Forum* 3, no. 4: 32–38.

Armstrong, Isobel. 1982. *Language as Living Form in Nineteenth-Century Poetry*. Totowa, N.J.: Barnes and Noble.

Arnold, Matthew. 1960. *On the Classical Tradition*. Vol. 1 of *The Complete Prose Works of Matthew Arnold*, ed. R. H. Super. Ann Arbor: University of Michigan Press.

———— 1965. *Culture and Anarchy*. Vol. 5 of *The Complete Prose Works of Matthew Arnold*, ed. R. H. Super. Ann Arbor: University of Michigan Press.

Assad, Thomas J. 1963. "Tennyson's 'Tears, Idle Tears.' " *Tulane Studies in English* 13: 71–83.

Auden, W. H. 1945. "Introduction." In *Tennyson*, pp. i–xxii. London: Phoenix House.

Auerbach, Erich. 1953. *Mimesis: The Representation of Reality in Western Literature*. Princeton: Princeton University Press.

Bagehot, Walter. 1859. "Tennyson's Idylls." In *Collected Works*, ed. Norman St. John-Stevas, II, 174–207. Cambridge, Mass.: Harvard University Press, 1965.

——— 1864. "Wordsworth, Tennyson, and Browning; or, Pure, Ornate, and Grotesque Art in English Poetry." In *Collected Works*, ed. Norman St. John-Stevas, II, 321–366. Cambridge, Mass.: Harvard University Press, 1965.

Baker, William E. 1967. *Syntax in English Poetry, 1870–1930*. Berkeley: University of California Press.

Ball, Patricia. 1968. *The Central Self: A Study in Romantic and Victorian Imagination*. London: Athlone Press.

Basler, Roy P. 1944. "Tennyson the Psychologist." *South Atlantic Quarterly* 43: 143–159.

Baum, Paull F. 1948. *Tennyson Sixty Years After*. Chapel Hill: University of North Carolina Press.

Bayley, John. 1978. "The Dynamics of the Static." *Times Literary Supplement* March 3: 246–247.

——— 1980. "The All-Star Victorian." *New York Review of Books* December 18: 42–49.

——— 1981. "Tennyson and the Idea of Decadence." In *Studies in Tennyson*, ed. Hallam Tennyson, pp. 186–205. London: Macmillan.

Bergonzi, Bernard. 1969. "Feminism and Femininity in *The Princess*." In *The Major Victorian Poets: Reconsiderations*, ed. Isobel Armstrong, pp. 35–50. London: Routledge and Kegan Paul.

Bidney, Martin. 1985. "Victorian Vision in Mississippi: Tennysonian Resonances in Faulkner's *Dark House / Light in August*." *Victorian Poetry* 23: 43–57.

Bishop, Jonathan. 1962. "The Unity of *In Memoriam*." *Victorian Newsletter* 21: 9–14.

Bloom, Harold. 1971. *The Ringers in the Tower: Studies in Romantic Tradition*. Chicago and London: University of Chicago Press.

——— 1973. *The Anxiety of Influence*. New York: Oxford University Press.

——— 1975. *A Map of Misreading*. New York: Oxford University Press.

——— 1976. *Poetry and Repression: Revisionism from Blake to Stevens*. New Haven and London: Yale University Press.

Boyd, Zelda, and Julian Boyd. 1977. "To Lose the Name of Action: The Semantics of Action and Motion in Tennyson's Poetry." *PTL: A Journal for Descriptive Poetics and Theory* 2: 21–32.

Brashear, William. 1969. *The Living Will: A Study of Tennyson and Nineteenth-Century Subjectivism*. The Hague: Mouton.

——— 1977. *The Gorgon's Head: A Study in Tragedy and Despair*. Athens, Ga.: University of Georgia Press.

Brie, Friedrich. 1959. "Tennysons Ulysses." *Anglia* 15: 441–447.

Briney, John O. 1973. "Alfred Tennyson's *The Lover's Tale*: An Interpretation." Ph.D. diss., Michigan State University.

Brooks, Cleanth. 1944. "The Motivation of Tennyson's Weeper." Rpt. in *Critical Essays on the Poetry of Tennyson*, ed. John Killham, pp. 177–185. New York: Barnes and Noble, 1960.

Browning, Elizabeth Barrett. 1983. *The Letters of Elizabeth Barrett Browning to*

Mary Russell Mitford, ed. Meredith Raymond and Mary Rose Sullivan, 3 vols. Waco, Tex.: Armstrong Browning Library of Baylor University.

Bruns, Gerald. 1978. " 'The Lesser Faith': Hope and Reversal in Tennyson's *In Memoriam.*" *Journal of English and Germanic Philology* 77: 247–264.

Bryant, Jacob. 1799. *Some Observations upon "The Vindication of Homer."* Eton: Pote and Williams.

———— 1807. *A New System; or, An Analysis of Antient Mythology*, 3rd ed, 6 vols. London: Walker.

Buckler, William E. 1980. *The Victorian Imagination: Essays in Aesthetic Exploration.* New York and London: New York University Press.

Buckley, Jerome H. 1960. *Tennyson: The Growth of a Poet.* Cambridge, Mass.: Harvard University Press.

———— 1967. "Tennyson's Irony." *Victorian Newsletter* 31: 7–10.

Bush, Douglas. 1937. *Mythology and the Romantic Tradition in English Poetry.* Cambridge, Mass.: Harvard University Press.

Butler, H. M. 1911. "Recollections of Tennyson." Rpt. in *Tennyson: Interviews and Recollections*, ed. Norman Page, pp. 43–51. London: Macmillan, 1983.

Byatt, A. S. 1969. "The Lyric Structure of Tennyson's *Maud.*" In *The Major Victorian Poets: Reconsiderations*, ed. Isobel Armstrong, pp. 69–92. London: Routledge and Kegan Paul.

Carr, Arthur J. 1950. "Tennyson as a Modern Poet." Rpt. in *Critical Essays on the Poetry of Tennyson*, ed. John Killham, pp. 41–64. New York: Barnes and Noble, 1960.

Cervo, Nathan. 1982. "Imitation in 'The Lady of Shalott.' " *Victorian Newsletter* 61: 17–19.

Chambers, D. Laurance. 1903. "Tennysoniana." *Modern Language Notes* 18: 230.

Chandler, James K. 1982. "Romantic Allusiveness." *Critical Inquiry* 8: 461–487.

Chesterton, G. K. 1913. *The Victorian Age in Literature.* New York: Henry Holt.

Chiasson, E. J. 1954. "Tennyson's 'Ulysses': A Re-Interpretation." Rpt. in *Critical Essays on the Poetry of Tennyson*, ed. John Killham, pp. 164–173. New York: Barnes and Noble, 1960.

Colley, Ann C. 1983. *Tennyson and Madness.* Athens, Ga.: University of Georgia Press.

Collins, John Churton. 1901. "Introduction." In *The Early Poems of Alfred Lord Tennyson*, pp. vii–xlii. London: Methuen.

Conrad, Peter. 1982. "The Victim of Inheritance." *Times Literary Supplement* May 15: 529–530.

Creese, Walter L. 1977. "Imagination in the Suburb." In *Nature and the Victorian Imagination*, ed. U. C. Knoepflmacher and G. B. Tennyson, pp. 49–67. Berkeley and Los Angeles: University of California Press.

Croker, J. W. 1833. Unsigned review. Rpt. in *Tennyson: The Critical Heritage*, ed. John D. Jump, pp. 66–83. London: Routledge and Kegan Paul, 1967.

Culler, A. Dwight. 1975. "Monodrama and the Dramatic Monologue." *PMLA* 90: 366–385.

———— 1977. *The Poetry of Tennyson.* New Haven and London: Yale University Press.

Culver, Marcia. 1982. "The Death and Birth of an Epic: Tennyson's 'Morte d'Arthur.' " *Victorian Poetry* 20: 51–61.

Daiches, David. 1961. "Imagery and Mood in Tennyson and Whitman." In *English Studies Today, Second Series*, ed. G. A. Bonnard, pp. 217–232. Berne: Francke.

Day, Aidan. 1980. "G. S. Faber and Tennyson: A Note on the Question of Influence." *Notes and Queries* 27: 520–522.

———— 1983. "The Spirit of Fable: Arthur Hallam and Romantic Values in Tennyson's 'Timbuctoo.' " *Tennyson Research Bulletin* 4: 59–71.

DeMott, Benjamin. 1962. "The General, the Poet, and the Inquisition." *Kenyon Review* 24: 442–456.

Devlin, Francis P. 1978. "A 'Cinematic' Approach to Tennyson's Descriptive Art." *Literature/Film Quarterly* 3: 132–144.

Dietrich, Manfred. 1976. "Unity and Symbolic Structure in Tennyson's *The Princess*." *English Studies in Canada* 2: 182–202.

Dodsworth, Martin. 1969. "Patterns of Morbidity: Repetition in Tennyson's Poetry." In *The Major Victorian Poets: Reconsiderations*, ed. Isobel Armstrong, pp. 7–34. London: Routledge and Kegan Paul.

Donahue, Mary Joan. 1949. "Tennyson's *Hail, Briton!* and *Tithon* in the Heath Manuscript." *PMLA* 64: 385–416.

Donoghue, Denis. 1968. *The Ordinary Universe: Soundings in Modern Literature*. New York: Macmillan.

Drew, Philip. 1964. " 'Aylmer's Field': A Problem for Critics." *The Listener* April 2: 553–557.

———— 1973. "Tennyson and the Dramatic Monologue: A Study of *Maud*." In *Tennyson*, ed. D. J. Palmer, pp. 115–146. Athens, Ohio: Ohio University Press.

Duncan, Edgar Hill. 1959. "Tennyson: A Modern Appraisal." *Tennessee Studies in Literature* 4: 13–30.

Dyson, Hope, and Charles Tennyson. 1969. *Dear and Honoured Lady: The Correspondence between Queen Victoria and Alfred Tennyson*. London: Macmillan.

Eagleton, Terry. 1978. "Tennyson: Politics and Sexuality in *The Princess* and *In Memoriam*." In *The Sociology of Literature*, ed. Francis Barker et al., pp. 97–106. Essex: University of Essex.

Eliot, T. S. 1950. *Selected Essays*. New York: Harcourt.

Elton, Oliver. 1924. *Tennyson and Matthew Arnold*. Rpt. New York: Haskell, 1971.

Emerson, Ralph Waldo. 1973. *The Journals and Miscellaneous Notebooks of Ralph Waldo Emerson*. Vol. 10, ed. Merton M. Sealts, Jr. Cambridge, Mass.: Harvard University Press.

———— 1975. *The Journals and Miscellaneous Notebooks of Ralph Waldo Emerson*. Vol. 11, ed. A. W. Plumstead and William H. Gilman. Cambridge, Mass., and London: Harvard University Press.

———— 1978. *The Journals and Miscellaneous Notebooks of Ralph Waldo Emerson*. Vol. 14, ed. Susan Sutton and Harrison Hayford. Cambridge, Mass., and London: Harvard University Press.

Empson, William. 1947. *Seven Types of Ambiguity*, rev. ed. New York: New Directions.

———— 1984. "Empson on Tennyson." *Tennyson Research Bulletin* 4: 107.

Fichter, Andrew. 1973. "Ode and Elegy: Idea and Form in Tennyson's Early Poetry." *ELH* 40: 398–427.

Findlay, L. M. 1981. "Sensation and Memory in Tennyson's 'Ulysses.' " *Victorian Poetry* 19: 139–149.

Fleissner, R. F. 1973. "Like 'Pythagoras' Comparison of the Universe with Number': A Frost-Tennyson Correlation." In *Frost: Centennial Essays*, ed. Jac L. Tharpe, pp. 207–220. Jackson: University Press of Mississippi.

Fletcher, Pauline. 1979. "Romantic and Anti-Romantic Gardens in Tennyson and Swinburne." *Studies in Romanticism* 18: 81–97.

Foakes, R. A. 1958. *The Romantic Assertion: A Study in the Language of Nineteenth Century Poetry*. New Haven: Yale University Press.

Ford, George H 1977. "Felicitous Space: The Cottage Controversy." In *Nature and the Victorian Imagination*, ed. U. C. Knoepflmacher and G. B. Tennyson, pp. 29–48. Berkeley and Los Angeles: University of California Press.

Francis, Elizabeth A. 1976. "Tennyson's Political Poetry, 1852–1855." *Victorian Poetry* 14: 113–123.

———— 1980a. "Introduction." In *Tennyson: A Collection of Critical Essays*, ed. Elizabeth A. Francis, pp. 1–17. Englewood Cliffs: Prentice-Hall.

———— 1980b. "Last Poems." In *Tennyson: A Collection of Critical Essays*, ed. Elizabeth A. Francis, pp. 189–214. Englewood Cliffs: Prentice-Hall.

Fredeman, William E. 1972. " 'The Sphere of Common Duties': The Domestic Solution in Tennyson's Poetry." *Bulletin of the John Rylands Library* 54: 357–383.

Fricke, Donna G. 1970. "Tennyson's 'The Hesperides': East of Eden and Variations on the Theme." *Tennyson Research Bulletin* 1: 99–103.

Fuller, Gerry William. 1976. "The Aesthetic Significance of Tennyson's Revisions for the 1842 *Poems*." Ph.D. diss., Catholic University of America.

Gallant, Christine. 1977. "Tennyson's Use of the Nature Goddess in 'The Hesperides,' 'Tithonus,' and 'Demeter and Persephone.' " *Victorian Poetry* 14: 155–160.

Gaskell, Philip. 1978. *From Writer to Reader*. Oxford: Clarendon Press.

Gillett, Peter J. 1977. "Tennyson's Mind at the Work of Creation." *Victorian Poetry* 15: 321–333.

Golffing, Francis. 1966. "Tennyson's Last Phase: The Poet as Seer." *Southern Review*, n.s., 2: 264–285.

Goodman, Paul. 1954. *The Structure of Literature*. Chicago: University of Chicago Press.

Goslee, David F. 1976. "Three Stages in Tennyson's 'Tiresias.' " *Journal of English and Germanic Philology* 75: 154–167.

Gransden, K. W. 1964. *Tennyson: In Memoriam*. London: Edward Arnold.

Gray, J. M. 1980. *Thro' the Vision of the Night: A Study of Source, Evolution, and Structure in Tennyson's "Idylls of the King."* Montreal: McGill-Queen's University Press.

Green, Joyce. 1951. "Tennyson's Development during the 'Ten Years' Silence.' " *PMLA* 66: 662–697.

Greene, Michael E. 1980. "Tennyson's 'Gray Shadow, Once a Man': Erotic Imagery and Structure in 'Tithonus.' " *Victorian Poetry* 18: 293–300.

Griffiths, Eric. 1983. "The Worth of Change: The Arthur Hallam Letters." *Tennyson Research Bulletin* 4: 72–80.

Groom, Bernard. 1939. *On the Diction of Tennyson, Browning, and Arnold.* Oxford: Clarendon Press.

Gunter, Richard. 1967. "Structure and Style in Poems: A Paradox." *Style* 1: 93–106.

Hair, Donald S. 1981. *Domestic and Heroic in Tennyson's Poetry.* Toronto: University of Toronto Press.

Halio, Jay. 1961. " 'Prothalamion,' 'Ulysses,' and Intention in Poetry." *College English* 22: 390–394.

Hallam, Arthur. 1943. *The Writings of Arthur Hallam,* ed. T. Vail Motter. New York: Modern Language Association.

——— 1981. *The Letters of Arthur Henry Hallam,* ed. Jack Kolb. Columbus: Ohio State University Press.

Hill, James L. 1968. "Tennyson's 'The Lady of Shalott': The Ambiguity of Commitment." *Centennial Review* 12: 415–429.

Hinchcliffe, Peter. 1983. "Elegy and Epithalamium in *In Memoriam.*" *University of Toronto Quarterly* 52: 241–262.

Hollander, John. 1975. "Tennyson's Melody." *Georgia Review* 29: 676–703.

Holmes, Richard. 1975. *Shelley: The Pursuit.* New York: Dutton.

Homans, Margaret. 1979. "Tennyson and the Spaces of Life." *ELH* 46: 693–709.

Horne, R. H. 1844. "Alfred Tennyson." Rpt. in *Tennyson: The Critical Heritage,* ed. John D. Jump, pp. 153–165. London: Routledge and Kegan Paul, 1967.

Hough, Graham. 1951. " 'Tears, Idle Tears.' " Rpt. in *Critical Essays on the Poetry of Tennyson,* ed. John Killham, pp. 186–191. New York: Barnes and Noble, 1960.

Houghton, Walter. 1951. *The Victorian Frame of Mind, 1830–1870.* New Haven: Yale University Press.

House, Humphry. 1955. *All in Due Time.* London: Rupert Hart-Davis.

Howitt, William. 1838. *The Rural Life of England,* 2 vols. London: Longman.

Hughes, Linda. 1979. "From 'Tithon' to 'Tithonus': Tennyson as Mourner and Monologist." *Philological Quarterly* 58: 82–89.

Hungerford, Edward B. 1941. *The Shores of Darkness.* New York: Columbia University Press.

Hunt, John Dixon. 1973. " 'Story Painters and Picture Writers': Tennyson's Idylls and Victorian Painting." In *Tennyson,* ed. D. J. Palmer, pp. 180–202. Athens, Ohio: Ohio University Press.

James, Henry. 1875. "Tennyson's Drama." In *Views and Reviews,* ed. LeRoy Phillips, pp. 163–204. Boston: Bell.

Jamieson, Paul F. 1952. "Tennyson and His Audience in 1832." *Philological Quarterly* 31: 407–413.

Johnson, E. D. H. 1958. "*In Memoriam*: The Way of a Poet." *Victorian Studies* 2: 139–148.

Johnston, Priscilla. 1978. "Tennyson's Demeter and Persephone Theme: Memory and the 'Good Solid Past.' " *Texas Studies in Literature and Language* 20: 68–92.

Joseph, Gerhard. 1968. "The Idea of Mortality in Tennyson's Classical and Arthurian Poems: 'Honor Comes with Mystery.' " *Modern Philology* 66: 136–145.

———— 1972. "Tennyson's Concepts of Knowledge, Wisdom, and Pallas Athene." *Modern Philology* 69: 314–322.

———— 1973. "Poe and Tennyson." *PMLA* 88: 418–428.

———— 1977. "Tennyson's Optics: The Eagle's Gaze." *PMLA* 92: 420–428.

———— 1978. "Victorian Frames: The Windows and Mirrors of Browning, Arnold, and Tennyson." *Victorian Poetry* 16: 70–87.

———— 1982. "Tennyson's Three Women: The Thought within the Image." *Victorian Poetry* 19: 1–10.

———— 1983. "Tennyson's Stupidity." *University of Hartford Studies in Literature* 15: 55–61.

Kennedy, Ian H. C. 1977. "*In Memoriam* and the Tradition of Pastoral Elegy." *Victorian Poetry* 15: 351–366.

———— 1978. "Alfred Tennyson's *Bildungsgang*: Notes on His Early Reading." *Philological Quarterly* 57: 82–103.

Kenner, Hugh. 1973. "Some Post-Symbolist Structures." In *Literary Theory and Structure*, ed. Frank Brady, John Palmer, and Martin Price, pp. 379–393. New Haven and London: Yale University Press.

Kiernan, Victor. 1982. "Tennyson, King Arthur, and Imperialism." In *Culture, Ideology and Politics*, ed. Raphael Samuel and Gareth Stedman Jones, pp. 126–148. London: Routledge and Kegan Paul.

Killham, John. 1958. *Tennyson and "The Princess": Reflections of an Age*. London: Athlone Press.

———— 1960. "Introduction: Tennyson, A Review of Modern Criticism." In *Critical Essays on the Poetry of Tennyson*, ed. John Killham, pp. 1–21. London: Routledge and Kegan Paul.

———— 1973. "Tennyson and Victorian Social Values." In *Tennyson*, ed. D. J. Palmer, pp. 147–179. Athens, Ohio: Ohio University Press.

Kincaid, James R. 1974. "Rhetorical Irony, the Dramatic Monologue, and Tennyson's *Poems* (1842)." *Philological Quarterly* 53: 220–236.

———— 1975. *Tennyson's Major Poems: The Comic and Ironic Pattern*. New Haven and London: Yale University Press.

———— 1977. "Tennyson's Ironic Camelot: Arthur Breathes His Last." *Philological Quarterly* 56: 241–245.

Kissane, James D. 1970. *Alfred Tennyson*. New York: Twayne.

Knowles, James. 1893. "A Personal Reminiscence." *Nineteenth Century* 33: 164–188.

Kolb, Jack. 1983. "Portraits of Tennyson." *Modern Philology* 81: 173–190.

Korg, Jacob. 1958. "The Pattern of Fatality in Tennyson's Poetry." *Victorian Newsletter* 14: 8–11.

Kozicki, Henry. 1979. *Tennyson and Clio.* Baltimore: Johns Hopkins University Press.

Krieger, Murray. 1967. *The Play and Place of Criticism.* Baltimore: Johns Hopkins University Press.

Laird, Robert G. 1976. "Tennyson and the 'Most Burlesque Barbarous Experiment.' " *English Studies in Canada* 2: 439–451.

Landow, George. 1974. "Closing the Frame: Having Faith and Keeping Faith in Tennyson's 'The Passing of Arthur.' " *Bulletin of the John Rylands Library* 56: 423–442.

Laury, J. S. 1959. "Tennyson's 'The Epic': A Gesture of Recovered Faith." *Modern Language Notes* 74: 400–403.

Leavis, F. R. 1932. *New Bearings in English Poetry: A Study of the Contemporary Situation.* Rpt. Ann Arbor: University of Michigan Press, 1960.

Leggett, B. J. 1970. "Dante, Byron, and Tennyson's 'Ulysses.' " *Tennessee Studies in Literature* 15: 143–159.

Lipking, Lawrence I. 1981. *The Life of the Poet: Beginning and Ending Poetic Careers.* Chicago and London: University of Chicago Press.

Lourie, Margaret A. 1979. "Below the Thunders of the Upper Deep: Tennyson as Romantic Revisionist." *Studies in Romanticism* 18: 3–27.

Mackail, J. W. 1926. *Lectures on Greek Poetry.* London: Longman, Green.

Madden, Lionel. 1973. "Tennyson: A Reader's Guide." In *Tennyson,* ed. D. J. Palmer, pp. 1–22. Athens, Ohio: Ohio University Press.

Malory, Thomas. 1971. *Works,* ed. Eugène Vinaver, 2nd ed. Oxford: Oxford University Press.

Mann, Robert James. 1856. *Tennyson's "Maud" Vindicated: An Explanatory Essay.* London: Jarrold.

Marshall, George O., Jr. 1963. "Tennyson's 'Ulysses' 33–43." *Explicator* 21, item no. 50. Unpaginated.

Martin, David M. 1973. "Romantic Perspectivism in Tennyson's 'The Lady of Shalott.' " *Victorian Poetry* 11: 255–256.

Martin, Robert Bernard. 1980. *Tennyson: The Unquiet Heart.* Oxford: Clarendon Press.

Mason, Michael. 1972. "The Dramatization of Sorrow." *Victorian Poetry* 10: 161–177.

———— 1981. "The Timing of *In Memoriam.*" In *Studies in Tennyson,* ed. Hallam Tennyson, pp. 155–168. London: Macmillan.

Mays, J. C. C. 1965. "*In Memoriam*: An Aspect of Form." *University of Toronto Quarterly* 35: 22–46.

McGann, Jerome J. 1982. "Tennyson and the Histories of Criticism." *Review* 4: 219–253.

McLuhan, H. M. 1951. "Tennyson and Picturesque Poetry." Rpt. in *Critical Essays on the Poetry of Tennyson,* ed. John Killham, pp. 67–85. New York: Barnes and Noble, 1960.

———— 1959. "Tennyson and the Romantic Epic." Rpt. in *Critical Essays on the Poetry of Tennyson,* ed. John Killham, pp. 86–98. New York: Barnes and Noble, 1960.

Meisel, Martin. 1977. " 'Half Sick of Shadows': The Aesthetic Dialogue in Pre-Raphaelite Painting." In *Nature and the Victorian Imagination*, ed. U. C. Knoepflmacher and G. B. Tennyson, pp. 309–340. Berkeley and Los Angeles: University of California Press.

Mermin, Dorothy. 1983. *The Audience in the Poem: Five Victorian Poets*. New Brunswick: Rutgers University Press.

Merriman, James D. 1969. "The Poet as Heroic Thief: Tennyson's 'The Hesperides' Reexamined." *Victorian Newsletter* 35: 1–5.

Miles, Josephine. 1942. *Pathetic Fallacy in the Nineteenth Century: A Study of a Changing Relation between Object and Emotion*. Rpt. New York: Octagon, 1965.

Mill, John Stuart. 1835. Review signed "A." In *Tennyson: The Critical Heritage*, ed. John D. Jump, pp. 84–97. London: Routledge and Kegan Paul, 1967.

Millett, Kate. 1969. *Sexual Politics*. New York: Avon.

Millhauser, Milton. 1971. *Fire and Ice: The Influence of Science on Tennyson's Poetry*. Lincoln: Tennyson Research Centre.

Mitford, Mary Russell. 1825. *Our Village: Sketches of Rural Character and Scenery*. London: Whitaker.

Mustard, W. P. 1904. *Classical Echoes in Tennyson*. New York: Macmillan.

Nash, Walter. 1972. "The Poetics of Idyll." Ph.D. diss., University of Nottingham.

——— 1975. "Tennyson: 'The Epic' and 'The Old "Morte." ' " *Cambridge Quarterly* 6: 326–349.

Nicolson, Harold. 1923. *Tennyson: Aspects of His Life, Character, and Poetry*. London: Constable.

Ostriker, Alicia. 1967. "The Three Modes in Tennyson's Prosody." *PMLA* 82: 273–284.

Packer, Lona Mosk. 1964. "Sun and Shadow: The Nature of Experience in Tennyson's 'The Lady of Shalott.' " *Victorian Newsletter* 25: 4–8.

Paden, W. D. 1942. *Tennyson in Egypt*. Lawrence: University of Kansas Publications.

——— 1965. "Tennyson's *The Lover's Tale*, R. H. Shepherd, and T. J. Wise." *Studies in Bibliography* 18: 111–145.

Palmer, D. J. 1973. "Tennyson's Romantic Heritage." In *Tennyson*, ed. D. J. Palmer, pp. 23–51. Athens, Ohio: Ohio University Press.

Pattison, Robert. 1979. *Tennyson and Tradition*. Cambridge, Mass.: Harvard University Press.

Peckham, Morse. 1962. *Beyond the Tragic Vision: The Quest for Identity in the Nineteenth Century*. New York: Braziller.

——— 1970. *Victorian Revolutionaries: Speculations on Some Heroes of a Culture Crisis*. New York: Braziller.

Peltason, Timothy. 1983a. "Supposed Confessions, Uttered Thoughts: The First-Person Singular in Tennyson's Poetry." *Victorian Newsletter* 64: 13–18.

——— 1983b. "The Embowered Self: 'Mariana' and 'Recollections of the Arabian Nights.' " *Victorian Poetry* 21: 335–350.

——— 1984a. "Tennyson, Nature, and Romantic Nature Poetry." *Philological Quarterly* 63: 75–93.

——— 1984b. "Tennyson's Philosophy: Some Lyric Examples." In *Philosophical Approaches to Literature*, ed. William E. Cain, pp. 51–72. Lewisburg: Bucknell University Press.

——— 1985a. *Reading "In Memoriam."* Princeton: Princeton University Press.

——— 1985b. "Tennyson's Fables of Emergence." *Bucknell Review* 29, no. 2: 143–170.

Pettigrew, John. 1963. "Tennyson's 'Ulysses': A Reconciliation of Opposites." *Victorian Poetry* 1: 27–45.

Pipes, B. N., Jr. 1963. "A Slight Meteorological Disturbance: The Last Two Stanzas of Tennyson's 'The Poet.' " *Victorian Poetry* 1: 74–76.

Pitt, Valerie. 1962. *Tennyson Laureate*. London: Barrie and Rockliff.

Pound, Ezra. 1934. *The ABC of Reading*. Rpt. New York: New Directions, 1960.

——— 1954. *Literary Essays of Ezra Pound*, ed. T. S. Eliot. London: Faber.

Preyer, Robert O. 1958. "Tennyson as an Oracular Poet." *Modern Philology* 55: 239–251.

——— 1966. "Alfred Tennyson: The Poetry and Politics of Conservative Vision." *Victorian Studies* 9: 325–352.

——— 1976. "The Burden of Culture and the Dialectic of Literature." In *Evolution of Consciousness: Studies in Polarity*, ed. Shirley Sugerman, pp. 98–105. Middletown: Wesleyan University Press.

Priestley, F. E. L. 1973. *Language and Structure in Tennyson's Poetry*. London: Deutsch.

Puckett, Harry. 1974. "Subjunctive Imagination in *In Memoriam*." *Victorian Poetry* 12: 97–124.

Pyre, J. F. A. 1921. *The Formation of Tennyson's Style*. Madison: University of Wisconsin Studies.

Rackin, Phyllis. 1966. "Recent Misreadings of 'Break, Break, Break' and Their Implications for Poetic Theory." *Journal of English and Germanic Philology* 65: 217–228.

Rader, Ralph. 1963. *Tennyson's "Maud": The Biographical Genesis*. Berkeley: University of California Press.

Rannie, D. W. 1912. "Keats's Epithets." *Essays and Studies by Members of the English Association* 3: 92–113.

Rawnsley, W. F. 1925. "Personal Recollections of Tennyson." Rpt. in *Tennyson: Interviews and Recollections*, ed. Norman Page, pp. 20–26. London: Macmillan, 1983.

Ray, Gordon N. 1968. *Tennyson Reads "Maud."* Vancouver: University of British Columbia.

Reed, John R. 1975. *Victorian Conventions*. Athens, Ohio: Ohio University Press.

Ricks, Christopher. 1972. *Tennyson*. New York: Macmillan.

——— 1981. "Tennyson Inheriting the Earth." In *Studies in Tennyson*, ed. Hallam Tennyson, pp. 66–104. London: Macmillan.

Robbins, Tony. 1973. "Tennyson's 'Ulysses': The Significance of the Homeric and Dantesque Backgrounds." *Victorian Poetry* 11: 177–193.

Robson, W. W. 1957. "The Dilemma of Tennyson." Rpt. in *Critical Essays on the Poetry of Tennyson*, ed. John Killham, pp. 155–163. New York: Barnes and Noble, 1960.

Rosenberg, John D. 1959. "The Two Kingdoms of *In Memoriam*." *Journal of English and Germanic Philology* 58: 228–240.

———— 1973. *The Fall of Camelot*. Cambridge, Mass.: Harvard University Press.

———— 1974. "Tennyson and the Landscape of Consciousness." *Victorian Poetry* 12: 303–310.

Rosenblum, Dolores. 1980. "The Act of Writing *In Memoriam*." *Victorian Poetry* 18: 119–134.

Rosenmeyer, Thomas G. 1969. *The Green Cabinet: Theocritus and the European Pastoral Lyric*. Berkeley: University of California Press.

Rowlinson, Matthew. 1984. "The Skipping Muse: Repetition and Difference in Two Early Poems of Tennyson." *Victorian Poetry* 22: 349–363.

Ryals, Clyde de L. 1962. "Point of View in Tennyson's 'Ulysses.' " *Archiv* 199: 232–234.

———— 1964. *Theme and Symbol in Tennyson's Poems to 1850*. Philadelphia: University of Pennsylvania Press.

Saintsbury, George. 1923. *A History of English Prosody*, 3 vols. London: Macmillan.

Sale, Roger. 1974. "Tennyson as Great Poet." *Hudson Review* 27: 443–450.

Schulman, Samuel E. 1983. "Mourning and Voice in *Maud*." *Studies in English Literature, 1500–1900* 23: 633–646.

Sedgwick, Eve Kosofsky. 1985. *Between Men: English Literature and Male Homosocial Desire*. New York: Columbia University Press.

Sendry, Joseph. 1966. " 'The Palace of Art' Revisited." *Victorian Poetry* 4: 149–162.

———— 1967. "*In Memoriam* and *Lycidas*." *PMLA* 82: 437–443.

———— 1980. "*In Memoriam*: Twentieth-Century Criticism." *Victorian Poetry* 18: 105–118.

Shaffer, Elinor. 1975. *"Kubla Khan" and "The Fall of Jerusalem": The Mythological School in Biblical Criticism and Secular Literature*. Cambridge: Cambridge University Press.

Shannon, Edgar F., Jr. 1952. *Tennyson and the Reviewers: A Study of His Literary Reputation and of the Influence of the Critics upon His Poetry, 1827–1851*. Cambridge, Mass.: Harvard University Press.

———— 1977. "Alfred Tennyson as a Poet for Our Time." *Virginia Quarterly Review* 53: 692–707.

———— 1981. "Poetry as Vision: Sight and Insight in 'The Lady of Shalott.' " *Victorian Poetry* 19: 207–223.

Shatto, Susan. 1978. "Tennyson's Revisions of *In Memoriam*." *Victorian Poetry* 16: 341–356.

———— 1980. "Tennyson's *In Memoriam*: Section 123 in the Manuscripts." *Library* 2: 304–314.

Shaw, Marion. 1973. "Tennyson and His Public 1827–1859." In *Tennyson*, ed. D. J. Palmer, pp. 52–88. Athens, Ohio: Ohio University Press.

Shaw, W. David. 1967. "The Transcendental Problem in Tennyson's Poetry of Debate." *Philological Quarterly* 46: 79–94.

———— 1971. "*In Memoriam* and the Rhetoric of Confession." *ELH* 58: 80–103.

—— 1976a. "Consolation and Catharsis in *In Memoriam.*" *Modern Language Quarterly* 37: 47–67.

—— 1976b. *Tennyson's Style.* Ithaca and London: Cornell University Press.

Sherry, James J. 1979. "Tennyson and the Paradox of the Sign." *Victorian Poetry* 17: 204–216.

Shires, Linda M. 1984. "Introduction." *Victorian Poetry* 22 (special issue entitled *The Dramatic "I" Poem*, ed. Linda M. Shires): 97–101.

Short, Clarice. 1967. "Tennyson and 'The Lover's Tale.' " *PMLA* 82: 78–84.

Sinfield, Alan. 1971. *The Language of Tennyson's "In Memoriam."* Oxford: Blackwell.

—— 1976a. "Tennyson's Imagery." *Neophilologus* 55: 466–479.

—— 1976b. " 'That Which Is': The Platonic Indicative in *In Memoriam* XCV." *Victorian Poetry* 14: 247–252.

—— 1977. *Dramatic Monologue.* London: Methuen.

Smith, L. E. W. 1963. *Twelve Poems Considered.* London: Methuen.

Spatz, Jonas. 1974. "Love and Death in Tennyson's *Maud.*" *Texas Studies in Literature and Language* 16: 503–510.

Spedding, James. 1843. Unsigned review. Rpt. in *Tennyson: The Critical Heritage*, ed. John D. Jump, pp. 139–152. London: Routledge and Kegan Paul, 1967.

Spitzer, Leo. 1950. " 'Tears, Idle Tears' Again." Rpt. in *Critical Essays on the Poetry of Tennyson*, ed. John Killham, pp. 192–203. New York: Barnes and Noble, 1960.

—— 1962. *Essays on English and American Literature*, ed. Anna Hatcher. Princeton: Princeton University Press.

Staines, David. 1982. *Tennyson's Camelot: The "Idylls of the King" and its Medieval Sources.* Waterloo, Ontario: Wilfrid Laurier University Press.

Stange, G. Robert. 1952. "Tennyson's Garden of Art: A Study of 'The Hesperides.' " Rpt. in *Critical Essays on the Poetry of Tennyson*, ed. John Killham, pp. 99–112. New York: Barnes and Noble, 1960.

—— 1973. "The Frightened Poets." In *The Victorian City: Images and Realities*, ed. H. J. Dyos and Michael Wolff, II, 475–494. London and Boston: Routledge and Kegan Paul.

Starzyk, Lawrence J. 1978. "The Will to Die: Tennyson's Poetics of Self-Transformation." *Humanities Association Review* 29: 21–36.

Stein, Richard L. 1981. "The Pre-Raphaelite Tennyson." *Victorian Studies* 24: 279–301.

Steiner, Wendy. 1982. *The Colors of Rhetoric: Problems in the Relation between Modern Literature and Painting.* Chicago: University of Chicago Press.

Sterling, John. 1842. Unsigned review. Rpt. in *Tennyson: The Critical Heritage*, ed. John D. Jump, pp. 103–125. London: Routledge and Kegan Paul, 1967.

Stevenson, Catherine Barnes. 1974. "The Aesthetic Function of the 'Weird Seizures' in *The Princess.*" *Victorian Newsletter* 45: 22–25.

—— 1980. "Tennyson's Dying Swans: Mythology and the Definition of the Poet's Role." *Studies in English Literature, 1500–1900* 20: 621–635.

Stevenson, Lionel. 1948. "The 'High-Born Maiden' Symbol in Tennyson." Rpt. in *Critical Essays on the Poetry of Tennyson*, ed. John Killham, pp. 126–136. New York: Barnes and Noble, 1960.

Stokes, Edward. 1964. "The Metrics of *Maud*." *Victorian Poetry* 2: 97–110.

Storch, R. F. 1971. "The Fugitive from the Ancestral Hearth: Tennyson's 'Ulysses.' " *Texas Studies in Literature and Language* 13: 281–297.

Sturman, Christopher. 1984. "Annotations by Tennyson in a Newly Discovered Copy of *Poems, Chiefly Lyrical*." *Tennyson Research Bulletin* 4: 123–138.

Tapsall, Peter. 1968. "Senator Robert Kennedy: A Lincolnshire Appreciation." *Tennyson Research Bulletin* 1: 2–3.

Tennyson, Alfred. 1969. *The Poems of Tennyson*, ed. Christopher Ricks. London: Longman.

—— 1981. *The Letters of Alfred Lord Tennyson*, ed. Cecil Y. Lang and Edgar F. Shannon, Jr., vol. I. Cambridge, Mass.: Harvard University Press.

—— 1982. *In Memoriam*, ed. Susan Shatto and Marion Shaw. Oxford: Clarendon Press.

Tennyson, Charles. 1949. *Alfred Tennyson*. New York: Macmillan.

Tennyson, Emily. 1974. *The Letters of Emily Lady Tennyson*, ed. James O. Hoge. University Park and London: Pennsylvania State University Press.

—— 1981. *Lady Tennyson's Journal*, ed. James O. Hoge. Charlottesville: University Press of Virginia.

Tennyson, Hallam. 1897. *Alfred Lord Tennyson: A Memoir*, 2 vols. New York: Macmillan.

Thesing, William B. 1977. "Tennyson and the City: Historical Tremours and Hysterical Tremblings." *Tennyson Research Bulletin* 3: 14–22.

Tillotson, Kathleen. 1953. "Rugby 1850: Arnold, Clough, Walrond, and *In Memoriam*." *Review of English Studies* 4: 122–140.

Timko, Michael. 1974. "Arnold, Tennyson, and the English Idyl: Ancient Criticism and Modern Poetry." *Texas Studies in Literature and Language* 16: 137–146.

——1978. " 'The Central Wish': Human Passion and Cosmic Love in Tennyson's Idyls." *Victorian Poetry* 16: 1–15.

Tobias, Richard C. 1971. "Tennyson's Painted Shell." *Victorian Newsletter* 39: 7–10.

Tobin, J. J. M. 1976. " 'Ulysses': A Possible Source in Horace." *Notes and Queries* 23: 395.

Tucker, Herbert F. 1982. "Tennyson's Narrative of Desire: *The Lover's Tale*." *Victorian Newsletter* 62: 21–30.

—— 1983. "Strange Comfort: A Reading of Tennyson's Unpublished Juvenilia." *Victorian Poetry* 21: 1–25.

—— 1984. "From Monomania to Monologue: 'St. Simeon Stylites' and the Rise of the Victorian Dramatic Monologue." *Victorian Poetry* 22 (special issue entitled *The Dramatic "I" Poem*, ed. Linda M. Shires): 121–137.

Turner, Paul. 1976. *Tennyson*. London: Routledge and Kegan Paul.

Ward, Arthur D. 1974. " 'Ulysses' and 'Tithonus': Tunnel-Vision and Idle Tears." *Victorian Poetry* 12: 311–319.

Weiner, S. Ronald. 1966. "The Chord of Self: Tennyson's *Maud*." *Literature and Psychology* 16: 175–183.

Welch, James Donald. 1976. "Tennyson's Landscapes of Time and a Reading of 'The Kraken.' " *Victorian Poetry* 14: 197–204.

Whiting, George Wesley. 1964. "The Artist and Tennyson." *Rice University Studies* 50, no. 3.

Wilkinson, L. P. 1969. "Tennyson and Dryden's *Aeneid*." *Times Literary Supplement* October 9: 1159.

Wiseman, Christopher. 1978. " 'Tithonus' and Tennyson's Elegiac Vision." *English Studies in Canada* 4: 212–223.

Wordsworth, Ann. 1981. "An Art That Will Not Abandon the Self to Language: Bloom, Tennyson, and the Blind World of the Wish." In *Untying the Text: A Post-Structuralist Reader*, ed. Robert Young, pp. 207–222. Boston: Routledge and Kegan Paul.

Wordsworth, Jonathan. 1974. " 'What Is It, That Has Been Done?': The Central Problem of *Maud*." *Essays in Criticism* 24: 356–362.

Index

Abercrombie, Lascelles, 19
"Achilles over the Trench," 339
Action. *See* Agency
Adams, Michael, 27
Aeschylus, *Eumenides*, 444n31
Agency, 14–19, 35, 47, 73–74, 83, 84,
 109, 246–247, 307, 309, 311; endorsed,
 246–247, 304–305; lack of, 14–19, 23,
 35, 38, 47, 83, 84, 115, 349; super-
 natural, 47. *See also* Character; Power
Ainger, Canon, 442n8
"Akbar's Dream," 21
Alienation, 124, 125, 135, 197–208, 213–
 214, 220–221, 226, 231–232, 244, 378,
 387, 401, 404, 412. *See also* Marginality;
 Solitude
Allan, in "Dora," 304–305, 306, 308, 311
Allen, Peter, 440nn8,10, 443n21, 444n30
Allingham, William, 26, 136, 345
Allusion, idyllic, 289–293, 311–313, 358
Alraschid, Haroun, in "Recollections of
 the Arabian Nights," 79, 84, 85, 86
Altieri, Charles, 238, 438n3
Ambiguity, 106, 108, 122, 148, 195–196,
 247–248, 395
Ambivalence, 22–23, 76, 81–82, 131
"The Ancient Sage," 74, 199, 441n17,
 449n22
Anderson, Warren D., 27
Antigone, 196
Aphrodite, 160, 162, 284
Apollo, 147–148, 150, 171, 257, 449n20
Appleman, Philip, 386
Arabian Nights, 441n18, 444n23
"Armageddon," 34, 40–51, 53–54, 55, 57,
 60–61, 62, 63, 80, 150, 181, 218,
 449n22; compositional history of, 40–41
Armstrong, Isobel, 378, 381, 383
Arnold, Matthew, 14, 321, 440n9,
 452n23; *Culture and Anarchy*, 391; *Em-*
pedocles on Etna, 14; *On Translating Ho-*
mer, 447n12
Arthur, legend of, 317, 318, 320, 328,
 333–334, 453n30
Assad, Thomas J., 369
Atmosphere, 14, 18–19, 72, 73, 74; poetic,
 139
Auden, W. H., 6, 23, 26
Audience, 103–104, 138, 232; and lan-
 guage, 88–89, 394
"Audley Court," 276, 300, 450n4
Auerbach, Erich, 313, 314
Aurora, in "Tithonus," 243, 244, 246–
 257, 258, 260, 266; gift of immortality,
 252–257
Autonomy, 121–122, 192, 308, 422. *See*
also Responsibility
"Aylmer's Field," 13

"Babylon," 65
Bagehot, Walter, 17, 314, 329, 452n23
"Balin and Balan," 453n34
Baker, William, 438n3
Ball, Patricia, 405
Basler, Roy P., 411
Baum, Paull F., 7, 148, 246, 450n5
Bayley, John, 15, 276, 279, 443n15
Beattie, James, 161
Beauty, 163–164, 261, 417
Bedivere, in "Morte d'Arthur," 325–332,
 336–341, 453n32
Belief, crisis of, 55–57, 59–61, 403–404
Bergonzi, Bernard, 352
Bidney, Martin, 438n4
Bible, 42, 90, 153, 171, 229, 236, 304,
 311, 313
Bildungspoesie, 349, 350
Bishop, Jonathan, 186
Blake, William, 42, 349, 445n1
Blame, 411. *See also* Responsibility.

Bloom, Harold, 71, 121, 168, 173, 228, 441nn16,3, 447n8

Boccaccio, Giovanni, 99, 441n1; *Decameron,* 442n4

Bower, imagery of, 77, 165, 181

Boyd, Zelda, 17, 337

Brashear, William, 44, 438n4, 439n3, 442n11, 445n31

"Break, Break, Break," 13, 346, 362, 364

Brie, Friedrich, 212

Brimley, George, 451n17

Briney, John O., 441n1

Brooks, Cleanth, 5, 8, 363

Browning, Elizabeth Barrett, 450n12

Browning, Robert, 15, 59, 62, 73, 191–192, 198, 207, 210, 268, 316–317, 322, 343, 450n5; *The Flight of the Duchess,* 348; "My Last Duchess," 280; *The Ring and the Book,* 321; *Sordello,* 348

Bruns, Gerald, 30, 378, 394, 405

Bryant, Jacob, 55, 448n19; *A New System; or, An Analysis of Antient Mythology,* 257

Buckler, William E., 186, 211, 292, 354, 440n9, 444n30, 454n3

Buckley, Jerome H., 37, 96, 304, 443n16

Burr, A.H., *Dora,* 452n25

Bush, Douglas, 443n16

Butler, H. M., 367, 440n15

Byatt, A. S., 417

Byron, Lord, 64, 440n10; *Childe Harold's Pilgrimage,* 89, 222; *Don Juan,* 348

Callimachus, *Aetia,* 450n8

Camilla, in *The Lover's Tale,* 97, 441n2

Capaneus, 446n4

Capitalism, 392, 401, 420. *See also* Economic imagery

Carlyle, Thomas, 304, 447n11

Carr, Arthur J., 17, 25, 65, 67, 316, 365, 439n3

Cassandra, 171, 444n30, 445n31

Cause and consequence, 407, 413

Chambers, D. Laurance, 438n8, 441n18

Chandler, James K., 443n19

Character, in AT's works, 14–19, 22, 23, 35, 47, 83, 84, 98, 115, 349

"The Charge of the Light Brigade," 27, 356

Chastity, in Classical myth, 135–136

Chaucer, Geoffrey, 14, 97; *Troilus and Criseyde,* 348

Chesterton, G. K., 450n7

Chiasson, E. J., 210

Christianity, 228–229, 387, 400

Class, social, 390–395, 410. *See also* Victorian culture

Classical myth, AT's use of, 134–136, 152–153, 171–172, 196–197

Claudian, *De Raptu Proserpinae,* 439n5

"The Coach of Death," 34, 439n5

Coleridge, Samuel, 51, 54, 110, 404, 440nn10,13, 450n8; "Dejection," 110, 222; "Frost at Midnight," 144; "Kubla Khan," 57–58, 131, 356, 440n13; "The Nightingale: A Conversation Poem," 144

Colley, Ann C., 426

Collins, John Churton, 60, 440n9, 443n19

"Come Down, O Maid," 362, 370–376, 421

"The Coming of Arthur," 321, 440n12

Condition of England question, 407

Conrad, Peter, 242, 287

Context, 193–195, 209–210, 211, 214, 216, 220–221, 232–233, 244–246, 263–265, 295–302, 384–386; and allusion, 289–293, 311–313; and desire, 194–195, 232–233; rejection of, 232–233, 379; and self, 232–233, 263–264, 386, 393. *See also* Culture

Crabbe, George, 452n24

Creese, Walter L., 450n7

Croker, J. W., 160, 299

"Crossing the Bar," 13, 18, 48

Culler, A. Dwight, 14, 22, 44, 74, 156, 275, 301, 317, 409, 438n2, 452n24, 453n29, 455n13

Culture, 193–195, 209–210, 214, 216, 220–221, 232–233, 244–246, 295–302, 384–386, 393–394, 398–406, 415–430; critique of, 401–406, 409, 415–430; in idylls, 295–302; mediated by language, 420; nature mediated by, 292–295, 357–358; role of, in conditioning love, 297–300, 357–358, 415–424, 427–429; and self, 232–233, 386, 393, 398–405; transmission of, 318–322, 330, 336–337, 342–345

Curse, 114, 207–208

Daiches, David, 441n3

Danaë, 370

Dante, 121, 232, 445n1; *The Divine Comedy*, 146, 230, 319

Day, Aidan, 33, 155

Death, 22, 64, 77, 82–83, 105, 106, 137, 144, 152, 161–162, 164, 165, 168–170, 233–234, 251, 261, 263, 265–267, 282–283, 339–341, 364, 386, 388, 396, 421; commonality of, 381–383; and culture, 381, 393, 428; and the deep, 260–261; fear of, 208; as immortality, 82, 262; and love, 86–87, 109–111, 124, 168, 170–171, 282–283, 285, 286, 374, 424; and sexuality, 91, 109–111, 133–134, 267, 281, 284, 296–297; and time, 286, 365; wish for, 259

Deep, the, 20, 217, 241, 260–261

DeMott, Benjamin, 444n30

"De Profundis," 441n19

Desire, 25, 85–87, 96, 113, 126, 146–154, 193–194, 229–230, 261, 287, 368–369, 426; cultural conditioning of, 418–421; frustration of, 98, 100; objects of, 95–96, 153–154; rejection of, 85, 86–88, 250–254, 258–259, 262–267; role of imagination in, 95–97; and self-annihilation, 115, 228, 261–262; sublimated, 284. *See also* Passion; Sexuality

Determinism, psychological and physical, 14–18, 35, 307, 309, 376, 412–413. *See also* Character; Doom; Fatalism

The Devil and the Lady, 35–40

Devlin, Francis P., 156, 450n11

Dickens, Charles, 275

Dietrich, Manfred, 354

Dionysus, 445n31

Dodsworth, Martin, 22, 62, 242, 443n20

Donahue, Mary Joan, 251

Donoghue, Denis, 14, 404

Doom, 20, 21, 22, 27, 40, 47, 64, 69–70, 91, 125, 144–145, 154, 188, 198, 254, 266, 285–286, 321, 407, 412, 414, 415, 432; cultural, 432–433; idyllic, 308

"Dora," 302–317, 343, 344, 452nn23,25, 26, 453n28

Dramatic monologue: context in, 193–195, 197–198, 210, 211, 214, 220–221, 226, 230–231; form of, 190–195, 208–209, 210, 265–269; and identity, 199, 263; vs. idyll, 157, 194–195, 270–271, 277–278; vs. monodrama, 410. *See also* Lyric

Drew, Philip, 15, 272, 417

"The Druid's Prophecies," 65

Duncan, Edgar, 233

"The Dying Swan," 88, 90–91

"The Eagle," 13

Eagleton, Terry, 352, 389, 454n5

Economic imagery, 213, 220, 221, 230, 235, 307, 391–392, 400–401, 410–411

"Edwin Morris," 300, 450n4

Ekphrasis, 284–285, 330, 450n11

Elegy, 178–179

Eliot, T. S., 23, 73, 293, 314, 378, 443n16

Elton, Oliver, 352, 406

Emerson, Ralph Waldo, 438n1, 447n10, 450n5

Emotion, 59–61, 65–66, 107, 363; and identity, 217–218; primacy of, over thought, 59–61, 218. *See also* Desire; Passion

Empson, William, 84, 202, 372

Enlightenment, the, 63, 401

"Enoch Arden," 16, 300, 301, 450n11

Epic: AT's revisionism toward, 317–322, 340–343; as cultural transmission, 318–322; in idylls, 290–291, 317–322, 338–345

"The Epic," 317, 318, 320, 453n29

Equivalencies, 82, 279, 283

Eris, 166, 170

Eros, 147, 174, 245, 279, 287

Eternal process, 21–22

Eternal recurrence, 22

Euripides: *Bacchae*, 445n31; *Hippolytus*, 135; *The Phoenician Women*, 196

Eustace, in "The Gardener's Daughter," 280, 290, 291, 296, 451n19

Excalibur, in "Morte d'Arthur," 326–331, 335

Experience, 18, 41, 219, 220, 222, 243, 316–317; authenticity of subjective, 379, 405; rejection of, 215–216, 223, 240, 266

Fable, 53–54, 56, 59, 60–63, 70, 71, 89, 127, 160, 218

Fatalism, 14–17, 23, 33–34, 38–40, 46–47, 64–67, 432; and agency, 38–40, 47, 66–67, 68, 98, 108–109, 244, 286; cultural, 411–412, 415; as curse, 108–109; evocation of, through language, 24–25, 26, 40, 47–48, 68, 128–129; in idylls, 307–311, 359; and self-annihilation, 115. *See*

Fatalism (*cont.*)
  also Agency; Character; Determinism,
  psychological and physical; Doom;
  Passivity
Fate, 38–40, 188, 197–198, 246, 254, 359
"Fatima," 117, 145–153, 154, 171, 174,
  218
Faulkner, William, *Light in August,* 438n4
Feminism, 353, 355, 358–360. *See also*
  Woman Question, the
Fichter, Andrew, 62, 152, 387
Findlay, L. M., 212
Fire, imagery of, 112, 113, 148, 150,
  169–170, 173
FitzGerald, Edward, 206–207, 441n19,
  444n26, 447n11, 450n9, 452n23,
  454n12, 455n14
Fletcher, Pauline, 130, 369, 417, 452n21
"The Flower," 441n20
Foakes, R. A., 397
Ford, George H., 19, 299, 451n15
"Forlorn," 442n7
Formalist criticism, 126
Fox, W. J., 448n16
"A Fragment," 440n12
Francis, Elizabeth A., 437n1, 450n5,
  454n1
Fredeman, William E., 183, 304
Freud, Sigmund, 229; "The Theme of the
  Three Caskets," 162
Fricke, Donna G., 130
Frost, Robert, 346
Fuller, Gerry William, 182

Gallant, Christine, 130
"The Gardener's Daughter," 16, 278–302,
  312, 314, 315, 329, 343, 344, 375,
  442n7, 450nn4,5,8,9,11, 451nn18,19
"Gareth and Lynette," 22
Gaskell, Elizabeth, 451n15; *Cranford,*
  294–295, 345
Gaskell, Philip, 155
"Geraint and Enid," 321
Gillett, Peter, 437n1
God, 47, 48, 65, 119, 229, 257, 268, 313,
  389, 405
The Golden Supper, 98, 441n1
"The Golden Year," 274–275, 276, 301,
  450n4
Golffing, Francis, 15
Goodman, Paul, 320
Goslee, David F., 194, 204, 447n6
Gosse, Edmund, *Father and Son,* 444n23

Gransden, K. W., 14
Gray, J. M., 333
Green, Joyce, 183, 443n16
Greene, Michael, 251
Grief, 381–385, 388
Griffiths, Eric, 396
Groom, Bernard, 370, 438n1
Guilt, 15–16, 65, 414
Gunter, Richard, 372

Hair, Donald S., 444nn29,30, 450n8,
  452n26
Halio, Jay, 246
Hallam, Arthur, 20, 56, 60, 73, 86, 138,
  139, 144, 154, 174, 177, 182, 237, 328,
  437n3, 442n12, 443n21, 444n30, 445n4,
  454n2; effect of death of, on AT, 154,
  177–180, 182, 184, 185–188, 265–267,
  405, 439n8; influence of, on AT, 178,
  183–184, 186–187, 440n8
Hallam, Ellen, 451n14
Hardy, Thomas, 346
Hatred, 166, 167, 170, 174
Helen of Troy, 162, 171
"Hendecasyllabics," 443n20
Hera, 160, 161
Hermeneutics, 268, 314, 345, 371, 395–
  397
Herrick, Robert, *Hesperides,* 136
Hesiod, *Theogony,* 135
Hesperides, myth of, 135–137, 443n16
"The Hesperides," 117, 126–137, 142,
  156
"The Higher Pantheism," 199
Hill, James L., 442n11
Hinchcliffe, Peter, 186
History, 197, 201–202, 301, 393, 405. *See
  also* Context; Culture; Self, empirical
  conditioning of
Hollander, John, 76, 454n4
Holmes, Richard, 152
"The Holy Grail," 18, 321, 437n1
Homans, Margaret, 365, 453n34
Homer, 121, 213, 284, 343; *Iliad,* 167,
  437n2, 441n15, 442n13; *Odyssey,* 230,
  232, 249–250, 443n18
Horace, 216; *Odes,* 447n11, 449n20
Horne, R. H., 14, 453n30
Hough, Graham, 365
Houghton, Walter, 451n17
House, Humphry, 226
Howitt, William, 454n10
Hughes, Linda, 240, 258

Hungerford, Edward B., 440n12, 448n19
Hunt, Holman, 442n9
Hunt, John Dixon, 275, 279, 301, 310

Ida, Princess, in *The Princess*, 15, 352, 353, 357, 358, 360, 361, 367, 368, 369, 375
Identity, 141, 149, 155, 218, 219, 228, 230–231, 265, 370–371. *See also* Self
Idyll: allusion in, 289–295; bourgeois nature of, 270–274, 301, 307, 344; as cultural transmission, 330, 336–337; vs. dramatic monologue, 157, 270–271; form of, 156, 158, 270, 289–295, 300–302, 303, 315–316, 350–351; formal constraints of, 274–277; vs. lyric, 382–383, 389, 392; relation to epic, 290–291, 317–322, 338–345; suppression in, 293–294; surface and depth in, 277–278, 293–294, 314–315, 328
Idylls of the King, 12–13, 16, 17, 154, 177, 179, 278, 301, 320, 322, 328, 333, 344, 347, 356, 374, 431, 444n30, 445n2, 453nn29,34, 455n13
"Ilion, Ilion," 449n20
Imagery: animals, 272; arch, 219–221, 226; dream, 79–81; garden, 386–287; lighthouse, 361; maiden, 103, 104; moon, 105, 112, 124; ocean, 20, 39, 124; phallic, 256; sun, 112, 145, 148, 150; technological, 275–276; urban, 407–408; wind, 145, 148. *See also* Economic imagery; Fire, imagery of; Light, imagery of; Mirror, imagery of; Rose, imagery of
Immortality, 22, 77, 78, 244, 252, 254–258; insufficiency of, 260; quest for, 249–250
Imperialism, 406, 421–422
Individualism, 409–410
Industrial Revolution, 25, 275, 400
In Memoriam, 13, 17, 19, 20, 60, 82, 91, 118, 154, 167, 172, 177, 179, 185, 188, 190, 219, 237, 266, 268, 278, 342, 347, 348, 376–406, 415, 437n1, 438n7, 445nn3,4, 448n13, 451n19, 452n20, 454n12; compositional history of, 13, 377–378
Insanity, 170–171, 426–428
"In the Valley of Cauteretz," 445n4
Irony, 104, 115, 191, 265
"I Wander in Darkness and Sorrow," 66–67, 71

James, Henry, 18, 429
Jamieson, Paul F., 443n21
Jerdan, William, 442n5
Johnson, E. D. H., 386
Johnston, Priscilla, 453n26
Joseph, Gerhard, 19, 162, 186, 316, 365, 445n32, 450n11, 453n31,. 454n4
Jowett, Benjamin, 33
Julian, in *The Lover's Tale*, 95, 97, 98, 121, 216

Kant, Immanuel, 72
Keats, John, 22, 34, 42, 46, 51, 54, 55, 71, 83, 131, 137, 160, 168, 261, 269, 329, 371, 372–373, 399, 440nn10,12, 454n8; AT's response to, 77–78, 133–134, 143; "Bright Star," 424; *Endymion*, 97, 441n18; "Epistle to J. H. Reynolds, Esq.," 439n7; *Hyperion*, 77, 323–324, 342, 440n12, 444n25, 455n17; *Isabella; or the Pot of Basil*, 441n16; "La Belle Dame sans Merci," 143; *Lamia*, 164; "Ode on a Grecian Urn," 169, 329; "Ode to a Nightingale," 26, 27, 83, 105–106, 168–169, 310, 388, 422, 424, 455n18; "Ode to Psyche," 62, 106, 165–166, 258, 264; "On First Looking into Chapman's Homer," 442n13; "To Autumn," 56–57, 76–77, 132, 133–134, 143, 292, 310, 365–366, 375; "When I Have Fears," 216, 424; "Why Did I Laugh," 424
Kennedy, Ian H. C., 237, 440n10
Kenner, Hugh, 438n1
Kiernan, Victor, 172, 449n2
Killham, John, 164, 228, 232, 243, 320, 327, 352, 355, 400, 405, 408, 437n1, 438n9, 441n18, 451n15, 452n21
Kincaid, James R., 164, 228, 232, 243, 320, 327, 400, 405, 455n13
Kingsley, Charles, *Alton Locke*, 455n14
Kissane, James D., 22, 74, 164, 305, 382, 449n21
Knowles, James, 367, 406, 453n1
Kolb, Jack, 22
Korg, Jacob, 437n2
Kozicki, Henry, 14, 442n11
"The Kraken," 362
Krieger, Murray, 450n11

"The Lady of Shalott," 52, 99–117, 146, 153, 154, 156, 164, 171, 181, 250, 258, 279, 286, 443n18
Laird, Robert G., 452n23
"Lamentation of the Peruvians," 65

"Lancelot and Elaine," 448n14
Lancelot, in "The Lady of Shalott," 111–116
Language: and atmosphere, 39–40, 74–75, 79; and desire, 74–76, 420; determinism of, 35–37, 39–40, 73–74; and equivalence, 81–84; evocation of death through, 82–84, 381; evocation of fatalism through, 24–25, 26, 128–129; inadequacy of, 380–381, 397; mediating function of, 292–294, 339–340, 394–397, 405
Laury, J. S., 320
Leavis, F. R., 8, 442n12
Leggett, B. J., 153, 246
Libertarianism, 412–413
Life, 82–83, 86, 188
"Life," 447n9
Light, imagery of, 43, 139, 145, 148, 150
Lipking, Lawrence, 445n1
Literary biography, form of, 9–10, 184–186
"Locksley Hall," 21, 452n22
"The Lord of Burleigh," 442n6
"The Lotos-Eaters," 13, 19, 444n24
Lourie, Margaret A., 17, 77, 96, 440n8, 443n21
Love, 82–83, 95, 97, 109, 113, 145–153, 161, 168, 226, 283, 372; cultural conditioning of, 297–300, 415–424, 428–429; and death, 87, 109–110, 281–286, 295, 374, 375, 424; not desire, 229; idyllic benevolence of, 279; impossibility of, 114–116; insufficiency of, 250; self-referential, 97–99; and solitude, 116–117. *See also* Desire; Relationship; Sexuality
The Lover's Tale, 94–99, 113–115, 120, 121, 142, 145, 150, 189, 216, 250, 279, 282, 329, 440n14, 441n19, 442n7, 451nn18,19, 454n1; compositional history of, 94–95
"Love Thou Thy Land," 342
"Lucretius," 13
Lucy, C., *The Reconciliation of Dora*, 452n25
Lyric, form of, 194, 356, 361–363, 389, 392, 394. *See also* Dramatic monologue, form of

Mackail, J. W., 304
Madden, Lionel, 437n1

Magus, in *The Devil and the Lady*, 18, 35–40, 49, 439n5
Malory, Sir Thomas, 320, 328, 331, 334, 335, 442n10, 453n32
Mann, Robert James, 455n15
Marginality, 49–50, 214–216, 220–226, 245, 263, 310. *See also* Alienation; Prophecy
"Mariana," 27–28, 52, 70–78, 81–82, 83, 87–88, 96, 143, 145, 181, 298, 362, 438n7, 441n16
"Mariana in the South," 117, 138–145; compared with "Mariana," 138–141, 144
Marriage, 281, 357, 370–371, 376, 398, 418
Marshall, George O., 211
Martin, Robert Bernard, 22, 51, 114, 438nn6,8
Mary, in "Dora," 305, 306, 307, 308
Mason, Michael, 186, 397, 450n5
"The May Queen," 118
Mays, J. C. C., 454n12
Maud, 12, 15, 16, 17, 21, 24, 52, 177, 179, 185, 266, 278, 347, 348, 350, 406–430, 431, 433, 437n1, 445n2, 450n4, 451n19, 455nn13,15; compositional history of, 12, 407–408
McGann, Jerome J., 438n8, 451n17, 454n5
McLuhan, H. M., 178, 275, 437n2, 438n3, 450nn8,11
Meaning, existential, 196, 197, 328, 329, 394, 397
Meisel, Martin, 442n12
Melancholy, 22–23, 25, 154, 158–159, 165–166, 198, 266
Memory, 25, 121, 228, 257, 259–260, 263, 282, 331–332, 364, 375; and self-dissolution, 259, 367
Menoeceus, in "Tiresias," 196, 197–198, 200, 201, 205, 208
"Merlin and the Gleam," 18
Mermin, Dorothy, 198, 233, 259
Merriman, James D., 127
"Midnight," 67–70, 72, 78
Miles, Josephine, 66
Militarism, 408, 416–418, 431–433
Mill, John Stuart, 437n3, 449n3
"The Miller's Daughter," 118
Millett, Kate, 454n5

Millhauser, Milton, 19, 316, 386, 450n3

"Milton: Alcaics," 438n9

Milton, John, 34, 42, 57, 64, 121, 127, 137, 143, 169, 343, 371, 439n7; *Comus,* 136, 142; *Paradise Lost,* 54, 55, 58, 63, 80, 132, 143, 236, 319; *Samson Agonistes,* 169, 444n28

Mimesis, 10, 108, 110, 281

Mirror, imagery of, 106, 107, 108, 111, 112, 113, 114–115, 141, 142–143, 163

Mitford, Mary Russell, 451n12; "Dora Creswell," 306–307, 312–313

Modernism: art/history distinction in, 5–6; AT's expression of, 23–24, 268–269; reception of AT, 3–9, 10, 431–434

Modernity, 55, 318, 408, 431

Monodrama, form of, 407, 409–410, 413, 414; vs. dramatic monologue, 410

Moralism, AT's, 118–119, 123, 210

Morality, AT's apathy toward, 14–15, 79, 81, 118–119, 120

"Morte d'Arthur," 52, 91, 317–345, 377, 453n29; as cultural transmission, 318–322; relation to epic, 317–322, 323–324

"Move Eastward, Happy Earth," 219

Mustard, W. P., 443n19

"The Mystic," 21, 88, 213–214

Narcissism, 47, 86, 365

Nash, Walter, 281, 289, 294, 405

Naturalism, 269, 387

Nature, 66–69, 77, 91, 105, 129, 156, 234, 242–244, 262, 292–294; and artifice, 156, 292–295; cultural determination of, 242, 292–295, 357–358, 423; in idyll, 295–302; linguistic mediation of, 292–294, 394, 396

New Criticism, 7, 8, 10, 268, 363

Nicolson, Harold, 6, 7, 19, 441n3

"Now Sleeps the Crimson Petal," 362, 369–370

"O Bosky Brook," 439n4

Oedipal complex, 415

Oedipus, 196

"Oenone," 117, 153–174, 181, 182, 208, 218, 284, 298, 324, 361, 393, 440n12, 442nn7,14, 443n22, 444nn24,30, 445n32

"On Sublimity," 49

Orestes, 445n31

Ostriker, Alicia, 73, 129, 443n20, 444n24

Other, and self, 45, 93–94, 96–98, 100–117, 122–125, 138, 142–152, 154–155, 167–168, 173–174, 197, 217, 226, 265, 385. *See also* Relationship

Ovid, 135–137; *Amores,* 137; *Heroides,* 171; *Metamorphoses,* 135

Packer, Lona Mosk, 442n8

Paden, W. D., 61, 65, 74, 81, 439n3, 440n12, 443n18, 444n23

"The Palace of Art," 117, 118–126, 131, 137, 161, 170, 173, 448n19

Palgrave, F. T., 345

Pallas, 160, 161, 444n27

Palmer, D. J., 100, 335

Paris, in "Oenone," 157, 164, 171–172; Judgment of, 158, 159, 160–162, 163, 444n30

Passion, 74–76, 82, 146–153, 159, 164, 167, 298, 426; and agency, 18–19, 74, 76, 149, 363; and passivity, 18–19; "phases of," in *Maud,* 409, 415, 421, 429. *See also* Desire; Relationship

Passivity, 15, 16, 18–20, 27, 47, 68, 83, 84, 115, 151, 248, 328; and passion, 18–19. *See also* Agency; Determinism; Victimage

Pathetic fallacy, 237, 244, 247, 383, 411

Patriotism, 199–208

Pattison, Robert, 14, 276, 288, 289, 442n11, 443n19, 444n30, 450n8, 451n15, 454n1

Peckham, Morse, 52, 270

Peltason, Timothy, 84, 86, 90, 110, 131, 289, 293, 363, 381, 396, 404, 448n17, 449n21

Pentheus, 445n31

"Perdidi Diem," 89, 439n6

Persephone, 453n26

Personality. *See* Agency; Character

Pettigrew, John, 212

Pitt, Valerie, 15, 17, 19, 23, 125, 275, 294, 355, 380

Plato, 61, 112

Poe, Edgar Allan, 445n32, 454n4

Poems (1832), 95, 98, 120, 131, 137, 150, 174, 178, 439n8, 448n19

Poems (1842), 177, 179–183, 185, 278, 377,

Poems (1842) (*cont.*)
441n19, 445n1, 447n11, 450n9, 452n23, 454n2, 455n14
Poems by Two Brothers, 64–70, 241
Poems, Chiefly Lyrical, 32, 73, 93
"The Poet," 88, 90, 96, 189
"The Poet's Mind," 52, 88
"The Poet's Song," 88, 189
Pope, Alexander, 32
Pound, Ezra, 6, 73, 134, 450n5
Power: of the past, 14; poetic, 41–42, 48, 54, 63–64, 187, 188, 197–209, 249, 389, 397; supernatural, 23, 25, 26–27, 38, 48–49, 77–78, 84, 145, 161, 164–168, 192, 199, 231–232, 256, 260, 264; technological, 274–276, 402
Preyer, Robert O., 26, 101, 172, 305, 454n3
Priam, 169
Priestley, F. E. L., 368, 411, 455n15
The Princess, 13, 17, 22, 153, 179, 278, 298, 301, 310, 348, 351–376, 377, 415, 420, 441n19, 449n19, 454nn7,11
Private code, vs. public code, 358, 406, 413, 418–419. *See also* Culture
Prophecy, 197–208, 220–221, 225, 229, 234–235, 236, 256, 263. *See also* Marginality
Puckett, Harry, 24
Pyre, J. F. A., 33

Quest, motif of, 18, 37–39, 49, 104, 142

Rackin, Phyllis, 382
Rader, Ralph, 454n3
Rannie, D. W., 281
"The Rape of Proserpine," 34
Rawnsley, W. F., 448n14
Ray, Gordon, 350, 409
"Recollections of the Arabian Nights," 78–87, 126, 416, 451n19; and "Mariana," 87–88
Reed, John R., 414, 454n3
Reform Bill of 1832, 213, 273, 299
Relationship, 93–95, 100–117, 122–123, 124, 138, 142–152, 154–155, 167, 173–174, 218–219, 265, 373; and beauty, 163–164; as confrontation, 154, 163–164, 167–168; in idylls, 314–315; impossibility of, 114–115; with the transcen-

dent, 168, 169, 261–262. *See also* Desire; Love; Other, and self
Repression, 120–122, 126, 254–260, 402
Responsibility, 15, 115, 158, 393, 414; abdication of, 15–16, 119, 210; acceptance of, 247, 255, 414
Richards, I. A., 6, 8
Ricks, Christopher, 15, 22, 41, 84, 142, 160, 213, 228, 257, 259, 286, 326, 343, 368, 370, 371, 437n1, 444n31, 451n19
Ritual, AT's secularized, 398–401
Robbins, Tony, 232, 448n18
Robson, W. W., 429
Roles, social, 308–309, 367
Romanticism, 20, 23, 34, 41, 69, 70, 96, 104, 131, 212, 292, 349, 389; appearance and reality in, 61–62; desire in, 95–96, 243, 267; doom in, 28–29, 321, 404; humanism of, 399, 405; and literary tradition, 54, 196; love in, 87, 267; modern reception of, 4, 7; originality in, 56–57, 127, 187–188, 288, 383, 405, 424; poetic power in, 41, 48, 63–64, 205, 249, 389; revisionism of, by AT, 28–30, 43, 51, 54, 64, 93, 95–96, 131–134, 142–143, 154, 172–174, 189, 212–213, 222, 225–226, 264, 349, 389, 428; secular religion of, 56, 228–229, 236, 403; self in, 93, 113, 116, 122, 135, 143, 167, 171, 190, 197, 228–229, 235, 371–372, 392, 405, 422; sensation in, 42, 189, 222; transcendentalism of, 249, 264
Rose, in "The Gardener's Daughter," 279, 281, 283, 284, 286, 289, 296, 297, 298, 299, 421, 450n7, 451n12, 452n21
Rosenberg, John D., 186, 217, 322, 334, 338, 401
Rosenblum, Dolores, 378
Rosenmeyer, Thomas G., 272, 275, 279, 281, 289, 300, 450n7
Rossetti, Dante Gabriel, 442n12
Rousseau, Jean-Jacques, 171
Rowlinson, Matthew, 133, 443n20
Ruskin, John, 4, 311, 313
Ryals, Clyde de L., 233

Saintsbury, George, 182, 444n24
"St. Simeon Stylites," 16, 191, 265, 446n1
Sale, Roger, 7
Savary, J., *Letters on Egypt,* 78
Schulman, Samuel, 427

Science, 63, 315–316, 401–402, 433

Sedgwick, Eve Kosofsky, 301, 352, 359, 416, 452n19, 454n5, 455n16

Self: alienated, 124, 125, 135, 211, 213–214, 220–221, 226, 231–232, 244, 265, 378, 387, 401, 404, 412; annihilation of, 22–23, 25, 229–231, 233, 235–236, 263, 348, 363–365, 374; and death, 121–122, 168, 227, 255; deep, 214, 380, 384, 389, 390–391, 393; empirical, abandoned, 62, 206–208, 227–228; empirical conditioning of, 25, 192, 232–233, 261–263, 305, 376, 378–379, 385, 386, 389, 390–391, 403–404, 422; as event, 385; identity of, 141, 149, 155, 218, 219, 228, 230–231, 263–266, 370–371; knowledge of, 213–218, 223; narrative, 304–305, 380; prophetic marginality of, 197–208, 214–216, 220–226; and other, 93–94, 96, 100–117, 122–125, 138, 142–152, 154, 163, 167–168, 173–174, 197, 217, 226, 265, 385; Romantic, 167, 171, 227–229, 371–371; vs. Soul, 62, 119, 120, 125, 267; and the unconscious, 362. *See also* Agency; Character; Identity; Other, and self

Sendry, Joseph, 386, 437n1, 442n12

Sensation, 19–20, 41–45, 48, 71, 78, 146; auditory, 45, 80, 90–91; crisis of, 42–45, 112, 113; tactile, 139, 218; and thought, 58–61; visual, 19–20, 41–42, 48, 80, 218

Sexuality, 77, 87, 91, 107–108, 109, 131, 134, 144, 162, 284, 368; and death, 91, 109–110, 134, 281, 284, 296–297; politics of, 375–376; rejection of, 85, 86–88, 250–254, 258–259, 262, 267. *See also* Desire; Feminism; Love; Passion

Shaffer, Elinor, 440n12, 450n8

Shakespeare, William, 71, 74, 121, 438n6; *Cymbeline*, 448n17; *Hamlet*, 350, 411, 447n13; *A Midsummer Night's Dream*, 292

Shannon, Edgar F., 347, 442n8, 444n27, 448n16, 454n2

Shatto, Susan, 186

Shaw, Marion, 270

Shaw, W. David, 14, 17, 47, 243, 253, 378, 381, 420, 430, 438nn3,4,9, 449n21, 450n3

Shelley, Percy Bysshe, 22, 34, 42, 51, 54, 87, 169–170, 269, 371, 433, 440n10, 441nn20,1; AT's response to, 132–133, 142, 149–156; *Adonais*, 236–238; *Alastor*, 122, 147, 443n21; *Defence of Poetry*, 89; *Epipsychidion*, 113; "Hymn of Apollo," 150; "Hymn to Intellectual Beauty," 56; "Mont Blanc," 238; "Ode to the West Wind," 132–133, 146, 149, 152, 174; *Prometheus Unbound*, 87, 151, 159, 254, 260; "To a Skylark," 103, 112–113, 291; *The Triumph of Life*, 149–150, 252

Sherry, James, 17, 63, 72

Short, Clarice, 441n1

Sight, imagery of, 20, 42–45, 47, 55, 61–62, 78–79

Sinfield, Alan, 17, 24, 164, 298, 438n3, 444n30, 455n15

"Sir Launcelot and Queen Guinevere," 446n2

Smith, L. E. W., 210, 443n16

Social critique, 401–406, 409, 415–430

Society. *See* Context; Culture; Social critique; Victorian culture

Solitude, 47–50, 135, 138, 142, 160, 197, 207, 213–214, 265–266, 398–399; and commitment, 96, 100–117, 138; and love, 265; self-imposed, 122–125, 126, 158; *See also* Alienation; Marginality

Soul, 16, 120–121, 122, 387; vs. self, 119, 120, 121, 125, 267

Sound, imagery of, 20, 42–45, 47, 61, 72–73, 90–91

Spatz, Jonas, 409, 411, 415

Spedding, James, 310, 454n2

Spenser, Edmund, 343; *The Faerie Queene*, 136, 319, 348; *Shepheards Calender*, 312

Spitzer, Lee, 22, 365, 450n11

Staines, David, 453n32

Stange, G. Robert, 130, 427, 443n16

Starzyk, Lawrence J., 62, 449n21

Stein, Richard L., 442n9

Steiner, Wendy, 450n11

Sterling, John, 80, 120, 450n3, 451n17, 452n23, 453n30

Stevens, Wallace, 346

Stevenson, Catherine Barnes, 90, 352

Stevenson, Lionel, 103

Stokes, Edward, 406

Storch, R. F., 15, 448n18

Swinburne, Algernon Charles, 32

Tapsall, Peter, 448n18

"Tears, Idle Tears," 19, 310, 362–367, 420

Technology. *See* Power, technological; Science

Telemachus, in "Ulysses," 210–213, 226, 229, 232, 325

Tennyson, Alfred: amoralism of, 14–15, 34; bad faith of, 353–354; careerism of, 51–52, 180–183, 184–185, 229, 277–278, 347–348, 390; conservatism of, 15, 113, 344; continuity of poetry of, 179–183; effect of Hallam's death on, 178–184, 188, 190, 265, 266, 267; egotism of, 46; modernism of, 23–24, 268–269; modern reception of, 3–9, 10, 431–434; myopia of, 19; and philosophy, 60; poet of aftermath, 13–14; poet of sensation, 20–21; power obsession of, 41–42; privacy vs. publicity in career of, 51–52; prodigy, 31–35; Romantic aspirations of, 41, 49, 51, 57, 61–64, 70, 76, 82–83, 84, 123, 174, 181, 225, 264, 349; and tradition, 57–59; transcendentalism of, 46; Victorianism of, 8

Tennyson, Edward, 454n8

Tennyson, Emily, 409, 429, 451n14

Tennyson, Hallam, 27, 449nn19,22,23, 452n22

Theocritus, 313

Thesing, William B., 427

Tillotson, Kathleen, 452n23

"Timbuctoo," 21, 40–41, 43, 44, 51–64, 70, 80, 89, 96, 131, 154, 157, 181, 188, 218, 317, 440nn9,12,14, 443n21, 444n24

Time, 21, 78–80, 84, 248, 263, 279–280, 287, 396–397; and death, 287–288, 365; equivalence of past and future, 194, 282, 387; uniformity of, 98, 287

Timko, Michael, 298, 452n23

"Tiresias," 192–209, 211, 232, 261, 266, 278, 442n14, 446n1, 447n6, 448nn15,19

"Tithonus," 21, 91, 167, 192, 232, 239–269, 278, 440n12, 442n14, 444n29, 449nn19,20,21,22; compositional history of, 239–241; relation of, to "Ulysses," 239–241

Tobias, Richard C., 112, 442n8

Tobin, J. J. M., 449n20

"To J. S.," 219

"To Poesy," 88, 439n6

"To the Queen," 321

"To Virgil," 29–30, 438n9

Trench, R. C., 118

Tucker, Herbert F., 439n5, 441n1

Turner, Paul, 443n19, 450n10

"Ulysses," 18, 20, 52, 167, 209–238, 266, 277, 324, 325, 346, 366, 438n7, 444n29, 446n1, 447nn7,8,9,10,11,12, 448nn14, 16,18; compositional history of, 209–213; relation of, to "Tiresias," 209–211

"Vastness," 445n4

Victimage, 27, 296–297, 331, 426. *See also* Passivity

Victorian culture, 25–26, 301–307, 386, 387, 401, 425, 431–432; Aesthetic movement in, 72; AT's affirmation of, 389–401; AT's critique of, 401–405, 415–430; capitalism in, 221, 392, 401, 420; skepticism of, 387, 393

Violence, 353, 355, 356–357, 375

Virgil, 28–30, 216, 318, 355, 438n9, 445n31, 446n4; *Aeneid,* 135, 146, 204–205, 219, 319, 445n31, 446n4, 453n33

Virgin Mary, in "Mariana in the South," 138–139, 141

"Walking to the Mail," 189, 271–275, 352

Ward, Arthur D., 232

Weiner, S. Ronald, 415

Welch, James Donald, 396

"Whispers," 447n7

Whiting, George Wesley, 450n11, 452n25, 454n7

Whitman, Walt, 441n3

Wilkinson, L. P., 453n33

Will. *See* Agency

Wimsatt, W. K., 8

Wiseman, Christopher, 243, 449n21

Woman, as rose, 420, 421

Woman Question, the, 144, 352. *See also* Feminism

Wordsworth, Ann, 186

Wordsworth, Jonathan, 411, 430

Wordsworth, William, 42, 51, 54, 59, 60, 67, 110, 180, 223–226, 349, 367, 397, 433, 440n10, 448n14, 450n8, 452n23; poet of reflection, 59–60; "The Brothers," 452n23; *The Excursion,* 319, 440nn10,11; "Intimations Ode," 56, 58–59, 110, 143, 172–173, 223–224, 343, 397–398, 421, 448n13; "Michael," 452n23; "The Old Cumberland Beggar," 452n23; "Peter Bell," 440n11;

Wordsworth, William (*cont.*)
  The Prelude, 319, 321, 348, 381; *The Recluse,* 58; "Resolution and Independence," 264; "The Simplon Pass," 242; "The Solitary Reaper," 90, 104; "Tintern Abbey," 58–59, 209, 225, 226, 235, 323, 366, 403–404; "To the Cuckoo," 104, 291; "Yarrow Unvisited," 56

World War I, 431–432

Yeats, W. B., 6, 180, 198, 226, 346, 444n30, 445n1

Zeus, 370, 446n4